AMERICAN POLITICS

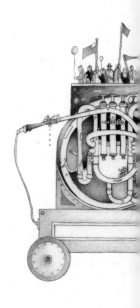

AMERICAN POLITICS

DENNIS J. PALUMBO
City University of New York
Brooklyn College

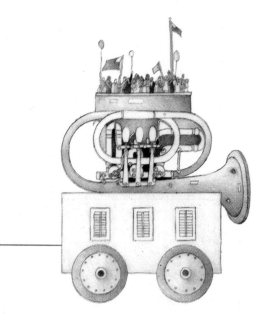

APPLETON-CENTURY-CROFTS
New York
EDUCATIONAL DIVISION
MEREDITH CORPORATION

73 74 75 76 77/ 10 9 8 7 6 5 4 3 2 1 0
Library of Congress Card Number: 72-91353

PRINTED IN THE UNITED STATES OF AMERICA

390-69126-7

ACKNOWLEDGMENTS

Illustrations

Cartoons

Page 9: Drawing by Stan Hunt; © 1972 The New Yorker Magazine, Inc. *Page 26:* Drawing by W. Miller; © 1971 The New Yorker Magazine, Inc. *Page 45:* Cartoon by Henry Martin; copyright 1971 Saturday Review, Inc. *Page 51:* Drawing by Weber; © 1972 The New Yorker Magazine, Inc. *Page 91:* Cartoon by Mort Gerberg; copyright 1972 Saturday Review, Inc. *Page 93:* Drawing by Lorenz; © 1971 The New Yorker Magazine, Inc. *Page 116:* Editorial cartoon by Pat Oliphant. Copyright The Denver Post. Reprinted with permission of Los Angeles Times Syndicate. *Page 130:* Drawing by Shirvanian; © 1969 The New Yorker Magazine, Inc. *Page 160:* Cartoon by Frank Baginski; © 1971 Frank Baginski. Courtesy Official Detective. *Page 173:* Cartoon by Joseph Farris; copyright 1971 Saturday Review, Inc. *Page 192:* Cartoon by Smilby; copyright 1970 Saturday Review, Inc. *Page 215:* Drawing by Richter; © 1971 The New Yorker Magazine, Inc. *Page 252:* Cartoon by J. B. Handelsman. Reproduced by special permission of PLAYBOY Magazine; copyright © 1972 by Playboy. *Page 264:* Drawing by J. Mirachi; © 1971 The New Yorker Magazine, Inc. *Page 272:* Cartoon by Henry Martin; copyright 1972 Saturday Review, Inc. *Page 292:* Cartoon by Al Ross; copyright 1970 Saturday Review, Inc. *Page 331:* Drawing by Ross; © 1971 The New Yorker Magazine, Inc. *Page 348:* Cartoon by Chon Day; © 1970 Chon Day. Courtesy D.A.C. News. *Page 358:* Cartoon by Bruce Cochran. Reproduced by special permission of PLAYBOY Magazine; copyright © 1971 by Playboy. *Page 379:* Drawing by B. Tobey; © 1971 The New Yorker Magazine, Inc. *Page 406:* Drawing by W. Miller; © 1971 The New Yorker Magazine, Inc. *Page 413:* Editorial cartoon by Pat Oliphant. Copyright The Denver Post. Reprinted with permission of Los Angeles Times Syndicate. *Page 465:* Cartoon by Joseph Farris; copyright 1971 Saturday Review, Inc. *Page 494:* Cartoon by Andrew Habbick; copyright 1969 Saturday Review, Inc. *Page 501:* Drawing by Dana Fradon; © 1970 The New Yorker Magazine, Inc. *Page 510:* Drawing by Whitney Darrow, Jr.; © 1971 The New Yorker Magazine, Inc. *Page 521:* Cartoon by Jack Markow; © 1969 Jack Markow. *Page 561:* Drawing by Booth; © 1971 The New Yorker Magazine, Inc. *Page 577:* Drawing by Minter; © 1971 The New Yorker Magazine, Inc. *Page 595:* Editorial cartoon by Pat Oliphant. Copyright The Denver Post. Reprinted with permission

(Continued after Subject Index, back of book)

CONTENTS

PART 3 THE PEOPLE IN POLITICS

Appendixes

Indexes

PREFACE

Much has been happening to the study of political science in recent years. In fact, the same thing might be said about political science today that a nineteenth-century poet once remarked about the heart of a young girl: it has, alas, been changing too fast. Within a relatively short time, political scientists have sharply shifted their focus from the question of ideal government that has preoccupied them since Plato wrote his *Republic*. This shift has resulted from two major revolutions: the behavioral and the post-behavioral. Instead of asking, "What is the best form of government?" political scientists in the behavioral revolution began to ask, "How are political decisions actually made?" The post-behavioral revolution has gone beyond the study of both questions. It is activist, and it concerns itself with how things can be made better, how injustice can be righted and inequities corrected, rather than with an understanding of the political process.

The post-behavioral activists have succeeded in injecting a new vitality into a social science constantly threatened by obsolescence in a rapidly changing world. Yet, activism as an orientation presents special difficulties to political science because it does not have a fixed point or question to guide it. It is certain only in its rejection of traditional institutions and ideals, such as pluralism, liberalism, and the welfare state and, in its more extreme form, objectivity and rationality. From the activist position, then, a great many existing works on American politics are outmoded, for most of them are based on political pluralism and extol its virtues. It is high time, the activists say, to rewrite all the texts on American politics. Being antirationalist, however, they do not believe in texts; thus some books have appeared that are known as "antitexts" or "nontexts."

This book has tried to take account of the recent revolutions in the study of politics. In fact, it goes further, for it incorporates behavioral questions with traditional institutional descriptions and is also concerned with how conditions can be improved. At the same time, it does not fail to point out possible shortcomings of pluralism and liberalism in present-day America.

Plan of the Book

Part 1: Introduction to American Politics

Part 1 explores the meaning of democracy in a changing society. Some of the contradictions and confusions in the American definition of democracy are considered: the liberal tradition in the United States, the constitutional framework of our system of government, the issues of social justice and political liberties, and the problems confronting minority groups today.

Part 2: Structures of Power and Decision-Making

Part 2 describes the American pluralist system of government and how it operates. It examines the peculiar balance of forces inherent in American politics, and the ways in which various branches of the federal government, the states, and the cities interact according to the political "rules of the game." The focus is on the major structures of power and decision-making: federalism, Congress, the President, the bureaucracy, and the courts.

Part 3: The People in Politics

Part 3 focuses on the behavioral reality of how political decisions are made, examining the effect of public opinion on the political process; the function of interest groups in decision-making; and the history and role of political parties in our system of government. Finally, in a discussion of the election processes, campaigns and voting behavior are examined.

Part 4: Public Policy

Part 4 takes up the question of public policy, both foreign and domestic. lt reaches into economic affairs, urban renewal, welfare, environmental pollution, defense, and national security. This section addresses itself to the activists in considering how our government might be improved.

Features of the Text

Intermingling of Approaches

Although each part of the book emphasizes a different aspect of politics, there is throughout an intermingling of the traditional, the behavioral, and the activist points of view.

Readability

A textbook has no value unless it can be read and understood by students. A poorly written and unnecessarily difficult textbook is a hindrance to the instructor as well as to the student. On the basis of this principle, every effort has been made to produce a book that is stylistically readable without sacrifice of content. A major aim has been to turn out a work that the student can understand and relate to his own experience.

Current Issues

Efforts have also been made to give each topic a distinctly contemporary focus, not simply in order to capture and maintain the student's interest, but because, in a very real sense, political science has no meaning if it does not grapple with forces that affect us now, in the very midst of our present-day political reality. In keeping with this effort, many current sources have been used, along with classics in the field, to help the reader understand and evaluate important recent developments. For instance, the book contains up-to-date materials on such contemporary issues as the environment, race relations, and the effects of the media on political behavior.

Graphs, Tables, and Illustrations

All the statistical material in this text has been designed to make it attractive, graphic, and comprehensible. The book contains a large number of photographs, which give visual impact and support to the text.

Suggested Readings

Each chapter ends with a list of suggested readings. Care has been taken to select books which will be of interest to the student and will add to his understanding of topics discussed in the chapter. Each work cited is briefly described and evaluated.

Alternative Sequencing

This book has been planned for flexible usage by the instructor. Chapters may be used in any sequence, so that the instructor can coordinate assignments from the textbook with his own needs and approach to the subject. For example, Part 2, "Structures of Power and Decision-Making"; and Part 3, "The People in Politics," could be covered in reverse order by those who wish to deal with the role of the people in the political process first. Alternatively, the public-policy chapters now at the end of the book could be covered before Parts 2 and 3 by those who wish to emphasize the outcomes of the system before discussing political institutions and processes.

Acknowledgments

Authoring a book is satisfying to one's ego, but in fact, authorship to a great extent rests on the ideas, research, help, and encouragement of a number of people. In the present case, the usual "without whom" acknowledgments must be augmented substantially, for a large part of what is worthwhile in this book is due to the superb editorial work of Mary Schieck, who was the chief editor. In addition, Trudy Emanuel's fine work as assistant editor has made a substantial contribution to many of the chapters. I should also like to express thanks to the many students who helped shape the ideas in this book; unfortunately, these have been too many to name individually here.

D. J. P.

1

INTRODUCTION TO AMERICAN POLITICS

It is often said that the United States has become more democratic over the course of history. A number of factors support this claim. Over the years, there has been a steady increase in the proportion of the population that can vote; today, universal suffrage, for all practical purposes, has been achieved. Educational opportunities have also been greatly expanded, as demonstrated by the fact that 75 percent of all young people graduate high school and 50 percent go on to college. In addition, there has been a general increase in affluence and the standard of living: more than 50 percent of all families have incomes of ten thousand dollars a year or more, and more than 20 percent have incomes of fifteen thousand a year or more. And, finally, American citizens have increasingly exercised their right to condemn the government openly and to organize in protest of government policy, as evidenced by the much-publicized marches on Washington during the late 1960s.

Yet, all is not right with American society. The late 1960s saw greater conflict, dissension, and turmoil than any other decade in many years. The environment is rapidly deteriorating. And hunger, poverty, and discrimination are present amidst material affluence. These contradictions and inconsistencies in American political life are reflected in widespread political apathy and alienation. Public distrust of politicians has increased. Certain moral values and beliefs have lost the position of high esteem they once occupied. The meaning and relevance of democracy itself has come into question. Many people maintain that the present system is incapable of solving the pressing problems facing the nation today. Some go so far as to argue that solutions can be found only through nondemocratic means.

The contemporary crisis in American politics is a crisis in democratic theory. How is democracy to be defined in a complex industrialized state such as our own? Part 1 of this book explores the meaning of democracy in a changing society, considering the American definition of democracy in the light of some of its contradictions and confusions; the liberal tradition in the United States; the constitutional framework of our system of government; the issues of social justice and political liberties; and the problems confronting minority groups today.

1
DEMOCRACY IN A CHANGING SOCIETY

There is a certain point in life when one suddenly becomes aware of having lived through history. Previously it was one's parents only who were endowed with a historical perspective. They remembered Franklin D. Roosevelt, the Second World War, the Depression. But as one grows more experienced in the world, one realizes that political events are not something exclusively of the past; they encompass everything down to the present moment and include all of us. Americans of college age today have lived through the Kennedy years, the Johnson years, and the Nixon years. They have experienced the Vietnam War, the rise of black power, and a multitude of other political changes.

It is an inescapable fact that American society has dramatically changed in the recent years, perhaps more rapidly and more profoundly than ever before. These changes have placed enormous strain on, and offered innumerable challenges to, the machinery of government. Certain institutions have been taxed to the breaking point in the effort to contain the bewildering onslaught of alteration. Other innovative programs have bloomed quickly in response to new needs.

The process by which a nation copes with change and regulates the forces that affect the lives of its citizens is called politics. Politics, to quote Harold Lasswell's simple but effective definition, is the method by which we answer the question "Who gets what, when, and how?"[1] Simple as this definition seems, politics in practice is, as we shall see, extremely complex.

In the course of his life the average citizen performs countless acts which affect the lives of other citizens, while he, in turn, is affected by the acts of other individuals. To protect all citizens from the consequences of those acts that infringe on the rights and political obligations of others, a whole network of laws and institutions has developed at the national, state, and local levels. Such laws and institutions pertain to everything from the practices of large corporations and government agencies down to standards of auto safety, building regulations, and the licensing of pets. The ways in which our laws are made, enforced, and changed, as well as the method by which those who make and enforce them are elected or appointed to office, are all part of the subject we call politics.

Political Culture

An American, seeing a child about to drown, would most likely make some effort to save him. If he did not, he would almost surely have guilt feelings about his failure to act; it would seem to him that he had shirked his moral obligation. A Buddhist, on the other hand, might act quite differently in the same situation. Imbued with a powerful sense of the predestination of all earthly events, he might consider it inadvisable to interfere with what has been ordained by Providence for purposes beyond his ken, especially when saving the child would be tantamount to taking full responsibility for it ever after.

The way we react in certain situations, the choices we are likely to make, are profoundly influenced by the culture in which we have been raised. What seems natural and honorable to us may seem foolish or disgraceful to a person of another culture, and vice-versa. Culture may be defined as the learned patterns of behavior, beliefs, and attitudes that are shared by members of a particular society.

---

[1] Harold Lasswell, *Politics: Who Gets What, When, How* (New York: McGraw-Hill, 1936).

Culture may be a source of pride and cohesiveness to people, but it may also cause them to cling stubbornly to certain inherited notions long after the objective situation has rendered these notions inoperative. Politics is as much a part of culture as our language, dress, and codes of etiquette. We like to think that our political ideas are founded upon pure rationality, that they are logical methods of dealing with the problem of government. To a certain extent this is true, but it may be shown that in some ways our political presuppositions are every bit as culturally determined as the way we hold our knife and fork.

Today many people are openly challenging the traditional values and beliefs of American political culture. They claim that these values are no longer applicable to the present, or that they were prejudicial from the start. In order to understand these charges we must first try to see them in their social and historical context by exploring some of the basic political values that have come to characterize American political culture.

Public opinion in the United States has come to be deeply divided on important issues. Demonstrations against the Vietnam War, for example, have often spurred counterdemonstrations stressing support for the government.

American Political Values

Political values are basic beliefs which members of a society share concerning what is right and wrong in politics. They are like the "givens" in a mathematical proof, the "truths" which a people hold to be "self-evident," and from which all the rest of their political system, at least in an ideal sense, may be shown to follow. In America, five of the most fundamental of these values are individualism; equality; the right to life, liberty, and property; limited government; and the rule of law.

Individualism

The emergence of individualism as a potential value is usually traced to the work of the English philosopher John Locke. At its heart lies the belief that individual satisfaction and fulfillment are of primary value in a society—that morality consists in treating persons as ends rather than means. So basic is the doctrine of individualism to the American consciousness that there are few documents of American thought in which it does not find expression. It is contained in the writings of Jefferson; in the wording of the Constitution and the Declaration of Independence; in the works of American poets and philosophers such as Whitman, Emerson, and Thoreau; and in the recent protester's slogan "I am a human being; do not fold, spindle, or mutilate."

Nor is individual self-fulfillment regarded as a favor conferred upon citizens through the benevolence of those in authority; it is, rather, thought to be a basic right, exercised through individual participation in the political process. The individual is considered a rational being capable of making intelligent and responsible decisions on how and by whom he is to be governed. Indeed, few images elicit as comfortable an emotional response from Americans as that of the ordinary citizen casting his vote at the polls, for it is here, by directly affecting the political process, that the individual in a democratic state affirms his basic dignity.

Equality

Another of the truths that Americans hold to be self-evident is that all men (and, more recently, women) are created equal. This does not mean that all citizens are assumed to be equal in abilities or prestige, but rather that all are equal under the law, enjoying equal rights. There are many inconsistencies associated with the doctrine of equality. For example, some of the Founding Fathers who affirmed this ideal were themselves slave owners and thus guilty of flagrantly denying the doctrine of equality by treating their fellow human beings as property, without rights or power of self-determination. Nevertheless, the idea that no class or racial group was created to serve another remains strong in the system of American values, and though many groups have had to fight bitterly in order to secure the rights promised them, the ideal of equality continues to inspire such groups, assuring them that what they demand is indeed rightfully theirs.

Natural Rights: Life, Liberty, and Property

Americans believe that the rights to life, liberty, and property are "unalienable" or natural rights; that is, they are accorded to each man by virtue of his humanity, rather than as a result of his membership in any society or political state. The rights to life, liberty, and property, preceding as they do the laws of government, cannot be abridged by government without due process of law. Drawing from a strong English heritage, Americans have tended to view government, ideally, as a trustee of human rights whose very reason for existence is the preservation of private property and individual liberty. As a people, we are impatient of any institutionalized restraint of these rights.

Limited Government

Unlike other philosophies, such as socialism or communism, American political thought is built around the concept of limited government. Attempts to use government for the special purpose of regulating or conferring benefits on individuals or private institutions are traditionally viewed with suspicion. Like the ideal of equality, the concept of limited government is surrounded by a great deal of controversy—especially since, over the years, the economic affairs of the United States have become increasingly complex, requiring government to step in again and again in order to maintain full employment and economic stability. Many Americans, however, still criticize such practices, insisting that "government is best which governs least."

Rule of Law

A strong commitment to the rule of law is deeply embedded in the American political tradition. Because men are seen as essentially corruptible, laws are believed to be necessary for the successful governing of society. Laws, in fact, are typically viewed as transcending the self-interests of individuals and embodying society's collective judgment of what constitutes the public good. A fundamental reason legal mechanisms are accorded such esteem in American politics is the allegedly impartial means they provide for reconciling even the most deeply rooted conflicts. Legal standards are believed to have the qualities of neutrality and consistency that contribute to equitable enforcement and a stable society.

The Ideal and the Actual

It has been said that one's view of a situation is profoundly conditioned by the culture in which he has been raised. The term *culture* is a flexible one and may be used not only to point out differences between the social patterns of one country and another, but between different segments of a population as well. Since members of different social, economic, racial, educational, and age groups undergo profoundly different experiences—which, in turn, color their ways of looking at things—they may be said to belong to different cultures, or, to use a term from sociology, *subcultures*.

An Indian from an impoverished southwestern village, a black from an urban ghetto, and a middle-class white from a suburban neighborhood are sure to place different demands on American government and to have very different perceptions of our national goals and ideals. And an American who has experienced the Depression and spent his formative years under the administration of Franklin Roosevelt is certain to see things differently from someone who has grown up during the Eisenhower or Kennedy years. Differences between generations are, seemingly, part of human nature—gaps between subcultures have always been apparent in a nation that draws upon so many heritages. But today we seem to be approaching a renewed recognition of diversity. As a nation, we have become so fragmented into conflicting interest groups that it has become somewhat incongruous to speak in terms of a single "American culture" at all.

Although most of us would agree that the American political ideals outlined above are desirable ones, few would claim without qualification that they accurately describe reality. Some would vehemently affirm that we have fallen far from some, if not all, of these ideals; others might say that the ideals have been misguided from the start; and still others that they are merely empty, hypocritical phrases masking basic injustices in the American system. We shall now examine some of the arguments of those who claim that the ideals of the American political system are frequently contradicted in practice.

Individualism: Is It Possible in a Mass Society?

Individualism as a value in American culture has not been repudiated, as the examples of those who strive to establish their own identity and "do their thing" amply attest. Yet many observers charge that life in a highly industrialized, mass society engenders feelings of alienation and estrangement that threaten individual development and fulfillment. In the political realm, alienation may be reflected in a conscious rejection of the political "rules of the game," as people become disenchanted with the results of those rules.

The reasons for political alienation in American society are many and complex. Some claim that the enormous growth of bureaucracy in the twentieth century has given rise to feelings of ineffectiveness and frustration, as people find access to government increasingly difficult. Others contend that the two-party system does not provide individuals with viable political alternatives—that the government carries out the same policies concerning employment, welfare, poverty, and the like, regardless of whether the Democrats or the Republicans are in control. This lack of choice, they claim, contributes to a rejection of established political procedures.

"Who is *he*? He keeps muttering that he doesn't hear America singing anymore."

New Yorker, *March 4, 1972*

Still other observers blame American apathy on the prevalence of technological specialization in our society. The perceptive nineteenth-century French observer of American culture, Alexis de Tocqueville, anticipated this situation when he pointed out the probable consequences of forcing workmen, in the interests of efficiency, to concentrate on simple, repetitive tasks while denying them the satisfaction of taking responsibility for a finished product.[2] More recently, Lewis Mumford has argued that the standardization of work due to mechanization has resulted in a decline in the importance of the individual in the production process. Accompanying this decline, moreover, is a reduction in the individual's own sense of personal identity and worth. Mumford stated:

> . . . the worker has scarcely any direct part in the process of production; he is, so to say, a machine-herd, attending to the welfare of a flock of machines which do the actual work: at best, he feeds them, oils them, mends them when they break down, while the work itself is as remote from his province as is the digestion which fattens the sheep looked after by the shepherd.[3]

If economic life has become remote and meaningless for the average worker, it is possible that political life has become similarly unrewarding for the average citizen. Most people in the United States are simply not socialized to participate in politics. They are encouraged to vote, but not much else. The act of casting his ballot in a free election becomes for the citizen of an individual state merely the isolated, impersonal process of pulling a lever in a voting booth, nothing more. In spite of his prerogative of exerting his will upon the machinery of government, he may remain cut off, alienated, frustrated by a pervasive feeling of impotence.

Equality: Some More Equal than Others?

If today a spokesman for the United States government were to conduct a nation-wide speaking tour in which he praised the historical success of the American pursuit of equality, probably he would win a very spotty reception. Some of his audience, notably those belonging to the "silent majority," would welcome his remarks with hearty affirmation. But on the college campuses, in the ghettos, in many cities in the East, and in the pockets of poverty that mark many of our rural regions, it is likely that his audiences' reactions would vary from lukewarm to hotly indignant. The fact is that in recent years many Americans have become painfully aware that inequality, not equality, seems to characterize much of American society; and they have grown, in varying degrees, incensed at what they perceive to be their government's reluctance to quickly remedy that situation.

Unequal access to the voting booth has traditionally been a source of indignation. Although in theory America enjoys universal adult suffrage, it was not long ago that harassment and threats by whites prevented black voters from casting their ballots in many southern states. And only recently have discriminatory poll taxes and literacy tests, which effectively barred many Americans from freely exercising their right to vote, been abolished.

Even more common today is the accusation that the United States does not enjoy economic equality. Though long celebrated as a land of plenty, America, upon closer inspection, is riddled with poverty. A government pamphlet, "Poverty

---

[2] Alexis de Tocqueville, *Democracy in America*, vol. 2 (New York: Vintage, 1945), p. 168.
[3] Lewis Mumford, *Technics and Civilization* (New York: Harcourt Brace Jovanovich, 1962), pp. 410–411.

This scene from the Mississippi Delta illustrates the gap between the ideal of economic equality and the reality of poverty in the United States.

and Deprivation," published in 1960 by the Conference on Economic Progress, concluded that thirty-eight million Americans lived in poverty, while another portion, of roughly equal size, lived in a slightly better but still substandard state which the study labeled "underprivileged." Together these two categories comprise about one-third of the population of the country.[4] Although the number of poor is somewhat less today—about twenty-four million in 1972—they still represent a substantial portion of the population.

Perhaps more disturbing to our sensitivities is the apparent permanence of poverty. Data indicates that over the last several decades there has been little improvement in the distribution of income in the United States after taxes. In 1936, the bottom fifth of all families (ranked according to income) received about 4 percent of total income, and their share is exactly the same today. Similarly, there has been little change in the share of income received by the top fifth of all families—the figure ranges between 46 and 42 percent over the same time period.[5]

[4] Quoted in Dwight MacDonald, "Our Invisible Poor," in *American Economic History, Essays in Interpretation*, edited by Stanley Coben and Forest G. Hill (Philadelphia: Lippincott, 1966), pp. 563–589.
[5] Gabriel Kolko, *Wealth and Power in America* (New York: Praeger, 1962).

In addition to the evidence of inherent inequalities in the American system, there are the claims by blacks, Puerto Ricans, Indians, and Mexican-Americans that they are victims of institutionalized discrimination—that the very structures of our social institutions assure that they will be deprived of jobs, decent living conditions, the right to a fair trial, free speech, power of self-determination, and so on, regardless of whether or not they are victims of individual discrimination. Americans often believe that everyone in our country is well off, for they have experienced a great increase in affluence since the end of World War II. The suburban commuter, speeding on a train through a central-city ghetto, does not really witness the conditions that exist there; therefore, he may not appreciate the full meaning of the claims made by those who live in poverty. Although poverty may have diminished somewhat in recent years, there can be no doubt that we are far from achieving economic equality.

Natural Rights: Which Rights Are Natural?

The Framers of the Constitution, such men as Hamilton and Madison, gave high priority to the individual's right to hold property. As time went by, however, it became clear that property rights often came into conflict with other ideals such as liberty and equality.

The case of slavery presents an early example of this controversy. There is no doubt that the slave owner, in exercising his right to buy, sell, and use his property (the slave) as he saw fit, violated the liberty and equality of the slave. Yet because a man's right to property was considered inviolable according to the American value system, slave owners felt justified in staunchly resisting abolitionist attempts at effecting emancipation. It was not until the end of the Civil War that the injustice was officially recognized and this particular "property right" abridged.

The same collision between conflicting ideals occurs today in the controversy over discrimination versus civil rights. A man who owns a restaurant, for example, may feel that, since his ownership is sanctioned by the sacred right to property, he may manage the restaurant as he likes and serve whomever he wishes, according to his personal preferences. Such was the position held by Lester Maddox, former governor of Georgia, who tenaciously fought to bar black customers from his Pickrick Restaurant in Atlanta during the early 1960s. But a black man who wants to be served at the restaurant feels similarly justified in his desire because it is upheld by the sacred principle of equality. A direct conflict of interests develops. If the restaurant owner is forced to serve the black customer, he then loses, to some degree, his right to property. If the black customer is refused service, then, in this situation, he is effectively less equal than the customers who are served.

The clash between property rights and liberty or equality has arisen again and again throughout American history. Because conflicting values are concerned, the problem can only be resolved by delicately balancing each. At times in American history, preference has been given to the individual's right to property, as in the nineteenth-century issue of slavery. Now, with recent civil-rights legislation, welfare systems, protection of defendants' rights, and concern over economic security, the emphasis has shifted to the ideal of equality. For example, up until the 1930s, the federal government outlawed attempts by workers to form unions on the grounds that such attempts amounted to illegal conspiracies which abridged the property rights of industrialists. Today, however, the courts uphold many

*Demonstrations demand that the individual values of equality
and freedom replace the protection of property.*

laws that protect the rights of the working man, including those protecting his
freedom to organize unions. Yet it must be recognized that this shift in emphasis
represents no permanent solution to the dilemma; the basic theoretical conflict
between property and individual rights still exists, and the overwhelming difficulty
encountered by government in enforcing civil-rights legislation in sensitive areas
such as housing only serves to draw attention to its persistence.

The Threat to Limited Government:
Bad Things in Big Packages

"Big government," "big business," and "bureaucracy" are the catchwords of many a modern editorial. They are, as concepts, interrelated. Government is in a sense a very big business—the biggest spender and employer in the nation. It is, moreover, a growing concern. The number of civilians employed by the federal government has more than doubled since 1940, while expenditures have more than quadrupled during the same period.[6] In the fiscal year 1972–1973, federal government expenditures will total more than $230 billion, which is greater than the total amount spent by households, businesses, and government combined (our Gross National Product) only twenty-five years ago.[7]

As government grows larger, it becomes, like most other organizations, more bureaucratic in structure. And as government spends more each year, its relationship to the economy—and to the businesses that dominate the economy— becomes more complex. In fact, the growth of big government is historically related to the growth of big business. Both are, in part, responses to technological advances which made possible the appearance of a truly mass society. And, to some extent, the growth of government is a response to increased needs for control of big business and the economy in general.

During the nation's early years, small businesses presided over local markets, occasionally making regional inroads; a healthy competition between local enterprises was assumed to operate in the public's favor. Insofar as government addressed itself to business, it played a largely protective role, mainly in international matters. Thus, Congress passed laws to provide tariffs and subsidize shipping interests and railroads in order to encourage the growth of the country's infant industries. By the late nineteenth century, however, many business firms, particularly those in steel, railroads, coal, iron, and other industries essential to economic growth, had expanded to national scale, and seemed capable of imposing their wishes on the economy. It was suddenly possible for a single firm—directed, perhaps, by a single strong-willed entrepreneur—to effectively curtail competition in an industry, thereby affecting large segments of the population. Thus, for example, Andrew Carnegie, the son of a Scottish immigrant, was able to control large segments of the steel industry through the clever creation of trusts; and the Vanderbilt family, by the turn of the century, had managed to accumulate twenty-one thousand miles of railroad lines.[8]

Small businessmen and farmers appealed to the government to protect their interests by breaking up some of the giant monopolies—and, indeed, this seemed like the democratic thing for government to do. In 1890, in pursuance of a stubborn attachment to the traditional laissez-faire position of many Americans, the Sherman Anti-Trust Act was passed to restore competition by breaking up some of the large trusts. The targets of the Act were the huge holding companies and corporate giants which, by that time, virtually monopolized entire industries. But enforcement of the antitrust laws has been very uneven throughout Ameri-

---

[6] *Statistical Abstract of the United States, 1969* (Washington, D.C.: Department of Commerce, 1969), pp. 397 and 407.

[7] *Economic Report of The President,* January 1972.

[8] Gustavus Myers, *Ending of the Great American Fortunes* (New York: Messner, 1939), p. 275.

Ecologists argue that granting tax advantages to multibillion-dollar oil companies deprives the public of environmental cleanup funds while subsidizing polluters.

can history. Teddy Roosevelt was notorious for his trust-busting activities, as was Woodrow Wilson. But few administrations since have seriously tried to break up the large corporations that control major industries, such as the automobile, steel, and communications industries.

For an institution with so much power and influence, big business seems singularly resistant to regulation on behalf of the general public. Many believe that the large corporation is simply not accountable to the public. As a Ralph Nader study has pointed out,

Highly concentrated corporations in tightly knit industries, with but a few rivals, are insulated from the public because their wealth buys legal and scientific apologists, because they are generally bigger and more powerful than government agencies making half-hearted attempts at confrontation, and because they can direct consumer choices away from environmental issues.[9]

Because big business is not truly accountable to the public or amenable to government regulation, it cannot be made to allocate its funds toward goods or services which, though not immediately profitable, are believed necessary for the public welfare. As a result, providing such services has become the business of the government. As economist John Kenneth Galbraith noted, "Services that are unneeded by the industrial system, and which, unavoidably, the state must render, suffer from a negative discrimination. Soap and dentrifices are accorded importance by the industrial system. . . . Public clinics, which may do more for health, are the beneficiaries of no similar promotion. They suffer accordingly."[10]

---

[9] John C. Esposito, *Vanishing Air,* introduction by Ralph Nader (New York: Grossman, 1970), p. 299.
[10] John Kenneth Galbraith, *The New Industrial State* (New York: Signet, 1967), p. 352.

Consequently, critics of American society argue that one of the greatest challenges to the democratic system seems to involve either making big business more responsive to social needs, or making big government more efficient in providing for them. With either alternative, it is hoped that decisions affecting the allocation of resources can be premised on cooperative, humanistic values, as well as on those of profit, comfort, and immediate gratification. This hope, of course, presupposes individual, as well as political, reform.

Rule of Law, or Rule of Violence?

Americans profess to respect the rule of law and to favor peaceful change over violent revolution. In practice, however, they often tend, both literally and figuratively, to shoot first and ask questions later. There seems to be something in the American consciousness that respects physical force as an ultimate solution to any argument. The civilized gentlemen of Boston, Philadelphia, and New York who wrote our Constitution and declared their defiance of England in elo-

The strength of police preparedness in response to late-sixties campus and ghetto revolts has intensified fear of spiraling violence in American life.

quent prose may be central to our heritage, but our hearts thrill more to names like Earp, Hickok, Crockett, and Boone than they do to Madison, Jay, and Dickinson. In our own time, the record of violence in America is disturbing. The assassinations of John and Robert Kennedy, Malcolm X, Medgar Evers, and Martin Luther King, Jr., sickened the nation. So has the more general violence which in the late 1960s erupted in the ghettos, on college campuses, in the nation's capital, and, sporadically, in cities all over the country. Certainly, we are not alone in venting our frustrations and aggressions in violent acts. But America's history of violence is nothing in which we can take pride.

Thus, although professing a firm commitment to the rule of law, Americans on numerous occasions have turned to violence as a means of achieving a desired end. Sometimes this violence has been carried out in the name of national causes, such as the Revolution or the Civil War; sometimes it has been in response to injustices that our laws seemed to perpetuate, such as the labor riots of the nineteenth century or the black riots of the 1960s. But at other times violence in America has been brutal or senseless, as with the massacre of Indian tribes or with the Kent State University killings.

The Nature of Democracy

The disparity between the ideal and the actual in American political culture is also reflected in concepts about the nature of democracy. *Democracy* is a word singularly resistant to precise definition. Most people agree that they are in favor of it, and that the United States is a leading example of one, but they do not agree about just what a democracy is. One person says that a democracy is a state where each citizen receives equal representation; another that a democracy allows each person to do whatever he likes, provided he does not injure anyone else; a third claims that democracy is a system in which there is justice for all; and still another that democracy is a condition in which wealth is equally distributed.

One problem involved in attempting to define democracy is the strong emotional attachment that most Americans have toward the term. Adherents to a diversity of political philosophies all insist on labeling themselves "democratic," because democracy in the political realm is virtually synonymous with good. For example, although a member of the New Left and a member of the John Birch society would both profess a belief in democracy, it is likely that, were they to compare their beliefs, they would immediately find themselves in disagreement.

Yet however difficult it may be to arrive at an objective definition of *democracy,* most political theorists agree that it is worthwhile to persist in trying to define this elusive term, for the simple reason that any theoretical discussion must begin with some workable understanding of basic concepts. Therefore, we will try, if not to arrive at a final definition of the term *democracy,* then at least to explore some of the meanings that various thinkers have ascribed to it.

Democracy is derived from the Greek words *demos,* meaning "the people," and *kratis,* meaning "authority." To the ancient Greeks, *democracy* literally meant "government by the many." Democracy as it was practiced in the city-state of ancient Athens, or in more recent times in the New England town meeting, or in many present-day experimental communities, is the embodiment of what is meant by "government by the people." It is a form called "direct democracy" in which the people themselves make all decisions. Representation is not necessary, because each citizen is able to voice his opinions and directly make the binding political decisions for his society. However, direct democracy is certainly not practicable for a modern state, because of the enormous difference in size between even the smallest of present-day countries and a Greek city-state, a New England village, or a commune. Thus, although direct participation may be a desirable quality in government, we must eliminate it from the list of practical alternatives for a modern nation, simply on the grounds that it is unrealistic, given contemporary conditions.

Clearly then, in attempting to define democracy, we must decide on our criteria for selecting a definition. Are we looking for a description of how decisions are made in a political system generally agreed to be democratic, or for an idealized description of what ought to be? Either approach, taken by itself, may be seen to contain difficulties. If we start by describing the procedures of a representative democratic government, which one shall we choose? The United States is commonly considered a democracy, but are we to admit the People's Democratic Republic of Korea, where things are done quite differently, into the same category, simply on the basis of its inclusion of the word *democratic* in its national title? And if we do not, how do we know we are not simply being subjective, defining *democracy* in terms of what is familiar to us, according to what is acceptable in our own cultural context? The alternate approach, that of beginning with an idealized set of conditions, is equally problematic. On what are we to base these requirements? Clearly no definition can exist as pure abstraction. Our ideas must originate somewhere, and, even if we begin with the assumptions of other political theories, we will be tying our definition to the political experiences and events which shaped their ideas.

Before attempting to define *democracy,* we must also confront several other problems. One is the question of how narrowly we are to consider the term *political.* For example, if equality is considered to be a defining feature of democracy, are we referring only to such things as equal voting rights and equal protection under the laws, or are we also referring to economic and social equality? The lines separating the provinces labeled "political," "economic," and "social" tend to blur, further complicating the process of definition.

A third theoretical problem is whether a definition of democracy should focus on political procedures or on the outcome of those procedures. Strictly, we might say that *democracy* refers only to certain methods of decision-making. But suppose the representatives of a people, duly elected by democratic means, were to institute programs detrimental to some racial or religious minority. Would the result be democracy? And if not, why not? In other words, are we to consider only the procedures of a political system in order to define what is democratic, or must we also consider the quality of the outputs of that system? Is *democracy* merely a label for one political system among many, or must it, of necessity, involve a value judgment?

To answer these questions, we will begin by considering two ways in which different political theorists have defined democracy. Both of these definitions are essentially ideals; that is, they are abstracted from actual experience and do not purport to account for everything that has happened or could happen in the political system as it actually exists. Nevertheless, they do remain within the bounds of what is realistically possible. The two definitions differ in that one (the traditional) focuses narrowly on the realm of political procedures, while the other (the egalitarian) encompasses the social and economic spheres as well as the political, and is concerned with specific policy rather than with political procedures.

The Traditional Definition of Democracy

Because direct control of government by the people is not feasible, given the conditions of most modern states, today's democracies are forced to resort to a second-best method, namely, representation and elections as a means of granting the people ultimate control over political decision-makers. It must be noted that the key word here is *control*, and not merely *influence*. A king, a dictator, or an oligarchy may be sensitive to the needs and wants of the people and be dedicated to ruling with the people's interest in mind. However, unless the form of government provides mechanisms insuring popular control by the people, there can be no guarantee that the rulers will adhere to their benevolent policies, or that the inheritors of their authority will not put into effect policies quite different from those desired by the people.

The most effective way to insure popular control of decision-makers, short of a system of physical or economic rewards and punishments, is for the people to choose the political leaders they want to represent them. According to the traditional definition of democracy, this power is best exercised through the institutionalization of free and relatively frequent elections. This does not mean that the voters have direct control over policy issues at elections (although, in certain cases, such as referenda, they do have such control). However, in a democracy, popular influence upon policies is widespread and may take many legitimate forms, such as the influence of organized interest groups.

One Man, One Vote Ideally, democracy is a system in which each person's view is counted equally. In fact, however, it is not possible to insure that every citizen in a democracy will have equal political influence. The publisher or editor of a newspaper will have more influence than the citizens who read it. A well-informed and articulate person will have more influence than one who does not possess these qualities, particularly if he has access to some means of public expression. A political candidate who has vast sums at his disposal will have the advantage over one who is running his campaign on a shoestring. The problem of public influence is an enormously complex one, and though many seeming injustices exist, it is doubtless true that an attempt to enforce complete uniformity of influence would result in more freedoms lost than gained. What we can insure is a basic form of political equality, guaranteeing each citizen equal voting power.

According to the traditional definition of democracy, every adult citizen has the right to vote, each citizen casts one vote, and every vote is counted equally. In essence this makes the voting booth a place of absolute equality, where each person may express his preferences in privacy, according to his judgment alone, and with exactly the same effect as every other citizen. Thus, it is hoped, the equality of the voting booth offsets the welter of conflicting, unevenly weighted influences that exist on the other side of the curtain.

Free Elections Voting equality in itself is not enough to insure democratic representation. This is so because votes in themselves, no matter how freely cast or honestly counted, are only so much raw material in the electoral process. Unless the people are presented with a meaningful choice of candidates, an election is no more than a deceptive simulation of popular control.

In order for an election to be meaningful, there must be a free choice among alternatives; candidates must be free to run for office, to make their policies known publicly, and to criticize the present officeholders, as well as the candidates against whom they are running. Moreover, voters cannot be coerced or intimidated (to an extent, the secret ballot provides a guarantee of this right), and they must have free access to competing ideas and viewpoints. These freedoms can be summarized as the fundamental political freedoms of speech and assembly, and the freedom to petition government for redress of grievances. It is only when these freedoms are assured that elections in a democratic state can function as open forums through which the opinions and wishes of the people can be honestly determined, rather than as prearranged shows of popular support to bolster the power of those already in authority.

Majority Rule and Minority Rights In a democracy, political power is won through the vote of a majority or, in some cases, a plurality.[11] But once the election is over and the votes counted, the decisions of that majority must be binding on all citizens, whether they contributed to it or not. No matter how disagreeable or unwise the minority may find the policies of the majority, it must abide by them. Otherwise the election will again have no meaning. On the other hand, it is necessary to guard against majority tyranny; the opposition cannot be abolished, or silenced, by the majority, nor can it be denied the right to work through peaceful means to change policy or to replace the majority in office. In this way, a balance is struck between unified, effective leadership and free, responsible dissent.

The Egalitarian Definition of Democracy

So far, in describing the traditional definition of democracy, we have concentrated on the procedures of government. Implicit in the traditional definition is the faith that, given a government which abides by the rules of free elections, majority rule, and minority rights, a maximum state of equality will result, bringing the greatest good to the greatest number. Moreover, the traditional definition assumes that only under the operation of these procedures will there be progress, as people learn from experience and improve in making decisions. Implicit also in this definition is the conviction that to bring about material well-being in a way which transgresses the procedural rules would be to remove those safeguards which protect a people from tyranny, exchanging long-term benefits for mere panaceas. To put it another way, the traditional definition of democracy emphasizes means rather than ends.

The egalitarian definition reverses this balance. It holds that democracy is a political system that maximizes the goal of equality, but this definition is less prescriptive concerning the means by which equality is to be brought about. It is more critical of the substance of policy than of the procedures of government. Since it is concerned with the outputs of government as opposed to the inputs, it also widens the sphere being considered, to include social and economic conditions as well as political considerations.

Those who define democracy in egalitarian terms would contend that the question of how benefits are to be distributed among the people is the most fundamental issue in a democracy. Unless there is a high degree of equality in the basic social,

---

[11] A plurality exists when the number of votes cast for a candidate (in a contest of more than two candidates) is greater than the number cast for any other candidate, but not more than half the total number of votes cast.

economic, and political conditions, a society can hardly be called democratic. Since the United States, as we have seen, is far from perfect in this regard, supporters of the egalitarian position would contend that their viewpoint is more pertinent to the needs of Americans than the remote and theoretical concerns of the traditionalists.

In actuality both views are important, and partisans of either would probably admit that each is incomplete without the other. While it is true that no system of constitutional freedoms can guarantee citizens equality in the actual conditions of their lives, and that many injustices can occur in a state which meticulously follows democratic procedures, it is also true that a nation which is willing to use any means in order to achieve equal outcomes cannot rightfully be called democratic.

American Politics: How Democratic?

The two definitions of democracy considered so far are abstract. The political reality in the United States is somewhat different: there are certain limits on the freedoms of speech and assembly; voting is sometimes meaningless when little difference exists between the two candidates: and there is a significant amount of inequality in income, living standards, education, and justice. In turning to actualities, then, we must try to determine just how democratic America really is. There are essentially two basic schools of thought regarding an evaluation of the American political system. One such school of thought is that of pluralism — which is essentially a "group" interpretation of American politics.

The Pluralist Viewpoint

Because most Americans share common interests with some other members of society, whether on the basis of race, religion, profession, or economics, their natural tendency is to form groups to protect those interests. As a member of a group, the individual is better able to bring his particular needs, concerns, and grievances before a wider audience and eventually to win the attention of governmental decision-makers. Pluralist theory approves of citizens' membership in groups, for otherwise they would constitute an ill-directed mass, susceptible to the emotional appeals of demagogues. Pluralism also encourages a citizen's belonging to more than one group. If a person's loyalties are multiple, he will most likely be cross-pressured on certain issues by the different groups to which he belongs. This cross-pressuring will better enable him to see the other side of an issue, to soften an otherwise hard-line position, and to reach agreement through a process of compromise.

Compromise, in fact, is the keynote of the pluralist theory. It presupposes a system in which power is widely dispersed, not only in government, but also in society. Conflict between groups is considered natural and desirable, as long as it is carried out according to an accepted system of bargaining and negotiating. Policy decisions resulting from this process must necessarily represent compromises between the different groups concerned and, as such, may be considered to be a public consensus and, therefore, agreeable to all.

One important by-product of the bargaining-compromise process is that all groups involved must be committed to the "rules of the game." Since, in a pluralist society, the bargaining-compromise process offers the most effective method of bringing about change, a group wishing to further its interests will, theoretically, think twice before taking unfair advantage which will alienate it from the other groups. This adherence to a common set of ground rules tends to stabilize society while keeping open as many avenues of change as possible.

Although pluralists believe that political power should be widely dispersed, they do not insist that it be evenly distributed throughout society. Some will always devote more time, energy, and resources to politics than others, and thus exert greater political influence. But as long as the same groups do not dominate in all areas of public and private life, the system will be a democratic one. Pluralists maintain that this condition is achieved in the United States.

In some respects the pluralist system may be said to be the political complement to the capitalist free market economy. Like capitalism, it thrives on rivalry among competitors governed by a basic, minimal set of rules. It advocates equal opportunity but not necessarily equality, and, like capitalism, it encourages the individual to use the resources at his disposal in order to secure the benefits he desires. Finally, it assumes that a self-balancing mechanism functions within the political system, closely akin to the "invisible hand" that is said to guide a capitalist economy. As long as various groups are allowed to compete with one another on a relatively equal basis, approximation of the democratic ideal will prevail.

Pluralist Democracy in America: Myth or Reality?

Like the free market economy which it resembles, pluralist doctrine has come under attack in recent years by critics who hold that it is not an accurate description of how the political system in the United States actually operates. These critics charge that the American political process is an inadequate system that masks inherent injustices in society and hinders beneficial change. Sociologist C. Wright Mills was one of the first to draw attention to the inconsistencies between classical pluralist theory and the actual political situation in contemporary America. Mills saw America not as a collection of diverse interest groups maintaining a balance of power among themselves, but as a highly stratified society in which a minority of organized, powerful, and frequently irresponsible elites secures most of the important decision-making functions for itself, while encouraging a state of impotence in the levels below. "At the top," he wrote, "there has emerged an elite of power. The middle levels are a drifting set of stalemated, balancing forces: the middle does not link the bottom with the top. The bottom of this society is politically fragmented, and increasingly powerless."[12]

Central to the critique of pluralism is the accusation that the most powerful groups in American society, far from representing a great diversity of interests, are severely biased in their points of view, and in actuality, serve to prevent many urgent problems from surfacing into the arena of articulate debate. These problems, chiefly those that affect the alienated and disadvantaged, remain unvoiced, often unformulated. Those who suffer feel them acutely enough; yet the organizations that are available to these people are not structured in such a way as to allow them to gain a fair hearing in the public forum. Because their problems remain unvoiced, the public, which hears little of them, is free to assume that they are of little consequence—and the situation is thus perpetuated.

In addition, critics of pluralism point to the fact that only a small portion of the population is actually interested in participating in politics. This minority

---

[12] C. Wright Mills, *The Power Elite* (New York: Oxford University Press, 1959), p. 324.

*Government building programs have not always provided
for those dislocated by the clearance of old structures.*

is made up chiefly of those from the higher social, economic, and educational
levels; they are the people who read newspapers and journals perceptively, who
form opinions about the forces and events that shape their lives, and who join
parties and interest groups in the hope of applying pressure on those in authority.
The rest of the population are rather apathetic, exerting little or no force in the
bargaining process. A number of studies of local communities such as Atlanta,
Georgia, and Muncie, Indiana, have concluded that a small group of people tend
to control all of public policy in these towns. For example, sociologist Floyd Hunter
concluded that 40 men ran Atlanta at the time he made his study (1952). More
recent research on community power structures focuses on the institutional
aspects of power which tend to benefit a small elite and systematically exclude
the poor from participation in public decisions.

There is a group of political observers, however, who, while admitting that the
mass of society wields no appreciable power in the decision-making process and
that public policy is largely guided by an influential few, still see no cause for
disillusionment or despair; instead, they hope to improve the system from within,
while retaining inequalities in the structure. Although they differ from one
another in some of their ideas, these critics all share the conviction that those
who form the elite—the top executives, labor leaders, heads of large secular and
religious organizations—ought not to be deposed, but rather encouraged or forced
to be "their better selves."

Some of the proponents of this view argue that even if elites do dominate, they
are still competing elites, and thus their dominance does not really deny the
pluralist demand that decisions be made through group interaction, bargaining,
and compromise. Susanne Keller, for example, maintained that "these elites

critically examine—and thereby check each other's actions and decisions. Thus limited power leads to limited abuses."[13]

Moreover, other observers have become disillusioned with the political knowledge and judgment of the common man. They see in such phenomena as the McCarthyism of the fifties evidence that the average citizen is not sufficiently schooled in democratic theory to recognize flagrant abuses to his freedoms: given the opportunity, he will easily fall under the sway of an unscrupulous demagogue. These critics point to studies which show that democratic ideals have not sunk very deeply into the consciousness of those of limited education.[14] They suggest that our political ideals may be safer in the hands of an educated, responsible elite, and that the democratic process may indeed be more successful without the participation of the uninformed, politically ambivalent masses.

Competing Ideologies of the 1970s

One of the virtues of pluralism is that it is an open-ended rather than a closed system. It allows for the formation of new groups as well as debate between already existing ones. If, in recent years, we have seen an apparent failure on the part of established groups to deal with the problems of the people they claim to represent, we have also seen the founding of many new groups to fill these needs. Some of these new groups, like the black militants, have emerged out of a long history of acknowledged social injustice; their rise to power, though alarming to some, is clearly the result of the chronic neglect, by other groups, of certain urgent and serious problems. Other groups, like the women's liberation advocates, have arisen in response to injustices so deeply imbedded in the social order that they have escaped the notice of the public and have been accepted without question as part of the status quo.

A number of these new groups have been lumped together by political commentators under the collective title "The New Left." The New Left is a diverse and eclectic movement which has included such organizations as SDS and the Weathermen, numerous antiwar groups, student groups, black liberationists, advocates of women's liberation, and ecology groups. In general, the New Left condemns the uses to which science and technology have been put. In doing so, it rejects the materialistic base of American society—especially the overconsumption of frivolous goods and services at the expense of more fundamental human needs. In the political system, the New Left attacks the clumsy, unresponsive nature of the bureaucratic state. It sees man as atomized and alienated.

In response to these alleged failures of American society, the New Left advocates several alternative goals. One is that of community; members of the New Left seek to replace the traditional American values of competition and self-interest with those of cooperation and brotherhood. In this sense, the goals of the New Left are idealistic and humanistic.

As an alternative political organization, the New Left advocates a system of decentralized, participatory democracy. In SDS's Port Huron statement, the first

---

[13] Susanne Keller, *Beyond the Ruling Class: Strategic Elites in Modern Society* (New York: Random House, 1963), pp. 273–274.

[14] See, for example, James W. Prothro and Charles M. Grigg, "Fundamental Principles of Democracy: Bases of Agreement and Disagreement," *Journal of Politics* XXII (May 1960), pp. 276–294.

New Left manifesto, the authors proclaimed: "We would replace power rooted
in possession, privilege, or circumstance by power and uniqueness rooted in love,
reflectiveness, reason, and creativity. As a social system we seek the establishment
of a democracy of individual participation."[15] Thus the New Left is attempting
to provide alienated individuals with a direct voice in the decision-making process.
Their primary aim is to allow the people of a society to control its political institutions. To bring about this goal the New Left proposes to redirect the focus of
the electoral system from the national to the community level. Majority rule would
remain the principle of decision-making, but the boundaries of the constituencies
would be narrowed in order to enable all to participate in decisions. The result
would be that groups which are now in a minority on a city, state, or nationwide
scale might become majorities within their own communities and, therefore,
able to control the forces that affect their lives.

---

[15] Quoted by Arnold S. Kaufman in "Participatory Democracy: Ten Years Later," in *The Bias of Pluralism*,
edited by William E. Connolly (New York: Atherton Press, 1969), p. 203.

*"Look, Son, I'm a far-right conserva-
tive and you're a far-left radical.
O.K.? So let's you and me go out
and beat up some liberals."*

New Yorker, *September 4, 1971*

Essentially members of the New Left are criticizing the "liberal" (or pluralist) ideology that dominates American political thinking. They are not the only group that has attacked liberalism from a leftist ground. Communists have long berated liberalism as the last desperate effort of capitalism to save itself. What is interesting in the New Left criticism is that it has adopted some of the arguments formerly employed by conservative critics of liberalism—the argument in favor of decentralization of authority being a primary example. The New Left challenge, moreover, has been much more successful than the former Communist challenge. Today, even the most cynical critic of New-Left ideology must admit that it constitutes a real force for change, drawing as it does on the powers of a more general dissatisfaction.

The New Left, however, has not gone uncriticized. Many maintain that adherents to its ideology are too romantic and unrealistic in the alternative values they propose. Liberals, for example, often argue that the goals of political decentralization and participatory democracy are quixotic and largely oblivious to certain important considerations which must figure into any serious proposal to revamp the American democratic process. William Pfaff, in criticizing the New Left, asked:

How is economic rationality to be reconciled with a serious decentralization of economic authority? How is the administration of very large, horizontally integrated and interdependent social groups accomplished if real power is radically decentralized? The solution surely involves a challenge to the existing priority of values in our society. The pursuit of GNP, growth, "development," and popular affluence may simply be inconsistent with the forms of social organization which people profess to want. Are the people of the big industrial states really ready to accept the consequences of what they say they want? There are formidable problems of political and economic theory as well as of political practice involved here which the publicists of the New Politics . . . hardly have begun to acknowledge.[16]

---

[16] William Pfaff, "The Decline of Liberal Politics," *Commentary* (October 1969), pp. 49–50.

In general, liberals acknowledge that the existing political, economic, and social order has serious failings. However, they maintain that the established political institutions and procedures, which allow for orderly change, are preferable to the chaos that would ensue if traditional values were abandoned.

To deal with the challenge of the New Left to the liberal tradition in America represents more than simply an attempt to make this book "up to date." As we have said, the study of politics transcends the classroom and the confines of academic debate; it is the very stuff of our daily existence; it affects the way we live now. In the course of this book we shall try to answer questions such as those proposed by the New Left. We shall provide a framework for evaluating to what extent democracy exists in the United States, whether or not a power elite exists, if liberalism is any longer a viable alternative, and what the prospects are for peaceful and progressive change in American politics.

SUGGESTED READING

Bachrach, Peter. *The Theory of Democratic Elitism: A Critique* (Boston: Little, Brown, 1967). Tracing the origins ofthe theory of "democratic elitism," the author presents a scholarly critique of this theory and suggests some alternative principles of democracy.

Braybrooke, David. *Three Tests for Democracy: Personal Rights, Human Welfare, Collective Preference* (New York: Random House, 1968). The author argues that the United States and Canada fail to be democratic societies by the three tests he formulates.

Connolly, William E., ed. *The Bias of Pluralism* (New York: Atherton, 1969). A collection of essays critical of pluralism and calling for an increase in participatory democracy and social change.

Dolbeare, Kenneth M., and Patricia Dolbeare. *American Ideologies: The Competing Political Beliefs of the 1970s* (Chicago: Markham, 1971). A well-organized overview of the major political ideologies of the 1970s and how they relate to one another. The discussion includes capitalism, liberalism, reform liberalism, black liberation, the New Left, American Marxism, and conservatism.

Downs, Anthony. *An Economic Theory of Democracy* (New York: Harper & Row, 1957). An economist sets up logical requirements for democratic government and examines various aspects of the model from the point of view of economic theory.

Galbraith, John Kenneth. *The New Industrial State* (New York: Houghton Mifflin, 1967). Written by one of America's leading liberals, this book sets out to show that the Soviet Union and the United States are getting more and more alike through the development of technology and bureaucracy.

Goodman, Paul. *People or Personnel* and *Like a Conquered Province* (New York: Random House, 1968). Collection of essays presenting suggestions for changes to improve the quality of life and develop a sense of community.

Harrington, Michael. *Toward a Democratic Left: A Radical Program for a New Majority Party* (Baltimore: Pelican, 1968). A discussion of how a new democratic coalition may be formed, written by the Chairman of the American Socialist Party.

Hartz, Louis. *Liberal Tradition in America* (New York: Harcourt Brace Jovanovich, 1955). The author interprets the evolution of American political thought since the Revolution. Various stages in the evolution of the liberal tradition are analyzed.

Keniston, Kenneth. *The Uncommitted* (New York: Harcourt Brace Jovanovich, 1965). The author shows how youth is alienated in the United States, defining alienation as a rejection of the dominant values in society.

Marcuse, Herbert. *One-Dimensional Man: Studies in the Ideology of Advanced Industrial Society* (Boston: Beacon Press, 1964). Essays arguing that American capitalism is oppressive and calling for people to drop out of the system as a way of changing it.

Mayo, Henry B. *Introduction to Democratic Theory* (New York: Oxford University Press, 1960). A readable discussion of the meaning of democratic theory, touching upon the nature of politics, the problems of defining democracy, Athenian direct democracy, political equality, the majority principle, and other selected aspects of political theory.

Megill, Kenneth A. *The New Democratic Theory* (New York: The Free Press, 1970). Radical democratic theory in which the author calls for a new democratic coalition of the poor, blacks, students, and the young, to begin a new society in which there is participatory democracy.

Mills, C. Wright. *The Power Elite* (New York: Oxford University Press, 1956). In paperback. Analysis of American society, including the author's view that government is controlled by a number of elite groups (military, industrial, and political), and that these groups tend to consider each other's views in decision-making.

Wolfe, Robert P. *In Defense of Anarchism* (New York: Harper & Row, 1970). In paperback. A well-written book presenting a critique of democratic theory. The author attempts to resolve the conflict between the state and the individual and concludes that the "moral autonomy of the individual" cannot be made compatible with the "legitimate authority of the state."

2

FRAMEWORK OF AMERICAN POLITICS: THE CONSTITUTION

To most students of American government the Constitution is a symbol of continuity, a durable but flexible testament of an established order. Yet, for its time, the Constitution was a revolutionary document, one which Richard Henry Lee, a Revolutionary leader, thought was "evidently calculated totally to change, in time, our condition as a people." Lee, criticizing the document, noted that

Whether such a change can ever be effected in any manner; whether it can be effected without convulsions and civil wars; whether such a change will not totally destroy the liberties of this country—time only can determine. . . .[1]

Obviously, the change which Lee feared has been effected: that a civil war eventually occurred is fact; that other "convulsions" have occurred is probably debatable; that liberties have expanded, instead of diminishing, is a matter of historical record. But all this has evolved through time, as Lee anticipated, and with time has come both overwhelming reverence and slight suspicion for the document that created our system of government.

Underlying the reverence of Americans for the Constitution is the idea that all power must be regulated by law, and the suspicion that without the protection of the law, freedom and security may well not exist. Much of the public distrusts elected officials—who are fallible and thus corruptible—and relies solidly on the institutions of government and on the checks and balances set up by the Constitution for political solutions to the problem of authority.

There are, in contrast, many others who distrust the people as a whole. Interestingly enough these elitists, too, place their faith in the checks of the Constitution, which they perceive as safeguards against the fickle popular will. In this chapter and those that follow, we shall try to determine if the Constitution, as originally written and as applied over nearly two centuries, is a democratic or an elitist document, and if the nation that is governed by it is democratic or elitist in nature.

The Declaration of Independence

Any consideration of the Constitution must take into account the Declaration of Independence, for that document contains much of the philosophy which underlay the thinking of many of those who were involved in the drafting of the Constitution. As Ralph Barton Perry has written:

While the Federal Constitution represented a different mood and emphasis, it did not reject the doctrine of the Declaration of Independence. In the last analysis, the sovereignty lay in the will of the people—if possible their thoughtful will, but nonetheless their will.[2]

The Declaration of Independence drafted by Thomas Jefferson, however, was by no means representative of the unanimous will of the people. War with Britain had broken out following an encounter between several companies of British troops and a band of militia and minutemen at Lexington, Massachusetts, on April 19, 1775. Although resentment had smoldered for many years, few Americans talked openly about separation. But attitudes were changed by the hardships of war, the terrible casualties at Bunker Hill, and the cutting off of colonial foreign

---

[1] Paul L. Ford, ed., *Pamphlets on the Constitution of the United States* (Brooklyn, N.Y., 1888), p. 283.

[2] Ralph Barton Perry, "The Declaration of Independence," in *The Declaration of Independence and the Constitution,* edited by Earl Latham (Boston: Heath, 1956), p. 8.

The members of the committee to draft the Declaration of Independence were (left to right) Thomas Jefferson, John Adams, Benjamin Franklin, Robert Livingstone (seated), and Roger Sherman.

trade by the British. Demands for separation became outspoken, but many maintained a stubborn loyalty, even after the appearance of Thomas Paine's pamphlet *Common Sense,* which inflamed passions by its fiery language calling on Americans to sever ties with a corrupt and tyrannical monarchy. Thus began a bitter debate. While fellow Americans were still arguing the merits of independence, the Second Continental Congress, the representative body of the thirteen colonies, appointed a committee to draft a formal declaration of separation from the mother country. The committee consisted of five representatives, including the actual author of the document, Thomas Jefferson.

Like many Americans of his day, Jefferson had read John Locke, the great seventeenth-century philosopher of the Enlightenment, who saw democracy as a contract under which governments were obliged to protect the "natural" rights of the people. Taking his cues from Locke, the highly idealistic Jefferson wrote in the Declaration: ". . . to secure these rights, Governments are instituted among men, deriving their just powers from the consent of the governed. . . ." Locke had written that people are born with the right to "life, liberty, health . . . ," and to this he added, "and of outward things," meaning the right to property. Jefferson adapted the phrase, so that the Declaration reads, "We hold these truths to be self-evident, that all men are created equal, that they are endowed by their Creator with certain unalienable Rights, that among these are *Life, Liberty and the Pursuit of Happiness.*"

Jefferson also adapted Locke's position on the duty to abolish governments that do not protect these rights. The Declaration thus asserts, ". . . it is their [the people's] right, it is their duty to throw off such government and to provide new Guards for their future security."[3] It should be noted, however, that many historians regard the American Revolution as quite different from other revolutions, such as those in France and Russia. Crane Brinton has viewed the American rebellion as only partly a "social and class" revolution, but predominantly a "territorial-nationalist" revolution, like the Irish revolution.[4] In other words, the Revolution in America did not change the social or economic structure of the country. Since it did, however, change the political structure, it can be viewed as almost purely a political revolution.

The second major part of the Declaration of Independence enumerates grievances against King George III — suprisingly enough not against the English Parliament, which was actually responsible for the acts the colonists resented. Although the Continental Congress had criticized the sovereignty of Parliament earlier in the decade, it did not do so in the Declaration. Such statements would have appeared to attack the concept of representative government, which they upheld as an ideal. Instead they directed their criticism at the symbol of a tyrannical monarchy in the person of the weak king. The document declares that a free people could not be ruled by such a monarch:

The history of the present King of Great Britain is a history of repeated injuries and usurpations, all having in direct object the establishment of an absolute Tyranny over these states. To prove this, let Facts be submitted to a candid world. . . . A Prince, whose character is thus marked by every act which may define a Tyrant, is unfit to be the ruler of a free People.

The concluding portion of the Declaration presents a formal statement declaring the united colonies "Free and Independent States." This decision, to form an

---

[3] Jefferson commented some years after independence on the relationship between the American Revolution and the Declaration of Independence:

When forced to resort to arms for redress, an appeal to the tribunal of the world was deemed proper for our justification. This was the object of the Declaration of Independence. Not to find new principles, or new arguments, never before thought of, not merely to say things which had never been said before; but to place before mankind the common sense of the subject, in terms so plain and firm as to command their assent, and to justify ourselves in the independent stand we are compelled to take.

Quoted in Clinton Rossiter, *Seedtime of the Republic* (New York: Harcourt, Brace & World, 1953), p. 355.
[4] See Crane Brinton, *The Anatomy of Revolution* (New York: Vintage, 1952), pp. 22–36.

independent republic, was the "one truly revolutionary decision" of the colonists.[5] Discussion in the Revolutionary period led far afield into areas other than those incorporated into the Declaration. Slavery was questioned, as was the disestablishment of official religions, the rightness of hierarchy in society, and the place of "rabble" in the republic.[6] Jefferson had written into the document antislavery views which the other committee members had not deleted. He was, however, forced to eliminate them from the final draft, on the South's insistence. Also deleted were passages that denounced the British people.

The Articles of Confederation and Their Weaknesses

When the Second Continental Congress met in June 1776, Virginia's Richard Henry Lee submitted not only a resolution calling for a formal declaration of separation from the British throne, but another one calling for the establishment of a permanent federal government. Lee, a radical of his era, was fearful of too strong an executive or too centralized a government and favored great independence for each state. Even colonial "states' righters," however, were able to see the need for the protections offered by centralization. The document that resulted was the Articles of Confederation, under which the United States was governed from 1781 until the adoption of the Constitution in 1789. The Articles avoided creation of a strong central government; free of British control, most Americans did not want to repeat their experiences as colonials of a distant and despotic government. The Articles, therefore, leaned heavily toward preserving the power and rights of the former colonies, now sovereign states, and grudgingly granted a limited authority to the central government. Consequently, they were full of shortcomings.

Among the most important of these shortcomings was the failure of the Articles to give Congress the power to regulate commerce. This left each of the states free to set up its own tariff system and caused serious feuds among them over foreign trade. The tariffs established by manufacturing states to protect their goods from foreign competition were unsuccessful because nonmanufacturing states imported large quantities of foreign goods which they shipped to other states for sale at very low prices. A state that wished to protect its own infant industries against cheap foreign imports had no alternative but to establish tariff barriers against commerce with other states. A competing system of interstate tariffs and other trade barriers developed, and the central government lacked the authority either to abolish or to regulate them. If one assumes that a primary cause of the Revolutionary War was the stifling effect of British policy on colonial trade and manufacturing, one can understand why the various business groups were reluctant to support a new political system that failed to defend their interests. Moreover, the Articles offered no procedure for settling disputes between the states or disputes between a state and the central government.

Another hindrance to successful commerce was the lack of a sound, uniform money system. While the Articles did restrict coinage to the central government,

---

[5] Clinton Rossiter, *Seedtime of the Republic,* p. 314.

[6] See Bernard Bailyn, *The Ideological Origins of the American Revolution* (Cambridge, Mass.: Harvard University Press, 1967), especially Chapter VI, pp. 230–320.

they did not empower it to issue paper money, but left this up to the individual states. The monies in circulation, therefore, differed tremendously in value.

The financial resources of the central government itself were meager, to say the least. Although the Articles gave Congress power to borrow money, they denied it the right to levy taxes. Taxing power, therefore, resided solely with the state legislatures, and Congress had to rely on the states to collect and forward taxes. By 1787 some states were already overdue in payment of their share of the Revolutionary debt and the expenses of the central government. When Congress attempted to use its borrowing power, loans became increasingly difficult and expensive to negotiate; potential lenders regarded a Congress without taxing power as a poor credit risk. By the mid-1780s, the government was in default on interest payments due on some bonds, and disgusted patriots were selling their war bonds at one-tenth of their face value.

The cumbersome procedures for decision-making established by the Articles were another notable flaw. The consent of nine of the thirteen states was needed before Congress could legislate on any subject; and the unanimous consent of Congress and all the states was required to amend the Articles. Without an executive and judicial branch in the central government, the interpretation, administration, and enforcement of congressional decisions depended on the good will of the individual states. Moreover, the inability to assume that laws would be properly enforced, had detrimental effects on some of the new nation's international dealings. Under the Articles, Congress could make peace and declare war, and handle most other foreign affairs. But the weakness of the central government made it virtually impossible for the new nation to deal effectively with foreign nations in such matters as trade agreements. As long as other nations knew that Congress lacked power to enforce its will on the individual states, agreements could not be negotiated.

Finally, some believed that the Articles of Confederation did not embody the political ideals for which the Revolution was assumed to be fought. John Quincy Adams, an advocate of strong central government and a past member of the committee that had drafted the Declaration of Independence, offered this comment on the similarity between that document and the Articles of Confederation:

> *There was no congeniality of principle between the Declaration of Independence and the Articles of Confederation. The foundation of the former was a superintending Providence—the rights of man, and the constituent revolutionary power of the people. That of the latter was the sovereignty of organized power, and the independence of the separate or disunited States. The fabric of the Declaration and that of the Confederation were each consistent with its own foundation, but they could not form one consistent symmetrical edifice. . . . The cornerstone of one was* right*—that of the other was* power.[7]

The Move toward Reform

In 1785 representatives of Maryland and Virginia met to work out trade and navigation differences concerning their common borders, the Potomac River and the Chesapeake Bay. Recognizing the possibilities in such interstate negotiations, the Virginia legislature issued a call to *all* the states to convene in Annapolis,

---

[7] Alpheus T. Mason and Richard H. Leach, *In Quest of Freedom: American Political Thought and Practice* (Englewood Cliffs, N.J.: Prentice-Hall, 1964), pp. 95–96.

Maryland, in 1786 to discuss uniform trade regulations. Judged by attendance, the Annapolis Convention was a failure, for only twelve delegates from the five leading commercial states appeared. Yet in what it ultimately achieved, it was of enormous significance. Prodded by Alexander Hamilton of New York, the delegates adopted a report that defined not merely the trade problems, but all the defects of the Articles of Confederation, and called on Congress to meet again in Philadelphia in May of the following year, inviting the states to send delegates for the purpose of correcting the inadequacies of the Articles.

The first reaction to the proposed Annapolis Convention was lukewarm. A few historians have argued that even then some states suspected that what Hamilton actually had in mind was not a mere revamping of the old Articles, but the design of a completely new government with a very strong central power base. These states were, therefore, reluctant to support the Philadelphia meeting. But by the fall and winter of 1786–1787, certain dramatic events had focused attention on the inability of the individual states to deal with their problems and thus succeeded in frightening men of property who exerted a major influence in Congress and in most state legislatures.

The crisis arose out of an economic decline, which made it difficult for many farmers to meet their mortgage and tax payments. In Rhode Island the debtors

Angered by the policy of imprisoning debtors, the farmers of Massachusetts organized Shays's Rebellion.

gained control of the legislature; issued a tremendous amount of paper money, which became almost valueless; and subsequently made it an offense for businessmen or creditors to refuse this paper money at face value in payment of debts. Rhode Island's Supreme Court, controlled by the propertied classes, ruled that the new laws were in violation of the state constitution. But the trend to more leniency toward debtors continued to spread. There was talk in other states of extending the time limit for payment of mortgages, and of banning imprisonment for debt.

Apparently these moves did not come quickly enough to satisfy the debtors. In Massachusetts a band of farmers facing imprisonment for debt were led by Daniel Shays, a former Revolutionary War officer, in a rebellion in which they blocked the doorways to courthouses to prevent the judges from foreclosing their property. Shays's Rebellion was promptly put down by a band of mercenaries• hired by local well-to-do citizens.

But the occurrence of armed rebellion and the violation of property rights were enough to propel fifty-five delegates, representing twelve of the states, to journey to Philadelphia in the spring of 1787.

The Illustrious Men of the Constitutional Convention

The unusual qualifications of the fifty-five delegates to the Constitutional Convention who met in Philadelphia in the summer of 1787 were widely recognized at home and abroad.[8] The French chargé d'affaires, writing to a friend, said that he had "never seen, even in Europe, an assembly more respectable for the talents, knowledge, disinterestedness and patriotism of those who compose it." Jefferson called them "an assembly of demigods," Franklin *"une assemblée des notables,"* and the *Daily Advertiser* of New York "the collective wisdom of the Continent."[9] Who were these Founding Fathers? What special qualifications did they bring to the task of writing the Constitution? Were they truly representative of the new nation?

Socially, most of the Framers came from "respectable if not always substantial"[10] families. Sixteen of the fifty-five could be characterized as aristocrats, many belonging to the first families of the nation. Their average age was forty-three, but the range was wide, from the twenty-six-year-old Jonathan Dayton of New Jersey to eighty-one-year-old Benjamin Franklin of Pennsylvania. Most were well educated: in an age when a college education was rare even among the wealthy and

---

[8] Seventy-four delegates had been appointed to the Convention by the various states, but only fifty-five finally attended. In New Hampshire, for example, four delegates were appointed, but only two appeared, the discrepancy influenced in part, perhaps, by the fact that the states were responsible for paying the expenses of the delegates, and New Hampshire's treasury was bare at the time. This information, along with much of the other description of Convention delegates that appears in this chapter, comes from Catherine Drinker Bowen, *Miracle at Philadelphia: The Story of the Constitutional Convention, May to September 1787* (Boston: Little, Brown, 1966). The material just cited is on p. 12. The actual size of each state's delegation was left up to the individual state and varied in size from the two-man New Hampshire delegation to the eight-man group from Pennsylvania. Rhode Island, pursuing a path characterized by no less than George Washington as "scandalous conduct," sent no delegates.

[9] Quoted in Clinton Rossiter, *1787: The Grand Convention* (New York: Macmillan, 1966), p. 138. Much of the vivid description of the convention delegates comes from this source.

[10] Rossiter, *1787: The Grand Convention*, p. 142.

prominent, more than half held degrees, mostly from American colleges, but also from Oxford and St. Andrews universities in Britain. Clinton Rossiter labels forty-six of the founding fathers as being somewhere between rich and comfortable, and only nine of modest or less-than-modest means. Many were investors in the usual assets of the day—land and slaves. The delegates are hard to classify by occupation, since many had two or three vocations. More than a dozen were primarily large planters or farmers, about an equal number lawyers, and eight were merchants. Only two were small farmers, and of these, one augmented his income by practicing law and surveying. Without exception, each of the delegates had some experience in government, having been "on the public payroll," either state or national, at one time or another.[11] In addition, thirty delegates had been in the Revolutionary armies; indeed, George Washington could look around the Convention Hall and see a dozen men who had served with him at the battles of Trenton or Monmouth or Yorktown.

As a group, they represented the elite of the new nation in political experience, family background, education, wealth, and occupation. Each delegate was distinguished in some way; some, by the impact of their personalities and influence, left an indelible impression on the nation's history.

Among them, George Washington, at fifty-four, was the best-known American. His reputation was based not only on his triumphant leadership of the Revolution and his position as one of the richest men in the country; he was also respected as a man of unassailable personal integrity. Standing six feet tall—in an age when the average height of American men was about five feet, five inches—handsome and commanding, he fully looked the part of a leader. Washington's intellectual gifts, however, were not outstanding,[12] and, making only two speeches throughout the entire Convention, he certainly did not dominate the proceedings. Nevertheless, his presence as chairman, a position to which he was unanimously elected, was enough to give great public acceptance and prestige to the work of the Convention from its very beginning. It was already assumed he would be President of the new nation.

James Madison has been described as "a priceless member" of the Convention. "Scrawny and pale, a bookworm and a hypochondriac," at first glance he seemed unimposing.[13] However, he had already demonstrated practical and intellectual gifts that presaged the brilliant contributions he was to make during the Convention. He had served in Congress (where he established a reputation as one of its hardest-working members) and in the lower house of the Virginia legislature and had also helped write Virginia's constitution. During the course of his career he had introduced measures pertaining to such issues as separation of church and state, public education, and the formation of new states. He was also one of the leading figures behind the organization of the Annapolis Convention that preceded the Philadelphia meeting. Madison's extensive practical experience in government was backed by vast theoretical knowledge. He had spent the period

---

[11] Forty-two of the delegates were incumbent or former members of the Congress, where they had learned to recognize the shortcomings of the Articles of Confederation.

[12] Washington's Vice President and successor, John Adams, once told the painter Gilbert Stuart, "Washington got the reputation of being a great man because he kept his mouth shut." From Samuel Eliot Morison, *The Oxford History of the American People* (New York: Oxford University Press, 1965), p. 347.

[13] The quotations are from Forrest McDonald, *Formation of the American Republic 1776–1790* (New Orleans: Pelican Publishing Co., 1965), p. 156.

James Madison   **Alexander Hamilton**

before the Convention reading widely about constitutions of either city-states or national confederations, going all the way back to early Greek and Italian times.[14]

Alexander Hamilton was already one of the most controversial figures in America at the time the Convention started. John Adams called him "the bastard brat of a Scotch Pedlar," while Talleyrand lavishly praised him as the greatest of the "choice and master spirits of the age."[15] Only in his mid-thirties, Hamilton had already established a reputation as a pamphleteer during the early days of the Revolution, as an administrator who was Washington's aide during much of the War and frequently wrote Washington's public statements, and as a politician who led the movement for the Annapolis Convention. Born in the West Indies, he lacked strong ties to any single state. Because his wartime activities made him aware of the difficulties of operating under a weak Congress, Hamilton strongly favored a powerful central government and maneuvered to head the Convention in this direction. However, the voting procedures that were established at the Convention limited his effectiveness and caused him personal embarrassment: Each state voted as a unit, and Yates and Lansing, who were Hamilton's co-members from New York and strong states'-righters, in every single instance were able to override Hamilton. Frustrated by this, Hamilton stayed away from Philadelphia during much of the Convention; but later on, back in New York, although working against great odds, he played the dominant role in achieving ratification of the Constitution.

---

[14] Catherine Drinker Bowen writes of Madison's laborious study:

> At [Madison's] request, Jefferson, who was serving as Minister to France, had sent [him] books from Paris. Madison asked for whatever "may throw light on the general constitution . . . of the several confederacies which have existed." The books arrived by the hundreds: thirty-seven volumes of the new Encyclopédie Méthodique, books on political theory and the law of nations, histories. . . . There were biographies and memoirs, histories in sets of eleven volumes. . . . Madison threw himself into a study of confederacies ancient and modern, wrote out a long essay comparing governments, with each analysis followed by a section of his own.

From Bowen, *Miracle at Philadelphia*, p. 14.

[15] Bowen, *Miracle at Philadelphia*, p. 7.

Gouverneur Morris   **Benjamin Franklin**

Two members from Pennsylvania are particularly deserving of comment.
Gouverneur Morris, born in what is today the Bronx in New York City, had moved
to Pennsylvania following a break with his family, who supported the British
cause during the War. (His half-brother was a major-general in the British army.)
An aristocrat in his political outlook, he distrusted government based on the power
of the common people. He was a tall, handsome man, lively and talkative, who
entertained dazzlingly in his bachelor's quarters in Philadelphia. His reputation
as a ladies' man was undiminished by the loss of a leg after he was run over by a
carriage in Philadelphia. Morris spoke brilliantly and often (173 speeches during
the less than four-month period of the Convention!). He was responsible for much
of the language in the final draft of the Constitution.

In world reputation, Benjamin Franklin, another Philadelphian, outshone any
other American of his day. As inventor, publisher, author, diplomat, politician,
and patriot, he had made his mark. One of the lesser-known facts about this
extraordinary man is that, during the early days of the new nation, in 1776, he
lent the government four thousand pounds of his own money, a sum that would
equal $17,760 in American money today. Because Franklin was eighty-one at the
time of the Convention, some historians have suggested that he was almost senile.
True, he was too frail to read his own speeches at the Convention (his fellow
delegate, James Wilson, read the famous call for unanimous approval of the Constitution that concluded the Convention), but his enormous prestige and diplomatic
skills even at that time doubtless contributed significantly toward smoothing out
the differences among the delegates and attaining results.

The Founding Fathers at Philadelphia were among the most illustrious men
in America, but there were others absent from the Convention who also had a
profound influence on the new nation. Some authorities claim that the original
revolutionaries were not represented at the Convention: only eight delegates were
signers of the Declaration of Independence. It is true that some of the firebrands
—Patrick Henry, Sam Adams, Tom Paine—were not present. In many cases, however, their absence seemed a matter of choice. Patrick Henry, for example, was
nominated by the Virginia legislature but refused to attend a meeting which he
believed was designed to produce an aristocratic document that would reduce the
powers of the states; he preferred instead to remain at home and fight ratification.
Tom Paine was off in Europe trying to raise money to promote his new invention,
an iron bridge. No delegates attended from Rhode Island; its state legislature
was busy issuing worthless paper money, and its politicians evidently were busy
exploiting their offices to enrich themselves—two activities likely to be discouraged

under a strong central government.[16] The frontier—the "back country" or western parts of Massachusetts, Pennsylvania, Virginia, and the Carolinas—was largely unrepresented, partly because there were no "name" politicians from those areas and partly because the frontier lacked interest in eastern political matters in general, and in a national government in particular. In addition, certain outstanding Americans were absent on business elsewhere: Jefferson was in France, and John Adams in London representing the United States in arranging trade agreements and loans. Various other distinguished gentlemen—Governor Samuel Huntington of Connecticut, the Lees of Virginia—stayed home to take care of their own affairs and the governing of their individual states. And finally, there were no direct representatives of the very poor, indentured servants, and blacks, who collectively represented a large majority of the population.

The Intentions of the Framers

Over the years, in search of a fuller understanding of the Constitution, historians have speculated about the intentions of the Convention delegates. One rather oversimplified attitude toward the Founding Fathers was prevalent during the nineteenth century. The delegates were seen as a group of "wise and virtuous men who stood splendidly above all faction, ignored petty self interest, and concerned themselves only with the freedom and well-being of their countrymen."[17] Indeed, this interpretation still prevails in a great many primary- and secondary-school textbooks.

In 1913, however, the appearance of Charles A. Beard's *An Economic Interpretation of the Constitution* questioned this idealized view. Beard claimed that economic self-interest was a strong motivating force behind the Constitution, that the Founding Fathers were primarily interested in providing a stable political climate in which their property could be protected. For example, he found old Treasury records showing that many Federalist leaders—members of the Philadelphia Convention as well as the state ratifying conventions—owned substantial amounts of Continental securities whose value would increase if a strong central government with effective taxing powers emerged. He did *not* claim that the Convention delegates single-mindedly pursued personal gain; rather, he suggested that political positions are inevitably affected by economic interests, and that this reality should be recognized in evaluating the intentions of the Framers. A second thesis developed by Beard was that the entire process of writing and ratifying the Constitution was essentially undemocratic and nonrepresentative, for only a limited number of interests were represented at the Convention, and the right to vote on the passage of the finished document was limited to property owners (meaning that suffrage extended only to those with property).

By the 1940s, many historians were "debunking" the Founding Fathers. Merrill Jensen restudied the Anti-Federalists—those who fought the Constitution and the establishment of a strong centralized government—and concluded that they had been vilified by history. Jensen saw them not only as the instigators of the Revolution but as the true democrats of the era, who represented the sentiments of

---

[16] See Rossiter, *1787: The Grand Convention*, pp. 87–89; and Bowen, *Miracle at Philadelphia*, p. 13.

[17] Stanley Elkins and Eric McKitrick, "The Founding Fathers: Young Men of the Revolution," *Political Science Quarterly*, vol. 76, no. 2. (June 1961), p. 183.

the majority in the nation against the elitist Federalists, a well-organized minority who triumphed with the adoption of a constitution which imposed a powerful central government upon the unwilling masses.[18]

In recent years, however, the conclusions of both Beard and Jensen have been questioned. Robert E. Brown produced figures to show that the right to vote during the Convention was more widely held than was contended by Beard (who considered it to be held by about 5 percent of the population), and that, in fact, Beard's own figures prove that it was more widely held. Beard had noted that some 97 percent of the people lived in rural areas, owning "a wide distribution of real property," and that these small farmers were qualified to vote as freeholders, even if they were debtors. Brown found, further, that in as many as eight or nine states the vote was not limited only to freeholders.[19]

Forrest McDonald did not totally disagree that economics played a role at the Constitutional Convention, but he challenged Beard's premise that national political differences were based on a clash between "personalty" (personal property) and "realty" (land) interests. In state after state, Federalists could not be distinguished from Anti-Federalists by the size of their property holdings, said McDonald. Nor could the economic interests involved in the creation of the Constitution be seen as a homogeneous group; rather, they were representative of specific business interests in specific places. In addition, the states themselves, each still a sovereign unit with its own interests and political leanings, had a strong influence on their respective delegates. States uneasy about their ability to survive independently were quick to ratify; those confident they could make it on their own held out longest. Thus, consideration of many factors led to a state's position at the Convention: the need for military protection in case of a war with the Indians (the situation in Georgia), the shaky political and financial structures of the individual states (New York was in good shape, but New Jersey and Massachusetts were near bankruptcy). The relative importance of various factors, then, led to divergent viewpoints. (A New Jerseyite could see that the only chance for repayment of his New Jersey bonds was in the assumption of his state's indebtedness by a strong federal government, while such a consideration would be minor to the New Yorker.)[20]

John P. Roche, placing economics aside, was impressed by the politics of the founders. He disagreed sharply with those scholars who have characterized the Federalists as out-and-out conservatives, reminding us that, *for their time,* "not only were they revolutionaries but also they were . . . superb democratic politicians . . . committed (perhaps willy-nilly) to working within the democratic framework, within a universe of public approval."[21] One must, of course, consider that what was revolutionary then may not appear to be revolutionary now, as what is revolutionary now may not seem so in 150 years.

---

[18] See Merrill Jensen, *The Articles of Confederation: An Interpretation of the Social-Constitutional History of the American Revolution, 1774–1781* (Madison, Wisconsin: University of Wisconsin Press, 1959) and *The New Nation* (New York: Knopf, 1950).

[19] See Robert E. Brown, *Charles Beard and the Constitution: A Critical Analysis of an Economic Interpretation of the Constitution* (Princeton, N.J.: Princeton University Press, 1956), pp. 38–39.

[20] See Forrest McDonald, *We the People: The Economic Origins of the Constitution* (Chicago: University of Chicago Press, 1958).

[21] John P. Roche, "The Founding Fathers: A Reform Caucus in Action," *The American Political Science Review,* vol. 55, no. 4 (December 1961), p. 799.

Although the argument about the Founding Fathers' motivations is still unsettled, and will probably flare up periodically as new primary sources are uncovered, it may safely be assumed that there was no single motive at work. We cannot ignore Beard's analysis of economic motivations, but today, with deeper awareness of the complex bases on which men act, we recognize that their actions must have been based on a variety of reasons, either conscious or unconscious. Was Hamilton the leading advocate of a strong central government because he owned government bonds and speculated in western real estate, or did he take this position because he had been snubbed repeatedly by the proud and antinationalistic first families of New York? John Lansing, owner of forty thousand acres of land in Schoharie County, New York, an aristocrat to his fingertips, with an obvious vested interest in preserving his property through a strong central government, nevertheless obstinately represented the antinationalistic element at Philadelphia. Why did he do so? It can be suggested only that then, as now, people acted from a variety of motives. The question of motives goes deeper than history and is not always of greatest importance. We know that people operate out of subconscious desires as well as conscious intentions. An elite structure may be created by people or groups who do not realize that they are doing so. Certainly the Framers cannot be regarded as totally selfless, but then again, they should not be denied credit for making use of an historic opportunity to create a constitution that has proved viable for two hundred years.

The Political Attitudes of the Framers

Sources of Conflict

When the delegates finally assembled in Philadelphia in May 1787 and proceeded to actually design a government, it became apparent that certain political conflicts needed resolving. From a reading of the basic source material about the Convention, primarily Madison's notes and an edited version of primary sources compiled by Max Farrand, we can identify the basic matters on which the delegates differed.[22] For example, many disagreed sharply on the role of the people in the new government; the more aristocratic distrusted the judgment of the lower classes and sought to limit the franchise. Elbridge Gerry of Massachusetts claimed that "the evils we experience flow from the excess of democracy."[23] Pierce Butler of South Carolina "thought an election by the people an impracticable mode" and Gouverneur Morris of Pennsylvania, advocating a very limited franchise, stated, "Give the votes to people who have no property, and they will sell them to the rich who will be able to buy them."

---

[22] Early in the Convention, the delegates decided to keep proceedings secret, without producing an official record of day-to-day deliberations. It was hoped that this practice would make compromise easier, as a delegate would not have to fear repercussions from his constituents.

Thus the only records we have of "who said what" are notes that individual delegates kept. The most complete set of notes are Madison's; apparently he went home after each session and kept a running record of the debates, which were eventually published in 1840, after his death.

[23] This quotation, as well as the others following by representatives at the Constitutional Convention, appear in Max Farrand, *The Records of the Federal Convention of 1787* rev. ed. (New Haven, Conn.: Yale University Press, 1966), vols. 1–4. These volumes represent the most complete edition of primary sources of the Convention. They include, in addition to Madison's debates and the records of other delegates, the official journal kept by William Jackson, the Convention's secretary.

Fortunately, the more democratic members of the Convention did not let these remarks go unanswered. "No government could long subsist without the confidence of the people," said James Wilson of Pennsylvania. On a practical basis, Oliver Ellsworth of Connecticut pointed out that "the people will not readily subscribe to the national Constitution if it should subject them to be disenfranchised," and John Dickinson of Delaware, arguing on more idealistic ground, said he considered the people "the best guardians of liberty."

Two Views of Representation   Another area of political disagreement among the Framers involved representation in the new legislature. In assigning membership, should influence be divided according to the total population of a state (thus favoring the more populous states), or should the states be equally represented (thus protecting the smaller ones)? Early in the Convention, Governor Edmund Randolph of Virginia submitted the Virginia Plan for a two-house (bicameral) legislature, with representation in the lower house proportionate to population, and membership in the upper house to be selected by the members of the lower house. The plan denied to smaller states assurance of seats in the upper house, since lower-house members from the more populous states could band together to exclude them. In addition, it provided for the national executive to be selected by this bicameral legislature, thus giving the bigger states even more potential power. In answer to the Virginia Plan, the smaller states offered the New Jersey Plan, which envisioned a single-house (unicameral) legislature, with equal representation for each state.[24] Eventually, the Connecticut Compromise was offered and accepted by both sides. This provided for an upper house (Senate), in which all states would have equal representation; and a lower house (House of Representatives), where representation would be determined on the basis of population. It is thus evident that the conflict between large states and small states grew out of their opposing self-interests and was not political in the sense of "democrat" versus "anti-democrat."

North versus South   In addition, the delegates were divided on sectional lines. The southern states were deeply concerned about the status of slaves. No one argued that slaves should be allowed to vote, but the southerners wanted them counted in apportioning seats in the House of Representatives, while delegates from the nonslave states maintained that only the free population should be considered in determining the size of the House delegation. This controversy was resolved by the three-fifths compromise, an arrangement that allowed three-fifths of the slaves in each state to be counted in apportioning House seats. Having arrived at this agreement, some delegates who objected to slavery on grounds of conscience were still unhappy about the question of slave trade. They demanded a constitutional prohibition on any future importation of slaves, and they were joined by the delegates of Maryland and Virginia, not on moral grounds but because these states already had so many slaves they needed no more. However, under pressure from South Carolina and Georgia—which were less developed and still in need of farm labor—a further compromise was adopted. Under its terms Congress could not prohibit slave trade for twenty years, until 1808, by which time it was assumed the need for slave labor would be fully satisfied.

---

[24] The New Jersey Plan also included what turned out to be a vital element in the final Constitution, the Supremacy Clause. This gave the Supreme Court the right to hear appeals from state judges and established the laws of the national government as supreme law of the land.

"If they had crowned George Washington king, none of this would be happening now."

Saturday Review, *March 27, 1971*

Another question that separated the North from the South concerned matters of foreign trade; it was resolved when the South held out for, and obtained, substantial securities. The southern states were essentially exporters of raw materials to Europe and importers of finished goods. They feared that northern interests might attempt to protect northern infant industries by arranging trade treaties that permitted the imposition of heavy import tariffs on goods from abroad, thus increasing the price of such imports in the South. Moreover, they suspected that, in an effort to balance the federal budget, the northerners might devise an export tax on southern raw materials.[25] The Constitution allayed southern fears by providing that no tax or duty be levied on articles exported from any state, and that a two-thirds majority in the Senate (where the southern states would be well represented) be required for ratification of treaties.

Areas of Consensus

The attention paid by many historians to the areas of conflict at the Convention has obscured the fact that the disagreements were primarily procedural and that the delegates agreed, in the main, on basic principles. Considering the similarity of background, experience, and interests of the Founding Fathers, it is not surprising that there were significant areas of consensus. There was agreement on the desirability of a stronger national government, with special emphasis on one that could effectively protect the property of its citizens. Almost all delegates

[25] The South still maintained the traditional colonial relationship in which raw goods were exported to the mother country and returned as finished goods. The North had moved away from this to its own manufacturing.

recognized the necessity for a republican government, instead of a hereditary monarchy or aristocracy.[26] Philosophically, most of the men at Philadelphia believed that ultimate sovereignty rested with the people, that government was based on a social contract among free men, each of whom had, under the laws of nature, a right to life, liberty, and property. These ideas, expressed originally in the work of John Locke, were incorporated by this time into all the state constitutions, and it was assumed that they would also underlie the federal Constitution. Yet despite the familiarity of delegates with Locke's theory of social contract, they were not prepared to institute a totally democratic system. Rather, most of them came to Philadelphia with a strong basic distrust of "rule by the people," believing that the people were too volatile, too uninformed, and too easily led astray to be trusted with the job of government. Madison himself, although less conservative than others, asserted the need "to protect the people against the transient impressions into which they themselves might be led . . ." and warned that the "people . . . were liable to err . . . from fickleness and passion."

In general, the overriding concern of the delegates, however, was the danger of concentrating too much power in any single authority, whether it be the masses, a too-powerful Chief Executive, or any group within the new government. Because of this concern, the delegates subscribed to the ideas of Montesquieu, who had prescribed the fragmentation of power among different branches of government as the most effective way of keeping any one group from tyrannizing the others.

Power Relationships of the Constitution: "A Harmonious System of Mutual Frustration"

In order to write the Constitution, the Founding Fathers had to anticipate how both citizens and public officials would attempt to wield power under the new governmental structure. The study of other constitutions had convinced them that specific controls had to be established for the benefit of the population. First, they wanted to give the central government sufficient power to control factions, especially majority factions. And second, they wanted to establish checks to insure that the new government itself be controlled.

The Bridling of Factions: Controlling the People

A recurrent theme in writings about the Constitution is the paradox that confronted the Framers: Entrusted to establish a government of the people, they believed the people could not be trusted to govern themselves. Having survived a long, painful struggle against England's oppressive power, the Framers recognized that a representative government was essential if America's hard-won liberty was to be preserved. On the other hand, they feared that at some point representative government might come to be dominated by powerful interest groups (referred to then as factions) whose dominance would put an end to its representative character, creating in effect a tyranny by the majority. In writing the Constitution, the Framers sought means to prevent such majority tyranny.

---

[26] Farrand quotes even Gerry of Massachusetts, one of the most aristocratic of the delegates and one of those most fearful of democracy, as saying: "There were not 1/1000 part of our fellow citizens who were not against every approach towards monarchy."

*After long debates and despite conflicting aims, the Framers
finally signed the Constitution on September 17, 1787.*

Madison expressed his apprehensions over the unbridled power of factions
when he described them as "citizens who are united and actuated by some common
impulse of passion or interest, adverse to the rights of other citizens." If factions
were allowed to gain control over government through their voting power, measures
would be decided "not according to the rules of justice . . . but by the superior
force of an interested and over-bearing majority." However dangerous factions
might be, Madison realized that banning them would put an end to liberty. Therefore, the problem was how to "secure the public good and private rights against
the danger of factions, and at the same time to preserve the spirit and form of
popular government."[27] In other words, it was necessary to design a political system
that would retain an elected republican government, but at the same time effectively
control the potential power of interest groups, protecting the minority against
dominance by an oppressive majority.

The Self-Control of Government: Federalism,
Separation of Powers, Checks and Balances

In addition to a control of factions, government itself needed to be controlled—
and these controls were established by (1) a *federal system* that provided a division

---

[27] From *The Federalist*, No. 10. The Federalist Papers, quoted throughout this section, are a set of newspaper
essays written by Madison, Jay, and Hamilton. They were published under the pen name Publius in various
New York newspapers in 1787 as part of the campaign to get New York State to ratify the new Constitution.
They can be found edited by Jacob E. Cooke (Middletown, Conn.: Wesleyan University Press, 1961).

of specified powers between the states and the national government, and (2) a *separation of powers* into three branches of government, assigning the legislative function to Congress, the executive function to the President, and the judicial function to the courts. But the Convention delegates felt that separation of powers in itself was not sufficient to prevent tyranny; the possibility remained that the electorate might permit the different branches of the government to combine their power. They therefore devised a system of *checks and balances,* as defended in *The Federalist,* No. 51. The interior structure of the federal government would be organized so that the "several constituent parts may, by their mutual relations, be the means of keeping each other in their proper place." To accomplish this, ". . . each department should have a will of its own . . ." and ". . . those who administer each department [should have] the necessary constitutional means and personal motives to resist encroachments on the other."

Thus, the Founding Fathers established in the Constitution the groundwork for a pluralist system of government. They distributed power among all the constituent parts of the government—as the means for preventing any single faction from acquiring too much power. And as an additional restraint, they made certain that no one branch would monopolize a particular function. In other words, although the Constitution places major responsibility for each of the three basic functions of government under the jurisdiction of a different branch, it also provides for a sharing of functions through the system of checks and balances. The President, for example, is primarily the Chief Executive, but he also has significant legislative power vested in him through his power to veto acts passed by Congress. And he functions in the judicial area as well through his power to nominate judges and pardon convicted criminals. Legislators may create new executive agencies, and control their funds. Judges, by judicial interpretation, define the written words of the law and thus participate in formulating legislation. These are but a few examples of how power is legally checked and balanced within a system of separated powers. As a result, change does not occur unless by consensus among the branches of government. If one of the branches has an objection, it can usually apply a check to prevent the change.

Legal checks and balances, moreover, are accompanied by political checks. Though the situation may be somewhat different today, the Framers provided for each of the branches of the government to be responsible to a different constituency: the House of Representatives to the people, the Senate to state legislatures, the President to electors, and the judges to the President with the consent of the Senate. In addition, each of these officials was to serve a different length of time: Supreme Court Judges hold office for life; Senators for six years; the President for four; Representatives to the House for two. This check makes it impossible for all of them to be ousted at one election.

Historian Richard Hofstadter has commented on the involved system of checks and balances. In his view, the delegates saw a well-designed government as one that would "check interest with interest, class with class, faction with faction and one branch of government with another in a harmonious system of mutual frustration."[28]

---

[28] Richard Hofstadter, *The American Political Tradition* (New York: Vintage, 1948), p. 9.

This cartoon from the Massachusetts Centinel celebrated ratification of the new Constitution by eleven out of the thirteen states.

Evaluating the Original Constitution: Was It a Democratic Document?

The Framers not only feared power in the hands of factions but, as we have seen, they were also apprehensive over the acquisition of too much power by the people. Assuming that they proceeded to write a document designed to limit the power of the people, can we regard the Constitution as a truly democratic instrument? Was it regarded as such during its own time? How democratic is it by today's standards?

The Anti-Federalist Movement

In 1787, when the new Constitution was offered to the state conventions for ratification, the Anti-Federalists, who opposed it, claimed that the document was essentially undemocratic.[29] Certainly, it was a far less radical document than the Declaration of Independence, whose emphasis was on human rights and freedoms, whereas the Constitution placed its stress on governmental procedures and power relationships. Despite this contrast, the Constitution and the Declaration have been regarded "as parts of 'one consistent whole,' and as a logical sequence in one continuous effort."[30] What, then, contributed to the Anti-Federalist claim? The speeches, letters, and publications of the Anti-Federalists leave the impression that they thought the Constitution provided for an aristocratic government; although the "titles, stars and garters" of the British aristocracy had been tossed out, a new elite based on "birth, education, talents and wealth" seemed to be in

---

[29] The name *Anti-Federalist* is deceiving. In reality, the *Anti*-Federalists were very much *for* a federation, but a federation such as was provided in the Articles of Confederation, where the sovereignty of the individual states received primary emphasis. The so-called Federalists, on the other hand, were those who favored the new Constitution, one that provided a strong central government rather than a mere federation of states. Nevertheless, early in the game, the supporters of the new Constitution cleverly assumed the name *Federalists,* leaving their opponents on the defensive.

[30] Alpheus T. Mason and Richard H. Leach, *In Quest of Freedom: American Political Thought and Practice*, p. 95.

Table 2-1   **Ratification of the Constitution**

State	Vote	Date
Delaware	Unanimous (30)	December 7, 1787
Pennsylvania	46 to 23	December 12, 1787
New Jersey	Unanimous (39)	December 18, 1787
Georgia	Unanimous (26)	January 2, 1788
Connecticut	128 to 40	January 9, 1788
Massachusetts	186 to 168	February 16, 1788
Maryland	63 to 11	April 26, 1788
South Carolina	149 to 73	May 23, 1788
New Hampshire	57 to 47	June 21, 1788
Virginia	89 to 79	June 25, 1788
New York	30 to 27	July 26, 1788
North Carolina	Rejected 193 to 75 on August 4, 1788	
	Finally ratified	November 21, 1789
Rhode Island	34 to 22	May 29, 1790

Source: David G. Smith, The Convention and the Constitution: The Political Ideas of the Founding Fathers *(New York: St. Martin's Press, 1965), pp. 33–34.*

the offing.[31] The Anti-Feder lists asserted directly and by implication that the Constitution, with such provisions as separation of powers, indirect election of the President and senators, presidential veto, checks and balances, and judiciary with life tenure, was designed by an American aristocracy to keep the common people from participating actively in government.

An aroused Anti-Federalist movement called upon the public to resist ratification, warning the people that they must not "consider themselves as a grovelling, distinct species, uninterested in the general welfare."[32] They warned that the government, under the new Constitution, would be run by "men that had been delicately bred, and who were in affluent circumstances,"[33] hence unable to understand or sympathize with the needs of the great body of ordinary people. More to the point, the Anti-Federalists maintained that the Constitution was undemocratic because it centralized power in this national government rather than in the states, and because it lacked a bill of rights to guarantee the fundamental freedoms of all citizens. Moreover, the Anti-Federalists believed that the delegates had exceeded their authority in writing the Constitution in the first place, for the original call to the Philadelphia Convention was not to write a new Constitution, but simply to amend the Articles of Confederation; the delegates' actions in Philadelphia were interpreted by Anti-Federalists as a warning of how they would continue to usurp more power if they assumed political control.

Viewed by different eyes, however, the Constitution was essentially a democratic document. The new American government it established was certainly more representative than that of any contemporary European government, and the American power structure radically more inclusive and accessible than its European equivalent at the time.

---

[31] Quoted in Gordon S. Wood, *Creation of the American Republic 1776–1787* (Chapel Hill, N.C.: University of North Carolina Press, 1969), p. 489.

[32] Wood, *Creation of the American Republic 1776–1787*, p. 490.

[33] Wood, *Creation of the American Republic 1776–1787*, p. 490.

"*From here it's just a bunch of stripes and stars. It doesn't say 'America.'* "

New Yorker, *April 8, 1972.*

The Constitution in Retrospect

By *today's* standards, however, the original Constitution can be seen as essentially elitist. As far as political equality is concerned, the failure to abolish slavery in the Constitution, and the absence of a national system of universal suffrage do not meet with today's definition of a truly democratic government. Perhaps it is unrealistic and unfair, however, to judge the 1787 Constitution exclusively in terms of mid-twentieth-century goals. Historian Gordon S. Wood has argued that the first concern of the Federalists of that time was to save a failing experiment. Their efforts were directed at preventing republicanism from being destroyed:

> *To the Federalists the move for the new central government became the ultimate act of the entire Revolutionary era; it was both a progressive attempt to salvage the Revolution in the face of its imminent failure and a reactionary effort to restrain its excesses. . . . The Federalists hoped to create an entirely new and original sort of republican government—a republic which did not require a virtuous people for its sustenance.*[34]

Major Changes in the Constitution

If we accept that in 1787 the Framers were concerned primarily with setting up a working government to insure the republican experiment, and that they therefore wrote a document that reflected the needs of the times as they saw them, we can better understand their failure to include the guarantees and procedures which we today consider essential to democratic government. They produced, however, a Constitution capable of meeting new needs and attitudes, through the rather slow and difficult process of amendment. Although one amendment was ratified

---

[34] Wood, *Creation of the American Republic 1776–1787*, p. 475.

in as little as two weeks, most have taken far longer. Congress, in fact, stipulates a reasonable length of time for ratification, which has usually been seven years.[35]

Despite its difficulties, the process of amendment has effected change. Although the original Constitution stands as a document that is not very democratic, some believe that it, along with the amendment process, has enabled the American government to grow increasingly democratic over the years. For this, credit belongs to the Framers and their ingenuity in writing a Constitution that is not always specific and can therefore be reinterpreted with the changing times.

In addition to changes made by means of formal amendments to the original document, and perhaps more important, informal changes have occurred by various means: reinterpretation by the courts; elaboration through enactment of new laws by Congress; adoption of new practices by the President, and the growth of political institutions unmentioned in the Constitution. Some contend that these informal changes have been the primary means by which our Constitution and our political system have achieved the flexibility necessary to survive.

The Bill of Rights

Even before the original Constitution was ratified, pressure began to build for formal amendment. One of the issues raised in 1787–1788 by the Anti-Federalists to oppose ratification was the failure of the Constitution to include a bill of rights. The concept of a bill of rights was very popular during the period; eight of the new state constitutions included such guarantees, and the Anti-Federalists found the issue an effective rallying point. The Federalists responded with two arguments. They claimed that the Constitution did indeed protect the individual liberties of citizens: for example, by prohibiting ex-post-facto laws (thereby preventing punishment for acts which were not illegal at the time they were committed),[36] guaranteeing jury trials, and providing for the writ of habeas corpus[37] (a protection against illegal imprisonment). Moreover, the Federalists argued that under the Constitution, the powers of the national government are limited only to those items actually enumerated in the document. Therefore, they said, since the ability to limit freedom of speech or of the press is not specifically listed among its powers, the federal government obviously cannot carry on such activities, and it is therefore unnecessary to attach a bill of rights. The weakness of this argument was made apparent as the struggle for ratification dragged on.

By May 1788, three months after the Constitution had been submitted to the states, New Hampshire became the ninth state to ratify it. In theory, this was

---

[35] The Constitution defines the amendment process. Each amendment must be proposed and subsequently ratified. An amendment may be proposed either by a national convention called by Congress at the request of two-thirds of the states (a method which has never been used) or by a two-thirds vote in each house of Congress. Ratification requires approval by the states, either by three-fourths of the state legislatures, or by three-fourths of special ratifying conventions held in each state. With the exception of the Twenty-first Amendment (repeal of prohibition), all amendments have been ratified by state legislatures.

The Constitution includes only two restrictions on amendments. The first, stating that the slave trade could not be outlawed before 1808, has long been meaningless. The second prohibits any amendment that would deprive any state of its equal representation in the Senate.

Although about 5,000 amendments in all have at one time or another been introduced in Congress, only twenty-six have finally achieved ratification.

[36] *Ex post facto:* arising from the fact, but acting retroactively.

[37] *Writ of habeas corpus:* A document calling for the appearance of a person before a court or judge to determine a question of illegal restraint upon liberty, or illegal imprisonment.

sufficient to establish the new government, but it was apparent that without the large states of Virginia and New York (who, along with Rhode Island and North Carolina had not as yet ratified), the new Union could not succeed. At this point, the Federalists let it be known that they would support the addition of a bill of rights to the Constitution as soon as the new Congress was established, and with this understanding, Virginia and New York ratified—New York by the very narrow margin of 30 to 27—and the other states soon followed.[38]

The Bill of Rights, which some authorities consider important enough to describe as "the second half of the Constitution," was proposed in Congress in 1789 and finally adopted two years later. Madison, a member of the House of Representatives and floor manager for the measure, had a difficult job maneuvering it through a maze of demands and obstructions. He had to deal, on the one hand, with various interests and the innumerable items they wished included; and on the other, with diehard Anti-Federalists who reversed their tactics and decided to fight the passage of any bill of rights, hoping this would lead to the downfall of the new government.

The first ten amendments to the Constitution comprise the Bill of Rights. Designed to guarantee the civil liberties of the people, they forbid Congress to make laws interfering with freedom of speech, the press, religion, and public assembly. They state that the citizen cannot "be deprived of life, liberty or property without due process of law," or be required to testify against himself in a criminal trial. They affirm the citizen's right to protection from the state against "unreasonable" searches and seizure, and contain assurance of trial by jury and against the imposition of unreasonable bail. They insure the "right of the people to keep and bear arms" as "necessary to the security of a free State," and guarantee against enforced quartering of soldiers in households, a much-resented practice under the British colonial government. The last two amendments state that the rights of the people are not restricted only to those enumerated in the first eight amendments and that powers not delegated to the federal government are reserved to the states or the people.

Despite the apparent victory for the Anti-Federalists, Richard Henry Lee was displeased with the final form of the Bill of Rights. Upon reading it he proclaimed: "How wonderfully scrupulous have they been in stating rights. The English language has been carefully culled to find words feeble in their nature or doubtful in their meaning."[39]

Although the Bill of Rights developed into a democratizing force, its provisions were enforced, until very recently, only against unjust action of the national government. At the time it was ratified, it was not meant to restrict the power of the police and the courts of the state and local governments. The states, in fact, continued to deny due process, so that some citizens, for example, were tried twice for the same crime, or forced to incriminate themselves. Some states even

---

[38] In addition to the lack of a bill of rights, which biased many nonaristocrats in New York against the new Constitution, the opposition to ratification also came from big landholders in the state. The Constitution prohibits any state from "lay[ing] any . . . duties on imports," and, previously, New York had financed itself largely through the imposition of import taxes on merchandise coming in at New York City. The big landowners feared that once this income was unavailable to the state, property taxes would soar. Because it was very important for the Federalists to pick up whatever support they could, their concession on a bill of rights was an important factor in achieving eventual ratification in New York.

[39] Quoted in Merrill Jensen, *The Making of the American Constitution* (New York: Van Nostrand-Reinhold, 1964), pp. 149–150.

upheld hanging, certainly a cruel and unusual punishment. The provisions of the first eight amendments have very slowly, piece by piece, come to apply to state and local governments as well as to the federal government. It took until the end of the Chief Justice Earl Warren's tenure in 1969, however, for this extension to evolve.

The Rise of Political Parties

Shortly after the adoption of the Bill of Rights, another major force for the democratization of the American political system began to emerge. This was the development of the political party, an important means, not mentioned in the Constitution, for citizens to participate in the governing process. The Founding Fathers had discussed factions extensively, but they did not foresee the growth of political parties. In fact, most of the men at the Convention strongly opposed parties. "If I could not go to heaven but with a party," Jefferson said, "I would not go there at all."[40]

Nevertheless, division along party lines began with the original Federalist-versus-Anti-Federalist controversy over the Constitution, and by the late 1790s, 90 percent of the members of Congress claimed affiliation with either the Federalists or the Republicans, who had formed out of the Anti-Federalists. The Federalists supported financial, trade, and shipping interests and favored a strong central government, and the Republicans supported agrarian interests and states' rights. As early as 1796, the presidential election was fought on party lines, with John Adams as the Federalist candidate, and Thomas Jefferson running as a Republican.

Party loyalty stalemated the 1800 election and pointed up that parties had become a force to be reckoned with in American politics.[41] Implicit in the ratification of the Twelfth Amendment, which provides for separate election of the President and Vice President to avoid a repeat of the 1800 election, was recognition of the political party as a democratizing agent in the election of the President. Since that time, with the exception of the uncontested 1820 election won by Monroe, all our presidential elections and almost all congressional and state elections have been party contests, although the names of the parties nominating candidates for office have changed.

Voters began to go to the polls in increasing numbers in the late 1820s, the percentage of the voting electorate increasing until the election of 1840 drew an unprecedented 80.2 percent of white adult males, as yet the only eligible voters, to the polls. Interest was engendered in the first half of the century by the emergence of the two-party system: the eagerness of citizens to exercise their democratic rights by voting has been attributed in no small measure to the excitement

---

[40] Quoted in Morton Borden et al., *The American Profile* (Lexington, Mass.: Heath, 1970), p. 64.

[41] The original Constitution envisioned a system in which presidential electors from each state, voting their independent judgments, would each vote for two preferred candidates, with the man who received the most votes becoming President, and the next most popular candidate, Vice President. By 1800, however, the electors had become political appointees, each of whom voted a straight party ticket. In the 1800 election, the Republicans ran Jefferson for President and Aaron Burr for Vice President. Solidly partisan, the seventy-three Republican electors gave them each the same number of votes, which, according to the rules in the original Constitution, entitled either man to be President. When the question of who was to be President was turned over to the House of Representatives, it took thirty-six ballots finally to elect Jefferson. (From Morison, *Oxford History of the American People*, p. 356.)

generated by the party organizations in political contests at a time when there were few other public entertainments.

The Framers' failure to recognize the democratic value of parties, like their omission of a bill of rights, was a major oversight. The Framers ignored the fact that parties provide a potentially influential means for the people to have an impact on government. Throughout the world, the rise of democracy is associated with the rise of political parties. In the United States, political parties have served democracy by broadening opportunities for citizens to participate in the governing process. Citizen participation influences party platforms and candidates, and gives the public the opportunity to form a new party if it is dissatisfied with the existing ones.

Yet the parties will have to go far to match the peak years of mass participation in elections of the late nineteenth century, when two-thirds of the electorate consisted of regular voters. Voting began to decline sharply after 1900, reaching a low in the postwar years of the early twenties, when only 25 percent of those eligible to vote cast ballots; and gradually rose until, in the sixties, an estimated 44 percent of the electorate could be considered core voters. But the percentage of those who voted declined as the proportion of the total population eligible to vote increased. In 1965, Walter Dean Burnham ascribed the absence of large numbers of Americans at the polls to a serious ailment at the heart of the American body politic. He wrote:

The concentration of socially deprived characteristics among the forty million adult Americans who today are altogether outside the voting universe suggests active aliena-tion—or its passive equivalent, political apathy—on a scale unknown anywhere else in the Western world.[42]

In recent years party attempts to gain the support of minority groups may have drawn some alienated citizens into politics. The competition for votes has focused in large part on blacks. This is particularly true in urban areas where the size of the black community makes its vote significant in winning elections. In the Cleveland 1967 election for mayor, Carl Stokes won when 85 percent of the eligible black voters turned out. The average turnout for city elections is 25 percent. The Cleveland election results indicate that the alienated can be stimulated to vote when the election is directly meaningful to them. Also of recent significance was a nationwide campaign to enroll young voters, between eighteen and twenty-one years of age.[43] In most communities this drive was spearheaded by the parties, particularly the Democrats, who believed they would attract most of the new voters. Whether or not the bid for the votes of blacks and eighteen-to-twenty-year-olds will result in a massive increase in voting remains to be seen.

Over the years, party procedures have become more democratic. Until 1824, presidential candidates were chosen by congressional caucus. Under this system the members of Congress from a particular party held a meeting, or caucus, through which they chose their party's candidate. A candidate without a strong base of power in Congress had no chance of winning. By the 1830s, however, strong state party organizations had developed, and the choice of presidential candidates was

[42] Walter Dean Burnham, "The Changing Shape of the American Political Universe," *American Political Science Review*, vol. LIX, no. 1 (March 1965), p. 27.

[43] The Twenty-sixth Amendment to the Constitution extended the franchise to include citizens eighteen years of age and over.

made by a national convention made up of delegates chosen by the state and county parties. Means of further democratizing the convention system have been a much-discussed consideration. In addition, the parties have instituted direct primaries enabling citizens to show their preferences for candidates; they were the first organized political opinion polls of the people.

Jacksonian Democracy

The preceding discussions of the Founding Fathers emphasized the elitist bias and lack of confidence in the common man that influenced their conception of democratic government. For the four decades between Washington's election to the Presidency in 1789 and Andrew Jackson's inauguration in 1828, this elitist tradition persisted, with presidential candidates being chosen by an inside group, the congressional caucus, derived from another in-group, the "Virginia-Massachusetts" dynasty.[44] By 1828, however, the nation was ready for an expansion of its power base, and important changes occurred not only in the philosophy of government of those in high office but also in the very practice of politics.

This change was effected by Jacksonian democracy, which evolved in reaction to the political and economic privilege of the earlier period. Jackson himself was in some ways typical of the new frontier society. The son of an impoverished farmer, his education was scanty. As a self-made man, with a record of success in such a wide range of careers as law, farming, business, and the military, he had an unshakable belief in the virtues and abilities of the common man. Moreover, he had suffered an early business failure which he blamed on powerful eastern financial interests, a group who he later claimed "bend the acts of government to their selfish purposes."[45] Moreover, in 1824, although he received a majority of the popular vote, Jackson was defeated for the Presidency in the Electoral College by what he described as corrupt bargaining between two eastern establishment candidates, John Quincy Adams and Henry Clay.[46] It was not until 1828 – by which time the congressional caucus had been replaced by the convention system, and the right to vote had been widely expanded – that Jackson was elected President.

What were the principles underlying Jacksonian democracy? Basic was a belief in the ability and right of the ordinary citizen to participate in government. "The duties of . . . public officers are . . . so plain and simple that men of intelligence may readily qualify themselves for their performance," said Jackson, adding, ". . . no one man has any more intrinsic right to official station than another."[47] This is a far cry from the views expressed some forty years earlier at Philadelphia when delegate Roger Sherman suggested that "the people . . . [should] have as little to do as may be about the government," and delegate William Livingstone loftily described the people as "unfit to retain the exercise of power in their own hands."[48]

---

[44] Washington, John Adams, Jefferson, Madison, Monroe, and John Quincy Adams – four Virginians and two citizens of Massachusetts – were all members of the original "Eastern Aristocracy" which had dominated politics in the United States since before the Revolution.

[45] Quoted in Walter E. Volkomer, ed., *The Liberal Tradition in American Thought* (New York: Putnam's, 1969), p. 156.

[46] A somewhat similar situation occurred in 1962, when President Kennedy nominated his brother Robert for Attorney General, an appointment that aroused charges of nepotism.

[47] Quoted in Volkomer, *The Liberal Tradition in American Thought,* p. 151.

[48] Quoted in Hofstadter, *American Political Tradition,* p. 4.

Andrew Jackson not only appealed to the common people as a candidate but drew them into the work of governing after his election to the Presidency.

Along with the Jacksonian belief in equal political opportunity for all went a conviction that the old political elite must be prevented from using its power to achieve unfair economic advantage. "Many of our rich men in 1832 have not been content with equal protection and equal benefits, but have besought us to make them richer by Act of Congress," said Jackson in vetoing the extension of the Bank of the United States charter.[49] In other words, Jacksonian democracy represented not only a campaign by an increasingly well-organized and self-confident majority to wrest the political rights from an elite minority, but also an attempt to keep this minority from using excessive and abusive economic power.

Within this philosophical framework, the Jacksonians effected several important changes:

1. They were instrumental in substituting the convention system for the congressional caucus.

---

[49] Quoted in Volkomer, *The Liberal Tradition in American Thought,* p. 157.

2. Jackson was the first President to design and practice the role of a strong Executive, in which he governed for the people as a whole, protecting their rights against vested minority interests in Congress and elsewhere.
3. They introduced the *spoils system,* which encouraged greater participation of citizens in government by rewarding members of the winning political party with government jobs. Although currently in disrepute, the spoils system initially had a democratizing effect, because it offered, for the first time, opportunities for "outsiders" to help run the government.

The fight against economic privilege took the form of various Supreme Court decisions under Roger B. Taney, the Chief Justice under Jackson. These decisions limited the economic power of the old elite and upheld the interests of the public when they came into conflict with the business establishment.[50]

One should note, however, an important area in which the Jacksonians failed to achieve their end: they fought hard but unsuccessfully to abolish the Electoral College and replace it with direct election of the President. More recently, Senator Birch Bayh (D.-Ind.), mindful of the close popular vote in the 1968 Nixon-Humphrey election, attempted once again to introduce a similar constitutional amendment, but his efforts, too, ended in failure.

Expanding the Size and Power of the Electorate

One of the most obvious examples of the adjustments made by our political system to meet new situations is in the change in size and power of the electorate since the Constitution was first written. The original document gave actual, *direct* power to the voters only in the right to elect members of the House of Representatives; it provided for *indirect* election of the President and senators. Qualifications for voting, which affected the size of the electorate, were left to the states, with each state setting its own rules. Generally speaking, in the early days of the Republic, most states had tax-paying or property qualifications of various kinds: for example, Virginia required ownership of twenty-five acres of improved land or fifty acres of unimproved land, and North Carolina gave the vote only to those who paid taxes.[51] The exact number of those eligible to vote in the late 1700s is disputed, but, in view of the limits imposed by property qualifications and denial of the franchise to such groups as indentured servants, slaves, and women,[52] suffrage by today's standards, was extremely limited.

Over the years, however, the percentage of the population eligible to vote has increased significantly. The growth of the electorate can be explained by a number of factors. First, the states themselves extended the franchise. For example, in 1816–1821, six new states entered the Union with constitutions that provided for universal white male suffrage, and in 1810–1821, four of the older states revised their voting requirements, dropping most property qualifications. The states' gradual elimination of barriers to the right to vote has been an ongoing process.

---

[50] In the Charles River Bridge Case, Taney ruled that the rights of the promoters of the original Charles River Bridge could not be protected at the expense of the public, and that a second bridge, the Warren Bridge, should be built despite the fact that the Charles Bridge promoters would suffer losses due to competition.

[51] See Robert E. Brown, *Charles Beard and the Constitution,* for a full discussion of state voting qualifications at the time of the ratification of the Constitution.

[52] One exception is noteworthy. In New Jersey, during the 1770s, a woman could vote if she met the same property qualifications as a man. See Morison, *The Oxford History of the American People,* p. 277.

The New Woman

Mrs. O.H.P. Belmont speaks at a suffragist tea.

Help us to win the vote

A curbside fund raiser, clutching a contribution basket, draws a bemused crowd.

I am sick to death of this shriek for women's rights. It is doing more harm than good among women. I wish all women felt as I do; I have more rights now than I can properly attend to.
MAY IRWIN, ACTRESS

We couldn't make a worse mess of it than the men, and we might do better.
AN ASPIRING WOMAN VOTER

I am suffering enough now and am really too busy to bother with the suffrage movement at all.
AN ANONYMOUS HOUSEWIFE

I believe in woman's suffrage wherever the women want it. Where they do not want it, the suffrage should not be forced upon them.
THEODORE ROOSEVELT

If anything is coming to us, we want it.
AN ANONYMOUS WOMAN

I would rather die and go to hell than vote for woman suffrage!
MEMBER OF THE MISSISSIPPI HOUSE OF REPRESENTATIVES

Feminist activity at the beginning of this century centered on the struggle for enfranchisement.

In fact, many states actually took the lead in expanding the franchise even before constitutional amendments or federal government action forced them to do so: Wyoming provided equal voting rights for women during the first session of its first territorial legislature in 1869, 51 years before constitutional amendment forbade denial of voting rights on the basis of sex; and the vote for eighteen-year-olds was approved in Georgia in 1943, 27 years before similar action took place in Congress.

Table 2-2   **The Twenty-six Amendments**

The Bill of Rights (1791)
  1. Prohibition of laws restricting religion, speech, press, peaceful assembly, and the right to petition the government.
  2. Right of the people to keep and bear arms.
  3. Right of homeowners or proprietors to refuse the quartering of soldiers on their premises.
  4. Right of the people to security of person and property against unwarranted searches and seizures.
  5. Protection against double jeopardy; self-incrimination; and the taking of life, liberty, and property without due process of law.
  6. Right to a speedy, public, and impartial jury trial in criminal cases.
  7. Right to a trial by jury in civil cases in which more than $20 is in question.
  8. Prohibition against requiring excessive bail or fines, and inflicting cruel and unusual punishment.
  9. Protection of rights "retained by the people," though not enumerated in the Constitution.
 10. Reservation to the states, or the people, of all powers neither delegated to the national government nor prohibited to the states.

Later Amendments
 11. Prohibition against the extension of federal judicial power initiated by an individual against one of the states, except with the consent of that state, or by foreign citizens or subjects (1798).
 12. Prescriptions for separate election of a President and Vice President (1804).
 13. Abolition of slavery (1865).
 14. Right of all citizens to "equal protection of the laws." Prohibitions against a state's taking of life, liberty, or property without "due process of law" and against state laws abridging the "privileges and immunities" of citizens. Provision to bar persons who have "engaged in insurrection or rebellion" from public office. Provision to prohibit the questioning of the public debt (1868).
 15. Guarantee of the right of citizens to vote by prohibiting the states from denying this right because of "race, color, or previous condition of servitude" (1870).
 16. Power of Congress to levy income taxes (1913).
 17. Provision for direct popular election of senators (1913).
 18. Prohibition against manufacture and sale of intoxicating liquors (1919),
 19. Guarantee of woman suffrage by prohibiting the states from denying the right to vote "on account of sex" (1920).
 20. Rescheduling of congressional and presidential terms so that congressmen begin to serve on January 3, and the President and Vice President on January 20 (1933).
 21 Repeal of Eighteenth Amendment (1933).
 22. Prohibition against any future Presidents being elected to that office more than twice; stipulation that anyone succeeding to the Presidency and serving more than two years may be elected to the office in his own right only once (1951).
 23. Guarantee of the right of citizens residing in Washington, D.C., to vote in presidential elections (1961).
 24. Guarantee of the right of all citizens over the age of twenty-one to vote in national elections by prohibiting denial of this right by the states because of failure to pay poll taxes or other taxes (1964).
 25. Establishment of procedures for succession to the Presidency and for determining presidential disability (1967).
 26. Guarantee of the right to vote to citizens eighteen years of age or older, by prohibiting the United States or any state from denying this right "on account of age" (1971).

A second method used to increase the number of voters has been through constitutional amendment. In this connection, it should be noted that, although it is usually assumed that the various amendments "give the right to vote" to different groups, the amendments do not order the states to extend the franchise; they merely forbid the states to refuse the vote to a special group for a special reason. The Fifteenth Amendment (1870) forbids the states to deny the vote to a citizen on account of race, color, or previous condition of servitude; the Nineteenth Amendment (1920) forbids denial on grounds of sex; and the Twenty-fourth forbids denial for failure to pay a poll tax. The Twenty-third Amendment (1961) is somewhat different in form: the original Constitution made no provision for presidential electors from the District of Columbia, so that citizens living there had no voice in choosing the President. The Twenty-third Amendment corrects this deficiency.

Recently, a third method has been created to expand the electorate. In 1970, Congress voted to permit eighteen-year-olds to vote in federal elections. President Nixon and many legal experts suggested that the law, as written, was unconstitutional, because the Constitution apparently gives the states, rather than the federal government, the right to set voting qualifications. Nevertheless, after the President signed the bill there was no court challenge, and the act was eventually ratified on June 30, 1971, as the Twenty-sixth Amendment to the Constitution.

In addition to extending the size of the electorate, various constitutional amendments have also increased the power of the electorate. The Seventeenth Amendment (1913) took election of senators out of the state legislatures and provided, instead, for direct senatorial elections by the people. Passage of the Twentieth (Lame-Duck) Amendment (1933) insured more representative government by providing that new congressmen take their seats within two months after election, changing the date from March 4 to January 20. This measure abolished the "lame-duck" session of Congress, in which defeated incumbents served for thirteen months after their defeat.[53] The Twenty-second Amendment (1951), which prohibits the election of a President for more than two terms, was intended to protect the basic democratic form of our government, but it is questionable whether in the last analysis it actually does democratize political procedures. It reflects the thinking of a long line of political scientists, as far back as Jefferson, who wanted the Constitution to limit each President to only one term. They were concerned that a popular President might be elected time and time again, until the Presidency degenerated into an "elected monarchy."[54] For a long time, it appeared as if the precedent set by Washington, who refused a third term, would remain unchallenged. But in 1940 and 1944, President Franklin D. Roosevelt, prompted in part by the troubled international situation, ran for and won third and fourth terms. Consequently, the Twenty-second Amendment was hastily proposed and ratified in an attempt to prevent another President from running for office more than twice. Because it will keep future voters from reelecting a President for a third term even if they wished to do so, it has been suggested that this amendment has antidemocratic implications; also, that it is likely to reduce the power of the Presidency, since an incumbent who cannot be reelected loses much of his political clout on Congress and the administrative bureaucracy—perhaps not altogether a loss to the democratic process.

---

[53] It also provides for inauguration of new Presidents in January rather than in March.

[54] These are Jefferson's words, as quoted in Volkomer, *The Liberal Tradition in American Thought,* p. 89.

Changes in the Role
of the National Government

In recent years, some of the most important changes in our political system have come about through reinterpretation of the functions of various political institutions. In the 1787 Constitution, the functions were barely suggested. Some of these changes can be viewed as beneficial in that they have increased participatory democracy and provided protection for the rights of the less powerful groups within our society. We are therefore especially concerned with how they have come about. Of particular significance have been three developments: general increases in the authority of the national government vis-à-vis the states, changes in the role of the federal judiciary, and the increased power of the Office of the President.[55]

Increases in the Power of the Federal Government

We have seen that the Founding Fathers originally designed a federal system, in which only certain stated powers were given to the national government, the rest being retained by the states. The system was further defined by the Tenth Amendment, which stated, "The powers not delegated to the United States by the Constitution nor prohibited by it to the states, are reserved to the states respectively, or to the people." Nevertheless, over the years, Supreme Court decisions have generally interpreted the Constitution with emphasis on "implied powers," ruling that in addition to the relatively small number of stated powers expressly granted to the national government in the Constitution, the national government also has implied powers (under Article I, Section 8) to engage in whatever other activities are necessary and proper in order to carry out its duties.[56] Under this interpretation, first put forth by Chief Justice John Marshall in 1819 in the case of *McCulloch* v. *Maryland,* the federal government has become involved in many areas of national life.

The power of the federal government was again widened by a constitutional amendment, the Sixteenth, in 1913. Originally, the Constitution prohibited Congress from imposing any "direct" taxes, unless they were apportioned among the various states on the basis of population;[57] in other words, the tax burden had to be levied equally on each person. The Sixteenth Amendment, by nullifying an 1894 Supreme Court decision that a tax on income was unequal and therefore unconstitutional, permitted federal taxation on a graduated basis. With laws requiring wealthy persons to pay taxes at a higher rate than the poor, the term "equality" came to have an economic dimension. Moreover, it is apparent that without such taxing powers, the federal government would be unable to finance the vast scope of activities, from moon shots to job-retraining programs, in which it now engages.

---

[55] These three institutions, the federal system of government, the judiciary, and the presidency, will be discussed in more detail in Chapters 5, 9, and 7, respectively. We mention them here to show how our political system has managed to adapt to the social, economic, and technological changes of the last two hundred years within the framework of government outlined in the original Constitution.

[56] Article I, Section 8, reads: "The Congress shall have power to make all laws which shall be necessary and proper for carrying into execution the foregoing powers, and all other powers vested by this Constitution in the government of the United States, or in any department or officer thereof."

[57] See Article I, Section 8.

Changes in the Power of the Judiciary: Judicial Review

Perhaps no other power has contributed more toward the evolution of the United States system of government than the power of judicial review. Judicial review gives the Supreme Court the right to determine whether or not a law is in conflict with the Constitution—and thus, whether or not it is valid. Although nowhere in the Constitution is this right specifically stated, it was spelled out early in our history in a Supreme Court decision by Chief Justice John Marshall (*Marbury* v. *Madison*, 1803). In sum, Marshall argued that the Constitution was the "supreme law of the land" (i.e., superior to the laws passed by Congress) and that it is the courts that have the responsibility and the authority to decide if a particular piece of legislation is in accord with the Constitution. A piece of legislation not in accordance with the Constitution is no law at all; hence it is null.

Because judicial review operates on a continuing basis, it provides a way for our political system to take a "second look" at laws and institutions in the light of new circumstances. The process offers an orderly procedure for laws to adapt to changing social and economic pressures.

The Ascendancy of the Presidency

The growth of presidential power since the early days of the republic has occurred without any constitutional change. Reflected in the aggressive leadership of such Presidents as Andrew Jackson, Abraham Lincoln, Theodore Roosevelt, Woodrow Wilson, Franklin D. Roosevelt, and Lyndon Johnson, the role of the President has grown so that he has become more than the Chief Executive of the nation; instead, in recent administrations, he has also been the chief legislator, responsible for a significant number of new laws introduced each year into Congress; the political leader and spokesman for his party; and the chief foreign-policy maker.

As the only national official chosen by all the people, the President often stands as the spokesman for the entire country, in contrast to congressmen or senators, who individually represent only a part of the total electorate. This is why some contemporary political scientists have interpreted the increasing power of the Presidency as a democratizing force, through which the voice of the people (frequently unheeded in the legislature because of greater influence of special-interest groups on congressmen) can be expressed. There are others, however, who have questioned the direction of this growth of presidential power.

The Constitution establishes the rules by which the country's politics are played. Some say that the rules are too rigid, outdated, and biased in favor of the well-organized and powerful. Enough outspoken people have been discouraged to call for an entirely new constitution. Essentially, these people believe that the Constitution is not adequate to cope with conditions in the last third of the twentieth century.[58] The great gap that exists between the ideals expressed in the Declaration and put into law in the Constitution, and the realities of life for many Americans who have been denied equal opportunity and equal treatment under the law, has made the question "Is the system still working?" the central political issue of our times.

---

[58] An ongoing project of updating the Constitution exists under the direction of Rexford Guy Tugwell at the Center for the Study of Democratic Institutions in Santa Barbara, California. A discussion of specific recommendations of the 150-member staff can be found in Fred P. Graham, "Study Center Offers New U.S. Constitution," *New York Times*, September 8, 1970.

SUGGESTED READING

Beard, Charles A. *An Economic Interpretation of the Constitution of the United States* (New York: Macmillan, 1935). First published in 1913, this classic regards the conflict over the Constitution as the result of divergent economic interests. The author concludes the Founding Fathers' concern was the protection of their realty and securities and that the entire process of writing and ratifying the Constitution was undemocratic and non-representative.

Becker, Carl. *The Declaration of Independence: A Study in the History of Political Ideas* (New York: Vintage, 1942). In paperback. Dealing with the literary, historical, and political significance of the document, Becker has carefully analyzed the concepts expressed in the Declaration, which convey the American character of political freedom. He discusses the origins of these concepts and explains their meanings at the time of the American Revolution and throughout subsequent American history.

Bowen, Catherine D. *Miracle at Philadelphia: The Story of the Constitutional Convention, May to September 1787* (Boston: Little, Brown, 1966). A highly readable account of the Constitutional Convention, with great insight into the personalities of the Framers.

Brown, Robert E. *Charles Beard and the Constitution* (New York: Norton, 1965). Analysis and point-by-point refutation of Charles Beard's economic interpretation of the Constitution. Among the conclusions reached by Brown is that the right to vote on ratification of the Constitution was far more widely held than Beard contended.

Eidelberg, Paul, *The Philosophy of the American Constitution: A Reinterpretation of the Intentions of the Founding Fathers* (New York: The Free Press, 1968). In paperback. An analysis of the deliberations leading to the construction of the Constitution. The author discusses the mixed intentions of the Founding Fathers, and notes that the Founders' commitment to, but fear of, democracy prompted them to establish a mixed regime — that is, a government combining democracy and oligarchy both philosophically and structurally.

Hamilton, Alexander, James Madison, and John Jay. *The Federalist Papers,* edited by Clinton Rossiter (New York: New American Library, 1961). In paperback. These papers, originally a series of newspaper articles published in New York City under the pen name Publius, were written in an attempt to influence ratification of the Constitution. Although the papers are somewhat difficult to read, the authors touch upon almost every problem of government that is of current interest: government by discussion and reason or government by violence; war, militarism, and civil liberty; conduct of foreign relations; the powers of Congress; and so on.

Jensen, Merrill. *The Making of the American Constitution* (New York: Van Nostrand-Reinhold, 1964). This book concerns itself solely with the origins of the Constitution, its writing, and its adoption. Conveying a view of eighteenth-century problems as the men of the time saw them, the book is mainly narrative with short quoted excerpts. In addition, the book contains a section of selected readings covering such items as the Virginia Resolutions, the Constitution, and the Bill of Rights.

MacDonald, Forrest. *We the People: The Economic Origins of the Constitution* (Chicago: University of Chicago Press, 1958). A critique of Beard's economic interpretation of the Constitution. MacDonald demonstrates that there was no consolidated economic interest at work in framing the Constitution and that Beard's argument concerning the personal financial advantage of the Framers of the Constitution is the weakest point of his argument. MacDonald then provides additional information on the reasons for various states' and various interests' support of the Constitution.

————. *E Pluribus Unum: The Formation of the American Republic 1776–1790* (Boston: Houghton Mifflin, 1965). An account and re-creation of the fourteen years during which a viable government was secured. The story of the shaping of the Articles of Confederation is told state by state; a discussion of the Philadelphia Convention follows.

Rossiter, Clinton. *Seventeen Eighty-Seven: The Grand Convention* (New York: Macmillan, 1966). In paperback. Rossiter calls 1787 the most fateful year in the history of the United States. The political method of the Framers and the historical justification for such a method is discussed. The author's underlying theme is that the Founding Fathers did indeed rescue the country from "chaos" by creating a Constitution that "preserved liberty for themselves and future generations." The book contains many anecdotes and personal sketches about the Founding Fathers.

Schlesinger, Arthur M., Jr. *The Age of Jackson* (Boston: Little, Brown, 1945). In paperback. This book examines American democracy generally, and in particular Andrew Jackson, whose impact on his age had a permanent influence on American democracy. In this interpretive account of a period of American political and economic crises, the crises of Jackson's era seem simplistic in the twentieth century. Nevertheless, an examination of them provides a sense of what it is that is democratic in the American tradition, and Schlesinger's constant view toward the future gives new exigencies to the meanings of an earlier age's crises.

Smith, David G. *The Convention and the Constitution: Political Ideas of the Founding Fathers* (New York: St. Martin's Press, 1965). In paperback. Smith writes of the philosophies of government underlying the formation of the Constitution, and examines some of the unfavorable political and social characteristics of the eighteenth century, which he terms the "Disharmonious Society." He also discusses the motives and struggles of the Founding Fathers, the question of federalism, and concludes by analyzing how well the original plan continues to serve today.

Tocqueville, Alexis de. *Democracy in America*, edited by A. Hacker (New York: Vintage, 1945). In paperback. This book, originally published in Paris in 1835, remains a valuable reading experience for the student of American government. De Tocqueville discusses the structures and problems of government and then offers a philosophical examination of social, economic, and political change.

3
EQUALITY AND DISCRIMINATION IN THE UNITED STATES

In 1776, a group of revolutionaries presented a stirring ideal to the new American republic in words that generations of school children were taught to repeat with pride:

We hold these truths to be self-evident, that all men are created equal, that they are endowed by their Creator with certain unalienable Rights, that among these are Life, Liberty and the pursuit of Happiness. . . .

Almost two centuries later, Alvin F. Poussaint, a black psychiatrist, told about an encounter he had with a white policeman as he was leaving his office in Jackson, Mississippi:

[The] policeman yelled, "Hey boy! Come here!" Somewhat bothered, I retorted: "I'm no boy!" He then rushed at me, inflamed . . . "What d'ja say, boy?" Quickly he frisked me and demanded, "What's your name, boy?" Frightened, I replied, "Dr. Poussaint; I'm a physician." He angrily chuckled and hissed, "What's your first name, boy?" When I hesitated he assumed a threatening stance and clenched his fists . . . I muttered in profound humiliation, "Alvin."

He continued his psychological brutality, bellowing, "Alvin, the next time I call you, you come right away, you hear? . . . Now boy, go on and get out of here or next time we'll take you for a little ride down to the station house!"[1]

Unlike most of his fellow black Americans, Dr. Poussaint was given an opportunity to educate himself for a profession; this opportunity, however, did not exclude him from one of the most demeaning forms of discriminatory treatment —treatment contradicting the American credo that all men are created equal and have an equal opportunity to participate in American life.

Discrimination in the United States Today

Many minority groups are discriminated against in the United States today—not only black Americans, but Puerto Ricans, American Indians, and Mexican-Americans, among others. And women, although not a statistical minority, are often confronted with bias in a male-dominated society.

Fundamental areas of discrimination include employment, education, and housing. The unemployment rate for minority-group workers is often twice that of white males. Moreover, members of minority groups are frequently restricted to the least attractive and worst-paying jobs in our economy; they often earn less money than the average male worker at the same job. During the 1971–1972 school year, almost two decades after the Supreme Court ruled that "separate educational facilities are inherently unequal," most black children in the United States were attending primary and secondary schools that were more than half black, and over 11 percent were still in all-black schools.[2] In college and graduate school, opportunities for women to pursue a higher education are restricted; for example, in 1970, scholarship and financial aid for college students averaged

---

[1] Alvin F. Poussaint, "A Negro Psychiatrist Explains the Negro Psyche," The *New York Times* (August 20, 1967), p. 53.

[2] For the 1971–1972 school year, 72 percent of the black children in the North and West and 56 percent in the South were attending schools which were primarily black. J. Egerton, "Report on Southern School Desegregation," *Saturday Review* (April 1, 1972).

$760 annually for men and only $518 for women.[3] Inequality in housing continues: about three-fourths of our black population lives in central cities, much of it in decaying slums;[4] and a survey of the thirty-one largest metropolitan areas in the Southwest showed that the homes of Mexican-American families are two to three times more likely to be dilapidated than those of other Americans.[5]

Within the last ten years, a considerable effort has been made — through Supreme Court decisions, new state and federal legislation, and stricter enforcement of laws already on the books — to eliminate discrimination in employment, housing, and public accommodations, and to assure voting rights to all Americans. Nevertheless, members of minority groups are far more likely than the average American to be poor, uneducated, and unhealthy. And most minorities still lack significant political power.

Institutionalized Discrimination

Twenty years ago, American liberals optimistically predicted that once the procedural and legal bars to equal opportunity were removed, discrimination would disappear; that once minority-group members were given the same opportunities as middle-class whites to take civil-service tests, or enroll in college, or purchase a home, they would soon enjoy the same kinds of jobs and education and housing. Today, it is more widely recognized that a major obstruction to the progress of blacks and other racial minorities is the built-in or institutionalized discrimination that permeates American society.

Institutional discrimination results from the "normal functioning of institutions . . . often without conscious or deliberate intent."[6] Unlike individual discrimination, which arises from subjective elements in human personality, institutionalized discrimination has its origins in the established organizations and procedures of our society; as such, responsibility for it is often difficult to pinpoint. As Stokely Carmichael and Charles V. Hamilton wrote:

When white terrorists bomb a black church and kill black children, that is an act of individual racism, widely deplored by most segments of the society. But when in that same city — Birmingham, Alabama — five hundred black babies die each year because of the lack of proper food, shelter and medical facilities, and thousands more are destroyed and maimed physically, emotionally and intellectually because of conditions of poverty and discrimination in the black community, that is a function of institutional racism. . . .[7]

Carmichael and Hamilton spoke of the conditions of poverty and discrimination — sometimes referred to as the "culture of poverty" — that prevent the escape of low-income minority members from the urban slum ghetto. In our society, jobs that pay well usually require education or high scores on job-placement tests, but the conditions of ghetto life place these achievements out of the range of

---

[3] *Time* (March 20, 1972), p. 91.

[4] Speech by Attorney General Nicholas Katzenbach, at the St. Louis Conference on Equal Opportunity in Housing, 1965.

[5] Julian Samora (ed.), *La Raza: Forgotten Americans* (Notre Dame, Ind.: University of Notre Dame Press, 1966), pp. 186–187.

[6] Richard C. Edwards, Michael Reich, and Thomas E. Weisskopf (eds.), *The Capitalist System: A Radical Analysis of American Society* (Englewood Cliffs, N.J.: Prentice-Hall, 1972), p. 288.

[7] Stokely Carmichael and Charles V. Hamilton, *Black Power: The Politics of Liberation in America* (New York: Vintage, 1969), p. 4.

the minority urban poor. Thus, in theory, civil-service tests or college-entrance exams provide equal job or educational opportunities for all; but in practice, these tests may result in fewer minority placements. Chicanos, Puerto Ricans, Indians, and blacks often do poorly on standardized tests, either because they have attended poor schools in the ghetto, or because the tests themselves are culturally biased.[8] One of our most cherished democratic institutions, the impartial test, conceived to assure fair play, has thus instead discriminated against certain segments of our society.

Fighting Discrimination:
The Changing Pattern of the Seventies

Discrimination against minorities is hardly a new development in American life. The earliest immigrants in the 1800s, the Irish and Germans, encountered as much bitter opposition as the later Slavs and Italians; native-born Americans often refused to work on the same jobs with foreigners and accused them of coming to the United States to become public charges. Several ugly racial and religious riots erupted in eastern cities between 1820 and 1860. During the 1900s, immigrants from southern and eastern Europe were described by author Kenneth Roberts in a widely approved *Saturday Evening Post* series as "human parasites" who would produce "a hybrid race of good-for-nothing mongrels."[9] Throughout most of our history, Jews, Italians, and Poles have suffered from job and social discrimination, on religious as well as ethnic grounds.

However, the response of these earlier groups to discrimination and their search for equal rights differed considerably from that of today's underprivileged minority groups. In the past, minority groups attempted to overcome discrimination by acculturation—that is, through adoption of American ways. Middle European names were Americanized, and the customs and language of the homeland were soon forgotten. American-born children of immigrants were often embarrassed when their parents spoke only their native language and carried on the culture of the old country; generally they made a great effort to disassociate themselves from their parents' ethnic background. Recent studies have shown, however, that minority groups have not completely assimilated into American society; they merely adopted some American customs, but continued to live in separate neighborhoods and associate predominantly with their own groups. As a result, most minorities have not achieved equal status over the years; the relative position of the various groups is much the same today as when the immigrants arrived.

Many of today's minorities, indeed, have decided that they are no longer willing to discard their ethnic identity as the price of equality. This is particularly true of those who are distinguished from the mainstream by color and other racial characteristics. Many middle-class white Americans are bewildered by such be-

---

[8] For example, a ghetto child might be mystified by an IQ-test question that asks him to indicate which picture does not belong in a group of four pictures showing a book, a record, a puzzle, and a pair of shoes. Unlike a middle-class child, he might be so unfamiliar with the first three as recreational devices as to be unable to place them in a single category. Children who score poorly on standardized tests are stigmatized as "slow learners"; they are not expected to succeed, and the school and the society often give up on them early in the game. Hence, the IQ tests have been called discriminatory by many authorities, and some tests have been struck down by the courts as unconstitutional.

[9] Samuel Eliot Morison, *The Oxford History of the American People* (New York: Oxford University Press, 1965), p. 897.

The black civil-rights movement since the early 1960s has passed from its initially moderate and philosophical phase to its present radical and action-oriented position.

havior, especially when it is expressed by the more militant "black power," "red power," and "Chicano power" advocates, for they have grown up with the concept of acculturation as the accepted American path toward equal rights.

Minority Groups in American Society

During recent years, the leading American minority groups have been increasing in number relative to the rest of the population: nonwhites grew from 10.1 percent of the population in 1940 to 12.4 percent in 1970;[10] today in the United States there are 25.5 million nonwhites (blacks, American Indians, Japanese, Koreans, Chinese, Filipinos, Polynesians, Asian-Indians), and 10 million persons among the Spanish-speaking minorities (Mexican-Americans, Puerto Ricans, Cubans, and those from Central and South America and the Caribbean). The total of over 35 million represents about one out of every six Americans.

Who are the minority groups in American society? What problems do they face, and what remedies are they seeking?

Puerto Ricans

The Puerto Rican minority consists of about 1.5 million citizens, of whom 1.2 million live in Chicago, New York City, and smaller communities near New York—cities such as Newark, New Jersey; Hartford, Connecticut; and New Haven, Connecticut.[11] Puerto Rican ties with the United States go back to 1898, when Americans occupied the island during the Spanish-American War. Since 1917, Puerto Ricans have enjoyed full American citizenship, although the island is a commonwealth and not a state. As citizens, Puerto Ricans pay taxes, are subject to the draft, serve in the United States armed forces, vote in presidential elections, and may come and go freely between the island and the mainland. As immigrants to the mainland, Puerto Ricans are latecomers, for the major exodus from the island did not occur until 1945–1959. At that time, some five hundred thousand emigrated from their homes to escape poverty brought about by a high birth rate and high levels of unemployment.[12] They were lured by job opportunities in the booming postwar American economy. Since the mid-sixties, as jobs have declined and housing and education deteriorated in the northeastern cities, immigration has fallen substantially, and there has been a net outflow of an estimated 145,000 or more Puerto Ricans from the continental United States back to the island.[13]

A Puerto Rican in the United States finds language a formidable obstacle to employment, housing, and education. Spanish-speaking children, in particular, have had a very difficult time in English-speaking schools, and this difficulty has produced a high incidence of school failure, school dropout, unemployment, poverty, drug addiction, and crime, all interrelated. In New York City, for example, only one out of five Puerto Rican adults has finished high school;[14] the unemployment rate for Puerto Rican workers in 1969 was three times the rate for the city's white workers and twice that for the city's black workers;[15] and 65 percent of the Puerto Ricans lived in poverty.[16]

---

[10] *Statistical Abstract of the United States, 1971* (Washington, D.C.: Department of Commerce, 1971).

[11] *U.S. News & World Report* (August 13, 1970), p. 66.

[12] M. Maldonado-Denis, "The Puerto Ricans: Protest or Submission," *Annals,* vol. 382 (March 1969), p. 27.

[13] Maldonado-Denis, "The Puerto Ricans," p. 27.

[14] *U.S. News & World Report* (August 13, 1970), p. 61.

[15] U.S. Department of Labor, Bureau of Labor Statistics, *Regional Reports,* no. 19 (May 1971), p. 1.

[16] The *New York Times* (March 22, 1971).

A changing concept of the role of minorities in our society is reflected in certain official policies toward the Puerto Rican minority. During the early post–World War II era, Puerto Ricans were expected to conform to the traditional American pattern of acculturation: education was conducted in English, voting was restricted to those who could pass English literacy tests, and candidates for government jobs (such as the police force in New York City) had to meet exactly the same requirements as other applicants. In recent years, however, attempts have been made to recognize the special problems of the Puerto Rican population. For example, New York State has approved literacy tests in Spanish, New York City now provides bilingual education, and the height requirement for admission to the New York City Police Academy has been reduced for the benefit of Puerto Ricans, who are often short.

It is difficult to predict what path the Puerto Rican community will take to attain equal status. Most Puerto Ricans appear willing, at least to some extent, to accept American values and behavior patterns. Yet there is a small but vocal minority, represented, for example, by the militant Young Lords in New York City, which condemns acculturation. Instead, they advocate new emphasis on traditional Puerto Rican values and culture, with the more extreme advocating complete independence from the United States for Puerto Rico as the only way to preserve the Puerto Rican way of life. Whether they live in the United States or on the island, most Puerto Ricans, however, prefer either a continuation of the present commonwealth status for the island, or a move toward statehood. But despite its small size, the independence movement is significant as a facet of the growing ethnic self-awareness of the Puerto Rican people.

American Indians

There are perhaps as many as one million American Indians in the United States;[17] about half live on reservations—primarily in Alaska, Arizona, New Mexico, Oklahoma, South Dakota, and Montana—and the rest in cities across the nation. Of all our minorities, American Indians are probably the most neglected. A study of American Indians in the 1970s referred to them as the "poorest of the poor,"[18] and the statistics are indeed appalling. The average annual family income is $1,500—less than one-fifth of the national average, and $4,000 below the median income of black families. Their unemployment rate runs close to 40 percent; more than half the Indian school children (double the national average) drop out of school; fifty thousand Indian families live in "grossly substandard homes,"[19] described as "worse than [those] found in Appalachia or any slum."[20] One statistic has the most tragic implications of all: the suicide rate of Indian teenagers, one hundred times that of white adolescents, reflects the despair with which young Indians view their world.[21]

---

[17] This figure is controversial. The Interior Department population estimate for 1970 was 650,000 Indians; another authority (Alvin Josephy) estimates Indian population at 800,000 and the Americans for Indian Opportunity, a private group, estimates 1 million.

[18] Alvin M. Josephy, Jr., *Red Power: The American Indian's Fight for Freedom* (New York: McGraw-Hill, 1971), p. 3.

[19] Josephy, *Red Power*, p. 3.

[20] Josephy, *Red Power*, p. 207.

[21] Josephy, *Red Power*, p. 3.

Indians on reservations are served by the Bureau of Indian Affairs (BIA), created in 1824 and now part of the Department of the Interior. The Bureau is considered the trustee of the reservation lands belonging to the Indians, and is responsible for providing public services, such as education and health care.

In all, the federal government spends about half a billion dollars a year in helping reservation Indians; but Indians who live away from the reservations receive no assistance from the Bureau. President Nixon described three-fourths of these urban Indians as living in poverty.[22]

The relationship between the federal government and the Indians goes back to the Northwest Ordinance (1787), which stated that "the utmost good faith shall always be observed towards the Indians, their lands and property shall never be taken from them without their consent. . . ." Until 1871, the federal government dealt with individual Indian tribes as it would with separate foreign nations. Through a series of treaties and money payments, it obtained Indian lands, but internal Indian matters were theoretically left to the authority of the autonomous tribes. In 1871, however, Congress voted that no Indian tribe would thereafter be recognized as an independent power, and serious attempts were made to bring Indian affairs under the direct control of Congress. Jurisdiction for crimes committed within the tribe, for example, was transferred from tribal councils to the federal courts.[23] Traditional Indian life was further disrupted by the Dawes (or Allotment) Act of 1887, by which Indian lands were subdivided among individual Indians (rather than held in trust for the entire tribe); these lands were thus made available for eventual purchase by outsiders. As a result of the Dawes Act, between 1887 and 1934 the Indians lost 86 million of their 138 million acres of land. Soon there were thousands of landless Indians, with no training or skills to enable them to earn a living in white society; and the urban Indian problem, as we know it today, developed. The allotment system was finally abolished under the Indian Reorganization Act of 1934, which also encouraged tribes in various ways to reassume responsibility for self-government, and to purchase former Indian lands in the open market as they became available.

In 1952, the Eisenhower administration adopted a highly controversial program intended to end, once and for all, the "special relationship" between the government and the Indians. Its key points were "relocation" (encouragement of Indians to move from the reservations to urban areas) and "termination" (elimination of the "special" services and protection offered by the federal government to the Indian tribes). Many Indian groups, however, felt that what was being "terminated" was the federal responsibility and the special rights that were owed the Indians under earlier treaties (such as the right to fish or hunt in certain areas regardless of existing Game and Fish Commission rules).[24] Moreover, many Indians believed that, without federal protection, they would be unable to maintain their cultural

---

[22] President Nixon's message to Congress, July 8, 1970.

[23] Congress was reacting to public opinion which had been aroused by several Indian raids (the Custer Massacre, the Chiricahua uprising under Geronimo, etc.) and had lost confidence in the willingness of Indian tribes to respect treaties. Current research, however, suggests that treaty violations were frequently by whites, rather than Indians, and that Indian leaders such as Geronimo or the Nez Percé Chief Joseph often embarked upon military adventures only as a last resort, after other attempts to obtain their treaty rights had failed.

[24] See Murray L. Wax, *American Indians: Unity and Diversity* (Englewood Cliffs, N.J.: Prentice-Hall, 1971), pp. 147–148 for discussion of termination policy and Indian response to it.

identity and tribal lands. By the late 1950s, the policy of termination was largely abandoned by the BIA. Current federal policy seems to be directed toward improving the lot of Indians and helping them retain their cultural identity.

What do the Indians want today? How do they plan to achieve their goals? In a letter sent by seventy-eight Indians who occupied Alcatraz Island in San Francisco on November 20, 1969,[25] and again in the 1970 statement of the Indian members of the National Council on Indian Opportunity,[26] Indian groups set forth their desires. In the statement of the National Council, Indians spoke of the need for hard-surfaced roads, government-guaranteed loan programs, better rapport with the banking community, consumer-education programs, and improved housing, schools, and medical care. Similarly, the Alcatraz Indians demanded solutions to their "water problems, land problems, 'social problems,' job opportunity problems."[27] Both groups emphasized two other factors: the importance of "self determination and control over their own destiny,"[28] and their desire to retain their own cultural identity.

Slowly, a new direction in Indian affairs is emerging. The federal government, for example, has encouraged greater Indian participation in the BIA (in 1970 an Indian was appointed commissioner of the Bureau), and it has released additional funds for specific projects like Head Start and Neighborhood Youth Corps. Among Americans as a whole, there is new recognition of the dignity and worth of Indian culture.

Mexican-Americans

About five million Mexican Americans live in the United States today, primarily in the Southwest, with the largest concentration in California, Arizona, Texas, New Mexico, and Colorado. Calling themselves Chicanos, many are migrant farm workers, although the majority live in urban slums in large cities (Phoenix, Tucson, Denver, Albuquerque, Dallas, Houston, Los Angeles, Santa Barbara). Generally, they obtain less education than whites, whom they refer to as Anglos, in the same communities, and 26 percent are actually illiterate.[29] (Mexican-Americans average 8.1 years of education in the Southwest as compared to 12 years for whites and 9.7 years for nonwhites.)[30] In addition, job opportunities for Chicanos are restricted: in proportion to their population, four times as many Anglos are found in professional and technical occupations as Chicanos;[31] the unemployment rate for Chicanos is often twice that of Anglos;[32] and in 1970, 28 percent of all Mexican-American families had incomes below the poverty line.[33]

Discrimination against Mexican-Americans has its roots, some sociologists say,

[25] These Indians, most of them college students, acted under an old federal law which permits Indian tribes to reclaim land originally owned by them but taken by the federal government, if the government no longer uses it.

[26] This is a presidential council consisting of the Vice President, seven Cabinet members, the director of the Office of Economic Opportunity, and eight Indian members.

[27] Josephy, *Red Power*, p. 188.

[28] Josephy, *Red Power*, p. 194.

[29] The *New York Times* (October 18, 1971), p. 1.

[30] *U.S. News & World Report* (July 13, 1970), p. 67.

[31] Samora, *La Raza*, p. 100.

[32] Samora, *La Raza*, p. 188.

[33] U.S. Bureau of the Census, *Current Population Reports*, Series P-20, no. 224 (October 1971), p. 7.

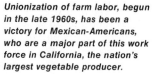

Unionization of farm labor, begun in the late 1960s, has been a victory for Mexican-Americans, who are a major part of this work force in California, the nation's largest vegetable producer.

in the language barrier. Because many of the children learned to speak only Spanish at home, in the past they were segregated in slow "special classes" or even in separate schools. In Driscoll, Texas, for example, a majority of the Chicano children routinely had to spend three years in the first two grades.[34] All through his school career, similar problems confront the Chicano child whenever testing and classification are done in English. As an extreme example, a Los Angeles elementary school teacher testified before the House Committee on Education and Labor that her district, acting on the results of such intelligence tests, had placed certain Spanish-speaking pupils in classes for retarded children.[35] More common in the upper grades is the practice of automatically placing Spanish-speaking children in vocational or industrial-arts programs, on the assumption that they cannot do academic or college-preparatory work. Thus, they are barred from many higher paying jobs and, in effect, confined to a life of poverty.

---

[34] Samora, *La Raza,* p. 97.

[35] Samora, *La Raza,* p. 98, quoting hearings before the Select Committee on Education of the Committee on Education and Labor, House, 88th Cong., 1st Sess., Los Angeles, August 12, 1963, p. 26; statement of Mrs. Ninfa Nieto.

In the past, the Mexican-American community made relatively few organized attempts to fight discrimination. On the federal level, there is one senator of Spanish-speaking extraction (Joseph Montoya of New Mexico), and only a handful of representatives. On the state level, in 1970 only one member of the California state legislature was a Chicano, although Chicanos constituted more than 11 percent of the total state population.[36] Recently, however, Mexican-Americans have shown a new interest in politics. A Chicano party, *La Raza Unida* (literally, the United Race), headed by José Angel Guiterrez, has appeared on the ballot in several Texas elections and has managed to elect several town and city officials. Other Chicanos have attempted to work through the existing party system. For example, the election of Republican Senator John Tower of Texas in 1966 was attributed by some to dissatisfaction on the part of Chicano voters with the Democratic candidate; also, the one-hundred-thirty–member delegation from Texas to the 1972 Democratic Convention included eighteen Mexican-Americans, the first time that Chicanos have had more than token representation.[37]

But political action is only one facet of the new Chicano activism. *La Causa* (The Cause), the farm movement led by Cesar Chavez, which was started to unionize Chicano migrant vineyard workers in California, has now taken on larger implications. The grape strike, which lasted from 1965 to 1970 and produced a nationwide boycott of California grapes, was marked on both sides by a deep bitterness of a kind not seen in recent times in the American labor movement. Finally, in 1970, the grape owners recognized Chavez's United Farm Workers Union, raised wages (from $1.10 an hour to $1.80 an hour, plus 20¢ a box), and the strike was over. Since then, Chavez has attempted to unionize other Southwestern agricultural workers, notably lettuce pickers, with varying degrees of success. To many observers, Cesar Chavez is important not only because of his specific economic accomplishment for Chicano migrant workers, but because he has raised self-awareness among Chicanos and shown them the importance of unified action. In the past, Mexican-Americans often stood by quietly while other minority groups organized. Today, however, there is a "brown beret" group in Los Angeles, a Mexican-American Political Association, and a Chicano political party (*La Raza Unida*).

Women

Although women make up slightly more than half the population of the United States, they, like the ethnic minority groups, have experienced various kinds of discrimination. In Texas, for example, state law makes it more difficult for a married woman than for her husband to acquire, own, or dispose of property; in Chicago, San Francisco, and other large cities, unmarried working women, regardless of their incomes, often find that landlords will not rent apartments to them; before 1963, the Harvard Business School would not admit women; and until a few years ago, Connecticut law prohibited the serving of alcoholic beverages to women seated at bars. The most economically oppressive form of discrimination against women is practiced in employment. Women generally are restricted to the less attractive, poorest-paying jobs, 64 percent of all women workers holding

---

[36] Stan Steiner, "Chicano Power," *New Republic* (June 29, 1970), p. 16.
[37] The *New York Times* (June 15, 1972).

jobs as sales clerks, service employees, and household servants, whereas only 20 percent of all male workers are employed in these occupations.[38]

Although there are still some legal bars to equal treatment of women in the job market (state or local laws may prohibit employment at night, on overtime, or in certain jobs officially designated as unsuitable for women), women are primarily the victims of institutionalized discrimination. For many years, the standard excuse for paying women less than men for similar work was that women "do not need the money," an idea supported by the old stereotype of the woman who enters the labor market because she is bored with housework. A government survey of the labor force in 1967, however, showed that more than half of all working women at that time were either "unmarried, separated from their husbands or married to men earning less than $3,000 a year."[39] In other words, they were working for the same reason men work: to support themselves and their families.

Women are often subtly discouraged from entering many fields. Young girls are generally taught by parents and teachers that women should be either mothers, teachers, or nurses; children's textbooks rarely portray women as being employed outside the home; instead, women are often characterized as passive spectators of male competition and achievement. Young women may hesitate to enter occupations they have been taught to view as "unfeminine" — so that, although 40 percent of those scoring high on certain engineering aptitude tests are women, women make up only 2 percent of the nation's engineers.[40] Similarly, women are often discouraged from pursuing the higher education needed for more prestigious jobs. For example, although roughly the same number of girls as boys graduate from high school, many fewer women obtain bachelors' and higher degrees. Less than 1 percent of tenured full professors at major American universities are women.

The Federal Equal Pay Law now prohibits employers from paying women less money than men for the same job, but the law works only in theory. In 1972, for example, the Pacific Telephone Company was forced to pay more than half a million dollars make-up pay to three hundred women who were employed as "plant service clerks" doing the same work as male "line assigners," but had received as much as $45 less pay a week. Nevertheless, some employers apparently find ways of circumventing the law. In a survey of starting salaries for 1971 graduates by major field, for instance, Northwestern University found that male accounting majors received an average of $845 a month, and women, $793. The University Placement Office contended that this was not an example of unequal pay for equal jobs, but rather reflected the fact that companies offered women different jobs that happened to pay less.[41]

Whether the Equal Rights For Women Amendment, recently passed by both the House and the Senate and (in 1972) in the process of ratification by the required three-fourths of the states, will really deter discrimination against women is questionable. Many feel that women's best vehicle for achieving equal rights is the women's liberation movement. By pressing for such services as day-care

[38] U.S. Department of Labor data in M. Suelzle, "Women in Labor," *Trans-Action,* vol. 8 (December 1970).
[39] U.S. Bureau of the Census, *Current Population Reports,* Series P-60, no. 75, Table 47, p. 105.
[40] *U.S. News & World Report* (September 8, 1969), p. 46.
[41] *New York,* May 1972.

centers and legal abortion, and by consciousness-raising activities that improve the self-image and aspiration level of women, feminists hope to prepare women for equal status with men in a society free of institutionalized discrimination.

Blacks

In 1903, W. E. B. DuBois, the black sociologist, warned that "the problem of the 20th century is the problem of the color line."[42] Sixty-five years later, the National Advisory Commission on Civil Disorders warned: "Our nation is moving towards two societies, one black, one white—separate and unequal."[43] There have been certain recent improvements—a rising black middle class now exists in the United States, and educational opportunities for blacks are significantly wider than they were twenty years ago. Blacks are now represented, if only in token numbers, at the highest levels of business and government. Yet discrimination against blacks in the United States today is as prevalent and as persistent as that against any other group.

Blacks represent a very large minority group: the 1970 official government figures show 22.6 million, or 11.2 percent of the population; but because of inaccurate counting in the census, the figure may actually be as high as 30 million, or 15 percent.[44] As late as 1910, 91 percent of the United States black population lived in the South, primarily in rural communities. But today, 70 percent live in metropolitan areas, most concentrated in the 12 largest central city ghettos in the nation.[45] Despite some emigration of the black middle class, black populations continue to grow within the central-city areas.

What is life like for the more than 12.5 million blacks who live in our central cities? The Kerner report estimated that two-thirds live in neighborhoods characterized by substandard housing and widespread urban blight. For the nation as a whole, the nonwhite unemployment rate is about twice that of whites: in the ghetto, the "subemployment" rate (unemployment plus underemployment[46]) has been estimated as high as 33 percent, with perhaps five hundred thousand "hardcore" unemployed—those who are unable to find a steady job, usually because they lack a basic education. Black men are about three times as likely as white men to hold dead-end unskilled jobs. For such persons, the future is even more bleak, for most new-job opportunities will probably be suitable for skilled workers and will be located outside the central cities; many blacks, then, will have neither the skills nor the access to them.

About 40 percent of the central-city blacks have incomes below the poverty

---

[42] As quoted in John Hope Franklin and Isidore Starr (eds.), *The Negro in 20th Century America* (New York: Vintage, 1967), p. ix.

[43] *Report of National Advisory Commission on Civil Disorders* (New York: Bantam, 1968), p. 1. This commission was established by President Johnson in the aftermath of the series of riots which swept through black ghettos of our major cities in 1967; it was headed by Governor Otto Kerner of Illinois and was charged with investigating causes of these civil disorders.

[44] Senator Robert Kennedy's researchers estimated that census takers missed 10 percent of the total black population, and 20 percent in the ghettos. The Moynihan Report suggested substantial undercounting, running as high as 19.8 percent among blacks under age 28. Data from Nat Hentoff, "Reflections on Black Power," in *The Politics of Confrontation*, edited by Samuel Hendel (New York: Appleton-Century-Crofts, 1971), p. 41.

[45] Most of the following data are taken from *The Report of the National Advisory Commission on Civil Disorders (Kerner Report).*

[46] Underemployment refers to a situation in which the individual is employed, but at a level below his full capacity.

line; they live in a culture of poverty characterized by crime (Kerner reported that a low-income black district in one city had thirty-five times as many serious crimes as a high-income white district in the same city); poor health and poor sanitation (most of the 14,000 cases of rat bite in the United States in 1965 occurred in ghetto neighborhoods); and poor education, with many black children falling farther behind whites in essential verbal and reading skills with each school year completed.

The sense of despair and hopelessness that has been created by segregation and poverty in the black central-city ghettos has dangerous implications for our entire society. Blacks who no longer believe that the existing system provides a way for them to obtain full participation in American society and a share in the material benefits enjoyed by the white middle class, have reacted with alienation and hostility to white society. The typical rioter in 1967, for example, was a black male teenager, a high-school dropout, either unemployed or underemployed. Thus, the Kerner Commission Report warned that if nothing was done to reverse present policies, "large-scale and continuous violence could result, followed by white retaliation, and ultimately the separation of the two communities into a garrison state."[47] It foresaw that a continuing racial polarization would ultimately destroy the basic democratic values in American society. In other words, segregation and discrimination are harmful not only to blacks but "they now threaten the future of every American."[48]

Racial Discrimination in the United States: A Case Study of Black Americans

Historical Background

Suppression of blacks in America began in 1619, when a Dutch trading ship brought the first slaves to the colony at Jamestown, Virginia. In 1790, there were an estimated 750,000 blacks in the United States (about 20 percent of the total population), of whom 700,000 were slaves.[49] Slave labor was of considerable economic importance during the colonial period. Tobacco, rice, and indigo, the major export crops of the southern colonies, were grown with slave labor; trading and shipbuilding, the leading northern industries, were closely tied to the slave trade with Africa. Thus, in the eighteenth century, slave labor sustained the wealth of the northern as well as the southern colonies.

Slavery was a touchy problem at the Constitutional Convention. Delegate George Mason warned against the "pernicious effect" of slavery, claiming that it would "bring down the judgment of Heaven on a country."[50] But others insisted that their states could not do without slaves, and the final version of the Constitution implicitly accepts the institution of slavery. The Constitution did, however, give Congress the right to ban further importation of slaves after 1808.

---

[47] *Kerner Report,* p. 22.

[48] *Kerner Report,* p. 22.

[49] Bureau of the Census, *Historical Statistics of the United States, 1789–1945* (Washington, D.C.: Department of Commerce, 1945), Table B13–23.

[50] Rodney P. Carlisle, *Prologue to Liberation: A History of Black People in America* (New York: Appleton-Century-Crofts, 1972), p. 73.

In the years preceding the Civil War, the expansion of cotton production gave new importance to the role of the black slave in the United States economy. After the invention of the cotton gin by Eli Whitney in 1793, cotton production skyrocketed: three thousand bales were produced in 1790, one hundred thousand in 1800, and by 1840, two million bales of cotton were grown annually. In 1840, cotton exports accounted for 57 percent of the dollar value of all United States exports. If the value of tobacco exports at that time is added to the value of cotton, these two slave-produced crops totaled 66 percent of the nation's exports.

The pre–Civil War period was marked by a series of slave rebellions – perhaps as many as two hundred fifty[51] – including Gabriel Prosser's Plot (1800), the Denmark Vesey Plot (1822), in which several thousand slaves were involved, and Nat Turner's Revolt (1831). In every case, the uprisings were put down with great brutality. For instance, Prosser and thirty-five of his followers were hanged, and after the Vesey Plot failed, thirty-seven participants were executed.

The pre–Civil War position of the black slave in American society was spelled out in the Supreme Court's *Dred Scott* decision of 1857. Scott, a former Missouri slave, claimed that he had become a free man by virtue of his four-year residence in Illinois (a free state) and Wisconsin (a free territory). His owner at the time of the trial, John Sanford, agreed with Scott, but decided to take the case to the Supreme Court in the hope that the Court would rule that former slaves could acquire their freedom by living in a free state or territory, thus providing abolitionist groups with a major new tool for freeing individual slaves. The Court ruled, however, that Scott had no right to sue for freedom for, in the words of Chief Justice Taney, black Americans were "not intended to be included under the word 'citizens' in the Constitution."[52]

After the Civil War, passage of the Thirteenth Amendment (1865) outlawed slavery in the United States; the Fourteenth (1868) gave the former slaves citizenship (thus negating the *Dred Scott* decision), and the Fifteenth gave blacks the right to vote. The Civil Rights Acts of 1866 and 1875 were further attempts by radical Republicans to insure equal rights for blacks: the 1866 Act (passed over President Andrew Johnson's veto) stated that blacks were entitled to equal treatment before the law and gave the federal Freeman's Bureau the power to set up special courts to defend the rights of former slaves, and the 1875 Act forbade discrimination in public places and on public carriers.

For a time, it appeared that federal protection of the civil rights of black citizens would prove effective, but the picture soon changed. For example, although many former slaves voted during the early Reconstruction period and actually managed to elect twenty-two southern blacks to the House and two to the Senate, by 1910 every one of the former Confederate states had disenfranchised its black citizens. In the civil rights cases of 1883 the Supreme Court struck down the Civil Rights Act of 1875 as unconstitutional, holding that the Fourteenth Amendment protected only against infringement of civil rights by the states, and not by private individuals.

The decision of the Court in *Plessy* v. *Ferguson* (1896) was even more devastating.[53] In 1890, Louisiana had passed a law requiring railroads to furnish "sep-

---

[51] This estimate comes from Herbert Aptheker, who defined a rebellion as any uprising involving ten or more slaves reported in the newspapers or similar records of the time. Carlisle, *Prologue to Liberation*, p. 43.

[52] *Dred Scott* v. *Sanford*, 19 How. 393 (1857).

[53] *Plessy* v. *Ferguson*, 163 U.S. 537 (1896).

arate but equal" accommodations for white and "colored" passengers. In 1892, Homer Adolph Plessy[54] took an empty seat in a "white" coach on a train leaving New Orleans, but he was ordered by the conductor to move to the "colored" coach. He refused, was then forcibly ejected from the train, locked up in the New Orleans jail, and convicted before a Judge Ferguson on a charge of violating Louisiana law. Plessy took the case to the Supreme Court, arguing that the Louisiana law violated the "equal protection" clause of the Fourteenth Amendment, which provides that no state shall "deny to any person within its jurisdiction the equal protection of the laws."

In a seven-to-one decision, the Court ruled that "separate but equal" public accommodations, schools, and so forth were constitutional. As a result, Jim Crow laws multiplied throughout the south. Blacks were separated not only in trains, schools, and hospitals, but at drinking fountains, pay windows, and even churches. In Atlanta, Georgia, blacks were required to visit the local zoo at different times from whites.

After World War I, blacks began to migrate to northern cities, a trend that accelerated rapidly after World War II. In 1939 President Franklin D. Roosevelt created a Civil Liberties Unit in the Department of Justice (later to become the Civil Rights Section), and established the first Committee on Fair Employment Practices, which had some effectiveness in eliminating discrimination in employment in companies and labor unions working on government contracts. In 1948, President Harry Truman banned racial segregation in the armed forces. Although this action did not affect certain southern state National Guard and Reserve units, it was a first major step toward elimination of discrimination in the military.

The Civil Rights Movement: 1950 to Mid-Sixties

Much of the impetus for the civil-rights advances of the last twenty years has come from the Supreme Court, beginning with the 1954 landmark decision in *Brown* v. *Board of Education,* which abolished constitutional sanction for the "separate but equal" doctrine and Jim Crow laws.[55] The case concerned Linda Carol Brown, an eight-year-old black child who lived only four blocks from the "white" Sumner Elementary School in Topeka, Kansas. Because Kansas law permitted Topeka to provide "separate but equal" public schools, Linda was forced to attend a segregated school twenty-one blocks from home, first crossing a dangerous railroad bridge, and then taking an overcrowded school bus which was often late. When Mr. Brown and the parents of twelve other black children asked the Sumner School principal to admit their children, he refused. Mr. Brown's case was taken to the Supreme Court, where Thurgood Marshall, then Chief Counsel for the NAACP (and since 1967 a Supreme Court Justice) argued it. In *Brown* v. *Board of Education* the decision written by Chief Justice Warren declared that segregation in the schools by race is "inherently unequal."

The 1954 decision did not in itself attempt to enforce desegregation, but in 1955 the Court heard further arguments and subsequently ruled that local school districts must proceed to end segregation "with all deliberate speed." Communities in some non-southern and border states (Arizona, Wyoming, Kansas, Virginia,

---

[54] Plessy was seven-eighths white, and appeared white. He had been chosen by the "Citizens Committee to test the Constitutionality of the Separate Car Law" to provide a test case. The Committee had advised the East Louisiana Railroad of its intention.

[55] *Brown* v. *Board of Education of Topeka,* 347 U.S. 483 (1954).

Missouri, among others) desegregated at once. But considerable resistance arose in the Deep South (Alabama, Georgia, Louisiana, and Mississippi), abetted in some cases by local public officials who deliberately defied the law. In September 1957, violence erupted when nine black teenagers tried to enter the all-white Central High School in Little Rock, Arkansas, armed with a federal court order instructing the school to admit them. President Eisenhower, who until then had been cautious in giving his support to the Supreme Court decision, federalized the Arkansas National Guard and sent in a thousand paratroopers. Violence broke out again in 1962 when James Meredith, a black student, tried to enter the University of Mississippi, and again in 1963, when two blacks tried to enroll at the University of Alabama at Tuscaloosa. In the Meredith case, President Kennedy sent federal marshals and sixteen thousand troops to restore order; at Tuscaloosa, he had to federalize the Alabama National Guard.

Once "separate but equal" had been declared unconstitutional in regard to educational facilities, it was only a question of time until attempts would be made to throw out Jim Crow practices in other areas. In December 1955, Rosa Parks, a black seamstress, refused to give up her seat in the "white" section at the front of a bus in Montgomery, Alabama. She was arrested and fined ten dollars, but her action precipitated a one-year boycott of Montgomery's bus system, under the leadership of a twenty-seven-year-old recent graduate of Boston University Divinity School, Dr. Martin Luther King, Jr. The boycott attracted nationwide attention by dramatizing the use of nonviolent resistance as a tool for acquiring civil rights. Following the successful Montgomery boycott, King and Reverend Ralph Abernathy founded the Southern Christian Leadership Conference (SCLC). The chief black civil-rights group, until that time the NAACP (National Association for the Advancement of Colored People), always relied primarily on legal action. Now the SCLC prompted, instead, the use of resistance by nonviolent direct action, and attempted to mobilize the moral indignation of blacks and whites. Using these methods, the SCLC became the leading force, and King the leading spokesman, for civil rights throughout the late fifties and early sixties.

The next important attack on Jim Crow took place in Greensboro, North Carolina, when black college students conducted a sit-in at a Woolworth's lunch counter where the management followed local practice by refusing to serve them. Out of this confrontation and others like it the Student Nonviolent Coordinating Committee (SNCC) developed, and over the next few years it was to use similar tactics — sit-ins, peaceful picketing, boycotts — to desegregate theaters, parks, hotels, and other public facilities throughout the South. In 1961, CORE (Congress of Racial Equality) also used such methods to desegregate interstate bus companies. Freedom Riders, groups of black and white youths, attempted to integrate buses, waiting rooms, lunch counters. The confrontations were intended to be peaceful, but in Alabama and Mississippi, riders were beaten and stoned, and one bus was overturned.

During the early sixties, the SCLC and SNCC also became active in voter-registration campaigns. In the spring of 1963, Dr. King mounted a major effort to register voters in Birmingham, Alabama, but local police and firemen attacked those who attempted to register. Newspaper photos and TV films of Birmingham Police Commissioner "Bull" Connor and his men using police dogs and clubs against the demonstrators shocked the nation. The black community reacted to violence with violence; riots erupted throughout the city, and, finally, when the white community was endangered, federal troops were sent in.

When Freedom Riders traveled from city to city in the South,
federal troops guarded their buses to forestall any conflicts.

After months of violence, Martin Luther King led a peaceful march of 250,000 blacks and whites to Washington in August to demonstrate for passage of a strong civil-rights act. It was here, in front of the Lincoln Memorial, that King delivered his now-famous "I have a dream" address:

> *I have a dream that one day this nation will rise up and live out the true meaning of its creed: "We hold these truths to be self-evident, that all men are created equal."*
> *. . . when all of God's children, black men and white men, Jews and Gentiles, Protestants and Catholics, will be able to join hands and sing in the words of the old Negro spiritual: "Free at last! free at last! thank God almighty, we are free at last!"*

The New Militancy

The March on Washington was inspirational, but it marked the end of a phase of the civil-rights movement that was primarily middle class, southern, nonviolent, and interracial. From this time on, as nonviolence failed in many cases and the federal government did not take action, a more militant leadership emerged. In subsequent years, the Civil Rights movement has tended to exclude whites, and to become militant, northern, and urban. Many blacks today feel that the enormous American commitment in Vietnam has been made at their expense— that money has been spent for the war, rather than for schools, housing, and health services, and that black combat deaths, as a percent of the black population, were greater than those of whites. Moreover, a new awareness of their rich African cultural heritage is emerging among American blacks to whom cultural assimilation no longer appears attractive. As James Baldwin said, "Do I really want to be integrated into a burning house?"[56]

The new militancy exploded in a series of riots in Watts, a section of Los Angeles, in August 1965, which lasted six days and ended in 34 deaths and 3,952 arrests. Subsequently, rioting occurred in Cleveland, Detroit, Newark, Chicago, St. Louis, San Francisco, and elsewhere. The Kerner Commission in 1968 concluded that these riots were largely spontaneous, and not the result of a nationwide conspiracy. Various organized black militant groups, however, were springing up across the country. As early as 1966, Stokely Carmichael of SNCC made black audiences aware of the phrase "black power" as he traveled on a freedom march through Mississippi; later that year, in Oakland, California, Bobby Seale and Huey Newton formed the Black Panther Party for Self Defense (the Party's third spokesman, Eldridge Cleaver, joined them in 1967). The Panthers were formed to act against violations of the rights of black citizens by the police. Since then, the organization has produced a ten-point program stressing the rights of blacks to self-determination and resistance to white economic exploitation. However, of the program as a whole, the violent assertions have drawn the greatest public attention. "The Black Panther never attacks first, but when he is backed into a corner, he will strike back viciously,"[57] reads the party literature—a very different approach from Martin Luther King's advice to accept an unjust white society "openly, lovingly."

From its inception, the Black Panther Party has met with considerable opposition. Party leaders have been caught up in a series of raids, shootouts, and arrests: Huey Newton was convicted of manslaughter of an Oakland policeman in 1968 and Bobby Seale of conspiring to incite riots at the 1968 Democratic Convention in Chicago; Fred Hampton was killed in a police attack on Panther headquarters in Chicago in 1969. Some view the Panthers and similar Black Power groups as a serious threat to the American system; the late director of the FBI, J. Edgar Hoover, called the Panthers the "most dangerous and violence-prone of all extremist groups."[58] Others, however, argue that police harassment of the Panthers has frequently been unjustified and marked by serious excesses. For instance, the federal grand jury investigating the shootout in Chicago in which Fred Hampton died found that the police had fired more than eighty shots into the apartment, while the Panthers had fired only one.[59]

---

[56] Skolnick, *The Politics of Protest*, p. 155.
[57] Skolnick, *The Politics of Protest*, p. 152.
[58] The *New York Times* (August 14, 1970).
[59] The *New York Times* (May 23, 1970)

Government Action
to End Discrimination

Discrimination in Education

Government moves against discrimination in education, as in other areas, have come from several sources: the courts, the Congress, and the President. The federal government has been brought into conflict with the states on the issue of school desegregation. Another part of the problem has been regulation of the private sector.

In the early years following the decision by the Supreme Court in *Brown* v. *Board of Education* (1954), and its subsequent ruling in 1955 instructing local school districts to desegregate with "all deliberate speed," various methods were devised by white southerners to evade school integration. In the words of one writer, the political leaders of some states launched "the most callous and unconscionable campaigns of frustration, evasion, circumvention, defiance and distortion of the law that twentieth-century America has ever known."[60] The Board of Supervisors of one Virginia county passed a resolution vowing never to operate public schools "wherein white and colored children are together";[61] the Arkansas General Assembly approved a law against compulsory attendance at racially mixed schools, and Senator Herman Talmadge of Georgia proposed a constitutional amendment which would restore the "separate but equal" educational formula.

All over the Deep South, state legislatures repealed compulsory school attendance laws, closed schools, provided tuition grants to private (white) schools, and refused to cut off appropriations to segregated schools. In one extreme case, for example, the Board of Supervisors of Prince Edward County, Virginia, refused to levy school taxes and closed the public schools in 1959–1964. During this time, many of the white children in the county attended private white schools, supported primarily by tuition grants and tax credits authorized by the General Assembly of Virginia and the Supervisors of the county; black children, on the other hand, had no schools at all. The situation persisted for five years, until the Supreme Court ruled (*Griffin* v. *School Board of Prince Edward County*) that the Prince Edward's support of private education was unconstitutional; accordingly, the federal district court ordered the county officials to appropriate funds for a desegregated public school system.[62]

Little Rock, Arkansas, erupted into violence as the governor of the state attempted to defy the court. Shortly after the *Brown* decision was announced, the Little Rock school board drew up a long-range desegregation plan. Early in September 1957, as a first step, nine black teenagers were scheduled to enter the formerly all-white Central High. To prevent their entry, Governor Orval Faubus, acting with support from the state legislature (although no request had come from the local school authorities) sent units of the Arkansas National Guard to the school. For three weeks, guardsmen "stood shoulder to shoulder at the school

---

[60] Spicer, *The Supreme Court and Fundamental Freedoms,* 2nd edition (New York: Appleton-Century-Crofts, 1967), pp. 183–184.

[61] Spicer, *The Supreme Court and Fundamental Freedoms,* p. 185.

[62] *Griffin* v. *School Board of Prince Edward County,* 377 U.S. 218 (1964).

The admission of James Meredith to the University of Mississippi in 1962 necessitated the presence of federal guards to put down disturbances and protect Meredith, the first black student ever to attend "Old Miss."

grounds and . . . forcibly prevented the nine Negro students from entering."[63] On September 20, the Arkansas National Guard was withdrawn on orders from the federal District Court; two days later the black students entered the school under the protection of the Little Rock Police Department and the Arkansas State Police. By that time, public opinion was so aroused that large, unruly crowds gathered about the area, threatening the safety of the students, and President Eisenhower was forced to send regular army troops to the school. These troops, plus federalized national guardsmen, remained there throughout the balance of the year, as did eight of the nine black students. Six months later, however, the Little Rock school board petitioned the federal district court, requesting permission to send the black students in Central High School back to segregated schools; they claimed that public hostility made it impossible for the board to run a sound educational program at the school. The board also requested that all further steps in its original desegregation plan be postponed for two and a half years.

The issue finally reached the Supreme Court in 1958, in the case of *Cooper* v. *Aaron* (Cooper was a member of the Little Rock School Board who wished to postpone desegregation; Aaron was one of the black children). The Court's ruling was unanimous. Little Rock was to proceed at once to desegregate its public schools despite the "chaos, bedlam and turmoil." The Court ruled that "law and order are not . . . to be preserved by depriving the Negro children of their constitutional rights." Moreover, the ruling included a statement by justices of their

---

[63] Quoted in *Cooper* v. *Aaron*, 358 U.S. 1 (1958).

unequivocal opposition to all devices developed by state and local officials to circumvent desegregation, whether they involved violence (as in the Little Rock
case) or legal maneuvers.

The Supreme Court's vigorous stand in the *Griffin* and the *Cooper* decisions
made it clear that the Court would not permit legal maneuvers to water down
the *Brown* ruling. Over the next few years the Court would hear other cases pertaining to the timing or methods used to achieve desegregation, but the basic
question of whether a school district could defy federal court orders to desegregate was no longer at issue.

Major congressional action to implement the Supreme Court desegregation
decisions did not occur until passage of the Civil Rights Act of 1964. When the
Act was proposed by President Kennedy in June 1963, in the aftermath of the
Birmingham riots, its chances of passage appeared slim. With the assassination
of President Kennedy on November 22, 1963, there was uncertainty over what
position President Johnson (a southerner from Texas) would take on the proposed legislation. Almost immediately, however, Johnson, in a special address
to Congress, declared strong support for the measure, suggesting that no more
fitting memorial could be created for the late President than passage of the Civil
Rights Act. Less than a year later (June 1964), the bill was approved by Congress.

The Civil Rights Act of 1964 dealt with many aspects of discrimination, including voting rights, public accommodations, and employment. Here, however,
we are concerned only with the provisions dealing with public education. Under
the Act, the Attorney General was authorized to file civil suits to compel desegregation of public schools in cases where the school board refused to act. In addition, federal funds were to be withheld from school districts which did not comply
with federal guidelines on integration.

The education provisions of the Civil Rights Act of 1964 reflected in part a
growing impatience with the speed of integration, particularly in some southern
districts. By 1964, ten years after the *Brown* decision, only 1.17 percent of the
black students in the eleven states of the Deep South were attending schools
with whites.[64] By 1968, despite the provisions of the 1964 Civil Rights Act, only
20 percent of all Southern black children were enrolled in desegregated schools.
At this point, the Supreme Court once again stepped in. In its earlier ruling on
the pace of desegregation (the second *Brown* decision in 1965) the Court had
called for "all deliberate speed"; now the Court announced (*Alexander* v. *Homes
County Board of Education*) that "all deliberate speed . . . is no longer acceptable." Instead, it declared that "the obligation of every school district is to ter-
minate dual school systems at once and to operate now and hereafter only unitary
schools."[65]

Many school-board members (and constitutional lawyers, too) were uncertain
about the meaning of the Court's phrase "at once"—after all, it is a physical im-
possibility to devise instantly a complex desegregation plan with new district
lines, transfer of faculty members, and many other details. Nevertheless, the
Court's decision forced many dilatory school boards to take action. At the beginning of the 1971 school year, it was estimated that less than 8 percent of all black
students in the South were still attending classes in all-black schools.

---

[64] See *Harvard Law Review*, "The Supreme Court, 1969 Term," vol. 84 (November 1970), p. 35.
[65] *Alexander* v. *Holmes County Board of Education,* 396 U.S. 79 (1969).

The preceding discussion has been limited to schools segregated by law—as, for example, in pre-1954 communities in the South where the school board operated two sets of schools, one for black students and one for whites. In many of the major cities of the North and West, however, although segregation of races has never been a legal requirement, schools are nevertheless segregated in fact, with most children attending schools that are nearly all black or all white. Such *de facto* segregation, or racial imbalance in the schools, is largely the result of housing patterns or economic factors—that is, many neighborhoods have become predominantly or all black, and in racially mixed areas the more affluent whites send their children to private or parochial schools. Most highly affluent areas, and their public schools, are virtually all white. In some cities segregation has persisted because of a commitment on the part of school officials to maintain "neighborhood schools." In the case of the West Side of Manhattan, the public schools are predominantly black because, with over 40 percent of the borough black, it is difficult to engineer desegregation.

In recent years, some black parents have complained that *de facto* segregation has deprived their children of the integrated educational opportunities mandated by the Supreme Court, and have tried to force local school boards to work toward racial balance. Some communities (such as New York City) have used a "freedom of choice" or "open admission" system, under which black parents have been permitted to enroll their children in predominantly white schools outside their home district if they so desired. Only a few, however, have chosen to do so, about 1 or 2 percent. In other areas (Hartford, Connecticut, for example) schools in all-white suburbs have voluntarily agreed to admit a few black children from the inner-city ghetto, and these children have been bused in daily. By the early 1970s, however, it had become clear that in many northern communities meaningful racial balance was an impossible goal under the neighborhood school system.

Although busing has been an accepted procedure in many rural parts of the United States for fifty years, it has taken on emotional overtones in the context of racial integration. In 1970, the Supreme Court heard a controversial case involving busing as a method of desegregation. In *Swann* v. *Charlotte Mecklenburg Board of Education*, the Court upheld a North Carolina federal district court which had ordered the local school board to rezone school districts to eliminate segregation, and to provide bus transportation for students as required.[66] The Court's decision did not, however, include specific guidelines; although the Court authorized the use of busing as a "remedy" (particularly where school districts had a history of officially segregated schools), it did not insist on the use of busing to achieve racial balance in every school in the district.[67] Moreover, it specifically stated that busing should not be ordered if the distance involved was so great as to risk the children's health or impair their education. Nevertheless, the *Swann* decision did give high-court sanction to busing as an acceptable tool, and very shortly, all over the nation, district courts were ordering local school boards to

---

[66] *Swann* v. *Charlotte Mecklenburg Board of Education,* 401 U.S. 1 (1970).

[67] In the *Swann* case, 29 percent of the students in the school system were black, but the Court accepted a plan under which some schools were permitted to remain all white, high schools were to range from 17 to 36 percent black, junior high schools from 9 to 33 percent black, and elementary schools from 3 to 4 percent. Thus, it was clear that racial balance (as opposed to integration) was not the Court's intent. (See *Harvard Law Review,* "The Supreme Court, 1970 Term," vol. 85 (November 1971), pp. 77 and 83.)

"*. . . And I say to you, if the Good Lord had intended us to be bused, he wouldn't have given us legs!*"

Saturday Review, *April 8, 1972*

devise comprehensive integration plans which would involve widespread use of busing.

Although some groups—the NAACP, for example—have generally supported busing to eliminate *de facto* segregation, there has also been widespread opposition from both blacks and whites. Critics point to recent studies that show that racial integration may not be essential to educational quality. Even within the black community, there no longer appears to be a clear consensus in favor of integration,[68] with many leading blacks now more interested in achieving community control than desegregation of local schools. Over all, opposition to busing has been strong: Congress included a moratorium on further busing in the 1972 Aid to Education Act; in his major address to the nation which called for the busing moratorium, President Nixon suggested that rather than bus children out of districts with inferior schools, we concentrate on upgrading schools in central cities, "so that the children who go there will have just as good a chance to get quality education as do the children who go to school in the suburbs";[69] and still other opponents have called for a constitutional amendment to forbid busing.

---

[68] In a 1969 school case heard by the Supreme Court, CORE (Congress of Racial Equality) submitted a brief in which it opposed integration.
[69] The *New York Times* (March 17, 1972), p. 22.

Busing became a political issue in the 1972 presidential campaign. But many busing advocates seem to disregard the hard reality that in most large cities the total school population is generally about 60 to 80 percent black and balance is impossible to achieve. Busing between cities and suburbs is a possible but highly improbable solution. The problem, therefore, appears to call for a redefinition of integrated education as more than the mere physical presence of blacks and whites in the same school. It would mean, among other things, a redefinition of education so that blacks would no longer be judged by white standards.

Discrimination in Employment

When the Senate was debating passage of the Civil Rights Act of 1964, Hubert Humphrey (D.-Minn.) spelled out the importance of the equal employment section. "What good does it do a Negro to be able to eat in a fine restaurant if he cannot afford to pay the bill?" asked Senator Humphrey. "How can a Negro child be motivated to take full advantage of integrated educational facilities if he has no hope of getting a job where he can use that education?"[70]

Title VII of the Civil Rights Act of 1964 made it illegal for employers or unions with more than twenty-five employees or members, and engaged in interstate commerce, to discriminate among workers on the basis of race, religion, sex, age, or nationality. The Act also created an Equal Employment Opportunity Commission (EEOC) whose job it was to persuade those who did not comply with the provisions voluntarily to do so; it gave the injured party or the Attorney General the right to sue in the courts if noncompliance persisted. In 1972, responding to complaints that overall effectiveness of the Act was limited because the EEOC lacked sufficient authority (only the injured party or the Attorney General could bring suit), Congress gave the Commission additional powers, including the right to sue for compliance and damages. The Commission responded almost immediately, filing suits against several major unions and employers. Among them was General Motors, which was accused of discriminating against women at its assembly plant in St. Louis, both in hiring and in promotion practices.

In addition to the 1964 Civil Rights Act, a primary federal government weapon in helping minority groups realize equal employment opportunities has been a series of presidential executive orders that require the millions of contractors and subcontractors who do business with the federal government not to discriminate in employment practices. Enforced vigorously by the Department of Labor, these executive orders have been used, for example, to threaten Columbia University, Harvard, Cornell, the City University of New York, and the University of Michigan with loss of government contracts if they did not move to provide more and better jobs for blacks, Puerto Ricans, and women.

To date, however, Title VII has had little effect as measured by the relative incomes of black and white workers. In 1972, the median family income for whites was $10,240; for blacks, $6,000 — indicating no change in their relative incomes.

---

[70] As quoted in Lucius J. Barker and Twiley W. Barker, Jr., *Freedoms, Courts, Politics: Studies in Civil Liberties* (Englewood Cliffs, N.J.: Prentice-Hall, 1965), p. 243.

"As an equal opportunity employer, I have to tell you that you're both fired."

New Yorker, *September 18, 1971*

Discrimination in Public Accommodations

Title II of the 1964 Civil Rights Act bars discrimination in places of public accommodation engaged in interstate commerce. The law applies to most motels and hotels,[71] and such places as restaurants, lunch counters, movie houses, gas stations, and stadiums. It states that an injured person or the Attorney General may bring suit to force compliance.

Title II was tested almost immediately after passage, when an Atlanta motel owner, Moreton Rolleston, Jr., claiming that the Act was unconstitutional, announced that he would continue to refuse to rent rooms to blacks. The case (*Heart of Atlanta Motel* v. *United States,* 1964) soon reached the Supreme Court, where the constitutionality of the Act was upheld in a unanimous decision. The Court based its ruling on the interstate commerce clause, asserting that racial discrimination in places of public accommodation affected interstate commerce by "discouraging travel on the part of a substantial portion of the Negro community," even if the particular establishment in question is a local one.[72] The Court also used the commerce clause in a second public-accommodation case,

[71] Excluded are places occupied by the owner that provide temporary accommodations for fewer than six guests—for instance, small boarding houses.
[72] *Heart of Atlanta Motel* v. *United States,* 379 U.S. 241 (1964).

Katzenbach v. *Ollie McClung* (1964), ruling that Ollie's Barbeque, an Alabama restaurant with an almost exclusively local clientele, was nevertheless subject to Title II because a considerable amount of the food served there came from out of state.[73]

As a result of these court rulings, as well as strong enforcement of Title II by the Attorney General's Office in the Justice Department, large public hotels and restaurants across the nation no longer discriminate against blacks or Chicanos, although discrimination continues in public motels and eating places in many smaller towns in the South and Southwest. In regard to quasi-public establishments, however, the constitutional position is not quite so clear. In a 1961 case, for example, the Court held that racial discrimination by a private restaurant operating in premises leased from the Wilmington, Delaware, Parking Authority (an agency created by the Delaware Legislature) was unconstitutional on the grounds that the relationship between the Parking Authority and the State of Delaware placed the "power, property and prestige" of the state behind the discrimination; thus, the discriminatory practices of the restaurant were illegal under the Fourteenth Amendment.

The Court ruled quite differently, however, in 1972, when K. Leroy Irvis, the black majority leader of the Pennsylvania House of Representatives, was taken as a guest to Moose Lodge No. 107 in Philadelphia, and refused service at the bar and in the dining room. Irvis brought suit, (*Moose Lodge 107* v. *Irvis*) charging that because the State of Pennsylvania had provided the Moose Lodge with a liquor license, his rights under the Fourteenth Amendment had been violated. The Supreme Court decided against Irvis, declaring that a state's regulation of liquor licenses "does not sufficiently implicate the state in the discriminatory guest policies" of the licensee, so as to make the state responsible for the discrimination.[74] The decision left private clubs free to discriminate against guests.

The *Irvis* case is interesting for the far-reaching results it may have. It closes the door on a legal maneuver which had been effective in the lower courts in forcing "private" establishments—such as country clubs and fraternal orders—to stop discriminatory practices. Civil-rights groups had hoped that they could use state involvement (through liquor licenses) to provide the Fourteenth Amendment guarantee of "equal protection," but the *Irvis* decision has dampened such hopes.

Discrimination in Housing

The Supreme Court began to take a stand against racial discrimination in housing as early as 1917, when it ruled that residential segregation ordinances passed by local municipalities were unconstitutional under the Fourteenth Amendment.[75] A few years later, however, the Court ruled that arrangements between private individuals under which property owners agreed not to rent or sell their property to blacks or others were constitutional, since no state action was involved.[76] Such agreements, known as "restrictive convenants," were widely used from that time on, although they lost much of their effectiveness in the late 1940s, when the

---

[73] *Katzenbach* v. *Ollie McClung,* 379 U.S. 294 (1964).
[74] *Moose Lodge 107* v. *Irvis,* 92 S.Ct. 1965 (1972).
[75] *Buchanan* v. *Warley* 245 U.S. 60 (1917).
[76] *Corrigan* v. *Buckley* 271 U.S. 323 (1926).

Court determined that although these private covenants were constitutional, it was unconstitutional to enforce them in state courts.[77]

During the 1960s, in a series of presidential executive orders, President Kennedy ordered federal agencies involved in housing activities to refrain from supplying funds or other help to segregated building projects. The 1968 Civil Rights Act made an even broader attempt to eliminate racial discrimination in housing. The Act barred discrimination in the sale or rental of about 80 percent of all housing in the nation by making it illegal for most private individuals to refuse to sell or rent to any person because of race, color, religion, or national origin.[78] Under the Act, an injured party may file a complaint with the Secretary of Housing and Urban Development (HUD) and, if not satisfied, sue for relief in the courts. In addition, the Attorney General may initiate suits, if he believes that a major seller or renter is engaging in discriminatory practices.

At the same time that Congress was acting to outlaw discrimination in housing through passage of the 1968 Civil Rights Act, the issue was in effect settled by the Supreme Court. In this case (*Jones* v. *Mayer Co.*, 1968), a St. Louis company had refused to sell a home to a black couple, Mr. and Mrs. Jones. The Joneses claimed that such action was illegal under the Civil Rights Act of 1866, an almost-forgotten 102-year-old statute. The Act of 1866 provided that "all citizens of the United States shall have the same right . . . as is enjoyed by white citizens . . . to purchase, lease, sell . . . real and personal property." This 1866 law had been generally overlooked, because it involved an attempt to regulate private dealings between individual buyers and sellers; in 1883,[79] the Supreme Court had struck down similar Reconstruction-period Civil Rights Acts, arguing that the Fourteenth Amendment protected only against infringements of civil rights by the states and not by private individuals. In its 1968 decision, however, the Supreme Court did not use the Fourteenth Amendment in ruling in favor of the Joneses and upholding the Civil Rights Act of 1866. The Court relied instead on a broad and novel interpretation of the Thirteenth Amendment.

In the post–Civil War period, Justice John Marshall Harlan, then sitting on the Supreme Court, had argued that the Thirteenth Amendment—which prohibits slavery within the United States and gives Congress the power to enforce this prohibition—also gives Congress the power to legislate against the "badges of slavery." The rest of the Court, defining slavery much more narrowly, did not agree with Harlan's interpretation. But in 1968, in the *Jones* v. *Mayer Co.* decision, the Court adopted Harlan's argument, asserting that racial discrimination which prevented blacks from buying homes on the same basis as whites was indeed a "badge of slavery"; therefore, under the Thirteenth Amendment, Congress had the power to enact any legislation necessary and proper to eradicate such badges.[80]

---

[77] *Shelley* v. *Kraemer* 334 U.S. 1 (1948) and *Barrows* v. *Jackson* 346 U.S. 249 (1953). In these cases, the Supreme Court ruled that the enforcement of a restrictive covenant in a state court would make the *state* a party to the action, and would therefore be unconstitutional under the provisions of the Fourteenth Amendment.

[78] The 1968 Civil Rights Act exempts private individuals who own less than four houses and sell or rent them on their own, without the services of a real estate agent; homes with fewer than five apartments, in which the owner also lives; and housing operated by religious organizations or private clubs on a noncommercial basis.

[79] *Civil Rights Cases,* 109 U.S. 3 (1883).

[80] *Jones* v. *Mayer Co.,* 392 U.S. 409 (1968).

Although the *Jones* ruling did not arise from a direct test of the constitutionality of the Civil Rights Act of 1968, nevertheless, after the decision it was clear that the courts, in upholding the Civil Rights Act of 1866, would also support the open-housing provisions of the 1968 Act. In addition, the case was significant in a broader sense because it provided civil-rights advocates with a new tool — the Thirteenth Amendment — to use along with the Fourteenth Amendment and the interstate commerce clause in future attacks against discriminatory practices arising in the private sector. As yet, however, the 1968 Act has been put to little use, and there is the possibility that it may be watered down by future court decisions.

Voting Rights

For a brief period immediately following the Civil War, it appeared that the Fourteenth and Fifteenth Amendments might be used successfully to insure the voting rights of black Americans. Soon, however, it was clear that the former Confederate states were embarking upon campaigns to "systematic disenfranchisement" of their black citizens. By 1900, these efforts to deny voting rights had proved almost completely effective. Among the devices introduced was the white primary, in which blacks were prohibited from participating in the Democratic party primaries, the outcome of which, in most southern states, has generally been tantamount to election. Southern whites argued that because the primary was not a general election, it was not subject to the constitutional requirements set by the Fourteenth and Fifteenth Amendments. Early Supreme Court decisions (such as *Newberry* v. *United States,* 1921), appeared to support this argument,[81] and the white primary became an effective means of disenfranchising blacks. For example, the original Texas White Primary Law of 1924 was invalidated by the Supreme Court in 1927 (*Nixon* v. *Herndon*) on the grounds that the state, by passing such a law, had become involved in a "direct and obvious infringement of the Fourteenth Amendment's equal-protection clause."[82] But a few years later, the Supreme Court held that the Democratic State Convention could deny blacks the right to vote in its primaries because it was acting as a private group (*Grovey* v. *Townsend,* 1935).[83] It was not until the 1940s that the Court finally outlawed the white primary by declaring that because party primaries in effect served as "instruments of the state" in the electoral process, blacks could not be disenfranchised in the primaries.[84]

Several other methods for keeping blacks from voting were also quite common. For example, many states invoked a "grandfather clause," under which a person who was a legal voter before 1866 (or his descendants) would be exempt from strict educational or property qualifications for voting. The Supreme Court ruled in 1915 (*Guinn* v. *United States*) that such clauses were a violation of the Fifteenth Amendment.[85]

Literacy tests were also used to disenfranchise black voters. An early post–Civil

---

[81] *Newberry* v. *United States,* 256 U.S. 232 (1921).

[82] *Nixon* v. *Herndon,* 273 U.S. 73 (1927).

[83] *Grovey* v. *Townsend,* 295 U.S. 45 (1935).

[84] *United States* v. *Classic,* 313 U.S. 299 (1941); *Smith* v. *Allwrights,* 321 U.S. 649 (1944).

[85] *Guinn* v. *United States,* 238 U.S. 347 (1915).

War Mississippi statute, for instance, required a voter to read and interpret the state constitution as a prerequisite for voting, and as recently as 1946, Alabama adopted the Boswell Amendment to its state constitution, under which a potential voter was required to "understand and explain" any article of the United States Constitution to the satisfaction of local voting registration officers. Sponsors of the amendment hoped that since it did not specifically mention blacks, the courts would let it stand; nevertheless, a district-court decision (upheld later by the Supreme Court) held that the provision violated the Fifteenth Amendment, because, as a rule, only blacks were forced to take the test.[86]

In 1890, when the Mississippi legislature called for a convention to prepare a new state constitution, its avowed purpose was to secure white supremacy. The first device approved was a two-dollar poll tax for all voters. The tax implicitly discriminated against blacks, who constituted the poorest segment of the population. Over the years, at one time or another, most of the Southern states adopted similar taxes, and the Supreme Court upheld them as constitutional. Finally, in 1964, the Twenty-fourth Amendment outlawed the poll tax as a qualification for voting in federal elections, and in 1966 the Supreme Court, reversing its earlier rulings, declared that its use was also illegal in state elections.

Congressional action to insure equal voting rights began under the Eisenhower administration with the Civil Rights Acts of 1957 and 1960. These provided, among other things, that the federal government itself could go to the courts to seek relief against actual or threatened interference with the voting rights of any citizen. A few years later, Title I of the Civil Rights Act of 1964 attempted to deal with the use of discriminatory literacy tests: it prohibited registrars from giving different tests to different applicants, and it eliminated all literacy tests as a requirement for registration in those cases where a potential voter had completed the sixth grade.

Despite this legislation, most civil-rights leaders were not satisfied with the progress in enfranchising the black citizens of the South. The early voting-rights measures were largely dependent upon court action for enforcement, which involved slow case-by-case handling of violations. Moreover, even after a court handed down a favorable decision, local officials were often able to circumvent it by substituting a whole new set of discriminatory tests, thus necessitating additional time-consuming court hearings.

In March 1965, as part of a voter-registration drive in Alabama, Martin Luther King set out on a fifty-mile march from Selma to Montgomery, accompanied by civil-rights supporters from all over the country. Governor George C. Wallace of Alabama sent state troopers to the scene, whose brutality in trying to break up the march was widely publicized.[87] Prodded by President Johnson and an outraged public, Congress responded five months later with the Voting Rights Act of 1965. The Act suspended the use of literacy tests, "good character" vouchers, and other devices in those areas where they were used to keep blacks from voting; it also provided for the appointment of federal examiners to aid in voter

---

[86] *Davis* v. *Schnell,* 81 F. 872 (1949).

[87] At least forty marchers were hurt, including a white Unitarian minister from Boston, Reverend James J. Reeb, who died of skull injuries received in an attack on a Selma street. Mrs. Viola Liuzzo, a white woman from Detroit, was shot and killed in an auto by white ambushers as she was shuttling blacks back to Selma from Montgomery.

Activists confronting police in riot gear, like these in the Alabama voter-registration drives of 1965, became an increasingly familiar sight as both the decade and political activism advanced.

registration in these communities.[88] In such localities, the Attorney General was given immediate authority (without going through the courts) to suspend all required tests, and to send in federal examiners appointed by the Federal Civil Service Commission to register voters. In practice, the law meant that neither local ordinances and prejudices, nor the inherent delays of the court system, could be used to deny the vote to black citizens. The 1965 Voting Rights Act was challenged almost immediately in the courts, and in *South Carolina* v. *Katzenbach* (1965), the Supreme Court upheld its constitutionality under the Fifteenth Amendment.[89]

---

[88] These communities were defined to include any area where such tests were in effect on November 1, 1964, and where less than half the voting-age population had participated in the 1964 presidential election. Principally involved were Alabama, Georgia, Mississippi, Louisiana, South Carolina, Virginia and thirty-four counties in North Carolina.

[89] *South Carolina* v. *Katzenbach*, 383 U.S. 310 (1966).

In 1970 (in a measure that received national attention mostly because it also lowered the voting age to eighteen), amendments to the 1965 Voting Rights Act extended the Act to 1975 and suspended the use of literacy tests, providing that persons otherwise qualified to vote need only to have lived in the election district at least thirty days before voting in a presidential election.

The cumulative effect of the various court decisions and Civil Rights Acts (and in particular, the Voting Rights Act of 1965), has been to enfranchise many blacks. It has also made the black vote an important factor in many elections. By 1970, there were over six hundred blacks holding elective office in the South; major cities such as Cleveland, Ohio; Gary, Indiana; and Newark, New Jersey have chosen black mayors; and 454 of the 3,085 delegates to the 1972 Democratic Presidential Convention (or almost 15 percent)were black.[90]

Poverty in America:
A Partner of Discrimination

While laws against discrimination may have the effect of opening up economic opportunities to many of the minorities who have been discriminated against, the elimination of discrimination cannot be regarded as the ultimate remedy for poverty, which has many causes. Moreover, legal measures aimed at the immediate removal of discrimination in schools or housing, or even employment, are insufficient to deal with the problem of poverty, for the roots of the problem go back to opportunities denied and indignities suffered two to three generations ago.

In discussing poverty, a distinction must be made between absolute and relative poverty. Absolute poverty pertains to a living standard at or below the minimum budget for the necessities of life—in 1972, four thousand dollars for an urban family of four. Relative poverty refers to a group's position in relation to the others; thus, those among the lowest 20 percent of all income earners might be said to be in poverty. This is what is meant by "relative deprivation," and it is evident when comparing the incomes of black and other racial minorities with those of the white middle class.

Who Are the Poor?

An early attempt to define exactly what was meant by "poor" was made in 1964 by the President's Council of Economic Advisers, which set the poverty level at a family income of less than three thousand dollars. Since that time, figures have been adjusted to allow for inflation and the size and location of a particular family. In 1970, the Social Security Administration set the poverty level for a non-farm family of four persons at $3,968. Using this definition, there were about 25.5 million persons at or below the poverty level in the United States in 1970, or about 13 percent of the population. Although in absolute numbers there are more white families living in poverty, the incidence of poverty is much higher among blacks and other minority groups than among whites. In 1972, 32 percent of black families were classified as poor, compared with 10 percent of white.

Interpreting the statistics on poverty can be a difficult task. The actual number

---

[90] Only 5.5 percent were black in 1968. The *New York Times* (August 9, 1971), p. 33.

of poor people has been declining in recent years — from over 39 million in 1959 to 25.5 million in 1970. Moreover, the poorest families in our society now earn about 57 percent more than they did ten years ago, even after allowing for inflation. A recent study reported that the average income of the lowest fifth of all families in the United States, calculated in 1970 dollars, had increased from $1,956 in 1958 to $3,085 in 1968.[91] Nevertheless, poverty remains a fundamental American problem: in the richest country in the world, after more than twenty years of unprecedented prosperity, in which the nation's production quadrupled,[92] one out of every eight citizens still lives in poverty.

Equally revealing are the data on inequality of income distribution in the United States. Statistics show that although poor families have made some gains in terms of income, the basic inequality in distribution of income has persisted over a long period of time. Such a trend is undesirable for several reasons. First, as one observer has suggested, economic "inequality is a major source of social instability and unrest. . . . [It] gives rise to feelings of inferiority which in turn generate inadequacy and self-hate or anger . . . anger results in crime, delinquency, senseless violence. . . ."[93] Secondly, the figures offer evidence that despite a widespread feeling among many Americans that the government has already taken substantial action to eliminate poverty by redistributing income, that is, by progressive income taxes, and through payments to welfare mothers, unemployed workers, the aged, and other low-income groups, these measures have accomplished very little to correct inequality in income distribution. And the distribution of wealth is even more unequal than the distribution of income, with one-half of 1 percent of the population in control of 33 percent of all wealth. Indeed, it appears likely that although the conditions of poverty are sometimes hidden in the United States because of overall prosperity, it is probable that much more could be done than has been done.

Recent Government Attempts at Alleviating Poverty

In 1964, responding to President Johnson's first State of the Union Message, in which he asked for a "war on poverty," Congress passed the Economic Opportunity Act. The Act recognized that despite the overall prosperity enjoyed by most Americans, there were many who were still very poor; its objective was to "eliminate the paradox of poverty in the midst of plenty," with particular emphasis on educating and training the young and the black for jobs. The Act created the Office of Economic Opportunity, which established and funded a series of antipoverty programs:

Job Corps The Job Corps was designed to provide disadvantaged young people between the ages of fourteen and twenty-one with job skills. The programs were carried out at a series of camps. In many cases, their actual operation was contracted out to private organizations; for example, the Camp Kilmer, New Jersey, facility was operated by the Federal Electric Corporation. The Neighborhood Youth Corps was the urban counterpart of the Job Corps.

---

[91] L. Upton and N. Lyons, of the Cambridge Institute, as quoted in Tom Wicker, "The Rich Get Richer," the *New York Times* (June 29, 1972), p. 39.

[92] Gross National Product was $285 million in 1950 and will approximate $110 trillion in 1973.

[93] Herbert Gans, as quoted in Tom Wicker, "The Rich Get Richer."

In 1965 President Johnson took a coffee break with trainees at the Catoctin Center Job Corps Camp in Thurmont, Maryland, near the presidential retreat at Camp David.

VISTA Volunteers in Service to America, also known as the "domestic Peace Corps," recruited Americans to serve in problem spots in the United States such as urban poverty areas or Indian reservations in the Southwest, or with the retarded and mentally ill.

The Community Action Program The Community Action Program was perhaps the most controversial of all OEO programs. Local public and private groups established Community Action Agencies in more than a thousand communities, with the aim of encouraging "maximum feasible participation" on the part of the poor themselves. Each CAA was to decide and organize its own programs, within general guidelines and funds from OEO. Typical programs have included Head Start (which has given preschool children educational and health-care services), Upward Bound (a program to help prepare disadvantaged high school children for college), day-care centers, the Legal Services Program (a program designed to offer adequate legal aid to the poor), and a Comprehensive Health Services Program (an attempt to find new ways of delivering total health care to the poor, especially in urban areas). In many CAA communities, however, insufficient funds and inadequate staffs resulted in a failure to coordinate resources to aid the poor, and, as a consequence, the benefits were limited.

Evaluation of Government Action

The merit of many of these antipoverty programs is open to question. Some people complain that they were poorly conceived; many students dropped out of the Job Corps, for example, and others claimed that they were being trained for jobs in the private sector that did not exist. Moreover, for the OEO programs in general, it is questionable whether federal-government funding was ever really adequate. Often, the original government appropriation was relatively small, and there were substantial cutbacks in individual cases in later years; President Nixon, for example, closed down fifty-nine Job Corps centers in 1969. Recently, attention has focused somewhat on a shift from antipoverty programs – with their emphasis on breaking the cycle of poverty by equipping the disadvantaged to work – to income-maintenance programs, which eliminate poverty by assuring every family a minimum income (see Chapter 15).

Equality in America: the 1970s

Although the Declaration of Independence states that "All men are created equal," our survey of the American experience has shown that throughout our history, minority groups have been deprived of equal rights, often with legal sanction of various government bodies. In recent years, and particularly since the *Brown* decision of 1954, major strides have been made to eliminate discrimination through court action and legislation. Nevertheless, it is apparent that although significant legal discrimination no longer exists in the United States today, the "badges of discrimination" endure. Legally, blacks may rent where they wish, but because of continuing poverty, many are forced to live in urban slums. Similarly, legal attacks on discriminatory bars to employment continually open up new fields for minority groups, but often, because of the persistence of the traditional cycle of poverty, they are unable to qualify. Thus, it now appears that although we cannot slacken in our attempts to combat discrimination through legal means, we must also recognize the close connection between the fight on poverty and the fight for equal rights.

Although poverty in the United States has been substantially reduced since 1960, there remain serious inequities and problems that threaten the stability and even the continued existence of the American system. The great surge in affluence has put severe pressure on the environment, raising the question of whether it will be possible to continue increasing the standard of living. At the very time this question was raised, the deprived groups in the United States became more conscious of the disparities in income and wealth, and they are demanding their share now. The limits to how much change can be produced through legal means add further to the frustration of the poor and dispossessed. Some of these problems will be considered in the next chapter.

SUGGESTED READING

Berger, Monroe. *Equality by Statute: The Revolution in Civil Rights,* rev. ed. (Garden City, N.Y.: Doubleday, 1968). In paperback. A historical and legal analysis of all major civil-rights legislation from the Reconstruction period until 1965.

Burnette, Robert. *The Tortured Americans* (Englewood Cliffs, N.J.: Prentice-Hall, 1971). An interesting introductory discussion of the position of American Indians in the United States.

Carmichael, Stokely, and Charles V. Hamilton. *Black Power: The Politics of Liberation in America* (New York: Random House, 1968). In paperback. Diagnosis of the plight of American blacks, with suggestions for a political solution. The authors argue that American blacks suffer depressed political, social, and economic conditions because of the white power structure.

Deloria, Vine, Jr. *Custer Died for Your Sins: An Indian Manifesto* (New York: Macmillan, 1969). In paperback. An enlightening commentary on Indian affairs, discussing the differences between Indian problems and those of blacks and other minorities.

Dorsen, Norman (ed.). *Discrimination and Civil Rights: Cases, Text, and Materials* (Boston: Little, Brown, 1969). In paperback. Judicial decisions and materials dealing with racial discrimination, organized in terms of issues such as voting, education, employment, housing, and public accommodations.

Du Bois, W. E. B. *The Souls of Black Folk* (Chicago: A. C. McClurg, 1903). Classic study of black identity by one of the early advocates of black pride and distinction.

Elkins, Stanley. *Slavery: A Problem in American Institutional Life* (New York: Grosset and Dunlap, 1959). Classic study of American slavery and its impact on the black man.

Essien-Udon, E. V. *Black Nationalism: A Search for Identity in America* (New York: Dell, 1964). Traces the history of black nationalism in the United States including a discussion and analysis of Marcus Garvey's Back to Africa movement, the Black Muslims, and other important stages in the black search for identity.

Flexner, Eleanor. *Century of Struggle: The Woman's Rights Movement in the United States* (New York: Atheneum, 1968). In paperback. Scholarly account of the feminist movement, with central attention given to the seventy-year struggle for suffrage and the personalities within the movement.

Josephy, Alvin M. *Red Power: The American Indians' Fight For Freedom* (New York: McGraw-Hill, 1971). Discusses the objectives and tactics of young, college-educated Indians heading the "Red Power" movement and the conditions to which they are reacting.

Lewis, Anthony, and the *New York Times*. *Portrait of a Decade: The Second American Revolution* (New York: Random House, 1964). In paperback. Developments in civil rights from 1954 to 1964, emphasizing legal changes and supplemented by excerpts of articles from the *New York Times*.

Millett, Kate. *Sexual Politics* (Garden City, N.Y.: Doubleday, 1970). In paperback. Arguing that the relationship between the sexes is and has been a political one, this book is a useful introduction to current women's liberation literature.

Moynihan, Daniel P. *The Negro Family: The Case for National Action* (Washington, D.C.: Department of Labor, 1965). The famous Moynihan Study that attributes much of the black man's current problem to his former condition of slavery, which destroyed the family structure.

Parsons, Talcott, and Kenneth Clark (eds.). *The Negro American* (Boston: Beacon Press, 1965). A book of essays conveying major aspects of Negro history, demography, and politics, and containing proposals for policy and change.

Samora, Julian (ed.). *La Raza: Forgotten Americans* (Notre Dame, Ind.: University of Notre Dame Press, 1966). Collection of essays discussing the history and contemporary problems of Mexican Americans, as well as current political movements and attempts toward change.

Silen, Juan Angel. *We, The Puerto Rican People: A Story of Oppression and Resistance,* trans. by Cedric Belfrage (New York: Monthly Review Press, 1971). Denouncing United States colonialism, which he contends takes the form of total economic penetration, the author supports independence for Puerto Rico.

Wagstaff, Thomas. *Black Power: The Radical Response to White Society* (Beverly Hills, Calif.: Glencoe Press, 1969). Collection of essays covering both historical and contemporary aspects of black power and showing some of the historical origins of contemporary developments.

4
JUSTICE AND
POLITICAL FREEDOM

"Eternal vigilance is the price of liberty"; this saying, byword of civil libertarians, is direct, yet far from clear. Whose liberty is to be protected, and whose rights? Society's or the individual's? The dominant group's or the minority's? In the sixties and the seventies, the search for answers to these questions began with mounting urgency in a nation where demonstrations proliferated over such issues as the Vietnam War and minority rights.

The Bill of Rights was added to the original Constitution to protect the citizen against the arbitrary power of the federal government. After the Civil War, the Fourteenth Amendment was intended to provide the same protection against state and local governments, and extended the citizen's protection against arbitrary federal action. Thus, in theory, in a nation of free men, the rights of all are equally protected under the law. But, in practice, freedom has been limited by law and there have been great inequities in the application of the law.

Through its rulings the Supreme Court has both extended and curtailed some of these inequities by reinterpreting and redefining our constitutional rights. But the best constitutions can serve only as guidelines for the fallible humans who govern, and the courts, although they can define rights, cannot guarantee ultimate protection of them. In the end, it is only the people themselves who can guarantee protection: state-ordered school desegregation, for example, cannot be enforced if the majority of people do not want to abide by court decisions.

In the struggle between opposing forces for what each deems right, the epithet of *rebel* has often been hurled at those who seek redress for their grievances through changes in the existing order. These rebels, both leftists and rightists, mild or extreme in their sentiments, are all part of the free political atmosphere that has always existed in America.

Indeed, the United States has a heritage of revolutionary sentiment, and many American thinkers have espoused doctrines of unrelenting individuality. Jefferson believed that the revolution should be renewed by each successive generation. Henry David Thoreau, after spending a night in jail for refusal to pay a poll tax, wrote the essay "Civil Disobedience," which has become a classic on the role of dissent in society. Thoreau, like the men who signed the Declaration of Independence, believed that the law of conscience is higher than the law of the state and urged disobedience against bad laws, even at the risk of imprisonment. If many men resisted in this manner, he argued, the government would not be able to uphold unjust laws, and right would prevail. Thoreau's essay served as an inspiration for at least two important nonviolent revolutions: the Indian liberation movement led by Mohandas K. Gandhi, and the civil rights movement of Dr. Martin Luther King.[1]

Black and student revolutionaries as well as practitioners of civil disobedience in the movements that began in the sixties have faced a similar challenge. Since the relatively tame and dignified civil rights and antiwar protests in the early part of that decade, we have witnessed a dramatic "radicalization" of our country's dissenters. Those who organized peaceful protest after the model of Thoreau were often bitterly disappointed when their efforts resulted either in transient or illusory reforms or in violent reprisals. Protesters who were shoved in a mass into police vans and sprayed with mace and tear gas found it difficult to maintain

---

[1] See Martin Luther King, Jr., "Letter from Birmingham Jail," in *Protest,* edited by Gregory Armstrong (New York: Bantam, 1969), pp. 97–113.

At Harvard University in 1969, antiwar students constructed this mock military graveyard, a universal image of waste linking Vietnam to past wars.

the philosophical calm displayed by Thoreau in his quiet cell in Concord.[2] Many abandoned their ideas of peaceful social change to become ideological and tactical extremists.[3] A minority of student and black radicals declared their opposition to the entire American system and began to justify such methods as riots, bombings, and violent demonstrations as necessary to shock the American public into a recognition of the evils inherent in society.

Edward C. Banfield, an urban specialist, argued that black ghetto residents, aware that they are victims of white man's oppression, believe they have a "kind of license to break the law." In a chapter entitled "Rioting Mainly for Fun and Profit," Banfield contended that a large part of the increase in crime is due to this belief among blacks that they have the right to redress unjust and oppressive laws.[4]

[2] For a description of the violent police reaction on the Kent State and Jackson State campuses and recommendations to eliminate further killings at student protests see *The Report of the President's Commission on Campus Unrest* (Washington, D.C.: Government Printing Office, 1970).

[3] Ralph W. Conant has categorized civil protest in order of severity: civil disobedience, rioting, insurrection. See Ralph W. Conant, *The Prospects for Revolution* (New York: Harper's Magazine Press, 1971).

[4] Edward C. Banfield, *The Unheavenly City: The Nature and Future of our Urban Crisis* (Boston: Little, Brown, 1970) pp. 185–209. For an interesting, readable account of an urban riot see Tom Hayden, *Rebellion in Newark* (New York: Vintage, 1967).

Eldridge Cleaver, a member of the Black Panthers and a spokesman for the radical black community, advocates crime, even crimes of violence such as rape, as valid forms of political protest for blacks.

What has contributed to this radical belief? Is the system as unjust as some claim? Evidence reveals that the unjust application of laws in America's criminal justice system is a chief contributor to the widespread disenchantment among political dissidents. The police station and the courtroom, instead of being strongholds of civil liberties, are, instead, often sites of grave injustice.

Current Problems in the Struggle for Civil Liberties

Many civil libertarians today have expressed the fear that our civil liberties are being eroded in the local courtrooms of America. Describing such a courtroom, a lawyer wrote of what he saw in symbolic terms:

> [*The place was a dingy*] *courtroom in which the men and women with business to do were mostly past caring, and the men and women—litigants—upon whom this business was to be done were mostly past hoping. Someone, in a forlorn battle to preserve the trappings of justice, had put a large plastic bag over the American flag in the corner to keep it clean. The bag itself had yellowed and was covered with grime. And in back of the judge's bench—not a bench, really, just the most comfortable chair in the house—an incomplete set of large aluminum letters proclaimed*
> IN GOD WE   RUST[5]

A number of highly questionable practices are prevalent today in our system of justice. These practices include plea bargaining, discriminatory arrests, excessive bail, and preventive detention. Although some observers claim that the first of these helps to cope with the backlog of court cases, the others have evolved under pressure for convictions or as the result of discrimination by public officials against racial minorities and the poor.

The Practice of Plea Bargaining

A common procedure in dealing with court backlog is the practice of negotiating pleas in exchange for lesser charges: a suspect is induced by the prosecuting attorney and by his own counsel to plead guilty to a lesser charge than the one he was originally accused of, and is promised a lesser penalty. This system, known in some circles as "copping a plea," results in ninety percent of all convictions.[6] There is, however, no guarantee that the judge will go along with the promise of minimal penalty and, in any case, the defendant is left with a conviction on his record when he may well be innocent. Still, this practice was confirmed twice by the Court as recently as 1970.[7] In one case a man entered a guilty plea and was sentenced for kidnapping; the Supreme Court upheld the conviction even after the defendant claimed he had been coerced into pleading guilty to

[5] Michael Tiger, "Forward: Waiver of Constitutional Rights: Disquiet in the Citadel," *Harvard Law Review,* vol. 84: November 1, 1970, pp. 5–6.

[6] *Crime and the Law, 1971* (Washington, D.C.: Congressional Quarterly, 1971), p. 36.

[7] *Brady* v. *United States,* 396 U.S. 809 (1970); and *Parker* v. *North Carolina,* 397 U.S. 790 (1970).

*Civil libertarians have argued that police readiness to arrest
minority-group members often amounts to discrimination.*

avoid the death penalty. In the second case, the defendant's plea of guilty, which
led to changing a death sentence to life imprisonment, was upheld as admissible
as evidence. In both cases, legality was affirmed, as counsel had been present
in the courtroom.

The practice of plea bargaining raises several issues.[8] Chief among them is
the replacement of a jury trial with the defendant's own assessment of his guilt,
not always a more reliable judgment. Many defendants have been known to enter
a plea of guilty and privately claim innocence. Others, many of them poor, simply
waive this right out of ignorance or impatience. The total number of innocent
people who have pleaded guilty is undetermined, but the occurrence itself is far
from unknown. Although "there are questions about the reliability and accuracy
of convictions after trial, so too there are questions about the reliability and accuracy of guilty pleas. The difference is that we are honest about the uncertainties
in the trial process."

Plea bargaining often results in a "double loss": rehabilitation is affected because it depends in part on the criminal's perception of the judicial system; and
deterrence of crime suffers because so many criminals are able to avoid jail sen-

---

[8] The following arguments are espoused by Peter L. Zimroth, "101,000 Defendants Were Convicted of Misdemeanors Last Year. 98,000 Had Pleaded Guilty—To Get Reduced Sentences," *New York Times Magazine*
(May 28, 1972), pp. 14ff.

tences. "The guilty plea system," therefore, "undermines, if it does not destroy, the effectiveness and rationality of criminal sanctions."[9]

Undeniably, plea bargaining works in relieving the backlog of the court; but it also "pressures the innocent to admit guilt. . . . rewards the guilty. . . . covers up information about criminal law-enforcement practices, [and] tends to nullify or weaken rules designed to protect all of us from illegal police action."[10] Out of the fear that the judicial system would collapse without plea bargaining, we have permitted the undercutting of values essential to a fair and equitable criminal-justice system: adherence to the rule of law, concern for the safety of society, and regard for the individual accused by the state. In fact the jury trial, which was instituted to protect the accused, is seldom used: only ten percent of all convictions are the results of trial by jury.

Police Discrimination in Arrests,
Bail, and Preventive Detention

Further evidence of injustice in our system of law enforcement involves discrimination in police arrests. Police in ghetto areas such as Harlem are uniformly distrusted by the residents precisely because the police distrust the residents. There are, for example, innumerable instances in which police have acted arbitrarily, overreacted, and discriminated on the basis of the dress and manners of ghetto youths.[11] Studies indicate that ghetto residents are more likely to be arrested than members of the middle class, particularly if the complainant in the case is middle class.

Both bail and preventive detention have been used as means of punishment, despite the fact that the Eighth Amendment prohibits this. The purpose of bail is to insure completion of a trial and at the same time to acknowledge the defendant's innocence until proven guilty. The judge, assigning bail, rightfully considers the diverse factors of the nature of the crime in question and the defendant's financial status. But in setting bail he may unfairly consider the defendant's character and past record, and the likelihood that he has committed the crime.[12] In 1966, Congress passed the Bail Reform Act, which provided federal judges greater leeway in releasing the accused on personal recognizance in all noncapital cases. In capital offenses, however, bail could be denied and the accused lawfully jailed until trial.

The new law had its greatest impact in Washington, D.C., where all criminal cases are under federal jurisdiction. It also aroused the greatest public reaction there. It was believed that much of the crime in the District of Columbia was

---

[9] Zimroth also claims that "bargains are usually struck in an atmosphere more appropriate to a thieves' market than to a judicial proceeding." The result is that sentences are meted out with no relation to the defendant's background or potential for rehabilitation, but rather according to "how much trouble the defendant can make for the prosecutor." Zimroth, "101,000 Defendants," p. 44.

[10] Zimroth, "101,000 Defendants," p. 44.

[11] See Paul Chevigny, *Police Power: Police Abuses in New York City, N.Y.* (New York: Vintage, 1969), Introduction, and Chapter 1.

[12] For a case study of the use of preventive detention see Charles E. Ares, Anne Rankin, and Herbert Sturz, "The Manhattan Bail Project: An Interim Report on the Use of Pre-Trial Parole," in *The Politics of Local Justice*, edited by J. R. Klonoski and R. I. Mendelsohn (Boston: Little, Brown, 1970), pp. 78–95.

being committed by defendants who had been released pending trial. Among the remedies suggested was preventive detention: the denial of bail to any defendant whose release threatened to endanger the community. Supported by Attorney General John Mitchell, this proposal aroused strong opposition from civil libertarians, who quickly pointed out that it amounted to imprisoning a man for crimes he had not necessarily committed.

Preventive detention has been widely used against protesters and rioters, in either its direct form or indirectly through the setting of extravagantly high bail. Jerome Skolnick pointed to the self-defeating nature of the process: participants in protests and riots express alienation from society and government; their prolonged exposure to the judicial system and its weaknesses through preventive detention only heightens this alienation.[13]

The poor clearly suffer most from the bail system, while bondsmen, insurance companies, and crime syndicates benefit. Posting of bail is a hardship on the defendant's family and friends, and if bail cannot be posted, the imprisoned man loses a chance to assemble a strong defense. Since he must appear before the court as a prisoner, he is often induced to plead guilty because the time he spends waiting for a trial need not be deducted from his sentence. It is a fact that persons released on bail are less likely to be convicted and, if convicted, are more likely to receive shorter sentences than those who have awaited trial in jail.[14] Therefore, those who cannot post bail are discriminated against.

But there is much to be said in favor of the bail system. Some means is needed to insure that the accused show up for trial. The issue, then, is not whether bail should exist—clearly it must. The more important question is how to make it nondiscriminatory.

The observer of the system of criminal justice today might well conclude that the dissent among minorities and protestors is justified, for the inadequacies are great. To remedy inequities in the system of justice, two approaches are available: the adherence to procedural safeguards and the guarantee that all Americans equally enjoy the fundamental freedoms of the First Amendment.

Due Process of Law

The concept of due process is stated for the federal courts in the Fifth Amendment and for the state courts in the Fourteenth. It assures that no citizen shall "be deprived of life, liberty, or property, without due process of law." The phrase appears simple, but its meaning is complex, and its interpretation has often been difficult.

No concept is mentioned more frequently in our judicio-legal process than "due process

---

[13] Conversely, Skolnick also noted, were defendants to be released pending trial, it is hardly likely that they would return to the scene of a riot. See *The Politics of Protest* (New York: Simon and Schuster, 1969), pp. 300–313.

[14] Skolnick, *The Politics of Protest*, pp. 310–311. For a critical discussion of who loses in the United States bail system, see Ronald Goldfarb, *Ransom: A Critique of the American Bail System* (New York: Harper & Row, 1965), pp. 32–91. Another description of the problem is "The Bail Problem: Release or Detention Before Trial," in *Law and Order Reconsidered: A Staff Report to the National Commission on the Causes and Prevention of Violence* (New York: Bantam, 1970), pp. 455–497.

of law," for either its presence or its absence; its banner is now raised in more appellate cases at the level of the United States Supreme Court than any other.[15]

Procedural due process refers to the process of the law used in the courts. It is used to assure every individual equal legal rights in all processes used from the moment of arrest to conviction. In recent years, the struggle for procedural due process has been at the center of the civil-liberties movement. Cases that involve guarantee of the rights of accused criminals represent the strongest challenge to government to behave equitably and without prejudice, despite precedent. Civil libertarians argue that if the government can stand up to such a test, other liberties are assured of protection.

Procedural Safeguards of Liberty

The oldest protections of individuals against the state in criminal cases are the writ of habeas corpus, prohibition against *ex post facto* laws, and prohibition of bills of attainder. All three date back to the English Magna Carta and were written into the Constitution in 1787.

A writ of habeas corpus is a written instruction that protects the individual against arbitrary arrest and punishment by demanding that authorities holding a prisoner bring him before a judge and there state the reasons for his arrest. If they cannot establish a valid reason for the arrest, the accused is then freed. During World War II, two civilians filed petitions for writs of habeas corpus after being convicted by a military tribunal in Hawaii. The military officers argued that martial law had been established and the writ of habeas corpus suspended, and, moreover, that the military trials were valid. However, the military was overruled, and the civilians were issued writs ordering their release.[16]

An *ex post facto* law is a law that imposes penalties on acts that were not considered criminal when performed, or increases the punishment for a crime after it has been committed. Bills of attainder are acts of Congress that single out specific persons or groups and order their punishment without a jury trial. In 1943, the House Committee on Un-American Activities prompted Congress to declare three government employees subversive and unfit for government service, and to deny the payment of their salaries. The three men sued the government, claiming that this treatment was tantamount to a bill of attainder, or conviction, and thereby unconstitutional. They won their case.[17]

The Bill of Rights expanded the Constitutional protections for those accused of crimes. Specifically, the Fourth Amendment concerns itself with the way evidence is acquired, providing procedures for search, seizures, and warrants. The Fifth Amendment provides for indictment by a grand jury for capital crime, re-

---

[15] Henry J. Abraham, *Freedom and the Court,* p. 79.

[16] *Duncan* v. *Kahanamoken,* 327 U.S. 304 (1946).

[17] *United States* v. *Lorett,* 328 U.S. 303 (1946). The Court again declared an act of legislation to be the equivalent of a bill of attainder, and thereby unconstitutional, in *United States* v. *Brown,* 381 U.S. 437 (1965). In 1959, Congress made it a crime for a Communist party member to be an employee of a labor union; it did not, however, set forth a general rule but designated the names of members of the party and imposed the punishment of them specifically. The Court ruled this act was a bill of attainder, and that "Congress possesses full legislative authority, but the task of adjudication must be left to other tribunals."

quiring that a large jury (more than twelve persons) find enough evidence to merit taking a case with a death penalty to trial; prohibits double jeopardy, making it impossible for a person to be tried for the same crime twice; prohibits self-incrimination; and states that due process of law must be followed in depriving a person of life, liberty, and property. The Sixth Amendment provides for speedy, public trial by an impartial jury in the state and district where the crime was committed; states that the accused must be informed of the charges against him; provides for confrontation between witnesses and defendant, stating the process for their summoning; and provides the right to counsel. The Eighth Amendment outlaws excessive bail, excessive fines, and cruel or unusual punishment.

To understand the significance of Supreme Court decisions in any of these areas, it is important to note in each case the size of the majority vote, and the reasoning of the justices. Differences in judicial interpretation occur because the guarantees in the Bill of Rights are very broadly stated. Careful attention should also be paid to concurring and dissenting opinions, for very often these minority opinions may eventually become majority views.

Unreasonable Search and Seizure

The Fourth Amendment guarantees "the right of the people to be secure in their persons, houses, papers, and effects, against unreasonable searches and seizures." In general, a home cannot be searched without a warrant, issued on the basis of probable cause that the items to be seized are located there. A warrant must also be authorized by an unbiased judge.

In 1971, local police in the state of New Hampshire, acting on suspicion that Edward Coolidge had shot and stabbed to death a fourteen-year-old girl, searched his home and car and found evidence, in the car, that linked the suspect with the victim. He was tried and convicted on this evidence. Upon appeal, the Supreme Court overturned the conviction on the grounds that the warrant under which the search of the car had been carried out was defective because it had been issued by the police and the prosecuting attorney rather than by a neutral and detached judge.[18]

There are, however, certain circumstances under which search and seizure without a warrant is considered "reasonable" and therefore permissible. Until recently, a police officer could search anywhere in a home without a warrant when in the act of making a lawful arrest. But in 1969, the Court ruled that warrantless search at the time of arrest must be confined to the suspect and his immediate surroundings—wherever he could reach to destroy evidence or obtain a concealed weapon.[19]

Another situation in which search without a warrant is allowed is one in which the search involves a vehicle—for the simple reason that the vehicle might be driven away before the authorities have time to obtain a warrant. Police can also search a person on the street, a practice known as frisking, if they believe he is going to commit a crime or has a concealed weapon.

In 1970, a controversial "no-knock" home entry law was passed in Washington, D.C. Although police were still required to obtain a warrant before searching a

---

[18] *Coolidge* v. *New Hampshire,* 403 U.S. 443 (1971).
[19] *Chimel* v. *California,* 395 U.S. 752 (1969).

home, the law made it possible for them to enter the home without knocking.
It was deemed that such an unannounced police entry would enable officials to
apprehend criminals who might escape or to obtain evidence that might otherwise be destroyed. The law was specifically aimed at drug users, because of their
practice of flushing evidence down toilets. It also was deemed a safety measure
for the police involved in the seizure or arrest. Opponents of the bill, however,
charge that it is an unconstitutional invasion of privacy.

In addition to rulings concerning the conduct of searches and seizures, the
Supreme Court has also ruled on the use of illegally obtained evidence. In 1914,
the Court ruled that evidence obtained through illegal search and seizure could
not be used against the accused in federal prosecutions.[20] This principle, however,
was not made applicable to state prosecutions until the 1961 case of *Mapp* v.
Ohio. The defendant, a woman named Dollree Mapp, was suspected of operating
an illegal betting operation. Upon searching for evidence to substantiate this
claim, pornographic pictures were found on her premises and Ohio officials attempted to convict her. The Supreme Court ruled that the materials seized were
obtained without a warrant and, therefore, were inadmissible in court.[21] More
recently, however, the court has ruled (*Harris* v. *New York*, 1971) that in specific
situations, certain types of illegally obtained evidence could be used against the
accused.

"Dissolving the Walls and Windows": The Threatened Right to Privacy

Infringement on privacy through the covert use of mechanical devices began
as far back as the Civil War, when telegraph messages were wiretapped by Union
and Confederate forces.[22] This practice, plus the widespread use of photography
and telephone tapping, flourished in the pre–World War I period, and during the
decades that followed. Private and public use of such practices abounded: lawyers
in divorce cases, for example, widely utilized the techniques; the FBI, the
Treasury Department, the Post Office, and congressional committees admitted
to the practice. FBI Director J. Edgar Hoover maintained that the use of wiretaps
aided in criminal conviction, and the public, passively, generally accepted the
practice, probably underestimating the extent of surveillance. Today, however,
the same public is beginning to grow uneasy and to raise questions. People now
have no way of knowing if their phones are being tapped; thanks to long-distance
photography and hidden camera devices, neither can they tell if they are being
watched, anywhere and at any time. Suddenly, privacy is being recognized as
a precious right in jeopardy. Technology has progressed so far, and police zeal is
so great, that surgically inserted "electronic beepers" have been suggested for
round-the-clock monitoring of parolees who volunteered to have them put in.
The reward for volunteering to carry one would be a reduced sentence.[23]

The laws have taken an ambiguous stand on wiretapping – they have favored
the civil liberties of the suspect and yet have reflected the government's concern

---

[20] *Weeks* v. *United States,* 232 U.S. 383 (1914).

[21] *Mapp* v. *Ohio,* 367 U.S. 643 (1961).

[22] See Alan F. Westin, "Dissolving the Walls and Windows," *Privacy and Freedom* (New York: Atheneum, 1967),
pp. 172–211.

[23] *Time* (June 1, 1972).

"I'm certainly glad you asked that question—yes, J. Edgar Hoover enjoys my absolute and complete confidence. . ."

Los Angeles Times *Syndicate*

with strict enforcement of criminal law. The Federal Communications Act of 1934 stated that a person not authorized by the sender must not "intercept any communication and divulge or publish the existence, contents, substance . . . of such intercepted communication to any person." Following these guidelines, the Court recently has tried to limit wiretapping by government to strictly defined national security cases.

In 1928, in *Olmstead* v. *United States*,[24] it was ruled that wiretapping was not considered seized evidence and was thus permissible in court. But the Olmstead case was overruled in 1967, in *Katz* v. *United States*,[25] in which the Court held that a warrant was required to use an electronic eavesdropping device attached to a telephone booth. In 1969, in a further ruling on wiretapping, the Court declared that if the government tapped illegally, it had to disclose to the defendant all transcripts obtained by the wiretapping; lawyers would thus be able to determine if any information used against their clients had been obtained unconstitutionally.[26]

In the Omnibus Crime Control and Safe Streets Act passed by Congress in 1968, electronic eavesdropping by the police and prosecutors was made legal under certain circumstances, where a wiretap warrant was obtained in advance; however, the act made it a crime for any unauthorized person to tap telephone wires or use bugging devices. It authorized the Attorney General to do so for a specified range of federal offenses and with court permission. It also granted state prose-

---

[24] *Olmstead* v. *United States,* 277 U.S. 438 (1928).
[25] *Katz* v. *United States,* 389 U.S. 347 (1967).
[26] *Alderman* v. *United States,* 394 U.S. 165 (1969).

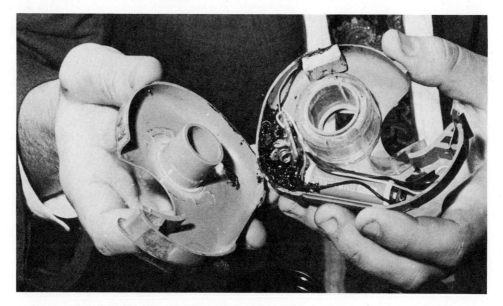

Cellophane-tape dispenser, when opened, reveals a bugging device.

cuting attorneys the right to apply for court permission to use eavesdropping devices where a major crime was involved. John N. Mitchell, then the Attorney General in the Nixon administration, nevertheless conducted wiretaps on suspected subversives without warrants, claiming the President's "inherent power" to do so.[27]

In 1971, in *United States* v. *White,* the Court held that the Fourth Amendment warrant requirement did not apply to the use of "bugged informers." This decision left law-enforcement authorities free to equip informers with devices to record or transmit conversations between unknowing suspects without prior legal permission. In a five-to-four decision, the Court argued that a person assumes the risk of misplacing his confidence whenever he speaks to another. The majority pointed out that conversations simply overheard had been accepted as evidence in the past, and that the risk of instantaneous disclosure by means of a bugged informer was no different. Justice Harlan, in his dissent, asserted that the practice would have a "chilling effect" on personal relationships. But the majority of the judges did not find the "chilling effect" as undesirable as the restriction on evidence.[28]

In June of 1972, the Court, in a unanimous decision, ruled that government officials could not use wiretapping against domestic radical groups without first obtaining a warrant. The justices argued that the Fourth Amendment was designed precisely to prevent law-enforcement officials from violating the privacy of citizens—unless a "neutral and disinterested magistrate" should decide that

[27] Fred P. Graham, "Wiretaps: Want to Bug? Tell it to the Judge," the *New York Times* (June 25, 1972), Sec. 4, p. 4.
[28] *United States* v. *White,* 401 U.S. 745 (1971).

it is necessary.[29] With this ruling the Court struck down the former government practice of wiretapping without a warrant in cases believed to endanger "national security." The Court reserved judgment on whether or not the wiretapping of foreign agents without a warrant is constitutional—giving rise to speculation over whether the government will try to tap radicals on the ground that they have links with foreign governments.

Despite all the court attention given to wiretapping and bugging regulations, neither the public nor high government officials feel there is effective restriction of the practice. Just after the June 1972 decision, a reporter wrote, "Henry Kissinger is so sure he's being wiretapped he wisecracks that he won't have to write his memoirs—he'll just publish the FBI's transcript of his telephone calls." The same source reports that the Assistant Attorney General had to have his office "swept" for listening devices, and that Secretary of State William Rogers tells friends he "can't discuss foreign policy over the telephone."[30]

Freedom from Self-Incrimination

Freedom from self-incrimination means that the burden of proof in cases of suspected criminal action is on the government—not on affirmation or denial of guilt by the suspect. A suspect has the right not to testify against himself. If, however, he agrees to be a witness, he must stand before cross-examination. Judges have been especially diligent in explaining to jurors that a defendant's refusal to testify does not imply guilt.

It should be noted that the majority of cases, about 90 percent, are decided on the basis of a confession. The usual practice of the police in the past was to arrest a suspect, grill him for hours until he confessed, or use much of what he said during the interrogation as testimony against him in court, or, finally, to make a deal to reduce the charge if the suspect pleaded guilty. Promised, "we'll go easy on you if you confess," many indigent suspects found it to their advantage to plead guilty to a lesser charge even if they had not committed a crime.

In certain cases, the government, instead of bringing charges against a witness, prefers to have him answer questions, and grants him immunity. The Organized Crime Control Act of 1970 provides that evidence, information, or even leads gained in immunized testimony—testimony authorized by a government agency, under the consent of the Attorney General, a majority of either the House of Representatives or the Senate, or two-thirds of the members of a congressional committee—cannot be used in any state or federal prosecution. No state may grant this total immunity. All a state can do in regard to immunity is to protect specific evidence revealed in state proceedings from use as evidence in federal courts.

In May 1972, the Supreme Court upheld the 1970 Crime Control Act's immunity provision. In the majority opinion (5 to 2) in *Kastigar* v. *United States*, the judges ruled that a defendant may be forced to testify under threat of a contempt-of-court citation.[31] Although the forced testimony or information derived from it may not be used against the witness in a criminal case, Justice Thurgood Marshall pointed out in his dissent that the witness could still be convicted on "independent

---

[29] *United States* v. *United States District Court for the Eastern District of Michigan et al.*, 403 U.S. 930 (1971).

[30] Graham, "Wiretaps: Want to Bug?"

[31] *Kastigar* v. *United States*, 402 U.S. 971 (1971).

evidence" acquired by the police. Marshall expressed apprehension over illegal police practices in acquiring evidence; as long as only the police are required to know if the new evidence is independently gathered or not, he feared insufficient protection for the accused.

Protection against self-incrimination was extended to defendants in state courts in 1964, in *Mallory* v. *Hogan*.[32] But even this procedural safeguard left unresolved the issue of the use of pretrial confessions in the courts. Before 1957, any coerced confession was held to be inadmissible evidence in court, and since that time the Court has made a series of decisions that have placed in doubt *any* confession obtained by pretrial interrogation. These recent decisions have often been linked with the defendant's right to counsel, a provision of the Sixth Amendment, which should aid the accused in his determination to confess his guilt or plead not guilty.

The Right to Counsel

The average citizen's knowledge of the law and its complexities is too limited to help him when he gets into trouble with the police. Under the Sixth Amendment, a suspect has the right to counsel: he is entitled to professional legal advice to define his rights and the limitations on authorities. The provision of counsel was upheld in federal courts in 1938,[33] but as of that date only applied to suspects convicted of capital crimes in state courts.[34] Not until the sixties was the right to counsel in all cases tested: the hero was Clarence Gideon, a perennial jailbird described as a "born loser," who had started a life of crime after running away from home as a boy, and had served four prison terms for burglary and larceny.[35]

Gideon was arrested in 1961 for breaking into a poolroom. In refusing a request for counsel, the Florida judge offered his apologies, explaining that state law only provided for counsel when the defendant is charged with a capital offense. Upon appeal to the Supreme Court in 1963, Gideon won his right to counsel in the now-famous case of *Gideon* v. *Wainwright*, and since that time this right has been secure in state and federal courts for all criminal offenses. In the last decade, however, the right to counsel has come into prominence as one of the most controversial issues in the federal courts.

In 1957, the Supreme Court held void a confession obtained after half an hour of police interrogation, on the grounds that the defendant had not been informed of his right to silence or his right to counsel, and had not been arraigned immediately before a magistrate.[36] Seven years later, it was similarly held that a confession was invalid if the suspect "had requested and been denied an opportunity to consult with his lawyer, and the police have not effectively warned him of his absolute constitutional right to remain silent."[37]

In 1966, in *Miranda* v. *Arizona*,[38] it was ruled that no conviction, state or federal, could stand on the basis of evidence acquired by the police in "custodial interrogation" unless the following conditions had been met: the suspect had to be

---

[32] *Mallory* v. *Hogan,* 378 U.S. 1 (1964).
[33] *Johnson* v. *Zerbst,* 304 U.S. 458 (1938).
[34] *Powell* v. *Alabama,* 287 U.S. 45 (1932).
[35] *Gideon* v. *Wainwright,* 372 U.S. 335 (1963).
[36] *Mallory* v. *United States,* 354 U.S. 449 (1957).
[37] *Escobedo* v. *Illinois,* 378 U.S. 478 (1964).
[38] *Miranda* v. *Arizona,* 384 U.S. 436 (1966).

warned that what he said could be used against him in court; he had to be told that he was entitled to have his attorney present during the questioning, that an attorney would be provided for him if he could not afford one himself, and that he could stop the police interrogation at any stage. If the suspect answered questions in the absence of an attorney, it rested on the prosecution to demonstrate that he had deliberately waived his rights to remain silent and have counsel present. The absence of these conditions was ruled sufficient to overturn a conviction even if independent evidence would establish guilt.

In 1968, parts of *Miranda* were reversed in the Omnibus Crime Control and Safe Streets Act passed by Congress. The act made "voluntariness" the sole test of the admissibility of a confession—with the stipulation that the suspect be arraigned before a magistrate within six hours of arrest. The act is a step backward in the viewpoint of most civil libertarians. As the Court pointed out in *Miranda,* it is virtually impossible to provide a precise legal definition for "voluntary" confession—so intimidating are the techniques and pressures used in police interrogations. The Court noted, in its decision, "that the blood of the accused is not the only hallmark of an unconstitutional inquisition." Indeed, "the modern practice of in-custody interrogation is psychologically rather than physically oriented."

In June of 1972, the Court handed down another decision that reflected a move away from the Warren Court philosophies. All four of President Nixon's appointees, joined by Justice Potter Stewart, concurred that only suspects who have been indicted are entitled to counsel. It has been suggested that the new decision which grants counsel after indictment is an arbitrary decision which often denies legal advice at "critical stages" of the judicial process, such as the time when an individual must appear in a police lineup.[39] It also reverses parts of the *Miranda* decision which granted counsel to any person detained by the police whether he had been indicted or not. For these reasons many find the new decision detrimental to civil liberties.[40] The suspect's need for legal advice soon after arrest has long been recognized by those who have seen mistaken identifications result from such police lineup tricks as placing a black suspect in a line of whites, or a youth among a group of old men.

Trial by Jury: A Vehicle for Equal Protection

The Sixth Amendment states that in all criminal cases the accused is entitled to a trial by jury, in which all evidence is presented to a panel of citizens who rule on the guilt or innocence of the defendant. In reality, however, only about half of those accused of crimes avail themselves of this right.[41]

There are three basic requisites to this right: that the trial be speedy, that it be public, and that it be impartial. An impartial trial requires both the absence of press sensationalism and an impartial selection of jurors. In the selection of the jury, discrimination on the basis of race, creed, or sex is forbidden—a principle affirmed in 1954 when evidence proved that no person of Mexican or Latin

---

[39] The lineup was defined as a "critical stage" of the judicial process in both *United States* v. *Wade,* 388 U.S. 218 (1967) and *Gilbert* v. *California,* 388 U.S. 263 (1967).

[40] Fred P. Graham, "Line-ups: Now You're on Your Own When the Finger Points," the *New York Times* (June 11, 1972), Sec. 4, p. 6.

[41] Stuart S. Nagal, "The Tipped Scales of American Justice," in Klonoski and Mendelsohn, *The Politics of Local Justice,* p. 118.

American extraction had been selected to serve on the county jury of a particular Texas county for twenty-five years.[42] Yet it is incorrect to assume that factors such as ethnicity or sex by themselves can determine the impartiality of a jury. In 1970, for example, Angela Davis, a philosophy instructor at the University of California, and a black activist and member of the Communist party, was accused of being an accessory to conspiracy, kidnapping, and murder of a judge and bailiff. It was thought by many that the all-white jury composed of seven women and five men would not hand down an unbiased decision. After a twenty-two-month trial and thirteen hours of deliberation, the jury unanimously found her not guilty on all counts.

Until recently most trial juries consisted of twelve persons and reached decisions by a unanimous vote. Then a few states began using smaller juries and accepting less-than-unanimous decisions. In 1970, the Supreme Court upheld this practice, calling the number twelve a "historical accident." And in May 1972, the Court, with Nixon's appointees voting together, ruled in favor of less-than-unanimous decisions in state courts, a verdict that was called "a constitutional development that could eventually turn the American jury into a committee. . . ."[43] Justice William O. Douglas, in his dissent, asserted that the majority had been swayed by a "law and order judicial mood," and Hans Zeisel, an academic authority on the jury system, agreed. Both men contended that the the practice of accepting only unanimous verdicts was a means of tolerance built into our system, and are now fearful that dissenting minorities may not be scrupulously protected.

Cruel and Unusual Punishment

Although no one has been executed by civil authority in the United States since 1967,[44] six hundred men and women on death rows in the United States felt they were saved from execution on June 29, 1972, when the Supreme Court handed down one of the most important decisions of the Court's history: it ruled capital punishment "cruel and unusual punishment," and thus a violation of the Eighth Amendment. The vote of five to four pitted the five holdovers from the Warren Court against the four Nixon appointees. Numerous states had already outlawed capital punishment, but before the 1972 ruling the Court had twice rejected challenges to the constitutionality of procedures by which the death penalty was imposed.[45] Justice Potter Stewart, in the majority opinion which outlawed capital punishment, stated that the death penalty is "so wantonly and so freakishly imposed" that those who are sentenced to death receive excessively harsh treatment. "These death sentences are cruel and unusual in the same way that being struck by lightning is cruel and unusual." The dissenting position held that the majority had usurped the prerogative of the state legislatures; Justice Lewis F. Powell, Jr., condemned the decision for its disregard of the principles of "federalism, judicial restraint, and—most importantly—separation of powers."[46] The Supreme Court ruling on capital punishment, however, has yet to be applied to

---

[42] *Hernandez* v. *Texas,* 347 U.S. 475 (1954).

[43] Fred P. Graham, "Jury Trial: Now the Vote Need Not Be Unanimous," the *New York Times* (May 28, 1972), Sec. 4, p. 6.

[44] The most recent available statistics are through 1970, which report none from 1968 to 1970. *Statistical Abstract of the United States, 1971,* (Washington, D.C.: Department of Commerce, 1971), p. 159.

[45] *McGautha* v. *California,* 402 U.S. 183 (1971); and *Crampton* v. *Ohio,* 402 U.S. 183 (1971).

[46] The *New York Times,* June 30, 1972, pp. 1 and 14.

the states. In some states, capital punishment remains on the books in cases involving murder of police officers and prison guards.

Substantive Due Process and the Protection of Property

There is a definite tension between the liberties of the individual and the protection of property. For example, a factory owner may feel that he is entitled to hire, fire, and pay his employees as he sees fit, on the basis of his right to operate his private property in whatever way he wishes. The owner's right to property, however, may conflict with the individual rights of the workers—their right to be treated in a fair manner and to receive an adequate wage for their labor. Similarly, the owner of a private club may believe that his right to property grants him the privilege of determining qualifications for membership; but when these qualifications systematically exclude certain racial, religious, or ethnic groups, he is infringing on their individual freedom to join whatever clubs they choose.

From about 1888 to the early 1930s, the chief concern of the Supreme Court was the protection of property. Repeatedly, the Court ruled that legislation providing for minimum wages, maximum working hours, and child-labor restrictions were violations of property rights. Sixteen New Deal laws protecting the individual were struck down between 1934 and 1936. In 1937, however, the Court changed its emphasis from protection of property to protection of the individual, in a trend that has not been reversed since.

Some authorities make the distinction between *procedural* due process and *substantive* due process. The protection of property has primarily been maintained through the use of substantive due process. This form of protection refers to the actual content of the law, and holds that laws which are unreasonable may be unconstitutional. It is generally agreed that procedural due process has played a greater role in the courts because of the vagueness of the standard of reasonable-

Senator Joseph R. McCarthy's early 1950s Senate hearings gave official sanction to anti-communist hysteria. Repeatedly, allegations of subversion were made with blatant disregard for the civil liberties of those accused. McCarthy is at the right.

ness in substantive due process, and because the nature of the grievances brought before the Court deal more with procedural safeguards than with the content of laws.

First Amendment Freedoms

The First Amendment freedoms are essential to a free and democratic people, because the oppressed, denied these rights, have no means of correcting injustice short of violence and revolution. Probably the most pressing among these freedoms is that of speech, which became one of the chief issues in the civil-rights rebellion of the sixties. The First Amendment asserts:

Congress shall make no law respecting an establishment of religion, or prohibiting the free exercise thereof; or abridging the freedom of speech, or of the press; or the right of the people peaceably to assemble, and to petition the Government for a redress of grievances.

Freedom of Speech

Even such ardent defenders of liberty as John Stuart Mill conceded that there were limitations to what an individual could be permitted to say.[47] As Justice Oliver Wendell Holmes wrote in the now-famous example, a person does not have a right to cry, "Fire!" in a crowded theater; one does not have a right to libel, slander, or defame other persons or groups. It is in the area of political speech, however, that the greatest difficulty has been encountered in determining the limits of free speech, and in this area, a ruling principle has been the "clear and present danger" doctrine, by which the courts have refused to allow revolutionary speech designed to instigate violent overthrow of the government.

Restrictions on freedom of speech occurred early in our nation's history. In 1798, during the panic that arose when the United States moved toward war with France, the Sedition Act made it illegal to publish or utter "false, scandalous or malicious" criticism of high government officials. In the twentieth century, the Sedition Act of 1918, as a reaction to wartime tensions and the Bolshevik Revolution, again made it a crime to criticize the government or its policy. Both of these acts were aimed at such overt action as the distribution of leaflets and speeches encouraging revolution.

The Smith Act of 1940 (tested in *Dennis* v. *United States*) made it illegal to advocate or teach violent overthrow of the government, or to be a member of any group with such intention. Aimed at the Communist party, this act was passed a year after the Nazi-Soviet Anti-Aggression Pact. To these precedents of restrictions on free speech was added the government loyalty program of 1947, which included a Loyalty Review Board to check on government employees. The Board was established by executive order of President Truman and extended under the Eisenhower administration. In 1950, in response to rising public fear of the spread of communism, the Internal Security or McCarran Act, barred Communists from working for the federal government and made the process of naturalization

---

[47] See John Stuart Mill, *On Liberty,* edited by Albursey Castell (New York: Appleton-Century-Crofts, 1947).

harder and deportation easier. The most recent restrictive measure in this area was the Communist Control Act of 1954, which denied the Communist party rights enjoyed by other political parties and also denied the benefits of the nation's labor laws to unions with Communist officers and employers who hired Communists in labor negotiations.

Certain provisions of the government loyalty program and the Internal Security Act have been overturned by the Supreme Court. Among these was the Summary Suspension Act, which originally provided for the dismissal of federal employees as security risks in jobs bearing on the national security, and which was broadened during the Eisenhower administration to apply to *all* federal employees. The Supreme Court ruled against the latter practice, stating that the Act could be applied only to individuals in "sensitive positions."[48] And in the 1960s, those provisions of the McCarran Act which denied passports to Communist party members, required members of the Communist party to register, and prohibited their employment in United States defense facilities were overturned by the Court.

The era of the "Red scare" in America has passed, but there are now dissident groups other than communists that appear to be a threat to the existing system. The fear of such groups was reflected in a Supreme Court decision in April 1972, dealing with the administration of loyalty oaths. The majority opinion, held by four of the seven judges and delivered by Chief Justice Burger, overruled a federal district court decision by holding loyalty oaths constitutional for employees of the state of Massachusetts.[49] The oath, which includes a pledge to oppose any overthrow of the government by force or violence, was not deemed in violation of the First Amendment, on the grounds that it only requires individuals to swear not to resort to illegal action. The dissenting opinion viewed the oath requirement as a flagrant violation of free speech.

Tests of Free Speech: Clear and Present Danger, Preferred Position, Absolutist Position Probably the most important principle concerning free speech was enunciated in 1919, when Justice Oliver Wendell Holmes, Jr., wrote the unanimous decision in *Schenck* v. *United States.* Schenck had been convicted of circulating pamphlets advocating resistance to the draft. In the opinion of the Court, he had the right to express his belief that the draft was wrong, but the issue was whether he had the right to provoke people to illegal seditious action. The Court ruled against Schenck, declaring that his words provoked a "clear and present danger," activity harmful to the national interest. Or, as Holmes wrote, using the criterion that was to be quoted many times thereafter as a test for the legality of public utterances:

The question in every case is whether the words used are used in such circumstances and are of such a nature as to create a clear and present danger that they will bring about the substantive evils that Congress has a right to prevent.[50]

With the Schenck case and *Abrams* v. *United States* that same year, the justices of the Court began to take increasing leeway in interpreting the law on the basis of philosophical attitudes and their own insights into men and the times. Abrams,

---

[48] *Cole* v. *Young,* 351 U.S. 536 (1956).
[49] *Cole, State Hospital Superintendent, et al.* v. *Richardson,* 403 U.S. 917 (1971).
[50] *Schenck* v. *United States,* 249 U.S. 47 (1919).

an anarchist-socialist, was convicted of sedition after he had distributed leaflets calling for acts of resistance against United States military intervention in Siberia. He had called for a protest in the form of a general strike, and a Court majority saw a "clear and present danger" in the strike. However, Holmes and Justice Louis Brandeis dissented in an opinion written by Holmes:

When men have realized that time has upset many fighting faiths, they may come to believe even more than they believe the very foundation of their own conduct that the ultimate good desired is better reached by free trade in ideas—*that the best test of truth is the power of thought to get itself accepted in the competition of the market, and that* truth is the only ground *upon which their wishes can be safely carried out. That at any rate is the theory of our Constitution.* It is an experiment, as all life is an experiment. *Every year if not every day we have to wager our salvation upon some prophecy based upon imperfect knowledge. While that experiment is part of our system, I think that we should be* eternally vigilant against attempts to check the expression of opinions that we loathe and believe to be fraught with death unless they so imminently interfere with the lawful and pressing purposes of the law that an immediate check is required to save the country.[51]

The Brandeis-Holmes position in the Abrams case added the notion of imminence to the clear and present danger doctrine in an effort to define the doctrine more precisely. The concept of imminence was further clarified in 1925 in the case of *Gitlow* v. *New York.* Publication of Gitlow's "Left-wing Manifest" was judged to be a threat because a "single revolutionary spark may kindle a fire that, smouldering for a time, may burst into a sweeping and destructive conflagration." In the court ruling, Brandeis defined imminence as occurring when "the incidence of the evil apprehended is so imminent that it may befall before there is opportunity for full discussion."[52]

Although obvious in intent, the clear-and-present-danger position has not always triumphed. In balancing the interests of the society against the freedom of the individual, some justices see the need for more, rather than less, restriction. In the 1951 case of *Dennis* v. *United States,* the judges preferred to protect the public instead of Dennis's free speech.[53] The court ruling provided for the first time a legal basis for the idea that the Communist party is a criminal conspiracy dedicated to overthrowing the government of the United States by force and violence. The Court ruled that the eleven top leaders of the American Communist party were guilty of teaching and advocating sedition and of organizing their party to overthrow the United States government *at some time in the future.* It was the Court's reliance on the reasoning implied by these last few words (that an indefinite amount of time, during which no action occurs, can still be threatening to society) which resulted in some experts calling this court ruling an application of clear and probable danger, instead of clear and present danger. Justice Felix Frankfurter delivered the opinion; both he and Justice John Marshall Harlan, Jr., frequently used this reasoning.[54]

---

[51] *Abrams* v. *United States,* 250 U.S. 616 (1919), discussed in Henry J. Abraham, *Freedom and the Court: Civil Rights and Liberties in the United States* (London: Oxford University Press, 1967), pp. 159–161.

[52] *Gitlow* v. *United States,* 268 U.S. 652 (1925).

[53] *Dennis* v. *United States,* 341 U.S. 494 (1951).

[54] The balancing-of-interests doctrine reached its height in 1959 when Justice Harlan delivered the opinion in *Barenblatt* v. *United States,* 360 U.S. 109 (1959).

Turning in draft cards as an antiwar protest became civil disobedience rather than the exercise of free speech after a 1968 Supreme Court ruling.

The balancing of interests as applied in *Dennis* is considered a politically conservative interpretation, one that limits an individual's civil liberties. A more liberal interpretation is the preferred position of First Amendment freedoms, advocated by Justice Harlan Fiske Stone and stated in a 1945 case:

Only the gravest abuses, endangering paramount interests, give occasion for permissible limitation [of speech]. The usual presumption supporting legislation is balanced by the preferred place given in our scheme to the great, the indisputable democratic freedoms secured by the First Amendment. . . . That priority gives these liberties a sanctity and sanction not permitting dubious intrusions."[55]

Carried even further, the preferred position results in the absolutist position — the stance that *any* law that limits speech is unconstitutional. Supreme Court Justices Hugo Black and William O. Douglas formulated this theory during the era of anticommunist hysteria, in response to the jailing of alleged subversives. It is, however, currently a controversial opinion which usually loses to the more realistic one that total freedom is detrimental in any society.

Weighing individual rights against the public order, then, continues to be a major challenge to the courts. In the past few years some antiwar demonstrators, when required to defend themselves in court, have based their defense on the symbolic use of free speech. Is this a legitimate use of the free speech clause? The Court has made its position clear, drawing the line where it deems appropriate. In 1968 the Court ruled that the burning of a draft card was not the symbolic speech claimed by the defendant, and hence not subject to First Amendment protection.[56] In another case, in 1969, however, it ruled that wearing a black armband (as Mary Beth Tinker did in her junior high school in Iowa) was a peaceful protest and a legitimate exercise of symbolic free speech.[57]

---

[55] *Thomas* v. *Collins*, 325 U.S. 516, pp. 529–530 (1945).
[56] *United States* v. *O'Brien*, 391 U.S. 367 (1968).
[57] *Tinker* v. *Des Moines School District et al.*, 393 U.S. 503 (1969).

Freedom of the Press

Daniel Webster expounded the benefits of a free press in these lofty words:

Given a free press, we may defy open or insidious enemies of liberty. It instructs the public mind and animates the spirit of patriotism. Its loud voice suppresses everything which would raise itself against the public liberty, and its blasting rebuke causes incipient despotism to perish in the bud.[58]

To preserve freedom of the press, the Court has been reluctant to place any prior restraint on the publication of possibly objectionable material, because prior restraint is censorship. But if the government waits until after publication, the damage has already been done; subsequent fines, even if very large, cannot usually correct it; despite this, the Court has seldom allowed prior restraint.

The first case to strike down prior restraint occurred in 1931 and held a Minnesota state law unconstitutional for violation of freedom of the press as protected by the due-process clause of the Fourteenth Amendment. The law in question was the so-called "Minnesota gag law," which enabled the courts to "padlock" articles that were deemed scandalous, malicious, defamatory, or obscene. This stipulation meant that the press could be restrained by an injunction from publishing any such material. The injunction could be lifted only when the judge who issued it was convinced that the publication would not be objectionable in the future.

The case involved a series of articles that charged public officials with gross negligence in failing to bring charges against a gangster involved in gambling, bootlegging, and racketeering. Among others, the chief of police was charged with illicit dealings with the gangsters, and the mayor with inefficiency and dereliction. Both the right of the press to make such charges and its future freedom were upheld. Chief Justice John Evans Hughes pointed out:

Charges of reprehensible conduct, and in particular of official malfeasance, unquestionably create a public scandal, but the theory of the constitutional guaranty is that even a more serious public evil would be caused by authority to prevent publication. . . . There is nothing new in the fact that charges of reprehensible conduct may create resentment and the disposition to resort to violent means of redress but this well-understood tendency did not alter the determination to protect the press against censorship and restraint upon publication.[59]

In this particular case, *Near* v. *Minnesota,* in which the charge was slander, the press won. Recently the press triumphed again; in a dramatic confrontation with the Nixon administration, the *New York Times* was charged with violation of the national security.[60] The *Times* published large portions of the Pentagon Papers, *A History of the U.S. Decision-Making Process on Vietnam Policy,* which was labeled classified information by the Pentagon and leaked to the press by Daniel Ellsberg, a former Pentagon official and government consultant. Attorney General John Mitchell obtained injunctions to halt any further publication of the papers by the *Times* or the *Washington Post,* which had also printed some of the classified documents. The issue of a credibility gap was highlighted by the papers, which revealed that information released to the public by administration officials re-

[58] Quoted in *Saturday Review* (November 13, 1971), p. 86.
[59] *Near* v. *Minnesota,* 285 U.S. 697 (1931).
[60] *New York Times Co.* v. *United States,* 91 S.Ct. 2140 (1971).

The Supreme Court's 1971 ruling lifting a government restraint on the publication of the Pentagon Papers was hailed as a victory for freedom of the press and a major gain for those demanding less government secrecy on national-security matters.

garding the conduct of the war was at variance with what had actually happened. In fact, the credibility of several administrations was impaired by the disclosures.

Eighteen days after the injunction was issued, a majority of the Court ruled that the government's charges should be dismissed. Three dissented: Justice John M. Harlan, who wrote the dissenting opinion; Chief Justice Warren Burger, and Justice Harry A. Blackmun. The majority opinion held that the government did not provide sufficient proof to justify the prior restraint. It should be noted that the majority did not take the position that the press should be totally free from restraint, but held that there are instances in which such action would be justified.

Prior Restraint and Television Television has remained freer from government control than the press. Censorship, which has come primarily from the media themselves, is only indirectly regulated by the government. The Supreme Court in 1969 maintained that broadcasters had to present both sides of important public issues—the fairness doctrine. "It is the right of viewers and listeners," Justice Byron R. White maintained, "not the right of the broadcaster, which is paramount."

Moreover, under the First Amendment, a broadcaster may not "monopolize a radio frequency to the exclusion of his fellow citizens."[61]

Film Censorship Until the fifties, movies were considered entertainment and not sources of public information, and were therefore subject to censorship by state and local boards.[62] In 1952, in the case of *Burstyn* v. *Wilson,* it was ruled that a New York State board did not have the right to censor a movie on the grounds that it was sacrilegious.[63] Since then, most state censorship boards have been disbanded. While prior restraint is constitutional in cases of obscenity, reviewing boards must prove, in order to utilize constraint, that obscenity, measured by precise standards, is in fact present.[64]

Informal censorship takes place, however, generally as a result of interest-group pressure in local areas. For example, about 10 percent of Americans read no advertisements for X-rated films in their daily papers because of self-imposed censorship by the publishers reflecting local pressures. However, there is little pressure for film censorship today, but rather increased tolerance for public expression of previously taboo ideas.

Obscenity Formulating a legal definition of obscenity has been extremely difficult. It has become increasingly clear that the evaluation of material as obscene is subjective, and the consensus of the courts has been that an individual's civil liberty should not be subject to the personal bias of politically appointed censors. Yet, the courts have ruled that purely pornographic materials should be regulated.

Several important rulings have been made on obscenity, and the court's opinions indicate efforts to reach a precise definition of obscenity. The *average-man* test was evolved in 1957 in the case of *Roth* v. *United States:* obscenity was said to exist when "to the average person, applying contemporary community standards, the dominant theme of the material taken as a whole appeals to prurient interests." Such prurient material, when "utterly without redeeming social importance,"[65] was ruled not subject to the constitutional protection of free speech or free press. In 1960, the ruling in John Cleland's *Memoirs of a Woman of Pleasure (Fanny Hill)* v. *Attorney General of Massachusetts* produced a threefold test: A book would be considered obscene if (a) it appealed to "prurient interest in sex"; (b) it was a patent offense to contemporary community standards; and (c) there was a total absence of "redeeming social value." The local decision which had ruled *Fanny Hill* obscene was reversed.[66]

---

[61] *Red Lion Broadcasting Co., Inc.* v. *FCC,* 395 U.S. 367 (1969). In the case of *The Selling of the Pentagon,* a program on the Columbia Broadcasting System which was highly critical of the government, an unsuccessful attempt was made to confiscate the unused portions of the documentary for the purpose of drawing up legislation against "deceitful editorial devices." See *Newsweek,* July 26, 1971, "The Selling of Congress."

[62] Films were held not to be part of "the Press of the country" in *Mutual Film Corporation* v. *Ohio Industrial Commission,* 236 U.S. 230 (1915).

[63] *Burstyn* v. *Wilson,* 343 U.S. 495 (1952).

[64] *Freedman* v. *Maryland,* 380 U.S. 51 (1965).

[65] *Roth* v. *United States,* 354 U.S. 476 (1957).

[66] *Memoirs* v. *Massachusetts,* 383 U.S. 413 (1966). In this area, legal precision has clearly worked in the direction of greater liberalization: in the presence of the slightest "social value" the protection of the First Amendment can be invoked. The courts, admitting the existence of obscenity, were at the same time admitting (once again) a preferred position in First Amendment freedom.

"If you are under eighteen years of age and unaccompanied by an adult, please move on to the next painting."

New Yorker, *December 13, 1969*

The Court has not been entirely averse to regulation where there has been no reasonable doubt of the obscenity of the material in question. Hence, Ralph Ginzburg, the publisher of *Eros* magazine, was convicted, not on the basis of the obscene content of the material involved but on the way it had been advertised — for "titillation" rather than "intellectual content."[67] Since Ginzburg's conviction community standards of obscenity have changed, so that if the case was to be tested today, a conviction would be highly unlikely. The Court also ruled in a 1968 decision against the sale of pornographic material to minors.[68]

Although there will be wavering in legislation and enforcement as long as there are pressures by forces for and against government control of obscenity, a basic trend toward liberalization of censorship can be discerned. The *Report of the U.S. Commission on Obscenity and Pornography* of 1970 is the strongest evidence for this trend, and at the same time the strongest basis for its establishment on legal and philosophical grounds. A surprise to the administration which initiated it (President Nixon rejected the report as "morally bankrupt"), the report ignored religious and moral objections to explicit sexual materials, concluding that they did not affect the rate of sex crimes:

---

[67] *Ginzburg* v. *New York*, 383 U.S. 463 (1966).
[68] *Ginzburg* v. *New York*, 390 U.S. 629 (1968).

Empirical research designed to clarify the question has found no evidence to date that exposure to explicit sexual materials plays a significant role in causation of delinquent or criminal behavior among youth or adults. The Commission cannot conclude that exposure to erotic materials is a factor in the causation of sex crime or sex delinquency.[69]

The Court has weighed the sociological as well as the legal ramifications of the possession of pornographic literature. In 1969, it rejected the attempt of the state of Georgia to forbid the possession of obscene materials on the ground that this amounted to "unwarranted governmental intrusion into one's privacy," and noted that "given the present state of knowledge, the state may no more prohibit mere possession of obscenity on the ground that it may lead to antisocial conduct than it may prohibit possession of chemistry books on the ground that they might lead to the manufacture of home-made spirits."[70] The end result of the entire obscenity controversy is that there is little legal censorship, except over hard-core pornography, which manifestly has no social value whatsoever. And even in such cases, it must be proved that the distributor of the pornography knowingly sold it as such.[71]

Libel and Slander   Libel (defamatory writing) and slander (defamatory language) are not legal. However, in a free society, criticism of those who govern is a necessity for free elections. In 1964 an attempt to distinguish criticism from libel was made when the Supreme Court ruled that the *New York Times* was not guilty of libel in carrying an advertisement criticizing officials of Birmingham, Alabama, for their treatment of a group of black student protestors. The court held that to prove libel, it must be shown that a statement about public officials was made with malicious intent—that is, in the knowledge that the statement was false or in reckless disregard for the facts. The advertisement in question did contain some factual errors, but this fault was ruled insufficient grounds for libel. In blunt language, the Court ruled that, in a democratic society, "debate on public issues should be uninhibited, robust, and wide-open, and . . . may well include vehement . . . attacks on government officials."[72]

Freedom of Assembly

It would be simple for authorities to prohibit unpopular groups from assembling by pleading fear of a riot, if the law did not carry restraints against such an action. In general, the rule has evolved that individuals can assemble as long as they do not interfere with traffic, take over buildings and disrupt facilities, or in any other way obstruct the normal habits of people in the surroundings. Frequently, however, an additional problem arises when the speaker provokes the audience. This situation requires law-enforcement officials to be able to distinguish between permitting the speaker to arouse an emotional but safe response in an audience and allowing him to provoke a riot.

---

[69] *Report of the Commission on Obscenity and Pornography* (Washington, D.C.: Government Printing Office, 1970), p. 27.

[70] *Stanley* v. *Georgia,* 394 U.S. 557 (1969).

[71] *Smith* v. *California,* 361 U.S. 147 (1959).

[72] *New York Times Co.* v. *Sullivan,* 376 U.S. 254 (1964). From 1964 to 1970, constitutional standards of libel differed depending on who was being libeled: in general, there was greater immunity from charges the more prominent the figure involved. But since *Rosenbloom* v. *Metromedia,* 403 U.S. 29 (1971), the same standard, that which evolved in *New York Times Co.* v. *Sullivan,* is applied for all subjects.

Most recent decisions involving freedom of assembly have depended on circumstances, and especially on specific local statutes. In *Feiner* v. *New York,* the Court upheld the conviction of a university student who refused to stop speaking publicly on civil rights after he was ordered to do so by police, who feared an open fight.[73] But in *Edwards* v. *South Carolina,* the conviction of a group of black civil-rights demonstrators was overturned because the evidence for a potential riot—there were some "possible troublemakers" in the crowd that assembled around the demonstrators—was deemed vague and insufficient. The Court specifically held that

a function of free speech under our system of government is to invite dispute. It may indeed best serve its high purpose when it induces a condition of unrest, creates dissatisfaction with conditions as they are, or even stirs people to anger.[74]

In recent years localities have generally been unsuccessful in appealing assembly cases to the Court because of the vagueness of their local laws. For example, in 1971, the conviction of a group of people for assembling on a sidewalk and conducting themselves in a manner annoying to passersby was overruled for vagueness. Justice Stewart stated that the city is indeed "free to prevent people from blocking sidewalks, obstructing traffic, committing assaults, or engaging in countless other forms of antisocial conduct." But it can only do this through "ordinances directed with reasonable specificity toward the conduct to be prohibited . . . it cannot constitutionally do so through the enactment and enforcement of an ordinance whose violation may entirely depend upon whether or not a policeman is annoyed."[75]

Religious Liberty

It has been claimed that freedom of religion is the basis of American society.[76] Religion has a symbolic importance for civil liberties. It is the realm in which the element of individual freedom, which has already been identified as the core of the civil-liberties question, reigns supreme. A sectarian belief often appears, to the nonbeliever, to be highly arbitrary and idiosyncratic. But to the believer it is a deeply held conviction—a response to a higher law (like Thoreau's law of conscience) and the very opposite of a subjective whim. It has been pointed out that "religion, like love, is so personal and irrational that no one has either the capacity or justification to sit in judgement."[77]

---

[73] *Feiner* v. *New York,* 340 U.S. 313 (1951).

[74] *Edwards* v. *South Carolina,* 372 U.S. 229 (1963).

[75] *Coates* v. *Cincinnati,* 402 U.S. 611 (1971). Protest at public facilities is a different matter when it interferes with the duties of authorities. In *Brown* v. *Louisiana,* 383 U.S. 131 (1965), a civil-rights demonstration in a public library was defended, as it did not interfere with the library's need for quiet. However, in *Adderly* v. *Florida,* 385 U.S. 39 (1966), the conviction was upheld of a group of students who demonstrated at a jailhouse against the jailing of their fellow students and the general condition of segregation in the jail. Justice Hugo Black argued that jails cannot be open to the general public because they are built for security reasons, and that a state is entitled to "even-handed enforcement of its general trespass statute . . . to preserve the property under its control for the use to which it is lawfully dedicated." In the eyes of the students, theirs was a political protest held in a political arena; but to the majority of the Court, "political" prisoners (the arrested students) were the same as any others, and the state was merely asserting its punitive role.

[76] Milton R. Konvitz, *Fundamental Liberties of a Free People* (Ithaca, N.Y.: Cornell University Press, 1957), pp. 3–9.

[77] See Henry J. Abraham, *Freedom and the Court: Civil Rights and Liberties in the U.S.* (New York: Oxford University Press, 1967), p. 172.

And yet, court judgment has been required in some cases to rule on religion, as in dealing with the polygamy of Mormons or the issues of draft resistance and refusal to salute the flag by Jehovah's Witnesses. Although the United States has a religious majority, Protestantism, ours is a country in which the secular view often prevails, and religious minorities must on occasion seek justice from the nation's highest legal authority, the Supreme Court. In the last twenty-five years, religious issues have made the Court both villain and hero to those involved in religious litigation.[78]

The provisions of the Constitution designed to protect religious liberty are Article VI, which forbids religious tests as qualifications for public office, and the First Amendment, which declares that "Congress shall make no law respecting an establishment of religion, or prohibiting the free exercise thereof." These laws insure that, although there may be a religious majority in the United States, it can never be an official majority with powers of constraint, and that religious minorities will be treated on an equal legal basis with the majority.

Free Exercise of Religion The claims of the individual versus the claims of society in the area of religion first surfaced in the case of *Reynolds* v. *United States* in 1879.[79] Reynolds, a Mormon, was convicted of practicing polygamy, which had been outlawed in the territory of Utah by congressional statute. Mormon doctrine at that time sanctioned the practice, but the conviction was upheld. In subsequent rulings, religious sects with particular medical beliefs have had to yield to public requirements for vaccination. Such rulings do not mean that religious sects cannot deviate from the accepted norm: deviation is forbidden only where the interests of society are imperiled, as was deemed the case in the vaccination and polygamy cases.

The religious tenets of the Jehovah's Witnesses have often served to test this liberty to deviate. In two cases, *Minersville School District* v. *Gobitis* of 1940, and *West Virginia Board of Education* v. *Barnette* of 1943, the slow, painstaking process of legally accommodating the unorthodox beliefs of religious minorities to the requirements of the society at large can be seen. The Gobitis case arose out of the refusal of two schoolchildren of the Jehovah's Witnesses to salute the American flag because they were taught by their religion that it was a "graven image." The local court upheld their right, but the school board protested and carried its objections to the Supreme Court. The board's right to require the salute was upheld. In his majority decision, Justice Felix Frankfurter pointed out that the issue was local and educational and should be decided by the local and educational authorities; moreover, he wrote, patriotism was a legitimate educational aim, constituting "that unifying sentiment without which there can ultimately be no liberties, civil or religious." The local board would aim to instill patriotism by whatever means it saw fit, and should enforce its aim in such a way that no doubts were raised about its legitimacy in the minds of the majority of students involved.[80] The Court decision was supported by the wave of public patriotism that had arisen at the time in reaction to Hitler's advance and the apparent threat to democracy, and scores of demonstrations against the Jehovah's Witnesses marked the climate of opinion.

---

[78] See Milton R. Konvitz, *Expanding Liberties: Freedom Gains in Postwar America* (New York: Viking, 1966), p. 3.
[79] *Reynolds* v. *United States*, 98 U.S. 145 (1879).
[80] *Minersville School District* v. *Gobitis*, 310 U.S. 586 (1940).

Three years later, however, the Gobitis decision was reversed in *West Virginia Board of Education* v. *Barnette*. The issue was the same but the local penalties were now greater: Jehovah's Witness children who would not salute the flag were expelled, and heavy fines were issued. The opinion of the Court was delivered by Justice Robert Jackson, who placed the issue in broad perspective: the refusal of the Jehovah's Witness children to salute did not interfere with the rights of others: on the contrary, requiring the salute was an interference not only with religious liberty but with the entire realm of spiritual liberty, including freedom of speech. Speaking eloquently for the majority, Justice Jackson maintained:

If there is any fixed star in our constitutional constellation, it is that no official, high or petty, can prescribe what shall be orthodox in politics, nationalism, religion, or other matters of opinion or force citizens to confess by word or act their faith therein. If there are any circumstances which permit an exception, they do not now occur to us.

We think the action of the local authorities in compelling the flag salute and pledge . . . invades the sphere of intellect and spirit which it is the purpose of the First Amendment to our Constitution to reserve from all official control.[81]

The religious practices of the Amish, an agricultural religious community which wishes to remain separate from the rest of society, have also come into conflict with the laws of the secular society. Members of this faith were often fined or jailed for not sending their children to school beyond the eighth grade on religious grounds. In May 1972, prompted by the appeal of three Wisconsin Amish parents, the Supreme Court ruled that compulsory school attendance past the eighth grade was illegal. This was hailed in a news account as "a milestone in the development of free exercise of religion clause."[82] Three of the justices found it significant that the Amish practice of requiring their children to attend school only up to age fourteen or fifteen falls short of Wisconsin's schooling requirement by only a year or two.

Another controversy over the free exercise of religion has arisen over protection of the rights of atheists. Belief in God seems to pervade our society, judging from our coins, which all bear the phrase "In God We Trust"; public gatherings where invocations and benedictions are recited; and courtroom procedure itself, which requires witnesses to swear on the Bible. Yet the Supreme Court has also upheld freedom *not* to believe in God. In 1961 the refusal of Roy Torcaso, a notary public, to declare that he believed in the existence of God, as required in the Maryland oath of office, was upheld: freedom of belief clearly implied freedom of nonbelief, and theistic test oaths were thereby declared invalid.[83]

---

[81] *West Virginia Board of Education* v. *Barnette,* 319 U.S. 624 (1943). The precedent established in this case held for another religious sect in *Sherbert* v. *Verner,* 374 U.S. 398 (1963), when the Court ruled that the denial of unemployment compensation to a Seventh Day Adventist who refused a job which would require her to work on Saturday was illegal: Governmental imposition of the choice between the job and foregoing benefits "puts the same kind of burden upon the free exercise of religion as would a fine imposed against appellant for her Saturday worship."

[82] Marvin M. Karpatkin, "Support for the Religious Dissenter," the *New York Times* (June 4, 1972), Sec. 4, p. 6. Also see a discussion of the problem by Stephen Arons, "Compulsory Education: The Plain People Resist," *Saturday Review* (January 15, 1972), pp. 51–57.

[83] *Torcaso* v. *Watkins,* 367 U.S. 488 (1961). Justice Black specifically classified atheism as a belief deserving the First Amendment protection, in his opinion. He pointed to religions in this country which do not teach what would generally be considered a belief in the existence of God, such as Buddhism, Taoism, Ethical Culture, Secular Humanism, and others.

In a recent Supreme Court case that pitted minority religious practices against secular law, the Amish won a major First Amendment right: their traditional agricultural way of life was supported in a decision that upheld their practice of education only through the eighth grade.

The conscientious objection is a prime illustration of the conflict between protection of freedom of conscience and the needs of society—in the objector's case, between pacifism and the need for military defense. Three pacifist cases were tried between 1900 and 1938, and in one of them the Court declared that, because "we are a Christian people," the laws of the land (and its military practices) are necessarily not inconsistent with the will of God.[84] In all three cases the Court held that there was no constitutional right to be exempt from military service because of religious conviction. Yet it was also ruled that Congress held the power to grant and withdraw at any time the privilege of exemption should it be granted on the grounds of conscientious objection.

Until recent years, conscientious objectors were generally treated harshly by courts and draft boards, which took a narrow and skeptical view of the religious principles of conscientious objection. But in the Selective Service Act of 1967, the requirement that conscientious objectors hold a "belief in relation to a Supreme Being" was eliminated, allowing exemption for those who, "by reason of religious training and belief," are "conscientiously opposed to participation in war in any form."[85] In 1970, the Court went even further, declaring that the objection to military service can be moral and ethical, not necessarily based on religious training, the criterion in the past.[86] However, in 1971, it was held that objection to a particular war—in this case, the Vietnam War—as distinct from war in general was not valid.[87]

---

[84] *United States* v. *Macintosh,* 282 U.S. 832 (1931).

[85] In the case of *Clay* v. *United States,* 39 L.W. 4873, 783 (1971), Mohammed Ali, the heavyweight boxing champion, protested against a five-year prison sentence for resisting the draft, on the basis of his Black Muslim beliefs. It was held that this was a matter of genuine religious conviction.

[86] *Welsh* v. *United States,* 398 U.S. 333 (1970).

[87] *Gillete* v. *United States,* 401 U.S. 437 (1971).

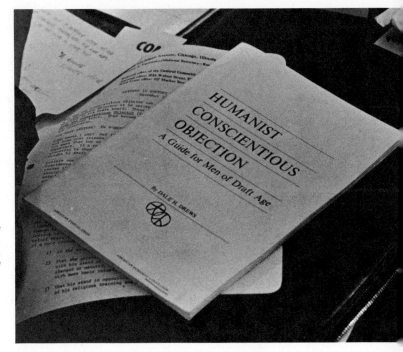

This booklet is available to help those who oppose war defend their belief so that they are not drafted into the armed forces, even though the basis of their opposition may be ethical but not religious.

The Establishment Clause: The Wall of Separation Although the First Amendment prohibits the establishment of any one religion in this country, some minority groups have claimed that the government gives preference to the practice of Christianity and in effect has legally established it as a national religion. The existence of *blue laws* prohibiting Sunday business throughout the United States is the factor that has contributed most to this belief. In the cases that have been tried in the last decade, the Court has maintained that, despite the obvious religious origins of the blue laws, their function today is simply to provide the community a day of rest, amusement, and family togetherness.[88]

The Establishment Clause has come to mean more than a guarantee against the establishment of a state religion. The Court has interpreted it as also meaning a guarantee against the preference of any one religion by the government and against government involvement in religious practices—a concept summed up in Jefferson's phrase "a wall of separation between Church and States."

Interpretation of the wall of separation has varied considerably among the justices on the Court, and sometimes within the minds of the individual justices themselves, who have, on occasion, reversed their positions. For example, a very narrow majority in the case of *Everson* v. *Board of Education of Ewing Township* in 1947 found that the State of New Jersey had not breached the wall by granting state money grants for bus fares of parochial-school children as well as

---

[88] Legally recognizing the changed rationale, New York City in 1961 replaced its Sunday Law with a Fair Sabbath Law, which allowed family-operated businesses to stay open on Sunday if (as in the case of many Jewish-run businesses) they were closed on Saturday.

public-school children.[89] The decision held that the benefit incurred was to the child, not the church. However, the following year, the use of school facilities for religious instruction was declared illegal, although in the case before the Court separate classes were conducted for Protestants, Catholics, and Jews, and teachers were employed by the respective religious groups out of the groups' own funds.[90] The Court ruled that this practice afforded aid to sectarian groups and thus represented a violation of separation of church and state.

Four years later, in *Zorach* v. *Clauson,* the Court by a seven-to-two decision upheld a ruling that permitted children to leave school during regular class hours to attend religious instruction at religious institutions. Justice William O. Douglas, speaking for the Court, pointed out that this case involving released-time instruction differed from previous cases in that it did not involve use of the school buildings for the instruction. He went still further, stressing that separation of church and state should not mean hostility between the two. "We are a religious people," Douglas wrote, and "we find no constitutional requirement which makes it necessary for government to be hostile to religion and to throw its weight against efforts to widen the effective scope of religious influence."[91]

The sympathetic attitude displayed by the Court in the Zorach case did not last. In one of the most controversial decisions of its history, the Court ruled, in the 1962 case of *Engel* v. *Vitale,* that a short, nondenominational prayer recited at the beginning of each school day in New York public schools was unconstitutional.[92] This decision was followed in the next year by *Abington School District* v. *Schempp,* in which the reading of short excerpts from the Bible to replace morning prayers in schools was outlawed.[93]

Since the precedent of *Everson* v. *Board of Education of Ewing Township,* in 1947, child benefit has justified the granting of many forms of aid to parochial schools, including transportation, lunch subsidies, counseling services, and aid for school construction.

In addition, under the Federal Aid to Education Bill of 1965, aid goes to *all* schools in the country in poverty areas whether they are secular or religious schools. The only restriction has been against use of federal money for that portion of the education that is strictly religious. Thus in 1968 in *Board of Education* v. *Allen* it was held that the State of New York must lend textbooks to parochial as well as to public schools. The Court decision emphasized that the

---

[89] *Everson* v. *Board of Education of Ewing Township,* 330 U.S. 1 (1947).

[90] *McCullom* v. *Board of Education,* 333 U.S. 203 (1948).

[91] *Zorach* v. *Clauson,* 343 U.S. 306 (1952).

[92] *Engel* v. *Vitale,* 370 U.S. 421 (1962). The uproar that followed the decision was not surprising. Religious groups that traditionally oppose the liberalism of the courts were joined by anticommunists and even movie stars. Billy Graham denounced the decision's "godlessness" and a governors' conference meeting in Pennsylvania also publicly disagreed with the decision. The emergence of the "silent majority" of the late 1960s was foreshadowed when, after this decision, there were resentful cries of "fairness, for a change, for the majority"—the Court defended, it was said, only minorities. Ugly subcurrents of anti-Semitism (several of the defendants were Jewish) and racism ("they've put the Negroes in the schools and taken God out") emerged. But the decision had constitutional, philosophical, and historical grounds, and, accordingly, it had its defenders. And the defenders were most clearly not atheists. Justice Tom Clark pointed out that religion was so sacred, such an "inviolable citadel," that even those outside who wished to aid it were intruding. President Kennedy pointed out laconically, and with quiet dignity, that now we could simply be all the more religious in our homes and churches. (L. J. Barker and T. W. Barker, *Freedom, Courts, Politics: Studies in Civil Liberties* (Englewood Cliffs, N.J.: Prentice-Hall, 1965), pp. 1–33.

[93] *Abington School District* v. *Schempp,* 374 U.S. 203 (1963).

texts, chosen by the state, for secular studies in the parochial schools were all secular books, and that the maintenance of quality in this aspect of parochial education was a matter of public concern.[94]

Since the beginning of the 1970s, a new interpretation of government neutrality toward religion has been evolving. This interpretation represents a compromise; it aims at avoiding hostility as well as excessive involvement with religion. In *Waltz* v. *Tax Commission,* the Court upheld a New York statute granting property-tax exemption to land owned by religious organizations and used solely for religious worship. While it was argued that church property exemptions are merely part of a general scheme of exemptions granted to nonprofit organizations which the state finds to be "beneficial and stabilizing influences in community life," it was also specifically pointed out that to tax church property would be to involve the government quite directly with religion.[95] It was deemed best for government not to be involved.[96]

Nationalization of the Bill of Rights

The Bill of Rights, even if interpreted completely liberally, would not have meant much in the early part of this century, for at that time it was interpreted as applying only to actions of the federal government. The basis for this stance was the ruling in the 1833 case of *Barron* v. *Baltimore,* in which the Court ruled that the Bill of Rights did not apply to the states. With this case as precedent, a person could be retried in a *state* court for a crime of which he had been acquitted in a *federal* court. This decision was never directly overruled. It was not until the courts began to adopt the position that the Fourteenth Amendment was meant to make the Bill of Rights a restriction on states, as well as on the federal government, that a liberalization of the Bill of Rights began. The amendment reads that no "state [may] deprive any person of life, liberty or property without due process of law. . . ." It was first applied in 1925 in *Gitlow* v. *New York,* a free-speech case.

Over the years there have been basically four interpretations of the proper way to apply the Bill of Rights to the states through the Fourteenth Amendment. The four doctrines are the fair-trial rule; the theories of selective and total incorporation; and the superfair-trial rule, also known as the incorporation-plus approach.[97]

As late as 1917, there were some justices, such as Frankfurter, who preferred a "case-by-case" or "fair-trial" rule. This method of interpretation required a judge to ask whether the government's action "shocked the conscience" or violated "common standards of civilized conduct." If this was found to be the case, the defendant was not convicted.

---

[94] *Board of Education* v. *Allen,* 392 U.S. 236 (1968). In a similar vein, the Court upheld, in *Tilton* v. *Richardson,* 39 L.W. 1857, 153 (1971), that government funds could be granted for buildings used for nonsectarian purposes in religious schools.

[95] *Waltz* v. *Tax Commission,* 397 U.S. 664 (1970). A discussion can be found in *Harvard Law Review,* "The Supreme Court, 1969 Term," vol. 84, no. 1, p. 127.

[96] In *Lemon* v. *Kurtzman,* 39 L.M. 4845, 89 (1971), the Court ruled against state involvement in religious practices, declaring, in this case, that funds from cigarette taxes could not be used to supplement parochial-school teachers' salaries.

[97] All four positions are discussed in Abraham, *Freedom and the Court,* pp. 73–78, which is also the source of the quotations.

Table 4–1   **Nationalization of the Bill of Rights**

Year	Amendment and Provision	Case
1925	1—Freedom of Speech	*Gitlow* v. *New York*
1931	1—Freedom of Press	*Near* v. *Minnesota*
1932	6—Right to counsel in capital cases	*Powell* v. *Alabama*
1934	1—Freedom of Religion	*Hamilton* v. *Regents of University of California*
1937	1—Freedom of Assembly	*DeJonge* v. *Oregon*
1947	1—Separation of church and state (establishment of religion)	*Everson* v. *Board of Education*
1961	4—Protection from unreasonable search and seizure	*Mapp* v. *Ohio*
1962	8—Protection from cruel and unusual punishment	*Robinson* v. *California*
1963	6—Right to counsel in all criminal cases	*Gideon* v. *Wainwright*
1964	5—Protection from self-incrimination	*Mallory* v. *Hogan*
1965	6—Right to confront witnesses against one	*Pointer* v. *Texas*
1967	5—Right to speedy trial	*Klopfer* v. *North Carolina*
1967	6—Guarantee of compulsory process to obtain witnesses for defense	*Washington* v. *Texas*
1968	6—Guarantee of trial by jury in all criminal cases	*Duncan* v. *Louisiana*
1969	5—Prohibition of double jeopardy	*Benton* v. *Maryland*

In 1937, however, in the case of *Palko* v. *Connecticut*, the Court distinguished between fundamental and formal freedoms: Fundamental freedoms were defined as those without which "ordered liberty" cannot survive (examples are freedom of thought and speech), and formal freedoms as those "without which justice would not perish" (an example is trial by jury). In this decision, fundamental freedoms were incorporated into state law, but formal freedoms were not.[98] The selective incorporation of the *Palko* case formulated by Justice Benjamin N. Cardozo has been called the concept of the "Honor Roll of Superior Rights" and is the test of incorporation most widely applied today.

A third position, total incorporation, was first espoused by Justice John Marshall Harlan the Elder, in the last third of the nineteenth century. The doctrine, which sees every provision in the Bill of Rights as binding on the states through the Fourteenth Amendment, was unsuccessfully championed by him from 1877 to 1911. Justice Hugo Black, a long-standing liberal member of the Court, was a more recent advocate of this interpretation.

A fourth position advocates an extension of total incorporation. Referred to as the corporation-plus approach, it not only incorporates all of the Bill of Rights

---

[98] *Palko* v. *Connecticut*, 302 U.S. 319 (1937).

but holds that in some cases it may be ruled that due process is being denied even when a specific Bill of Rights freedom is not in question. First espoused by Justices Frank Murphy and Wiley B. Rutledge in the late 1930s and 1940s, it was eventually embraced by Justice William O. Douglas in the early 1950s. Henry J. Abraham called Douglas's position the "superfair-trial" rule and noted that the title of an essay written by Douglas is "The Bill of Rights is not Enough."

As Table 4–1 indicates, the Fourteenth Amendment has by today incorporated every provision of the Bill of Rights, except the Second and Third Amendments, permitting the public to keep and bear arms and prohibiting the peacetime quartering of soldiers in homes; and the phrase of the Fifth Amendment which provides for indictments by grand jury. The First Amendment freedoms were incorporated by 1947; the rights of those accused of crime were nationalized more slowly, and were complete only by 1969 – a great triumph for the Warren Court.

SUGGESTED READING

Abraham, Henry J. *Freedom and the Court: Civil Rights and Liberties in the United States* (New York: Oxford University Press, 1967). In paperback. Examination of the Supreme Court's role in the development and implementation of civil liberties. Abraham attempts to evaluate the basic problem of distinguishing between individual and community rights.

Chevigny, Paul. *Police Power: Police Abuses in New York City* (New York: Pantheon, 1969). In paperback. A study of the "routine denials of due process of law," by false arrest, unlawful search, and "summary punishment" by policemen. The author seeks to discover what is wrong with law enforcement in the streets, and the reasons behind these ills.

Emerson, Thomas I. *The System of Freedom of Expression* (New York: Random House, 1972). A formulation of the legal foundations for an effective system of freedom of expression. Emerson bases his ideas on cases and retains a detailed technical analysis of Supreme Court decisions.

Hand, Learned. *The Bill of Rights* (Cambridge, Mass.: Harvard University Press, 1962). Discusses the functions of United States courts, particularly the Supreme Court, in the context of civil liberties questions. While the power of a court to annul federal or state statutes and executive acts is not found in the Constitution, it was a practical necessity that logically fell upon the courts. The author discusses the conditions under which this power should be exercised, and the desirability and practicality of its use on extreme occasions.

Hendel, Samuel (ed.). *The Politics of Confrontation* (New York: Appleton-Century-Crofts, 1971). In paperback. An anthology of short readings dealing with the issues and techniques of civil disobedience, violence, the role of the university ROTC on campus, student power, and other areas of political protest.

Konvitz, Milton R. *Expanding Liberties: Freedom's Gains in Postwar America* (New York: Viking, 1966). In paperback. A study of human liberty in the twenty-five years since World War II, concentrating on newly attained freedoms. Konvitz asserts that the advances in First Amendment freedoms and civil and human rights came not necessarily because of their own worth, but as a result of various political actions.

Krislov, Samuel. *The Supreme Court and Political Freedom* (New York: The Free Press, 1968). In paperback. An examination of the Supreme Court's actual and potential role as the defender of the freedom of expression. The author considers the theoretical relationship between the Court and the public, as well as the evidence on how the system works.

Kurland, Philip B. *Politics, the Constitution, and the Warren Court* (Chicago: University of Chicago Press, 1970). Critical essays on the contributions of the Warren Court, discussing the relationships of Congress and the President, federalism and egalitarianism to the Warren Court. Also analyzes other problems that face a political court.

Lewis, Anthony. *Gideon's Trumpet* (New York: Random House, 1964). The story of Clarence Earl Gideon's struggle to exercise his right to counsel and an examination and interpretation of the role of the Supreme Court itself.

Meiklejohn, Alexander. *Political Freedom: The Constitutional Powers of the People* (New York: Oxford University Press, 1965). In paperback. Consisting of two parts, this book presents the text of *Free Speech and its Relation to Self-Government* which was published in 1948, as well as a collection of papers written between 1948 and 1958 which develop Meiklejohn's original argument.

Pritchett, C. Herman. *The American Constitution*, rev. ed. (New York: McGraw-Hill, 1968). An excellent text of the major aspects of constitutional law, covering both the Constitution itself and the Bill of Rights.

Shapiro, Martin. *Freedom of Speech: The Supreme Court and Judicial Review* (Englewood Cliffs, N.J.: Prentice-Hall, 1966). In paperback. Discussion of the role of the Supreme Court in relation to the freedom of speech. The author challenges the judicially modest interpretation of the role of the Supreme Court which would keep the Court out of politics, and argues that one of its unique functions is to defend those interests which can find no defenders elsewhere.

Skolnick, J. H. *The Politics of Protest* (New York: Ballantine, 1969). In paperback. An outspoken report prepared for the National Commission on the Causes and Prevention of Violence. The author contends that protest and violence in America have arisen from resistance to needed social change. Of greatest concern are the antiwar movement, student protest, and black militancy, as well as the official and unofficial reactions to these areas.

Thoreau, Henry D. *The Variorum Civil Disobedience,* introduction and annotations by Walter Harding (New York: Twayne Publishers, 1967). A highly readable essay on the relation of the individual to the state. Thoreau proposes that there is a law of conscience, a "higher law" than the law of the land, that should be obeyed if the two laws conflict. He adds that one must assume the full consequences of disobedience, and thus draw public attention to the unjust law and bring about its repeal.

Wirt, Frederick M., and Willis P. Hawley (eds.). *New Dimensions of Freedom in America* (San Francisco: Chandler, 1969). In paperback. A collection of articles treating various aspects of liberty and freedom from both philosophical and pragmatic perspectives. Various authors discuss such topics as freedom of expression, freedom of religion, racial equality and the law, due process of law, and prospects for the future.

2

STRUCTURES OF
POWER AND
DECISION-MAKING

In the 1950s, a student of American politics was taught that the American pluralist system of government was synonymous with democracy—that our system was the best and perhaps the only way to conceive of democracy. In recent years, however, the American pluralist political system has been increasingly criticized by many observers because its rules tend to benefit the middle class and are biased against the poor. These critics view pluralism as a system in which the articulate, well organized, and rich tend to win whenever political decisions are made. Pluralism, the critics argue, is a system of politics in which only the informed, educated, and highly motivated are seen as being capable of making rational decisions for the promotion of the general welfare. Thus, though pluralism is a system of "gentlemanly politics" in which individuals put aside their own self-interest to make decisions that benefit all the people, it can also be viewed as an essentially elite system because only a few have the financial background and personal characteristics that enable them to perform leadership functions.

In addition, many critics of the American political system attack the consequences of elite rule. Pluralist theory holds that elites are supposed to be concerned with the good of the whole community rather than with their own personal advancement. Consequently, pluralist politics makes it difficult, in theory, for the merely self-interested to pursue their own fortunes, because there are many ways an aroused public or, more likely, other competing elites can prevent them from taking advantage of the system. Critics of pluralism, however, contend that the existence of competing elites does not dispel the upper-class bias of the political system.

Part 2 of this book describes American political institutions and how they operate, focusing on the major structures of power and decision-making: federalism, Congress, the President, the bureaucracy, and the courts. Throughout Part 2, the questions of who dominates in the decision-making process and who benefits from the existing political system are emphasized. Also central to this part is the problem of responsible government: To whom should the various branches of government be responsible? Are political leaders held sufficiently accountable to the will of the people? If political decision-makers do indeed form an elite that is biased in favor of the interests of the upper middle class, how can government be made more responsive to all its citizens?

5

FEDERALISM: THE NATION, THE STATE, AND THE METROPOLITAN AREA

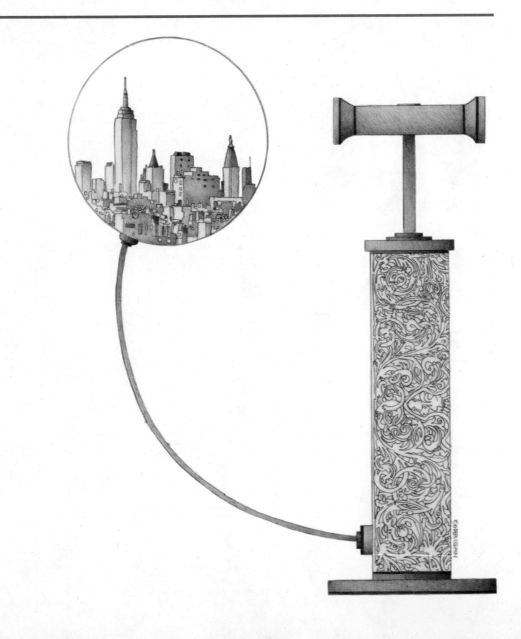

Because federalism is a complex and evolving form of government, a simple definition of it is difficult. Most political scientists would agree, however, with a skeletal definition: federalism is a form of government which involves two or three major levels; each level derives its powers directly from the people and operates within its own sphere of authority as outlined in a constitution; a judiciary is the final authority in cases of controversy.[1] It is within this framework that we will discuss the federal nature of the United States political system, recognizing that the exact structure of the state-nation relationship has changed over the years, and that further changes, or perhaps a drastic reworking of the entire nature of the relationship, are possible within the near future. In recent years, the federal form of government has become increasingly popular, with perhaps half of all the earth's territory governed by systems at least nominally federal (for example, the United States, the U.S.S.R.,[2] India, Australia, Brazil, Mexico, Switzerland, Canada), and with many of the post–World War II countries opting for such an arrangement (including Nigeria and the Congo). Nevertheless, we should recognize that alternatives do exist. A people may choose a *unitary* government, in which all political power is legally vested in a central government (examples are Israel and Great Britain). Or a league, alliance, or *confederation*[3] may be established, under which individual governing units (city-states, nations) agree to permit a central body to handle certain aspects of their political lives, but with such authority derived from and dependent on the consent of the individual units. In ancient times, various Greek city-states operated under such a system; the thirteen states under the Articles of Confederation provide another example; and today the British Commonwealth and the European Economic Community (Common Market) operate as such.

Why Did the United States Choose Federalism?

Speculation over why the United States chose the federal form of government in 1787 has existed since that date. Current political thought suggests that such a choice is never abstract or accidental; rather, under certain circumstances, it becomes the only possible logical choice. R. C. Wheare, in his classic discussion of federalism, theorized that a federalist state will emerge whenever four preconditions exist: simultaneously, the community must experience both a strong desire and a strong capacity for union, as well as an equal desire and an equal capacity to establish or retain regional governments. In Wheare's analysis, all these conditions could be found in late eighteenth-century America.[4]

Given a *desire* for political union, Wheare argued, the *capacity* for establishment of an effective national government depends to a large extent on similarity of political and social institutions among the constituent states. For example, he suggested that one reason behind the failure of early attempts in the 1930s

---

[1] See Richard H. Leach, *American Federalism* (New York: Norton, 1970), p. 1.

[2] It should be noted at the outset of a discussion on federalism that federalism is not to be equated with democracy. The U.S.S.R., for instance, has a federal form of government but is not a democracy.

[3] As we will discuss later in this chapter, the meaning of the word *confederation* has changed in the last two hundred years; we use it here in its modern political sense.

[4] R. C. Wheare, Federal Government (London: Oxford University Press, 1953), pp. 37ff.

to form a federation of states in British India was that some of the states were autocratic bodies governed by hereditary princes, while others enjoyed representative government. In eighteenth-century America, on the other hand, all the states had republican forms of government and were unquestionably committed to maintaining them. Wheare also stated that a common race, language, religion, national background, and social institutions, while not an absolute requirement for a successful union, are helpful, and we might observe that Americans did to a considerable degree share a common language and similar culture. Such cultural homogeneity does not exist between the northern Nigerians and the Biafrans, for example, who have had so much difficulty living together within the postwar Nigerian federation; or between the Hindus and the Muslims in India.

Despite these forces pushing toward the formation of a strong national government, pressures were also building up to retain meaningful state governments. In 1790, for instance, Americans had a strong sense of loyalty to their states, and at that time "most citizens of the United States, if asked their country or nation, would have answered, not 'American,' but 'Carolinian,' 'Virginian,' 'Pennsylvanian,' 'New Yorker,' or 'New Englander.'"[5] In addition, they recognized that there were major economic differences between the commercial North and the agricultural South. And finally, strictly from a logistical point of view—given the state of transportation and communication technology of the day—the distances from one part of the country to another were huge, and regional bases of government seemed a sensible solution to the geographical spread between New England and the Deep South.

It appears clear from a review of conditions in America in 1787 that federalism would represent a satisfactory solution to the particular problems confronting the new nation; nevertheless, no one went to Philadelphia with a preconceived determination to create a federalist government. Federalism, as such, was never presented to the delegates in one package as a coherent system; it was never debated as a possible alternative to another system. Instead, it was the bundle of compromises that evolved between the "states' righters" and those favoring a strong central government. The first of these compromises concerned representation in Congress. The compromise was the result of the Virginia Plan, which in its early and most extreme form could have reduced the individual states to mere administrative districts; and the New Jersey Plan, which was not very much more than a rehashing of the old Articles of Confederation. Almost everybody at Philadelphia accepted the necessity of creating some kind of strong central government to provide protection against foreign dangers, and in maintaining a system where "republican liberty" was assured. The question was one of means, rather than ends.[6] The debate continued for weeks, and "so hot did [it] become that at one point [Benjamin] Franklin suggested turning to prayer, but the lack of funds to pay for a minister, plus the doubtful tactic of admitting the necessity of an appeal to the almighty, put a stop to the proposal."[7] Finally, the Connecticut Compromise (our present two-house system, with one house

---

[5] Samuel Eliot Morison, *History of the United States,* vol. 1, p. 10, as quoted in Wheare, *Federal Government,* p. 39.

[6] See Martin Diamond, "What the Framers Meant by Federalism," in *A Nation of States,* edited by Robert A. Goldwin (Chicago: Rand McNally, 1963), pp. 24–41.

[7] Merrill Jensen, *The Making of the American Constitution* (Princeton, N.J.: Van Nostrand, 1964), p. 59.

elected according to population and the other with two members from each state) emerged. Once this initial compromise between the two groups had been reached, they went on to develop the series of further compromises out of which the system we now call American federalism evolved.

Original source reading on the background of federalism presents a serious roadblock: semantics. In 1787, the word *federal* did not mean *national* as it does today in the term *federal government*. In fact, it had an almost opposite meaning: the Founding Fathers used the word *federal* as we would use the word *confederate*—that is, to mean a loose "sort of association or league of sovereign states."[8] Thus, at the Constitutional Convention, the federalist position was one opposed to the nationalist (or strong-central-government) position, and the "federal" system advocated was one in which the day-to-day nuts and bolts of government operations would remain in the hands of the individual states, except for a few matters primarily involving foreign affairs. Indeed, Madison made this point quite clear in *The Federalist*, No. 39, where he described the final version of the Constitution as "neither a national nor a federal Constitution, but a composition of both." In other words, he saw the new government as a compromise between a unitary government (what he meant by "national") and a confederal government (what he meant by "federal").

The Constitutional Formula for Federalism

Federalism, like all other areas of the American political system, evolves and changes. Nevertheless, a first step in describing the present relationship between the states and the national government is to consider the original fixed terms of the arrangement, as stated in the Constitution and its amendments.

The National Government and Its Powers

Enumerated Powers In Article I, Section 8, the Constitution lists certain specific powers expressly reserved to the national government. These enumerated powers include the right to coin money, declare war, raise and support armies, regulate commerce with foreign nations and among the states, and establish uniform rules of naturalization.

Implied Powers Following the list of enumerated powers is one final clause, in which Congress is given the authority "to make all laws which shall be necessary and proper for carrying into execution the foregoing powers." This is called the "elastic clause," because it gives Congress the power to act in many areas not specifically mentioned earlier in Section 8, but permissible where such action is deemed necessary to carry out the enumerated powers. For example, combining the elastic clause with the enumerated power to regulate interstate commerce, Congress has passed innumerable laws, including those setting car safety standards, wages and working hours, drug safety requirements, and even laws providing equal time for all candidates on television. In each case, the guiding principle has been that since the product or service involved passes in interstate

---

[8] Diamond, "What the Framers Meant by Federalism," p. 27.

commerce, Congress has the implied power to regulate almost any phase of its manufacture or distribution.

Inherent Powers The Supreme Court has ruled that the national government has certain additional powers, which are neither enumerated in the Constitution nor implied from the enumerated powers. They are called "inherent powers" and are understood to be part of the essential character of any government, just because it is a sovereign state. Thus, although the Constitution doesn't specifically mention the right to conduct foreign relations with other nations, this is assumed to be an inherent right of any national government.

Significance of the Tenth Amendment A rapid reading of the Constitution (especially by one not familiar with the actual functioning of the American government) would suggest that even if a fairly broad interpretation of the elastic clause is assumed, the powers of the national government are somewhat limited. After all, the Tenth Amendment clearly states that "all powers not delegated to the United States by the Constitution, nor prohibited by it to the States, are reserved to the States respectively or to the people," and for years, many pieces of congressional legislation were declared unconstitutional because they dealt with matters "not delegated to the United States by the Constitution," and thus, in theory, "reserved to the states." For example, during the early twentieth century, national laws regulating child labor were declared unconstitutional by the Supreme Court on these grounds, as were some of the early New Deal statutes. Changing Supreme Court interpretations of the Tenth Amendment, beginning in 1937, have left it almost meaningless as a device to restrain national government authority. However, the language of the Amendment has apparently found a permanent home in the vocabulary of contemporary "states' righters," as evidenced by the speeches of Governor George C. Wallace of Alabama, who, attempting in 1963 to keep black students out of the University of Alabama in defiance of a federal court ruling, spoke of education as one of the powers reserved to the states.

The Supremacy Clause In addition to spelling out to some extent the limits of national and state government powers, the Constitution attempts to handle the problem of dual authority; that is, of those areas where the Constitution and/or national law might be different from state law. Article VI is unequivocal: it states that "The Constitution . . . and the laws of the United States . . . shall be the the supreme Law of the Land." In other words, neither state nor local officers may interfere with federal law. We have experienced vivid examples of this point of view in recent years, as various southern state educational officers have had no choice, despite local laws and practices, but to carry out school-desegregation orders of the federal courts.

Federalism: The Effect of Later Amendments Major changes in the original relationship between the national government and the states have been brought about by several of the amendments. To some, the Sixteenth Amendment is probably the most significant of all, because by giving the national government the right to impose a graduated income tax, it has provided the national government with an enormous source of revenue and power. Without the income tax, national tax collections would be a small fraction of what they are (in a typical year, the income tax accounts for about 90 percent of all federal government revenue!) and without income, the scope of federal activities would have to be indefinitely more limited than it is today.

Another important amendment has been the Fourteenth, which prohibits a state from depriving any person of life, liberty or property without due process of law and from denying any person the equal protection of the law. It also gives the national government the power to deny a state some of its House seats in direct proportion to the number of citizens who are denied the right to vote in presidential elections. This amendment has been the major source for expanding the civil liberties of the Bill of Rights to the fifty states.

There are still other relevant amendments to the operation of federalism. The Fifteenth forbids the states to deny the right to vote *in any election* on the basis of race, color, or previous condition of servitude. The Nineteenth and Twenty-sixth forbid similar discrimination by the states on the basis of sex or age, provided a citizen is over eighteen years old.

The Rights of the States

The Constitution gives the states the right to certain national government guarantees. Among these guarantees are "a republican form of government,"[9] the protection of the states from invasion and domestic violence, the maintenance of the boundaries of each, and equal representation in the Senate. The federal guarantee of protection against "domestic violence" states that application by the (state) legislature or executive is required to obtain this protection. Since the Korean War, Supreme Court decisions pertaining to the National Guard have enabled the President to "nationalize" it in an emergency and use it in a state even if the state has not requested it. In 1957, for example, President Eisenhower sent troops to Little Rock, Arkansas, to handle difficulties caused by integration of the schools.

Relations among the States

Article IV of the Constitution provides that the states give "full faith and credit" to the laws, judicial decisions, and records of every other state; that the citizens of each state "shall be entitled to all privileges and immunities of citizens in [all other] states," and that fugitives from justice who flee to another state be "delivered up" "on demand" to the state from which they have fled. These require-

---

[9] The Dorr Rebellion in Rhode Island in 1841–1842 is the only example in United States history in which the national government was called upon to act under this constitutional provision. At the time, Rhode Island was still using its unamendable seventeenth-century charter as a state constitution, and a large part of the growing urban population was unable to vote because of property qualifications. After trying unsuccessfully for years to get the state legislature to write a new constitution, Thomas H. Dorr organized the People's Party, which called a constitutional convention; the convention wrote a new constitution providing for universal manhood suffrage; submitted it to popular vote, where it was ratified by a large majority; and elected a new state government with Dorr as governor. In the meantime, however, the established legislature, operating under the charter, had elected its own state government, and appealed to President Tyler, who ruled that the old government was legal. Some years later, the Supreme Court gave final approval to Tyler's action (*Luther* v. *Borden* 7 How. 1 [1849]), by ruling that Dorr's activities represented an extralegal rebellion, and that Tyler's appeal for national aid was valid, as the national government must guarantee to each state a republican form of government. (See Samuel Eliot Morison, *The Oxford History of American People* [New York: Oxford University Press, 1965], p. 430.)

This dam on Norris Lake in Tennessee is one of twenty-seven dams under the Tennessee Valley Authority, organized as a compact among the states of the Tennessee River Basin.

ments appear clear-cut, but in reality they provide some ticklish areas of constitutional interpretation. The "full faith and credit" clause suggests that every state is obliged to honor the laws of every other state. This provision is relatively uncomplicated today, its application causing problems only in regard to the divorce laws of some states, such as Nevada, which have not been recognized as binding elsewhere. Similarly, the requirement that every state grant to all citizens the privileges and immunities of its own citizens is usually honored with few complications. The extradition clause mentioned contains no provision for enforcement; it has generally been left to the discretion of the governor in the state to which the fugitive flees, and, in some widely publicized cases, governors have refused to order extradition of fugitives from particularly unsavory penal institutions.

A combination of many of these constitutional problems arose several years ago, in the "Baby Lenore" case, when a New York couple, ordered by a New York court to return their foster child to its natural parent, moved to Florida, where the laws in such cases appeared to permit them to keep the child. Under the Constitution, was Florida obligated to give "full faith and credit" to the laws of New York? Or was it required to offer the same "privileges and immunities" of its own citizens to the former New Yorkers, and permit them to retain custody of their child? And what would have been the moral obligation of the Florida governor if New York had requested extradition of these "fugitives" from its laws?

One other constitutional provision covering relations between the states deserves special mention. Article I, Section 10 includes a requirement that states obtain congressional approval before "enter[ing] into any agreement or compact with another state." In the early years of the republic, most such interstate compacts involved establishment of boundary lines between states; within the last fifty years, however, interstate compacts have often been used as effective vehicles for handling problems which, while they affect several states, are not nationwide in scope. In 1921, for example, the Port of New York Authority agreement was drafted by New York and New Jersey and approved by Congress. Under the original compact, bridges, tunnels, and harbor improvements were built and operated. In 1953, the same two states received congressional authority to establish a Waterfront Commission, this time *not* primarily to build facilities, but to cope with the problems of "the thug, the racketeer . . . the labor goon [who] have flourished," and the "pilferage and extortion [that have] imposed so great a toll."[10]

Interstate compacts appear to offer special possibilities in the fight against pollution, for it is obvious that no one state can clean up its rivers, if a neighboring state permits continued fouling. As early as 1940, six of the states bordering the Ohio River (West Virginia, Ohio, Indiana, New York, Illinois, and Kentucky) obtained congressional approval for the Ohio River Water Sanitation Compact, and they were joined in 1948 by Virginia and Pennsylvania. The Compact created a commission charged with planning those actions needed to combat pollution in all the waters in the signatory states which flow ultimately into the Ohio River and its tributaries, and gave the interstate agency the power to enforce its rulings in the courts of *any* of the eight states.[11] Unfortunately, the compact, which seems to hold great potential for solving the water-pollution problem, has not realized much of an improvement.

The Supreme Court: Arbiter of the Federal System

Even as bargaining between those who favored strong national government and those who opposed it was continuing in Philadelphia in 1787, it was apparent that, regardless of the exact terms of the final division of power, the Constitution would have to include some procedure for settling jurisdictional disputes once the government was in operation. James Monroe saw the problems clearly: "There is a division of sovereignty between the national and state governments," he wrote. "How far then will they coalesce together? Is it not to be supposed that there will be a conflict between them?" He then went on to discuss the need for "a third essentially distinct branch to preserve a just equilibrium, or to prevent such encroachments."[12] In the final version of the Constitution, the Supreme Court was assigned to play this role of umpire between the states and the

---

[10] From a report of the House Judiciary Committee hearings, 1953, as quoted in Weldon V. Barton, *Interstate Compacts in the Political Process* (Chapel Hill, N.C.: University of North Carolina Press, 1967), p. 47.

[11] Barton, *Interstate Compacts in the Political Process*, p. 36.

[12] James Monroe, as quoted in Walter H. Bennett, *American Theories of Federalism* (University, Ala.: University of Alabama Press, 1969), p. 86.

national government, with responsibility for determining the constitutional limits within which each should operate. The Court has achieved this through rulings over the years in three ways.

A Broad Construction of the Constitution:
McCullough v. *Maryland*

The Supreme Court's interpretation of the "elastic clause" has perhaps played the dominant role in shaping the form of American federalism, and the 1819 ruling *McCulloch* v. *Maryland* was the landmark decision in defining the clause. The case had its origins in 1791, when Congress granted a charter to the Bank of the United States, giving it special rights to issue paper money and to hold federal-government deposits. Although the constitutionality of the Bank was not challenged at this time, some people feared that such a bank would provide strong competition for state-chartered banks, and objected to its establishment, claiming that nowhere in the Constitution was the power specifically given to Congress to charter it. In 1819, however, confronted by a business panic and recession which many believed were caused in part by "the monster,"[13] as some called the Bank, several states, including Maryland, decided to drive its offices from their states. To accomplish this aim, Maryland assessed the Bank for $15,000 in taxes. McCulloch, the cashier of the Bank's Baltimore branch, refused to pay.

Maryland's case was based on the claim that the Bank was unconstitutional, and this was the first issue that Chief Justice John Marshall dealt with in his decision. He agreed that "the powers of the [national] government are limited, and that its limits are not to be transcended." But, he went on to say,

> . . . we think the sound construction of the Constitution must allow to the national legislature that discretion, with respect to the means by which the powers it confers are to be carried into execution, which will enable that body to perform the high duties assigned to it. . . . Let the end be legitimate, let it be within the scope of the Constitution, and all means which are appropriate, which are plainly adapted to that end, which are not prohibited, but consist with the letter and spirit of the Constitution, are constitutional.[14]

Here is the heart of the "elastic clause" interpretation, under which all the implied powers involved in a broad construction of the role of the national government flow. If the end is legitimate, and if the particular action taken by the national government is essential to carry out the stated aim, then the action itself is legitimate, *whether or not it is specifically authorized in the Constitution.*

Marshall's decision in *McCulloch* v. *Maryland* is an early and classic example of how the Supreme Court, through its constitutional interpretation, has delineated the division of power between the states and the national government. Although the Court's specific interpretations change over time, the primary trend has tended toward rulings emphasizing national supremacy at the expense of the states. The implied-powers construction was used, for example, to permit

---

[13] The feelings of many Americans, especially westerners, toward the Bank are seen graphically in these words from a speech of the time by Senator Thomas Hart Benton of Missouri: "All the flourishing cities of the West are mortgaged to this money power. They may be devoured by it at any moment. They are in the jaws of the Monster. A lump of butter in the mouth of a dog—one gulp, one swallow, and all is gone!" Quoted in Morison, *The Oxford History of the American People*, p. 403.

[14] *McCulloch* v. *Maryland*, 4 Wheat. 316 (1819). Morison, *The Oxford History of the American People*, p. 402.

establishment of the Federal Reserve System; to authorize New Deal social legislation such as unemployment insurance and social security, as well as economic legislation such as wage and hour laws in the 1930s; and to promulgate various consumer-protection laws such as truth in lending and auto-safety standards in the 1960s.

Supremacy of the National Government

Marshall's opinion in *McCulloch* v. *Maryland* did not stop at the issue of implied powers. Having ruled that the initial creation of the Bank by Congress was legal, he then went on to rule on the question of whether Maryland had the right to tax the Bank. The Bank, said Marshall, was a "creature" or "instrumentality" of the national government, and Maryland had no right to tax it, for "the power to tax involves the power to destroy . . . [and] if the right of the states to tax the means employed by the general government be conceded, the declaration that the Constitution, and the laws made in pursuance thereof, shall be the supreme law of the land, is empty and unmeaning declamation." In other words, if a state did have the power to tax (or destroy) a national government instrumentality, this power would suggest that the states, rather than the national government or the Constitution, were the supreme power.

During his years as Chief Justice, Marshall's Court continued to produce rulings that reaffirmed the principle of national supremacy outlined in *McCulloch* v. *Maryland*. In *Martin* v. *Mott* (1827), for example, it ruled that no state could refuse to send its militia for national service when requested to do so by the President.[15] Although the *McCulloch* ruling is the earliest application of supremacy law, an equally significant application occurred after the Civil War when, in 1869, in *Texas* v. *White,* the Court ruled that no state could leave the union once it had been admitted. "The Constitution . . . looks to an indestructible union, composed of indestructible states," reads the Court's decision—making it clear that, although the states may be called sovereign entities, in our federal system they have permanently relinquished one essential characteristic of a sovereign state: the right to withdraw from the union into which it has entered.

Judicial Review

As early as 1802, Marshall had established the right of the Supreme Court to judicial review of laws and lower federal-court decisions;[16] within the next few years he was to extend this principle to apply to state laws and actions. In 1816 his court[17] ruled that state-court decisions were subject to review by the Supreme Court,[18] and in 1824, he declared that certain state laws were unconstitutional.[19] This process of judicial review of state-court rulings and laws continues today and has been used extensively in recent years in the civil-rights area, with the Supreme Court in most cases forcing the states to abandon their conservative stands on voting practices, education, segregation of public facilities and, most recently, women's rights.

---

[15] *Martin* v. *Mott,* 12 Wheat. 19 (1827).
[16] *Marbury* v. *Madison,* 1 Cr. 137 (1802).
[17] Marshall himself did not rule in this case, because he owned some of the property involved.
[18] *Martin* v. *Hunter's Lessee,* 1 Wheat. 304 (1816).
[19] *Gibbons* v. *Ogden,* 9 Wheat. 1 (1824).

The Court Defines Federalism

Early American Federalism Before examining the nature and operations of federalism today, it is helpful to look at how federalism was viewed in the earliest days of the Republic. Alexander Hamilton and John Marshall supported and acted upon what one political scientist calls a "nation-centered" view of federalism[20] The two men saw the Constitution as emanating directly from the people, with the national government created by this Constitution as the most important repository of political power in the United States. As Marshall expounded in *McCulloch* v. *Maryland,* the national government "is the government of all, and acts for all." Opposed to this view was the "state-centered" version of federalism developed by Thomas Jefferson and John C. Calhoun. It held that the Constitution had resulted from state action, and that primary emphasis in the Constitution focused on setting limits to the powers of the federal government, with the understanding that all remaining powers were reserved to the states, where they would be used to serve the interests of the citizens and protect their liberties. The basic difference in philosophy between the two schools of thought can be appreciated by contrasting the broad view of the role of the national government implied in Marshall's statement above, with the state-centered approach of Madison, expressed in *The Federalist,* No. 45:

> *The powers delegated by the proposed Constitution to the federal government are few and defined . . . [and] will be exercised principally on external objects. . . . The powers reserved to the . . . states will extend to all the objects which, in the ordinary course of affairs, concern the lives, liberties and properties of the people.*[21]

Dual Federalism By the end of the nineteenth century the United States had expanded from thirteen to forty-five states. This orderly expansion of the country was due in part to the federal system; annexing states would probably have been more difficult without the uniform nation-state relationships provided for by the federal system. By this time in the nation's history a synthesis had emerged from the two conflicting views of federalism described. This synthesis, known as "dual federalism," holds that there exist concurrently two centers of power, state and national, each with its own proper sphere of jurisdiction, each dominant within its own area, and the two centers equal in authority since both receive their powers directly from the people. The tricky part of dual federalism, however, lay in the fact that as it developed, through Supreme Court interpretations and rulings, there appeared to exist, in addition to the two stated spheres of influence, a third or "jurisdictional no-man's land"[22] in which neither the federal government nor the states would legislate. This situation developed because the states felt that they were forbidden to regulate under the doctrine of national supremacy, and the federal government felt that it should not regulate because of the Tenth Amendment's reservation of power to the states and the current interpretation of the interstate-commerce clause.

As a result of these interpretations, big-business interests were able to operate

---

[20] Both the "nation-centered" and "state-centered" views are presented in Leach, *American Federalism,* pp. 10–13.

[21] James Madison, John Jay, Alexander Hamilton, *The Federalist Papers* (New York: New American Library, 1961) pp. 292–293.

[22] Leach, *American Federalism,* p. 13.

for many years without regulation from either source.[23] In 1918, for example, the Supreme Court struck down Congress's attempt to restrict child labor in the states by insisting that employment practices were an area reserved to the states under the Tenth Amendment.[24] The *Schechter Poultry* case of 1935 is the most famous of the cases deferring to business. Schechter Poultry Corporation ran a wholesale slaughterhouse in Brooklyn, buying its live poultry from commission men in New York, and selling slaughtered poultry to local retail dealers. The company was convicted of violating the wage-and-hour code of the National Industrial Recovery Act (1933), through which Congress in the Depression years had attempted to spur economic recovery and employment by permitting the establishment of mandatory wage and hour standards in various industries. Upon appeal to the Supreme Court, Schechter's activities were analyzed as follows: 96 percent of the poultry sold in New York City did come from out of state, but the actual slaughtering and selling done by the defendant was strictly a local matter; that is, once the defendants made their purchases, "the interstate transactions in relation to that poultry then ended." On the basis of these facts, the Court concluded that although the original source of the poultry involved interstate commerce, the persons employed by Schechter were "*not* employed in interstate commerce [and] their hours and wages [had] no direct relation to interstate commerce. . . . Where the effect of intrastate transaction upon interstate commerce is merely indirect, such transactions remain within the domain of state power."[25] On these grounds, the Court ruled unanimously that the National Industrial Recovery Act was unconstitutional, because Congress lacked the power to regulate local (intrastate) transactions which affect interstate commerce only in an indirect manner. Since a large proportion of the business operations in the United States fell under this description, the *Schechter* ruling, in effect, tied the hands of the Roosevelt administration in its attempts to use federal power to solve economic emergencies.

The Reality of Today's Federalism

Most current political scientists disagree with an analysis of the development of American federalism that emphasizes the early rivalry between the states and the national government, and the subsequent evolution of dual federalism. Instead, they would support the view of Daniel Elazar, who contended that cooperation between levels of government has been the dominant theme throughout our history:

Federalism in the United States, as practiced, *has traditionally been cooperative, . . . dual federalism as a demarcation of responsibilities has never worked* in practice, *and . . . governmental activities in the nineteenth century, as in the twentieth, were* shared *by the federal and state governments* in collaboration *despite formal pronouncements to the contrary.*[26]

Elazar uses the case of the Dismal Swamp Canal to illustrate the state-national–

---

[23] The problem was further complicated by the fact that effective state regulation was also impossible because of the power of big business interests in state legislatures and state courts.

[24] *Hammer* v. *Dagenhart,* 247 U.S. 251 (1918).

[25] *Schechter Poultry Corp.* v. *United States,* 295 U.S. 495 (1935).

[26] Daniel Elazar, *The American Partnership* (Chicago: The University of Chicago Press, 1962), p. 24. Italics added.

government cooperation dating back to the earliest days of the republic. The swamp is a marshy region located in Virginia and North Carolina. Preliminary work on draining it dates back to 1763 (George Washington was a member of the original surveying party). From 1790 to 1823 the actual canal was built, the planning and building stages marked by cooperation between state and federal officials; and at completion, actual ownership of the canal devolved on both Virginia and the federal government.[27]

Cooperative Federalism: The Marble-Cake Analogy

It appears, then, that clear-cut areas of responsibility for the three levels of government do not in fact exist. Government operations cannot be so neatly pigeonholed. Morton Grodzins used the analogy of a marble cake to symbolize the interrelated nature of the cooperative federalism practiced in the United States today. He viewed our federal system not as a tidy three-layer cake, with each layer distinct and separate, but rather as a marble cake, in which the three levels of government mix and combine in whirls and swirls and blendings of colors, so that it is impossible to know where one begins and the other ends. "So it is with federal, state and local responsibilities, in the chaotic marble cake of American government."[28]

The mixture of governments is visible at every turn, with almost no local-government function not involving a combination of federal, state, and local government activity in one way or another. Education is one example. There are about twenty thousand school districts in the United States; these local districts raise some of their own funds, hire their own teachers, and organize curricula, but they also obtain financial support from the state, which sets teacher qualifications and dictates standard textbooks and course content. The county may act as collection agency for the school taxes levied by the district, and it frequently establishes safety requirements for school buses, buildings, and playgrounds. In addition, the county (or the city) may be requested to provide school crossing guards if grade-school children must use busy intersections, or police protection in troublesome high schools. The federal government supplies school-lunch programs, money to hire special reading and language teachers, aid to vocational and agricultural education programs,[29] and funds for school libraries.

The roots of this sort of partnership, as Elazar has illustrated, date back to the late 1700s. The greatest impetus to its development, however, dates from the passage of the Sixteenth (income tax) Amendment in 1913. The federal government proceeded almost at once to share its new source of revenue with the states by proposing the first grant-in-aid program (an agricultural extension service), which provided grants of money to states willing to participate. Then, during the New Deal, cooperative federalism began to develop to its fullest potential. Faced with unprecedented economic problems (including a 25-percent unemployment rate), President Roosevelt stated his position clearly:

---

[27] Daniel Elazar, *The American Partnership*, pp. 36–54.

[28] Morton Grodzins, "Centralization and Decentralization in the American Federal System," *A Nation of States*, edited by Robert A. Goldwin (Chicago: Rand McNally, 1963), p. 3.

[29] The original impetus for establishing our system of free public education was probably the national government, which, beginning as early as 1785, has supplied some 145 million acres of federally owned lands to local governments for primary and secondary education. (See Grodzins, "Centralization and Decentralization in the American Federal System," p. 3.)

Whether it be in the crowded tenements of the great cities or on many of the farm lands of the nation, you and I know that there dwell millions of our fellow human beings who suffer from the kind of poverty that spells undernourishment and underprivilege. If local government, if State Government, after exerting every reasonable effort, are unable to better their conditions, to raise or restore their purchasing power, then surely it would take a foolish and shortsighted man to say that it is no concern of the national government itself.[30]

Operating from this position, he worked at bailing the country out of the Depression.

Growth of National Power

Why Has the Power of the National Government Expanded? In keeping with the Grodzins-Elazar theory that government functions are shared, it is still possible to claim that the national government's powers have increased; they have increased absolutely—as have the powers of all levels of government—not relative to state powers, nor at their expense. This expansion of federal powers is primarily due to the tremendous expansion of our modern industrial society. Many contend that since problems, such as those involving the physical environment, do not stop at state borders, their regulation cannot be accomplished effectively on a purely local or state-by-state basis. Others assert that, with a mobile population such as ours, and population centers that ignore state lines, (such as Washington, D.C., metropolitan area, which includes parts of Virginia and Maryland as well as the District of Columbia), social and economic problems within the states must also become the concern of the central government. Similarly, because production and distribution, and even modern credit transactions, are rarely handled on a local basis, regulation of these activities cannot be handled locally. Fifty years ago, receiving credit was probably a matter between a local merchant and a local customer. Today, however, an automobile loan will usually involve a local customer and a national corporation such as the General Motors Acceptance Corporation, with headquarters many states away. In such a case the home state simply cannot offer meaningful protection to its citizens; instead, the consumer must turn to the national government in an effort to protect himself from organized business interests.

Finally, in any attempt to understand why the central government's power has grown, the progressive income tax on which the federal government was first to capitalize cannot be ignored. The income tax is possibly the best of all currently available money-raising devices, because of its wide acceptance, its responsiveness to economic growth, and its ease of collection through withholding. Although most of the states have turned, in recent years, to imposing their own income taxes in an attempt to increase available funds, the federal government, already entrenched in this sphere, has made it difficult for states to introduce meaningfully high rates. Instead, they continue to rely on the traditional sales and property taxes for their major source of money.

Not only has the federal government preempted the best source of funds by issuing the first income tax, but, as far as this or any other tax is concerned, the federal government is in a better position to impose or increase a tax than are the states. Federal tax burdens are nationwide; no one part of the country can escape

---

[30] Speech by Franklin D. Roosevelt, Little Rock, Arkansas, June 10, 1936, cited in *The Public Papers and Addresses of Franklin D. Roosevelt*, vol. 5 (New York: Random House, 1938), p. 210.

them. State taxes, on the other hand, may meet special resistance from citizens of the state who fear they will be unable to compete with those from other states who are not so taxed. If cigarette taxes are increased in Ohio, consumers who live near the Pennsylvania-Ohio border can cross it, make their purchases in Pennsylvania, and transport the cigarettes illegally back to Ohio. Although such action is common, it is also illegal, and some people get caught and punished.

The Constitutional Basis for Expansion of National Power While the power of the federal government vis-à-vis the state and local governments has not expanded very much in regard to the amount of money it raises and spends (see Table 5–2) or in regard to the kinds of subjects with which it deals, there are three areas in which the federal government has greatly expanded its activities, and these contribute to the image of a growing national government.

THE COMMERCE CLAUSE. Some of the constitutional provisions and interpretations which have enabled the central government to expand its powers have already been mentioned. One of these, the "commerce clause," found in Article I, Section 8 of the Constitution, has been used to justify more new federal government activities than any other. The right of Congress "to regulate commerce . . . among the several states" has been construed to refer to almost anything affecting goods that move in interstate commerce. Under this construction, the national government has regulated the wages, hours, working conditions, and union activities of workers who make, ship, or sell goods, as well as the hiring practices of their employers. It has ruled on the ingredients that go into the goods, the TV advertising that sells them, and the banks that finance them. Moreover, the courts have also

Best Cartoons of 1971, edited by Lawrence Lariar (New York: Dodd, Mead, 1971).

ruled that Congress may write civil-rights legislation under the commerce clause, because discrimination in places of public accommodation impedes the flow of goods in interstate commerce by making it difficult or embarrassing for some citizens to travel around the country conducting business.[31]

THE POWER TO MAKE WAR. Modern warfare, whether fought with conventional or nuclear weapons, is total warfare and involves every phase of a community's economic life, as well as full utilization of all its resources (educational facilities, transportation, raw materials, and so forth). In light of this fact, the constitutional powers "to make war" and "to lay taxes . . . for the common defense" have been interpreted to include almost every conceivable activity. Some of the programs substantiated by the war-making clause include the support of language courses at universities, subsidies for our merchant marine, stockpiling of critical raw materials (zinc, quicksilver), and, of course, a wide variety of foreign military- and economic-aid programs.

POWER TO TAX AND SPEND FOR THE GENERAL WELFARE. The constitutional provision giving Congress the power "to lay and collect taxes . . . to provide for the . . . general welfare" has resulted in literally reams of legislation, granting appropriations in such diversified areas as student loans, hospital construction, crop-reduction programs, and the support of museums and symphony orchestras. Because Congress has the power to fund a program or withhold money, it has the opportunity to determine the shape of much of American life. Moreover, once Congress does decide to provide money for a project, it can stipulate both technical and broad policy standards and regulations that must be followed in spending it. Over the years Congress has used its taxing power as an instrument of social control.

Direct Aid and Grants-in-Aid

Federal assistance reaches the people through many channels. Some programs, such as Social Security and Medicare, are handled directly by the national government, with Washington setting standards, determining levels of assistance, and distributing the money. Most programs, however (about 99 percent), involve *grants-in-aid,* also known as categorical agents, furnished by the federal government to states or localities to be used for specific purposes. Grants-in-aid cover thousands of projects from Head Start to urban renewal, from mental health to environmental protection to urban mass transportation, law enforcement, and welfare. In 1970, these grants amounted to about $24 billion[32] and provided about one-fifth of all the funds spend by state and local governments.[33] Until 1973, all grant-in-aid programs have been written "with strings attached"; that is, they are available to a state or locality only if it agrees to provide a "matching requirement" toward the total cost of the project. In some cases, the matching rate is the same for each grant in each locality; in others, differential rates are used so that relatively poorer states have lower matching ratios than wealthier ones. For example, the federal government now pays half of New York's and California's

---

[31] *Heart of Atlanta Motel* v. *United States,* 379 U.S. 241 (1964).

[32] *Special Analysis: Budget of the United States, Fiscal Year 1973* (Washington, D.C.: Government Printing Office, 1972), p. 241.

[33] *Special Analysis: Budget of the United States, Fiscal Year 1973,* p. 242.

Figure 5–1   **Federal Aid to State and Local Governments**

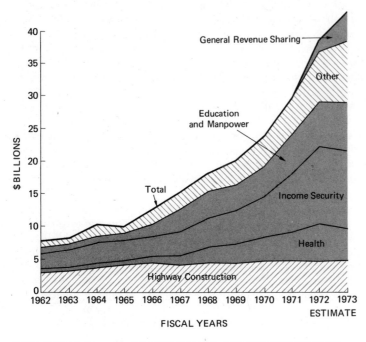

Source: Special Analyses of the United States Government, Fiscal Year 1973 *(Washington, D.C.: Government Printing Office, 1972), Special Analysis P, p. 239.*

welfare programs but supplies up to 83 percent of the cost for lower-income states such as West Virginia, Arkansas, and Tennessee. Most legislation provides that grant funds be allocated on a *formula* basis; that is, monies are distributed to all eligible communities on the basis of some formula such as the population, the wealth of the community, or the number of poor people.[34] Project grants are a relatively new development: these are monies appropriated to solve specific problems, such as the Head Start program, aimed at intellectual enrichment of preschool ghetto children. A community which wants these funds must design a program and apply for a grant from the prescribed appropriate federal agency, which then assesses whether or not the program meets its requirements and deserves funding.

Criticisms of Grants-in-Aid Criticism of cooperative federalism centers on the grants-in-aid programs. It is, by now, common for critics to point to the built-in inefficiencies and expenses that go with the creation of fifty sets of state administrators each time a new program is introduced, and to other administrative difficulties, such as the delays and uncertainties caused by unnecessarily detailed and

---

[34] For example, under the Elementary-Secondary Education Act of 1965, funds were available to the states on the basis of the number of school children in low-income families. See Walter W. Heller, *New Dimensions of Political Economy* (Cambridge, Mass.: Harvard University Press, 1966), p. 142.

costly application requirements.[35] In addition, despite attempts made by varying the matching-fund requirements, there are still inequities in the services provided by the different states with federal money. Some southern states, for example, are still unwilling or unable to meet even the modest matching funds required for certain educational programs, so that citizens of these states do not participate at all in the federal allocation of these funds.[36]

Perhaps the most significant objection of all, however, concerns the basic matching-funds concept. Many grant programs are designed for new activities which the local government body has not supported previously. Although many of these projects are worthy, they put the local government in a quandary, especially if it is operating on a tight budget and has no surplus funds. It must either ignore the new program, or else drop an old activity (which may be even more essential) in order to obtain the funds needed to meet the matching requirements. For example, a school board may find itself in the unenviable position of either firing teachers throughout the district in order to afford participation in a new matching-funds program to stock its libraries, or else foregoing the new program. Since there is always pressure to take grants when they are offered, this system keeps a local board from establishing its own priorities and using total available funds most sensibly. This criticism has frequently been lodged by states' righters, who claim that federal grants interfere with the rights of local government to tackle their problems alone, and attempt to force them to accept federal standards in areas such as employment.

The Pros and Cons of Central Control

Neither the original constitutional formula for federalism, nor the formula as modified by amendments and judicial interpretation, has produced a final division of power between the national and state governments which has been accepted as the last word by all. Throughout our history, the two opposing viewpoints (those supporting the supremacy of the central government, and those opting for a major role for the states) have disagreed, and each finds it easy to quote apparently unassailable constitutional references to support its side. It is interesting, however, to note that the actual lineups have changed over the years, even if the arguments are pretty much the same: no longer do we find the big states opposing the small ones; instead we find that support for states' rights in recent years comes from segregationists, from big business, and from special-interest groups, all of whom have discovered that it is often much easier to control state legislatures, state officials, and state courts than national institutions, and who therefore believe that state regulation of their areas of concern will be more beneficent

---

[35] A management survey of six Ohio departments that use federal money showed that just to meet federal reporting requirements, 98,077 report submissions must be made each year, an effort consuming 539,000 man hours or the equivalent of almost 259 full-time employees. That manpower alone costs $2.6 million annually. Ohio Welfare Department employees, the survey showed, spent half their time just filling out federal forms.

[36] For example, in 1972, the federal government was paying 75 percent of the cost of certain birth-control services extended to the poor, with the states paying the remaining 25 percent. A number of states, however, had failed to set up programs, claiming they could not afford the 25-percent matching requirement. In an attempt to remedy the situation, in May 1972 the Senate Finance Committee voted to provide 100-percent federal-government financing of the cost of providing birth-control devices for low income women of childbearing age.

than federal regulation. In addition to these rather conservative states' righters, a new form of decentralization movement has emerged and is supported by an entirely different ideological group—the New Left. This group battles for the cause of community control, and while its position is not exactly the same as the traditional states'-rights position, it shares with the states' righters a desire to break down the large federal bureaucracy to more manageable, smaller units. Consumer groups, labor unions, and environmental-protection groups, on the other hand, favor the expansion of national-government power, as many of them believe that state governments will not be responsive to their desires.

The States' Rights View Despite the fact that, as we have seen, much of the power of the national government is exercised in a decentralized manner through the states and localities, there is a large and vocal group of Americans who resent the intrusion of federal power into areas formerly controlled by the states. They fear that the "federal octopus" now "threaten[s] the very existence of the states"[37] and that soon, as Senator Everett M. Dirksen once phrased it, "The only people interested in state boundaries will be Rand McNally."[38]

Senator Barry Goldwater (R.-Ariz.), a leading conservative spokesman and the Republican candidate for President in 1964, summarized the traditional states'-rights position on the central government's usurpation of power as follows:

The federal government has moved into every field in which it believes its services are needed. The state governments are either excluded from their rightful functions by federal preemption, or they are allowed to act at the sufferance of the federal government. Inside the federal government both the executive and judicial branches have roamed far outside their constitutional boundary lines. . . . The result is a leviathan, a vast national authority out of touch with the people, and out of their control.[39]

This states'-rights argument is based on the thesis that the states are closer to the people than the national government, that state government is more responsive to the immediate needs and desires of people because citizens can hold sanctions over local officials more easily than over federal ones. States' righters also contend that government should be limited in what it does; if the national government continues to absorb responsibilities formerly exercised by the states and the private sector, individual liberty will disappear. As one writer has warned,

If the central government can aid our disabled, and pension our old people, and succour our illegitimate children; if it can build our highways and lay our sewers and vaccinate our children and finance our college student, it can dominate our lives in such a way that freedom is lost altogether. . . . The power to control follows the Federal dollar as surely as that famous lamb accompanied little Mary.[40]

The same conservative concluded that "the [federal] scholarship program that begins with a subtle hint of what should be learned will yet end in effective control of what shall be taught, and to whom, and by whom, and in what sort of buildings."[41]

---

[37] Morton Grodzins, "Centralization and Decentralization in the American Federal System," p. 4.
[38] As quoted in Terry Sanford, *Storm over the States* (New York: McGraw-Hill, 1967), p. 37.
[39] Barry Goldwater, *The Conscience of a Conservative* (Shepherdsville, Ky.: Victor Publishing, 1960), p. 20.
[40] James Jackson Kilpatrick, "The Case for 'States' Rights,'" in Goldwin, *A Nation of States,* p. 103.
[41] Kilpatrick, "The Case for 'States' Rights,'" p. 104.

*Senator Barry Goldwater (R.-Ariz.)
is a leading states' rights advocate.*

In a more constructive approach to the problem of states' rights, several leading governors have spoken out recently, not only emphasizing the particular advantages which the states provide as governing bodies, but also offering some positive suggestions for restoring their vitality vis-à-vis the federal government. Former Governor Terry Sanford of North Carolina spoke of "federalism at its best," where the states permit an opportunity for "experimentation, change and local leadership in controversial matters." He suggested that in the states "new ideas can come to the surface close to home where local leadership can put them into practice with the confidence of the people."[42] Some of the major social and economic advances in the nation have begun with small-scale experimentation on the state level. The state of Wisconsin enacted the first unemployment insurance act in 1932, three years before the federal government acted; Wyoming permitted woman suffrage fifty years before the Nineteenth Amendment; California pioneered with the concept of government responsibility for all those who wished to obtain higher education.[43] Governor Nelson A. Rockefeller of New York, rather than merely decrying the eclipse of state power by national power, proposed a cure. He ascribed the decline of the states to their being afraid to collect adequate taxes on their own. The Governor wrote:

If a state government lacks the political courage to meet the needs of its people by using its own taxing power—if it prefers to escape by letting the national government do the

---

[42] Sanford, *Storm over the States,* pp. 4 and 5.
[43] In mid-1972, Governor William T. Cahill of New Jersey offered the first meaningful plan to use a broader-based tax (the income tax) to replace the traditional property-tax base for support of public education. The plan, although defeated, represents a beginning attempt to solve the national problem of burgeoning school costs; it was introduced by a *state,* on a *state* basis.

taxing and then return the money to the state—the leadership of this state puts itself in an exceedingly poor position to weep over the growth of federal power. The preservation of states' rights—in short—depends upon the exercise of states' responsibilities.[44]

This fresh approach to states' rights envisions the problems not merely as a need to "hold the line" and fight off new ventures by the federal government, but as a movement that can succeed, through state leadership, in solving its citizens' problems.

The Case for More Centralization Does the future of American federalism lie in a swing toward greater states' rights? Most liberals would disagree; instead they would point to the recent creation of regional governments that transcend state boundaries and to the forces in American life which appear to call for more, rather than less, activity on the part of the national government. The reality is that nationwide problems and population mobility make the old states' rights arguments meaningless. For example, traditionally, education has been considered strictly a local matter, but today when thousands of southern blacks immigrate annually to northern cities such as Chicago or Newark, the quality of the education they have received in the South is surely of concern to Illinois and New Jersey. In addition, many question the old assumption that local government is always closer to the people than the federal government. This was probably so in nineteenth-century America, when most citizens lived in small, rural areas, but today, with population centered in large urban areas, there is evidence that the reverse is true.[45] If closeness is to be measured by participation in elections, many more Americans vote in national elections than in local elections. The position of liberals has been that the federal government is more responsive to the people and that it has provided for the needs of the aged, the unemployed, the poor and the nonwhites better than have the states. Liberals would assert that in general the states'-rights argument has not been used, as claimed, to protect *all* a state's citizens against a distant, arbitrary national government, but rather as a device to perpetuate inequities in the system, to permit a powerful minority to tyrannize the majority, and to permit special business interests to be the outstanding beneficiaries of the system.[46] As one authority has phrased it, "Legislatures are inefficient and corrupt, . . . they procrastinate on public business while habitually kowtowing to private economic interests, legislators . . . line their own pockets, scratch their own backs and roll their own logs."[47]

Other liberal arguments for further centralization are offered in the light of the weaknesses of the states. Under existing tax arrangements some believe the states lack the financial resources to handle many problems: Governor Rockefeller and Mayor John V. Lindsay of New York have been pleading for years with Washington to assume the full costs of welfare. Not only do the states lack money, cry these critics, but they also lack the ability to act in the economic sphere. As early as 1939, Harold J. Laski, in a well-known article on the role of the states, announced that the "epoch of federalism [was] over" and called the "form of the federal state unsuitable" and "ineffective" to control the "giant capitalism" that

---

[44] Nelson A. Rockefeller, *The Future of Federalism* (Cambridge, Mass.: Harvard University Press, 1962), p. 24.

[45] See Morton Grodzins, "Centralization and Decentralization in the American Federal System," pp. 9–15.

[46] See William H. Riker, *Federalism: Origin, Operation, Significance* (Boston: Little, Brown, 1964), pp. 152–153.

[47] Frank Trippett as quoted in Leach, *American Federalism*, p. 122.

Support for decentralization used to mean support for the status quo and hence a conservative position, but in urban schools today, centralization has become such a dominant reality that decentralization has become a cause for those who seek change.

characterized the American economy.[48] State legislatures, for example, have always been particularly vulnerable to corporate interests.

Liberals also argue that cumbersome state constitutions add to the problem by making it time-consuming for states to adjust to changing circumstances[49] and by restricting the ability of governors to act and lead: governors may be limited to only one term; their powers may be fragmented among other elected officials, and very often control of budget or long-range planning is out of their hands. Furthermore, state legislatures are often notoriously malapportioned: in 1962 when the Supreme Court announced the first of its one-man–one-vote rulings,[50] which are now forcing the states to reapportion, twenty-seven states had not redistricted their legislatures in 25 years, and eight states had not redistricted in more than 50 years![51]

---

[48] Harold J. Laski, ''The Obsolescence of Federalism'' in *The New Republic* (May 3, 1939), pp. 367 and 369.

[49] Louisiana's constitution includes 253,830 words as compared to the national constitution's 6,000; by 1968 it had been amended some 460 times! (See Leach, *American Federalism*, pp. 118–119.)

[50] *Baker* v. *Carr*, 369 U.S. 186 (1962).

[51] Sanford, *Storm over the States*, p. 35.

In response to the growth of national power that has in fact occurred in the United States in the past decade, some have become dissatisfied with the traditional liberal view. This group holds that the bureaucracy of the federal government has become too large and that, consequently, it has fallen short of fulfilling the needs of many disadvantaged Americans. The group argues that the only way to improve things is through community control—that is, by even greater decentralization than that advocated in the states' rights position. Urban education has become a prime target of these New Left advocates; they prescribe that large city school systems be broken into smaller units so that the people in the immediate areas surrounding the schools will have greater control over the content and quality of their children's education.[52]

Decentralization within the American Political System

Despite the fact that the activities of the national government have grown tremendously, we have seen that sharing of functions exists: the belief that growth has occurred at the expense of state and local governments is more myth than reality. The American system, in practice, is highly fragmented and decentralized. Local governments do exert a major influence in the governmental process, and this influence is due in large part to the American party system.

In order for a congressman to achieve election, he must obtain the support of his *local* party and *local* constituency, and to maintain this support he is required to make major efforts in Washington to see that national power is used in his district in a way that suits local citizens. Such efforts can involve either constant prodding of the federal bureaucracy which administers federal laws to insure that his constituents are pleased, or, more commonly, an arrangement written into the laws, through which the exercise of national power is channeled through the states and localities.

In the United States, the party system is primarily a county, district, and state system. National parties such as the National Democratic party and the National Republican party conduct only limited activities revolving around presidential candidates. On a continuing basis, however, the fifty state parties are the real sources of power to governors and state legislators, and county and district organizations the source of power for city politicians. Candidates for the House and the Senate rely on state parties for the collection and dispensation of campaign funds and for providing workers and know-how at election time. The state and local political party is important to a congressman not merely because it provides him with a nomination and a campaign effort and funds, but also because it is the source of most of the rewards available in American political life: state and local patronage vastly exceed federal patronage. In fact, many state and local posts hold more prestige and power than national government posts.[53]

---

[52] For a full discussion of the politics, experiments and successes and failures of decentralized and centralized city school systems see Marilyn Gittell and Alan G. Hevesi, editors, *The Politics of Urban Education* (New York: Frederick A. Praeger, Publishers, 1969).

[53] Mayor Lindsay of New York City left the House of Representatives, where he represented a constituency of some four hundred thousand voters and had a handful of patronage jobs to distribute, to become mayor of a city of eight million with twenty-eight thousand non–civil-service jobs at his disposal. Similarly, it is doubtful whether the House or even the Senate would have much to offer Mayor Daley of Chicago or Governor Rockefeller of New York.

The decentralized party system, then, insures that congressmen maintain a vital and continuing interest in national programs implemented on the state and local level in a manner satisfactory to their local constituencies.[54] The following story, related by Alben Barkley, long a congressman and senator from Texas before becoming Harry Truman's Vice-President, illustrates the pressures felt by congressmen to provide these services:

I called on a certain rural constituent and was shocked to hear him say he was thinking of voting for my opponent. I reminded him of the many things I had done for him as prosecuting attorney, as county judge, as congressman, and senator. I recalled how I had helped get an access road built to his farm, how I had visited him in a military hospital in France when he was wounded in World War I, how I had arranged his loan from the Farm Credit Administration, how I had got him a disaster loan when the flood destroyed his home, etc., etc.

"How can you think of voting for my opponent?" I exhorted at the end of this long recital. "Surely you remember all these things I have done for you?"

"Yeah," he said, "I remember. But what in hell have you done for me lately?"[55]

The Changing Face of Modern Federalism

Creative Federalism   In an attempt at meeting some of the objections to federal granting operations, President Johnson introduced in 1964 the concept of "creative federalism." It differs from cooperative federalism in that it includes a role for private centers of power, along with local, state, and national government. Johnson visualized private industry, nonprofit foundations, labor unions, local community groups, and so forth, working together with the three levels of government: for example, as part of his administration's antipoverty program, large corporations such as RCA and Western Electric were hired by the federal government to run some Job Corps centers, which were set up around the country to train young men and women in specific skills. Creative federalism also emphasized the importance of developing both leadership and programs from the grassroots, so that ideas and administration came not only from top administrative levels but also from local sources, both private and public. A system of Community Action Agencies was introduced in 1964 in which local groups, including representatives of such diverse interests as church groups, local antipoverty and self-help organizations, city government agencies, and block associations would join together to design programs. Under the Community Action Agencies, services such as day-care centers and storefront legal-aid offices were established where needed, with funds provided on a matching basis from the federal government. In addition, the Johnson administration also concentrated on various innovations designed to coordinate the hundreds of different local projects the federal government was supporting in one way or another.[56]

During Johnson's last year in office, Congress approved a new version of the grant-in-aid program: bloc grants. These are sums of money given to the states

---

[54] See David B. Truman, "Federalism and the Party System," in *American Federalism in Perspective,* edited by Aaron Wildavsky (Boston: Little, Brown, 1967), pp. 81–108.

[55] Quoted in Morton Grodzins, "American Political Parties and the American System," in Wildavsky, *American Federalism in Perspective,* p. 121.

[56] Howard S. Rowland, *The New York Times Guide to Federal Aid for Cities and Towns* (New York: Quadrangle, 1972). The author notes that $40 billion will be available as of July 1, 1972, for 656 major urban aid programs administered by 64 federal agencies.

Table 5-1   **Federal, State, and Local Expenditures**[a]

Selected Fiscal Years 1946–1970
(Millions)

Year	Total	Federal Expenses	% of Total	State Expenses	% of Total	Local Expenses	% of Total
1946	$ 79,707	$ 66,534	83	$ 6,162	8	$ 7,011	9
1950	70,334	44,800	64	12,774	18	12,761	18
1954	111,332	77,692	70	15,802	14	17,837	16
1958	134,931	86,054	64	23,337	17	25,530	19
1962	176,240	113,428	64	29,210	17	33,601	19
1966	224,813	143,022	64	39,114	17	42,677	19
1970[h]	334,485	210,565	63	63,533	19	60,387	18

[a] Grants-in-aid are counted as expenditures of the first disbursing unit. Total expenditures include insurance trust expenditures.
[b] Data for 1970 estimated by Tax Foundation.
Source: Expenditures are adapted from the Bureau of the Census and Facts and Figures on Government Finance, 16th Edition (New York: Tax Foundation, 1971), p. 17.

on a matching-grant basis to be used in solving general problems, rather than for a very specific purpose as had previously been the categorical grants-in-aid practice. The first set of bloc grants was authorized under the Omnibus Crime Control and Safe Streets Act (1968); it was intended to improve law enforcement. Each state received a sum of money which it then distributed to state and local government bodies to be used for such purposes as "development of public protection devices, recruiting and training of law enforcement personnel, public education, projects to prevent and control civil disturbances, training special law enforcement units to combat organized crime . . . improve police community relations . . . improvement of courts and corrections systems. . . ."[57] Although the bloc grants do give the states somewhat more flexibility in using federal money to meet local needs, criticism has revolved around the fact that it is the *states* who are given the funds to distribute. Once again, the cities feel shortchanged.[58]

Fiscal Federalism In the 1970s it has become evident that one of the most important problems now facing our federalist system is that of the fiscal relationships between the national, state and local governments. The problem revolves around the fact that the demands for state and local services have expanded tremendously and show signs of continued growth, but the traditional allocation of tax resources has given the national government better access to revenues.[59] In short, the states and localities have the problem; the national government has the money! If we examine government expenditures in the United States during the post–World

[57] U.S. Government Organization Manual 1971–1972 (Washington, D.C.: Government Printing Office, 1971), p. 198.
[58] For an analysis of Creative Federalism see Harry N. Scheiber, "The Condition of American Federalism: An Historians's View," in U.S. Senate Study by Subcommittee on Intergovernmental Relations of the Committee on Government Operations (Washington, D.C.: Government Printing Office, 1966), pp. 14–22.
[59] Walter Heller estimated that property, sales, and gross receipts levied by local governments barely keep pace with the growth of the economy, rising a trifle less than 10 percent for each 10 percent rise in Gross National Product, while income taxes increase 16–18 percent for every 10 percent rise in GNP. See Heller, New Dimensions of Political Economy, p. 127.

Table 5-2   Federal-aid Outlays in Relation to Total State-Local Revenue

Fiscal Year	Amount (millions)	Federal Aid as a Percent of Combined State-Local Total Revenue
1959	$ 6,669	12.3
1960	7,040	11.6
1961	7,112	11.0
1962	7,893	11.3
1963	8,634	11.6
1964	10,141	12.4
1965	10,904	12.4
1966	12,960	13.2
1967	15,240	14.2
1968	18,599	15.8
1969	20,255	15.3
1970	23,954	15.9
1971	29,844	17.9
1972 estimate	39,080	21.1
1973 estimate	43,479	21.1

Source: "Special Analysis P," 1973 Budget (Washington, D.C.:
Government Printing Office, 1972), p. 245.

War II period, we see that the total cost of all government has increased over four fold, but that state and local government expenditures have increased at a significantly faster rate, about 1000 percent, than national government spending, which has increased by just less than 300 percent.

The increase in local and state spending reflects both the growing urbanization of America, with its need for more police, more roads, more garbage and sewage disposal facilities, and the like; and the higher level of expectation on the part of our citizens for such necessities as good schools and for such "luxuries" as local recreation facilities and libraries. Although the federal government has helped to some degree with grants-in-aid and now supplies about 21 percent of all monies spent by states and localities, the major responsibility for supplying these services has fallen on the states and local governments.

In theory, local government has an alternative. It can accept its limited resources and provide limited service. Governor Ronald Reagan of California advocates this practice. His method is substituting private enterprise for the government's.[60] It appears, however, that no matter how attractive, in principle, the idea of "minimum budgets with no frills" is, most Americans suffer from what can be called a "deep-seated schizoid condition"[61] when it comes to the role of government: they distrust it as a spending agency and would prefer to leave most of the national income, untaxed, in private hands; but at the same time they expect and demand an ever-increasing number of expensive services from government.

---

[60] Leach, *American Federalism*, p. 199.
[61] Both quoted phrases are from Frederick C. Mosher and Orville F. Poland, *The Costs of American Government: Facts, Trends, Myths* (New York: Dodd, Mead, 1964), p. 2, as quoted in Leach, *American Federalism*, pp. 199–200.

What, then, are some of the alternatives available to states and localities as they attempt to increase their revenues? One possibility lies in systemization of local taxes, which now lack overall plans as a result of organized public pressure. Another is consideration of new kinds of taxes, a task requiring some creativity, as few things remain untaxed at present. In addition, some attempt could be made to obtain direct federal-government payments for many expenses which it in effect "mandates" on certain local communities. In all, however, these suggestions are at best stopgaps, and the fundamental problem remains: the benefits of public policy must be redistributed so that local government—and especially bankrupt cities which are now heavily populated by the poor in the wake of middle-class desertion—can systematically and continuously receive major amounts of federal tax collections.

Nixon's Federalism: Revenue Sharing In the mid-sixties Walter Heller, previously chairman of the Council of Economic Advisers under Kennedy and Johnson, devised a plan through which federal monies could be channeled to localities. Entitled *revenue sharing,* it called for the federal government to "distribute a specified portion of the federal income tax to the states each year on a per capita basis, with next to no strings attached."[62] The plan would solve two of the major problems of grant-in-aid programs: the matching requirement, and the narrowly specified usage of the funds. Heller saw the dollars for revenue sharing coming from the "fiscal dividend" of at least $15–20 billion that would become available for other federal-government spending once the Vietnam War was over.

President Nixon formally recommended the first revenue-sharing plan in a message to Congress in August 1969. In this message he spoke of the increasing remoteness of the federal government from the people, accompanied by the federal government's usurpation of initiative from the states. Then, in noting the unprecedented quantity of programs instituted in the last five years, he stated, "Federal expansion has passed its peak . . . the American people . . . are turning away from the central government to their own local and state governments to deal with their local and state problems."[63]

Nixon's General Revenue Sharing Plan was designed to provide additional funds to the state and local governments so that they, rather than Washington, could deal with these local problems. It called for a program under which a set amount of federal revenues would be returned annually to the states to be used as the states and local government wished. A first-year (fiscal 1971) allocation of only $500 million was envisioned, but the plan called for $3.7 billion in 1972, $5.3 billion in 1973, and a proposal that at some time in the future there be an automatic return of 1.3 percent of the federal personal income-tax revenue to the states to provide growing sums to them in proportion to growing national income.[64]

---

[62] Walter W. Heller, *New Dimensions of Political Economy*, p. 145.

[63] Text of Revenue Sharing message to Congress, August 13, 1969, quoted in *Nixon, The First Year of His Presidency* (Washington, D.C.: Congressional Quarterly, 1970) pp. 79A–80A.

[64] From *U.S. Budget in Brief, Fiscal Year 1973*, p. 69. In addition to this General Revenue Sharing the President also called for six Special Revenue Sharing programs, which would provide state and local governments with funds in special broadly defined functional areas (transportation, education, urban and rural community development, manpower training, and law enforcement). These funds could be spent only within the specified areas, but there would be no matching-fund requirements, nor would federal approval of specified projects be necessary. See "Special Analysis P," *1973 Budget*, p. 243 ff.

"I'm initiating a revenue-sharing program. I want you to share your revenues with me."

Saturday Review, *June 12, 1971*

In June 1972 the House of Representatives passed a $5.3-billion revenue-sharing bill, allocating $1.8 billion to the states and the remaining $3.5 billion to cities and towns according to complicated formulas reflecting, in part, degree of urbanization, extent of local or state tax funds, and amount of poverty. Thirty-eight thousand local governments—all general-purpose localities—were included in the plan. Depending on the amount of tax increase instituted by each state, federal funds can rise as much as $300 million a year to a total of $3 billion in 5 years. Counties also receive money unless, as in Connecticut, they levy no taxes themselves. The passage of the House bill was a victory for President Nixon and the governors and mayors of the country, despite the fact that the plan is considerably different from the President's original proposal. The Senate passed a similar bill in October 1972, and it was signed into law by President Nixon that same month.

Consideration of the new bill by the House Ways and Means Committee and the Senate Finance Committee reflects the widespread criticism of revenue sharing which explains the long delay in action. Much of the controversy revolves around a distrust of the states—that they will waste the money, or that they will use the money to cut current taxes rather than to finance new improved services. In particular, the cities believe they can not trust state governments to respond to urban needs. Epitomizing the feelings of many urban leaders, former Mayor John Collins of Boston declared in the mid-sixties that "tax sharing is the most dangerous idea in America today."[65] Other objections involve the feeling that it

---

[65] Leach, *American Federalism*, p. 216.

is wrong to divorce tax collection from spending: by relying on federal funds, local government units and officials will only become less efficient and less responsive, as they will no longer be forced to obtain voter approval of taxes before they embark on new programs. Many liberals object to the absence of federal standards to insure equitable use of the funds, while others simply are reluctant to foot a new large spending commitment. A May 1972 Brookings Institution study reported that merely to maintain current federal-government civilian programs, even assuming the winding down of the Vietnam War, will require all planned government revenues, plus a large $12-billion tax increase package.[66]

ALTERNATIVE SOLUTIONS TO REVENUE SHARING. Several solutions to fiscal federalism other than revenue sharing have been suggested. One is to augment the present system of tax credits, under which a taxpayer receives some credit on his federal income-tax return for state and local taxes paid. This would permit the states to increase their own taxes with less outcry from local citizens, since part of the additional state-tax burden would be offset by a reduced federal-tax obligation.[67] Another suggestion includes further consolidation of grant programs similar to bloc grants. Governor Nelson A. Rockefeller advocates such a policy, which would give states and localities more flexibility in the use of federal monies, even if total federal dollar contributions do not increase substantially. Still others argue that a large-scale major plan is needed for monitoring the federal system. A plea for such a plan was made by Senator Edmund Muskie during Johnson's administration and was again advocated by the Brookings Institution in 1969.[68]

Other solutions to fiscal federalism are merely administrative in nature. The Nixon administration has continued the earlier efforts of President Johnson to improve the administration of the many federal government programs involving the states and localities. Early in his term, President Nixon created the Office of Intergovernmental Relations, under the direct supervision of the Vice President, to strengthen the channels of communication among the various levels of government. Perhaps most important was the appointment of an Urban Affairs Council, which is intended to coordinate all domestic government activities the way the prestigious National Security Council does for foreign affairs. A very practical first step was to reorganize the field offices of the five offices most concerned with welfare and social programs (the Departments of Health, Education and Welfare; Housing and Urban Development; and Labor; the Office of Economic Opportunity;

---

[66] The *New York Times* (May 25, 1972), p. 32. For various arguments against revenue sharing, see William G. Fredericks, "No to Revenue Sharing," *National Review*, vol. 23, no. 27, pp. 754–757; William Anderson, "The Myths of Tax Sharing," *Public Administration Review*, vol. 28, no. 1, pp. 10–14; and Leonard Opperman, "Aid to the States: Is Revenue Sharing the Answer?," *Review of Politics*, vol. 30 (January 1968), pp. 43–50.

[67] For example, under current federal tax rules, an Illinois taxpayer who pays $2000 in local and state taxes may subtract this amount as a deduction from his income before computing federal income tax due. Thus, if his income was $20,000 before state taxes (on which he might owe a federal tax of $4000), his taxable income after deducting state taxes would be only $18,000, on which he would owe about $3300 in federal taxes. In other words, of the $2000 he paid in state taxes, his actual expense was only $1300, since he achieved a $700 federal state-tax savings because of the state-tax deduction. Advocates of tax-credit systems suggest making these federal-tax savings even more attractive; for example, a system could be devised whereby a taxpayer could obtain an actual credit against federal taxes (rather than just a deduction) for a large percentage of state and local taxes paid.

[68] See Edmund S. Muskie, "Creative Federalism in 1968: A Legislator's View," *State Government*, vol. 41, no. 4, pp. 249–250; and James Sandquist and David Davies, *Making Federalism Work* (Washington, D.C.: The Brookings Institution, 1969), pp. 246, 273, 275.

and the Small Business Administration), so that they now all have common regional headquarters and common boundaries for their districts. This means that if a community wishes help in solving a problem that involves several government agencies administering several grant-in-aid programs, acquiring this help is far simpler. One survey reported that because of the new system, the time required to process a typical loan application for federal money was cut in half, and in one case HUD was able to process a mayor's request for a rehabilitation loan in five days, rather than the usual three months.[69]

The Metropolitan-Area Problem

Concentration of Population in Metropolitan America

In the preceding discussion of the relationships between local government and national government, there have been frequent references to the special problems of urban America. In this section these problems will be described, with a stress on how an effective system of government can be provided for urban areas. Can an answer be found within the framework of our traditional national-state-local federalism, or are the problems of metropolitan America so different or so enormous that new forms of government must be created in order to handle them?

The first step is to understand the statistics of the situation. It is widely recognized that the United States is no longer a nation of farmers; however, to visualize America simply as a nation of big-city dwellers is equally inaccurate. As early as 1949, the Bureau of the Census, recognizing this problem, coined the phrase *metropolitan area* to designate the unit within which most of us live; and since that time has issued social and economic statistics in terms of "standard metropolitan statistical areas" (SMSAs). An SMSA is "an integrated economic and social unit with a large population nucleus." Generally consisting of a central city with a population of at least fifty thousand, and the metropolitan area around it, it may include two or more central cities in one area, although generally within one state, such as the Greensboro–Winston-Salem–High Point, North Carolina SMSA. It may cross state lines, like the Delaware–New Jersey–Maryland SMSA, which includes counties in all three states. As of July 1, 1971, there were 243 SMSAs in the continental United States, 88 of which had total populations of fifty to two hundred thousand, and 155 with populations in excess of two hundred thousand.[70]

In 1970, two-thirds of all Americans lived within SMSAs, and while the total population of the United States increased some 12 percent from 1960 to 1970, SMSA population grew by 16.6 percent. These figures by themselves, however, do not give an accurate picture of how American population patterns have changed in the last ten or fifteen years. Prior to 1950, it was the population increase *within the cities themselves* that characterized American demographics. Today, however, the central cities are no longer growing explosively; their growth rate for

---

[69] John Fischer, "The Easy Chair: Can the Nixon Administration be Doing Something Right," *Harpers Magazine* (November 1970), pp. 22–37.

[70] There are 4 more SMSAs in Puerto Rico, with San Juan's population over two hundred thousand. All of these figures are drawn from Bureau of the Census, *Metropolitan Area Statistics* (Washington, D.C.: Government Printing Office, 1971), p. 829.

Figure 5–2   **Rural vs. Metropolitan U.S. Population, 1970**

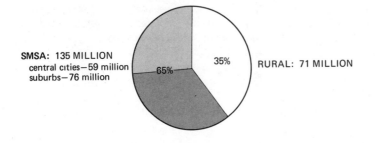

SMSA: 135 MILLION
central cities—59 million
suburbs—76 million

65%

35%

RURAL: 71 MILLION

1960–1970 was only 5.2 percent, or less than the rate for the United States as a whole, and sixty-nine of the central cities in the 155 larger SMSAs actually lost population during the period. Thus, it is the population boom *outside the central city, but within the SMSA,* which registered an astounding 28.3-percent increase from 1960 to 1970, the significant figure with which we must now deal. To put it another way, America is neither rural nor urban today; it is primarily suburban, with the largest number of our citizens living in the outlying areas that surround our central cities.

Fragmentation of Government within the SMSA The federal government's definition of an SMSA as an "integrated economic and social unit" implies a certain commonality of interest between the central city and the suburbs that surround it. The people who live in Beverly Hills, California, for example, but commute to work, shop, or study in Los Angeles, are clearly not spending *all* of their time in a city or *all* of it in a suburb. Such individuals are in the position of understanding the common interests of both areas and the logic of cooperation. Services such as public roads and transportation, and water- and air-pollution regulations, would be more desirably managed by one coordinated metropolitan-area government. In reality, however, the governmental units of our SMSAs are fragmented beyond belief, incredibly complex, and unable to successfully govern these increasingly troubled areas with efficiency and imagination.

   Leach called this fragmentation "ridiculous, if not . . . macabre."[71] In 1971, there were well over eighteen thousand units of government within the 243 SMSAs; with the average SMSA enjoying the dubious delights of government by ninety-one different units, including overlapping and/or contiguous cities, townships, and counties; plus, for example, innumerable special fire-protection, library, sewage, school, water-supply, and highway districts. Within the Chicago metropolitan area alone there are twelve hundred twenty government bodies, and the citizens of one Chicago suburb, Park Forest (itself created barely twenty years ago), are governed by and pay taxes to thirteen local units—two counties, three townships, five school districts, a forest-preserve district, a mosquito-abatement district and the village board of trustees.[72]

---

[71] Leach, *American Federalism*, p. 147.

[72] Figures on Chicago and Park Forest, Illinois, are from Merriam, "The Future of American Federalism," *State Government,* vol. 44, no. 4 (Autumn 1971), p. 239.

A result of this fragmentation was envisioned as early as 1922 by Chester C. Maxey, who saw the "political disintegration" of metropolitan areas as "gravely impeding all progress and comprehensive public undertakings."[73] Thirty years later, in 1968, echoing this pessimism, the federal Advisory Commission on Intergovernmental Relations concluded that "because of the metropolitan area problem, the federal system itself [is] on the brink of destruction."[74] Some people, such as these critics, believe because that cooperation and coordination are lacking under the present fragmented system of local government, present-day services are expensive and inadequate, and reflect little comprehensive planning. Moreover, the existing system has encouraged the division of metropolitan America into two artificial parts, the central city and the suburb, to the long-term advantage of neither.

The City versus the Suburbs

During the first sixty years of the twentieth century, the standard complaint of big-city mayors was that urban districts were continuously shortchanged at the state capitol because of malapportionment in state legislatures favoring rural areas, despite the growing population of the cities. This traditional political struggle between the city and rural America is for all practical purposes no longer an important factor; the Supreme Court has forced reapportionment so that representation is now equitable. The result, however, has been a new division of power, for it is the cities and the *suburbs* who now find themselves in conflict, with the voters of suburbia often aligning themselves with those of rural areas against the city.

To understand the bitterness of the conflict between the cities and their suburbs, it is necessary to examine the reasons behind the growth of the suburbs. To a large extent growth has come in reaction to the deterioration that has marked the central city since the Depression and World War II with abandoned housing, poor schools, drugs, pollution, and high crime. These problems have accelerated in recent years, because for the first time in our history the cities are no longer performing their former role of taking in immigrants from other cultures and successfully providing them with the economic skills and American social values. Instead, blacks (and in certain metropolitan areas, Puerto Ricans and Chicanos), who have been subject to many generations of our society's discrimination, leaving them with an accumulation of health, educational, and employment problems, have flocked to the cities. The cities are simply unable financially to provide the very expensive services these residents require. This new influx of nonassimilated, troubled newcomers is only half the problem: the response of the established city dwellers has vastly complicated the situation.

Middle-class New Yorkers, for example, confronted with public schools in which most of the children are reading at several years behind grade level, have reacted by leaving the central city for its environs. This pattern has been repeated again and again in such cities as Cleveland, Cincinnati, Philadelphia, and Detroit. From 1960 to 1969, the black population of the central cities increased by 2.7 million;

---

[73] O. Warren, *Government in Metropolitan Regions: A Reappraisal of Fractionated Political Organization.* (Sacramento: Calif. The Regents of the University of California, 1966), p. 6.

[74] Quoted in Leach, *American Federalism,* p. 152.

during this same period, the white population of the cities declined by 2 million, while the white population of the suburbs increased by 14 million.[75]

These new suburbanites feel strongly that, having escaped the housing, education, and recreation problems of the city, they no longer wish to be involved in them. They are not eager to see their state taxes increased to pay for housing, transportation, compensatory education, health, or welfare plans which are designed primarily for central-city residents. Now that fair representation gives the suburban voter considerable power in his state legislature, such projects are frequently turned down. In addition, suburban communities try to keep out city problems by zoning restrictions that prohibit low-income housing and admit only "clean" corporate businesses rather than industry. Through these methods they avoid the environmental problems of noise and pollution and provide no impetus for the low-income individual to settle in the vicinity. These same suburban communities enact school programs that keep their children in the suburbs and central-city children in the city.[76] Because of the fragmentation of government discussed earlier, it is very easy for the suburbs to act in this way, for each local community has its own zoning board and own school district, which act to "protect" themselves.

Recently, however, some suburbanites have begun to realize they cannot ignore the central city. All too often, today's suburb is not the separate enclave, characterized by the lovely homes with manicured lawns seen on the Late Show in old Andy Hardy or Doris Day movies. Instead one finds what urban planners call "slurbs," suburbs which are really nothing more than extensions of the city, and which are now finding themselves caught up in many of the same problems as the central city. Moreover, even the distant suburbs find that crime does not stop at the city line, that inadequate city sewage-disposal plants pollute suburban beaches, and that drug peddlers abound at suburban high schools as well as at inner-city schools.

It is particularly unfortunate that help in solving the city-suburb problem has not been forthcoming from some of the most obvious sources. The states, by permitting the helter-skelter creation of new units of local government, have in fact been a primary cause of current difficulties. Very often, administrative procedures on the state level, or the state constitutions themselves, make it difficult for local governments to work together on area-wide problems should they so desire. In addition, the states have been reluctant to take over many local government functions that they could handle more efficiently on a statewide basis (for example, sewage collection and disposal, air-treatment systems, metropolitan-area transportation). Finally, central cities are particularly plagued by tax and debt-limits set years ago by the states before current population and cost-of-living explosions, and are thus unable financially to help themselves.

---

[75] Although it is hidden in this set of statistics, one should nevertheless note a comparable outflow into the suburbs that is in process for a particular slice of the *black* population: the growing black middle class. Reacting in most cases to the same stimuli which have resulted in the white escape from the central city, the black population of the suburbs increased by about a million from 1960 to 1969, or 37 percent, with black suburban populations exhibiting dramatic growth in some areas (68 percent in the North and West). See U.S. Census Bureau, *Current Population Reports, Special Studies, Trends in Social and Economic Conditions in Metropolitan Areas*, pp. 2, 8.

[76] Three of the many suburban areas that have zoned against low-income housing are Madison Township, New Jersey; Lima, Ohio; and Troy, Michigan. See *Newsweek* (November 15, 1971), p. 61.

The national government attempted to take steps to promote intragovernmental cooperation, but with little success. Among the large number of programs instituted were the Economic Opportunity Act of 1964 and the Model Cities Program, which were to emphasize metropolitan-wide and community-wide planning.[77] In addition, the Department of Housing and Urban Development (HUD) was established in 1965 to show particular sensitivity to the need for metropolitan-area coordination. An encouraging sign of national-government dedication to the problem was the Federal Housing Act of 1970: this Act, in addition to authorizing funds, instructed the President to develop a broad National Urbanization Plan, and to report back to Congress every two years on urban growth in the nation.[78]

The City and the State

The federal government, in addressing itself to urban problems, now has better lines of communication between itself and the cities than state governments do. The cities have found that the most effective way for them to obtain help is by going directly to Washington, and indeed, although some bloc grants are still given to the states for distribution to localities, many of the largest federal-aid programs, such as the Model Cities Program, and OEO's Community Action Program, now bypass the state completely and are given directly to the central cities or to localities within them. To obtain such aid directly, the cities have used their political power in the Congress or have formed their own pressure groups, often consisting of mayoral delegations to the President or to Congress. As a result of these independent activities, relationships between central cities and state officials have been distinctly cool, and have in some cases degenerated to public feuds, as a recent interchange between Governor Rockefeller and Mayor Lindsay of New York illustrates. The Governor, rejecting the Mayor's request for more state aid, lashed out at Mayor Lindsay, describing the City as "a place where housing can't be found, streets are unsafe, corruption undermines public trust, traffic is unbearable, no one can ever seem to get anything changed for the better because . . . there is [no] actual control over the functioning of city government."[79] He then went on to suggest that the city's administration, which prides itself on a liberal "reform" government, would be better run under the old-line political machines, which, Rockefeller claimed, ran the city more satisfactorily. In reply, the Mayor described the sad situation of their city-state relationship:

"All the gains the City of New York has made have been done by exerting substance, political power and the coalition of the Big Six Mayors [mayors of the six largest cities in New York State]. None of it has been done with any sense of graciousness on the Albany end, and certainly none of it has been done by any sense of willingness to see the city achieve."[80]

These remarks, unfortunately, epitomize the city-state problem. The states see the central city's troubles as a result of central-city inefficiency, lack of ability to

---

[77] To formulate these plans groups of area-wide officials, called Councils of Government (COGs) were formed and now exist in many SMSAs.
[78] Merriam, "The Future of American Federalism," p. 240.
[79] The *New York Times* (January 19, 1972), p. 20.
[80] The *New York Times* (January 19, 1972), p. 1.

Boston proper is one of the smallest cities in the United States geographically, but taken together with adjacent densely populated areas like the city of Cambridge, metropolitan Boston is relatively large. Shown here from Boston across the Charles River is Cambridge, with the Massachusetts Institute of Technology lit up in the center.

manage, and corruption, and thus feel justified in refusing to help. The cities, on the other hand, view their predicament as the result of forces beyond their control, for which both the state and the federal government must assume some responsibility.

Solutions to the Metropolitan-Area Problem

Metropolitan-Area Governments One suggested solution for the problem of metropolitan-area management is a form of area-wide government, called *metropolitan-federalism,* or *metro.* Metro attempts to achieve a government structure and process in which the whole community, both city and suburbs, cooperate in area-wide planning, and in providing those services which are obviously area-wide in scope.[81] Toronto, Canada, was one of the first cities to operate under such a system, installing an early version in 1953; today, metro-Toronto consists of five boroughs plus the city of Toronto and has achieved an outstanding record in building and operating subways, highways, sewers, water lines, and the like throughout the area. London has a somewhat similar system, including even more government functions. In the United States Metropolitan Miami (Dade

---

[81] See Daniel R. Grant, "The Metropolitan Government Approach," *Urban Affairs Quarterly,* vol. 3 (March 1968), p. 20.

County) and Nashville, Tennessee, are two examples. Dade County Metro (formed in 1957) includes Miami and twenty-seven other cities, each of which retains some local government functions, while others such as fire, police, and transportation are handled by the county metro, which also provides all government services for those who live in unincorporated parts of the county. Nashville formed a single metropolitan government for the 533-square-mile area of Nashville-Davidson County, which has been notably successful in equalizing public-education opportunities and in developing area-wide plans for constructing new water and sewer facilities. Jacksonville, Florida; Seattle, Washington; and Indianapolis, Indiana, have also attempted metropolitan-area governments to some extent.

Despite these positive examples, some authorities doubt that metropolitan-area government represents a final solution to the problem. They mention the deep-seated distrust between the suburbs and the central cities, the cleavage between the increasingly black-controlled cities and the white suburbs. Many urban planners say that although area-wide management may be potentially useful for small metropolitan areas, metro is politically unattainable for our largest cities because blacks in the cities fear the loss of much of their new-found power and suburbanites are reluctant to incur higher taxes. St. Louis, Missouri, and its environs has been the site of a failed attempt to form such a metropolitan government. Although there were many groups advocating its acceptance, the people defeated the plan.

Regional Governments A 1972 report by the Federal Commission on Population Growth and the American Future concluded that the urbanization of America was proceeding so quickly that, soon, even metropolitan-area governments such as Metro-Miami and Metro-Nashville would be inadequate to meet the needs of the new, still larger urban units that are emerging across America. The report suggested that by the year 2000, eight out of ten Americans would live within "huge webs of urbanization, . . . large, concentrated and continuous zones of relative high density" that will sprawl across hundreds of miles, including the Atlantic Seaboard Area (with a projected population of 57 million), the Lower Great Lakes Area (52 million), the Florida Peninsula Region (12.8 million) and the California Region (35 million). After criticizing present fragmentized local government arrangements "which border on chaos in some areas," the report called for the establishment of broad regional governments to handle such region-wide planning matters as the allocation and management of the environment.[82]

This concept of "regional" government has been discussed before under the name *megalopolis*, which was invented in 1961 by Jean Gottman to describe the batch of cities stretching for six hundred miles along the Atlantic coast from Boston to Washington. Others have expanded on his theme, assigning the name *Boswash* (Boston/Washington) to one megalopolis, *Chipitts* (Chicago/Pittsburgh) to another, and *SanSan* (San Francisco/San Diego) to a third.

Proponents of regionalism as the basis for government units see present state boundaries as artificial and claim that more and more of today's problems are of regional scope. Given the mobility of today's population, the product of a Pittsburgh school may well be a welfare case in Chicago, a hospital patient in Cleveland, and an unemployment statistic in Dayton in the course of his life.

---

[82] The *New York Times* (February 6, 1972), p. 1.

Surely it would be more efficient to have regional governments to grapple with the urban problems of all of Chipitts, instead of attacking them piecemeal.

The Future of Federalism

In a recent address by a leading political scientist, the speaker presented his own version of George Orwell's *Nineteen Eighty-Four* by reading the opening paragraph of a hypothesized report on "The Decline and Fall of American Federalism":

> *Death came to the American federal system not with a sudden blow, but gradually, over decades of slow disintegration. The seeds of decline were planted before World War II, sprouted in the post-war years, and grew steadily in the sixties and seventies. The signs were obvious for anyone wanting to see—there were cries of warning—but the majority saw no intrinsic value in maintaining the federal system and sought solutions to the Nation's overwhelming domestic problems outside traditional structures.*[83]

This chapter has surveyed many of the "signs" to which the speaker referred, and the past few pages have dealt with some of the structural changes in our federal system which have been offered as viable solutions to the problems now confronting us. Any of these would involve a comprehensive reworking of the traditional national-state-local government arrangements which have characterized American federalism to date, with the states, in most cases, assuming less and less importance. Is this indeed the only alternative left to us?

Robert Merriam, who delivered the gloomy words quoted above, does not think so. Like many other authorities, chief among them state governors, he argues that what we need is more federalism rather than less. He advocates a return to our original balanced system, with the states assuming greater responsibility for collecting tax money, reorganizing local governments in a rational manner, and planning and administering local problems. Under such a system, the power of the national government, which has been increasing over recent years as its areas of responsibility have increased, would be balanced in the future by the expanding power and responsibilities of the state governments. The result, claims Merriam, would be a government closer and more responsive to the needs of the people.

Other political scientists would concur that reorganizing governments should not be America's first priority at present; layers of metropolitan and regional government will not solve the more deep-seated national problems based on values and habits. Pollution, for example, cannot be eliminated by a new bureaucracy, regional government, or federal grant-in-aid; as later chapters in this book will discuss, there are limits to what can be accomplished through government.

SUGGESTED READING

Banfield, Edward C. and James Q. Wilson. *City Politics* (New York: Vintage, 1963). In paperback. An integrated view of city politics that conceives the principal problem of urban politics to be the management of conflict. Although the book has not been revised since publication, the authors' comments and descriptions of various urban situations and governmental structures remain useful.

---

[83] Merriam, "The Future of American Federalism," p. 238.

Bollens, John C. and Henry J. Schmandt. *The Metropolis, Its People, Politics, and Economic Life*, 2nd edition (New York: Harper & Row, 1970). This textbook is a good introduction to the problems of metropolitan areas in the 1970s. Taking the metropolis as its focus, it examines geographical, social, economic, political, and other aspects and makes some suggestions for metropolitan government that are already being tried.

Clark, Kenneth B. *Dark Ghetto: Dilemmas of Social Power* (New York: Harper & Row, 1965). Since the civil-rights struggle turned north in the middle of the 1960s, the large black urban population has been the recipient of special attention and some quickly assembled government programs. Kenneth Clark writes about these "dark ghettos," their sociology, pathology, and psychology, and some of the early governmental attempts at change.

Elazar, Daniel J. *The American Partnership: Intergovernmental Cooperation in the Nineteenth-Century United States* (Chicago: The University of Chicago Press, 1962). The author demonstrates that, contrary to widespread belief, virtually all domestic activities of government in the nineteenth-century U.S. were shared endeavors, much as they are today. He concludes that the widely held view that American federalism is a system of dual sovereignties – federal and state – has never worked in practice, although it has long been an official theoretical pronouncement.

————. *American Federalism: A View from the States* (New York: Thomas Y. Crowell, 1966). Examining federalism from the perspective of the states, Elazar conveys the political, legal, and cultural factors that are important in shaping the states' place as participants in the American federal system. He conceives federalism – an interdependent partnership of governments, publics, and individuals – as the animating principle of the American political process.

Elazar, Daniel J., R. Bruce Carroll, E. Lester Levine, and Douglas St. Angelo (eds.). *Cooperation and Conflict: Readings in American Federalism* (Itasca, Ill.: F. E. Peacock Publishers, 1969). Starting with the Grodzins thesis that American federalism is a political system in which many governments share functions, the authors assemble a picture of American federalism up to and into the 1960s that corroborates Grodzins's thesis and extends and deepens its central theme of negotiated compromise. The book presents numerous points of view including theory, historical perspective, areas of federal-state-local relationships, and the dynamics of decision-making. It is rich with materials oriented toward current issues confronting the federal system.

Goldwin, Robert A. (ed.). *A Nation of States: Essays on the American Federal System* (Chicago: Rand McNally, 1961). A series of essays that examine American federalism as it appears in civil rights, revenue-sharing, highway construction, race relations, agriculture, welfare programs, and so on. Their approaches and findings differ, but they all agree that the successful governing of America requires an understanding of federalism and that today there is a profound misunderstanding of its essential character.

Grodzins, Morton. *The American System: A New View of Government in the United States* (edited by Daniel J. Elazar) (Chicago: Rand McNally, 1966). Published after Grodzins's untimely death, the book supports his hypothesis of shared government functions with the results of wide-ranging original research. Grodzins rejects the federal system as a system of isolated governments with separated powers (similar to a layer cake), and instead offers his famous analogy of the American system of interdependent governments as a marble cake.

Jacobs, Jane. *The Death and Life of Great American Cities* (New York: Vintage, 1961). In paperback. Jacobs, an urban specialist, criticizes the ends to which funds at all government levels were used in the early days of the "urban crisis." She calls low-income projects, downtown business-district renewal, luxury housing, and other early priorities the "sacking of cities," and looks instead at the sociology and ecology of cities: what factors are vital to a city, what leads to decay? She provides insights into what governmental and private sectors of the community can and should do.

Leach, Richard H. *American Federalism* (New York: Norton, 1970). In paperback. Leach sets out various theories of federalism, ending, as most other authors do, with a variant of cooperative federalism. He attempts to put the various federal and poverty programs of the Great Society into perspective and to explain the Republican alternative of "new federalism." Leach provides an introduction to the recent thorny problems of finances — tax reform, revenue-sharing, and the uses to which local governments put federal grant-in-aid funds in their desperate need for hard cash.

Lyford, Joseph P. *The Airtight Cage* (New York: Harper & Row, 1966). Lyford takes us into a New York City neighborhood and shows the forces working or not working on it. The neighborhood is an "area X," in Lyford's terms, the object of government programs from all levels. He documents and describes the different populations, the social and political agencies, and the political activity of the citizens.

Martin, Roscoe C. *The Cities and the Federal System* (New York: Atherton, 1965). Martin examines the city-federal relationship in America which emerged only in the 1930s. He explores foundations of the ties between the two levels of government, as well as some of the early programs — slum clearance, airports, the federal highway program, and the various welfare programs. A sound foundation for current evaluation of this governmental relationship.

Riker, William H. *Federalism: Origin, Operation, Significance* (Boston: Little, Brown, 1964). Riker examines and demonstrates the ways in which federalism has affected the practices of political parties, the actions or inactions of the President and Congress, the legislative process, and the American political culture as a whole. He is sharply critical of federalism, particularly of its proven ability to frustrate majority will.

Sundquist, James L. *Making Federalism Work: A Study of Program Coordination at the Community Level* (Washington, D.C.: The Brookings Institution, 1969). An examination of the processes and problems of coordination at the local level that have resulted from a new phase of federalism in America. Sundquist finds that the extant community institutions were generally unequal to the demands of the new national programs for leadership, planning, and coordination at the local level. After examining and summarizing the workings of the federal system, he provides a structural model of a coordinated federal system necessary to solve the situation of stress in which we find ourselves today.

Wildavsky, Aaron (ed.). *American Federalism in Perspective* (Boston: Little, Brown, 1967). The editor of this series of essays seeks to place American federalism in a broad analytical context. The authors are concerned with conceptual analysis, general theory, and comparisons vis-à-vis historical-legal descriptions. Special attention is given to the interaction between party and federal systems and the nature of this relationship. The book as a whole concentrates on analysis and largely avoids the polemical literature on states' rights, centralization, and so forth.

Wood, Robert C. *1400 Governments* (Cambridge, Mass.: Harvard University Press, 1961). Wood looks at the results of federalism from the perspective of one metropolitan area, Greater New York City, and traces the interrelationships of some fourteen hundred governments, including federal, state, and local units, from regional giants such as the New York Port Authority to local school boards. The paradox is that while the governmental structure is so fragmented there is real economic interdependence within the metropolitan area.

6
CONGRESS

"In Republican government, the legislative authority necessarily dominates," James Madison asserted. Words like these made good propaganda, but, in fact, the Framers did not wish the Congress to dominate. The Constitution they wrote gave Congress, as the representative body, "all legislative power" and, in addition, control over the budget. But, newly delivered from what they saw as a tyrannical rule, the Framers were careful to limit the power of the legislature. As Edmund Burke, the great English parliamentarian, had put it, "Bad laws are the worst sort of tyranny." To protect the nation against tyranny by a Congress that represented the mass of the people, the Framers provided the safeguards of checks and balances. Yet the Congress they established was, in effect, coequal to the office of President, if not, as Madison's rhetoric suggested, the dominant branch of government.

The American government, however, has had to adapt to many changes in American life since the Constitution was written. In the process, a considerable shift of power has taken place. Americans living in the twentieth century have seen wars and internal crises give new dimensions to the President's power— under circumstances that have narrowed the legislative scope of Congress in ways undreamed of by the men who wrote the Constitution. During the past half-century, as the power of the Chief Executive has expanded to meet the demands of increased involvement in international affairs, and with the growth of governmental bureaucracy and large-scale industry, the legislative role of Congress has steadily diminished.

The United States has not been unique in its shift from the Legislative to the Executive branch. A shift has also been evident in most other Western democratic nations. Like our own Congress, the French National Assembly and the British and West German parliaments have also been called "rubber stamps" of their respective executives.

Although some observers have argued that the American Congress is more powerful than any other legislative body in the world,[1] the fact remains that its lawmaking power has been greatly reduced. Congressional initiation of legislation has declined to the point where today an estimated 80 percent of the bills enacted into law originate in the Executive branch of the government. In fact, since the establishment of the Bureau of the Budget in 1921, the President has set up the agenda for Congress. In recent times, moreover, Congress has been no more diligent in contributing to the final shape of legislation proposed by the Executive branch than it has been in initiating legislation. While Congress had a major influence upon the final content of 55 percent of the important laws passed between 1882 and 1909, between 1933 and 1940 it had a major influence on only 8 percent of legislation, and since then its record has not improved.[2]

One important reason for the waning of congressional power has been the development of specialization within the Legislative branch. Specialization has brought about a proliferation of committees, subcommittees, and even sub-

---

[1] Lewis A. Froman, Jr., *The Congressional Process: Strategies, Rules, and Procedures* (Boston: Little, Brown, 1967), p. 3.
[2] Samuel P. Huntington, "Congressional Responses to the Twentieth Century," in *The Congress and America's Future*, edited by David B. Truman (Englewood Cliffs, N.J.: Prentice-Hall, 1965), p. 24.

committees of subcommittees. And it has become increasingly difficult for any man or group of men to weld this fragmented collection of specialized domains into a cohesive legislative organ. Some critics of Congress, in fact, argue that Congress has become so weakened by fragmentation that its chief remaining influence in the policy-making area is now a negative one, as when it uses its power to delay or, less frequently, to block bills proposed by the President.

This argument is a persuasive one. One may wonder, in recalling the doggedness with which Congress opposed President Nixon's welfare reforms or the vigor with which the Senate Foreign Relations Committee attacked the Vietnam policy during the Johnson and Nixon administrations, about the correctness of a House Report in 1962 that compared Congress to "a sometimes querulous but essentially kindly uncle who complains while furiously puffing on his pipe, but who finally, as everyone expects, gives in and hands over the allowance, grants permission, or raises his hand in blessing. . . ."[3]

But if the legislative role of Congress has declined in recent times, this development has not had the effect on national policy that the Founding Fathers might have anticipated. Congress, and especially the popularly elected House of Representatives, is not, as the Framers feared, a hotbed of radicals. The delegates to the Constitutional Convention seemed to have been haunted by nightmares of streetcorner demagoguery, and this fear of the people was reflected in the Framers' decision to have senators appointed by the various state legislatures instead of by elections—a practice changed by constitutional amendment in 1913.

The Framers were needlessly worried. Congress has proved to be anything but impetuous, with the House even more conservative in recent decades than the Senate. For example, passage of the Medicare bill, signed into law by President Lyndon B. Johnson on July 30, 1965, was delayed by Congress for twenty years from the time it was first proposed by President Harry S Truman, who had fortunately survived to witness the signing and to benefit from the law.

Slow, meticulous consideration of legislation to avoid calamitous mistakes may have been functional in the nineteenth and early twentieth centuries when the country was somewhat simpler. But the cumbersome legislative process may be one of the reasons for the contemporary decline of the power of Congress; a fast-changing world simply does not allow time for the intricate parliamentary procedures of the past.

Unable to keep up with the times, many congressmen have tried to hold them back. One-party control in southern districts, and the seniority system have kept the House even more conservative than the Senate in recent decades. Before and since the 1940s, when a radio character named Senator Claghorn made his appearance on the Fred Allen Show, there have been many long-winded Claghorns in Congress, consistently conservative on all subjects. For a truer picture of Congress, however, we must take a wider view, examining not only the backgrounds of the various kinds of men who serve in it, but the traditions and procedures of both houses.

---

[3] House Report 1406, 87th Congress, Second Session (1962), p. 7, as quoted in Huntington, "Congressional Responses to the Twentieth Century," p. 24.

Recruitment of Congressmen

Who is Elected?: The Socioeconomic Backgrounds of Congressmen

In the routine of a recent comedian, Representative Abe Lincoln, in search of a new image, hires a press agent who advises him to remember in interviews that "first he was a rail splitter and *then* an attorney." The fact is that, while Americans still tend to have a soft spot for political candidates who have made it the hard way, few United States congressmen have ever had to split rails for a living. Instead, most national legislators have been the sons of successful business or professional men, and—in contrast to Lincoln, who learned his law by candlelight in a log cabin—have received extensive formal education. Like Lincoln, however, most come from rural or small-town backgrounds and most have been lawyers.

Experience in law is desirable because it develops familiarity with legal processes useful in legislative work. Since the beginning of this century, however, there has been a decline in the proportionate number of lawyers in Congress. Entry into politics by occupational groups other than lawyers has been seen as a tendency resulting from economic development and diversification.[4] In the Ninety-second Congress in 1971, the House had 301 lawyers, 172 bankers or businessmen, 72 professors, 49 farmers, 37 journalists, and 2 clergymen. Most had served an apprenticeship in local and state politics, and most were veterans.[5]

The twentieth-century trend toward an urban society, however, is not significantly reflected in the backgrounds of congressmen. "Sixty-four percent of the members of the United States Senate in 1959 had grown up in rural or small-town environments, while only 17 percent had been raised in medium-sized cities and 19 percent in metropolitan centers."[6] And congressmen tend to remain in the country; the average legislator maintains his residence a median distance of only 22 miles from the place of his birth. In contrast, a comparable group of business executives live a median distance of 314 miles from their birthplaces.[7]

In statistical profile, the average legislator is a fifty-three-year-old white Anglo-Saxon Protestant male lawyer. But even their mounting years does not prevent most legislators from noticing that there are few women among them—only twelve women representatives and one senator in the Ninety-second Congress, although women constitute a majority in the population. Moreover, in the same legislative session, the House had only twelve black members, and the Senate, one.[8]

The disproportionately small representation of women and racial minorities in Congress, under our system of government, does not mean that the needs of these groups are necessarily neglected. However, it has been a tradition in American politics to have the candidates on a ticket reflect the major ethnic groups in a

---

[4] Roger Davidson, *The Role of the Congressman* (Indianapolis: Pegasus, 1969), pp. 40–44.

[5] *Congressional Quarterly* (January 15, 1971).

[6] Malcolm E. Jewell and Samuel C. Patterson, *The Legislative Process in the United States* (New York: Random House, 1966), p. 102.

[7] Huntington, "Congressional Responses to the Twentieth Century," p. 12.

[8] *Congressional Quarterly* (January 15, 1971).

Abraham Lincoln's life style is far from the model for congressmen today.

community—Jews, Italians, Poles, all have been able to vote for a candidate of their ethnic origin on a "balanced ticket." Accordingly, other groups in recent years—women, blacks, Puerto Ricans, Chicanos—have legitimately requested that one of their own members represent them. In 1972, for example, the issue was raised by Representative Bella Abzug (D-N.Y.) who asserted that women, blacks, Puerto Ricans, and Chicanos are grossly underrepresented in Congress by spokesmen from their own groups. The view of Representative Abzug suggests a quota system, raising the question of whether a person can truly be represented only by someone with the same ethnic, social, and economic background. If this is the case, then very few Americans enjoy adequate representation in Congress, for only about 5 percent of the total population has a background similar to that of the typical congressman. It may also be argued that under a quota system, should blacks be expected to speak for blacks and whites for whites, a polarization dangerous to society might result. Moreover, a quota system makes it impossible for a minority group to exceed its percentage of the population, thus denying it the opportunity to use elected office as a means of social mobility.

The Nature of Congressional Elections

Decentralization and Localism Unlike the President, whose constituency is the entire nation, congressmen are elected from limited geographical areas. So it is not surprising that "If there is one maxim which seems to prevail among many members it is that local matters must come first and global problems a poor second—that is, if the member of Congress is to survive politically."[9] Congressmen are dependent upon the support of hometown interests for both their election and their tenure in office. In almost all cases, if a congressman does not take care of the interests of his home district by providing it with federal jobs and expenditures and doing a number of small favors for constituents, he will not be reelected. The activist voters in a district are more concerned with whether their congressman has obtained Small Business Administration loans, federal milk programs, or money for highways than with how he stands on global issues like foreign relations or nuclear disarmament. And congressmen are also subject to pressures from local interest groups, as well as being involved in a web of favors and influence extending from party county chairmen down to the boss of the tiniest local political precinct.

This localism is behind what is sometimes called pork-barrel legislation. The term refers to measures pushed by congressmen to impress the voters back home —sometimes without regard to the consequences elsewhere. A classic example is what frequently occurs when the President attempts to close outmoded air bases. Congressmen in whose districts these bases are located may react swiftly with stern warnings about the need for well-dispersed air power to protect the nation from imminent attack, igniting groundless fears. Air bases bring jobs and economic vigor to a community. So the congressman may be speaking less from patriotism or military zeal than for the interests of local pocketbooks. In this example "pork barreling" has also contributed to the growth of what has been called the military-industrial complex. Some observers, in fact, argue that the military-industrial complex is as much a haphazard product of this local self-interest as of collusion between the military and big business.

Although, as might be expected, senators remain highly sensitive to the wishes of local interests, their outlook is usually broader than that of representatives. Entire states, especially those that are heavily industrialized, are more likely than their separate House districts to approximate the makeup of the nation as a whole. Senators, then, must respond to more diverse interests.

Security of Congressional Seats Whatever the particular characteristics of the home district may be, studies show that voters are usually very accepting of congressmen, and have been returning them to office with increasing regularity.[10] Reflecting a continuing pattern, a recent study showed that incumbents were returned to the Senate in 80 percent of the contested elections; in the House, incumbents won 92 percent of the contested elections.[11] Thus, a newly elected con-

---

[9] Senator Richard Newberger, quoted in James N. Rosenau, *National Leadership and Foreign Policy* (Princeton, N.J.: Princeton University Press, 1963), pp. 30–31.

[10] Charles O. Jones, "Inter-Party Competition for Congressional Seats," *Western Political Quarterly,* vol. 12 (September 1964), pp. 461–476.

[11] Barbara Hinkley, "Seniority in the Congressional Leadership Selection of Congress," *Midwest Journal of Political Science,* vol. 13 (November 1969), pp. 613–690.

"Will I vote for Congressman Pickering? Young man, I am Congressman Pickering."

Saturday Review, *May 2, 1970*

gressman stands a good chance of parlaying his congressional service into a lifelong career. A difference seems to be developing, however, in the margins by which senators and representatives achieve reelection. Senatorial contests have become more closely fought, while House incumbents have had easier victories than the senatorial combatants.[12]

Increasing margins of victory in the House add to the already significant number of "safe seats" in that branch of Congress. (A safe seat is one to which the same man is repeatedly reelected with little serious opposition.) One observer sees lack of turnover in membership as partially responsible for the growing "institutionalization" of the House.[13] Unless an incumbent congressman antagonizes his supporters, he will usually be renominated by his party, and in safe districts this nomination means almost automatic reelection. During the decade from 1952 to 1962, when Eisenhower twice won the Presidency by a landslide and the Democrats (in 1958) won huge congressional victories, "over two hundred House districts remained unswervingly Democratic and over one hundred thirty unswervingly Republican. Party turnover was limited to the remaining ninety-odd

---

[12] H. Douglas Price, "The Electoral Arena," in Truman, *The Congress and America's Future,* p. 44.
[13] Nelson W. Polsby, "The Institutionalization of the House of Representatives," *American Political Science Review,* vol. 63 (March 1968), pp. 144–168.

districts. . . ."[14] Thus, approximately three-fourths of all representatives during this decade were retained consistently in office, in spite of political turbulence on the presidential level. And safe seats are not, as sometimes believed, a purely southern phenomenon. They occur throughout the country, with as many in the eight most populous industrial states as in the eleven states of the South.[15]

What makes seats safe? This is an important question, and the answer points to the importance of primary elections. One authority cites the fact that safe districts are usually characterized by a low voter turnout at primaries.[16] In one-party states and districts, winning the nomination in the primary of the dominant party is tantamount to election. The turnout in primaries for Congress, especially in an off year, is likely to be very low — perhaps as low as 15 percent of the eligible voters — thus leading to control by a small clique or party machine, such as the courthouse gang which gerrymanders, bribes, logrolls, cajoles, and uses other sundry devices to remain in power.

The public's ignorance about its congressmen may also contribute to safe seats. Most people do not even know the name of their representative, and if they do, they know very little else about him — especially about his legislative record. This leads some authorities to conclude that as long as a congressman seems conscientious, smiles readily, and confines his public kissing to babies, the voters will keep him in office.

Another factor that may contribute to a legislator's long congressional life is the practice of gerrymandering, which "is defined broadly as the drawing of district lines in such a way as to give an unreasonable or unfair advantage to one party."[17] The party that receives the unfair advantage is the one that controls that state legislature, since it is this body that draws up the districts in each state. Unlike states, which are the constituencies of senators, House districts do not have permanent boundaries. Gerrymandering, however, can be hazardous; the practice has even been known to backfire. But when practiced with skill and caution, gerrymandering can greatly prolong the congressional life of a legislator.

Actually the golden days of gerrymandering — when state legislators were able to enhance their interests by creating districts extremely unequal in population size — are gone. "Rotten boroughs," as the results of this practice were called, went out with the 1964 Supreme Court ruling in *Wesberry* v. *Sanders*, that "as nearly as practicable one man's vote in a congressional election is to be worth as much as another's." This ruling required districts to be as nearly equal in population as possible, the equality to be determined every ten years by the national census. The decision necessitated a wave of congressional redistricting in which gerrymandering became more difficult, presenting new challenges to the ingenuity of stage legislators.

The principle of one man, one vote, however, has not prevented state legislators from drawing district lines in such a way as to maximize the power of those in control. Often when a representative of the party in control in the home state is

---

[14] Price, "The Electoral Arena," p. 43.

[15] Price, "The Electoral Arena," p. 44.

[16] Lewis A. Froman, Jr., *Congressmen and Their Constituencies* (Chicago: Rand McNally, 1963), pp. 28–32.

[17] Jewell and Patterson, *The Legislative Process in the United States*, p. 70. The word *gerrymander* was coined from the name of Elbridge Gerry (1744–1814) and the word *salamander:* When Gerry was governor of Massachusetts, his opponents reshaped some election districts in the state, so that they were laid out in the form of a salamander on the map, to prevent his reelection to a third term.

insecure about his margin of support, his district will be redefined to exclude opposition-controlled areas and add areas of party support that can be spared from surrounding districts without danger to the other party-held seats. Especially hard-hit have been controversial women representatives. In 1972, Boston's freshman Democrat Louise Day Hicks, whose candid opinions had made important enemies in both political camps, found her district had been extended into the conservative but unfriendly suburbs, greatly endangering her chances for reelection. And outspoken Bella Abzug, the women's and minorities' advocate from New York City, discovered that she no longer had a district. It had been carved up and divided among surrounding districts. Forced to run in another district, she attempted to unseat incumbent liberal William Ryan, and failed.

The Effects of Safe Seats: Congressmen and Their Constituents What effect does a safe seat have upon a congressman's legislative record? The evidence on this point is unclear. Some authorities argue that it tends to reduce the number of activists in Congress; that "the congressman from a safe seat usually follows the easy alternative: he stays put. He placates the dominant social forces in the district; 'protects' his district against hostile outside forces; does a great many individual favors. . . . His main commitment is to the status quo."[18]

Safe seats do not always have such a stultifying effect. But congressmen who pursue policies strongly at odds with the views of their constituents might find their margin of support dwindling. Senator J. William Fulbright (D.-Ark.) has had to fight for what otherwise might have been a classic safe seat, making certain not to run counter to the basic racial and economic sensitivities of his state so that he may advance foreign-policy views that might sour the chewing tobacco of many of his own constituents, as well as infuriate Presidents.

There are a number of possible benefits from safe seats. Relieved of the necessity for taking politically expedient positions in hard campaigning, and secure in a lifetime career as a legislator, theoretically a congressman is in a position to take a longer view of the issues. Over the years he may also develop into an expert in a particular field of legislation, such as labor or education. The use to which a particular safe seat is put seems to depend largely on the motives of its occupant. But most political observers tend to agree that the disadvantages of safe seats outweigh their advantages to the nation.

Maintained in office, in effect, by the political apathy of a large segment of their constituencies, congressmen continue to represent their own attitudes, reinforcing them by mingling with people and reading publications that hold similar views. One congressman has been quoted as saying:

You know, I am sure you will find out a congressman can do pretty much what he decides to do and he doesn't have to bother too much about criticism. I've seen plenty of cases since I've been up here where a guy will hold one economic or political position, and get along all right; and then he'll die or resign and a guy comes in who holds quite a different economic or political position and he gets along all right, too. That's the fact of the matter.[19]

---

[18] James McGregor Burns, *The Deadlock of Democracy*, (Englewood Cliffs, N.J.: Prentice-Hall, 1964), pp. 243–244, quoted in Jones, "Inter-Party Competition for Congressional Seats."

[19] Lewis A. Dexter, "The Representative and His District," in Robert L. Peabody and Nelson W. Polsby, *New Perspectives on the House of Representatives* (Chicago: Rand McNally, 1969), p. 3.

Representative Edward I. Koch (D.-New York City) confers with some of his constituents.

Thus, blame is placed directly on the electorate. And congressmen may concur in this by pointing out that their voting records are clear for the public to see. Where constituents fail to express an interest in larger issues, or in the votes of their congressmen, the representative's ability to do political favors and his appearance of activity in the home district become the brick and mortar of his power base. Congressmen differ, however, in their estimations of the political value of favors for constituents. Some feel that securing a favor for one alienates ten others; others feel that each satisfied constituent soon tells his friends of the congressman's attentiveness. But doling out favors, a function of the Legislative branch unmentioned in the Constitution, continues to take up a large portion of the time of legislators and their staffs. It is an ingrained part of a system in which legislators are strongly resistant to changes which may shake their own security, and in which new leaders with fresh ideas are likely to be discouraged.

Dispersion of Power and Influence in Congress

When the snail, the slowest of all animals, becomes too large for its shell, it sheds it and grows a new one. Congress, also, tends to be sluggish; and although its functions have grown, Congress, unlike the snail, clings to its outgrown shell.

The buck starts here: the House initiates all appropriations bills.

We have seen how the entrenchment of its members has protected the status quo, but the basic structural awkwardness of Congress has been even more restricting. Bicameralism (the division into two houses), the committee system, and weak party allegiance are the three fundamental features of this structure.

To extend the system of checks and balances into the legislative branch of government, the Founding Fathers created two independent houses, or chambers, of Congress. Each chamber has the right to veto legislation passed by the other—making the two chambers, in theory, equal in power as well as separate. But equality does not necessarily mean sameness in every respect. As in the relationship between men and women, one authority argues, it is the differences between the House and Senate that prove most interesting.[20]

First is the difference in size between the chambers—the Senate being composed of 100 members and the House, of 435. This means that each individual senator has a power advantage over each individual representative: the ratio of power of each senator to the whole Senate is theoretically 1:100, while that of each representative to the whole House is 1:435. This relative power of senators to representatives would be true in practice if each senator and representative wielded the same amount of influence. In fact, however, power within the Senate, as well as the House, is very unequally distributed.[21] The difference in size be-

---

[20] Froman, *The Congressional Process,* p. 7.
[21] The House Speaker and the chairmen of important committees may exercise much greater influence than other representatives. And there is an equal disparity in power between the Senate Majority Leader and freshman senators.

tween the two branches of Congress contributes to a difference in the tone of House and Senate proceedings. The general tone of House activity remains quite faithful to the vision of the Founding Fathers, that of an assembly of clamorous, elbowing citizens. Moreover, because of its cumbersome size, House organization is structured more formally and hierarchically than the Senate. If it were not, it is unlikely that the House would be able to function.

The atmosphere of the Senate, with its aura of confidence, might be compared to that of the alumni club of a prestigious university. Fewer in number than representatives, senators achieve a higher status by becoming known to a larger public. An important source of the Senate's more dignified tone is the length of office of its members — six years, in contrast to the two-year term in the House. The longer term enables senators to develop into more statesmanlike figures than representatives, who are almost always thinking of reelection or running for office. The six-year term also gives senators more time to build a political image and a following back home. Senators receive higher pay than representatives, and they are more likely to be wealthy when they come into office, because it takes more money to campaign for election to the Senate than to the House.

Finally, there are certain differences in the constitutionally assigned functions of each chamber of Congress. Thus, the two bodies hold power in different areas. The House, for instance, is said to hold the power of the purse, for all appropriations bills must originate in that chamber. The Senate, on the other hand, holds power over treaties and presidential appointments, both of which must be approved by a two-thirds vote.

The Committee System

The operation of both the House and Senate depends heavily upon committees — twenty standing committees for the House, sixteen for the Senate, each specializing in a different subject area. These committees are the backbone of the congressional decision-making process. The popular image of fiery congressional debate before packed galleries, while the fate of the nation hangs in the balance, is largely myth. A bill's outcome is usually determined in committee well before it ever reaches the floor of Congress. Most bills do not even get this far. Only one quarter reached the floor, for example, in the House during the Eighty-second Congress (1951–1952) — the largest percentage of all, in a study covering selected Congresses from 1911 to 1967. In the Sixty-second Congress (1931–1933), a low of only one out of every twenty-eight bills was reported out of committee for general House debate.[22] All bills automatically begin their congressional journey by being referred to the proper committee. In order to reach the floor of Congress, a bill must then pass through the intense scrutiny of committee and conflicting personal interests, pressures, and ideologies. Few bills make it to the floor for a vote.

There is one preeminent justification for the often criticized committee system: it is the only workable means for Congress to fulfill the demands of its enormous

[22] Figures from U.S. Congress, *House Calendars and History of Legislation,* 89th Congress, 1967, pp. 324–325. These statistics are slightly inflated by the fact that several representatives will sometimes concurrently introduce identical bills into the House. This is a mere formality that occurs because, unlike senators, House members may not co-sponsor a bill. And several representatives may wish to share the credit for a particular proposal.

Herbert Stein, chairman of the Council of Economic Advisers, contributes his expertise in testimony before the Joint Economic Committee on Administration Policy.

work load. Each year, Congress is deluged with thousands of bills, so many that a senator or representative could not possibly amass enough information to judge each of them intelligently. Instead, in the majority of instances, he relies upon the expert opinion of the committee as a quick guide to decision-making. On its recommendation alone, he will frequently vote for a bill—especially when committee agreement is unanimous. Headline-grabbing issues that bring an avalanche of voter mail are the rare exception, so a congressman is not necessarily ignoring his constituency by following committee advice. Most bills, in fact, are made so difficult to read by technicalities, and are frequently so trivial in nature, that the average voter would find them either too difficult or too boring to read.

The concentrated expertise of the committees, aided by the employment of staff assistants, serves Congress in its efforts to keep watch on the increasingly complex workings of the administrative bureaucracies—an activity that has gone so far that it is argued that investigative probing has replaced legislation as the major activity of Congress. Between 1950 and 1962, each session of Congress conducted more critical investigations than all of the Congresses combined in the nineteenth century.[23] Special committees are formed for the development of the special expertise required to accomplish this function.

Committees perform another valuable function by holding open educational hearings to inform other legislators on issues of broad national concern. These forums help congressmen to gauge public reaction to the issue as well as to examine the problem itself. Usually they do so when the issue is too controversial and widely publicized for them to base their votes solely on the recommendations of a committee. On such issues, legislators may be called upon to make decisions that are based more upon party policy, constituent sentiment, or their own consciences. The 1972 hearings to explore the possibility of amnesty for draft resisters was this form of committee activity. They also demonstrated a frequent side effect of such hearings – they may bestow legitimacy on a previously taboo subject. Several months before the congressional hearings, draft-evasion amnesty was considered too hot to touch in open public discussions; in general, the issue was confined to such forums as underground coffee houses. Senator Fulbright's 1966 foreign-policy hearings served a similar purpose in opening up discussions about the legitimacy of the Vietnam War.

There are, however, fundamental objections to the committee system – in particular, the objection that it fragments the decision-making process. The multiple power centers created by the committee system make it very difficult for Congress to operate as a smooth-running legislative engine, especially in the absence of forceful centralized authority or strong party leadership.

Committee Leadership: The Seniority System Committees are usually headed by the longest-serving members, since chairmen rise to their positions through seniority. The party which holds the majority of the seats in that house of Congress will also hold the majority of committee seats and will make its ranking member in a given committee the chairman. The ranking member of the minority party on the committee may also wield substantial influence. He is, in a sense, second in command of the committee; if his party wins a majority in the chamber, he will assume the position of committee chairman. In addition, other ranking members of the majority party are important, for the committee chairman typically assigns them to leadership positions on various subcommittees. Influence on a committee, however, does not necessarily accrue to those with the most years of service. For many years, the chairman of the Education and Labor committees, of which Adam Clayton Powell (D.-N.Y.) was ranking majority member, gave subcommittee chairmanships to other members; until Powell finally became chairman, he was effectively shut out of power on the committee.[24]

A committee chairman possesses formidable *personal* influence from long years of congressional service. Besides personal influences, he also has *formal* power to set meeting times, determine agendas, preside over meetings, form subcommittees and decide who should serve on them, hire staff, and manage or delegate the management of bills on the floor of Congress. Possessing these formidable sources of influence, the chairman alone can block almost any bill. Chairmen do not generally act so arbitrarily, however, although they have often been charged with despotic use of their power. The role of the committee chairman vis-à-vis his committee members is more like that described by one authority, who said:

[23] George P. Galloway, *The Legislative Process in Congress* (New York: Thomas Y. Crowell, 1955), p. 166.
[24] Hinkley, "Seniority in the Congressional Leadership Selection of Congress," pp. 620 and 629.

A chairman who is the acknowledged expert in his field, whose skill in political maneuver is at least as great as that of his colleagues, and who exploits his prerogatives to the fullest can dominate his committee or subcommittee. But his dominance may well proceed with the acquiescence of the majority of the committee. They may, and usually do expect him to lead. Since a majority of any committee can make its rules, it is impossible for a chairman to dictate committee decisions against the wishes of a cohesive and determined majority of its members—at least in the long run. The acquiescence of his sub-committee chairmen will be especially crucial. On the other hand, since time is of the essence in legislative maneuver, a short run autocracy may be decisive in shaping House decisions.[25]

It is theoretically possible for a determined majority of committee members to override the wishes of the chairman, but there are strong congressional traditions against doing this. And the chairman's personal power makes such rebellion very dangerous for most committee members. Thus, a chairman's power usually remains secure. For example, the late Mendel Rivers (D.-S.C.) for many years had such a strong grip upon the House Armed Services Committee, and such close ties to the Pentagon, that his power in military matters was said to rival the President's. A former chairman of the House Rules Committee, Judge Howard Smith, a crusty and reactionary Virginian, succeeded in effectively blocking administration measures beginning in 1939—defying his own party's opposition in a power struggle climaxed by his monumental battle with President Kennedy, which led to the expansion in 1962 of the Rules Committee from twelve to fifteen members.[26] Kennedy was more fortunate with, but no less dependent on, the support of the powerful Wilbur Mills of Arkansas, chairman of the House Ways and Means Committee. "The President had to have Mills' support, and when he got it on the tax, trade, and debt-ceiling bills, those bills passed the House. Mills declined to support the President's medical-care bill, and it died that year in Mills' committee."[27]

Criticism has been leveled at the seniority system from several angles. First, as shown in Tables 6-1 and 6-2, it entrenches congressmen from safe districts. This means that, in addition to the likelihood that they are older men who have served in Congress many years, most committee chairmen have been either southern Democrats or small-town Midwest Republicans. Eleven out of sixteen Senate committee chairmen and nine out of twenty House chairmen in the Ninety-first Congress were southerners with safe seats—so safe that many of them had run unopposed in the preceding election. Generally, there have been few committee chairmen from urban industrial areas, but the Supreme Court redistricting decision and independent population shifts are starting to even the balance.

In addition, there is a built-in unfairness in a system which may determine a congressman's future power in Congress by his initial committee assignment. Hence, among equally experienced congressmen, a political or personal advantage places some in positions of greater potential power than others.[28]

Some argument can be made in favor of seniority, if not enough to outweigh

---

[25] Richard F. Fenno, Jr., "The Internal Distribution of Influence: The House," in Truman, *The Congress and America's Future,* p. 56.

[26] Charles O. Jones, "Joseph G. Cannon and Howard W. Smith: An Essay on the Limits of Leadership in the House of Representatives," in *Congressional Behavior,* edited by Nelson W. Polsby (New York: Random House, 1970), pp. 214–217.

[27] Neil MacNeil, *Forge of Democracy* (New York: McKay, 1964), p. 265.

[28] Hinkley, "Seniority in the Congressional Leadership Selection of Congress," pp. 620 and 629.

House Ways and Means Committee Chairman Wilbur Mills: Presidents seek his backing for their legislative proposals.

its flaws. Impartiality in awarding chairmanships has the virtue of circumventing the intrigue and favoritism which would otherwise be very likely to occur in the selection of a chairman. Seniority, by giving the chairmanship to the person with longest experience on the committee, at least increases the likelihood that he will be knowledgeable. There is also the somewhat questionable advantage that most chairmen come from safe districts, so they can, if they wish, ignore pressures by constituents in guiding their committees. Many critics of the seniority system have proposed that chairmanships be awarded on merit; the answer has been that congressional merit is, like beauty, a subject on which opinions differ. The seniority system allows the longevity of a chairman to delay for many years the assumption of the chairmanship by a younger man; but competence cannot be judged merely on the basis of age. Much of the anti-seniority sentiment has come from liberals who have seen the system consistently awarding chairmanships to conservatives.

The Party Structure in Congress

The third key pillar in the congressional structure is the party system. Studies suggest that when a congressman votes he looks first to the party. It determines his vote more consistently than any other single influence, usually outweighing constituent pressure. "For most of its members a party label stands for some things which they share in common—an emotional attachment, an interest in getting and keeping power, some perceptions of the political world, and perhaps certain broad policy orientations."[29] We have seen that Congress has become frag-

---

[29] Fenno, "Internal Distribution of Influence: The House," p. 62.

Table 6-1   Senate Leadership and Committee Chairmen

Position	Name	Age (in 1972)[a]	Year Entered Congress and/or Year Entered Senate	State (including population) in 1970	% of Vote in Last Election	ADA Rating[b]	Carswell Nomination[c]	Cut in Military Budget[d]
Senate Leadership								
Majority Leader	Michael J. Mansfield-D.	69	1943 & 1953	Montana (694,409)	61	75	–	+
Majority Whip	Robert Byrd-D.	54	1958	West Virginia (1,744,237)	78	3	+	+
Minority Leader	Hugh Scott-R.	71	1941 & 1959	Pennsylvania (11,793,909)	52	31	+	–
Minority Whip	Robert P. Griffin-R.	48	1947 & 1966	Michigan (8,875,083)	56	28	+	–
Committee Chairmen[e]								
Aeronautical & Space Sciences	Clinton P. Anderson	76	1941 & 1949	New Mexico (1,016,000)	53	31	abs.	abs.
Agriculture & Forestry	Herman E. Talmadge	61	1956	Georgia (4,589,575)	78	3	+	–
Appropriations	John L. McClellan	76	1935 & 1943	Arkansas (1,923,295)	unopposed	0	+	–
Armed Services	John C. Stennis	70	1947	Mississippi (2,216,912)	88	9	+	–
Banking and Currency	John J. Sparkman	72	1937 & 1946	Alabama (3,444,165)	60	13	+	–
Commerce	Warren G. Magnuson	66	1937 & 1944	Washington (3,409,169)	65	72	–	–
District of Columbia	Thomas F. Eagleton	42	1968	Missouri (4,677,399)	51	91	–	+

Committee	Senator	Age[a]	Year elected	State (population)	Percent[ ]	Liberal rating[b]	Carswell[c]	Military budget[d]
Finance	Russell B. Long	53	1948	Louisiana (3,643,180)	unopposed	13	+	–
Foreign Relations	J. William Fulbright	66	1943 & 1945	Arkansas (1,923,295)	59	66	–	+
Government Operations	Sam J. Ervin	76	1954	North Carolina (5,082,059)	61	13	+	–
Interior and Insular Affairs	Henry M. Jackson	59	1941 & 1953	Washington (3,409,169)	82	56	–	–
Judiciary	James O. Eastland	67	1943	Mississippi (2,216,912)	66	3	+	–
Labor and Public Welfare	Harrison A. Williams	42	1958	New Jersey (7,168,164)	54	94	–	+
Post Office and Civil Service	William G. McGee	57	1959	Wyoming (332,416)	(not available)	47	–	–
Public Works	Jennings Randolph	70	1958	West Virginia (1,744,237)	60	59	+	+
Rules and Administration	B. Everett Jordan	75	1958	North Carolina (5,082,059)	56	43	+	–

Source: Information from Michael Barone, Grant Ujifusa, Douglas Matthews, The Almanac of American Politics: The Senators, the Representatives—their Records, States and Districts, 1972 (Boston: Gambit, 1972).

Average age of all senators is 57.
[b] Americans for Democratic Action's Liberal rating; scale from 0 to 100.
[c] Carswell nomination: President Nixon's nomination of G. Harrold Carswell, a conservative, for Associate Justice of the Supreme Court. Debate centered around the adequacy of his judicial and ethical qualifications. Vote taken April 8, 1970; defeated 45-51 (+ = for Carswell; – = against Carswell).
[d] Cut in military budget: Military-spending limit, HR 17123, Department of Defense appropriations provided for a ceiling of $66 billion on all Department of Defense spending in fiscal 1972; would result in a $5.2 billion cut in proposed $71.2 billion budget. Vote taken August 28, 1970; defeated 31-42. (+ = for cut in military budget; – = against cut in military budget).
[e] Note that all committee chairmen, as well as subcommittee chairmen, are currently Democrats, as regulations stipulate that the majority party holds all chairmanships. The Democrats have been the majority party, and thus held chairmanships, since 1954.

Table 6-2   House Leadership and Committee Chairmen

Position	Name	Age (in 1972)[a]	Year Entered Congress	District	% of Vote in Last Election	ADA Rating[b]	No-Knock Vote[c]	SST Vote[d]
House Leadership								
Speaker	Carl B. Albert-D.	63	1946	3rd Okla.	unopposed	48	+	+
Majority Leader	Hale Boggs-D.	58	1947	2nd La.	69	48	+	+
Majority Whip	Thomas P. O'Neill-D.	59	1952	8th Mass.	unopposed	76	+	−
Minority Leader	Gerald P. Ford-R.	58	1949	5th Mich.	61	12	+	+
Minority Whip	Leslie C. Arends-R.	76	1935	17th Ill.	62	20	+	+
House Committee Chairmen[e]								
Agriculture	William R. Poage	72	1937	11th Tex.	unopposed	8	abs.	+
Appropriations	George H. Mahon	71	1935	19th Tex.	unopposed	8	+	+
Armed Services	F. Edward Hébert	71	1940	1st La.	87	4	+	+
Banking and Currency	Wright Patman	68	1929	1st Tex.	78	24	+	−
District of Columbia	John L. Macmillan	(not available)	1939	6th S.C.	65	4	+	+
Education and Labor	Carl D. Perkins	56	1949	7th Ky.	75	40	+	+
Foreign Affairs	Thomas E. Morgan	65	1945	26th Penn.	68	56	abs.	+
Governmental Operations	Chet Holifield	68	1942	19th Calif.	70	60	−	+
House Administration	Wayne Hays	60	1948	18th Ohio	60	32	abs.	+
Interior and Insular Affairs	Wayne N. Aspinall	75	1949	4th Colo.	55	28	abs.	+
Internal Security	Richard H. Ichord	45	1961	8th Mo.	54	12	abs.	+
Interstate and Foreign Commerce	Harley O. Staggers	64	1949	2nd W. Va.	63	52	+	+
Judiciary	Emanuel Celler	83	1923	10th N.Y.	73	80	−	−
Merchant Marine and Fisheries	Edward A. Garmatz	69	1947	3rd Md.	unopposed	52	+	+
Post Office and Civil Service	Thaddeus J. Dulski	56	1959	41st N.Y.	80	80	+	−
Public Works	John A. Blatnik	60	1947	8th Minn.	76	76	abs.	−
Rules	William M. Colmer	82	1933	5th Miss.	90	0	+	+
Science and Astronautics	George P. Miller	81	1945	8th Calif.	69	56	+	+
Standards of Official Conduct	Charles M. Price	67	1945	24th Ill.	68	56	+	+
Veterans' Affairs	Olin E. Teague	61	1946	6th Tex.	unopposed	8	+	+
Ways and Means	Wilbur Mills	62	1939	2nd Ark.	unopposed	12	abs.	+

Source: *Information from Michael Barone, Grant Ujifusa, Douglas Matthews, The Almanac of American Politics: The Senators, the Representatives—their Records, States and Districts. 1972 (Boston: Gambit, 1972).*

[a] Average age of all representatives is 49.
[b] Americans for Democratic Action's liberal rating; scale from 0 to 100.
[c] No-Knock: Police search authority, HR16196, D.C. Crime bill. Most controversial feature was "no-knock clause," granting police power to obtain a search warrant that would give them the right to enter a building without notice if giving notice might endanger officers or cause destruction of evidence. Vote taken March 19, 1970. Pass: 294–47. (+ = for no-knock; − = against no-knock).
[d] SST: Supersonic transport plane, HR8190, Second Supplement Appropriations bill. Provided $85.3 million for continued construction of two proto-types instead. Vote taken May 12, 1971; passed 201–197. (+ = for SST; − = against SST).
[e] Note that all committee chairmen, as well as subcommittee chairmen, are currently Democrats, as regulations stipulate that the majority party holds all chairmanships. The Democrats have been the majority party, and thus held chairmanships, since 1954.

There is not a moment to be wasted in the exchange of ideas during this typical visit of the New York State Democratic Party delegation to the House.

mented into various specialized committees. Party loyalty acts as one of the few central unifying forces in Congress, since it joins together the men who sit on these different committees. Parties also control the committee assignments of their own members; each party is allowed a number of committee positions proportionate to the total number of congressional seats it captured in the last election. This further strengthens the unifying effect of our two-party system—in sharp contrast to the fragmentation caused by the multiparty systems of most European legislatures.

While congressmen prefer to follow party policy whenever possible, Congress by no means has a disciplined party system such as that in Great Britain. In British politics, a member of Parliament can lose his seat if he defects from his party on a single vote. But in the United States the average congressman votes against his party roughly one-third of the time.[30] In other words, his vote conflicts with that of the *majority* of his fellow Democrats or Republicans on almost one out of three issues. As a group, southern Democrats and liberal Republicans are the most consistent defectors from party ranks.

. . . the unitary party label also masks a pluralism of geographical, social, ideological and organizational sources of identification, support and loyalty. . . . Different House members owe their election to different elements in the party coalition, and they can be expected, in the interests of survival, to respond to their own special local sources of support. Each party label therefore papers over disparate factional blocs and conflicting policy viewpoints. Inside the House as well as outside, the parties remain loose coalitions of social interests and local party organizations.[31]

[30] Froman, *The Congressional Process,* p. 6. This study covered the period from 1961 to 1964.
[31] Fenno, "Internal Distribution of Influence: The House," pp. 61–62.

Table 6-3　**Party Unity Votes**

	Total roll calls	Party unity roll calls	Percentage of total
Both chambers: 1970	684	219	32
Senate	418	147	35
House of Representatives	266	72	27
Both chambers: 1969	422	144	34
Senate	245	89	36
House of Representatives	177	55	31
Both chambers: 1968	514	172	33
Senate	281	90	32
House of Representatives	233	82	35
Both chambers: 1967	560	198	35
Senate	315	109	35
House of Representatives	245	89	36

Source: Congressional Quarterly Almanac *(Washington, D.C.: Congressional Quarterly, Inc., 1971), p. 1140.*

This is true for the Senate as well as the House. Thus, it is often impossible to determine exactly why a congressman votes as he does on a particular issue, or to separate the factors that influence him. His party affiliation and local support seem especially interdependent. A congressman receives his local support largely because he belongs to a particular party; he may also have chosen to run as a member of that party in order to capitalize on its local strength.

The finer details of legislative dynamics should come more sharply into focus in the following separate discussions of the two chambers of Congress, and, finally, in an examination of how all of these forces act when Congress responds to a legislative proposal from the President.

The Legislative Process

The House of Representatives

The size of the House of Representatives creates a two-pronged problem: before it can begin to function, the House must divide power and assign clearly defined tasks to each member; it must also guard against the crippling personal conflicts that might arise among 435 men of diverse temperament and ideology, often thrown into close contact for long periods of time while working at a strenuous pace. So the House must find ways to protect itself against internal conflicts. As with a space-exploration team, it does this by requiring each member to subordinate his personal feelings and emotions to the smooth functioning of the mission as a whole. This is effected by a hierarchically organized set of positions, procedures, and informal norms that defines the role of each congressman. At the controls is the Speaker of the House.

The Speaker of the House During the nineteenth and early twentieth centuries the position of Speaker offered an opportunity for almost unlimited personal control of the House. The autocratic reigns of Speakers "Czar" Thomas B. Reed of Maine from 1889 to 1891 and "Uncle Joe" Cannon of Illinois shortly after the turn of the century took full advantage of every opportunity to put their personal imprint on all the House activities of this period. The House finally revolted against Speaker Cannon in 1910, stripping some formal powers from the position of Speaker. Most important among these powers were the appointment of committee chairmen and the right to assign rules for House debate to a bill.[32]

Despite the reduction in its formal scope, the position of Speaker still remains the most powerful in the House—if its occupant has the political skill and personal influence to fully exploit its opportunities. The Speakership of Sam Rayburn (D.-Tex.), during periods of Democratic dominance from 1940 to 1961, while not tyrannical like those of Reed or Cannon, was clearly a forceful one, because of Rayburn's personal powers of persuasion. When "Mr. Sam" was against something, the House rarely overruled him. Joseph W. Martin, Jr. (R.-Mass.), for many years Republican Minority Leader while the Democrats held Congress and Rayburn was Speaker, became Speaker during the Eighty-third Congress (1953–1954) when the Republicans won control. Unlike Rayburn, Martin was reluctant to use excessive zeal, which, he said, lost votes. "Well, I had a program to get through and you don't give a fellow a crack on the jaw to make him agree with you. I believe in persuasion and conciliation."[33] Rayburn's two successors, John McCormick (D.-Mass.) and Carl Albert (D.-Okla.), have generally held much the same philosophy of leadership as Martin's.

What weapons does the Speaker possess? His power is both formal and—probably more important—informal. The Speaker's official authority stems from his role in directing certain House activities. He presides over House proceedings, deciding who will or will not be recognized; appoints special (but not standing) committees; determines, if there is a question, to which committee a bill will be initially sent; and, in addition, fulfills other parliamentary functions.

Informally, the Speaker is the leader of the majority party and has a crucial influence on party committee assignments. In this role he

avails himself of his own good personal relations with members, his reputation for fairness, for integrity, for trustworthiness and for political judgment. He extends his own capacities by using the talents of those friends and protégés whom he locates in every House group. Through them he maintains a line into every committee, every bloc, and every informal group. With them, "the Speaker's boys," he shares his party leadership and in return, secures a broader base of support than he might otherwise get. Through personal friendship—such as that which existed between Sam Rayburn and Joseph Martin —he maintains a line into the opposition party.[34]

The Speaker is nominated by a party caucus at the beginning of each congressional term. Technically, he must be elected by an open vote of the entire House. There is, however, a tradition of rigid party unity on this matter, so the man who is nominated by the party that holds the majority of House seats inevitably receives all of their votes and is elected Speaker.

---

[32] Because chairmen are the most powerful members of committees, the Speaker derived considerable power from his ability to appoint chairmen. If the Speaker did not assign an appropriate rule to a bill, he could virtually kill it. The power to assign bills was later given to the Rules Committee (described in the pages that follow), and subsequently made its chairman one of the most powerful members of the House.

[33] MacNeil, *Forge of Democracy*, p. 93.

[34] Fenno, "Internal Distribution of Influence: The House," p. 67.

Carl Albert (D.-Okla.) was elected in January 1971 to succeed John McCormick as Speaker of the House.

Party Leadership Positions in the House The top party leadership positions in the House—Majority Floor Leader and Majority Whip—usually have far less influence than the Speaker. The minority party also has a leader and a whip. Unlike the Speaker, these posts originate with party tradition; they have no formal or constitutional basis. The Floor Leader, as the name suggests, is in charge of the practical management of party policy. As a shepherd of sorts for party interests, he marshals either support or opposition for bills in the various committees, as well as guiding strategy on the House floor. The Majority Leader works closely with the Speaker, assisting him in many duties and often acting as his spokesman. Floor leadership is also the usual training ground for future House Speakers.

Assisting the floor leaders are the whips of each party.[35] The role of congressional whips in relation to other party members can be likened—on a more dignified level, it is hoped—to that of local leaders of party machines around the country, who have been known to distribute chickens, babysit, or even hustle their supporters out of bars in order to get them to the polls to vote. They also act as liaisons between the House leadership of each party and the rank-and-file members. As for the qualifications required for these House leadership posts, "Successful Speakers and majority leaders are men who appeal personally to their fellow House members and not men whose main appeal is to party elements outside the House. They have been men whose devotion to the House was considered greater than any devotion to ideological causes."[36] In other words, their respect for the House itself as an institution has outweighed even their concern for party or national interests.

The Majority or Minority Leaders in the House are chosen at conferences or caucuses of their respective parties. Each party has a *committee on committees* to appoint members to the twenty standing committees of the House.

---

[35] While there may be a certain analogy, the term *whip* does not literally refer to a long cord of leather—it comes from fox-hunting: the "whipper-in" keeps stray hounds from leaving the pack.
[36] Fenno, "Internal Distribution of Influence: The House," p. 63.

The House Rules Committee Looming in the path of every bill that enters the House is the Rules Committee—with power rivaling that of the Speaker or most other committees combined. Almost all bills must face this committee, whose conservative leadership has been the bane of liberal sponsors. The Rules Committee decides if, and under what conditions, a bill will be sent to the floor of Congress. These conditions include how much time will be allotted to a bill, whether amendments may be added, and if so, what kind—the functions previously performed by the Speaker, until the 1910 revolt against Speaker Cannon deprived the Speaker's office of some of its powers. By refusing to assign such "rules" for floor debate, the committee can in fact bury a bill.

Although it is true that the Rules Committee is often referred to as a "graveyard" for legislation, it should be remembered that committees in general serve a "burial" function for about 90 percent of all legislation introduced in Congress each session. What sets the Rules Committee apart from all other committees is that it has the power to bury or delay bills that legislative committees want to reach the floor. Historically, the power of the Rules Committee has been strong or weak, roughly in inverse relationship to the power of the Speaker and the party leadership. Its power started to grow after 1910 and the action taken against the autocratic power of Speaker Cannon. Still, in the early New Deal days the Rules Committee generally worked in tandem with the House leadership. This changed, however, when southern Democrats began their defection to a "conservative coalition" with Republicans—a coalition which is symbolized for most observers in the warfare waged between Speaker Rayburn and Democrat "Judge" Howard Smith, the long-time Rules Committee chairman from Virginia. Since the late 1930s, the Rules Committee has been controlled by southern congressmen—who tend to be even more locked into the status quo than many of their conservative counterparts outside the committee. This conservative control turns the Rules Committee into a formidable barrier for a President with liberal inclinations, and reformers have mounted a series of assaults on its powers.

An important factor contributing to the power of the Rules Committee since the New Deal has been the power of the chairman over the will of the majority on the committee. Besides the formal power of Rules Committee chairmen, there has been considerable personal influence based on the personalities of chairmen. For example, Judge Smith would conveniently be out of town when it suited his purposes, and Adolph Sabath (D.-Ill.), chairman from 1940 to 1952, once went to extreme lengths to get his way over the second-ranking Democrat on the committee, Eugene Cox of Georgia. At question was a resolution to change the rules of the committee so that any member could call up a bill for a vote in spite of the chairman's objection. Sabath cried out to Cox that passage of the resolution was certain to kill him for he had a weak heart. Cox was unmoved, whereupon Sabath collapsed at his feet. "My God," Cox exclaimed, "I've killed him." Several committee members leaped to Sabath's aid, carrying him to a couch in his office, where they left Clarence Brown of Ohio to watch him as they rushed off to get medical help. To Brown's astonishment, Sabath opened one eye and winked at him. "Why, you old rascal, there's nothing wrong with you!" Brown exploded. "Well," said Sabath smiling, "Mr. Cox didn't get his resolution, did he?"[37]

The House has two procedures to pry legislation out of the Rules Committee;

[37] MacNeil, *Forge of Democracy: The House of Representatives*, p. 103.

both have enjoyed little success. A discharge petition can be used to compel bills from the Rules Committee or any legislative committee. After a specified time has elapsed and 218 members have signed a petition, it must be agreed to by a majority on the floor and may then be called up by any signer. However, since 1937, though over two hundred petitions have been filed and a much smaller number have been placed on the Discharge Calendar (having accumulated the required 218 signatures), only a handful have passed the House and only two bills have become law in that way (the Fair Standard Act of 1938 and the Federal Pay Raise Act of 1960).

The second mechanism for forcing a bill out of the Rules Committee is Calendar Wednesday; it has been used successfully only twice since 1950 — most recently in 1960. At a specified time the committees are called in turn, and the chairman of a committee whose bill is held up by the Rules Committee can call up the bill under ground rules limiting debate to two hours and requiring that all work on the bill be completed that day. Calendar Wednesday has not been used often because of its unwieldy nature (a committee can bring up only one bill and has to wait its turn alphabetically) and because of its time constraints.

Other means of diminishing the power of the Rules Committee have been attempted periodically with varying degrees of success. Liberals inspired by the spirit of the "New Frontier," led by President Kennedy and aided by Speaker Rayburn, challenged the Rules Committee in 1961. They attempted to purge from the committee a southern Democrat, William Colmer (D.-Miss.), who had supported Richard Nixon in the presidential campaign. The combined might of his opponents was not enough to dislodge the rebellious Democrat. However, President Kennedy *was* able to add two seats to the committee, seats which were quickly filled with more sympathetic congressmen.[38]

Reformers again attacked the Rules Committee in 1965, riding on the landslide Democratic victory in the Johnson-versus-Goldwater campaign. A twenty-one-day rule was enacted which was instrumental in rerouting crucial "Great Society" legislation around the hostile Rules Committee and onto the floor. Under a twenty-one-day rule, if the Speaker recognized a committee chairman whose legislation had been bottled up in the Rules Committee for twenty-one calendar days, a majority vote could bring the legislation to the floor. The twenty-one-day rule was far more useful than other unwieldy procedures which remain on the books, such as discharge petitions or Calendar Wednesday. Although it was used successfully only eight times in the entire Eighty-ninth Congress — six in 1965 and two in 1966 — its influence was wider than these figures indicate. Threatening to use the twenty-one-day rule often produced reluctant Rules Committee action.[39]

The twenty-one-day rule, however, was short-lived; like a similar reform adopted in 1949, it was abolished two years later. The 1967 rejection was, however, accompanied by a partial limitation on what had been the almost arbitrary power of the committee's chairman to set meeting dates for the Rules Committee and

---

[38] Milton Cummings, Jr. and Robert L. Peabody, "The Decision to Enlarge the Committee on Rules: An Analysis of the 1961 Vote," in Peabody and Polsby, *New Perspectives on the House of Representatives,* pp. 253–280.

[39] Douglas M. Fox and Charles H. Clapp, "The House Rules Committee and the Programs of the Kennedy and Johnson Administrations," *Midwest Journal of Political Science,* vol. 14 (November 1970), pp. 667–672.

to table legislation without a majority vote.[40] Some authorities argue that these repeated assaults have taken a toll—that the obstructive power of the House Rules Committee has actually diminished in recent years. This is not certain; but even if its strength has been partially limited, the House Rules Committee still remains a central bastion of power, usually controlled by a southern conservative chairman. Although he is almost as powerful as the President, few people today know his name or what he stands for.

House Norms Entrenched custom in the House should not be viewed as a completely obstructionist force, however. A series of norms and informal traditions widely revered by House members prevent the process of legislating and bureaucracy-watching from being torn apart by irreparable personal conflicts. Fundamental among these is the apprenticeship-protégé system. Like future business executives, freshman legislators are expected to start at the bottom. In this apprenticeship period they are supposed to devote themselves to all of the less glamorous legislative tasks—quietly cultivating the good will of their constituents, carefully learning the procedural rules of the House, studying to develop expertise in a committee area, attending congressional sessions regularly but rarely speaking. Newcomers to the House must leave the spotlight to their congressional elders; cutting House sessions to appear on national TV, or to go junketing around the world, is a luxury of veteran legislators. Above all, the key to House advancement is cooperation—cooperation with party leaders, fellow legislators, and even important members of the opposition party. In this way a new representative can prove that he is a true "House man," dedicated to the institution and its maintenance. If he is successful in demonstrating this dedication to one of the more influential House leaders, or perhaps the general party leadership, a legislator will be raised to the informal status of protégé. This usually happens around the third term in office. It means he is a man to watch. He may then be assigned to one of the more prestigious committees or perhaps to a minor leadership post. At this point, visions of an eventual floor leadership or even the Speaker's chair will begin, with some justification, to glimmer in the mind of our upward-oriented legislator. Expectations of this sort help make bearable the possible discontent of junior members—born perhaps of seeing the positions of real power monopolized by men with long years of service. Such defined steps along the route to House leadership also help prevent no-holds-barred scrambles for power at all levels.

The apprentice-protégé system, however, does make junior legislators more fearful of endangering their congressional careers by "rocking the boat"—for instance, by proposing bold innovative legislation. Thus, this informal apprentice-protégé ladder also serves to reinforce the congressional status quo.

A final but very pervasive lubricant of House proceedings is usually termed "reciprocity." What reciprocity really amounts to is the time-tested practice of "you take care of me, I'll take care of you."

On this basis committees negotiate treaties of reciprocity ranging from "I will stay

---

[40] Douglas M. Fox and Charles H. Clapp, "The House Rules Committee's Agenda-Setting Function, 1961–1968," *Journal of Politics*, vol. 32 (May 1970), pp. 440–443.

out of your specialty if you will stay out of mine" to "I'll support your bill if you will support mine." Committee leaders share the desire to preserve their autonomy within the House and will come to each other's aid when they perceive a threat to the committee system in general. The survival of them all demands and produces a norm of mutual respect for one another.[41]

Reciprocity, or *logrolling*, works not only between committees but in relationships between individual congressmen. In the highly improbable circumstance, for example, that a bill legalizing undersized-trout fishing were to be proposed by a congressman from Maine, a Michigan congressman, in reciprocation for support of his own measure to require automatic window panes on all new automobiles, might agree to support the trout bill. Compromise then joins cooperation as the second of the two fundamental norms of the House—norms which reduce conflict, smoothing the ongoing operation of the institution as a whole. Similarly, bargaining and the other power distributions already described may promote harmony in House operations. Whether these procedures always work to the ultimate good of the nation is open to question. However, there is something to be said for the view of Jeremy Bentham that the "good of the nation" is the sum of individual good.

The Senate

Does an "Inner Club" Run the Senate? Some authorities have maintained that the Senate is ruled by an "inner club" or so-called establishment. This club is said to be made up of a traditional mix of southern Democrats and northern conservatives and certain other prestigious senators by dint of their personal qualities. Although these observers agree about who is in the club, they differ about the specific requirements for club membership. One view emphasizes the more visible lines of formal institutional power, especially committee chairmanships. According to Senator Clark,

. . . under a custom which has grown up over the years of following the rule of seniority in making committee assignments . . . the result has been that those who have been here longest have become chairmen of committees, and as such chairmen, have exercised virtual control over the distribution of favors including committee assignments and other prerequisites of office in the Senate, and largely—although not always . . . determine who shall be selected to posts of leadership in this body.[42]

Like William White, who covered the Senate for the *New York Times* and was a personal confidant of Lyndon Johnson when he was Majority Floor Leader, some writers insist that club membership is based more on *personal* qualities— that there is a "Senate type" of man who, because of his personal qualities, may wield considerable informal, as well as formal, influence. Illustrating this informal influence at its most extreme, White refers to a 1956 proposal to establish a joint committee for overseeing the Central Intelligence Agency. "Under their bleak and languid frowns the whole project simply died; a wind had blown upon it from the Inner Club and its erstwhile sponsors simply left it."[43] Whether or not its code of behavior does culminate in an "Inner Club" of such intimidating

---

[41] Fenno, "Internal Distribution of Influence: The House," p. 73.

[42] Joseph Clark and other senators, *The Senate Establishment* (New York: Hill and Wang, 1963), pp. 22–23.

[43] William S. White, *The Citadel* (Boston: Houghton Mifflin, 1957), Ch. 7.

Members of the press eagerly await the remarks of Senator Jacob Javits (R.-N.Y.), second from the right.

proportions, a tight web of informal norms and traditions does exert pressure upon all Senate members. The "Senate man" is, first, prudent. Like his House counterpart, he is expected to serve a patient apprenticeship, speaking little but learning a lot. Courtesy, helpfulness, and cooperation with other senators are also expected of each member. Senators, in the tradition of British members of Parliament, are ideally supposed to be able to share a congenial dinner with a man whom they may have opposed in a heated policy debate on the Senate floor a few hours earlier. Foremost among Senate norms is, as in the House, loyalty to the institution. The Senate man has "tolerance toward his fellows, intolerance toward any who would in any real way change the Senate, its customs or its way of life." He views the Senate as "a career in itself, a life in itself and an end in itself."[44]

Other observers claim that the picture of an inner club is a distortion; that Senate influence is much more evenly distributed, and that this description applies to both the formal and informal circuits of power. Senate ways, they point out, are diverse. *Formally,* some Senators amass influence by becoming experts in a particular policy area; others excel in backstage maneuvering; some are catapulted to national fame through committee investigations; others are quietly

[44] White, *The Citadel,* Ch. 7.

respected for their consistent success at pumping federal funds into their home states. *Personally*, the Senate also has "its sages, its clowns, its mavericks, its fools."[45] All easily fit into the expandable fabric of Senate life. Critics of the inner-club theory point out that while such mavericks do few of the things that senators are supposed to do, they too are able sometimes to build up their own independent bases of support, outside of the normal Senate channels. Former Senator Wayne Morse, the individualistic, outspoken party-switcher from Oregon, and the late Senator Joseph McCarthy (R.-Wis.) are the best-known more recent examples.

Leadership Structure in the Senate   Officially, the Vice President presides over Senate proceedings, with the Senate electing a president *pro tempore* to serve in his absence. This job is a mere formality, in no way comparing in power to the position of House Speaker. Senators feel that presiding is actually a tedious chore. A measure of the disesteem in which it is held is that when the president *pro tempore* is away, this job is often handed over to freshman senators. Their only consolation for presiding is the chance that a constituent may pop into the Senate gallery while visiting the Capitol; if he is innocent of Senate custom, the voter may be tremendously impressed by the speed with which his own senator has "risen to the top," seemingly to direct the entire drama.

The closest Senate parallel to the House Speaker is the Majority Floor Leader, who derives his strength more from personal influence than from any formal authority. A comparison of Lyndon Johnson with his successor, Democratic Senator Mike Mansfield of Montana, shows how different Senate Majority Leaders can be in their styles. Johnson's method of pressuring Senators to vote his way was known as "the treatment." Cornering the target, Johnson, over six feet tall, would usually tower over him, bombarding him with a vehement recital of facts, memos, and statistics—interlacing the information with pleading and veiled threats. The effect was almost hypnotic—leaving the victim stunned, and pliable enough to vote for a National Draft-Dodging Week—if that had been the issue. Under the guidance of his assistant Bobby Baker, Johnson also developed a personal information network that stretched throughout the Senate, not only informing him of the strength and weaknesses of each senator but also keeping him abreast of general sentiment in the nation. Further consolidating his power, Johnson personally had filled all of the other party policy posts within grasp of the Majority Leader. The net effect was to give him tremendous legislative leverage, bolstered by decisive influence upon Senate Democratic committee assignments.

In the shadow of such a dynamic predecessor it is not surprising that soft-spoken Mike Mansfield has been at times accused of weak leadership. He once replied, "I am neither a circus ringmaster, the master of ceremonies of a Senate nightclub, a tamer of Senate lions, or a wheeler and dealer."[46] His tenure represents a more democratic kind of leadership, with dispersion rather than concentration of power.

The Senate, like the House, also has a minority-party leader and whips for both parties. In order to operate more effectively, the Majority Leader will usually

[45] Nelson W. Polsby, *Congress and The Presidency* (Englewood Cliffs, N.J.: Prentice-Hall, 1964), p. 41.
[46] *Congressional Record* (November 27, 1963), p. 22862.

"My folks are in the gallery. If you can work it in, would you mind terribly calling me 'my esteemed colleague'?"

New Yorker, *July 31, 1971*

establish, if not personal friendship, at least a fairly close working relationship with the leader of the minority party. The Minority Leader, too, can be either colorful or quiet. The late Senate Minority Leader Everett Dirksen (R.-Ill.) had the rare senatorial distinction of making a hit record. On it, he did dramatic patriotic readings in a voice like honeyed gravel, crackling with righteous indignation as he often did on the Senate floor, surpassing even Lyndon Johnson in acting ability and rhetoric. Although a leading conservative, Senator Dirksen was at times pragmatic enough to cooperate closely with the Democratic administration. Originally opposed to President Johnson's nuclear-test-ban treaty with the USSR, Senator Dirksen later changed his position to help the Democratic Floor Leader muster support for its ratification. As the Senator explained, constituent mail seemed to be running in favor of the treaty—at the rate of forty-three to one.

Procedures in the Senate Senate proceedings, as we have seen, are usually less rigid than those of the House. But certain unwritten rules control the conduct of Senators. Freshman Senators, for example, are expected to stay in the background, listening and learning, with their mouths shut, a frustrating restraint for those eager to make a good showing before their constituencies.

Display of rather elaborate courtesy and the avoidance of personal attack, regardless of how hostile one might feel toward an adversary, is another Senate tradition. Often quoted is the cynical advice of the late Senator Alben Barkley to a freshman: "If you think a colleague stupid, refer to him as the 'able, learned and distinguished Senator,' but if you know he is stupid, refer to him as 'the *very* able, learned and distinguished Senator.' "[47] Such courtesy is not meaningless but serves to foster cooperation where chaos might otherwise rule.

Whereas the House has a formal tool—the Rules Committee—that can be manipulated to block legislation, the less formal Senate has a more direct device —the *filibuster*—that is blatantly intended for that purpose alone, and rests on the custom of elaborate courtesy. The notorious problems the filibuster can cause illustrate, perhaps, that the mere absence of complicated procedures does not necessarily make legislating any easier in the Senate than in the rule-ridden House. The size of Senate membership allows the Senate the luxury of virtually unlimited debate on any bill—in contrast to the House, where there is a strict time limit on speeches. This means that a determined minority, or technically even one man with superior lungs and stamina, can block progress on any bill simply by refusing to stop talking.[48] And the definition of what constitutes relevant discussion is very broad—reciting the telephone directory will do. This stalls all of the pending Senate business, as well as the bill in question. In hopes of overcoming a filibuster by wearing out its participants, proponents of a bill may keep the Senate going in continuous, round-the-clock sessions. Since, in order to end a filibuster, a quorum of fifty-one senators must always be ready to answer a roll call, the question is, Who is wearing out whom? Opponents of the filibuster are forced to spend the night on cots in the Senate hallway, or in their offices; as to an ancient Chinese torture chamber, they are summoned by gongs every two hours to answer roll call on the Senate floor. The filibuster group, on the other hand, can usually divide the chores so that each speaker (normally they speak for two hours at a time) will be well-rested and fresh. Thus, even the threat of a filibuster is frequently enough for a small minority to wring concessions from the Senate majority. Historically the filibuster is a favorite weapon of the southern Democratic-Republican coalition, especially against civil-rights bills; but they do not have a monopoly on it—liberals have also, on rarer occasions, used the filibuster for their own purposes. In 1964 a group of liberals, led by Senator Paul Douglas (D.-Ill.), successfully filibustered against a measure sponsored by Senator Dirksen (R.-Ill.) which would have delayed the congressional redistricting ordered by the Supreme Court. Tiring of the marathon, the Dirksen forces agreed to drop the measure, so the Senate could proceed with its business.

Technically, a filibuster can be stopped through *cloture*. According to Senate Rule XXII, if sixteen members sign a petition calling for a limit on debate, two days later the question is put to a vote; if two-thirds of the Senators vote for cloture, no Senator may then speak on the bill for more than one hour, after which it must be brought to a vote before the Senate. Obviously this is not a simple or frequently used maneuver. Cloture was voted only eight times out of forty-seven attempts between 1917, when the rule was first passed, and 1970. Rule XXII was made slightly easier to invoke in 1959: before that date the two-thirds vote applied to the entire Senate; now the assent of only two-thirds of the Senators present on the floor is required for cloture. But attempts to use it are still rare, and its success against a filibuster even rarer.

Like the House Rules Committee, the filibuster has come under heavy fire because it allows a small minority to tyrannize national legislative policy. Lib-

---

[47] Donald R. Matthews, *U.S. Senators and Their World* (New York: Vintage, 1960), p. 99.
[48] The individual record, over 23 hours, is held by Senator Strom Thurmond (D.-S.C.).

erals have been its most consistent critics—perhaps, in part, because this device is used most frequently against them. Filibustering also has its defenders. They claim it is a cherished refuge for the principle of minority rights; they also point out that simple majority rule is not always applicable—the Constitution requires two-thirds or even unanimous agreement on many issues considered by the Senate; one example is treaty ratification. Finally, proponents of the filibuster fall back upon the Senate tradition of cooperation and respect for the desires of other senators. They argue that, although senators may oppose a bill, they must find every measure which is passed at least within range of the tolerable. This minimal assent is necessary in the interests of Senate harmony—harmony which will also be required if the measure is to be followed up by appropriations to carry it out, or if there are later difficulties to be ironed out after it is in effect. When a group of senators is angry enough to filibuster, the proposal in question falls within range of the intolerable.

Decision-Making in Congress: Specialization and Stages

Congress is a place of wheels within wheels. Not only are there two essentially autonomous houses which share the legislative functions, but each house has its own set of committees and subcommittees, its own leadership structure, its own set of both formal procedures and informal norms of conduct. Despite the complex structure of power and decision-making in Congress shown by our discussion, we are able to draw a few broad conclusions about the legislative process.

Unquestionably, congressmen are confronted with an enormous work load; in the first session of the Ninety-first Congress, 21,553 bills and resolutions were introduced in the Senate and the House combined, followed by 7,487 in the second session.[49] Faced with such a huge quantity of legislative proposals, Congress had found it essential to specialize and to divide labor. Power in Congress is thereby dispersed widely among the various committees and subcommittees of each house. In the absence of strong party leadership, the individual committees tend to be highly autonomous; in most noncontroversial matters, the decisions made in committee are accepted by Congress as a whole.

The legislative process in Congress involves a number of different stages. As shown in Figure 6–1, every bill introduced in Congress must pass through a complex set of steps if it is to be enacted into law. Frequently, a bill is introduced in the House and the Senate simultaneously (with the broad exception of appropriations bills, which are introduced in the House). Once introduced, the bill is assigned to the appropriate committee in each house; typically, the committee chairman reassigns it to a subcommittee for investigation and debate. After the subcommittee stage, the bill is returned to the full committee for review, revision, and approval. If it is successfully voted out of committee, the bill is placed on the appropriate calendar in each chamber. In the House of Representatives, the Rules Committee determines the conditions under which a bill will be sent for debate on the floor. In the Senate, the order in which bills are called up for floor action is scheduled by the Majority Leader, working in conjunction with the

---

[49] Of course, this figure includes identical bills introduced in each house of Congress as well as different versions of essentially the same piece of legislation introduced by different members.

Figure 6–1   **How a Bill Becomes Law**

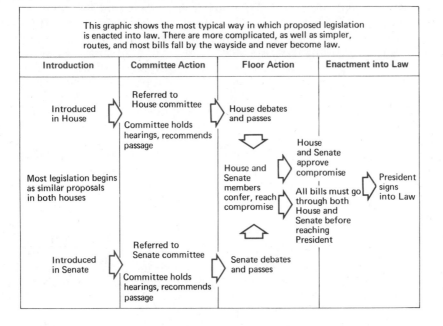

> This graphic shows the most typical way in which proposed legislation is enacted into law. There are more complicated, as well as simpler, routes, and most bills fall by the wayside and never become law.

Introduction	Committee Action	Floor Action	Enactment into Law

policy committee, the minority leader, and other key senators. When a bill is passed by one house of Congress, it is sent to the other house, which may pass the first chamber's bill, assign it to committee for consideration, or proceed with the passage of its own version of the bill. If the two pieces of legislation passed by the House and the Senate are essentially different, a conference committee of key members in each body may be convened. The job of the conference committee is to reconcile the fundamental differences in the two versions of the bill. When this is accomplished, the bill is presented again before the floor of each house. If approved, it is sent to the President to be signed into law.

The multi-stage nature of the legislative process allows many opportunities for delay of a bill to arise along the way. Negative action at any one stage may be sufficient to remove it from consideration indefinitely, a procedure referred to as *tabling* or *pigeonholing*. This complexity often provides a clear advantage to opponents of a bill. Many current criticisms of Congress focus on the institutions or procedures that make prolonged delay possible—the legislative committees or subcommittees in each chamber, the Rules Committee in the House, and the filibuster in the Senate.

How a Bill Becomes a Law: A Case Study of the Lockheed Loan Guarantee Bill[50]

Of the enormous number of bills considered by Congress each year, few are of great interest to most congressmen. The average congressman is a specialist in

---

[50] All information taken from *Congressional Quarterly* (May–August 1971).

only a single legislative area, and few issues that come before Congress are of significant interest to his constituents. As a result, reciprocity facilitates the passage of the majority of bills. The trading of votes among congressmen enables Congress to readily pass many noncontroversial pieces of legislation each session.

But the picture of how decisions are reached is not complete without an examination of the factors involved in highly controversial issues. When a bill is controversial, it involves or touches upon many powerful interests. The Lockheed Loan Guarantee Bill was one of the most hotly debated pieces of legislation before the 1971 session of the Ninety-second Congress; it highlights the intricate nature of decision-making in Congress and provides an excellent example of the problems and practices encountered in passing any important bill.

History of the Bill

The Nixon Administration, on May 13, 1971, sent legislation to Congress to guarantee up to $250 million in loans to major business enterprises which are failing. While the bill did not mention any companies by name, the administration's primary intention was to avoid the impending bankruptcy of the Lockheed Aircraft Corporation. Lockheed, as the nation's largest defense contractor, had recently incurred significant losses as a result of Defense Department penalties levied on cost-overruns on the C-5A military transport plane. It also faced commercial failure following the bankruptcy of Rolls Royce, the British manufacturer of jet engines for Lockheed's L-1011 Tristar Airbus. Lockheed needed the Tristar to stay in the commercial aircraft business, but to manufacture the Tristar it needed additional credit, especially after the engine prices were raised by the company that won the engine contract after the collapse of Rolls Royce. Lockheed, it was argued, could not stave off bankruptcy on its own.

Between the time of the proposal and the actual beginning of formal congressional activities, many influential persons outside of Congress made public statements in attempts to influence congressmen and the public for or against the bill. Among the bill's opponents was the chairman of the board of General Electric, manufacturer of the jet engine for the American McDonnell Douglas DC-10, which was in competition with the L-1011 Tristar. The support mustered in favor of the bill was quite impressive. President Nixon, at a news conference, argued that Lockheed's bankruptcy would cause additional unemployment in California, a state already overburdened with this problem. Secretary of Treasury Connally argued that the magnitude of the present investment in the Tristar, $1.4 billion, warranted continued investment, or at least protection of the current one. He pointed out that Lockheed had some 35,000 subcontractors who all would be affected by a Lockheed bankruptcy. George Meany, president of the AFL-CIO, also announced support of the bill.

Within Congress, opinion on the legislation was divided, with influential spokesmen for both sides. Senator William Proxmire, who had exposed the Lockheed C-5A military transport cost-overruns, vowed a fight against the bill because it seemed to reward the very inefficiencies that give rise to high production costs. Similarly, Senator Edmund Muskie, a Presidential hopeful, expressed misgivings over the bill and skepticism at rewarding mismanagement. Senator Hubert Humphrey, former Vice President and also a presidential contender, in principle opposed direct loans to large corporations, but came out in favor of the loan guarantee bill nevertheless. He argued that Lockheed had served the country well, thus deserving help in return; he also maintained that the project was financially feasible and money would not be lost.

From the beginning it was clear that proponents of the bill were lodged in key positions in Congress. Senator John Sparkman, Chairman of the Senate Banking, Housing and Urban Affairs Committee, the Senate committee which would handle the bill, said he favored it, because he supported the principle of government aid to large and vital corporations that are failing. The House Banking and Currency Committee would likely favor it as well, but wanted time to study the particulars. Senator Hugh Scott, Senate Minority Leader, favored the bill with the arguments that the loan guarantee would be cheaper than a government takeover and that losses were not expected anyhow. Representative Gerald Ford, House Minority leader, announced his support of the bill.

Interest-group pressure was also influential in winning support for the proposal. Senator David Gambrell (D.-Ga.) supported the bill; Lockheed C-5A is manufactured in Marietta, Georgia. Senator John Tunney, the liberal Democrat from California, also favored the plan; Lockheed's headquarters are in Burbank, California.

Senate Committee Action On June 7, 1971, the Senate Banking, Housing and Urban Affairs Committee began hearings and debate on the administration's proposal. As he had previously announced, Senator Sparkman, the chairman, favored the proposal, giving the bill a better chance to remain alive in the committee, receive a favorable hearing and prompt delivery for Senate debate. Numerous and diverse witnesses were heard. David Packard, Deputy Secretary of Defense, testified that without the loan guarantee Lockheed's bankruptcy was inevitable and that substantial unemployment would result. Another administration man, John Schaffer, administrator of the Federal Aviation Agency of the Transportation Department, argued for the bill on the basis that the Tristar would be a superb aircraft and a vital addition to the commercial aircraft field; it would also maintain the competitive and productive capacity of the United States airline industry. The bill was thus identified with the national interest. A host of airline executives, whose companies had already invested in the L-1011, and Lockheed subsidiary executives testified in favor of the bill. Also, bankers who represented a consortium of some twenty-four banks that had already loaned Lockheed $400 million argued for the bill's passage.

Among the opponents of the proposal, the Chairman of the Securities and Exchange Commission testified that Lockheed's management had concealed its financial problems from the investing public. Leonard Woodcock, president of the United Auto Workers of America, opposed the bill. Consumer advocate Ralph Nader and one of his associates testified against the bill, saying that the loan guarantee would only temporarily support a company that was basically unsound.

At such a stage in the congressional process the advantage lies with the committee chairmen, who have enormous power in their respective committees. The chairman, if he chooses to do so, can act as a virtual dictator. To be sure, the chairman is likely to listen to and consider the opinions of his colleagues and others, but he is not required to do so. Where the chairman stands on any particular bill, then, is crucial. Where he stood in the Lockheed case was made clear by the revised bill that subsequently emerged from committee.

Action on the Floor of the Senate On July 19, after much debate in committee, the Senate Banking, Housing and Urban Affairs Committee finally reported out a broader piece of legislation than the administration had proposed—a bill that would authorize an Emergency Loan Guarantee Board to grant loans up to a maximum of $250 million for any single business, and up to a total of $2 billion to major business enterprises, the failure of which would effect the national economy. Filibustering was begun on the floor of the Senate, led by Senator William Proxmire, with the aim of preventing passage of the bill before August 8, the beginning of the summer recess. Debate continued, with proponents of the bill fearful that continued debate would result in new amendments; amendments, in turn, would either kill the bill on the floor or result in differing House and Senate versions, thus necessitating a Conference Committee, which would further delay enactment of the bill.

On July 22, Majority Whip Robert Byrd announced that a motion would be entered on July 23 to invoke cloture and end debate. On July 26, the Senate rejected the first cloture motion in a roll-call vote of forty-two to forty-seven. Cloture, as noted earlier, requires a two-thirds yea vote and is always difficult to get. In this case, senators were not anxious to end debate, a gesture which would then force them to go on record for or against a bill and forfeit votes back home no matter which position they took. This circumstance favored the opposition.

A second motion for cloture was filed, on July 26, and a vote was scheduled for July 28. By a roll-call vote of fifty-nine to thirty-nine, the Senate again refused

United Auto Workers chairman Leonard Woodcock (right) told the Senate Banking Committee, chaired by John J. Sparkman (D.-La., left), that the proposed government loan probably would not save Lockheed.

to invoke cloture. Because Congress was due to begin summer recess August 8, proponents immediately filed a motion for a third attempt to end debate. On July 29, Senate opponents agreed with supporters and administration representatives to end debate if the bill was scaled down to the original $250 million administration request and brought to a vote. The deal collapsed when Lockheed supporters conceded they lacked enough support to pass the Lockheed-only bill. On July 30, the third cloture vote failed by a roll-call vote of fifty-seven to thirty-seven. A fourth cloture vote was scheduled for August 2. Action in the Senate was not finished by this date, but events in the House must be examined before the complete Senate passage can be detailed.

House Action After a two-month study, the staff of the House Banking and Currency Committee issued a report on July 8 recommending that the committee reject the proposed administration bill for several reasons: there was a substantial risk of default and loss; the bill gave preferential treatment to Lockheed; there was insufficient evidence that severe unemployment would follow a Lockheed bankruptcy; and the guarantee would be fundamentally inconsistent with a free-enterprise system. Hearings were held in the House Banking and Currency Committee, but apparently the staff report had little real effect in the Committee or the House as a whole. The committee chairman, Wright Patman (D.-Tex.), who earlier had expressed personal opposition to the proposal, reluctantly changed his position to support the bill, stating that he did not want the Democratic Party to be charged with being a "springboard for a depression." Patman's support increased the bill's chance of passage. The participants in the hearings were largely the same persons who had testified at the Senate committee hearings. On July 21, the House Banking and Currency Committee by a seventeen-to-fourteen vote accepted a bill offered by Robert Stephens (D.-Ga.) identical to the broader bill being considered in the Senate. The Committee then accepted the Senate's version as a substitute for its own, and voted to report the bill out of committee.

On July 30, the House took up the bill on the floor, and there the bill was stripped down to a $250 million guarantee authorization for Lockheed Aircraft Corporation only. It passed the House, July 30, by a three-vote margin, 192 to 189. A partisan breakdown of the vote shows that 90 Republicans and 102 Democrats voted for the bill, including 47 Southern Democrats. Of those who voted against the bill, 60 were Republicans and 129 Democrats.

Passage in the Senate By unanimous consent the Senate agreed to consider the House bill. This agreement was presumably facilitated by the belief of opponents that a bill pertaining only to Lockheed would be defeated. Debate was limited to two hours and twenty minutes for any amendments or motions. The order for a fourth cloture vote was withdrawn.

By a single vote, on August 2, an agreement was passed similar to the one which had failed on July 29. The Senate abandoned its own bill, and by a one-vote margin roll-call vote of forty-nine to forty-eight, cleared for the President's signature a bill which closely resembled the Administration's May 13 proposal. Since no amendments were added, the need for a conference committee was avoided.

The Lockheed Loan Guarantee Bill demonstrates the advantage gained by the supporters of a bill when they can speak of bread-and-butter issues, while their opponents can cite only hypothetical *if*s. There are many liberal senators and representatives who oppose military contractors and who seek a shift in national priorities; there are also many conservatives who remain firm in their commitment to capitalism and their opposition to "corporate socialism." Yet, in the final analysis, the conflict was won in the Senate by the decisive vote cast by the liberal and maverick Senator Lee Metcalf (D.-Mont.), who earlier told one of the major proponents of the bill, the liberal California Senator Alan Cranston, "I'm not going to be the one to put those thousands out of work." In this case, ideological principles and party alignment became secondary to the bread-and-butter issues at stake.

The passage of the Lockheed bill seems to indicate that even a highly controversial bill, when backed by the Administration, important interest groups, and both key committee chairmen in the Senate and the House, starts out with a good chance for eventual passage. The committee chairmen remain powerful figures in the congressional process. The Presidency, too, has prestige and vast resources which, when skillfully placed behind an important piece of legislation, can influence congressional votes. And in the Lockheed case, it appears that powerful interests—such as business and the military—gave significant leverage to proponents of the bill. Congressional opponents, on the other hand, did not have sufficient information about the possible effects of Lockheed bankruptcy, nor about the technical advantages of the Tristar. The bill combined matters of national security and employment, and the Congress tends to allow the President to lead on these matters. Finally, the bill embodied a fundamental principle of logrolling. Although not fully documented in this case, probably one of the major reasons liberal opponents supported the bill was the principle of *quid pro quo*— one thing in return for another; it is likely that debts were repaid on later bills.

SUGGESTED READING

Bailey, Stephen K. *The New Congress* (New York: St. Martin's Press, 1966). In paperback. An overview of the United States Congress, including a description of profound and recent changes in the national role and internal power relationships of this law-making body. The author's theme is that basic political, economic, and social changes in America, and in the world at large, have finally forced a series of adjustments in the structure and role of the Congress. Cumulatively, these adjustments are so profound as to merit the term *revolution* and to have produced a "New Congress," a Congress in which the principal movement is now irrevocably the cosmopolitan, centripetal pull of presidential and party influence, rather than the parochial, centrifugal force of congressional committees.

Barone, M., G. Ujifusa, and D. Matthews (eds.). *The Almanac of American Politics* (Boston: Gambit, 1972). In paperback. A political profile of every state and congressional district. Each profile is bolstered by statistical tables concerning many politically relevant factors of every state, district, and congressman. The book also includes district maps for every state. This is a basic handbook for candidates, campaign workers, and students of American politics.

Burns, James M. *The Deadlock of Democracy: Four-Party Politics in America* (Englewood Cliffs, N.J.: Prentice-Hall, 1967). In paperback. A history and analysis of the Madisonian and Jeffersonian models of American politics. Burns critically analyzes what he sees as a dangerous deadlock between President and Congress, the result of which is a loss of control of national politics by Americans and a lack of national purpose. He examines the use of power by Presidents, the splintering of parties, and the structure of coalition politics. Finally, he proposes a cure for the democratic deadlock.

Clapp, Charles I. *The Congressman: His Work as He Sees It* (Washington, D.C.: Brookings Institution, 1963). Exploration of all facets of a congressman's life: his work in committees, relationships with colleagues, party leadership, legislative functions, and office administration. It is an account of the congressman and the Congress, written essentially from the congressman's point of view.

Fenno, Richard F., Jr. *The Power of the Purse: Appropriations Politics in Congress* (Boston: Little, Brown, 1966). A description and analysis of the contemporary appropriations process in Congress. The author demonstrates that a committee-centered analysis is important for an increased understanding of Congress and that the exercise of the appropriations power constitutes the core of the legislative process. The study is a systems analysis with twin foci—the House Committee on Appropriations and the total appropriations process in which the Senate as well as the House plays a part. The problems of decision-making and committee integration serve as approaches for describing and explaining behavior inside the committee.

Froman, Lewis A., Jr. *The Congressional Process: Strategies, Rules, and Procedures* (Boston: Little, Brown, 1967). In paperback. A description and analysis of the organization, rules, and procedures of Congress and their effect on the formulation of public policy. Given the decentralized decision-making structures of both houses, Froman sees bargaining as the principal mechanism for coordination and coalition-building. He carefully assesses the impact of the rules and procedures of each house on legislative strategy and the substance of bills; relates decision-making structures to the problem of majority rule; and, finally, discusses problems dealing with congressional reform.

Manley, John F. *The Politics of Finance: The House Ways and Means Committee* (Boston: Little, Brown, 1970). A comprehensive study of the House Ways and Means Committee, through which is channeled most of the significant legislation that Congress is called upon to pass. The author examines the period from the New Deal to the Nixon administration, analyzing both the internal relations of the Committee and the Committee's relations with the House, the Senate, the President, and pressure groups. The author also examines the policy-making process in the Committee, as well as the crucial role of the chairman, Wilbur Mills.

Matthews, Donald L. *U.S. Senators and Their World* (New York: Random House, 1960). In paperback. A description of U.S. senators—who they are, how they behave, and why they behave the way they do. Matthews views the Senate as a group of people rather than as an institution, and he draws on extensive interviews with senators, Senate staff members, lobbyists, and Washington journalists in constructing a profile of the postwar senators' world.

Peabody, Robert L., Jeffrey M. Berry, William G. Frasure, and Jerry Goldman. *To Enact a Law: Congress and Campaign Financing* (New York: Praeger, 1972). In paperback. The authors use a case study of a single bill—the Political Broadcast Act of 1970—to explain the legislative process. They demonstrate the law-making process step by step—how a bill is conceived, the ways it can be subjected to interest groups' pressure, subcommittee and committee activities, House and Senate floor action, and a presidential veto. The case study illustrates the complexity of the legislative labyrinth and treats an important issue of American politics—namely, campaign reform.

Ripley, Randall B. *Majority Party Leadership in Congress* (Boston: Little, Brown, 1969). In paperback. The author examines twentieth-century majority-party leadership and analyzes the profound change in the relationship between congressional leaders and the President. The formally elected party leaders now confront a President who has his own legislative program, and their job is to mediate between powerful members of Congress and the President. Ripley suggests four main types of legislative leadership and explores ten representative Congresses as a means of assessing what combination of leadership techniques, size of majority, and other institutional and historical factors are likely to give legislative success to the majority party.

_____. *Power in the Senate* (New York: St. Martin's Press, 1969). In paperback. An analysis of the internal distribution of power in the Senate and the consequences of that distribution. The Senate is viewed as an institution and its internal processes are analyzed according to general models of power distribution and the transition from one pattern of power distribution to another in the years between 1945 and 1968. Finally, some of the consequences of different patterns of internal processes for policy are examined.

Robinson, James A. *Congress and Foreign Policy-Making* (Homewood, Ill.: Dorsey Press, 1967). In paperback. A study of the influence of Congress on the formation of United States foreign policy and the process by which that influence is effected. The author argues that Congress's role is primarily and increasingly to approve and finance executive actions. Among the significant explanations for this relationship is the changing character of information in modern policy-making. The Executive branch of government has substantial advantages in U.S. foreign policy-making, partly as a result of the bureaucratization which enables it to obtain and process intelligence.

Wilson, Woodrow. *Congressional Government* (New York: World, 1956). In paperback. A study of American politics, in which Congress is considered the central, predominant, and controlling power of the American system, with its primary power lying within the congressional committees. Wilson deplores congressional supremacy, which, he claims, perverts centralized power and thus effective leadership, and strict accountability for the use of power. Instead of congressional supremacy, Wilson proposes a strong parliamentary system in which a strong and responsible cabinet would lead the public and superintend all matters of government.

7

THE PRESIDENCY AS
THE CENTER OF POWER

Like most other countries of the world, the United States is experiencing a period of executive supremacy. The trend began when Franklin Roosevelt took strong action to pull the nation out of the Depression—or to give us, through his use of the media, the impression that such was the case. True, there had been Presidents in pre-Depression days who possessed great popular appeal and who assumed great power—Jackson, Lincoln, Wilson, and Theodore Roosevelt. But not before Franklin Roosevelt had the American public expected with such fervency that the man they selected to occupy the chief position in their government be not only a capable politician but something of a spiritual leader as well. As James Reston observed, "The White House is the pulpit of the nation and the President is its Chaplain." Despite this exalted position, Presidents are chosen haphazardly in America and the selection process, according to some, has not worked very well. For example, a poll of historians conducted by Arthur Schlesinger in 1962 found only five of the first thirty-four presidents could be considered great, while six were below average and two "outright failures."[1] Who among a nation of two hundred million becomes the President of the United States? What powers does he wield, and what are the consequences of his actions?

Who Becomes President

By what qualities do we judge a person who has declared his intention of running for the highest office of the land? The Constitution stipulates that he or she must be at least thirty-five years old, a natural-born citizen, and a resident of the United States for fourteen years. On the basis of these requirements, millions of Americans are theoretically qualified to become President. Yet there is an unwritten list of criteria which, though unofficial, is infinitely more demanding than the constitutional stipulations. What are some of these unofficial qualifications?

That any child can grow up to be President is a particularly cherished American belief, one that appeals deeply to the American sense of equality. Yet, in view of the records of American Presidents (see Table 7-1), it is difficult to see how this myth has perpetuated itself. Most American Presidents have been English in ancestry, with a sprinkling of Irish, Scots, Dutch, and German, and all but one have been Protestant. Not until the Kennedy election was the tradition of Protestant Presidents successfully challenged. (The only other Catholic ever nominated for President by a major political party was Al Smith, an experienced politician who, though heavily defeated in the Electoral College, carried about 40 percent of the popular vote.) Kennedy was successful in overcoming his religious handicap, but the probability is that some votes, although not necessarily a decisive number, will continue to be lost by a minority-religion candidate. The United States may be a land of opportunity in the sense that its political system is not totally controlled by an aristocratic minority. But, judging purely by statistics, if a boy happens to be poor and/or a member of a racial, ethnic, or religious minority, his chances of ascending to the office of Chief Executive are not very good. As recently as 1972, Senator Edmund Muskie, an unsuccessful candidate for the Democratic presidential nomination and a Polish Catholic, said he felt justified in declining to consider a black running mate. Such a choice, he said, would make victory impossible.

[1] The *New York Times* (July 29, 1962).

Richard M. Nixon was inaugurated as the thirty-sixth President of the United States on January 20, 1969.

It is also generally conceded that a woman cannot be elected to the Presidency. As far back as 1872 the Equal Rights Party offered as its presidential candidate Victoria Claflin Woodhull, a woman who had led an extraordinarily varied career as publisher, banker, and activist on behalf of woman suffrage, faith healing, spiritualism, and socialism. On the ticket as her vice-presidential running mate was the black leader Frederick Douglass. A vocal minority at that party's convention, displeased with the choice of Douglass, favored instead the Indian Chief Spotted Tail.[2] By any estimation neither ticket stood much of a chance in 1872.

One hundred years later most experts still contended that Representative Shirley Chisholm, another presidential hopeful, would be unacceptable to the average voter both on account of her sex and because she was black. In fact, Mrs. Chisholm herself privately spoke of the futility of her bid for office, saying that her purpose in running was to pressure the party into supporting reform in the interest of blacks and women. Women and blacks, then, regardless of their constitutional qualifications, are not likely to be successful candidates for the Presidency in the near future.

---

[2] For an interesting discussion of Woodhull's presidential bid, see Johanna Johnston, *Mrs. Satan* (New York: Putnam, 1967).

Much of the popularity that led to Dwight D. Eisenhower's being elected President in 1952 and 1956 stemmed from his huge success as Allied Supreme Commander, a post he held at the time of the 1945 New York victory parade pictured here.

About ten of our thirty-six Presidents have risen from modest beginnings. Andrew Johnson's father, for example, was a bank porter and sexton and he himself a tailor; Hoover's father was a blacksmith and Grant's a leather tanner. But the majority have come from the upper middle class. A few, such as George Washington, Franklin D. Roosevelt, and John Kennedy, have come from the upper class, and have enjoyed high social position and great wealth.

Presidential candidates in recent years have found that it takes a lot of money to run for the office because of the high cost of television and image-making. Kennedy spent almost $12 million on his campaign in 1960; Johnson over $13 million; Nixon almost $29 million in 1968.[3] Campaigning has become so expensive that nearly all candidates, even the richest, now require outside backing. The business community usually lavishes its funds on candidates sympathetic to them, and these candidates are almost always Republicans. Labor, on the other hand, almost always supports the Democratic party, somewhat offsetting the Republican advantage among big business. In addition, small contributors tend to support the Democrats.

---

[3] John H. Runyon, Jennifer Verdini, and Sally S. Runyon (eds.), *Sourcebook of American Presidential Campaign and Election Statistics, 1948–1968* (New York: Unger, 1971), p. 176.

Table 7-1 *What Manner of Man Becomes President?*

President	Ancestry	Father's Occupation[1]	Religion[3]	Education[4]	Own Occupation	Govt. Positions Held before the Presidency[6]
Washington	English	n.a.[2]	Episcopalian	Academy	Farmer, surveyor, military	st leg, Cont Cong, gen
J. Adams	English	Farmer	Unitarian	Harvard	Lawyer	st leg, Cont Cong, cab, dipl, vp
Jefferson	Welsh	Justice of the peace (college educated)	nondenominational	College of William and Mary	n.a.	st leg, Cont Cong, gov, dipl, cab, vp
Madison	English	Justice of the peace; farmer	Episcopalian	Princeton	Lawyer	st leg, Cont Cong, HR, cab
Monroe	Scots	n.a.	Episcopalian	College of William and Mary	Military attorney	st leg, Cont Cong, sen, dipl, gov, cab
J. Q. Adams	English	President of U.S.	Unitarian	Harvard	Lawyer	sen, cab[7]
Jackson	Irish	n.a. (Irish immigrant)	Presbyterian	Academy, law	Teacher	HR, gen, gov, sen
Van Buren	Dutch	Farmer, innkeeper	Dutch Reform	Academy	Lawyer	st leg, st atty gen, sen, gov, cab, vp
W. H. Harrison	English	Farmer (signer of Declaration of Independence)	Episcopalian	Hampden-Sidney College	Lawyer	HR, gov, gen, st leg, sen, dipl
Tyler	English	Governor; judge	Episcopalian	College of William and Mary	Lawyer	st leg, HR, gov, sen, vp[8]
Polk	Scots-Irish	Governor	Presbyterian	University of North Carolina	Lawyer	st leg, HR, gov.
Taylor	English	Port collector (relative of Madison)	Episcopalian	rudimentary tutoring	Military, tutor, farmer	gen[9]
Fillmore	English	Farmer, pioneer	n.a.	read law	Lawyer	st leg, HR, vp
Pierce	English	Governor	Episcopalian	Bowdoin College	Lawyer	st leg, HR, sen, gen
Buchanan	Scots-Irish	Storekeeper, farmer	Episcopalian	Dickinson College	Lawyer	st leg, HR, dipl, sen, cab
Lincoln	English	Carpenter	nondenominational	read law	Lawyer	st leg, HR
A. Johnson	English	Bank porter, sexton	nondenominational	Academy	Tailor, labor organizer	m, st leg, HR, gov, gen, sen, vp
Grant	English	Tanner	Methodist	West Point	Military	gen, cab[10]
Hayes	Scots	Farmer	Methodist	Kenyon College, Harvard Law School	Lawyer	gen, HR, gov
Garfield	English	Farmer, canal builder	Disciples of Christ	Hiram and Williams College	Professor	st leg, gen, sen
Arthur	Scots-Irish	Clergyman	Episcopalian	Union College	Lawyer, principal	gen, port coll[11]
Cleveland	English	Clergyman	Presbyterian	read law	Grocery clerk, lawyer	m, gov
B. Harrison	English	Congressman (grandson of President W. H. Harrison)	Presbyterian	Miami University	Lawyer	gen, sen

President	Ethnic Origin	Father's Occupation	College	Religion	Own Occupation	Offices Held
McKinley	Scots-Irish	Iron manufacturer	Allegheny College	Episcopalian	Lawyer	HR, gov
T. Roosevelt	Dutch	Port collector	Harvard	Episcopalian	n.a.	st leg, cab, gov, vp
Taft	English	U.S. Secretary of War, U.S. Attorney General	Yale	Unitarian	Lawyer	cab, judge[12]
Wilson	Scots-Irish	Clergyman	Princeton; Ph.D., Johns Hopkins	Presbyterian	Lawyer	gov
Harding	English	Doctor	Central College	Baptist	Lawyer, newspaper publisher	st leg, lt gov, sen
Coolidge	English	Storekeeper	Amherst College	Congregational	Lawyer	st leg, m, lt gov, gov, vp
Hoover	Swiss	Blacksmith	Stanford	Quaker	Engineer	cab
F. D. Roosevelt	Dutch	n.a.	Harvard	Dutch Reform	Lawyer	cab, gov
Truman	English-Scots-Irish	Farmer, livestock dealer		Baptist	Railroad timekeeper,[5] farm manager	sen, vp
Eisenhower	German	n.a. (college educated)	West Point	Presbyterian	Military	gen[9]
Kennedy	Irish	Financier	Harvard	Roman Catholic	Reporter	HR, sen
L. B. Johnson	English-French-German	State Legislator, rancher	Southwest Texas State Teacher's College	Disciples of Christ	Teacher	HR, sen, vp
Nixon	Irish	Small merchant, farmer	Whittier College, Duke Law School	Quaker	Lawyer	HR, sen, vp

1 As the modern concept of *working class*, with its urban- and industrial-society connotations, is hard to apply here (especially on the frontier), three measures which should help are included: father's occupation, religion, and education.

2 Information not available. When this notation appears under the *Own Occupation* heading, it indicates that no established occupation was discernible. Frequently this person entered elective politics at a young age.

3 The most prestigious denominations would include Episcopalian, Congregational, Presbyterian, Unitarian, and Dutch Reform; middle-class and lower-middle-class include Disciples of Christ, Methodist, and Baptist.

4 Most were college educated, quite atypical for American society. The term *read law* means that the individual studied law on his own and was apprenticed to a lawyer. He had no formal college or law-school education.

5 In the twentieth century Truman stands out because he did not attend college (the only President who didn't), but it must be noted that he failed to go to West Point only because his eyesight was too poor.

6 Offices held, their abbreviations, and the number of Presidents who held them:

I. *Elective Offices:* state legislator (st leg) — 19; House of Representatives (HR) — 16; senator (sen) — 16; governor (gov) — 15; vice president (vp) — 11; Continental Congress (Cont Cong) — 5; mayor (M) — 3; lieutenant governor (lt gov) — 2; state attorney general (st atty gen) — 1.

II. *Appointive Offices:* cabinet or sub-cabinet post (cab) — 12; diplomatic post (dipl) — 6; federal judge (judge) — 1; port collector (port coll) — 1.

III. *Military Rank:* general (gen) — 12.

In reading this part of the table, it should be noted that since this table concerns types of experience before ascendance to the Presidency, each position is marked only once, whether or not several terms were served. Generally speaking, there has been increasing specialization after the first generation of presidents who had been active in the revolutionary period and held a variety of elective and appointive offices. After that, appointive offices drop out, save for the sub-Cabinet positions of the Roosevelts, Arthur, and Taft.

7 John Quincy Adams served in the House after his term as President.

8 Tyler served in the Confederate House after his term as President.

9 Taylor and Eisenhower are the only Presidents who had only military careers before becoming President.

10 Beginning with Grant, all the Republican Presidents through Harrison had been generals in the Union Army.

11 Collector of the Port of New York is an important patronage position.

12 Taft served as Chief Justice of the Supreme Court after his term as President.

Sources: Robert Sobel (ed.), Biographical Directory of the US Executive Branch, 1774–1971 (Westport, Conn.: Greenwood Publishing Company, 1971); Luman H. Long (ed.), 1971 Edition, The World Almanac (New York: Newspaper Enterprise Association, Inc., 1971).

The Presidency, however, is won by votes, not just money. In many ways acquiring voter support is directly related to the amount of money spent on a campaign—if it is spent wisely. But some image makers and analysts contend that a candidate from a middle-class background or the illusion of one, with or without good financial resources, can attract the votes of the average voter who readily identifies with these roots. In 1840, for example, William Henry Harrison circulated campaign posters of himself standing before a log cabin when, in actuality, he was an affluent land owner with a splendid country estate in Ohio. Theodore H. White, although in the minority among political analysts, believed Richard Nixon in 1960 "found an echo" in the small villages of the farm belt where, among his "natural constituency, his idiom [was] their idiom." White attributes Nixon's success in these states (he won as much as 62.1 percent of Nebraska's vote) to his knowledge of small-town culture and the support this earned among these people, culminating in "the most solid and decisive expression of will of any of the major regions of the United States."[4]

What practical political experience is necessary to win the Presidency? From the record, a majority of our Presidents have been lawyers, and almost all have had political careers. The most frequently held previous office is state legislator, followed by senator and representative, governor, Vice President, and Cabinet member, in that order. Some, such as Jackson, Grant and Eisenhower, have been generals.

In addition to experience, a successful presidential candidate needs that intangible quality often called charisma. This quality can sometimes be the most crucial of all. For example, in 1932, columnist Walter Lippmann described Franklin D. Roosevelt as "a pleasant man who, without any important qualities of the office, would very much like to be president."[5] Nevertheless, Roosevelt's charm and buoyant self-confidence won him popularity with the people. Another example of popular appeal outweighing experience may be seen in the case of Warren G. Harding. Despite what many considered complete political incompetence, Harding succeeded in attaining the office of President if for no other reason than that he presented an amiable, dignified appearance and, to many people, simply "*looked* like a President."[6]

In contrast to Roosevelt and Harding, there are some cases in which superficial qualities such as looks, personality, and family life may well have contributed significantly to defeat. In 1956, for example, Adlai E. Stevenson lost the presidential election despite his experience in government, his wealth, and his personal charm. There is a reason to think his intellectualism and sophisticated wit did not have a broad enough appeal among Americans. Equally important to some was the fact that Stevenson had been divorced. Americans expect their national leaders to be family men, and they are likely to reject a candidate who does not project this image.

One political observer, in analyzing the Presidency, writes sarcastically:

[4] See Theodore H. White, *The Making of the President, 1960* (New York: Atheneum, 1961), pp. 332–333, 419–432.

[5] Quoted in Arthur M. Schlesinger, Jr., *The Crisis of the Old Order*, vol. 1 of *The Age of Roosevelt* (Boston: Houghton Mifflin, 1951), pp. 290–291.

[6] Sidney Warren, "How to Pick a President," in *American Government*, edited by Peter Woll (Boston: Little, Brown, 1969), p. 295.

President Franklin D. Roosevelt's admirers loved him as much for his forceful, charismatic personality as for his programs to end the Great Depression.

According to American folklore the ideal President is an authentic man of the people, undistinguished by wealth or achievement, unbeholden to any interest group or potentate.[7]

Unfortunately, several Presidents have been average in ability when exceptional talents are needed; some have also been average in achievement. History indicates, therefore, that when the American people are given a choice, it is not easy to predict whom they will select as their leader.

Changing Times and the Presidency

Generally speaking, periods of high concentration of power in the Executive Office have coincided with times of national emergency. Lincoln was practically a dictator during the Civil War, and Wilson guided the country through World War I with an almost fanatical confidence in his own infallibility.

The Great Depression of the 1930s, however, was a national emergency that marked the beginning of continued executive supremacy in the United States. The Congress, not having a center of leadership of firm party control, was unable to act, so the American people turned to the White House for aid. Through the National Industrial Recovery Act of 1933 the government became involved in

---

[7] R. Emmett Tyrrell, Jr., in the *New York Times* (July 8, 1972), p. 25.

regulating the economy, first by imposing price and wage controls and later by augmenting these with welfare measures such as social security. The proliferation of government programs designed to aid the economic and social problems of Americans set a trend that has not, as yet, been reversed.

The changing character of world politics since World War II has also been a contributing factor in the rise of American presidential power. From a position of isolation during the 1930s, the United States has moved in one generation to the position of the leading power in the world. Because the President holds supreme authority in the conduct of foreign relations, this change in the role of the United States has naturally contributed to a growth in the power of the Presidency.

But even more crucial than America's advance to prominence in world politics has been the change in the nature of international relations themselves. Prior to World War II, international politics was characterized by the competition of individual nation states, each pursuing its own self-interest and bent on securing and protecting its own territory. Wars were the result of the invasion of one country by another across territorial boundaries. Since World War II, however, the situation has changed. Now international relations are characterized by battles for ideological allegiance rather than territory. Each major power has been concerned with winning others over to its political-economic system, whether capitalism or communism. These struggles occasionally erupt in limited "national liberation" or "guerrilla movements" in underdeveloped areas. Major powers no longer engage each other directly, but instead give their assistance to smaller countries which, for one reason or another, they have promised to protect. It is a situation which, in the 1950s, earned the name "the Cold War."

Given such a situation, characterized by conflicts such as Korea, Lebanon, Cuba, and Vietnam, the traditional power of Congress to declare war becomes an anachronism. Wars are not declared, and the President, through his power of conducting foreign affairs, manages the international conflict as he sees fit. Many believe that the transfer of such power from Congress to the President represents a serious threat to the principle of democracy, since the President, by committing troops to a conflict, can involve the country in a *de facto* war, without even the indirect consent of the people as represented by Congress. It is, however, difficult to see any alternative to this type of presidential power. The possibility of nuclear war further confirms the primacy of the President in foreign relations. The decision to use nuclear power, if it were made, must be in a matter of minutes. Clearly Congress is totally unsuited to this task. Only the President, with the help of the special assistant who carries a briefcase containing the secret coding device for activating a nuclear attack, can realistically be entrusted with this dread responsibility. Thus, since the President controls this ultimate weapon, his power, in matters of foreign relations at least, far overshadows that of Congress.

Concepts of the Presidential Role

A presidential candidate, whatever his actual capabilities, attempts to show while campaigning that he holds a workable plan for America's future. But when his term of office is finished and he is assessed in the light of history, it becomes evident that some Presidents have shown true leadership by shaping events, while others have merely reacted to them. Herbert Hoover, for example, had extensive experience as a successful engineer, but his reaction to the Depression was extremely passive. His concept of his role as President in the Depression years was to sit tight and let things right themselves, and he was optimistic that times were not so bad after all. As he put it:

[The issue] is solely a question of the best method by which hunger and cold shall be prevented. It is a question to whether the American people, on one hand, will maintain the spirit of charity and self-help through voluntary giving and the responsibility of local government as distinguished, on the other hand, from appropriations out of the Federal Treasury for such purposes. My own conviction is strongly that if we break down this sense of responsibility of individual generosity to individual and mutual self-help in the country in times of national difficulty and if we start appropriations of this character we have not only impaired something infinitely valuable in the life of the American people but have struck at the roots of self-government. . . . That has been the American way of relieving distress among our own people, and the country is successfully meeting its problem in the American way today.[8]

Hoover's manner of administrating is exemplified by the way in which he handled national emergencies in the early thirties. After a drought in the Southwest in which many herds of cattle had died, the ranchers turned to Washington for aid. Hoover reacted by presenting a detailed plan, including provision of seed, fertilizer, and food. But he did not perceive the widespread unemployment in that area of the country as meriting any action on his part. Thus, many of his Democratic critics were soon pointing out that he could feed livestock, but not people.

Hoover was not unique in his view of the Presidency. William Howard Taft contended that the President's role was limited by a narrow reading of its constitutional prescription. He maintained:

The true view of the Executive function is, as I conceive it, that the President can exercise no power which cannot be fairly and reasonably traced to some specific grant of power or justly implied and included within such express grant as proper and necessary to its exercise. Such specific grant must be either in the Federal Constitution or in an act of Congress passed in pursuance thereof. There is no undefined residuum of power which he can exercise because it seems to him to be in the public interest.[9]

Dwight D. Eisenhower, although he served in office as recently as the 1950s, also upheld this view and refrained from initiating wide-scale programs as Franklin D. Roosevelt had before him.

There have been many Presidents who have been far less concerned than Taft and Hoover about overstepping their authority; instead, they held to the principle that in serving the public interest, they needed to refrain from doing only what the law expressly prohibited them from doing. Most of these men have served in times of national stress or since the Depression. An early advocate of such belief was Andrew Jackson, who claimed he was the embodiment of the general will. Although he was known to favor limited government, he occasionally acted contrary to this belief and raised the wrath of many who felt he overstepped the proper bounds of executive authority. After removing public deposits from the Bank of the United States, the charter for which he had vetoed, Jackson read these words to his Cabinet, expressing his conception of the President's role:

It would ill become the executive branch of the Government to shrink from any duty

---

[8] W. S. Meyers and W. H. Newton (eds.), *The Hoover Administration* (New York: Scribner, 1936), p. 63.

[9] W. H. Taft, *Our Chief Magistrate and His Powers* (New York: Columbia University Press, 1916), p. 139; quoted in Nelson W. Polsby, *Congress and the Presidency* (Englewood Cliffs, N.J.: Prentice-Hall, 1964), p. 24.

which the law imposes on it, to fix upon others the responsibility which justly belongs to itself. And while the President anxiously wishes to abstain from the exercise of doubtful powers and to avoid all interference with the rights and duties of others, he must yet with unshaken constancy discharge his own obligations and cannot allow himself to turn aside in order to avoid any responsibility which the high trust with which he has been honored requires him to encounter. . . .[10]

Wartime presidents such as Lincoln and Wilson have advocated similar principles; Franklin Roosevelt, Lyndon Johnson and John Kennedy are also good examples. These Presidents held that the Presidency was a "stewardship" for the people, and endeavored to steer the ship of state into new water rather than hold it steady on a predetermined course. Those who hold this view often justify their interpretation by the idea expressed by Theodore Roosevelt in the early 1900s: Roosevelt took the position that the executive power was "limited only by specific restrictions and prohibitions appearing in the Constitution or imposed by the Congress under its constitutional powers." He said that

. . . every executive officer, and above all every executive officer in high position, was a steward of the people. . . . [Roosevelt] declined to adopt the view that what was imperatively necessary for the Nation could not be done by the President unless he could find some specific authorization to do it.[11]

Presidents who have held Theodore Roosevelt's view of office as opposed to William Howard Taft's have also tended to be more dynamic leaders. Since the President is the only elected government official with a national constituency, such Presidents have considered themselves the true representatives of the people and have freely initiated policy for the national good as they perceived it.

The Men Around the President

Regardless of the concept a President holds of his role, he realizes that he alone cannot fulfill the demands put on him. The Presidency of the United States is, in fact, more of an institution than just a man, and, like all institutions, it functions regardless of who is the titular head. The different offices and officials that aid the President should be examined, then, with this fact in mind.

The Vice President

A total of eight Presidents have died in office, four in the twentieth century. Because of the very real possibility that the Vice President may become President, he should, ideally, be someone qualified to assume the Chief Executive's office. Despite the fact that many Vice Presidents have ascended to the Presidency (eight as a result of death of the President and nine elected in their own right, some after filling portions of terms left incomplete after a President's death), little is mentioned in the Constitution about the Vice President's role, a role that should presumably prepare him for this eventuality. The first Vice President, John

---

[10] James D. Richardson, ed., *A Compilation of the Messages and Papers of the Presidents, 1789–1910*, vol. 3 (Washington, D.C.: Government Printing Office, 1896), p. 10.

[11] T. R. Roosevelt, *Theodore Roosevelt: An Autobiography* (New York: Macmillan, 1913), pp. 388–389. Quoted in Polsby, *Congress and the Presidency*, p. 24.

Adams, unknowingly and accurately stated, "In this office I am nothing. But I may be everything."[12] In eight years he was the President, the "everything" he envisioned as his potential.

The constitution only briefly mentions the Vice President as successor to the President; he is not given any responsibility or constitutional power other than as President of the Senate, a relatively meaningless power since he votes only in the case of ties. This constitutional oversight has left very little prescribed business for the Vice President to do, and most Presidents have not vastly expanded their role. Alben Barkley, Truman's Vice President, used to joke about a family with two sons. The first son ran away to sea; the other became Vice President; and neither was ever heard from again.[13] The Vice President is basically the man in reserve, the potential inheritor of enormous power and responsibility, but, in his capacity as Vice President, he is one of the least integral parts of the executive machinery.

An inherent limitation to the power of the Vice Presidency arises from the nature of party politics. The Vice President is traditionally chosen to balance a ticket geographically and ideologically. When this balancing results in discrepancies in viewpoint between the President and the Vice President, the President will hesitate to entrust power to his Vice President. This was true of Kennedy and the southerner Johnson, and of Johnson and the northern liberal Humphrey; and during their first term in office it was also true of Nixon and Agnew, who represent different degrees of Republican conservatism.

The role of the Vice President has, nevertheless, expanded somewhat in recent years. Under Eisenhower, Nixon was kept better informed of the inner workings of government than were previous Vice Presidents because illness restricted Eisenhower's activities and made it prudent to prepare the Vice President to take over his office. Nixon's own experience under Eisenhower, and the intervening Kennedy assassination, encouraged him to involve his own Vice President in governmental operations. Spiro Agnew was given an office in the White House and made head of the Office of Intergovernmental Relations. But the duties of the Vice President are still not well defined, and the office is by no means a center of power.

The Cabinet

Under the Constitution, the President is responsible for the appointment of the heads of major executive departments; these officials make up the President's Cabinet. Various Presidents have reorganized the Cabinet structure, adding new departments and merging old departments into new, more inclusive ones. There has also been a good deal of variation in the ways in which Presidents have used their cabinets. In general, the rule holds that the President's Cabinet is whatever he chooses to make it.

There have been two extremes in the attitude of Presidents on the role of the Cabinet. One is that the President and the nation are best served by a strong Cabinet consisting of "the best minds" and serving to prevent "one-man government." This view, held by Harding, is known as the compensation theory, and is based on the belief that the Cabinet serves the President by providing him

---

[12] David Brinkley, "NBC Nightly News" (July 25, 1971).
[13] Quoted by David Brinkley, "NBC Nightly News" (July 25, 1972).

with collective knowledge, expert advice, and support.[14] The other view of the Cabinet's role, one that disregards collective decision-making, is epitomized by Lincoln's concise statement concerning an issue on which his Cabinet unanimously opposed him: "Seven noes, one aye—the ayes have it."

Harding's view of the Cabinet makes that body a check on the President—one that assures he will rely on expertise, avoiding one-man decisions based on insufficient information. Although, ideally, such a Cabinet is in the spirit of American democracy, it presents inherent problems. Any administrative group must be activated and coordinated. Thus, a strong leader—the new type of man the compensation Cabinet is meant to keep in check—is the kind needed to keep the Cabinet from being stagnant and uncreative. A strong leader, in fact, can compensate for the deficiencies in the perspective of individual department secretaries. Finally, a strong leader is needed to cope with rivalry between departments arising directly out of day-to-day governmental operations.

A compromise between the two prevailing Cabinet philosophies was attempted under the Kennedy administration. Kennedy followed Eisenhower, whose compensation Cabinet was modeled after an Army General Staff—meeting regularly, with a formal agenda and a Cabinet secretary. The Eisenhower meetings ran smoothly, the result of good planning and homogeneity; most of these Cabinet members had previous administrative experience in the business community. But these sessions were also bland and without serious differences, because of this homogeneity. Kennedy, realizing this, also took as his model the Roosevelt Cabinet. Franklin Roosevelt often played one member of the Cabinet off against another, so that he had the benefit of choosing among competing judgments. It was Roosevelt's belief that good ideas were more likely to come out of conflict than from a group of yes-men. Kennedy opted for a heterogeneous Cabinet, but unlike Roosevelt, he took the advice of its members. He did not demand unswerving loyalty—a mistake made by Truman—but he did insist upon team performance. He deployed the team in a way that guaranteed the utilization of each member's talents and expertise, minimizing internal conflict, and conserving energy. The fact that the Cabinet met regularly helped avoid the formality that had inhibited such meetings under previous administrations. Moreover, there was less pressure for conformity and agreement. Most often, Kennedy conferred with the individual department secretaries, such as Arthur Goldberg, Secretary of Labor; Robert Kennedy, Attorney General; or Abraham Ribicoff, Secretary of Health, Education and Welfare, with whom he worked out the initial stages of the poverty program. Kennedy met with the Cabinet as a body only when a matter involved *all* the departments of government. Since Cabinet members had been kept on their toes between meetings, they were generally well prepared to act in concert when called together by the President.

The White House Staff

Far more important than the Cabinet in influencing the President is the group of unofficial advisers known as the White House Staff. The first President to employ such an organization was Jackson, who feuded with his Cabinet and developed

---

[14] The quotations from Harding and the discussion of the compensation theory are drawn from Richard F. Fenno, Jr., "The President's Cabinet," in *The Presidency,* edited by Aaron Wildavsky (Boston: Little, Brown, 1969), pp. 491–512.

President Nixon has relied heavily on his national-security adviser, Henry Kissinger (right), for crucial foreign-policy dealings such as those with China arranged through Yugoslav Ambassador Cornelieu Bogdan (center).

an alternative group of advisers made up of trusted friends, which he referred to as his "kitchen cabinet." Subsequent Presidents have followed Jackson's example, although, since the White House Staff is an unofficial body, its structure and makeup is likely to vary considerably with each administration.

The White House Staff is necessary to the President as a body of specialists, undivided in their loyalties. Its members are generally more anonymous than members of the Cabinet. The proverbial "men behind the scenes" are often old friends of the President, in whom he feels complete confidence; their influence on him is sometimes enormous.

The functions of the White House Staff are various and extensive. The Staff manages the President's time, deciding who gets to see him and who does not. Its members brief the President on public opinion and write his speeches and press releases. They act as liaisons with Congress. And they affect other branches of the executive bureaucracy whenever they brief the President on the work done in the Executive branch and advise him on appointments. Finally, they advise him on security policy.

Frequently, one man is made overall coordinator of the White House Staff. Sherman Adams had astonishing power under Eisenhower, and Eisenhower freely admitted his dependency on him. Theodore Sorenson was Kennedy's right-hand man (though he shared the position with Robert Kennedy). The most conspicuous example of a 'President's man" in recent times has been Henry Kissinger, as specialist on national security under Nixon.

Kissinger—a Harvard professor with a flair for the intrigue of top-level political strategy—shared the headlines with Nixon during his trip to the People's Republic of China in 1972. He personally engineered the journey, preceded the President in a secret preliminary visit, and participated in Nixon's talks with Chou En-lai and Mao Tse-tung.[15]

---

[15] See sketch of Kissinger in *Newsweek* (February 7, 1972), "Mr. Nixon's Secret Agent."

A few months later, Kissinger also prepared the way for President Nixon's meeting with Soviet party chief Leonid Brezhnev in Moscow. During both of these secret negotiations, Kissinger was entrusted with enormous responsibility and was treated by his hosts accordingly. During the Moscow visit he spoke with Brezhnev for a total of fourteen hours, a longer interview than had been granted to any other Western diplomat.

The Executive Office

The White House Staff is one of sixteen agencies that constitute the Executive Office of the President. These agencies deal with domestic as well as foreign affairs; they are as general as the Office of Management and Budget, and as specific as the Special Action Office for Drug Abuse Prevention.

The origins of the Office of Management and Budget (OMB) go back to 1921, when the Bureau of the Budget was established to coordinate the haphazard budget requests for the various departments, thereby initiating a major change in the allocation of powers between the Executive and Legislative branches of government.[16] Franklin Roosevelt made this shift more definite when he transferred the Bureau from the Treasury Department into the Executive Office. Today's Office of Management and Budget—reorganized under its present name by President Nixon in 1970—is a six-hundred-man operation. Nixon described the reorganized agency as "the President's principal arm for the exercise of his managerial functions." While the Domestic Council, formed at the same time, was to be "primarily concerned with what we do: the Office of Management and Budget will be primarily concerned with how we do it, and how well we do it."[17] OMB prepares the federal budget—designates what funds Congress will allocate, and resolves competing claims from the various departments and agencies. It has responsibility for evaluating the performances of these departments and agencies to insure that they are fulfilling the aims of funded programs. OMB also reviews legislation in relation to the budget and monitors all government statistics. The President has acquired tremendous power through OMB, for through it he decides the funding priorities of the nation. The Chief of OMB occupies such an important high-level position that some claim the post is as crucial as Kissinger's.[18]

Another agency concerned with economic matters is the Council of Economic Advisers. Similar to the White House Staff in its closeness to the President, it is a three-man council (appointees must be confirmed by the Senate), which advises the President on such economic matters as taxation, the stemming of inflation, and unemployment. However, the independence of its thinking is not unlimited. Originally conceived as a highly independent body of experts, the Council members are now expected to support the President in testifying before Congress and to resign if they disagree with him. But in actuality, the President is rarely an economic expert, and will hesitate to assert himself in this area.

---

[16] Grant McConnell sees the creation of the Bureau of the Budget as a governmental change of constitutional importance—greatly increasing the power of the President. See *The Modern Presidency* (New York: St. Martin's Press, 1967), p. 41.

[17] *Congressional Quarterly,* vol. 28, no. 11 (March 13, 1970).

[18] The importance of such an office is enhanced by personal rapport: George Schultz, who held the office until he became Secretary of the Treasury, shares the President's calm, quiet, and even-tempered approach to people and politics alike. See character sketch in *Newsweek* (November 15, 1971).

Table 7-2   **Executive Office of the President**

Non-Cabinet Agencies Directly under the President

The White House Office	Office of Economic Opportunity
Council of Economic Advisers	Office of Emergency Preparedness
Council on Environmental Quality	Office of Intergovernmental Relations
Council on International Economic Policy	Office of Management and Budget
Domestic Council	Office of Science and Technology
National Aeronautics and Space Council	Office of Telecommunications Policy
National Security Council	Special Action Office for Drug Abuse Prevention
Office of Consumer Affairs	Special Representative for Trade Negotiations

Source: Executive Office of the President, Office of Management and Budget, *The U.S. Budget in Brief,* Fiscal Year 1973 (Washington, D.C.: Government Printing Office, 1972).

Another executive agency, the National Security Council, is composed of the President, Vice President, the Secretaries of State and Defense, and the Director of the Office of Emergency Preparedness. It was created in 1947, coinciding with the United States' emergence as a major power, to be the central machinery for advising the President and helping him coordinate U.S. military and foreign policy. The National Security Council has varied in significance with the different Presidents. Eisenhower used it extensively and regularly; Kennedy did not, establishing instead a larger but informal body called the Executive Committee of the National Security Council. Nixon, who had been a member of the Council under Eisenhower, has restored it to prominence.

Nixon, we have seen, also gave priority to the Domestic Council, which he created, along with the reorganized OMB, in 1970. It formulates domestic policy on broad questions as well as on specific issues—particularly those involving more than one federal agency—and it makes recommendations to the President. The President heads the Council, which consists of the Vice President, members of the Cabinet (but not the Secretaries of State and Defense), three counselors to the President, the Director and Deputy Director of OMB, and the Director of the Office of Economic Opportunity. The Domestic Council is not designed to work as a full committee; rather, members are assigned to subcommittees formed to deal with particular policy issues. In establishing the Council, Nixon said that it would assess national needs, identify alternative ways of achieving them, and respond to the President's need for quick policy advice on pressing domestic issues. In addition, it would, along with OMB, coordinate national priorities for the allocation of available resources.[19]

The Executive Office of the President also includes the Office of Intergovernmental Relations, the National Aeronautics and Space Council, the Office of Emergency Preparedness, the Office of Science and Technology, the Office of Telecommunications Policy, the Special Representative for Trade Negotiations, and the Council on International Economic Policy. These offices vary in size and importance, depending on presidential priorities and changing national and international events. Three other offices arose directly out of pressing concerns of the 1970s: the Special Action Office for Drug Abuse Prevention, the Council on Environmental Quality, and the Office of Consumer Affairs. The Executive Office is a highly flexible organization, which may be altered at any time to meet the changing needs of the nation.

---

[19] *Congressional Quarterly,* vol. 28, no. 11 (March 13, 1970).

The Special Action Office for Drug Abuse Prevention, for example, came into being when official sources reported that the number of *new* addicts — previously a steady figure — had more than doubled in 1969, rising from 7,219 to 14,606 new reported addicts.[20] In 1971 a special $155-million grant was allocated by Congress, and the SAODAP was assigned such tasks as investigating narcotics-producing plants; searching out ways to control worldwide opium production; developing methadone maintenance programs; expanding drug-education programs; providing special attention to the drug problems of veterans, many of whom had acquired drug habits while serving in Vietnam; and enforcing punishment for drug traffickers.

The Council on Environmental Quality was founded in 1970 in response to growing demands for federal action to halt environmental pollution. The Council reviews any federal project with potential effect on the environment and conducts research on pollution that focuses on whole industries — such as automobile air pollution or noise pollution by jets. It advises and assists the President in preparing an annual report on the state of the environment.

Of related concern, the Office of Consumer Affairs was created in 1971 to analyze and coordinate all federal activities in the field of consumer protection. Its creation owes much to the widely publicized crusades of consumer advocate Ralph Nader.[21]

Finally, the Office of Economic Opportunity represents the government's "war against poverty," as President Johnson called it when the agency was created in 1964 under his administration. During the first year of the Nixon Administration, it was extended, but later it suffered cutbacks and was threatened with dissolution. Affecting about twenty-six million impoverished Americans in cities and rural areas, OEO concerns itself with housing, job opportunities and training, day-care centers for working parents, and equality of educational opportunity.

Areas of Presidential Power

When Franklin Roosevelt took office in the 1930s he brought with him a great change in presidential style. His predecessor, Hoover, had been a solemn, remote figure, scarcely given to communication with his associates, much less with the public. Roosevelt's method was quite the opposite. He initiated a series of radio broadcasts, called "Fireside Chats," designed to reassure the people that they had a competent and caring leader, and to let them know what to expect from the Executive Office. Thus Roosevelt became the first President to astutely exploit modern communication methods in order to appeal directly to the people and to establish his own influence as symbolic head of the government.

With the advent of television, the President, as the titular head of government, received the golden opportunity to use free TV time for announcing programs. Presidents, aware that such appearances gain them public support and future votes, have used the opportunity freely. For example, President Nixon personally

---

[20] *Statistical Abstract of the United States, 1971* (Washington, D.C.: Department of Commerce, 1971), p. 79.

[21] The Agency is a prime example of presidential capitulation to public opinion despite personal inclination. Nixon, traditional defender of the free-enterprise system, self-consciously started his message to Congress with an assurance that the new agency would not interfere with this system, and termed his message a "Buyer's Bill of Rights" in order to place it indisputably in the constitutional tradition. See *Congressional Quarterly Weekly Report*, vol. 29, no. 9 (February 26, 1971).

announced to the nation, over live nationwide television, his wage-and-price-freeze program, troop withdrawals from Vietnam, and his trips to China and Russia. The President's live appearance on television, as elsewhere in public, has important psychological effects, perpetuating his image as both national leader and man of the people.

The President's image as national leader and man of the people is to a large extent real. In an age of specialization, the President must be a generalist. He is expected to operate in an almost unlimited number of areas and to be something of an authority in each of them. Government agencies such as the CIA provide the President with a continuous stream of inside information, allowing him to be one jump ahead, not only of the public, but also of most other members of the government who lack access to such sources. Thus, the President is the insider's insider. He is the one man in the government from whom we expect no secrets to be kept. Other government officials may have more detailed information in certain areas, but no one else has at his fingertips the vast amount of data which lies within the President's domain.

Another important source of the President's authority lies in his power to persuade. Prime-time television and other media outlets are at his disposal for policy statements, but it is the President's task to utilize successfully this powerful means of influence. Persuading the public is a delicate business, highly dependent on such unpredictable elements as personality, national mood, and mass psychology.

But perhaps more important than the President's ability to persuade the public is his use of the techniques of persuasion with other branches of government. Richard E. Neustadt, an authority on the powers of the Executive Office, defined this type of persuasion as "the power to bargain." Since the President is not an absolute ruler, he cannot simply order government officials to concur with his opinions. He must take into account and make allowances for their points of view. In other words, he must negotiate and bargain. However, the President's status and authority clearly give him the advantage over other government figures in the bargaining process. These people are aware that their ability to carry out their jobs and attain their ambitions rely heavily on the President's approval. Hence, as Neustadt says, their "needs and fear" give the President the advantage in bargaining. And, as a consequence, "from the veto to appointments, from publicity to budgeting, and so on down a long list, the White House now controls the most encompassing array of vantage points in the American political system."[22]

Foreign Affairs

Although the areas of presidential leadership frequently overlap, most are clearly identifiable. The one in which presidential power is most clear-cut, probably strongest, and certainly most dramatic, is foreign affairs.

The Constitution gives the President power to appoint all United States representatives abroad, and to negotiate and sign treaties with the advice and consent of the Senate. He has the power to recognize the ambassadors of foreign countries, and he is Commander-in-Chief of the U.S. armed forces throughout the world. In effect, the President is the director of United States foreign policy, and this

---

[22] Richard E. Neustadt, *Presidential Power* (New York: New American Library, 1964), pp. 45, 53, 61.

**President John F. Kennedy (hat in hand) is shown here with
President Charles de Gaulle of France on an official visit
Kennedy made in June 1961.**

position gives him an awesome amount of power over the lives and destinies not
only of Americans but also of world citizenry through his relations to the governments of foreign countries. This power is something the Founding Fathers could
not have foreseen, since the United States in their day was a small, young nation
seeking to avoid entanglements with ideologically hostile foreign powers. As the
United States grew into a world power, however, its relationship with these
countries changed. The two World Wars drew the United States fully into the
realm of international politics, so that today isolationism as a foreign-policy position has become entirely outmoded. For good or ill, the United States has emerged
as a major world power. In response to this change, the power of the Presidency
has become vastly extended. The President is now not simply the chief designer
of our foreign policy, but the guardian and defender of America's power and
prestige.

The President's authority in this area has come to him not only through constitutional prescription, but also through Supreme Court rulings that have given
him great latitude of action. Congress, the most likely partner for sharing this
awesome power, is not designed for quick decisive actions required in today's
foreign policy.

It has fallen to the President, then, acting with the advice of a small circle of
experts and advisers, to take such decisions upon himself. The resulting international agreements, reached between the President and his counterpart in a

foreign government without action by Congress, are called Executive agreements. The President's powers of executive agreement have been the source of some controversy within government. Questions regarding the use of executive agreement were raised in the Supreme Court case of the *United States* v. *Belmont* in 1937, in connection with America's recognition of the Soviet Union. The Supreme Court ruled that executive agreements have the same legal force as treaties, and that they do not lapse with a change in administrations. More than half of our international agreements in recent times have been reached through such presidential action, ranging in importance from relatively insignificant trading gestures to large-scale commitments like the destroyer-base agreement Franklin Roosevelt made with Great Britain, thus bringing the United States closer to entering World War II.

Decision-making by the Executive branch is also necessitated by the fact that much information regarding international affairs has become too complex, the possibility of exposure too dangerous, to be entrusted to numerous leaders in Congress. As the one person with access to all the intelligence data separately compiled by Central Intelligence, the State Department, and the Pentagon, the President has become the ultimate decision-maker in foreign affairs.

In some cases, top secrecy must be maintained in the making of military decisions. The Cuban missile crisis is one of the most dramatic examples of secrecy in military planning and its potential effectiveness. President Kennedy met secretly every day with his top advisers in the White House offices, while Congress, the nation, and the outside world were equally in the dark about a potentially explosive issue. The President's decision to form a blockade against the delivery of missiles to Cuba by the Russian fleet had to be based on incontrovertible and up-to-the-minute information about the deployment of the missiles; and he also had to be certain that the plan's effectiveness would not be undercut by any breach of secrecy.

The Military

Under the Constitution, the President is designated Commander-in-Chief of the armed forces and empowered to appoint all officers of the armed forces with the consent of the Senate. The role of Commander-in-Chief gives the President tremendous power in international affairs, while it also makes him a pivotal figure in the balance between civilian and military authority at home. As an elected civilian official—a representative of the people—the President acts as a check on the power of the military. This aspect of the executive role places tremendous pressure on the President, particularly in wartime. For example, when critics of President Johnson's policies in Vietnam attacked him for escalating the military effort while failing to deal with pressing problems at home, the President promised that both needs would be filled—that we would have both "guns *and* butter." Although we got neither successful military nor domestic policy, the statement does illustrate the dual nature of the President's responsibilities.

Sometimes the balance of power between the military and the civilian government erupts into open confrontation. Such an event occurred in 1951 when President Truman, exercising his power to dismiss officers as well as appoint them, dismissed General Douglas MacArthur, United Nations Field Commander. The General, who had been Supreme Commander of Allied Forces in Japan and Commanding Officer of American forces in the Far East, was appointed United Nations Field Commander in Korea when the Korean War broke out in 1950.

Through public statements issued after his meetings with Chiang Kai-shek, the Nationalist Chinese leader, General MacArthur implied support of the Chinese Nationalists and an involvement with the Nationalists in Korea. The variance with U.S. State Department policy was glaring. His political error was aggravated by military setbacks in Korea at the hands of Chinese Communists, which he blamed on Washington-dictated instructions. MacArthur began advocating maneuvers against the Chinese Communists on their own ground and calling for a victory to "Red China's undeclared war";[23] President Truman and the American allies would have been satisfied to protect South Korea from North Korean domination and keep the war limited. A letter from the General critical to his superiors was sent to the Minority Leader of the House of Representatives. Within a few days MacArthur was relieved of duty. Truman's act caused much public furor, since MacArthur was a popular hero, but the presidential decision held.

The President is not always so successful in defending civilian interests against the military, however. For example, with the publication of the *Pentagon Papers,* the public learned that all the hopeful reports of our military progress in Vietnam during the 1960s actually masked a deep pessimism on the part of the armed forces, and that the great buildup of troops was really their attempt to save an already calamitous situation.

In addition to deploying forces abroad, the President may, if necessary, use the military to control domestic disturbances. In 1961, for example, when James Meredith, an Air Force veteran and a black man, attempted to enroll in the University of Mississippi, violence erupted, resulting in injuries to hundreds and at least one death. To deal with the crisis, President Kennedy used the full extent of his formal and informal powers. He deployed federal troops and federalized the Mississippi National Guard. Moreover, he used the power of his office to override the resistance of the segregationist governor of Mississippi, and then availed himself of the TV networks to explain his actions to the nation. Kennedy saw the crisis as more than a racial issue; it was a test of his power to uphold the Constitution and his ability to maintain the domestic peace. Kennedy's personal feelings may have been stirred by the racial issue, but in sending federal troops he acted as the nation's Commander-in-Chief to put an end to domestic violence.[24]

While only Congress can declare war, raise armies, appropriate funds, and ratify international treaties, these powers today are not very important, and, in reality, Congress has relinquished most of its military power to the President, who can involve the country in war by executive commitments – deployment of forces and executive agreement. The President may also take action to move Congress in the direction of a declaration of war – as President Roosevelt did by the Lend-Lease policy of 1941, which provided arms and raw materials to countries already at war with the Axis powers.

Occasionally an activist President will openly challenge the power of Congress to control the military. Such an event occurred during the administration of Theodore Roosevelt, when the President sent the naval fleet halfway around the world to impress the Japanese and stave off war with the Philippines. Congress opposed his action. But in the end, when Roosevelt's aims were successfully achieved, Congress was forced to appropriate funds to pay for the fleet's return.

[23] Quoted in Neustadt, *Presidential Power,* p. 25.
[24] See Arthur M. Schlesinger, Jr., *A Thousand Days: John F. Kennedy in the White House* (Boston: Houghton Mifflin, 1965).

When military action is required, the production of war materials comes under presidential surveillance and control. In World War I, following the spectacular example of German mobilization of resources, President Wilson virtually took control of the national economy. In World War II, President Roosevelt instituted rationing of food and materials needed for the war effort, and confiscated land. But mobilization of the economy is not the only emergency power the President may assume during wartime. In World War II President Roosevelt issued an executive order aimed at preventing espionage and sabotage through which 112,000 West Coast residents of Japanese ancestry, 70,000 of whom were American citizens, were relocated to detention camps in the Midwest. This autocratic action, when challenged in the Supreme Court, was supported on narrow grounds, and the larger political issues were avoided. In short, the courts did nothing ". . . to restrain and next to nothing to mitigate an arbitrary presidential-military program suspending the liberties of some part of the civilian population."[25]

In 1969 Congress took steps to prevent arbitrary executive actions during war by restricting the President's war-making powers. In a heated debate over Vietnam, the Senate argued about constitutional issues and the nature of power. "The question," Senator Mike Mansfield said, "goes to the nature of the constitutional responsibilities of this body." Senator J. William Fulbright asserted that there was "almost no restraint" on the President's power "to commit the country to dangerous and often irreversible courses of action in foreign policy."[26]

Such reconsideration of the President's power to make foreign policy and military commitments represented a reversal of the Gulf of Tonkin resolution of 1964 – a resolution which gave the President a "blank check" to take whatever military action in Vietnam he felt necessary. The result was a senatorial resolution that any "national commitment" to a foreign power was henceforth to be subject to "a treaty, statute, or concurrent resolution of both houses of Congress specifically providing for such commitment." The Senate subsequently weakened the resolution, redefining "national commitment" to include armed forces but not financial support (as many senators urged). Finally, the resolution was presented as an admonition to the President, based on "the sense of the Senate." In other words, it was not binding. But the Senate made its point: it was seriously concerned and suspicious, and in this regard the senators were presumably representing their constituents. Congress had assumed a watchdog stance, which was reflected in the committees and subcommittees that continued to scrutinize and investigate every request for military expenditure and foreign aid.

Legislative Leadership

According to the Constitution, the President is required to report to Congress "from time to time" on the state of the Union. He may also recommend legislation, call either or both houses of Congress to session or adjourn them if they cannot agree on an adjournment time, and has the power to veto bills which the Congress has passed. Theoretically, the relation between the President and Congress is a balanced, mutually supportive one, allowing the President to impart to Congress information and advice derived from the many sources available to

---

[25] Clinton Rossiter, *The Supreme Court and the Commander in Chief* (Ithaca, N.Y.: Cornell University Press, 1951), pp. 52–53.

[26] *Congressional Quarterly,* Weekly Report, vol. 27, no. 26 (June 27, 1969), pp. 1111–1114.

President Nixon is pictured here in a 1970 visit to a joint session of Congress; Vice President Spiro T. Agnew (left) and former House Speaker John McCormack are in the rear.

him, upon which Congress can base legislative action. In addition, the two branches were intended to provide checks on each other's power. In practice, however, the system is a good deal more complex than these broad outlines imply.

Although technically Congress is the Legislative branch of government, the President has become the chief initiator of legislation. Since Franklin Roosevelt, each President has sent to Congress a detailed program of legislation. Yet, despite his position of power, the President cannot be certain that his legislative program will eventually be enacted; he often encounters major difficulties and sometimes defeat. The interplay of pressures between the President and Congress has taken on aspects of a ritualized tug-of-war.

The President whose party enjoys a substantial majority in Congress can usually expect success for his legislative proposals, particularly in the beginning of his term—the "honeymoon period." Such a President can count on the support of many congressmen of similar ideological bent, and on the political indebtedness of others. Kennedy and Johnson had the advantage of working with congressional majorities. However, the peculiar nature of party politics in the United States makes for subtle differences in the relationship of each President with the legislature. Johnson had more influence on Congress than Kennedy, as reflected by the greater success of his programs. This success resulted from the increased number of liberal northern Democrats carried into Congress with Johnson's landslide victory over Goldwater in 1964, as well as the psychological effects of the Kennedy assassination. Kennedy himself had more limited success, even though he had a majority in Congress. This was true because some of his liberal programs were killed by the coalition of southern Democrats and Republicans.

Presidents who find themselves facing a legislature dominated by the opposition party have a more difficult, but not a hopeless task. Such a situation is not uncommon; there have been six Presidents since 1900 who have been saddled with Congress under control of the opposition, and another three in the 1800s. Richard Nixon took office knowing that he would have to do battle with an opposition Congress. During his first term in office, however, he managed to make some headway in pushing through legislation, chiefly by exploiting the split between southern and northern Democrats. Eisenhower similarly took advantage of loose party discipline and the possibilities open to congressmen for crossing party lines. His bipartisan strategy was so successful that Democrats repeatedly provided him his necessary margins of victory—fifty-eight times in 1953, the administration's worst legislative year.[27]

In short, a President can manipulate predictable intra-party tensions to his own advantage. But the manipulation of bipartisan power is always difficult. Usually the outlook for a President facing a hostile Congress is bleak; of necessity, more compromise is involved than with friendly Congresses.

However, even if an opposition Congress refuses to pass the bills the Chief Executive recommends, the President still retains the power to kill legislation he disagrees with through his use of the veto. When the President vetoes a bill, he returns it with his objections to Congress. In response, Congress is able to override the veto by a two-thirds vote in the House and the Senate. A bill becomes law if the President neither signs a bill nor vetoes it within ten workdays of receiving it. But if Congress adjourns within this period, the President can kill the bill by taking no action on it—the *pocket veto.*

Few vetoes—about 3 percent of the total—have been overridden. In fact, the threat of a veto itself is so strong that most Presidents have not had to use it extensively. Franklin Roosevelt's total of 633 vetoes issued between 1933 and 1945 represent an all-time record; Kennedy and Johnson were close to the average, with 21 and 30 respectively. During his first term in office President Nixon had vetoed over twenty bills.

A limitation to the President's veto power is the lack of the item veto—the power to reject individual stipulations in a bill submitted for presidential approval. Knowing of this check, Congress frequently adds riders—which may be distantly related, or even totally unrelated, provisions for desired legislation—to a bill whose substance the President is sure to endorse. Examples of this strategy are numerous. One occurred recently when an amendment calling for the busing of black students to white schools was added to a popular aid-to-education bill. The bill narrowly passed both houses of Congress and was signed into law by the President. Its enforcement in some states caused such violent opposition, however, that President Nixon subsequently called for a moratorium on busing.

Nevertheless, in the struggle between Congress and the President, the President appears to have the advantage. He has more tools and techniques at his disposal than Congress has. Among the most effective are informal pressures. For ex-

[27] Reported in *Congressional Quarterly Almanac for 1953,* quoted in Louis W. Koenig, *The Chief Executive* (New York: Harcourt Brace Jovanovich, 1968), p. 146.

"Since most of our power was usurped by the Executive branch, I find I have more free time to devote to getting myself re-elected."

Playboy, *June 1971*
Copyright © 1972 by *Playboy*

ample, if a President wants to influence Congress's appropriations of funds or voting on a bill, he may invite certain congressmen to the Oval Room, or call them on the telephone, in order to apply unofficial executive pressure. The particular sales technique a President uses to promote his plans varies greatly with personality. Lyndon Johnson, for example, was well known for his aggressive, hard-sell approach. An experienced member of Congress, Johnson brought the tactics of that branch of government to the Presidency. He would wheedle, cajole, and bulldoze his listener until he got the response he was after. Richard Nixon, a lawyer and a veteran of the low-key Eisenhower administration, is more of a soft-sell President. His favorite line is "I know you have problems with this, and I will completely understand if you can't come with me. But if you can I'd appreciate it."[28]

A President may also use social pressures to punish uncooperative legislators. He may exclude them from White House functions or refuse to hear their opin-

---

[28] Rowland Evans, Jr., and R. D. Novak, *Nixon and the White House: The Frustration of Power* (New York: Random House, 1971), p. 107.

ions on issues. This type of presidential exile was practiced by Lyndon Johnson on Senator J. William Fulbright for his outspoken criticism of the Vietnam War, and by Eisenhower on Senator Joseph McCarthy for his immoderate anticommunist campaign and his attacks on the army. But whatever technique of informal persuasion a President uses, his influence is likely to have a telling effect, simply because of the enormous status and power of the office which he fills.

Another source of presidential power has grown out of the accepted practice of filling in details of legislation—a practice that arose in response to a practical need of Congress. Because many areas of legislation, such as labor relations and tariff agreements, are highly complex and require administrative expertise which Congress may lack, Congress may limit itself to setting guidelines or standards and relying on the executive bureaucracy to fill out the specifics.

Finally, the President can seek support for legislation through the three major addresses he now delivers to Congress: the State of the Union, the State of the World, and the National Budget. Fulfilling his mandate to address Congress on the state of the nation, the President has an opportunity in these messages to exert the power of persuasion in ways that have great impact. As clearly addressed to the nation as to Congress, these addresses are instantly televised and reported in the newspapers. They are usually intended to make Congress feel that this is what the nation, and not the President alone, wants and believes.

The President and the Judiciary

Under the Constitution, the President would seem to have wide-reaching power in the judicial area. He appoints federal judges with the advice and consent of the Senate, and he has actual judicial power himself: he can grant reprieves, pardons, and amnesty for offenses against the United States. However, in actuality, the President's power over the courts is, as we shall see, limited by a number of factors.

Appointment of federal judges is, of course, the President's most important power over the judicial system. While lower appointments to the federal courts are usually left to the Justice Department, the President has the opportunity to exert control over the courts through his appointments of the men at the top of the judicial hierarchy. Moreover, through his appointments of judges to the Supreme Court, the President can not only create conditions favorable to his administration, but also—since Supreme Court appointments are for life—help shape the course of future events.

However, Supreme Court appointments do not always turn out as planned. First, appointments of justices must be approved by the Senate. This process can frustrate a President's plans, especially when Congress is dominated by the opposition party, as was the case when the Senate rebuffed Nixon's nominations: In 1969 Clement Haynsworth was rejected because of conflict-of-interest charges, and in 1970 G. Harrold Carswell was denied the post because of his mediocre judicial record. Second, even when the President succeeds in seating a judge, there is nothing to insure that he will remain a "President's man." The President can only appoint judges; he cannot remove or discipline them. And once they are on the bench, they are far more likely to base their decisions on judicial tradition, the evolving tone of the Court, and their own opinions than on their loyalty to the President.

However, as independent as the Judiciary is, it is still constrained by the fact that it must depend on the other branches of government to enforce its decisions. Thus the fact that the Judicial branch is effectively powerless alone causes it to act within the confines set for it by prevailing political realities. It can fight the President, and it can hold out in that fight for a long while, but in the end it must at least compromise, for it is the Executive branch of government which ultimately carries out judicial decisions. This principle was recognized very early in the nation's history. For example, under Thomas Jefferson's administration, Chief Justice John Marshall returned a decision on the case of *Marbury* v. *Madison* which was unacceptable to the President. Jefferson's response was to declare: "Marshall made the decision, now let him enforce it."

Presidential Leadership in Party Politics

There is no mention of parties in the Constitution, but it is an established fact that American politics operates with two major parties. Each major party is essentially a decentralized set of local committees that choose delegates to the national nominating convention every four years. These delegates come together for the purpose of selecting their nominee for the Presidency. They elect a national chairman, who functions in the interim between conventions. The national chairman of the Republican Party in 1972 was Senator Robert Dole of Kansas. He is the nominal head of the Party, but, in fact, for the party occupying the White House, it is the man elected President who invariably is the real leader of his party. There is no equivalent of the President's position in the opposing party. The last defeated presidential candidate has power in his party, but it does not compare with the party influence of the President.

The President generally follows the suggestions of local party chiefs in making appointments to federal positions, thereby strengthening his political power through the use of patronage. Despite the fact that he is national leader, however, the President has little control over who is elected in state and local elections; it is simply not possible for him to be in all places at all times, or to master the issues that turn the tide at the local level. Sometimes, however, he can aid a party member substantially by publicly supporting him for congressional election or by being photographed with him so that the public identify the two men with each other. In presidential election years these actions, combined with presidential popularity, can result in the lower official's "riding the President's coattails" to victory. Presidential endorsement, however, carries little weight in a nonpresidential election year.

The Interaction of Presidential Responsibilities

While the areas of presidential leadership can be separated for analysis, they continuously intermingle, and at times even interfere, with one another. Clinton Rossiter, after describing all the areas, offered in summary the image of the Presidency as a "wonderful stew whose unique flavor could not be accounted for simply by making a list of its ingredients."[29] The President, attempting to respond to party demands, will feel the pressure of his responsibilities as arbiter of the national budget, or he will have to proceed more cautiously than his party would like, because he knows that if he does not, a reaction will be expressed in the

---

[29] Clinton Rossiter, *The American Presidency* (New York: Harcourt Brace Jovanovich, 1960), p. 41.

*Vice President Hubert Humphrey
(right) joined President Lyndon
Johnson here at one of the massive
barbecues at the LBJ ranch for
which Johnson's Presidency
was noted.*

courts or in Congress. In foreign affairs the President must fulfill his roles as chief ambassador and guardian of the nation's security, while taking care that his actions do not alienate important members of his party and thereby jeopardize his status as party leader. Presidential responsibilities, then, are rarely clear cut or easily executed; final presidential action in any one area of leadership is a culmination of consideration of all of them.

Presidential Style

Today, the average American has a much more intimate acquaintance with national leaders than did his grandfather, or even his father. Television brings the President into our living rooms, and we develop the feeling that we know him almost on a personal level. Best-selling books and magazine articles by and about members of his family and staff augment this sense of personal knowledge, filling us in on what food the President eats, what color he likes his wife to wear, and what he enjoys doing in his spare time. Calvin Coolidge, for example, was said to have napped at least once a day; some people claimed he suffered from narcolepsy. Numerous editorial statements that barrage us through the media provide ample help in judging his actions. Perhaps it is this transformation of the Presidency to a national seat of superstardom that has made us so aware of the phenomenon which has come to be known as presidential style.

No longer the final authority, former President Harry S Truman paid an informal visit to the U.S.S. Salem *off the French coast during a European vacation in 1958. While in office, Truman had been noted for his blunt language and down-to-earth style.*

According to Louis Koenig, who has written on the office of the Chief Executive, presidential styles fit generally into two schools. One school patterns its conduct on the intrinsic dignity of the office, after the model of George Washington. As different as Eisenhower and Kennedy were, Koenig believes they both veered toward this school. The other school is exemplified by the informal, uninhibited manner of such Presidents as Andrew Johnson, Harry Truman, and Lyndon Johnson.[30]

Although the President is the focal point of countless pressures and influences, in many cases he alone makes a final decision. Often this decision is determined by his character—the dynamics of his personal makeup—much more than by purely objective considerations. Also, the President's personality, along with his personal, social, and political loyalties and ties, determines the sort of people he will appoint to federal offices, who will largely determine the priorities of his administration. Finally, the personality of the President will influence, to a great extent, the entire tone of the country during the four years he holds office. Thus, the Kennedy years are often remembered for poetry readings and concerts at the

---

[30] Koenig, *The Chief Executive*, p. 341.

White House, and for carefree summer days of swimming and playing touch football on Cape Cod; the Eisenhower years are pictured as a time filled with leisurely rounds of golf and peaceful Camp David surroundings; the Johnson years are noted for informal Texas barbecues and "down home" gatherings of friends. Each period is distinguished by a particular mood. The national atmosphere emanating from the White House affects the way people view themselves, their problems and their hopes. Often a certain group or class may feel itself either favored or disenfranchised more on the basis of its response to the President's personality than because of anything tangible. As a result, the mood which the President projects may be a very real force in determining people's actions, and thus have a quite important effect on political matters.

Style of Decision-making

In analyzing presidential decision-making, it is important to remember that the President is not a computer programmed to consume vast quantities of complex data and come up with recommendations based on mathematical laws. Rather, he is a human being doing a very difficult job. As Theodore Sorenson pointed out, conflict is at the core of White House decision-making—conflict between departments and agencies, between the Executive and Congress, between interest groups in society.[31] Decision-making in the White House involves extraordinary difficulties; the problems are complex. There will always be some people who will be alienated by a decision; moreover, at any moment a plan may be rendered obsolete, or proven wrong, so that each White House decision is at best a calculated risk.

The President must also determine which decisions he must make personally. He will at times be tempted to make decisions which might be more properly vested in a lower-echelon agency (a temptation supported by the popular image of the omniscient President), and he may at times be tempted to delegate a decision that he alone should make (a temptation to yield to pressure from ambitious government officials anxious to assert their authority). President Truman used to say, "The buck stops here"; and often that is political reality: if, in arriving at a decision, the President has weighed what Sorenson defined as the "limits of permissibility," and the "limits of available information,"[32] then he can feel somewhat confident that the decision is a reasonable one.

Presidents have taken various approaches to decision-making. Nixon chose to surround himself with committees and councils, isolating himself from the minor irritations of government, and in this way conserving his time and energies for major concerns. In contrast, John Kennedy was known for throwing himself into "the thick of things" and constantly seeking alternatives so that he would not be imprisoned by the choices finally presented to him by his aides.

Two Case Studies in Presidential Style

Lyndon Johnson, the Persuader   The image the nation had of Johnson before he became President was that of a powerful congressional leader, and indeed he was.

---

[31] Theodore C. Sorenson, *Decision-Making in the White House* (New York: Columbia University Press, 1963), p. 15.

[32] Sorenson, *Decision-Making in the White House*, pp. 23ff.

Johnson himself expressed his devotion to legislative politics when he said in 1963, "for thirty-two years, Capitol Hill has been my home."[33] When he ascended to the Presidency, he continued to use many of the tactics to control Congress that he had learned to use as Majority Leader in the Senate.

After the Kennedy assassination, Johnson resolved to show that the United States had passed into the hands of a strong leader, who would sustain it in a dominant role among the nations of the world. As President, his key to achieving this control was congressional leadership, and the key to congressional leadership was the series of tactics Johnson had learned during his thirty-two years in Congress.

The tactics were various. To get a controversial bill passed, providing for purchase of Soviet wheat, he called congressmen into special session during the Christmas holiday and sought to restore their spirits with a huge Christmas Eve party. To insure passage of an equally controversial tax bill, he personally telephoned every member of the Finance Committee, asking them to hold back an amendment that threatened to drastically weaken it. In the case of the Civil Rights Bill, he avoided compromise by taking a firm stand and informing Congress that he would exert pressure to hold up other Senate business while outwaiting any resulting filibuster. In this way, he also made his sympathies clear to those inclined to question his sincerity, as a southerner, in the matter of civil rights.

In mustering support for the Economic Opportunity Act of 1964, Johnson made shrewd use of opposition legislators. He consulted with Republican congressmen constantly, and he relied on Senator Everett M. Dirksen "almost as if the Republican leader were the Democratic leader in the Senate."[34] He marshalled a mountain of statistical data justifying the Act, portraying it to conservatives with emphasis on the "Americanism" of its self-help features. At the same time, he appealed to liberals by associating the bill with a billion-dollar cut in defense expenditure in 1963, stating that the saved funds would pay for the war on poverty, the money going "from the haves to the have-nots."[35] He visited depressed areas, dangling funds before local officials. Thus Congress found itself yielding to pressures from a President who was also a master political tactician, and who almost always attained the legislative control he sought.

Richard Nixon, the Administrator A President's style is generally most striking where he has the greatest ability: Johnson's, in the legislator's role; Nixon's, in the administrator's. The Nixon ideal in government has been efficiency, following the model of big business; he has proposed major structural changes toward this end and devoted a vast amount of energy getting his master plan into operation.

In addition to creating the Domestic Council and OMB in 1970, and setting up new lines of authority to give the two offices greater prominence, Nixon created the Special Action Office for Drug Abuse Prevention, the Office of Consumer Af-

---

[33] Quoted in Rowland Evans and Robert Novak, *Lyndon B. Johnson: The Exercise of Power* (New York: New American Library, 1966), p. 380. A good discussion of Johnson in his role as legislator can be found on pp. 380–403 of Evans and Novak's book.

[34] Koenig, *The Chief Executive*, p. 147.

[35] This statement, with a good discussion of the inception and passage of the Economic Opportunity Act of 1964, can be found in John Bibby and Roger Davidson, *On Capitol Hill: Studies in Legislative Process* (New York: Holt, Rinehart and Winston, 1967), pp. 219–251.

When the 1964 Civil Rights Bill was finally passed, Everett M. Dirksen, then Senate Minority Leader (left center, shaking hands), quoted Hugo: "Stronger than all the armies is an idea whose time has come"; but President Johnson's persuasive powers, learned during years in Congress, also had much to do with the final passage of the bill.

fairs, and the Council on International Economic Policy. Further carrying out his bent for organization and reorganization, he greatly simplified application for grants-in-aid to localities, by forming ten regions with one central city in each. Previously, local governments had to make applications to agencies in various cities—to one city for an education grant, for example, and to another for housing. Nixon made it possible for grants to be obtained from many departments located in a single city.

Nixon's major plan for reorganization of the Executive branch, submitted to Congress in 1972, proposed cutting the eleven government departments to eight. While maintaining the Departments of State, Treasury, Defense, and Justice, he would create four new departments, with the goal of focusing on problems and concentrating responsibility for them. These would be: the Department of Natural Resources, comprising land, recreation, water, energy, and mineral resources; the Department of Human Resources, comprising health services, income maintenance and security, education, manpower, and social and rehabilitation services; the Department of Economic Development, comprising food and commodities, domestic and international commerce, science and technology, labor relations and standards, and statistical economic development; and the Department of Community Development, comprising housing, community development, metropolitan development and renewal, and transportation. By reorganizing the departments along these lines, Nixon claimed he would be focusing on problems and

President Nixon is shown here with administration officials and key congressional leaders. To the right of the President is Speaker of the House Carl Albert (D.-Okla.); to the left is Senator Mike Mansfield (D.-Mont.); Secretary of State William Rogers is directly opposite Nixon.

concentrating executive responsibility for carrying out the "great purposes of government."[36]

Some critics have suggested that the impetus for a reorganization may have resulted more from Nixon's passion for order and efficiency than from a basic reassessment of American goals. Opposition to the plan took several forms: disagreement with its substance; party politics (Representative Chet Holifield (D.-Calif.) called the Nixon plan "political grandstanding"); resistance to the practical difficulties involved (Holifield also noted that it would take "at least four years" for his House Government Operations Committee to process the necessary legislation); and the pressure of special-interest groups who did not wish to risk losing their good relationships with the existing bureaucratic structure.[37]

The Limits of Presidential Power

Presidential power may be defined as the capacity to make decisions and see them enforced. How this power is wielded depends upon the capacities of the Presi-

---

[36] *Congressional Quarterly Weekly Report,* vol. 24, no. 5 (January 29, 1971).

[37] *Congressional Quarterly,* vol. 30, no. 14 (April 1, 1972).

dent, the limitations set by the Constitution, and the public's acceptance or resistance to the use of power in a given situation.[38]

The Constitution is vague about presidential power in general, but precise on certain particulars. It provides the President with more exclusive power in foreign affairs than in the domestic arena. It gives him power over the military and allows him loopholes by which he can increase his power in times of crisis. In the Vietnam War, we have seen Congress and the public react against the unsanctioned use of power by the President. Both recognized the need for a strong Executive, yet both guard against his abuse of power.

The constitutional limits on the Presidency may be vague and open to a variety of interpretations, but they are not the only restrictions which the President faces. As we have seen, governmental activity is pervaded by conflict. In order to get done the things he feels are important, the President must continually wage war against a whole army of individuals and groups bent on defeating, changing, or delaying his proposals.

The strongest checks on the power of the President remain the powers of the other two branches of government, the Judiciary and the Congress. The Judiciary, as the final authority on the constitutionality of the law, is better able than Congress to set up legal obstacles in the President's path, restricting his power to act. As Clinton Rossiter has pointed out, in the light of the influence and prestige of the courts, it would be imprudent in the extreme for a President "to invite judicial condemnation."[39]

Congress, on the other hand, if sometimes outflanked in its attempts to limit the actions of an incumbent President, is often successful in passing legislation which restricts the actions of Presidents in the future. For instance, in 1972 the Senate passed the War-Powers Bill. If passed by the House in a similar form, the bill would empower the President to commit armed forces in an emergency but would require him to withdraw such forces within thirty days if denied approval by Congress. In that same year the House passed a strong anti-busing bill. If passed by the Senate with similar content, it could be quite restrictive to a President who favors busing.

Congress can also exert pressure on the President by passage of a resolution or opinion, by moral persuasion, or by making use of its powers of investigation. It may withhold funds for administrative proposals or cripple a measure, as the Senate Finance Committee did in early 1972 when it rejected Nixon's welfare reform program, the Family Assistance Plan, in favor of a plan that would withdraw benefits from 40 percent of the families on welfare and offer them low-paid jobs instead. Under the Constitution, as an extreme instrument to cut off presidential power, Congress can call for impeachment of a President who engages in "treason, bribery, or other crimes or misdemeanors"—an action taken only once in American history, against Andrew Johnson. Johnson's impeachment trial, which, historians now feel, was motivated chiefly by northerners who were incensed at the President's efforts to rebuild the South after the Civil War, ended in acquittal. But its political repercussions, and its humiliating effect on Johnson himself, have so stigmatized the process of impeachment that it has never again been used against an American President.

---

[38] For a good general discussion of presidential power and its roots in both men and events, see Robert S. Hirschfield, "The Reality of Presidential Power." *Parliamentary Affairs*, vol. 21, no. 4 (Autumn, 1968).

[39] Clinton Rossiter, *The American Presidency* (New York: Harcourt Brace Jovanovich, 1960), pp. 48–49.

The final responsibility for decision-making that rests with the President often makes his job a solitary one.

The federal system may also act to hinder the exercise of presidential power. Generally, the states try to control actions which affect their localities, often enlisting the aid of big businesses whose interests involve them in the conflict. Thus, in addition to the federal system, free enterprise — with its political arm, the pressure groups — serves to constrain presidential power.

The Civil Service system, a vast bureaucracy composed in part of appointees, but mostly of individuals who have reached their positions through an impersonal process of qualification and advancement, forms another important impediment to the President's actions. The bureaucracy is so large that it is not always possible for the President to extend his control over all of it. The President cannot control the speed, the techniques, or the intra-office embroilments of the vast pyramids of men and women who form the separate departments and agencies, any more than he can control party affiliations of most of them, and particularly those of civil-service employees. The President, in the area of his richest resource, personnel, knows his most continuous day-to-day frustrations.

The most direct limitation on presidential power, however, comes from the President's personal capabilities. Eisenhower, for example, relied heavily on his Cabinet and Vice President, partly out of inclination, perhaps because his military background had taught him to delegate responsibility along a chain of command, and partly because of his poor health. Harding acknowledged a limited capacity to understand and cope with the problems of the office.

Even strong, activist Presidents have been limited by their own concept of the range of their authority. According to Rossiter, a President's "conscience and training, his sense of history and desire to be judged well by it, his awareness of the need to pace himself lest he collapse under the burden—all join to halt him far short of the kind of deed that destroys a President's 'fame and power.' "[40]

Another factor limiting presidential power, which, though difficult to measure precisely, is nonetheless very powerful, is the force of public opinion. As Lincoln remarked, you can't fool all of the people all of the time. Particularly in a country like the United States, where access to political information is constitutionally guaranteed, a President must be very sensitive to tides of feeling within the electorate if he hopes to retain its good will and cooperation. American history is full of instances in which public opinion operated to restrain a President's actions. Strong antiwar sentiment and disapproval of presidential actions served to retard the course of the Mexican War in the 1840s. Powerful isolationist tendencies in the American public in the 1930s kept the United States out of World War II until the disaster at Pearl Harbor galvanized American feeling against the Axis Powers. More recently, public opinion played a major role in convincing President Johnson not to run for a second term, besides exerting a steady, growing pressure on both Johnson and Nixon to bring an end to the Vietnam War. On the issues of abortion reform and the legalization of marijuana, the President, aware of large areas of conservative feeling, has seen fit to retard legislation, despite pressure calling for liberalized laws.

The Credibility Gap

Given the crucial importance of public opinion, many Presidents have devoted themselves to seeking ways of guiding and molding it to their advantage. The media—newspapers, television news programs, and so forth—are the chief organs in our society for the formation of public opinion. Therefore, attempts at changing public opinion have concentrated on efforts to control these institutions. In recent years such activity has come to be known as "news management."

News management is hardly new. The term was coined during the Eisenhower administration, but charges of government manipulation of the media date back much farther. Even before George Washington took office, delegates to the Constitutional Convention warned colleagues against speaking to reporters, fearing a news leak might prevent the ratification of the Constitution. Lincoln withheld the Emancipation Proclamation for three months because his advisers told him it might cost the Republican Party the election.

It is difficult to pass judgment on news management, because the secrecy in-

---

[40] Clinton Rossiter, *The American Presidency,* p. 70.

"*That bow tie certainly doesn't do anything for his credibility.*"

New Yorker, *November 6, 1971*

volved is often said to be in the national interest. In the past, public opinion regarded secrecy of this sort as legitimate. However, certain events in the 1960s have served to reverse that judgment.

Heated criticism of the administration's management of the news began during John F. Kennedy's term of office, centering largely around the Cuban missile crisis. Kennedy and his advisers withheld all information upon which the decision to act was based. This suppression of data could be defended on the grounds that it was necessary for security and for the success of the venture, but the state of total ignorance which it imposed on the public gave many the feeling, as they fearfully awaited the Soviet Union's reply to Kennedy's ultimatum, that the government had entered a risky global gamble with their lives as the stakes. An earlier incident of news manipulation during the Kennedy administration occurred after the failure of the Bay of Pigs invasion in 1961. As with the Missile Crisis, Kennedy carried out preparations for the invasion in strict secrecy, but since in this case there was no victory to justify the news blackout, Kennedy subsequently attempted to use the media to rationalize the abortive attack. As a result, Kennedy's critics accused him of out-and-out falsehood, charging that suppression of information was as deceptive as an actual distortion of the facts, and as reprehensible.

However, the chief event of our times that has raised the question of news management and news manipulation has been the Vietnam War. The escalation and prolongation of that war under the administrations of Johnson and Nixon, despite emphatic promises by both Presidents that the conflict would soon draw to a close, have created a "credibility gap," a deep-seated, chronic suspicion on the part of many citizens about virtually all statements emanating from the Executive Office.

During President Johnson's term, Senator J. William Fulbright, Chairman of the Senate Foreign Relations Committee, condemned the administration's actions as "the arrogance of power." The charge persisted that the administration was taking us ever deeper into a war we could not win, without sufficient justification and at enormous cost in lives and resources, and national morale and prestige. This criticism and the notion of the credibility gap as a whole focused on the President and his actions, which, many argued, went beyond his mandate. Johnson was accused of withholding the truth by picturing the war as a crusade for democracy that we were winning. While critics pounded at the White House, other Americans assailed the critics for their disloyalty. These people believed that the public must trust their elected officials, who act on the basis of information that cannot be made public lest it endanger American security.

The credibility gap, long dismissed by defenders of the President as a paranoid delusion foisted on the public by malevolent agitators, received objective corroboration in 1971 with the publication of the Pentagon Papers. Publication of the secret papers at last provided official documentation for the charges against the administration. The Papers revealed the details of commitments, never before disclosed to Congress or the public, that had been made to the South Vietnamese regime, a government whose corruption was known but never officially acknowledged. Shocked readers learned the details of decisions to pursue almost hopeless military goals, because military withdrawal might be seen (by the world *and* by the opposition party) as a humiliating defeat for the administration. They also read about military carelessness, impetuousity, and refusal to acknowledge mistakes. And they learned that Johnson had made campaign promises he knew were impossible to fulfill. The Pentagon Papers showed that Kennedy was as much implicated as Johnson. From Truman through Johnson, every President "passed down the problem of Vietnam in worse shape than he had received it."[41] And every President was involved in the credibility issue. Each one had deceived the public about the central dilemma of continued commitment to a losing fight in the interest of our image. Johnson said to his wife in 1965, "I can't finish it with what I have got. So what the hell can I do?" But the information revealed in the Papers demolished the rationalization that the Presidents had been drawn deeper into the war by forces beyond their control—the so-called quagmire theory. The Papers made it evident that the Presidents had deliberately chosen their options. Outraged critics of the Vietnam policy demanded new controls over the Executive branch.

A deeper issue was brought out by the historian Hannah Arendt. Asserting that "the famous credibility gap has suddenly opened up into an abyss," Arendt placed the blame for the government's hopeless involvement in the Vietnam problem on its overreliance on professional "problem-solvers." She charged that these problem-solvers, though highly intelligent, are guided essentially by the mentality of Madison Avenue, being more concerned with image than with reality. "Where

---

[41] "The Lessons of Vietnam," the *New York Times* (July 6, 1971).

defeat was less feared than admitting defeat," she wrote, the government had deceived itself into believing that the cause was a just one, and that we were, in fact, winning a military victory. In this case, she pointed out, the problem to be focused on was not the dishonesty of the administration but its isolation—a self-imposed isolation that encouraged delusions to flourish unchallenged. Thus, she concluded, secrecy, designed to avoid criticism or accountability, had to be reconsidered in order to protect the President from self-deception, and the people from its effects.[42]

The credibility gap, and the mood of suspicion, disunity, and despair which attends it, is merely one aspect of the problem America faces today. Our society is internally divided by contradictory, seemingly irreconcilable forces. An optimist might interpret them as growth pains, signs of dynamic change signaling the emergence of a new order with new answers to all the old problems. But such optimism is not shared by many observers. Most of us acknowledge the problems that must be solved if our society is to survive, but find them so numerous that we hesitate, out of a sense of impotence, even to lend a hand. In such times, the ordinary citizen, knowing that it is his fate not to lead but to be led, looks for a deliverer. In a country where the Presidency has taken on such awesome power and influence, this burden falls largely on the Chief Executive.

Presidential power, then, has grown so much that it has probably permanently altered congressional-executive relationships. Whether or not the needs were subtly planted by the Framers of the Constitution, the Presidency now is supreme, and it is unlikely that Congress will ever be able to regain most of its lost power. Policy-making in America, as it exists today, is conducted by the branch of government that, except for the one man at the top, is not directly elected by the people. The question exists, then, whether the will of the people can be made effective in the context of executive power. Some answers to this question will be considered in the remainder of this book.

SUGGESTED READING

Barber, James David. *The Presidential Character: Predicting Behavior in the White House* (Englewood Cliffs, N.J.: Prentice-Hall, 1972). An important attempt to employ the findings of psychohistory and leadership studies to presidential character. Barber develops types of presidential leadership and writes at length about representative examples.

Binkley, Wilfred E. *President and Congress* (New York: Vintage, 1962). In paperback. A comprehensive historical survey of the Presidency and an appraisal of that office in its relation to Congress. The author examines the problem of the Constitutional Convention —namely, how the Presidency should be related to Congress—and the various solutions to it in the context of the American experience with these governmental institutions. He concludes that the problem of integrating the Executive and Legislative branches has not yet been solved.

Brown, Stuart Gerry. *The American Presidency: Leadership, Partisanship, and Popularity* (New York: Macmillan, 1966). In paperback. A series of related essays on the connections between presidential popularity and presidential leadership. The author examines instances to demonstrate the two principal kinds of popularity, partisan and unpartisan, and

---

[42] See Hannah Arendt. "Lying in Politics," in *Crises of the Republic* (New York: Harcourt Brace Jovanovich, 1972).

then to see how each fares in matters of constitutional controversy and crisis, in domestic policy, and in foreign affairs. The focus of attention is the intricate relationship between a President's popularity and his power to lead.

Corwin, Edward S. *The President, Office and Powers* (New York: New York University Press, 1957). In paperback. This monumental work is primarily a study in public law, with an approach that is historical, analytical, and critical. The main theme is the development and contemporary status of presidential power and the office of the Presidency under the Constitution, but the personal and political aspects of the Presidency are also covered.

Evans, Rowland, and Robert Novak. *Lyndon B. Johnson: The Exercise of Power* (New York: New American Library, 1966). In paperback. A serious political biography of the thirty-sixth President. On the basis of personal observations and numerous interviews, the authors show how LBJ sought, achieved, and dispensed power, particularly after he became Senate Democratic Leader in 1953. The book, then, also is a study of political power, especially the LBJ style of power politics in both the Senate and the Presidency.

Fenno, Richard F., Jr. *The President's Cabinet* (New York: Vintage, 1959). In paperback. A political analysis of the President's Cabinet which emphasizes functions and relationships rather than historical development. The author analyzes the Cabinet as a distinct institution, the close President-Cabinet relationship, and the patterns of influence between the President-Cabinet nexus on the one hand, and the larger political system on the other. He concludes that the Cabinet is a force of diversity, vis-à-vis unity, in the American political system.

Hargrove, Erwin C. *Presidential Leadership, Personality and Political Style* (New York: Macmillan, 1966). In paperback. A study of the problem of presidential leadership. The author demonstrates how presidential leadership grows out of crucial choices Presidents make about their role in the political system and, in turn, how these choices are influenced by the personalities of individual Presidents.

Kennedy, John F. *Profiles in Courage* (New York: Harper & Row, 1964). In paperback. John Kennedy chose several famous American politicians and, in case studies, discussed the political crises through which they emerged as courageous leaders. The book, highly readable, places the conditions of political leadership in historical perspective and reveals the late President's ability to evaluate true leadership with insight.

Koenig, Louis W. *The Chief Executive* (New York: Harcourt Brace Jovanovich, 1968). In paperback. A full-length study of the Presidency, rich in illustrative examples and historical insights. The Presidency is analyzed from its historic past into its troublesome present, and warnings and recommendations for the future of the office, an office which the author claims must be powerful, are set forth in a learned and readable style.

Neustadt, Richard E. *Presidential Power: The Politics of Leadership* (New York: Wiley, 1964). In paperback. In one of the most important books yet produced on the Presidency, Richard Neustadt analyzes the functions and authority of the Presidency and the politics of presidential leadership. The emphasis is that presidential power is the talent to convince, and that such talent is eminently personal. The author explores the politics of presidential power: what is it, how to get it, how to keep it, how to use it.

Rossiter, Clinton. *The American Presidency* (New York: Harcourt Brace Jovanovich, 1960). In paperback. An examination of the Presidency in terms of what the office is; what its powers, limitations, and tasks are; and what it should be. In a series of brief sketches of some of the more significant Presidents, Rossiter describes the evolution of the Presidency from a relatively weak office in relation to Congress, to a powerful institution that, although it cannot force its will on a reluctant Congress, likely will dominate Capitol Hill permanently.

Schlesinger, Arthur M., Jr. *A Thousand Days: John F. Kennedy in the White House* (Greenwich, Conn.: Fawcett Publications, 1965). In paperback. A personal memoir and a historical narrative of the Kennedy Presidency. The book combines a keen political insight with a wide-ranging account of the events, foreign and domestic, of the Kennedy Presidency and the Kennedy operating and decision-making style.

8
THE BUREAUCRACY

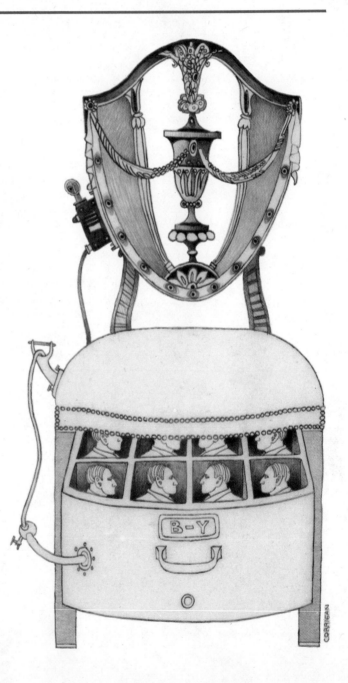

Within the great reaches of the American bureaucracy is an official called the "Associate Assistant Administrator in the Office of Assistant Administration for Administration."[1] Mind-boggling though it is, the title says much about the complexity of a system built of layers upon layers of policy-makers. This national bureaucracy of ours, with its three million civilian employees, has been called the fourth branch of government. Some people think it has grown into the most powerful branch of all, with perhaps the most profound effect upon the daily lives of Americans.

Contemporary Criticisms of Bureaucracy

Today the term *bureaucracy* is often used derogatorily – virtually as a synonym for *red tape*. Bureaucracies have become unpopular with people of various political ideologies, both conservative and liberal. In the 1930s, however, New Deal liberals had great hopes that economic conditions could be improved by government action. The bureaus and agencies established under the Roosevelt administration were the primary vehicle through which the "power of the mighty was to be put down, and the welfare of the humble exalted."[2] Thus, the Securities and Exchange Commission was created to control the power of the Wall Street establishment; the Tennessee Valley Authority to bring prosperity to a poverty-stricken rural and agricultural area; the National Labor Relations Board to protect the rights of workers. These federal agencies were established as instruments for significant change in the nation. Liberals applauded, but conservatives were disturbed, for this development, if not downright unconstitutional, certainly meant abandonment of the traditional "hands off" attitude of government toward business.

Since the sixties, however, the New Left and many liberals have joined conservatives in criticizing the bureaucracy as inflexible, stodgy, and unimaginative. Those interested in changing government policies in education, welfare, consumer protection, and foreign policy complain that the professional Washington bureaucrats do too little to solve the problems of the nation. One of these critics, economist John Kenneth Galbraith, when he was ambassador to India, wrote to President John F. Kennedy describing his difficulties with Department of State bureaucrats so bogged down by paperwork and indecision that they could not be prodded into action. Wrote Galbraith:

If the State Department drives you crazy, you might calm down by contemplating its effect on me. The other night I woke up with a blissful feeling and discovered I had been dreaming that the whole . . . place had burned down. I dozed off again hoping for a headline saying no survivors. I think I dislike most the uncontrollable instinct for piously reasoned inaction. When the Department does respond to telegrams it is invariably to recommend evasion of issues that cannot be evaded. The result, in the end, is that we get the worst of all available worlds.[3]

---

[1] From Martin Landau, "On the Concept of a Self-Correcting Organization," paper prepared for delivery at the Maxwell School, Syracuse University, under the auspices of the Albert Schweitzer Chair in the Humanities, April 13, 1972, p. 1.

[2] Francis E. Rourke, *Bureaucracy, Politics, and Public Policy* (Boston: Little Brown, 1969), p. 128.

[3] John Kenneth Galbraith, *Ambassador's Journal* (Boston: Houghton Mifflin, 1969), p. 177.

Liberals today generally feel that the bureaucracy tends to represent those with a vested interest in keeping things as they are, and that any improvement in the welfare of the less powerful groups in our society will come in spite of bureaucratic activities, rather than because of them. For example, Daniel P. Moynihan, former special adviser to President Nixon and staff member of the Harvard-MIT Joint Center for Urban Studies, expressed the disenchantment of the liberal establishment when he said that "liberals must divest themselves of the notion that the nation, especially the cities of the nation, can be run from agencies in Washington;"[4] and Robert F. Kennedy, campaigning for the Democratic nomination for President in 1968, made a similar point before an audience in the Watts section of Los Angeles, California: "I want the control over your destinies to be decided by the people in Watts, not by those of us in Washington."[5]

[4] Herbert Kaufman, "Administrative Decentralization and Political Power," *Public Administration Review*, vol. 29 (January/February 1969), p. 7.

[5] Kaufman, "Administrative Decentralization and Political Power," p. 7.

Administrative Organization

Growth of Bureaucracy

Some problems related to the bureaucracy are a direct result of the tremendous increase in the number of civilians employed by the federal government. In 1860, federal civilian employees totaled fifty thousand or about one out of every six hundred Americans. By 1970, the number had grown to three million, or about one out of every seventy. The enormous expansion of bureaucratic operations is dramatically illustrated by a comparison of today's Postal Service with its modest eighteenth-century counterpart. The following passage from a letter written by Thomas Pickering, Washington's first Postmaster General, to Secretary of the Treasury Hamilton, describes his plan for the first headquarters of the Post Office Department and asks for Treasury approval of a projected three-hundred-dollar annual budget:

After much inquiry, I have found a house which would accommodate my numerous family, and at the same time give me office room. The greatly extended *business of the department, I think, may be accomplished with the same help which has been used since the time of Mr. Osgood's appointment; to wit, an assistant and a clerk. For these, with their necessary writing-desk, table, boxes, cases, and papers, would sufficiently occupy 1 room; and another room would be convenient for myself. A servant also will be wanted to keep the rooms in order, make fires and perform other services. These services, however, not being constant, I would employ a domestic servant, but one selected with a reference to such public service. If for the two rooms for the General Post-Office, a cellar for wood, and the necessary attendance of my domestic servant, I might make a charge of about three hundred dollars. I would then engage the house referred to; but, previous to such engagement, I wish to obtain your opinion on the propriety of the charge.[6]*

Today, the Postal Service has over six hundred thousand full-time employees, staffing over thirty thousand individual offices across the country.[7]

Why has the bureaucracy expanded to its current size? C. Northcote Parkinson, a British humorist, has suggested that the growth of bureaucracies proceeds according to a fixed principle he calls Parkinson's Law: It is that "the work expands to fill the time available." The bureaucrat who operates by this principle always hires two assistants when only one is needed, and they, in turn, create work to fill time, so that each soon requires two aides, causing the agency to expand geometrically. When agencies can show that the conditions they are charged with remedying have gone from bad to worse, they ask for and receive larger appropriations. Consequently, the least successful agencies generally receive the greatest financial reward.[8]

In bureaucracies all over the world, our own included, Parkinson's Law operates with more truth than fancy. But there are, in fact, several valid justifications for the massive increase in federal employees in the United States during the last quarter of a century. First, the federal government has had to set up many agencies in areas once considered the primary responsibility of local government or private business. These agencies finance, regulate, and evaluate public education;

---

[6] Leonard White, *The Federalists: A Study in Administrative History* (New York: Macmillan, 1948), pp. 492–493.

[7] The Post Office is no longer a Cabinet-level department. Starting July 1, 1971, it began operating as an independent establishment of the Executive branch.

[8] C. Northcote Parkinson, *Parkinson's Law* (Boston: Houghton Mifflin, 1959).

Table 8-1   **Civilian Employment of Federal Executive Branch**

Year	Number (in thousands)	Rate per 1000 population
1940	1,033	8.0
1945	3,496	27.0
1950	2,052	12.7
1955	2,376	14.3
1960	2,403	13.1
1965	2,507	12.8
1970	2,891	14.1

Source: Statistical Abstract of the United States, 1971 (Washington, D.C.: Department of Commerce, 1971), p. 388.

establish and maintain public highways and transportation systems; operate a vast network of law-enforcement agencies; and establish and enforce standards for health care, welfare, and air pollution, besides performing other functions. Another factor in bureaucratic expansion is the rise of the United States as an international power, calling for the employment of a large number of civilian employees to help conduct foreign affairs and run military installations. In 1972, for example, approximately 1.1 million civilians were working for the Department of Defense. Finally, the size and scope of the federal bureaucracy has been broadened by a changing concept of the relationship between government and business. The change arose out of the development of gigantic business enterprises against whose power the individual citizen was relatively helpless. The government no longer takes a consistent laissez-faire attitude toward business; instead, it often acts to protect the rights of the individual as "the policeman over the economic giants who dominate our society."[9] To this end, many new regulatory bodies have been created in diverse areas, as exemplified by the Civil Aeronautics Board, the Federal Power Commission, the Federal Trade Commission, and the National Labor Relations Board.

It is important to note that the growth of bureaucracy has not been limited to the federal government. While the number of federal civilian employees increased by about 40 percent from 1950 to 1968 (from 2.1 million to 3 million), the number of state employees was up by 150 percent (from 1 million to 2.5 million), and the number of local government workers almost doubled.[10]

Growing bureaucracies—and complaints about them—are not, moreover, exclusive to the government. They are found in business, labor unions, colleges, and even religious organizations. There is evidence that, like government agencies, these private bureaucracies are also burdened by their enormous size. For instance, in 1972, the new chairman and chief executive of the thirty-six-thousand–employee Pan American World Airways ordered the elimination of over five hundred administrative and managerial positions in an attempt to make the organization more efficient.[11] And during the late 1960s, I. W. Abel replaced David J. MacDonald, the long-time president of the United Steel Workers of America, fol-

[9] Charles E. Jacob (ed.), Policy and Bureaucracy (New York: Van Nostrand-Reinhold, 1965), p. 33.
[10] Data from the Statistical Abstract of the United States.
[11] The Wall Street Journal (March 23, 1972), p. 2.

lowing a rebellion by USW members against an entrenched (and apparently unresponsive) union bureaucracy. Finally, the Catholic Church (with forty-seven million American communicants) has met similar difficulties. In a typical protest against Church bureaucracy, a committee of priests in the Archdiocese of New York, disturbed by the tendency of the Cardinal and his staff to make all decisions about selection of officials, programs, and budgets, has requested a stronger voice for the priesthood in such activities.[12]

Whatever the faults of large-scale organizations, they must be accepted as an essential component of modern industrial society. Within government and outside of it, the massive bureaucracy is here to stay.

Present Structure of the Bureaucracy

The federal bureaucracy is extensive and complex, as Figure 8-1 indicates. For purposes of study it can be divided into four broad agency categories: Cabinet departments, independent executive agencies, government corporations, and independent regulatory agencies. All are theoretically under the President's control. In addition, he is served by the Executive Office of the President, a group of White House staff members and special "offices;" they advise him directly in specific areas and help him organize, control, and coordinate the work of all the other agencies.

The diagram of the Executive branch shown here shows only the major divisions of the federal bureaucracy. Each agency has many subdivisions. For example, the staff of the Department of Commerce, set up "to foster, serve and promote the Nation's economic development and technological advancement,"[13] is headed by the Secretary of Commerce, a member of the Cabinet, and has—in addition to a general counsel—an ombudsman for business, an assistant secretary for administration, and six assistant secretaries who head a proliferation of administrations, bureaus, and offices in such diverse areas as business economics, the census, telecommunications, maritime affairs, commerce, and tourism, among others. An executive with the title of administrator heads a division dealing with oceanic matters. There are also numerous deputy assistant secretaries, and under them, directors for the individual agencies. These executives and their staffs brought the total personnel employed by the Department in 1971 to twenty-eight thousand; yet this number, large as it may seem, is only a fraction of the total number employed by a giant corporation. General Motors, for example, had nearly 775,000 employees in 1971.

Cabinet Departments The federal bureaucracy has eleven Cabinet-level departments. Only three—State, War (now Defense), and Treasury—existed in George Washington's administration, but over the years others have been added, with Housing and Urban Development (1965) and Transportation (1966) the most recent additions. The Postal Service, a Cabinet-level department since the eighteenth century, was recently given new status as an independent government corporation, and the Postmaster General is no longer a member of the Cabinet.

---

[12] Kaufman, "Administrative Decentralization and Political Power," p. 7.

[13] *U.S. Government Organization Manual 1971–72* (Washington, D.C.: Government Printing Office, 1972), p. 271.

Figure 8-1   **Executive Branch of Government**

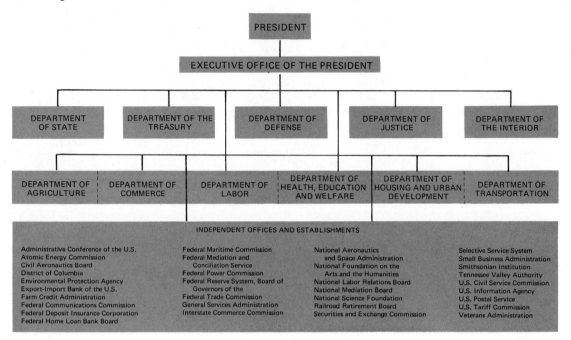

Independent Executive Agencies These agencies are very similar to Cabinet departments, but because they are not headed by a Cabinet member, they are known as "independent." The chief of each one is appointed by the President, reports to him, and may be dismissed by him. Some agencies—like the Veterans' Administration, with 150,000 employees—are bigger than most Cabinet departments. Others, like the National Aeronautics and Space Administration, the Small Business Administration, and the National Science Foundation, are substantially smaller.

Government Corporations Originally designed to allow independent administration in specific areas, government corporations were created as somewhat autonomous, corporation-like organizations, with ultimate control held by the federal government as the sole owner of all corporation stock. For example, the St. Lawrence Seaway Corporation was thus formed to construct and operate this important waterway; the Federal Deposit Insurance Corporation was established to insure savings accounts against loss. The newest addition to the government corporations is the Securities Investor Protection Corporation, established by Congress in 1970 to protect money and securities left by customers in brokerage accounts. At first, government corporations had considerable autonomy in determining their fees and investing their earnings, but in recent years they have been brought under more direct presidential control and must operate under annual congressional appropriations, as do other departments and agencies.

Independent Regulatory Agencies In recent years, much criticism has been directed at the independent regulatory commissions. They are distinguished from other federal administration agencies in that they are formally independent of all three branches of the government; in fact, they have been referred to collectively as the "headless branch of government." Their commissioners are appointed for established terms of office by the President with the consent of the Senate, but ordinarily, they cannot be removed by the President, and overlapping terms assure that the entire group will not normally be indebted to one President. Moreover, their day-to-day decisions usually cannot be appealed either to the President or to Congress. At times, however, when the public interest has been aroused, a congressional committee may investigate the work of a commission and attempt, through prodding or new legislation, to redirect its activities. For example, the investigations of Ralph Nader provoked congressional hearings on deceptive advertising and mislabeling in the drug industry, and ultimately led to stricter enforcement by the Federal Trade Commission.[14] But this kind of direct pressure on the independent regulatory agencies is relatively infrequent.

The commissions were granted autonomy to enable them to function as independent, expert regulators of powerful monopoly business interests such as railroads, public utilities, and stock exchanges. To regulate in the public interest, it was believed, they had to be free of control by politicians in both Congress and the White House. Moreover, it was strongly felt that because the commissions would be called on to deal with matters that were highly technical in nature, laymen in Congress or the White House would be unqualified to evaluate commission performance.

Profile of American Bureaucrats

How Are Bureaucrats Chosen?

Today, the overwhelming majority of government civilian employees obtain their jobs through competitive examinations administered under official Civil Service procedures. Of the nearly three million civilian jobs in the federal government in 1972, only about 15 percent were exempt from Civil Service, and many of these positions were with such agencies as the FBI or the State Department, which give their own examinations. In 1969, when President Nixon entered the White House, he had the power to replace with his own appointees only about two thousand officeholders in "key" jobs,[15] a figure representing less than 1 percent of the total number of government employees.

The Rise of Civil Service   The Civil Service has not always been the primary means of government employment. During the first hundred years of the republic, a victorious candidate could fill government posts with his own men. As Senator William L. Marcy of New York put it in 1832, "to the victor go the spoils."[16] He thereby christened the system brought to its fullest development by Andrew Jack-

---

[14] See Edward F. Cox, Robert C. Fellmuth, and John E. Schulz, *"The Nader Report" on the Federal Trade Commission* (New York: Richard W. Baron, 1969).

[15] Dom Bonafide, "Nixon's First-Year Appointments Reveal Pattern of his Administration," *National Journal* (January 24, 1970), p. 182.

[16] The same point of view was expressed almost a hundred years later by Warren G. Harding, when, in accepting the Republican nomination for President in 1924, he proclaimed "I believe in sponsorship in government."

son. Upon assuming office in 1828, Jackson used the spoils system to replace about one-third of the presidential appointees left from the previous (John Quincy Adams) administration, and some 10 to 20 percent of all other government officials, with his own men. Jackson acted partially out of his bitterness over what he termed a "corrupt bargain" made by Adams to steal the 1824 election from him. He also resented the monopoly over government jobs held by the powerful "Virginia-Massachusetts dynasty" in Washington since the founding of the republic. And finally, he saw no reason to believe that his own appointees would be any less competent than those they replaced. Jackson maintained that "the duties of public officers . . . are so plain and simple that men of intelligence may readily qualify themselves for their performance." This was probably truer in Jackson's time than it is now, when there is a greater need for technicians and specialists in government.

As time passed and bureaucracy mushroomed, so did public complaints about inept and dishonest government officials. By the 1870s it was said that the spoils system had gone so far as to include even scrubwomen.[17] The Presidents themselves became unhappy with the system, objecting to the time and effort required to choose successful job applicants and appease rejected ones. During Grant's administration (perhaps the most corrupt of all) the first Civil Service Commission was established, but no serious attempts at reform occurred until after 1881, when President Garfield was assassinated by a disappointed officeseeker, Charles Guiteau.[18]

In the wake of public outrage over the murder, George Pendleton, an Ohio congressman, sponsored the Civil Service Reform Act, passed in 1883. The Pendleton Act, as it was called, set up a Civil Service Commission and a fairly difficult competitive examination system; it also outlawed "kickbacks" paid by federal appointees. Initially, 12 percent of all federal jobs were placed under the Civil Service; this figure has gradually increased to the present total of 85 percent.[19]

Regardless of the existence of a Civil Service system, some degree of patronage appears inevitable in any government. Every incoming President wants his own supporters in key positions; in the first Nixon Cabinet, for example, three of the twelve members were long-time intimates of the President—Attorney General John Mitchell had been his law partner; Secretary of Health, Education and Welfare Robert H. Finch was his former campaign manager; and Secretary of State William P. Rogers had served as a member of Eisenhower's Cabinet when Nixon was Vice President. When these appointments were announced, few people ques-

---

[17] Samuel E. Morison, *Oxford History of the American People* (New York: Oxford University Press, 1965), p. 736.

[18] In the 1880 campaign, the Republican ticket teamed James A. Garfield with Chester A. Arthur for Vice President. Garfield represented the "reform" element within the party, which favored limitation of the spoils system and expansion of the Civil Service. Arthur was the candidate of the anti-reform, or "Stalwart" branch of the party, favoring continuation of the patronage system. Indeed, Arthur's only political post before nomination was Collector of the Port of New York, in which he was responsible for distribution of many of the patronage jobs in New York State. Guiteau's cry as he shot Garfield was, "I am a Stalwart and now Arthur is President." Garfield died, and Arthur became President, ironically becoming a proponent of Civil Service Reform.

[19] Morison, *Oxford History of the American People,* pp. 736–737. It is interesting to note that state and local patronage are much more widespread than patronage on the federal level. It has been estimated that in 1963 only thirteen thousand of Pennsylvania's eighty-one thousand state jobs were under State Civil Service, the rest being subject to appointment by the incoming governor.

tioned Nixon's selection of his close personal friends for the Cabinet, for it is generally recognized that a President needs top aides whom he trusts and with whom he can work easily. Among the enormous number of civilian jobs in federal government today, however, only a relatively few positions are filled by this kind of political appointment.

Who Are the Bureaucrats?

Statistics on federal employment indicate that many of the common clichés about the bureaucracy are misconceptions. The federal bureaucracy does *not* consist of a vast horde of people working in Washington, D.C. Actually, only 11 percent of federal employees are stationed in the Washington area; 86 percent are dispersed throughout the various states (in 1971, California alone had almost as many federal employees as Washington, D.C.), and the proportion located in foreign countries has at times reached 6 percent. Perhaps even more astonishing is the fact that more than half of all civilian employees work for defense-related agencies,

When a client is old as well as poor, can a bureaucrat who is young, middle class, or both really understand that client's problems?

while only a small percentage work for welfare agencies. In 1972, the Defense Department and the Veterans Administration had approximately 1.25 million civilian employees; Health, Education and Welfare (HEW) and Housing and Urban Development (HUD) together had only about 120,000.[20]

Federal government posts are extremely diverse. Many officials have highly technical responsibilities—as for example, the antitrust lawyers at the Justice Department, the water-pollution experts at the Environmental Protection Agency, the medical personnel at the Veterans' Administration Hospitals, the engineers at the National Aeronautics and Space Agency, and the engravers who design our money at the Bureau of Printing and Engraving in the Treasury Department. As suggested earlier, the complexity of modern life has created an increasing demand for government services. In the 1973 budget, for example, funds were requested to hire twenty-eight hundred more Transportation Department employees, primarily air-traffic controllers; eight hundred new employees for the Department of Housing and Urban Development to administer new subsidized housing programs; and eight hundred more Department of Labor employees to enforce occupational-safety and health programs passed by Congress. Surprisingly, however, the rate of growth in federal employment has not outstripped population growth. The ratio of federal employees to total U.S. population has remained remarkably constant during the post–World War II period. In 1947, federal employment statistics showed 14.4 civilian employees for every thousand Americans; in 1973 the ratio was about 13.1 per thousand. With the exception of the Korean War years, this has been the approximate ratio of federal employees to total population during the last twenty-five years.[21] Before then, an enormous spurt in federal employment had taken place when the welfare-state measures of the New Deal were implemented by the Roosevelt administration.

How Representative Are the Bureaucrats?

It is reasonable to assume that who a bureaucrat is will determine how he carries out his responsibilities and whose interests he will serve best. A middle-class administrator, for instance, might take a different view of his responsibilities than one from the upper or lower classes, not necessarily because he will deliberately discriminate in favor of his own kind, but because he will tend to establish rules and procedures that unintentionally have this consequence. We might also expect that a bureaucrat will be influenced by his religious and ethnic background. Considering the built-in biases of men, then, we may well wonder how representative our federal bureaucracy is of the general public.

Although it is relatively easy to obtain data about the geographical and occupational makeup of federal employees, it is much more difficult to draw conclusions about the representative composition of the bureaucracy. Some observers suggest that the bureaucracy, being at least nominally responsible to the Chief Executive, shares the presidential role of representing the broadest national constituency, instead of the more limited special interests represented by Congress. They maintain that the three million federal civilian employees, now recruited primarily through the Civil Service, probably serve as a better sample of the total U.S.

---

[20] *Special Analysis of the United States Government, Fiscal Year 1973* (Washington, D.C.: Government Printing Office, 1972), p. 107.

[21] *Special Analysis of the United States Government, Fiscal Year 1973*, pp. 106–114.

population than do members of Congress; therefore, they conclude, the bureaucracy is more likely to represent a wide diversity of interests than is the elite segment of the population serving in the House or the Senate.[22] For example, in 1969, only one black and one woman were among the hundred members of the Senate, whereas in the higher levels of the Civil Service (positions paying over $15,000) 6 percent of the jobs were held by women and 5 percent by nonwhite males.[23] Thus, it appears that groups underrepresented in Congress have, in the bureaucracy, a channel through which to express their views. One authority suggests that "the rich diversity that makes up the United States is better represented in its Civil Service than anywhere else."[24]

This description is not true, however, of the men who run the federal bureaucracy, according to a recent Brookings Institution analysis of a thousand federal executives serving at the highest levels in the Truman, Eisenhower, Kennedy, and Johnson administrations. The study concluded that most of these men (only twelve in the group were women) were white easterners from big cities, educated at better-known colleges, between forty and sixty years of age, and Protestants (especially Presbyterians and Episcopalians).[25] Most had backgrounds in big government, big business, or big law firms (44 percent had law degrees, but not all were practicing lawyers). From the Brookings study one may therefore conclude that, although the *three million* federal civilian employees are probably fairly representative of the total population, *the group at the top,* the top-level policy-makers, are anything but representative.

An analysis of President Nixon's appointments in his first year in office (1969) tends to confirm this conclusion. During the 1968 campaign, Nixon had declared: "I . . . want a government . . . drawn from politics, from career government service, from universities, from business, from professions—one including not only executives and administrators, but scholars and thinkers."[26] This implied that there would not only be a large-scale replacement of cliquish and generally like-minded bureaucrats who staffed the Johnson team, but that the new administration would be of a different kind—more broadly based. Because of Civil Service rules, however, the incoming President had relatively few posts available to distribute; therefore, a major turnover of government personnel was out of the question.

But what about the appointments that President Nixon did make during his first year in office? A look at the facts reveals few changes from patterns established by earlier administrations. Despite his campaign rhetoric, Nixon's party loyalty governed most of his decisions. He "cleaned out almost all Democrats in upper-echelon positions, replacing them—not unnaturally—with Republicans."[27] Moreover, despite his promise to include "scholars and thinkers" in government

[22] Norton E. Long, "Bureaucracy and Constitutionalism," in *The Politics of the Federal Bureaucracy,* edited by Alan A. Altshuler (New York: Dodd, Mead, 1968), pp. 17–26.

[23] John Kenneth Galbraith, "The Galbraith Plan to Promote Minorities," *New York Times Magazine* (August 22, 1971).

[24] Long, "Bureaucracy and Constitutionalism," p. 22.

[25] David T. Stanley, Dean E. Mann, and Jameson W. Doig, *Men Who Govern: A Biographical Profile of Federal Political Executives* (Washington, D.C.: The Brookings Institution, 1967), p. 9ff. The Eisenhower men were more likely than bureaucrats in other administrations to come from Midwest states, to have attended well-known prep schools, to be Protestants, and to be somewhat older.

[26] Bonafede, "Nixon's First-Year Appointments," p. 183; also Nixon's radio speech, September 19, 1968.

[27] Bonafede, "Nixon's First-Year Appointments," p. 183.

The backgrounds of federal bureaucrats are not always as diverse as those of the population they serve.

positions, Nixon selected 40 percent of his appointees from business and law (the same percentage as in the Johnson group), and only 7 percent from education (considerably less than the percentage in either the Johnson or Kennedy administrations). As in previous administrations, women and blacks continued to be very much underrepresented in the Nixon appointments, with women numbering only one out of six (most in lower-level posts) and blacks totalling only about 5 percent. About the only significant change in the Nixon appointments, as compared to the three previous administrations, was in geographic distribution: there were many more appointees from the South and far West and considerably fewer from the Mid-Atlantic states. In all, however, the federal appointees in the Nixon administration did not differ markedly in general complexion from those appointed by his predecessors, being preponderantly white and male, and from business or the legal profession.

If, as the facts suggest, top-level federal bureaucrats, as a group, are homogeneous and unrepresentative of the U.S. population as a whole, should this situation be deplored? Can we, or should we, expect upper-echelon bureaucrats, as individuals, to be representative? In a study of federal bureaucrats, Stanley, Mann, and Doig stated that "federal political executives . . . are representative of persons who have an affinity for public service and demonstrated ability to run larger enterprises. . . . Candidates for executive posts are selected . . . for their capacities for the job to be filled, their attitudes towards the President's programs and their ability to work with others. . . . Thus similarities in background must be expected."[28] The authors conclude that, in regard to the highest levels of government, an effort has been made to get the best people available, "even if their unrepresentativeness of the general population may result in occasional strains."[29]

[28] Stanley, Mann, and Doig, *Men Who Govern*, p. 80.
[29] Stanley, Mann, and Doig, *Men Who Govern*, p. 80.

Those who disagree with this view contend that, in the selection of high-level bureaucrats, women and members of certain minority groups are often discriminated against although they are well qualified to hold office. As a result, the views of women and certain minority groups are underrepresented in the policy-making process in favor of those that are biased toward the political establishment.

The issue here is similar to the one created by standards of admission to universities and other areas of institutional life. Under the merit system, minority groups are likely to be underrepresented because their education has not provided them with the necessary qualifications. Where a quota system is used, the admissions process becomes too much like the spoils system. Further, under a quota system, federal government jobs could not be used as a means of social and political mobility by blacks and other disadvantaged minority groups, as local government jobs were once used by the Irish, the Italians, and the Jews: in the classic political machine, almost all government employees were Irish (1870–1890) until disproportionate numbers of Italians and Jews moved into these jobs. Finally, to determine how representative the federal bureaucracy is, it is necessary to look not only at the backgrounds of high-level appointees, but at the bureaucratic decision-making process, and the kinds of policies enacted.

Administrative Decision-Making

The typical federal-government department or agency is not a monolith, where all the bureaucrats think and act alike. Rather, at every level, conflicts arise among those with opposing interests or viewpoints. For example, top political executives may see things quite differently from the career bureaucrats beneath them. A notable example occurred in 1971, when, to the surprise of most observers, an Anti-Trust Division case against the International Telephone and Telegraph Company was settled in the company's favor at the highest level within the Department of Justice. A lower-level career staff member refused to sign, however, because he thought it was a poor settlement from the government's standpoint.[30] Less dramatic examples take place routinely. "Guerrilla warfare" between careermen and "new broom" political appointees used to be commonplace whenever Postmasters General tried to streamline post office operations. It took place in the Department of Defense in the 1960s when army officers attempted to protect their traditional ways of doing business from Secretary McNamara's relentless efficiency experts. In most such battles the sides are evenly matched. The career bureaucrat knows how to get things done within his department by working "through channels," and if he disapproves of a new plan, he can often sabotage its implementation. On the other hand, the political appointee at the top has access to presidential power and prestige, which he may use to obtain cooperation from reluctant careerists. Moreover, the political appointee himself occasionally will be a man of such outstanding accomplishment that he can command respect and obedience from careerists within his department. (Examples are Francis Keppel, dean of Harvard Graduate School of Education, who was appointed head of the Department of Education; and Glenn Seaborg, a Nobel laureate, named chairman of the Atomic Energy Commission.)

[30] The *New York Times* (March 24, 1972), p. 18.

In addition to the conflicts between political appointees and career bureaucrats, there are those that arise between "specialists" (technicians) and "generalists" (administrators). The specialists—those with highly developed skills or knowledge —are often deeply committed to goals they have been trained to work toward. Foresters, for example, may be highly motivated toward forest conservation; social workers, toward the elimination of poverty; navy admirals, toward naval supremacy. Such specialists are likely to feel that the only important considerations are those that help them to reach their goals; they tend to be annoyed and frustrated by the "paper-shuffling" generalists who must measure alternatives from the standpoint of relative costs and priorities. A Secretary of Defense, for example, while recognizing the military effectiveness of atomic submarines, must also weigh the alternatives of additional aircraft carriers, bombers, or tanks, evaluating them within the context of foreign-policy objectives and budget requirements.

Finally, bureaucratic decision-making is further complicated by outside advisers or consultants who are often asked to participate in the process. The outside adviser offers expertise not available within a government agency; thus, a distinguished outside scientist may be asked to work with government people on special health or defense or transportation problems. Experts from the outside can often be more open-minded and innovative than regular department employees, who may have neither the perspective nor the independence to oppose or criticize accepted department procedures. However, as Ralph Nader has pointed out in many of his studies of federal agencies, the opportunities for conflict of interest multiply when an outside adviser is consulted by an executive agency. For example, Nader criticized the Food and Drug Administration for using outside consultants to evaluate new drugs when those consultants had done research for the pharmaceutical industry in the past, and might be hired by the industry again in the future.[31]

Two Schools of Thought in Decision-Making

Given the many different groups involved in the bureaucratic decision-making process, how are decisions actually reached? Very rarely by taking bold new steps. Essentially there are two schools of thought about how administrative decisions should be made—the *incrementalist* and the *rationalist*. In incremental decision-making, there are no sweeping innovations; instead, change takes place through compromises which emerge gradually through bargaining between conflicting interests.[32] According to the concept of sunk costs,[33] an important factor in incrementalism is the consideration that jobs might be affected and costs incurred by any large-scale change in the old way of doing things. Entrenched bureaucrats, set in their ways, tend to see a major revision of a program as a threat of disruption to their lives. The incrementalist school argues that it is impossible to achieve rationality in decision-making because of the factor of sunk costs; moreover, the argument goes, rationality is undesirable because the bargaining-and-trading process of incrementalism yields better decisions.

The rational, logical school believes decisions can be reached by clearly specify-

---

[31] The *New York Times* (April 3, 1972), p. 30.

[32] See Charles E. Lindblom, "The Science of Muddling Through," *Public Administration Review*, vol. 19 (Spring 1959), pp. 79–88.

[33] Herbert A. Simon, *Administrative Behavior*, 2nd edition (New York: The Free Press, 1957).

Mass-transportation experts often argue that highway building is a less rational use of federal funds than the upgrading of mass-transit systems.

ing objectives, all alternatives to these objectives, and the costs associated with each alternative. Then the alternative which potentially comes closest to the objective at the least cost should be selected. This is essentially the procedure followed in cost-benefit analysis, which was pioneered by economists.

A more sophisticated version of the rational approach to decision-making is known as PPBS. In an attempt to depersonalize the decision-making process, quantitative data were made the basis for decision-making in the Defense Department in 1961. Under Secretary Robert S. McNamara, the Department instituted PPBS—a planning-programming-budgeting system under which an agency could identify, rank, and determine the cost of its major goals; then, armed with this information, it could choose rationally among them. For example, given the goal of protecting the United States against foreign nuclear attack, the Defense Department, through PPBS, should be able to determine whether the best means would be a powerful retaliatory force of nuclear warheads, a radar network, a fleet of superbombers, or some combination of these. This approach is quite different from the earlier Department of Defense procedures, in which each branch of the military (Army, Navy, Air Force) worked up a line-item schedule of its projected requirements—that is, it specified what items it wanted to purchase (tanks, planes, and so on) rather than goals or objectives it wished to achieve. Today, the defense budget is prepared in terms of "missions"—such as limited war or air defense—and the relative effectiveness and cost of each solution is estimated and compared to the others.[34]

Since 1965, the PPBS approach has been used by many other executive agencies in an attempt to get the best use of each tax dollar spent by the government. There are obvious limitations to its use, however. Although it is relatively simple

[34] *Nation's Business* (August 1961), p. 62.

to "cost out" and compare the value of objectives in the military area, how can an agency compare the worth of an arthritis drug-research program with the benefits of a federally financed school-lunch program? Or the relative merits of clean water and air versus slum clearance? What is the decisive factor in choosing between a $20-million "mission" to eliminate rats in urban areas and a $20-million program for symphonies and art museums? In brief, whatever the merits of quantitative decision-making, it is of questionable value where both subjective and qualitative values are concerned.[35]

In addition, the older line-item system is one that is more easily controlled by congressmen, under the logrolling procedure. For support of a bill to buy a hundred planes, a congressman can extract a promise that some of those planes will be built in his district. Such deals are not as easy to effect when budget allotments are made in terms of overall missions. Thus, congressmen were consistent enemies and critics of McNamara's whiz kids who conceived PPBS.

The Hierarchy of Decision-Making

To a certain extent, bureaucratic decisions are implemented through a hierarchical process—that is, decisions reached at higher levels within the bureaucracy are passed down the line to the lower levels, where they are eventually either carried out or allowed to expire. As the bureaucracy widened, it became more dependent on the hierarchical structure as the only way in which control of lower-echelon employees could be maintained. For example, when a decision was made to encourage minority employment within the government, its implementation by every agency, department, and office was enforced by the hierarchical structure. Similarly, priorities established at higher levels in regard to funds or personnel have to be heeded at lower levels to be effective. It is useless for the Secretary of Health, Education and Welfare to announce that official Department policy is to encourage desegregation of local school districts, if lower-level bureaucrats continue to supply money to districts which refuse to integrate. To take another example, most observers believe that ultimate control of the Defense Department must remain not with the military professionals but with the civilians at the top of the hierarchy if our democratic form of government is to survive.

Although hierarchical chains of command theoretically dominate within the bureaucracy, some subordinate agencies are apparently independent of their nominal superiors—usually because of strong support from outside interest groups. A "managerial impotence" results, as described by a former director of the U.S. Employment Agency, in regard to his relationship to the Veterans Employment Division, nominally under his control:

I started as Director with a naive idea that I ran it, but I discovered that there was a part of the Service that no Director ran. This was the Veterans Employment Division, which did not even receive its mail in our mailroom. It had a special post office box downtown. When I tried to do something about the Division, I learned that it took orders mainly from the Employment Committee of the American Legion. From then on, I discussed the work of the Division regularly with a Committee of the American Legion in Indianapolis.[36]

Despite such cases, effective hierarchies are, in general, characteristic of the

---

[35] Daniel Seligman, "McNamara's Management Revolution," *Fortune* (July 1965).

[36] Rourke, *Bureaucracy, Politics, and Public Policy*, p. 104–105.

Decentralization may help to make the bureaucracy more accessible to the public than it is here.

federal bureaucracy as a means of making organizations responsible and workable. Since the 1960s, however, there has been an increasing demand for a return to a system of dispersed authority for greater effectiveness. The demand represents the belief that the only way to make our large, impersonal administrative agencies more representative is to decentralize them—to permit local, lower-level bureaucrats to make the decisions about policy and allocation of resources that are appropriate for their clientele. In many cities of the nation, for example, a movement toward decentralization of large bureaucracies has begun. Similarly, in various federal projects, attempts are being made to give more responsibility to local administrators, and to encourage participation by community people. Tenants are being given a voice in operating low-rent projects, neighborhood associations in designing urban-renewal programs, community lay boards in running local public hospitals.[37] Whether this trend will indeed produce more responsive administrators, or whether decentralization will result in new bureaucracies that are even larger and less efficient than the old ones is a debated issue.

Recent years have seen a growing recognition of the limitations of existing

[37] Kaufman, "Administrative Decentralization and Political Power," p. 6.

bureaucratic decision-making procedures. They are often slow, cautious, and the result of compromises on a limited range of alternatives, superimposed upon long-standing practices.

The Question of Bureaucratic Power

The question of bureaucratic power is an extremely important one in American politics. Many observers contend that the power of the federal bureaucracy has extended too far—that certain government agencies have become so autonomous that they are no longer responsive to the people. To understand the significance of these charges, let us examine the Army Corps of Engineers, not as a typical agency but as one that embodies many of the problems of bureaucratic power.

Case Study in Bureaucratic Power:
The Army Corps of Engineers

Created by Congress in 1802, the Corps of Engineers is part of the Department of the Army, under the Department of Defense.[38] It carries on various peacetime activities, as well as such wartime military tasks as building bridges and fortifications and managing landing operations. Its first job was to build and operate a military academy at West Point; during the 1800s it surveyed the West and helped build roads, canals, and national parks; at other times, it has constructed such major projects as the Panama Canal and the Apollo launching facilities at Cape Kennedy. Today, the Corps's primary civilian responsibility involves development of our water resources: it widens harbors, builds dams, improves internal waterways (canals), and develops flood-control projects. The Corps employs about 28,500 civilian workers, directed by about 450 officers, and spends about $1.6 million a year.[39]

Before it recommends any project to Congress, the Corps evaluates the needs of the area under consideration. Although hearings are held in the district concerned, and local interests are consulted to determine if there is sufficient justification for the work, critics charge that very often the Corps's district offices invent work to stay in business. Accordingly, some claim that the motto of the Corps should be "the only good river is a straight river."[40] The civilian workers are particularly sensitive to this criticism, for their careers depend on funds allocated to each district, which in turn depend on the number of projects authorized.

Once a project is under consideration by the Engineers, important local support for it generally develops.[41] Real-estate speculators, bankers, and construction firms angling for contracts, as well as other businessmen and working people, are eager for the benefits of a Corps project, such as flood control or a new harbor, which may infuse the community with millions of dollars on a short-term basis and offer promise of long-term prosperity. In theory, the Corps tries to listen to

---

[38] For an in-depth study of the power of the Army Corps of Engineers see Arthur Maass, *Muddy Waters: The Army Engineers and the Nation's Rivers* (Cambridge, Mass.: Harvard University Press, 1951).

[39] Data from The *New York Times* (February 20, 1972), p. 45n.

[40] The *New York Times* (February 20, 1972), p. 45n.

[41] The Corps itself simplifies the work of these special-interest groups by providing them with an outline of the eighteen steps a community should follow to drum up support for a project. In certain circles this publication is known as "The Eighteen Steps to Glory." From The *New York Times* (February 20, 1972), p. 45n.

all sides, but dissident groups are generally few and unorganized. They tend to base their objections on ecological grounds, and in most cases, the Corps has brushed them off as mere "butterfly chasers."[42]

Congress will not consider any project unless it is approved by the Chief of Engineers. But once the Corps does recommend a piece of work, pressures to authorize it build up in Congress. These pressures come from the Corps itself, from local interests—Chambers of Commerce, for example—from special-interest groups—barge-and-dredging companies, road-building firms, the cement industry—and, of course, from the congressmen in the affected districts. In Washington, before Congress as a whole votes on the project, hearings are held before the appropriate congressional committees (Public Works and Appropriations) at which all interested parties testify. These committees are usually dominated by sympathetic congressmen, whose districts include many water-control projects. Committee members and congressmen in general have a strong tendency to support any proposed project, first because of pressure from powerful interest groups,[43] and second because of a reluctance to turn down the project of a fellow congressman today, when his approval may be needed tomorrow for one of their own projects. This is the essence of "pork-barreling," and although disparaged, it is often at the core of congressional sanction for a project. There is an old Corps joke: "You know what a pork barrel is? It's a project in somebody else's district."[44]

Congress, as we can see, has lost much of its function in water-resources development to the Corps of Engineers and to special-interest groups and individual congressmen who support the Corps. This leads us to the question of the role of the Chief Executive, to whom, as Commander-in-Chief of the Armed Forces, the Corps is theoretically responsible. Beginning in 1883, Chester A. Arthur was the first of many Presidents to try to bring the Corps under Executive control. Both Warren G. Harding and Franklin D. Roosevelt, for example, attempted unsuccessfully to move the Corps into the Department of the Interior, where its activities could be supervised more closely. For years, the White House has objected that certain projects recommended by the Corps have not been compatible with the aims of other government agencies. For instance, the Department of Agriculture and the Department of the Interior have at various times protested against Corps plans that would result in soil erosion, and have urged a curb on Corps projects.

A recent attempt was made to coordinate proposed Corps of Engineers legislation with other government needs by requiring that Corps projects be submitted first to the Office of Management and Budget. Budget officials would then evaluate each project and transmit to Congress *only* those held to be consistent with the President's overall program. In the past Congress has consistently authorized almost all measures requested by the Corps, regardless of budgetary recommendations and the administration's objections. For example, from January 1941 through

---

[42] Widening of harbors and rivers often leads to serious erosion problems along the new banks of waterways; new dams can destroy traditional nesting places of wildlife; and, very often, the construction process itself can lead to serious environmental problems.

[43] The comprehensive, well-financed, and powerful water-resources lobby centers around a pressure group called the National Rivers and Harbors Congress. Contractors, building-supply companies, barge interests, and chambers of commerce support it, but it also counts among its members many congressmen. See Arthur Maass, "Congress and Water Resources," in *Bureaucratic Power in National Politics,* edited by Francis E. Rourke (Boston: Little, Brown, 1965), pp. 106–108.

[44] The *New York Times* (February 20, 1972), p. 45n.

September 1948, the Bureau of the Budget received 436 recommendations from the Corps of Engineers. It approved 360 for congressional action and opposed 76. The Corps then submitted the rejected 76 to Congress, where 62 were approved.[45]

The presidential veto has proved no more effective than budgetary means in controlling the Corps. Most Presidents have recognized that powerful interest groups may successfully pressure Congress to override the veto. This was shown by the experience of Chester A. Arthur, the only President ever to veto a piece of Corps legislation. In 1882, Congress overrode his veto. President Arthur noted in disgust that an extremely bad bill, such as the one he vetoed, might include projects for everyone, in almost every congressional district. "Thus," he observed, "as the bill becomes more objectionable, it secures more support."[46]

Although atypical of federal agencies in general, the operations of the Corps of Engineers raise certain important issues concerning the role and power of the bureaucracy in a democratic society. Some authorities have questioned whether the Corps is, in the broadest sense, promoting the general welfare, or whether its procedures instead favor the needs of only a small, special constituency. It is also significant that the Corps not only executes policy decisions – the traditional role of a bureaucratic agency – but makes the decisions. Moreover, the Corps seems to operate with few constraints on its power. Congress typically makes little attempt to control it, and the Chief Executive has often found it impossible to do so. With virtually independent status, the Corps of Engineers appears to respond to the needs of the general public only when a major confrontation arises, such as the current ones over the environmental issue.

Sources of Bureaucratic Power

The case study of the Army Corps of Engineers is an example of the degree to which autonomous power may be put to use by a government agency. It also raises important questions about the sources of bureaucratic power. By what means is the Corps able to wield such enormous power in the area of water-resources development? What factors contribute to the power of any government agency?

Bureaucratic Expertise Max Weber wrote, "The absolute monarch is powerless opposite the superior knowledge of the bureaucratic expert." In our own democracy, bureaucratic expertise is often no less formidable a source of power.[47] The highly technical nature of many governmental decisions is a primary reason for the development of bureaucratic expertise. The experts at the Corps of Engineers, for example, have the skills to solve flooding problems; they have the engineering know-how to determine whether it would be best to widen a riverbed channel, build a dam, or carry out drainage operations; and they can support their recommendations with data available only to professionals. But the expertise of the bureaucrat is not limited to technical matters; administrative and political skills also call for specialized knowledge. Members of the Corps of Engineers, in addition to their technical expertise, know how to present material at a congressional

[45] Maass, "Congress and Water Resources," pp. 110–111.
[46] The *New York Times* (February 20, 1972), p. 45n.
[47] Rourke, *Bureaucracy, Politics, and Public Policy*, p. 91.

hearing, and which newspapers, labor leaders, chamber of commerce members, and congressmen to phone in order to mobilize support for a given project. Therefore, when confronted with opposition, the Corps has "precision, speed, unambiguity, knowledge of the files, continuity, discretion, unity . . ." in its favor;[48] opponents, in contrast, whether a recently organized environmentalist group or a newly appointed presidential aide or Cabinet member, usually are weaker in these resources. Weber, an early student of bureaucratic structure, observed:

> *Under normal conditions, the power position of a fully developed bureaucracy is always overtowering. The "political master" finds himself in a position of the "dilettante" who stands opposite the "expert" facing the trained official who stands within the management of administrations.*[49]

Expertise has also developed from the division of labor in bureaucracies, permitted by increased size. The availability of personnel and organization allows a complex problem to be broken down into small manageable parts, with individual members assigned to specialize in single aspects. This development has made possible, for example, a Department of Agriculture expert on the effect of giving antibiotics to swine; a HUD expert who knows the historical relationship between changes in mortgage rates and changes in new construction in the Southwest; and a State Department diplomat who speaks Pashto (the native language of most Afghans) and is up to date on current political alignments within the Afghanistan parliament.

This kind of development may be all to the good, but bureaucratic expertise exerts a special power, one with potential danger, where there is no corresponding expertise elsewhere in government or private organizations. Americans may consult with private veterinarians when in doubt about Department of Agriculture statistics on the safety of penicillin injections for pigs, but they have no outside source of information against which to check most Central Intelligence Agency or Defense Department data. Thus, President Kennedy's only alternative during the Bay of Pigs incident in 1961 was to reject CIA evaluations of Cuban military strength. Such an alternative was extremely risky, however, so Kennedy accepted the advice of the experts, only to find that the Cuban defenses had been vastly underestimated. Similarly, for years the military fed overly optimistic reports about the situation in Vietnam to Presidents Kennedy, Johnson, and Nixon.

Recognizing the advantage of a monopoly of expertise, bureaucracies sometimes attempt to develop exclusive control over information. Thus, a hundred years ago, treasury officials of the State of Persia kept their records in a secret script, so that they alone could evaluate their handling of the budget;[50] likewise, U.S. State Department bureaucrats today routinely stamp military and other documents "Top Secret," so that only they will have access to certain information about the administration's conduct of the war.

The Mobilization of Support Regardless of its control over information, a bureaucracy as a rule needs active support from outside interest groups, as well as from Congress and the President, in its quest for authorization and funds for its projects.

---

[48] Max Weber, "Essay on Bureaucracy," in Rourke, *Bureaucratic Power in National Politics,* p. 6.
[49] Weber, "Essay on Bureaucracy," p. 11.
[50] Weber, "Essay on Bureaucracy," p. 11.

"It does frighten one. It is the special file on dissenters."

Saturday Review, *August 15, 1970*

SUPPORT FROM OUTSIDE INTEREST GROUPS.   Every federal-government agency attempts to gain public support for its policies and its work in general. The Department of Transportation, for example, promotes the idea that intercity rail service is essential, and that the Department's sponsorship of Amtrak has been eminently successful. During the 1930s, '40s, and '50s, the FBI was particularly effective in developing a positive image of itself, using TV shows; interviews with its director, J. Edgar Hoover; magazine articles about the exploits of FBI men; and guided tours through FBI headquarters in Washington. In addition, government agencies recognize the importance of cultivating special ties with special constituencies—those groups "whose attachment is grounded on an enduring tie of tangible interest"[51]—in other words, groups whose economic or social interests are the same as those of the agency.[52]

Such common interests are the basis on which support from outside groups is developed. The Department of Housing and Urban Development, for instance, is concerned with the improvement of housing, particularly in decaying inner-city areas. Its natural constituency includes municipal governments, builders, real-estate operators, and organizations representing the poor. These groups obviously have an interest in helping HUD obtain larger congressional appropriations, more

[51] Rourke, *Bureaucracy, Politics, and Public Policy*, p. 14.

[52] In considering the role of a government agency in developing public or special-interest support, it should be noted that, strictly speaking, public-relations activities of federal bureaucracies are legally limited. A 1913 act forbids such agencies from using public funds to compensate "any publicity expert unless explicitly appropriated for that purpose." In practice, however, most agencies neatly circumvent such restrictions; the typical government bureau will lack a "publicity expert," but "public-information officers," "education officers" and "publication officers" abound.

flexible building codes, and expansion of its authority and activities. The fact that a government agency and its special-interest groups offer opportunities for an interchange of jobs strengthens these ties. For example, HUD might logically look for urban planners, architects, and social workers from among the real-estate and social-service organizations that support it. Similarly, private firms or organizations frequently offer employment to competent federal bureaucrats with whom they have worked in government. A chairman of the Civil Aeronautics Board, Najeeb Halaby, later became chairman of the board of Pan American World Airways.

While some government agencies have "natural constituencies" with closely tied interests, other bureaucracies, like the State Department, lack such a constituency—a group of clients for which it can routinely do "tangible and significant favors." Sometimes the bureaucracy, recognizing the advantage of having a vocal outside support, will attempt to develop it. The State Department, for example, has encouraged the formation and growth of the prestigious Foreign Policy Association, the Citizens' Committee for Peace and Freedom in Vietnam (a group which supported President Johnson's policies), and various other private citizens' organizations.

Such support is often the strongest weapon an agency has in its bid for a larger slice of the federal budget. The American Farm Bureau Federation can lobby more expensively, and sometimes argue more effectively before congressional committees for Department of Agriculture projects, than the Department itself can.[53] Defense-related industries are often more effective than the Department of Defense in pressuring congressmen to vote for increased military expenditures. As Senator Barry Goldwater once observed, "The aircraft industry has probably done more to promote the Air Force than the Air Force itself."[54]

But support from outside interest groups can be a mixed blessing. There is always the danger that a close relationship between an agency and an outside client group will bring the agency under the client's control. Regulatory commissions, in particular, have tended to become "captive" agencies. The Interstate Commerce Commission has been called the captive of the railroad industry; the Food and Drug Administration, of the drug industry; various bureaus within the Department of Transportation have been charged with being too sympathetic to automobile manufacturers, and hence incapable of impartiality.

The experience of the Tennessee Valley Authority is a classic example of a two-way relationship between an administrative agency and special-interest groups. The TVA was created by Congress in 1933 to exploit the water resources of the Tennessee Valley and its tributaries. From its very beginning, the Authority endeavored to mobilize grass-roots support and participation. The TVA established governmental rather than private ownership and operation of power facilities; it

---

[53] Bureaucrats are often limited in their personal lobbying efforts by a 1919 federal statute that forbids use of any public funds appropriated to a government agency for activities "designed to influence . . . a member of Congress to favor or oppose . . . any legislation or appropriation . . ."; and a 1948 statute (62 Stat 792, 1948) reinforced these rules. Although, as will be shown later in this chapter, government agencies have found effective ways of circumventing such restrictions, this legislation can be potentially limiting to a bureau, and it is often useful to have a well-financed private group to carry the ball. See J. Leiper Freeman, "The Bureaucracy in Pressure Politics," *Annals of the American Academy of Political and Social Science*, vol. 319 (September 1958), p. 12.

[54] Quoted in Rourke, *Bureaucracy, Politics, and Public Policy*, p. 19.

involved a new form of organization, the relatively autonomous public corporation. Since such a corporation was a revolutionary concept at the time, it was essential for the Authority to mobilize public support in the area for the implementation of its policies. Aside from these purely practical considerations, however, the TVA was philosophically committed to a democratic approach; it believed that the people of the Valley should "direct their own destinies," and be offered "free choice rather than ready-made presentations elaborated in the fastnesses of planning agencies."[55] To this end, the Authority made every attempt to encourage grass-roots participation, making a special effort to work through local agencies and institutions already in the area. Cooperative relationships were maintained with municipal power boards, electric cooperatives, school boards, trade unions, contractors' organizations, and land-grant colleges. In general, this approach proved eminently successful, gaining the Authority widespread support in the Valley.

Some unexpected problems arose, however, from working with local special-interest groups. The Authority found itself in the position of having to support the status quo in certain instances, to please these groups. For example, although the Authority preferred a policy of nondiscrimination toward blacks, it could do little against the discriminatory practices of the agencies that comprised its constituency. Also, by accepting the support of the dominant American Federation of Labor (AFL) unions in the area, the TVA had to limit its affiliation with other labor groups. Similarly, in cultivating the support of the farm groups in the Valley, the TVA channeled much of its activity through the existing agricultural establishment within the land-grant college system, and did nothing to help the small farmers in the area.

It appears, then, that the TVA, because it needed the support of special-interest groups, was forced to compromise on some of its goals—to abandon the development of certain new institutions and procedures even if it considered such changes desirable.

Although the TVA accommodated itself to special requirements of its supporters, the Authority managed to retain an essential integrity and accomplish its major goals. But quite a different picture emerges from the relationship between another government agency, the Interstate Commerce Commission, and its constituency. As early as 1952, Samuel P. Huntington, a political scholar, suggested that the ICC was losing prestige, authority, and leadership in its role as the primary federal regulating agency for transportation. He attributed this decline to the fact that the ICC had only one major source of outside support, the railroad industry. As a captive of that industry, it had become vulnerable to attacks from other transportation groups, from government agencies aligned with them, and from the general public. Huntington suggested that the only solution for the problem was for the Commission to develop other sources of support, thereby freeing itself from domination by the railroads.[56] Some years later, in 1970, a Ralph Nader study group found that the situation had not changed; stating that the railroad industry had "captured" the ICC, the report recommended that the Commission be abolished and that a brand-new transportation regulatory agency be created.[57]

---

[55] Philip Selznick, *TVA and the Grass Roots* (Berkeley, Calif.: University of California Press, 1949), p. 37.

[56] Samuel P. Huntington, "The Marasmus of the I.C.C.: The Commission, the Railroads, and the Public Interest," *Yale Law Journal* (April 1952), pp. 467–508. (*Marasmus*, from the Greek *marasmos* ("waste"), means a gradual and continuous wasting away of the bulk of the body from morbid cause.)

[57] Robert C. Fellmeth, *The Interstate Commerce Commission* (New York: Grossman Publishers, 1970).

Part of the reason for the bad connotation of the word bureaucracy is the distaste most people have for being "processed."

The Nader report found substantial evidence of the close relationship between railroad and ICC officials. It pointed to job interchange between the Commission and the industry and suggested the existence of a system of "deferred bribes." For example, in the decade 1958–1968, all but one of the eleven commissioners who left the ICC took positions either as railroad officers or as ICC practitioners, representing the rails in their dealings with the ICC.[58]

Like a well-satisfied client, the railroad industry has heaped praise on the ICC. The Association of American Railroads has praised the "impartiality, deliberation, expertness . . . that have marked the history of the ICC"; the American Short Line Railroad Association has referred to the "fair intelligent treatment" given its members by the Commission; a trade magazine, *Railway Age,* praised the "collaboration" between the Commission and the industry.[59] In general, the railroad industry has energetically fought all attempts to bring the ICC under close control of other government bodies or to transfer any of its regulatory functions to other agencies.

Finally, the railroads' influence over the ICC is seen in the favoritism shown by the Commission to the industry. The Commission, which is responsible for regulation of motor and water carriers as well as rails, has consistently produced rate

[58] Fellmeth, *The Interstate Commerce Commission,* pp. 20–21.
[59] Huntington, "The Marasmus of the I.C.C."

schedules favoring the rails at the expense of other carriers and the public. Moreover, the Commission has made competition difficult for non-rail carriers in other ways—for example, by refusing to grant new routes to trucking firms.

The ICC represents an extreme case of the domination of a government agency by a special-interest group, but the potential exists in many agencies where close ties have developed with clients. Why has the National Highway Transportation Safety Administration been so lax in insisting that the automobile companies recall models with mechanical defects and other safety hazards? Why was the Securities and Exchange Commission so ready to agree to the decision of the New York Stock Exchange to raise commissions paid by small investors?

In each case, the regulatory agency appears to have become so closely identified with a special interest that it has lost sight of the public interest. According to Grant McConnell, who analyzed the life cycle of federal commissions, a "crusading spirit" initially characterizes commissions created in response to public outcry against an industry, but in time this idealistic spirit recedes as the public loses interest, so that the interests of client groups are once again able to predominate.[60]

SUPPORT FROM CONGRESS.   Government bureaucrats derive much of their power from their ability to muster support for their programs in Congress, particularly from congressmen who serve as chairmen of congressional committees or subcommittees. As Francis E. Rourke wrote, "There is in fact, no better lobbyist for any administrative agency than a legislator."[61] This statement was proven true in 1972, for example, when the Treasury found its way cleared in Congress for the passage of a potentially troublesome bill to increase the price of gold; its success was largely due to the efforts of Representative Henry S. Reuss (D.-Wis.), an acknowledged expert, who, merely by giving the measure approval, encouraged many confused or wavering congressmen to vote for the bill.

The close relationship between the Corps of Engineers and the committees which approve and fund its projects has already been mentioned; similarly, the military establishment has continued to enjoy excellent relationships with the Senate Armed Services Committee under Chairmen Richard Russell and John Stennis, and the House Armed Services Committee under Chairmen Carl Vinson, Mendel Rivers, and F. Edward Hébert.

The RS-70 Bomber Program offers a case in point of these important relationships.[62] In 1962, Secretary of Defense Robert S. McNamara, together with President Kennedy, determined that funds for the development of a manned supersonic bomber (the RS-70) should be drastically cut because of a shift in defense policy toward greater reliance on missiles. They decided to ask Congress for only $171 million (later raised to $227 million) to build test models, rather than the $491 million favored by the Air Force under the vocal leadership of its Chief of Staff, General Curtis LeMay. Vinson and Russell were chairmen of the House and Senate Armed Services Committees at the time, and under their leadership, Congress authorized $362 million for the program, despite objections from McNamara and the President. Although in the final analysis the Secretary of

---

[60] Grant McConnell, *Private Power and American Democracy* (New York: Alfred A. Knopf, 1966).

[61] Rourke, *Bureaucracy, Politics and Public Policy*, p. 28.

[62] Peter Woll, *American Bureaucracy* (New York: Norton, 1963), p. 127ff.

Defense had his way (he refused to spend the money, and although Congress can authorize funds, there is little it can do to force an agency to spend them), this example typifies the situation in which rapport with important committee chairmen can be a major source of bureaucratic power.

Conversely, agencies lacking such rapport with appropriate committee chairmen are often in trouble. Representative Otto Passman (D.-La.), chairman of the Foreign Operations Subcommittee of the House Appropriations Committee, has been an obstacle to bureaucrats in charge of foreign aid because of his persistent efforts to cut back funds for their programs.

Support from the Chief Executive The relationship between the federal bureaucracy and the President is complex and variable. Article II of the Constitution provides for strong direct control of the administrative bureaucracy by the President, and formal organization charts of the Executive branch make this control appear to be so. But since government agencies are also responsible to Congress, as well as to the client groups which support them, an agency with strong support from either of these sources can often afford to ignore presidential authority. Harry S Truman is reported to have pointed this out in a trenchant comment shortly before he left the White House in 1952. Speaking of President-elect Dwight Eisenhower, he said: "He'll sit there . . . and he'll say, 'Do this! Do that!' Poor Ike—it won't be a bit like the Army. He'll find it very frustrating."[63]

While agencies with strong outside support can often implement policy without the backing of the Chief Executive, agencies with no outside constituencies may be forced to rely heavily on presidential support as their only source of power. Most agencies, however, fall somewhere between these two extremes. Although they cultivate outside constituencies and congressional sponsors, they also feel the need for strong ties to the White House. The President's prestige and his access to the news media give him unique opportunities to influence public opinion and thus mobilize Congress. An agency seeking support for a project will therefore value presidential support for its goals. President Nixon's stand on busing in 1972 was a major factor in shifting the balance of power to the anti-busing groups within the Department of Health, Education and Welfare, and lowering the status and influence of the pro-busing groups.

The President can also exercise some control over bureaucrats through the Office of Management and Budget (OMB). OMB is a unit of the Executive Office of the President, and thus directly under presidential control. In fact, OMB (originally the Bureau of the Budget) was created as a means of giving the President greater control over government agencies. Every government agency must channel its annual request for funds through OMB (rather than directly to Congress); OMB reviews and evaluates all requests and then sends a single budget on to Congress. In theory, OMB could use these powers to enforce close control over bureaucratic agencies. In practice, however, agencies, like the Corps of Engineers, can overcome OMB limitations through independent submissions of projects to congressional committees; and others, like the Department of Defense, can use powerful congressional "friends" to sponsor larger appropriations than those recommended by OMB. A study by Aaron Wildavsky suggested, moreover, that budget officials are aware of the potential outside support available to specific

---

[63] Richard E. Neustadt, *Presidential Power* (New York: Wiley, 1960), p. 9.

agencies; therefore, they tend to be more generous with those agencies known to enjoy influential congressional relationships.[64]

Channels of Bureaucratic Influence

Bureaucracies, as we have seen, add to their power with expertise and outside influence. Our next concern is to determine how they use this power. Basically, there are two means: first, bureaucrats provide policy-makers with advice and recommendations; and second, they are often responsible for carrying out the decisions reached by policy-makers, a role which requires them to exercise discretion in choosing among alternatives.

Bureaucrats as Advisers The indirect influence of bureaucrats on policy-makers is most clearly seen in the work of such staff agencies as the Council of Economic Advisers, the Joint Chiefs of Staff, and the Office of Science and Technology. The United States Tariff Commission, to give another example, serves both the President and Congress as an advisory fact-finding agency on tariffs, commercial policy, and foreign trade. Such agencies work closely with the President, who relies on their technical expertise for advice in highly complex areas; often the recommendations they make on domestic economic problems, military affairs, scientific matters, or questions of international trade largely determine final presidential policy. Most of these agencies are *staff* agencies (those lacking decision-making power) created especially for the purpose of giving advice to the President. But the heads of the regular *line* agencies (agencies to which Executive power has been delegated), the Cabinet members, are also supposed to give advice to the President. Of course, most Presidents do not use the Cabinet in this way, which accounts for the rather large growth of the White House staff and of special advisory agencies such as the Council of Economic Advisers and the Joint Chiefs of Staff.

Most Presidents have been wary of depending on the evaluations and recommendations of any one set of experts. Historian Arthur M. Schlesinger, Jr., said in describing President Franklin D. Roosevelt's relationship with his advisers: "An executive relying on a single information system [becomes] inevitably the prisoner of that system." Roosevelt's method was to "check and balance information acquired through official channels through a myriad of private, informal and unorthodox channels. . . ."[65]

As suggested earlier, however, alternative sources of data are often impossible to find in certain areas. Roosevelt, for example, was forced to depend almost exclusively on the Joint Chiefs of Staff for military advice during World War II. And although several Presidents attempted to obtain independent evaluations of actual conditions in Vietnam, for the most part, they had to fall back on the military's view of the situation. The Vietnam experience provides a provocative case study of the President as the instrument of his intelligence services; it also brings to mind President Kennedy's comment concerning the CIA shortly after the Bay of Pigs fiasco: "All my life," he said, "I've known better than to depend on the experts. How could I have been so stupid. . . ."[66]

[64] Aaron Wildavsky, "Political Implications of Budgetary Reform," *Public Administration Review,* vol. 21 (Autumn 1961), pp. 183–190.

[65] Arthur M. Schlesinger, Jr., *The Coming of the New Deal* (Boston: Houghton Mifflin, 1959), p. 523.

[66] Theodore C. Sorenson, *Kennedy* (New York: Harper & Row, 1965), p. 305.

In their advisory role, bureaucrats do more than provide the Chief Executive with advice and recommendations. Much of the legislation introduced by the Executive branch originates in "agency bills" written by government agencies; in fact, the major part of a President's legislative program has its source in specific statutes drafted by various bureaus.

Bureaucratic Discretion in Executing Decisions The fact that the bureaucrats recommend legislation to Congress is far less controversial than their execution of laws after they have been passed. Administrators can exercise discretion in a wide range of situations – that is, they can choose how, when, and where to enforce legislation passed by Congress or executive policy decisions. In his day-to-day life the individual citizen is affected constantly by bureaucratic discretion – when a school superintendent determines acceptable class size, or when the town sanitation officer, assigned the job of providing "adequate" garbage service, decides to cut back collections from three times a week to two, or when a policeman decides which offenders to pursue more vigorously. In most such cases, unless there is an "enabling" law to specify how many or how often, administrators may use discretionary power.

In the federal bureaucracy, agencies must use discretionary power in order to properly exercise their functions as defined by the law. Such power was obtained, for example, by the Federal Power Commission when Congress gave it the legal right to fix rates for electric utilities, and by the Civil Aeronautics Board when a law permitted it to approve airline mergers.

With a rise in the number of regulatory agencies there has been an increase in rule-making (quasi-legislative) and adjudicatory (quasi-judicial) power lodged in administrative agencies. This situation departs from the American tradition of separation of powers in that a single agency not only makes the laws but also decides whether someone has broken them. Many argue that this development has created a dangerous concentration of power in administrative agencies, raising the question of whether administrative tribunals are fair and if the means of appeal against bad bureaucratic decisions are too complex.

Such appeared to be the case in 1972 when the New York City Housing Authority, acting on its discretionary power to screen out tenants who might commit violence, brought eviction proceedings against a man and wife of good reputation in a Harlem housing project because their son, who had gone to jail for attempted robbery, might someday return home. The case brought on a clash between the New York Civil Liberties Union and the Housing Authority over the criteria used by the authority to determine "desirability" of tenants, and the evictees faced the prospect of a difficult legal battle.

Most political scientists agree that enabling legislation can merely define the basic function of the agency; discretion must obviously be permitted in the use of its authority. The limits of the agency's authority are established by the enabling legislation, and it has no legal power to act in matters not placed under the jurisdiction of its authority. There is, however, a wide range of discretion, without which no governmental body can function. Discretion is required, for instance, by building officials who inspect houses, and by the Forestry Service to close parks when weather conditions are deemed conducive to forest fires.

In considering bureaucratic discretion, it is necessary to distinguish between normal discretion, inherent in the administrative process, and that given to an agency by Congress. It is the latter that some call dangerous; the former is considered inevitable and not dangerous as long as the agency is held accountable. Yet many say bureaucracies are not accountable and responsive, since they are often independent of the President and Congress; critics say they are powers unto themselves, indifferent to the opinions of the public.

Many independent regulatory agencies with quasi-legislative powers have been set up under federal legislation to adjudicate conflicting claims. One of these is the National Labor Relations Board, established by the National Labor Relations Act in 1935, whose primary duties are to determine if management has engaged in unfair labor practices, and to choose between unions contending as the bargaining agent for a particular company. Another is the Civilian Aeronautics Board, which, on occasion, chooses between two airlines competing for a route.

The Administrative Procedures Act of 1946 was an attempt to establish uniformity, fairness, and rules for adjudication by regulatory agencies, giving the victim of unfair administrative procedures the right to appeal to the courts for relief. Under this Act, the courts may review agency decisions and overrule them not only on the basis of legal jurisdiction but also on the basis of the facts in a particular case.

Following the passage of the Administrative Procedures Act, a complicated area of administrative law has developed, much of it concerned with the conditions under which interested parties may appeal rulings by adjudicating agencies. It is a complicated question, but experience under the law suggests that administrative agencies remain the final power in many important matters, including questions about loyalty and security. For example, when J. Robert Oppenheimer was removed from his position in the Atomic Energy Commission as a "security risk," the courts did little more than support an administrative decision which, it turned out, was based on meager substantive evidence. Philip M. Stern, Oppenheimer's biographer, wrote: "In the end Oppenheimer's judges found the physicist not only loyal but *unusually* discreet with secrets—but nonetheless ruled that 'the father of the A-bomb' was a 'security risk,' no longer entitled to his government's trust."[67]

Controlling the Bureaucracy

A recurring fear in American politics is that the bureaucracy has become an all-powerful and autonomous branch of the government, with the Chief Executive exercising no more than occasional supervision, and Congress kicking up an occasional fuss about some relatively unimportant area, while routinely approving most bureaucratic requests for authority and funds.

The image of the bureaucracy as an uncontrollable monster tends to be exaggerated; certain constraints on bureaucratic power, although not always strong or effective, do exist. Such constraints come, first, from other branches of government. Congress can limit agency activity through legislation, or by cutting back appropriations, or by the threat of investigation. Moreover, even the vaunted bureaucratic expertise is at times partially offset by a certain degree of congressional expertise, as in the case of Representative Emanuel Celler (D.-N.Y.), a fifty-year veteran of the House, and the foremost congressional expert on antitrust matters; or Representative Wright Patman (D.-Texas), chairman of the House Banking and Currency Commission and its pro on bank regulation. The President, too, can act to restrain the powers of his executive agencies, by limit-

[67] Philip M. Stern, *The Oppenheimer Case* (New York: Harper & Row, 1969), p. 5.

The growing popularity of foreign travel in recent years has lengthened lines and shortened tempers in passport offices.

ing their budgets (through the Office of Management and Budget), by replacing personnel, and by using the prestige of the White House to push for implementation of his policies. Judicial review provides another, though expensive and time-consuming, means by which bureaucratic power can be opposed.

It should be noted, further, that groups outside the government which are a source of support, hence strength, for a bureaucracy, may impose constraints on its power. Such constraints have already been discussed in the case of some of the regulatory agencies—the ICC, for example, which appears unwilling (if not unable) to regulate the rails. Interest groups may also impose counteracting constraints on an agency with *several* client groups, as in the case of the U.S. Forest Service, which serves in the conflicting roles of guardian of forest for exploitation by the lumber companies and watchdog of forest lands as a nonreplacable environmental and recreational resource. Because the Forest Service must balance its commitments, it is sometimes seriously hampered in its efforts to take conclusive action in a specific direction.

Journalists also provide some constraints on bureaucratic activities, such as the work of Ida Tarbell and Lincoln Steffens (the muckrakers of 1890–1910). The Drew Pearsons and Jack Andersons of recent years have succeeded in drawing considerable attention to questionable bureaucratic activities, but the effect on the bureaucracies themselves has been difficult to measure. For example, in 1972, when Jack Anderson publicized a possible kickback to the Republican Party in return for the Justice Department's dropping its antitrust suit against International Telephone and Telegraph, the exposure did not change the government's position in regard to the case.

In addition to *external* limitations on bureaucratic activities, certain *internal* constraints may also exist, such as interagency rivalry. During the 1950s, for example, competition among various branches of the military for funds fragmented the power of the Armed Services. The Air Force (which requires only a relatively small number of men) came out against conscription, while the Army attempted to rally support for the draft, bringing to mind the prophetic words of the Founding Fathers: "Ambition must be made to counter-act ambition."

In summary, it is clear that bureaucracy—particularly the federal bureaucracy— has become tremendously powerful. As Max Weber noted, bureaucracies are an essential and inescapable part of industrialized, urbanized, and large-scale society. They are not likely, therefore, to be dispensed with, as envisioned by the more romantic rebels of the New Left—not even Lenin believed they could be abolished. What must instead be asked about them is, How can the bureaucracies be made more responsive to the people? And how can they be made more effective and freer from red tape?

In reply to the first question, one important answer of recent years has come from Sweden, which invented the office of ombudsman. The ombudsman's function is to hear complaints from the public and see to it that the agency deals with those that are justified. It is too soon to estimate how successful this development will be. More important is the need to revise our theories about government, and the relationship of the people to government, which were devised in the nineteenth century when the Legislature was supreme and powerful, as is no longer true today. As for the means used to make agencies more effective, the proposals so far tend to be ambiguous and uncertain. One suggestion is that an institutionalized procedure of criticism should be set up in each agency to constantly question ends and means. According to a proponent of this idea, "The institutionalization of criticism would . . . permit policy makers, planners and program analysts to protect against undue specialization, the trained incapacity to think, premature closure of a field, ideology disguised as fact, and Gresham's law[68] of decision making."[69]

SUGGESTED READING

Berkley, George E. *The Administrative Revolution: Notes on the Passing of Organizational Man* (Englewood Cliffs, N.J.: Prentice-Hall, 1971). The author traces the shattering effect of technology on organizational structure and executive operations, as well as the growing convergence of public and private organizations. This book is an attempt to assess the impact of the administrative "revolution," which is only in its beginning stages and is already affecting both the public and private sectors.

---

[68] Gresham's law: The tendency of an inferior form of currency to circulate more freely than, or to the exclusion of, the superior currency, because of the hoarding of the latter. Named after Sir Thomas Gresham, an English financier.

[69] Martin Landau, "On the Concept of Self-Correcting Organization," p. 31.

Downs, Anthony. *Inside Bureaucracy* (Boston: Little, Brown, 1967). In paperback. An attempt to develop a useful theory of bureaucratic decision-making, which would enable analysts to predict some aspects of bureau behavior and to incorporate the role of bureaus into a more generalized theory of social decision-making. The fundamental premise is that bureaucrats, like other agents in society, are significantly motivated by their own self-interests; they seek to attain their goals rationally (efficiently); and their social functions strongly influence their organization's internal structure. From these central axioms the author deduces a set of basic hypotheses which partly explain bureaucratic activities.

Frankel, Charles. *High On Foggy Bottom: An Outsider's Inside View of the Government* (New York: Harper & Row, 1968). One man's reaction to life in the higher reaches of government. The author, a philosopher, served for more than two and a half years as Assistant Secretary of State for Educational and Cultural Affairs. In this book he describes the State Department and his impressions of what it is like to live and work inside the government. He also gives us an insider's explanations of many of Washington's bureaucratic mysteries.

Gawthrop, Louis C. *Bureaucratic Behavior in the Executive Branch: An Analysis of Organizational Change* (New York: The Free Press, 1969). An interpretation and explanation of organizational behavior, with a systematic analysis of the integral relationship between making decisions and resolving conflicts in the Executive branch of the U.S. government. The author examines the manner in which the Executive branch of the federal government resolves internal conflict, makes decisions, develops a sense of loyalty within its ranks, and responds to the internal and external forces of change. The overall focus of the study is on the development of an analytical model which can be used to explain the functioning of bureaucratic systems.

Howton, William F. *Functionaries* (Chicago: Quadrangle Books, 1969). After a description of the background of organization theory, the author presents his own theory of functionalization, which he contends is analogous and complementary to bureaucratization. Emphasis is on the analysis of the functionary social type in the military, in business, in government, and in voluntary associations and the relation of these roles to the workings of some key institutions in contemporary society.

Jacob, Charles E. *Policy and Bureaucracy* (New York: Van Nostrand, 1966). In paperback. An introduction to public policy and public administration, which emphasizes the politics and behavioral aspects of decision-making. The author neither discusses traditional administrative notions nor describes major institutions, but spends considerable time examining the sociological and political aspects of bureaucracy.

Kohlmeier, Louis M., Jr. *The Regulators: Watchdog Agencies and the Public Interest* (New York: Harper & Row, 1969). Description and analysis of the major independent administrative, or regulatory, agencies created by Congress to regulate or promote private industry for stated public purposes and the relationships of these agencies to all other federal laws and programs that concern the consumer interest. The author demonstrates how these agencies, which often become the promoters of the industries they were supposed to police, have failed in their purpose to protect the American consumer. He analyzes the regulatory agencies' frustrating presidential and congressional attempts at reform, as well as their tendencies to place their business interests above the public interest on their scale of priorities.

Lindblom, Charles E. *The Intelligence of Democracy: Decision Making Through Mutual Adjustment* (New York: The Free Press, 1965). Refutation of the general belief that political systems require some centralization of authority to coordinate otherwise disparate and conflicting policies. Instead, the author contends they rely on dispersion and fragmentation of power to achieve the efficiency ordinarily attributed to central coordination. The author systematically compares centrally directed decision-making and partisan mutual adjustment as processes for rational decision-making by political leaders. He argues that people can coordinate with each other without anyone's coordinating them, without a dominant common purpose, and without rules that fully prescribe their relations to each other.

Simon, Herbert A. *Administrative Behavior* (2nd ed.) (New York: The Free Press, 1957). In paperback. An attempt to construct a set of tools—concepts and a vocabulary—suitable for describing an administrative organization and its operation. Decision-making, and therefore human choice, is conceived as the core of administration. The book also describes and explains the nature of organization, the administrative process, the nature of decision, and the mixture of fact and value that enters into all decisions.

———; Donald W. Smithburg, and Victor A. Thompson. *Public Administration* (New York: Knopf, 1968). A description and explanation of how government is managed in all its executive branches. The book deals in depth with the activities of the executive branches of national, state, and local governments; the independent boards and commissions established by Congress and state legislatures; and the government corporations. The authors combine empirical knowledge of public administration with theoretical knowledge of human behavior and give serious attention to the relationship between politics and administration.

Wise, David, and Thomas B. Ross. *The Invisible Government* (New York: Random House, 1964). A full account of America's intelligence and espionage bureaucracies, which the authors label the Invisible Government. Composed of many people and agencies, the largest and most important of which is the CIA, this Invisible Government wields tremendous power and spends literally billions of dollars annually. The authors describe the activities of America's secret government, concluding with suggestions on how to make it more compatible with democracy.

9
THE COURTS, THE LAW, AND THE ADMINISTRATION OF JUSTICE

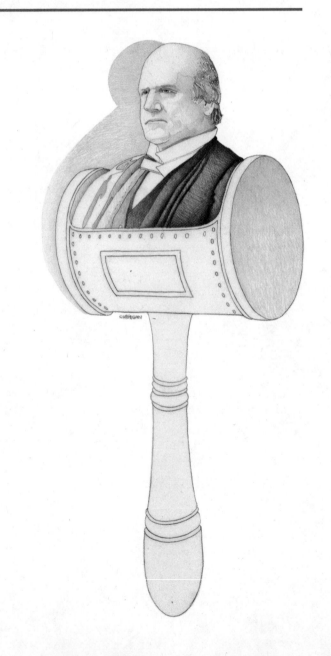

A major characteristic of American democracy is its reliance on law. In fact Americans prefer to think of their government as one of laws, rather than men and, since the nation's inception, the written law has held an honored spot. Lawyers have always abounded in the service of the United States government. At the Constitutional Convention, thirteen of the fifty-five delegates were lawyers and many of the others highly knowledgeable in jurisprudence. Today, three-fifths of the legislators serving in the Senate and the House of Representatives have had legal training, while recent statistics showed over forty-six thousand lawyers in the employ of government on all levels, almost twenty thousand by the federal government alone.[1]

The courts, as the instruments of administering law and justice, are also held in high prestige. Law and the value of adjudicating disputes are two concepts that hold a place in American life unlike that of most other democracies. Alexis de Tocqueville long ago observed that American courts were unlike any others. "Scarcely any political question arises in the United States that is not resolved, sooner or later, into a judicial question." This statement is particularly true with regard to the Supreme Court. In no other nation would a court become involved in such matters as ordering school integration or deciding whether children may be asked to recite prayers in public classrooms. Formulating complex social and political questions in legal terms which lead ultimately to court cases seems uniquely American.

The Meaning of Law

Carved into the imposing marble facade of the United States Supreme Court Building is the motto "Equal Justice under law." These words suggest that the law is indispensable for administering impartial justice. But what exactly is *the law*? In Britain there is no written constitution of laws to turn to, and lawyers rely on custom and a sense of fairness and justice. In the United States, however, these two elements, a written Constitution and judicial ethics, morality, and custom, are not so clearcut.[2] Indeed, even thoughtful students of jurisprudence find it difficult to delineate between the two. So imperceptibly do these elements shade into each other that to one expert, writing more than half a century ago, they appeared to be "different names for almost the same thing."[3]

For the purposes of our discussion, law can be defined as a system of rules for regulating conduct backed by the organized power of the community—in other words, by government.[4]

But law as applied in the courts—from the Supreme Court down to the justices of the peace—is by no means a homogeneous system. The modern law of the United States is a complicated fabric. Its texture is woven of many strands, including common law, statutory law, constitutional law, and administrative law (see Table 9–1). Even primitive customs and traditions reflecting a world found

---

[1] *Statistical Abstract of the United States, 1971* (Washington, D.C.: Department of Commerce, 1971), p. 153.
[2] For the view that the United States judiciary should rely less on the constitutional document and more on a moral sense of fairness and justice see Edward S. Corwin, *The Higher Law Background of American Constitutional Law* (Ithaca, N.Y.: Cornell University Press, 1955).
[3] James Coolidge Carter, *Law: Its Origin, Growth and Function* (New York: Knickerbocker Press, 1907), p. 320.
[4] Harry J. Abraham, *The Judicial Process* (New York: Oxford University Press, 1968), p. 9.

Table 9–1   **Types of Law and Their Definitions**

Common Law	Judge or bench-made law, evolving from application of precedents (past court decisions).
Statutory Law	Laws enacted by legislative bodies.
Equity	Law preventing serious injury either by forbidding action or requiring just compensation beforehand.
Constitutional Law	Law based on the text of the Constitution as well as the legal doctrines enunciated by the Supreme Court.
Administrative Law	Rules and regulations devised by commissions and other types of regulatory agencies to which Congress delegates authority to regulate public services.
Maritime Law	Laws relating to shipping and commerce on the high seas.
Private Law	Law concerning the obligations of one person to another and the settling of disagreements arising between them.
Public Law	Law involving disputes in which the government is a party.
Civil Law	Law relating to disputes among individuals or private groups; the plaintiff or aggrieved party must bring action against the defendant.
Criminal Law	Law relating to offenses against the public order; the government initiates court action.

only in history books still influence the American judges making decisions in this last third of the twentieth century.

Common Law and *Stare Decisis*

Common law, for example, is founded upon feudal practices of medieval England. Referred to as judge-made law or bench-made law, it evolved from decisions offered in settling actual cases. The continuous application of past decisions to fresh disputes in England resulted in the creation of Anglo-Saxon law.[5] In the United States, the development of an indigenous common law based on the common law of the mother country began in the seventeenth century. Today, each state, with the exception of Louisiana, has a common law of its own; Louisiana's law follows the Roman civil-law tradition and stresses legislative law at the expense of bench-made law. Federal courts have no common law of their own. A federal judge adjudicating an interstate dispute may use a precedent drawn from the common law of one of the states. Common law and precedent—a juridical principle expressed in the Latin phrase *stare decisis*, meaning "Let past decisions stand"—are inseparable. Indeed, precedent is the keystone of the common law.

The practice of judges adhering to decisions of the past gives a degree of stability and predictability to the administration of justice. As Oliver Wendell Holmes noted, "Imitation of the past until we have a clear reason for change, no more needs justification than appetite. It is a form of the inevitable to be accepted until we have a clear vision of what different things we want."[6] The rule is by no means an injunction to follow the past blindly. In cases that break new ground, the judge has the obligation to weigh carefully the advantage of hewing to the precedents of legal history against the need for judicially planned social and economic change. In regard to the responsibility to further progress,

---

[5] The classic compilation and analysis of this case-derived law was produced by the famed jurist Sir William Blackstone in his *Commentaries on the Law of England.*

[6] Oliver Wendell Holmes's statement quoted in "Holdsworth's English Law" in *Collected Legal Papers* (Boston: A. Harcourt, 1920), p. 290.

Supreme Court Justice Talbot Smith once observed that precedents are judge-invented and therefore may be judge-destroyed.

The Power of Judicial Review

Consider this brief scenario: The Congress enacts an economic measure prohibiting employers from hiring children under the age of sixteen. The President signs it into law and the vast and powerful machinery of the federal Executive branch moves to enforce it. Somewhere, a single individual construes the law as encroaching upon his rights as a citizen. He sues. The case reaches the Supreme Court, which rules in favor of the individual. The law is struck down as unconstitutional. An uneven struggle pitting a solitary citizen against the Congress, the President, and the federal bureaucracy has ended in victory for the individual.

The power of the courts to annul an act of the Legislature is called judicial review. It is a peculiarly American concept, although its roots are found in English law as far back as 1610, when the court triumphed over the will of Parliament. Uncomfortable with this situation, Parliament's supremacy over the judiciary was established and still exists today.

The Establishment of Judicial Review

How and when did the American courts gain the enormous power to override decisions of the Legislative and Executive branches? The Constitution is silent on the matter of judicial review. As occurred with many later principles of constitutional law, judicial review itself was forged through time. The political philosophy behind it had been around for some time – the Founding Fathers discussed it in their writings, and delegates to the Constitutional Convention debated the subject. But a confrontation between brilliant political adversaries among the nation's founders was required to bring the issue to the surface. It was during a clash between Jeffersonian Democrats and Federalists that judicial review, the safeguard of constitutional law, was established. And the case that established this right for the court was *Marbury* v. *Madison*,[7] which appeared on the Supreme Court's docket in 1802.

The Federalist faction, headed by President John Adams, had been handed a crushing defeat in the election of 1801 when Thomas Jefferson was elected to the Presidency. In the waning days of his term, Adams and the Federalist party, which dominated Congress, moved to entrench themselves in the judiciary. Dozens of federal judgeships were hastily created and filled with loyal Federalist appointees. The Jeffersonian faction was enraged by the court-packing, but it was powerless to take action against a perfectly legal maneuver. Upon taking office in 1801, Jefferson discovered that a number of commissions for justices of the peace in the District of Columbia, relatively minor posts, were undelivered. Adams had vacated his office before tying up all the loose ends. Jefferson instructed his new secretary of state, James Madison, to withhold seventeen commissions, including the judgeship of William Marbury. Finally, Marbury, joined by three other frustrated appointees, sued in the Supreme Court. Their strategy

---

[7] *Marbury* v. *Madison*, 1 Cr. 137 (1802).

was based upon a provision of the Judiciary Act of 1789 which extended to the Supreme Court the power to issue a *writ of mandamus. Mandamus,* Latin for *we command,* is an order requiring an official to perform a formal, nondiscretionary act. In other words, Marbury and the others requested a court directive ordering Madison to surrender their commissions, since they had been duly appointed to the posts.

The Chief Justice of the Supreme Court at the time was John Marshall, Jefferson's arch-rival. As President Adams's Secretary of State, Marshall had not only carried out the court-packing ploy but owed his own exalted position to one of those last-minute, lame-duck appointments by Adams. Many thought Marshall was in a bind. Could he, in view of the plain language of the Judiciary Act and his own background, refuse to issue the writ? The Jeffersonians expected Marshall to grant the order, and in this tense atmosphere there was talk of impeaching the Chief Justice of the Supreme Court.

But Marshall's decision confounded both friend and foe, Federalist and Jeffersonian alike. In the first twenty pages of a twenty-seven-page decision, Marshall expatiated on the basic justness of the Federalist position, agreeing that the plaintiff, Marbury, had a legal right to his post and castigating Jefferson and Madison for their "rascality." Then, in the remaining seven pages, Marshall, in what seemed like a reversal, informed Marbury the Court could not provide a remedy. While Marbury was entitled to a place on the bench, the provision of the Judiciary Act under which the suit had been brought violated the Constitution. Article III of the Constitution carefully delineates the jurisdiction of the Supreme Court. Since the Judiciary Act attempted by mere act of Congress, rather than by amendment, to broaden the Court's jurisdiction, it was unconstitutional.

Chief Justice John Marshall.

The closing pages of the decision, packed with keen analysis and close reasoning, launched a vehement controversy that racked the nation. Even if one granted Marshall's contention that the law of Congress was in conflict with the Constitution, should that be a decision of the Court? Could not other branches of government claim an equal right to interpret the Constitution? Had the Framers of the Constitution vested in the courts the power of upsetting legislation, as part of the system of checks and balances? If so, why did not the Constitution declare its intent?

Relying, in the absence of precedent, entirely on his powers of reasoning, the Chief Justice argued eloquently that such authority was given the Court:

> *It is emphatically the province and duty of the judicial department to say what the law is. Those who apply the rule to particular cases, must of necessity expound and interpret that rule. If two laws conflict with each other, the courts must decide on the operation of each. So if a law be in opposition to the Constitution . . . the court must determine which of these conflicting rules governs the case. This is of the very essence of judicial duty.*

After Marshall's landmark decision, fifty years elapsed before the Supreme Court again struck down a legislative measure in the Dred Scott case.[8] Chief Justice Roger Taney's ruling in 1857 to return a runaway slave, Dred Scott, to his master not only reinforced the Supreme Court's authority to interpret the Constitution, but even broadened it. Without the *Dred Scott* decision, Marshall's 1802 ruling could be interpreted to mean that the Supreme Court merely had the power to define its own domain under the provisions of Article III of the Constitution. But, building on the logic of the *Marbury* decision, Taney further established the Supreme Court's power to interpret the functions of the President and the Congress. Through *Dred Scott*, all federal activities were brought under the umbrella of judicial review.

The Current Controversy over Judicial Review: An Active or a Restrained Supreme Court

The most rancorous controversies in political life have swirled frequently around the highest tribunal in the land, the Supreme Court of the United States. Former Chief Justice Earl Warren was, no doubt, annoyed by the handful of critics advocating his removal from the bench, but Chief Justice John Marshall, the country's third Chief Justice, was bedeviled by a political party that actually wrote an impeachment plank into its campaign platform. Marshall's colleague, Justice Samuel Chase, narrowly missed impeachment only because a few senators decided to bolt their party and vote acquittal after the House had agreed on impeachment.

The controversy over the role of Supreme Court, then, is one that has existed since its inception. Created to be a barrier to the impassioned majority, the Court was instituted to protect the people against the excesses of democracy, and the power of judicial review has done just that. But some contend that nine judges with life tenure should not hold equal weight with a President elected by the nation, and a large Legislature elected from local constituencies. George W. Norris of Nebraska, a towering figure in the United States' senatorial history, a man

---

[8] *Dred Scott* v. *Sandford,* 19 Howard 393 (1857).

known for his gentle mien, rose to speak one day in the Senate. With unchar-
acteristic vehemence, he shouted:

*We have a legislative body, called the House of Representatives, of over four hundred
men. We have another legislative body, called the Senate, of less than a hundred men.
We have, in reality, another legislative body, called the Supreme Court, of nine men;
and they are more powerful than all of the others put together.*[9]

The crux of the legislative-judicial conflict boils down to the fact that, in applying
a law to a specific case, judges do make policy. Every law is limited by a finite
number of words yet it must be applied to a great number of situations. Of necessity, a law is couched in broad terms. Once a statute is enacted, however, cases
are bound to arise requiring interpretations of the language of the law. The
judge's role, to choose between alternatives open to him—to decide whether the
law covers a particular case or not—can be considered lawmaking. Similarly, the
application of the Constitution to current situations requires decisions that some
would call judicial policy-making.

Like the social scientists who analyze the behavior patterns of some group,
such as alcoholics, political scientists study the voting patterns of courts as well
as of individual judges, diagnosing whether a judge or a court is policy-oriented
or not. A policy-minded judge, or collectively, a court, takes advantage of the
latitude permissible under the law and uses that freedom to make decisions that
shape public policy.[10] Whether policy-making implies deliberate intent and planning by a judge or whether it is an unplanned side-effect or unconscious bent is
a debatable issue.[11]

Judicial policy-making has its advocates and opponents. Those subscribing to
the so-called mechanistic theory of judicial process say the Constitution plainly
describes the Supreme Court as an adjudicatory body and denies it any role in
formulating public policy. On the other side are proponents of what is called free
decision. The Court's machinery, including judicial review, they hold, should be
used to prod the legal establishment and legislators to keep pace with a dynamic
public policy.[12]

Congress generally supports the mechanistic theory. A study by Robert A. Dahl
showed that Congress does not accept Supreme Court superiority passively. Of
twenty-six measures held unconstitutional within four years of their enactment,
Congress capitulated to the Court and changed its position to conform with the
judicial decision only twice. It eventually acquiesced in eight other instances.
In twelve decisions, however, Congress succeeded in reversing the Court's policy,
and four other times it took tentative action against court rulings.[13]

The most direct rebuff Congress can use toward the Supreme Court is the

---

[9] *Congressional Record,* 71st Cong., 2nd Sess., vol. 72, part 4 (Feb. 13, 1930), p. 3566, as quoted in Glendon
A. Schubert, *Constitutional Politics* (New York: Holt, Rinehart and Winston, 1960), p. 177.

[10] Richard S. Wells and Joel B. Grossman, "The Concept of Judicial Policy-Making," in *Elements of the Federal Judicial System,* edited by Sheldon Goldman and Thomas Jahnige (New York: Holt, Rinehart and Winston, 1968), pp. 294–296.

[11] Wells and Grossman, p. 296.

[12] Arthur H. North, S.J., *The Supreme Court: Judicial Process and Judicial Politics* (New York: Appleton-
Century-Crofts, 1966), pp. 10–12.

[13] Robert A. Dahl, *Pluralist Democracy in the United States: Conflict and Consent* (Chicago: Rand McNally,
1967), p. 161.

amendment. Six to eight of the Constitution's amendments—depending on how they are viewed—were passed solely to overcome the Court. Among them is the Eleventh Amendment, broadening the original jurisdiction of the Supreme Court and reversing the 1793 decision in *Chisholm* v. *Georgia*[14] that enabled states to be sued in federal courts. Others are the Civil War amendments, the Thirteenth and Fourteenth, passed to protect Negro civil rights and abolish slavery. These amendments canceled the Court's *Dred Scott* decision and subsequent rulings. Finally, the Supreme Court's declaration in 1895 in the *Pollock* v. *Farmers' Loan and Trust Co.*[15] that declared various income-tax laws unconstitutional was reversed by the Sixteenth Amendment, which gave Congress the power to impose levies of all kinds.

The Supreme Court in the course of its 167-year history struck down ninety-four acts of Congress. In the long run, as one expert sees it, the Court avoids veering too far from the legislative course. When the Court dominates Congress, it is usually the symptom of a weak congressional majority, a superficial legislative coalition, or a transient alignment. The court has a slim chance of prevailing against a strong and determined lawmaking majority firmly committed to an important issue.[16]

While no one today seriously challenges the Supreme Court's power to use judicial review, a fundamental disagreement remains about how often judicial review should be utilized. As formulated by one constitutional scholar, the question is whether the Court should be an active, creative partner with the Legislative and Executive branches in shaping the nation's legal structure, or whether it should exercise self-restraint. By self-restraint, experts mean a passive role in which the Court leaves to the other branches of the government the "breaking of new ground."[17] There are those who believe that members of the Court, in interpreting law, must be guarded from infringing on the authority of the Executive and Legislature. These political scientists argue that judges should aim for judicial judgment and shun judicial will. Judicial judgment, in this view, means applying the law, but making only minimal changes and adaptations. Judicial will, on the contrary, disregards the constitutional limits on the Court's functions and freely legislates by court fiat. This use of judicial will is in essence the use of judicial policy-making and is the activist, as opposed to the restrained, use of the Court's power. Admittedly, there is a thin line between these two positions, and attempts to find its exact placement have produced eloquent spokesmen for both philosophies.

In contemporary courts, Justices Felix Frankfurter, John Marshall Harlan, and Harlan Stone have been forceful proponents of judicial restraint. Frankfurter's beliefs have been described as pragmatic, self-effacing, and "humilitarian." He repeatedly warned his colleagues against concentrating power in the Court and insisted that social improvement be left to the states and agencies of the federal government.[18] Similarly, Harlan, an intellectual and legal craftsman, warned

---

[14] *Chisholm* v. *Georgia*, 2 Dallas 419 (1793).

[15] *Pollock* v. *Farmers' Loan and Trust Co.*, 158 U.S. 601 and 157 U.S. 429 (1895).

[16] Dahl, *Pluralist Democracy in the United States*, pp. 154–156.

[17] Archibald Cox, *The Warren Court* (Cambridge, Mass.: Harvard University Press, 1968), p. 2.

[18] Wallace Mendelson, "The Case for Judicial Restraint," in *Basic Issues of American Democracy*, edited by Hillman M. Bishop and Samuel Hendler, 6th edition (New York: Appleton-Century-Crofts, 1970), pp. 322–333.

Justice Felix Frankfurter in 1939.

against the "mistaken view that every major social ill in this country can find
its cure in some constitutional principle and that this court should take the lead"
in promoting reform when other branches of government fail to act.[19]

It should be noted that Harlan Stone's argument for judicial restraint pertained
to economic and social problems. He advocated more active use of the Court in
guarding minority rights and freedom of speech and the press.[20]

While campaigning for the Presidency in 1916, Charles Evans Hughes often
proclaimed, "We are under the Constitution, but the Constitution is what the
judges say it is." While Hughes is not considered a leading activist, his succinct
statement has been used to sum up the position of judicial activists who seek
to apply the Constitution to solve economic and political problems. These judges
contend they are licensed to read meanings into the Constitution to suit the needs
and conditions of their time. A more sophisticated approach to activism emphasizes the Court's responsibility to take positive action as well as issue negative
rulings. "The judiciary," in the words of A. T. Mason, "like other agencies of government, should facilitate achievement of the great objectives mentioned in the

---

[19] *Time* (January 10, 1972), p. 14.
[20] Walter F. Murphy, *Congress and the Court* (Chicago: University of Chicago Press, 1962), p. 71.

Constitution's Preamble." The Warren Court, for example, became known for boldly tackling cases with political implications, the kind that earlier judges studiously avoided. To the activists, the Warren Court correctly interpreted the Constitution and used judicial review properly. A statement made in 1921 by Justice Benjamin Cardozo has been said to express the essence of the Warren Court's activist approach to judicial review: "We find the judiciary's chief worth in making vocal and available ideals that might otherwise be silenced. . . ."[21]

For many years an outstanding activist on the Court has been Justice William O. Douglas, who considers the Court to be the watchdog of constitutional liberties. Court decisions, according to Douglas, should subordinate legal technique to practical need. When the issue before the Court involves individual liberties or the Fourteenth Amendment equality guarantees, the libertarian end takes precedence over the legal means.[22] Enthusiastic protection of personal freedoms and concern for individual welfare have characterized court decisions since 1970.

The Supreme Court

The American judicial system is dual in nature: each state has courts of its own with power derived from its state constitution and statutes, and the federal government also maintains its own system. Although the two systems generally operate in separate domains, they form a hierarchical structure for the solution of constitutional (meaning the Constitution of the United States) and federal questions; at the summit of this institutional pyramid stands the United States Supreme Court. Any individual who believes that he has been treated unjustly in a state court in a case with a valid constitutional issue may appeal to federal district courts and eventually to the Supreme Court itself.

The Judges of the Supreme Court

The Constitution permits the President to select justices to sit on the Supreme Court with the advice and consent of the Senate. Appointments to the Court rank among the most important political decisions a White House occupant makes. This politicization of the Court exists because a President may mobilize the public opinion of the nation for some political program and elicit the support of Congress only to find a hostile Supreme Court blocking his most important proposals. It has therefore come to pass that party considerations are regarded as very important in the choice of a justice. Affiliation with the President's party, however, is not sufficient. Since the major American parties represent a coalition of various shades of opinion, a President must search beyond party membership. Careful scrutiny tries to ascertain a candidate's judicial philosophy and determine the positions a nominee would be likely to take on substantial issues. Such burrowing into a nominee's background, however, does not always assure selection of a justice who will be totally sympathetic to a President's program. Elevation to the highest court often has had the effect of changing a judge's outlook. Justice Hugo

---

[21] Both quotations are from Alpheus Thomas Mason, "The Warren Court and the Bill of Rights," in *The Supreme Court in American Politics,* edited by David F. Forte (Lexington, Mass.: Heath, 1972), p. 29.

[22] Fred Rodell, "The Case for Judicial Activism," in Bishop and Hendler, *Basic Issues of American Democracy,* pp. 316–321.

Justice William O. Douglas in 1970.

Black, for example, was at one time a member of the Ku Klux Klan. After appointment to the bench by Franklin Roosevelt, he earned a reputation as a strong liberal. The annals of American political history are filled with Supreme Court justices disappointing their sponsors. Lincoln found his expectations about a key nominee wrong, as did Eisenhower, who appointed Chief Justice Earl Warren, unaware that Warren would take very liberal stances during his tenure.

Next to the President, the Senate wields the greatest power in selecting a Supreme Court judge, since it can reject an appointment. Approval of a nominee may be withheld in the Senate for such reasons as 1) antagonism toward the President; 2) reservations about the nominee's ability, character, or position on a political issue; 3) political fickleness and lack of party allegiance, and 4) discouragement as a result of senatorial courtesy. The last of these reasons, senatorial courtesy, refers to the presidential act of consulting the senators from the candidate's home state, if they belong to the President's party.

Recent examples of the Senate's involvement in court appointments are President Nixon's stormy confrontations with the Senate over two successive appointments to the Supreme Court. The Senate withheld approval of Judge Clement Haynsworth, Jr., because of organized opposition by labor and civil-rights groups, while G. Harrold Carswell's appointment was refused because of charges that he was deficient in ability and supported racial segregation. It is evident, then, that although the President has the power to make judicial appointments, and the Senate the final power of approval, the will of both Executive and Legislature can be circumscribed from many directions, including pressure groups and public opinion. In the words of one expert, "The time has come to set aside the simplistic explanation that senators alone determine appointments to the federal bench. . . . The process is much more complicated and, indeed, much more interesting."[23]

What qualifies an individual to sit on the highest bench in the land? Logically, one would expect judges named to the Supreme Court to have a judicial background. The Constitution makes no such demands, and history shows that most of the outstanding Court members—John Marshall, Roger B. Taney, Charles E. Hughes, Louis Brandeis, and Felix Frankfurter—lacked prior judicial experience. In fact, one fourth of the Supreme Court's members have never served in court. Most, however, have been lawyers (although this also is not a formal prerequisite) and have displayed professional competence. What appears to be a more important qualification is political experience. With one exception, all Supreme Court judges have held some political office before appointment to the bench. Most justices are of middle- and upper-class origins; they have all been white with the exception of Thurgood Marshall, and, except for six justices, they have all been of Anglo-Saxon stock. Their religious affiliation has been predominantly Protestant; there have been six Roman Catholics and five Jews who have served.

The removal of a Supreme Court justice by impeachment, the only constitutional method for removal, is rare; only four judges were ever removed. Impeachment requires indictment by a majority of the House of Representatives and conviction by two-thirds of the Senate. In our nation's history, the House has initiated nine impeachment trials against judges, of which five ended in acquittals. The last conviction of a judge occurred in 1936. More recently, House Republican Leader Gerald Ford attempted to initiate impeachment proceedings against Supreme Court Justice Douglas over alleged misconduct involving a foundation's funds. The move died in committee.[24]

The Supreme Court Through Time

From the time it was constituted in the eighteenth century, to well into the twentieth, the Supreme Court remained a conservative institution, zealously pro-

---

[23] Harold W. Chase, "Federal Judges: The Appointing Process," *Minnesota Law Review*, vol. 51, no. 2 (December 1966), p. 221.

[24] See Paul N. McCloskey, Jr., *Truth and Untruth: Political Deceit in America* (New York: Simon and Schuster, 1972), pp. 192–196, on the move to impeach Justice Douglas and its relationship to other Nixon appointments to the Court.

tecting states' rights and property rights. For instance, John Marshall utilized the Court as a nationalizing force favoring Federalist principles which were usually financial and mercantilist in nature. His successor, Roger B. Taney, championed the cause of states' rights against the expanding federal government, avoiding strong support of personal freedoms. Although the Fourteenth Amendment was enacted to protect Negro rights in the Reconstruction era, the Supreme Court interpreted it to apply to corporations and defended rampant capitalism from government regulation. Later, during the freewheeling era of the robber barons, when financiers such as the Morgans and the Goulds seized control of a large portion of the economy, the Supreme Court again stood between the magnates and effective government controls. Antitrust laws and other regulations were curtailed by the Court.

Roosevelt Packs the Court The year 1937 marked a turning point for the Court. Franklin Roosevelt reshaped the court from a conservative, laissez-faire institution favoring property rights to a socially minded judicial body favoring the individual. In 1937, Roosevelt and the Supreme Court met in a head-on collision. When the justices, with their nineteenth-century ideas, refused to uphold the New Deal economic legislation, Roosevelt moved to assert the power of the Presidency. Flushed with the success of the previous year's reelection landslide, in 1937 he confidently introduced administrative and procedural changes in the federal court system for the purpose of alleviating court backlog and improving court efficiency. Although the plan was generally stated, it was aimed specifically at the Supreme Court and has come to be called Roosevelt's "Court-Packing Bill." The measure would have permitted the President to appoint an additional justice for each incumbent over seventy until the court was expanded to a maximum size of fifteen members. This change would have meant the addition of six new justices to provide some balance for the four (Pierce Butler, James McReynolds, George Sutherland, and Willis Van Devanter) who were solidly united against New Deal policies, and a fifth (Owen Roberts) who often sided with them. Roosevelt's aim was to bring to the judicial system "a steady and continuing stream of new and younger blood . . . to bring to the decision of social and economic problems younger men who have had personal experience and contact with modern facts and circumstances under which average men have to live and work."[25] The Roosevelt plan was defeated by Congress.

Nevertheless, Roosevelt's campaign won a victory. Just before the President's plan was sent to Congress, Roberts voted with the four more liberal justices to validate a state minimum-wage law.[26] Chief Justice Charles Evans Hughes was elated at Roberts's action, which he contended "saved the country." In effect, "the switch in time saved nine." From this point on, the Court's direction was the same as Roosevelt's.

The stalwarts of the liberal wing of the Roosevelt Court were Justices Louis Brandeis, Harlan Stone, and Benjamin Cardozo. Chief Justice Charles Evans Hughes often, but not consistently, joined them. When vacancies became available after the retirement of Van Devanter and Brandeis, Roosevelt appointed

---

[25] The *New York Times,* March 10, 1937, p. 15, as quoted in Robert Scigliano, *The Supreme Court and the Presidency* (New York: The Free Press, 1971), p. 45.

[26] *West Coast Hotel Co.* v. *Parrish,* 300 U.S. 379 (1937).

Chief Justice Earl Warren in front of the Supreme Court Building upon his retirement June 23, 1969.

Hugo Black and William O. Douglas, who joined the liberal wing. He also elevated Harlan Stone to the position of Chief Justice in 1941, a change applauded by New Deal supporters.[27]

The Warren Court   The Court continued on a progressive course after Roosevelt. President Eisenhower, a Republican, appointed a fellow Republican from California, Earl Warren, to be Chief Justice. The Warren Court compiled one of the most activist and liberal records in court history. The Warren era began with the school desegregation decision that ignited the civil rights struggle, *Brown* v. *Board of Education*.[28] That the school integration case would have a far-reaching impact on the race issue was understood by the Court. As Yale scholar Alexander Bickel has noted, "The judges were plainly conscious of entering upon a great and intricate new enterprise."[29] They were in this decision moving away from

---

[27] For a comprehensive study of President Roosevelt and the Supreme Court see C. Herman Pritchett, *The Roosevelt Court: A Study in Judicial Politics and Values, 1937–1947* (New York: Octagon, 1963).

[28] *Brown* v. *Board of Education of Topeka*, 347 U.S. 483 (1954).

[29] Alexander Bickel, *The Supreme Court and the Idea of Progress* (New York: Harper Torchbooks, 1970), pp. 5–6.

The members of the Supreme Court at the end of 1972 were: (seated, left to right) Potter Stewart, William O. Douglas, Chief Justice Warren E. Burger, William J. Brennan, Jr., and Byron R. White; (standing, left to right) Lewis F. Powell, Jr., Thurgood Marshall, Harry A. Blackmun, and William H. Rehnquist.

strict legal construction of the Constitution and following the Brandeis precedent of using sociological reasoning as the basis for its ruling.

A host of civil-liberties decisions followed, including a ban on Bible reading and prayer in public schools; reapportionment of voting districts on the basis of one man, one vote; restrictions on wiretap evidence; and loosening of curbs on obscene material. The trend also provided safeguards, through the Escobedo and Miranda cases, for those accused of crime.[30] The Warren Court became the target of attacks both inside and outside of Congress and was denounced for its "radicalism." A law expert, summing up the Court's achievements, saw it differently. The court, he wrote, was in "the mainstream of American history—a bit progressive but also moderate, a bit humane but not sentimental, a bit idealistic but seldom doctrinaire, and in the long run essentially pragmatic."[31]

---

[30] *Escobedo* v. *Illinois,* 378 U.S. 478 (1964), and *Miranda* v. *Arizona,* 384 U.S. 436 (1966).
[31] Cox, *The Warren Court,* pp. 133–134.

Table 9-2   **Justices of the Supreme Court, 1972**

Name	Political Affiliation	Appointed by	Year
William O. Douglas	Dem.	F. D. Roosevelt	1939
William J. Brennan, Jr.	Dem.	Eisenhower	1956(57)*
Potter Stewart	Rep.	Eisenhower	1958(59)*
Byron R. White	Dem.	Kennedy	1962
Thurgood Marshall	Dem.	Johnson	1967
Warren E. Burger (Ch. Jus.)	Rep.	Nixon	1969
Harry A. Blackmun	Rep.	Nixon	1970
Lewis F. Powell, Jr.	Rep.	Nixon	1971
William H. Rehnquist	Rep.	Nixon	1971

* The first date represents time of interim appointment, and the second, official appointment.

The Burger Court In campaigning for election in 1968, Richard Nixon candidly informed the voters of his plans to change the Supreme Court. Nixon appealed to voters disillusioned with Warren Court decisions, mainly on crime, and to those of conservative beliefs opposed to the "loose" interpretive methods of the Warren Court. Such displays of candor are rare. Presidents are reluctant, normally, to indicate their motives for designating nominees.

President Nixon was presented with the opportunity of redeeming his pre-election promise soon after taking office. He appointed Warren Earl Burger to replace the retiring Chief Justice Earl Warren, and Harry A. Blackmun succeeded Associate Justice Abe Fortas, who resigned. Later, two more Nixon appointees joined the Supreme Court, Lewis E. Powell, Jr., and William H. Rehnquist. All four of the Nixon justices appear to favor a strict interpretation of the Constitution, leading to more conservative opinions.

The conservative leanings of the Nixon justices are undisputed. But has Nixon, in appointing them, ended three decades of judicial liberalism and created a genuinely conservative court? Will the Burger Court nullify the many precedents established under the Warren stewardship? These are difficult matters to predict. The Burger Court, thus far, has been cautious, restrained, not at all eager to break sharply with the past, observed Chicago law professor Harry Kalven, Jr.[32]

But at the same time it appears clear that Nixon's four appointees, when joined by Potter Stewart and Byron R. White (two justices who dissented against many of the Warren Court's liberal decisions on crime), will form a majority that can effectively move away from liberal rulings on crime. Fred P. Graham, a journalist who has covered the Supreme Court for many years, has detected that there may well be a "backtrack . . . on procedural safeguards," but he has also foreseen that "more crucial battles are shaping up over individual liberties." The more crucial battles facing the Burger Court are those which pit the power of the Executive branch against the basic liberties of Americans. In Graham's view, "if the Supreme Court does not curb the Government, nobody else can."[33]

[32] Harry Kalven, Jr., "The Supreme Court, 1970 Term" in *Harvard Law Review,* vol. 85, no. 1 (November 1971), p. 5.
[33] Fred Graham, the *New York Times* (January 7, 1972), p. 8.

The Court at Work

The cases tried before the Supreme Court fall into two categories: since the Court has appellate jurisdiction and original jurisdiction, it hears both appeals and untried litigation. The preponderance of the cases are appeals reaching it from lower federal courts or state courts. The Constitution envisaged the Supreme Court as the highest appeals tribunal in the land. Rarely, however, does a case go directly from a state court to the Supreme Court. When one party in a state case believes a federal constitutional issue is involved, he may appeal to a lower federal court and then, if still dissatisfied, to the Supreme Court. More than 90 percent of the Court's workload consists of written appeals known as *writs of certiorari,* Latin for "made more certain" or "better informed." In current legal use it means "at the court's discretion." When the Court chooses to review such requests, it orders the lower court to forward the trial record for examination.

Under the Constitution, the Supreme Court is given original jurisdiction to hear disputes between the states or between the federal government and a state, and cases involving foreign diplomats. Such litigation, however, is infrequent; of the twenty such cases brought before the Court in the 1970 term, two complaints were denied, five disposed of, and thirteen remained on the docket for the following term. During that same term, which ended in June 1971, a total of 3,318 cases were brought to the Court. Of these, 2,838 petitions for review were denied or dismissed, 139 appeals were dismissed, 200 *per curiam* decisions (short opinions) were handed down, and 141 written opinions were offered.

The Court's sessions, which last from October through June, are held in a white marble building on Capitol Hill, modeled after the Greek temple of Diana at Ephesus. A special session may be convened when the Court is not in session, but only five have been called in this century, the last in July of 1972 when the Court was reconvened to deliver a verdict in the Democratic party dispute over credentials for admittance to their national convention. At the start of each day, the judges march into the hall in single file in the order of their seniority, the Chief Justice heading the procession. They and all in attendance remain standing while the court marshall intones: "Oyez, Oyez! All persons having business before the honorable, the Supreme Court of the United States, are admonished to draw near and give their attention, for the court is now sitting. God save the United States and this honorable court!"

Oral debate still plays an important role in the Court's decision-making, although written briefs are submitted. A lawyer receives half an hour to state his case. Supreme Court judges tend to have numerous questions, often interrupting a lawyer's argument to clear up a point. Five minutes before the allotted time is up, a white light flashes. A red light means *stop,* and a lawyer may continue only with permission of the Chief Justice. The Court also requires that lawyers be formally admitted to try cases before the Supreme Court, a rule that does not hold for lower district courts, since it is accomplished for the entire judiciary of each state when a lawyer passes its bar exam.

Fridays are set aside for the weekly Supreme Court conference. The judges, who meet in an oak-paneled room under a large portrait of John Marshall, discuss their votes on pending cases and applications for *certiorari* writs as they sit around a large rectangular conference table. The deliberations are secret. Each justice has a hinged docket book, a notebook that can be locked, in which he records his positions. From his seat at the south end of the table, the Chief Justice chairs the meeting. The Senior Associate Justice sits at the opposite end. Theoretically the Chief Justice is no more than a "chief among equals." However, he controls the agenda at these meetings and assigns, in most instances, the writing of the Court's decision.

Written decisions by the Court were the invention of John Marshall; in England, justices have always delivered decisions orally. In recent years Chief Justices limit themselves to the writing of landmark decisions, relying on other justices to produce the more routine decisions. If the Chief Justice does not side with the majority, the responsibility for producing the opinion falls to the ranking member of the majority.[34] Judges sometimes file dissenting opinions when they are with the minority and concurrent decisions if they agree with the majority stand, but for different reasons. Critics ask, "Why publish the lengthy reasoning that leads to a conclusion? Why bother with concurrent and dissenting opinions?" What may appear to be a futile exercise forms part of the Court's tradition and enlightens others of the legal reasoning employed by the Court. Such public education is influential as well as interesting. The minority views once held by Louis D. Brandeis, Oliver Wendell Holmes, William Douglas, and Benjamin Cardozo were later adopted by the Court. Milton Konvitz, in praise of the detailed decisions that laid bare the processes through which judges arrive at their conclusions, has asserted that "the quest for the decision is at least as important as the decision itself."[35] An American law professor instructing at Moscow University discussed majority as well as dissenting opinions in the famous Dennis case of 1951. Intrigued at first with the opportunity to read American opinions that were pro-Communist, the students later revealed puzzlement at a judicial process that permitted such freedom of judges.[36]

A Supreme Court ruling in itself will not insure implementation of the decision. Usually, the Court, instead of concerning itself with implementation of the decree, refers the matter to lower courts, which are permitted substantial latitude in interpreting the Supreme Court's decision. Some Court decisions depend, by their very nature, on the mass of government employees to implement them. The bureaucracy of the federal Executive or local elected and administrative officials can thwart a decision. Thus, the Court outlawed school segregation, but, long afterward, some local school boards disregarded the decision and maintained separate school facilities. Some school districts refused to comply until civil-rights activists obtained court orders mandating the officials to integrate specific facilities. As a rule, court decisions affecting the Executive branch in Washington are rapidly executed, while those involving the lower courts may be delayed, or circumvented.

The Court and Congress

Congress is the highest lawmaking body in the country; its members are elected by the people for this purpose. The Supreme Court, however, through judicial policy-making, also creates law. Here, then, are the elements for a classic contest

---

[34] For a complete discussion of the Chief Justice's powers and influence see David J. Danelski, "The influence of the Chief Justice in the Decisional Process of the Supreme Court," in Goldman and Jannige, *Elements of the Federal Judicial System*, pp. 147–160.

[35] Milton R. Konvitz, *Expanding Liberties: Freedom Gains in Postwar America* (New York: Viking, 1966), p. xvi.

[36] The *New York Times* (February 16, 1963; April 14, 1963), noted in Samuel Krislov, *The Supreme Court and Political Freedom* (New York: The Free Press, 1968), p. 219.

for supremacy, and, in fact, a historical rivalry has existed between the Court and the other branches of the federal government, especially Congress. Its roots are to be found in the early eighteenth-century philosophical differences between the Jeffersonian Republicans and the Federalists. The power of judicial review, as some see it, amounts to court supremacy, giving the courts the right to veto acts of Congress. Others disagree, citing the powers Congress wields over the Court, such as the ability to pass amendments and new legislation after the Court has found an earlier bill unconstitutional. In 1922, for example, the Court outlawed a "penalty" grain tax levied on those who avoided federal regulation.[37] The Congress, in rebuttal, passed further legislation reinforcing a tax.

There are means, however, by which the Court is directly under the control of Congress. Under the Constitution, Congress can alter the size of the court, limit its jurisdiction, and prescribe rules for courtroom procedure. The Senate can block new appointments and convict errant justices. So important is the Senate in filling a court vacancy that its mood is carefully gauged before an appointment is made. Potential nominees many times are bypassed because their appointment would not rest well with the Senate.[38]

In recent decades, following the explosive confrontations over the New Deal programs in the 1930s, only minor clashes have occurred between the Congress and the Supreme Court. In the 1940s, an attempt engineered by southern senators to force Roosevelt appointees off the bench failed. It died quietly in committee. A 1948 decision outlawing racially restrictive covenants (provisions in contracts barring the sale of homes to certain persons) spurred southern members of Congress to criticize court action on the floor. But it never went beyond verbal attacks. Also in the forties, Congress exempted certain businesses from antitrust provisions and amended several other statutes affecting commerce to head off anticipated decisions by the Court. Even in the 1950s, congressional factions, outraged by the Warren Court's liberalism, only condemned the Court publicly. An alliance formed of segregationists and Cold War hard-liners denounced the Court for destroying states' rights and protecting subversives.[39] In the mid-1960s a movement to impeach Warren failed, never gaining more impetus than the support of a few congressmen.

The Supreme Court exercises self-restraint in its role as monitor of Congress's activities. Traditionally, the Court avoids excessive intrusion into the affairs of Congress and shuns use of judicial review. In reviewing a particular case, the Court usually attempts not to formulate constitutional rules broader than the facts of the lawsuit. Even where the litigant cites a constitutional principle, the Court often will look for other grounds, such as poorly drafted legislation, on which to dispose of the case.[40] The court also has shown caution and a reluctance to intervene in investigations by Congress, although it has upheld contempt citations of witnesses where the congressional committee has adequate authorization and seeks information with a valid legislative purpose. But it has not sought to define legislative purpose and thereby restrict an investigating committee's scope.[41]

[37] *Hill* v. *Wallace,* 259 U.S. 44 (1922).

[38] Walter F. Murphy, *Congress and the Court,* pp. 333–334.

[39] These clashes between the two branches of government are discussed in Murphy, *Congress and the Court,* pp. 74–75, 86–91.

[40] Concurring opinion by Louis D. Brandeis to *Ashwander* v. *Tennessee Valley Authority,* 297 U.S. 288 (1936), pp. 346 ff.

[41] Samuel Krislov, *The Supreme Court in the Political Process* (New York: Macmillan, 1965), pp. 102–103.

The Court has become increasingly active in administrative law, an area it had all but abandoned after 1937 to the administrative agencies created by Congress. In 1946, Congress passed the Administrative Procedure Act. The law directs the Court to control the affairs of the administrative agencies. The Court has interpreted its mandate broadly, to include the right to overrule agency rulings when they show a deficiency in expertise.[42]

The Court and the President

Although the Constitution grants the President no direct authority over the Supreme Court, Chief Executives have, historically, found ways to influence the direction of the Court. The President's constitutional right to fill vacancies, as we have seen, allows him an indirect control over court policy. The justices placed on the Court are those who appear to share his political views. However, Presidents have other means at their disposal. After all, appointments to the Court average only about one in every two years.

A President's chances of persuading the Court are probably better if he employs subtle methods. A President can ask Congress to enact legislation nullifying a court decision, or by virtue of his power to appoint judges to the lower federal courts, speed up or brake implementation of a Supreme Court ruling. Certainly, his prestige and ability to take his case directly to the people are important factors in molding public acceptance or opposition to a court order. President Eisenhower's reaction to the school-desegregation decision, in which he spoke of his sworn duty to uphold the constitutional processes, smoothed the way for carrying out a difficult mandate for social change. On the other hand, President Nixon's challenge of the school-busing orders by lower federal courts has had its impact. His televised attack accelerated the campaign in and out of Congress to legislate against court-ordered busing to achieve racial balance.[43]

Under the Constitution, the Chief Executive enjoys virtually unlimited latitude in foreign policy matters. The Court traditionally has deferred to the President, respecting his role as the nation's foreign-affairs spokesman and maker of foreign policy. Thus, Justice Holmes once stated there was hardly any limit on the President's power to make treaties except for the required Senate approval.[44]

The executive prerogative to shape foreign policy was a key element in the dramatic confrontation between the court and the President in the famous Steel Seizure case of 1952.[45] To avert a shortage of military supplies needed for the Korean conflict, President Truman intervened in the steel labor dispute. The executive action of seizing and operating the steel mills was based on the President's powers as Commander-in-Chief as well as the obligation to honor NATO treaty commitments. In the back of the judges' minds loomed the disturbing precedent of a President expanding domestic powers through foreign involvement. The Court ruled the seizure illegal, basing its decision on the fact that the President could have utilized existing congressional statutes established for dealing with labor emergencies.

The Steel Seizure decision highlights the Court's concern with the President's circumvention of Congress. This concern is typical. The Court's tendency is to

---

[42] Krislov, *The Supreme Court in the Political Process*, p. 104.
[43] The *New York Times* (March 17, 1972), p. 22.
[44] *Missouri* v. *Holland*, 252 U.S. 416 (1920).
[45] *Youngstown Sheet and Tube* v. *Sawyer*, 343 U.S. 579 (1952).

view critically executive or legislative actions in which the branches conflict, while it has a history of upholding actions where Congress and the President concur.[46]

The Court and the Press

The Supreme Court functions within a democratic context, and, therefore, the way news media reflect its decisions affect its policies. In the opinion of some experts, court coverage is poor. Journalists, who usually are persons untrained in the law, interpret the technical court opinions from a layman's perspective. This treatment does indirectly influence the Supreme Court's thinking, especially since elected representatives of the public react to the Court and formulate their official opinions from information transmitted by the news media. At the very least, some authorities say, the choice of which judge writes a court opinion is made with an eye to the media. If what many consider to be a liberal opinion is offered by a conservative justice, public response to the decision will not be as divisive as if the author had been a liberal. For example, it was Justice Clark, usually a conservative, who wrote the 1963 court opinion which declared classroom reading of the Lord's Prayer and other Bible verses unconstitutional.

The Supreme Court, in the face of the public uproar that greeted the highly controversial school-prayer and apportionment decisions, maintained its traditional posture of aloofness and silence. But the shock tremors these decisions emanated seem to have jolted the Court slightly, and after a decent interval elapsed following the prayer ruling, Justice Clark broke the silence. In an untraditional gesture, he defended the Court. The press, Clark said, had created a misunderstanding by its inaccurate reporting and should shoulder the blame for the wave of criticism. Somewhat charitably, Clark added, the failure of the press was mitigated by two factors: the need to file a story under deadline pressure and the frantic scramble on the day of that decision to report on several other cases which broke simultaneously.

Does the Justice's analysis hold up under close scrutiny? Chester A. Newland's study suggests there is no basis for blaming a "misunderstanding" on the press. The harshest editorial criticisms appeared in the papers that published the most accurate reports of the decision. If a misunderstanding did indeed ignite a public controversy, the text of the justices' opinions and the public declarations of the courts' political opponents were as much at fault as the press. Whatever the flaws in court coverage, they are not due to haste, Newland concluded, but to the news-editing techniques that stress sensational material at the expense of substantive cases, and which blow up stories to lurid dimensions.[47]

Is the Supreme Court Elitist?

There are some observers of the American courts who would not support the favored weighting of the judiciary in American life. Thomas Jefferson did not find the judiciary wiser or better qualified to interpret the Constitution than the Executive or Legislative branches of government. The Supreme Court, in his view, had not proven itself to be more impartial or disinterested than the other

---

[46] Samuel Krislov, *The Supreme Court and Political Freedom* (New York: The Free Press, 1968), p. 101.

[47] Chester A. Newland, "Press Coverage of the U.S. Supreme Court," in Goldman and Jahnige, *Elements of the Federal Judicial System*, pp. 317–325.

branches. Henry Steele Commager, many years later, agreed with Jefferson and wrote: "Experience . . . justifies Jefferson's faith that men need no masters – not even judges."

But given that the Supreme Court exists, many are concerned that it is elitist in nature. The most prominent analysts of the legal structure seem to concur in this opinion. Yale law professor Fred Rodell, whimsically perhaps, claimed that the justices of the Supreme Court wield more "accountable-to-no-one-power" than the bosses of the Kremlin.[48] Justice Frankfurter proclaimed the Court "basically oligarchial" on one occasion[49] and on another voiced the opinion that Courts were outside the democratic structure: "Courts are not representative bodies, they are not designed to be a reflex of a democratic society."[50]

Certainly the composition of the Court through time has not been democratic, and the practice of life tenure is not a concept generally compatible with democracy. However, the Court, as constructed and as it operates, usually reflects the political tone of the day, changing its own tone as the spirit of the nation changes. At times, however, the Court's constitutional position enables it to act as the conscience of America, leading the way in protecting the population through new interpretations of the law.

United States Judiciary:
A Dual System of Courts

Justice in the United States is administered by a dual court system, the federal courts of the national government and the courts of the state and local governments functioning side by side. The two major judicial systems reflect the fact that under the federal structure each state is a sovereign political entity. In a strict sense there are fifty-one systems – the courts of all the states, and the federal courts.

The Federal Court System

At the top of the federal judicial pyramid is the United States Supreme Court, a body that accepts for consideration only select cases. All suits involving a federal law or a constitutional issue may theoretically be appealed to the Supreme Court, but in practice the Court hears only very serious cases in these two categories.

District Courts and Courts of Appeal Under the Constitution, Congress "may from time to time ordain and establish" inferior courts. Through the wide powers implied by this phrase, the federal government has set up a network of courts that handle the preponderance of federal cases. The Federal District Courts process over a hundred thousand cases a year. These trial courts hear cases involving infractions of federal law – patent and copyright matters and bankruptcy; civil rights, antitrust, postal, and counterfeiting offenses. Suits related to immigration laws and disputes between citizens of different states are also first heard in the District Courts. There are eighty-eight District Courts, with their jurisdictional lines usually coinciding with state boundaries, plus single courts for the District

---

[48] Fred Rodell, *Nine Men* (New York: Random House, 1955), pp. 3–4.
[49] *A.F. of L.* v. *America Sash and Door,* 335 U.S. 538 (1949), p. 555.
[50] *Dennis* v. *United States,* 341 U.S. 494 (1951), pp. 524–525.

*Figure 9–1   **America's Dual System of Courts***

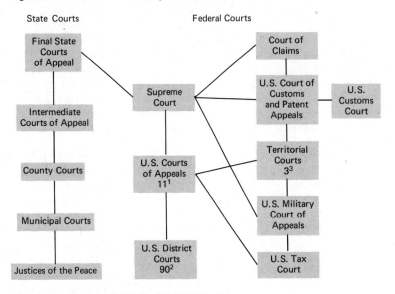

[1] One circuit court of appeals is for the District of Columbia.
[2] Includes district courts of Puerto Rico and Washington, D.C.
[3] The territorial courts of Guam, Virgin Islands, and Canal Zone, and the U.S. District Court in Washington, D.C., have mixed federal and local jurisdiction.

of Columbia, Canal Zone, Guam, the Virgin Islands, and Puerto Rico. Populous states such as New York are subdivided into several districts. Each federal district has at least one judge. The Southern New York District, the busiest, has twenty-four judges. Above the District Courts are the Courts of Appeals, which review rulings of the federal regulatory agencies and hear appeals from the lower federal tribunals. They handle about ten thousand cases each year. The United States is divided into eleven federal judicial circuits, each with its own Court of Appeals. A total of ninety-seven judges were serving on Courts of Appeals in 1970.

Special-purpose Courts For certain specialized cases Congress has established a number of special-purpose courts: the Court of Claims, the Court of Customs and Patent Appeals, the Court of Military Appeals, and the Customs Court. The Court of Claims was created in 1855 to deal with such cases as claims arising from government contracts, damage suits in condemnation of property, and negligence suits against federal employees. It has five judges. The Customs Court, with nine judgeships, reviews appraisals by federal customs collectors. Appeals from Customs Court decisions are taken to the Court of Customs and Patent Appeals, a five-member panel which also has jurisdiction over patent and tariff cases. The newest special court is the Court of Military Appeals, which Earl Warren has called the "civilian supreme court of the military." The court, composed of three civilian judges, is the highest appellate tribunal in court-martial proceedings. The court was created as part of a revised Uniform Code of Military Justice in 1950 in the wake of criticisms directed at the military system of justice.[51]

[51] For a description of the Court of Military Appeals and the controversy that led to its establishment, see Abraham, *The Judicial Process*, pp. 147–148.

Administration of the Federal Courts Under the Constitution, the judges in the federal-court system are, from the administrative standpoint, autonomous. Laws enacted in 1922 and 1939 introduced long-overdue coordination and administrative organization. The Judicial Conference of the United States, set up under the Judicial Act of 1922, runs the courts; it assigns judges and monitors operations. The Conference, whose members are ranking judges of the federal Courts of Appeals, is headed by the Chief Justice of the Supreme Court. In 1939, Congress created the Administrative Office of the United States Courts as an executive arm to the Judicial Conference. This "housekeeping" agency compiles budgets, audits accounts and statistics, and requisitions supplies. It is headed by a director appointed by the Chief Justice.[52]

Federal Judges All federal judges are appointed by the President and subject to confirmation by the Senate. This clear directive is, in practice, however, more complicated, and appointment of federal judges has widened to include screening by leaders of the President's party, the Department of Justice, and the American Bar Association's standing committee on the federal judiciary.[53] Moving from a federal district court judgeship to a judgeship on a circuit court of appeals is common, although such a line of advance from a court of appeals to the Supreme Court does not exist. As is true of Supreme Court justices, most federal judges have been active in politics and come from upper-middle-class backgrounds.

Legislators and the Congress control the number of judgeships. Since judgeships are highly important in the patronage system, party politics strongly influence the creation and abolition of judgeship positions.

In the federal court system, judges serve for life or specified lengthy terms stipulated by Congress. The security of tenure, in the opinion of many observers, protects the independence of the judiciary.[54] Those who disagree claim life terms provide security for incompetent judges and produce judicial autocrats who defy the will of the people.[55]

The need for better judges has recently prompted formation of seminars and summer study programs for members of the judiciary. Such programs are sponsored by the United States Judicial Conference, several states, and universities.[56]

State and Local Courts

The administration of justice in the United States remains, despite the growth of federal courts, largely in the hands of the states and localities, whose courts handle the bulk of all cases. Although state court systems vary a great deal, there are structural similarities, starting with the justice of the peace and culminating in a high tribunal.

Justices of the peace or magistrates, untrained in the law (except for those in some large cities), handle minor matters (cases involving less than two hundred dollars) and perform marriages. Municipal courts, also known as traffic courts, city courts and police courts, are staffed by judges possessing legal background.

---

[52] Peter Graham Fish, "Crisis, Politics, and Federal Judicial Reform: The Administrative Office Act of 1939," *Journal of Politics*, vol. 32, no. 3 (August, 1970), pp. 599–627.

[53] Chase, "Federal Judges."

[54] Abraham, *The Judicial Process*, p. 41.

[55] Glenn R. Winters and Robert E. Allard, "Judicial Selection and Tenure in the United States," in *The Courts, the Public and the Law Explosion*, edited by Harry W. Jones (Englewood Cliffs, N.J.: Prentice-Hall, 1965), p. 162.

[56] For a description of seminars and study programs for judges see Winters and Allard, "Judicial Selection and Tenure in the United States," pp. 172–177.

They process some criminal cases (misdemeanors) and civil suits involving sums between five hundred and a thousand dollars. County courts, the workhorses of the state judiciaries, have jurisdiction over larger civil disputes including probate and inheritance cases. Other courts, found on the level above the county courts in most larger states, are appeals courts, variously called appellate divisions, superior courts, state appellate courts, and intermediate courts of appeals. These courts hear appeals from the county and municipal courts. Final courts of appeals, also known as supreme courts, are the states' highest judicial authorities and have strictly appellate jurisdiction. They are the final courts for all matters derived from state constitutions or state laws. From these tribunals, the only further recourse for a dissatisfied defendant is the Supreme Court of the United States, and the Supreme Court will not generally hear a case unless "all remedies below" have been exhausted and a federal issue is at stake.

State Judges Two-thirds of state judges are elected by popular vote. Some states, finding this system inadequate, have experimented with finding a middle way between appointed and elected judges. The Missouri plan utilizes both. Under this system, judgeships are assigned by a nonpartisan panel composed of lawyers, citizens, and judge-select nominees, who are appointed by the governor. After an initial term on the court, the judge must be approved by the voters.[57]

How Justice Is Administered

For all the immense powers entrusted to the courts, they are still the most passive of the three branches of government; their scope, compared with that of the Legislative and Executive branches, is limited. Not every dispute of constitutional challenge comes within the jurisdiction of the courts. A dispute must be judicable to be considered for a court ruling. If a question is essentially nonlegal, involves powers assigned by the Constitution to another branch of government, or is not appropriate for handling by the Court, it is not judicable.

Since the business of the Court is adjudication, the courts cannot render a decision unless adversaries bring a dispute before the bench. Even the boldest challenge to the Constitution by Congress could not be touched by the courts themselves. The courts must wait for litigation embodying the constitutional principle to reach them. Since courts are empowered only to adjudicate, the Supreme Court will not advise the Congress or President on constitutional matters even when asked.

Challenging the constitutionality of a law requires a real case. Only a genuinely aggrieved individual who can show he has "sustained or is in danger of sustaining a direct injury" can bring a court action. A constitutional test cannot be brought by a person having only a general interest in a legislative matter. In a milestone decision given in 1892, the Supreme Court rejected an attempt to test an act by the Michigan legislature, because, the Court said, the suit was obviously contrived.[58]

Just as a citizen desiring to take an action to court must file a specific com-

---

[57] For a complete discussion of the Missouri plan see Abraham, *The Judicial Process*, pp. 35–47.

[58] *Chicago and Grand Trunk Railway Co.* v. *Wellman*, 143 U.S. 339 (1892).

"If you please, Mr. Justice, would you mind not saying, 'Of course, we could be wrong'?"

New Yorker, *February 27, 1971*

plaint, so the court must be specific when it acts. De Tocqueville wrote: "Judicial power . . . pronounces on special cases and not upon general principles. If a judge, in deciding a particular point, destroys a general principle by passing a judgment which tends to reject all the inferences from that principle . . . he remains within the ordinary limits of his functions. But if he directly attacks a general principle without having a particular case in view, he leaves the circle in which all nations have agreed to confine his authority."[59]

The Adversary Process

American justice is founded on the adversary process. A courtroom may be compared to a boxing ring with the judge in the role of the referee and each side battling, with the facts and arguments at its command, to vanquish the other. This adversary process is designed to bring out the truth from the clash of opposing viewpoints.

To be sure, the judge is not always the sole arbiter of a court dispute. Along with the judge, the jury—technically called the *petit jury*—frequently shares this responsibility. And it is the jury that makes the important determination of guilt or innocence. Under these conditions the judge's function is to preside over the trial—by no means an unimportant role, since he instructs the jury members in matters of law and screens out evidence inadmissible under the court's rules.

The Petit Jury

The jury is a chosen panel of ordinary citizens convened to participate in a trial and bring in a verdict. A venerable Anglo-Saxon institution, both praised and

[59] Alexis de Tocqueville, *Democracy in America* (New York: Vintage, 1945), Chapter 6.

damned, juries date back to twelfth-century England, when, under King Henry II, citizens were called to serve as judgmental panels in the courts.

Today, the United States is the home of the jury trial, with some hundred thousand juries impaneled each year. Federal law requires jury trials be provided in all criminal cases and in all civil cases where the sum involved is twenty dollars or more. In 1968, the Supreme Court ruled that state courts must provide jury trials in "serious" criminal cases, a designation defined two years later as any case in which the jail sentence imposed for conviction exceeds six months.[60] At least 80 percent of criminal trials by jury in the world take place in the United States,[61] a disturbing fact to some legal experts. The strength of the jury system is its attractive quality of direct democracy through public participation, but the system is faulted, some say, by the cross-section of the population, nonprofessionals in the techniques of justice, who are brought into the courtroom. Unexposed to the court's criminal system, juries are untrained in the law and unaccustomed to rigorous legal reasoning. A flamboyant defense attorney playing on their emotions may distract them from applying the law and meting out a just verdict to a criminal.

Not infrequently jury trials end in deadlocked panel and a mistrial. Most cases in the United States are tried under rules requiring a unanimous verdict by the jury members in the tradition of the classic concept of the Anglo-Saxon jury. Judges at times use subtle pressure to prod a jury into returning a verdict. Nevertheless, some three thousand jury proceedings end in nonunanimous decisions each year. Some legal experts, taking a libertarian view, see the mistrials or hung juries as a democratic safeguard protecting the dissent of a minority.[62]

Innocent until Proven Guilty

Few legal principles have influenced American justice so profoundly as the concept that the accused remains innocent until proven guilty beyond a reasonable doubt. Many fundamental rights common to citizens of Western democracies and rooted in Anglo-Saxon tradition, such as the right to cross-examine witnesses, the privilege to withhold self-incriminating evidence, and the writ of habeas corpus, are rooted in this common-law concept of the presumption of innocence. Because jurors, as already noted, are laymen and untrained in courtroom methods, lawyers often are fearful that pretrial publicity may create a mood detrimental to a fair trial. Aside from concern over prejudicing chosen jurors, media influence often makes securing unprejudiced panels in highly publicized crimes very difficult. Judges, aware of this, frequently question prospective jurors closely in such cases to determine whether information from the media could have implanted a bias in their minds.

---

[60] *Duncan* v. *Louisiana,* 391 U.S. 145 (1968) and *Baldwin* v. *New York,* 399 U.S. 66 (1970).

[61] Harry Kalven, Jr., and Hans Zeisel, *The American Jury* (Boston: Little, Brown, 1966), pp. 12–13.

[62] Kalven and Zeisel, *The American Jury,* p. 453. Less prevalent than the trial jury, or petit jury, is the grand jury, a body that determines neither guilt nor innocence, but only whether sufficient evidence to justify a trial has been produced. A petit jury delivers a verdict, a grand jury an indictment. Fewer than half of the states still use the grand jury in indictment proceedings, and even among these some have limited its scope to investigating official corruption, murder, and treason. The stronghold of the grand jury remains the federal judiciary, as the Fifth Amendment of the Federal Constitution guarantees grand-jury action to any person being brought to trial for a serious federal crime.

The Role of the Department of Justice

As the scope of the federal government has widened in the twentieth century, so has the quantity of litigation and the government's legal staff increased. Although the regulatory commissions and the Treasury Department and its Internal Revenue Service have large legal staffs, the Department of Justice is the chief legal arm of the federal government. The Cabinet post of Attorney General was authorized by Congress in 1789, but only after the Civil War did Justice emerge as a separate department.[63] Today, the Justice Department is a key agency in the federal government's political activities, and the Attorney General's position one of high importance as a chief presidential adviser. Since the appointment of Robert Kennedy by his brother, he and his successors, Ramsey Clark and John Mitchell, all have enjoyed the close confidence of the Presidents under whom they have served and have been in the public spotlight.

The chief responsibility of the Department is to represent the government in civil lawsuits and criminal cases in the federal courts. For every federal judicial district there is a United States attorney with functions similar to those of the local district attorney. But while local prosecutors, usually elected officials, operate autonomous offices, the United States attorneys, although appointed by the President with Senate approval, serve under the Attorney General. Those who are given these choice positions of political patronage prepare cases, negotiate with defendants, and prosecute in court.

Within the Justice Department, there are several divisions: the Bureau of Prisons, which operates federal correctional and community-treatment facilities; the Law Enforcement Assistance Administration; the Community Relations Division, which aids in the solving of racial conflicts; the Immigration and Naturalization Service; the Bureau of Narcotics and Dangerous Drugs. Other major divisions in the Department specialize in handling antitrust, civil-rights, criminal, tax, and internal-security cases.

The Attorney General and Solicitor General of the United States

The Justice Department is headed by the Attorney General, who is both a Cabinet officer and the President's chief legal adviser. It is often assumed incorrectly that the Attorney General is merely a law-enforcement official on a national level. In fact, he holds a sensitive political post in the Cabinet, and his policies often are affected by political considerations. A President's policies will determine, for example, how the Attorney General prosecutes antitrust, civil-rights, and anti-subversive cases. For example, in the case of the Chicago Seven, who led protest demonstrations at the 1968 Democratic National Convention while President Johnson still held office, Ramsey Clark, the Attorney General at the time, did not seek criminal prosecution; John Mitchell, who succeeded him under President Nixon, did.

Next to the Attorney General and his deputy, the Solicitor General is the most important figure in the Justice Department. The Solicitor General tries cases for

---

[63] Herbert Jacob, "Lawyers for the Federal Government," in Goldman and Jahnige, *Elements of the Federal Judicial System*, pp. 54–55.

the Justice Department in the Supreme Court. The prestigious post attracts top-notch legal experts, although the salary in 1972 was only $28,500 yearly.

In some quarters, criticism has been expressed in recent years that the Justice Department and the United States attorneys are too susceptible to political influence. Ramsey Clark has proposed selecting United States attorneys from the ranks of career civil servants instead of filling the posts on the recommendations of senators and congressmen. Such an appointment process as he has suggested, Clark says, would result in officeholders who are relatively immune to political pressures, and would develop nationally uniform standards of prosecution.[64]

The Controversial FBI

The most famous branch of the Justice Department is the Federal Bureau of Investigation, whose reputation rivals that of the Department itself. Through skillful promotion in the press, television, and Hollywood films, G-men, or the "Feds," have achieved an enviable public image as smoothly efficient and incorruptible crime fighters, and their organization, the FBI, has become synonymous with professionalism. The FBI operates fifty-nine field divisions and employs 17,000 persons, about half of them FBI agents. The others are technicians, secretaries, and clerks. The FBI assists other law-enforcement agencies in fighting violations of federal law. It operates through its highly respected fingerprint-identification and laboratory services, police-training school, and National Crime Information Center.

There have been many critics as well as admirers of the FBI. The agency's surveillance techniques, including wiretaps and files on political activities of government critics, are considered by some a potential danger to civil liberties. Attacks on the Bureau have mounted in recent years, but polls show that most Americans still have a favorable view of the agency. A similar controversy surrounded the FBI's long-time director, the late J. Edgar Hoover, who served as Bureau head for forty-eight years, a tenure unmatched in high-level federal service. Hoover's opponents, while crediting him with building up the agency and understanding the need for strong control of such an agency, claimed the agency's performance declined during the last years of his tenure. One critic, Victor S. Navasky, wrote:

> . . . for years Hoover overemphasized the threat of domestic subversion and underestimated the strength of syndicated crime; and at a time when the bureau wasn't doing anything about wholesale violations of civil rights, he dispatched so many undercover men to infiltrate the Communist party that, according to one agent's estimate, more than half the dues-paying members of the CPUSA [Communist Party of the United States of America] were FBI informants.[65]

Navasky went on to speculate about how much Hoover contributed to the "institutionalization of paranoia" in the United States. While favoring the FBI's independence from politics, he also asked for assurances that the Bureau in the future will be "more responsive to policy" and free from Hoover's "excesses." Navasky was skeptical of the fact that for ten years "not one penny" of the FBI's requested funds has been denied. In addition, he pointed out, only one hundred

[64] Ramsey Clark, *Crime in America* (New York: Simon and Schuster, 1970), pp. 189–191.
[65] Victor S. Navasky, "The FBI Must Be Depoliticized, Says a Critic," *Saturday Review* (May 27, 1972), p. 28.

To the mounting number of queries about his plans for retirement, J. Edgar Hoover answered, up to the time of his death, that he had no such plans. Here he stands in front of the Capitol in 1970.

blacks and no women are among the agency's nine thousand agents. Navasky is wary about the combination of duties the agency performs; he argues that the FBI should not concern itself with both federal criminal matters (most criminal matters are in the jurisdiction of the state courts) and international counterintelligence work.

Such a list of grievances would not be compiled by most Americans. A Gallup poll rated Hoover's performance "good" or "excellent,"[66] and leading political spokesmen such as James L. Buckley on the right, and Ramsey Clark on the left, have used the word *excellent* in describing Hoover's stewardship of the FBI and

[66] The *New York Times* (May 3, 1972).

Figure 9–2   **Violent Crime**[1]
U.S. 1933-1968

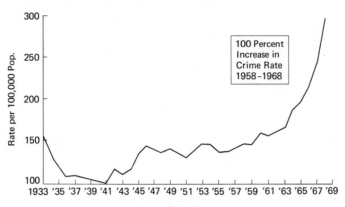

[1] Homicide, forcible rape, robbery, aggravated assault.

Source: Cited from Task Force Report, Crimes of Violence, *National Commission on the Causes and Prevention of Violence, in* To Establish Justice, to Ensure Domestic Tranquility: The Final Report of the National Commission on the Causes and Prevention of Violence *(New York: Bantam, 1970), pp. xxiv.*

the agency itself. Buckley exalted Hoover for "his nonpartisan vision of public service as one of the highest of vocations and, like all vocations, one infused with meaning and purpose only so far as its principles are not confused with those of other callings. Partisanship is needed in public affairs, but has no place in public service."[67]

Crime in America

Crime as an issue has moved to the forefront of American life, with the majority of the American people now believing that crime is among the most serious of our national problems. A federal-government survey revealed crime the second most frequently named domestic problem, exceeded only by racial difficulties.[68] The country, experts have found, is gripped by fear of violence, with half of the women and one-fifth of the men fearful of walking the streets at night even near their homes. In a third of the nation's households, guns are reportedly kept to provide protection against intruders, and in some urban neighborhoods a third of the residents questioned were seeking new homes outside of the city only to escape the high crime rate.[69]

The Extent of Crime

That these widespread fears are based on real conditions is shown by crime statistics. In 1960, murders, rapes, and other violent crimes reported in the

[67] James L. Buckley, "J. Edgar Hoover Was a Superadministrator, but What Is His Legacy? His Achievement Was 'Unparalleled,' Says an Admirer," *Saturday Review* (May 27, 1972), p. 28.

[68] Robert W. Winslow, *Crime in a Free Society—Selections from the President's Commission on Law Enforcement and Administration of Justice* (Belmont, Calif.: Dickinson Publishing Co., 1969), pp. 16–18.

[69] *To Establish Justice, To Insure Domestic Tranquility: A Final Report of the National Commission on the Causes and Prevention of Violence* (New York: Bantam, 1970), pp. 15–16.

United States totaled 285,000. There were 731,000 such violent offenses in 1970. Within a decade violent crime had jumped 157 percent. A similar upsurge of crime against property was reported for the same period. Auto thefts rose from 326,000 to 921,000, and property thefts generally more than doubled, climbing from 1,729,000 to 4,837,000.[70]

Alarmists, however, should take note that only an indefinite portion of the reported statistics represent an actual increase in crime. The increase in the statistics is largely due to better reporting ("statistical crime wave"),[71] and some is due to inflation: for years, the FBI has reported as a *major* crime the theft of anything over fifty dollars in value. As inflation pushes the prices of things up, more and more things get reported as crime that would have previously gone unreported. A further explanation for the increase is that the proportion of people in the eighteen–to–twenty-five age group – the group that commits the largest amount of crime – has greatly increased in recent years. Along with these clarifications of statistics, however, must also be included the fact that statistics comprise only reported offenses. The FBI and other law agencies agree that a large proportion of crimes go unreported.

The failure of citizens to report crimes to the authorities is in itself a serious problem. More than half the victims of criminal acts do not bother to report them, according to a survey by the National Opinion Research Center conducted for the President's Commission on Law Enforcement. The reasons given are a low opinion of police effectiveness, a reluctance to become involved in police and court procedures, and a fear of reprisal.[72]

Although criminal activity is a broad category including nonviolent offenses such as embezzlement, counterfeiting, bribes, and payoffs (antisocial activity generally classified as white-collar crime), it is violent crime that is most often reported and punished in the United States. Since the poor are most likely to commit crimes of violence, they are most likely to wind up in prison, while white-collar crimes are overlooked and even considered normal behavior by many.

Youths and juveniles are responsible for the major share of violent crimes committed. For example, youths under twenty-four accounted for 76 percent of the homicide arrests and 65 percent of the rape arrests in 1969.[73] Most alarming to experts is the soaring crime rate for juveniles between the ages of ten and fourteen. In this group, there was a 300-percent increase in arrests for serious assaults between 1958 and 1967 and a 200-percent increase in the robbery rate during the same period.[74]

The Cost of Crime

Crimes cost the economy $20.9 billion in 1965. Almost 10 percent of these costs were borne by the private sector for prevention services and equipment, insurance, lawyers, bail, and witness expenses. Government spent $4.2 billion of the total on enforcement and justice alone – nearly 92 percent of these costs being

---

[70] Cited from Federal Bureau of Investigation, *Uniform Crime Reports*, in *Statistical Abstract of the United States, 1971*, p. 146.

[71] See Daniel Bell, *The End of Ideology: The Exhaustion of Political Ideas in the Fifties* (New York: The Free Press, 1962), pp. 151–174, for the opinion that less crime existed in the 1960s than at any previous time in the history of the country.

[72] Winslow, *Crime in a Free Society*, pp. 31–32.

[73] FBI, *Uniform Crime Reports*, as cited in *Statistical Abstract of the United States, 1971*, p. 146.

[74] *To Establish Justice*, p. 19.

Figure 9–3   **Crime and Law Enforcement**
Total Serious Crimes,* U.S. 1968: 9,000,000

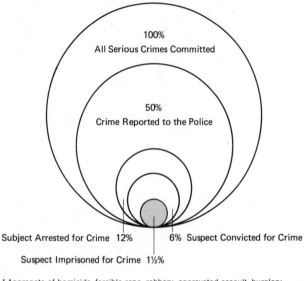

100%
All Serious Crimes Committed

50%
Crime Reported to the Police

Subject Arrested for Crime 12%   6% Suspect Convicted for Crime

Suspect Imprisoned for Crime 1½%

* Aggregate of homicide, forcible rape, robbery, aggravated assault, burglary, larceny over $50, auto theft. Based on estimates.

Source: To Establish Justice, to Ensure Domestic Tranquility: The Final Report of the National Commission on the *Causes and Prevention of Violence (New York: Bantam, 1970), p. xxviii.*

absorbed on the state and local levels. The federal government in 1971 spent $1.4 billion on crime reduction.[75]

Organized Crime

The federal government, since the famous Kefauver hearings in the 1950s, has been prosecuting those who operate organized crime to provide the public with illicit goods and services for which considerable demand exists – gambling, loan sharking, prostitution, and narcotics. Organized crime also participates in legitimate business and organized labor, using illegal means, such as terror tactics, monopoly, extortion, and tax evasion, to wrest control from legitimate owners and union leaders. Some people who have no contact with loan sharking, bookmaking and drug importing doubt that organized crime exists; but it is a reality, a big business, which grosses in a year twice the profits derived from all other types of crime. Gambling alone yields an estimated $20 billion a year. Even when the operations of organized crime have been persuasively documented, the public tends to be tolerant toward criminal syndicates. The President's Law Enforcement Commission has deplored the public's ambivalent attitude, which couples moral in-

[75] Figures on the 1965 costs of crime to the economy – public and private, state, local, and federal – from *The Challenge of Crime in a Free Society: A Report of the President's Commission on Law Enforcement and Administration of Justice* (New York: Avon, 1968), pp. 125 and 126. Federal crime-reduction figure for 1971 from Executive Office of the President, Office of Management and Budget, *Special Analyses, Budget of the United States,* fiscal year 1971, in *The Challenge of Crime in a Free Society,* p. 126.

dignation with virtual unconcern. "We regularly deplore the Mafia but regularly tolerate its activities. In fact, 'toleration' is too genteel a term; 'affection' would be more accurate," states a Commission report.[76]

Senator Robert F. Kennedy adamantly attempted to make the public aware of organized crime and get them to fight it. He wrote:

The racketeer is not someone dressed in a black shirt, a white tie, and diamond stickpin, whose activities affect only a remote underworld circle. He is more likely to be outfitted in a gray flannel suit and his influence is more likely to be as far-reaching as that of an important industrialist. . . . When the racketeers bore their way into legitimate business, the cost is borne by the public. When the infiltration is into labor relations, the racketeer's cut is paid by higher wages and higher prices — in other words, by the public. When the racketeer bribes local officials and secures immunity from police action, the price exacted by corrupt law enforcement — incalculable in dollars — is paid, again, by the public. In short, organized crime affects everyone. It cannot be the concern only of law enforcement officers. It must be the urgent and active concern of every citizen.[77]

Crime and drug traffic are closely intertwined. Underworld syndicates find drugs a lucrative field. The importing and wholesaling of narcotics — a $350-million-a-year-business — requires international connections and huge investment capital, which only organized crime can supply. The result of this illegal business leads to the making of addicts; individuals seeking money to purchase drugs account for much crime in large cities. No completely reliable data can be found to validate the frequently cited estimate that addicts commit 50 percent of all crimes.[78]

A type of offense that needs, perhaps, to be reexamined in terms of modern life is the violation of a morals law, or, as it is sometimes called, a "crime without a victim." Enforcing these laws clogs court calendars and, in the opinion of some, spawns police corruption. In 1969, for example, arrests for drunkenness totaled one million.[79] It is victimless crimes for which the underworld supplies goods and services; in fact, organized crime emerged during Prohibition when it provided illegal liquor for the public.[80] Some experts, although not a majority, think legalization of drugs, gambling, and prostitution might lead to the collapse of organized crime in the country.

Gun Control and Crime

Unlike many other industrialized countries, the United States has no national gun-control program. Experts are divided over the question of how much firearms contribute to the level of violence in the country. Gun sales have increased greatly within the last few years, and, while hunting and sport shooting are more popular than they were, clearly many civilians are acquiring guns for self-protection.[81] Gun dealers selling to civilians stocked some 6.1 million weapons

---

[76] Quotation, as well as statistics on organized crime, from *The Challenge of Crime in a Free Society*, p. 29.

[77] Quoted by Donald Cressey in *Theft of a Nation: The Structure and Operations of Organized Crime in America* (New York: Harper & Row, 1969), epigraph.

[78] For a complete discussion of drug and nondrug offenses committed by addicts see *The Challenge of Crime in a Free Society*, pp. 508–511.

[79] FBI, *Uniform Crime Reports*, as cited in *Statistical Abstract of the United States, 1971*, p. 146.

[80] For a short history of how crime became organized, see Bell, *The End of Ideology*, pp. 127–150.

[81] *To Establish Justice*, p. 146.

in 1969.[82] The National Commission on Violence has concluded that firearms increase violent crimes and disorders and cause many accidental deaths. So, although the possession of a firearm may seem to insure an individual's right to self-protection, the Commission recommended federal controls on hand guns, arguing against the belief that guns help civilians cut down crime: the householder, usually taken by surprise by the robber or intruder, has little chance to pick up his weapon in self-defense.[83]

The Role of the Police

The President's Commission on the Causes and Prevention of Violence has estimated that the United States has some 420,000 policemen, and that in 1967 police salaries cost the nation about $3.7 billion.[84] Nevertheless, police departments across the country are not only financially strapped and undermanned, but have staff problems aggravated by the trend toward shorter working hours, longer vacations, and more paid holidays. Moreover, police are not able to devote all their time to fighting crime. Police officers are expected to perform many community functions, from guiding bewildered strangers, directing traffic, and supplying first aid, to mediating marital disputes and helping children cross streets. As a result, police manpower is often spread too thin to be effective.

The law-enforcement officer pursues his vocation in a nation churning with social ferment, and, therefore, he is no stranger to frustration. The policeman often is the man in the middle when opposing forces in the social conflict clash. An angry community, victimized by rising crime, attacks him for incompetence and leniency toward offenders, while others attack his harshness and acts of "police brutality."

Increased police power and tremendously improved police efficiency are not likely to reduce crime. Murders, for example, are generally committed by people who, in the heat of passion, kill someone they know. Robberies and muggings occur at unpredictable times and places and it is simply impossible for the police to be everywhere at all times. Law enforcement can only be effective if the population as a whole respects and obeys laws and cooperates in enforcing them in their communities.

An aid in improving law enforcement, especially in the inner cities heavily populated by minority members, would be to require human-relations training for policemen and to create large community-affairs sections in the police departments. In the words of the Commission: "The police are, indeed, prejudiced against minorities. And the minority groups are equally prejudiced against the police." In short, better communications could dispel mutual suspicions and misunderstanding. The President's Crime Commission has suggested sweeping reforms that include guidelines for police conduct on and off duty, training of police in the legal background of their work, study of the psychology and social

---

[82] Cited in *Statistical Abstract of the United States, 1971,* No. 226 from National Shooting Sports Foundation, Riverside, Conn. (unpubl. material); Department of Commerce, Bureau of the Census, *U.S. Imports, General and Consumption, Schedule A, Commodity and Country,* Report FT 135; and National Commission on the Causes and Prevention of Violence, Task Force Report, *Firearms and Violence in American Life.*

[83] *To Establish Justice,* p. 149.

[84] The statistics on the role of the police and the source of most of this information is *Law and Order Reconsidered, Report of the Task Force on Law and Law Enforcement to the National Commission on the Causes and Prevention of Violence* (New York: Bantam, 1970), pp. 285–307.

problems of nonconformists and minority groups, and higher education as a requirement for police recruitment.[85]

As most police departments lack adequate management and organization systems, the Commission urged immediate remedial action to lay the groundwork for instituting needed reforms and regulating police misconduct.[86] Discovering that police jurisdictions in the United States are badly fragmented and that there exist many special-function policing agencies, the Commission suggested that merging these jurisdictions or, at least, pooling their resources, would improve police services vastly, without infringing on local government autonomy.[87]

Although these are difficult times for police, the public overwhelmingly stands behind them. Surveys show most people believe police are fair in treating minority groups and nonconformists. Half of the blacks in the high-crime city of Washington agree.[88]

The Flaws of the American System of Justice

The administration of criminal justice leaves many experts dissatisfied; one of them called it a "nonsystem of criminal justice." It is not the laws themselves or the rights guaranteed to criminals that they criticize, but the way the machinery works, so that inconsistency and lack of uniformity result. The system has three main components. The initial step is law enforcement, the functions of policemen and sheriffs. Then there is the judicial process, utilizing judges, prosecutors, and defense lawyers. Finally, there exists the correctional system, consisting of prisons and prison officials, probation and parole officers. The people employed in each of the three stages approach the criminal and crime differently from those in the other groups; instead of a criminal-justice system with clearly defined goals, the President's Commission on the Causes and Prevention of Violence has complained, we have a fractionalized and compartmentalized process.[89] Offenders are moved through the system as if on a conveyor belt from one stage to the next, and each step of the way society's representatives tackle criminal behavior according to different criteria.

The Backlog of the Courts

No matter how democratic and fair our nation's laws that protect the accused, laws in themselves will not assure true justice. The fair execution of them is equally crucial. The concept of "innocent until proven guilty" and the constitutional guarantee of a speedy trial are familiar terms to the public. However, it is generally not known that in practice many defendants will not receive prompt justice because most American courts are inefficiently operated and incapable of disposing their caseloads expeditiously.[90] In Washington, D.C., for example, an accused felon must wait an average of nine and a half months for a trial in the

---

[85] *Law and Order Reconsidered*, p. 263.

[86] *Challenge of Crime in a Free Society*, pp. 287–300.

[87] *Challenge of Crime in a Free Society*, pp. 301–309.

[88] Winslow, *Crime in a Free Society*, p. 28.

[89] *Law and Order Reconsidered*, p. 264.

[90] *Law and Order Reconsidered*, p. 557.

Blind justice stands guard with sword and scales on the exterior of a court building in Brooklyn, New York.

federal court.[91] In many states, delays in criminal cases average ten to eighteen months. Persons suing to recover injury damages, according to one comprehensive study, face a median delay of twenty and a half months.[92] In New York City, where felony indictments average twenty-five thousand per year and courts dispose of only twenty thousand cases annually, the courts sometimes are clogged with ten-thousand-case backlogs. Worse still, some 25 percent of the many accused of crime are too poor to raise bail and are kept in jail for more than six months

---

[91] *Annual Report of the Director of the Administrative Office of the United States Courts 1968* (Washington, D.C.: Government Printing Office, 1969), as cited in *Law and Order Reconsidered*, p. 557.
[92] Institute of Judicial Administration, *Calendar Status Study — State Trial Courts of General Jurisdiction — Personal Injury Cases* no. 269 (1968) as cited in *Law and Order Reconsidered*, p. 557.

because of the court logjam.[93] Efforts by the New York State Chief Judge to impose a ninety-day trial requirement failed.[94] The jammed court dockets not only frustrate the defendant eager to be cleared of charges but, as Ramsey Clark pointed out, reduce the probability of convicting the guilty since, as time goes by, memories fade and witnesses disappear. In civil cases, the lawyers and law firms permitted to take too many more cases than they can handle at once are to blame for much delay.[95]

Few courts in the United States have trained administrative personnel. The management techniques tested and proven in private enterprise – data processing and similar modern managerial innovations – are rarely employed by the judiciary. One bright spot is an ambitious long-range Criminal Justice Project launched by the American Bar Association in 1964 to bring the courts out of the horse-and-buggy era. More than seventy-five judges, lawyers, and legal educators have joined the modernization study project. A top American Bar Association priority is establishing a set of nationwide uniform court procedures for criminal cases so that judges, prosecutors, and defense lawyers everywhere would know what may be expected of each in the courtroom. In the opinion of the President's Commission on the Causes and Prevention of Violence, the federal government should assist the states financially in streamlining court management through grants.

Changes in civil-law procedures advanced by experts to relieve court congestion include appointing special court officers for quasi-judicial duties; limiting payment for physical injuries; "no-fault" auto insurance to compensate collision victims without trials; shortening the duration of trials, and, most dramatically, eliminating juries in civil cases.[96] Where such methods have been tried, however, they have brought no more than very limited success.

The management-oriented Commission on the Causes and Prevention of Violence has claimed that lobbying by lawyers, coupled with public pressure, could by 1975 result in substantive court modernization that would provide executive offices in the metropolitan and regional courts staffed by management specialists and centralized administrative offices to coordinate each state's court system. There should also, by 1975, be citizens' panels within the states to work in tandem with state legislatures in expediting trials. These improvements should result in speedy justice that safeguards the defendant's rights.[97]

One result of the court delay, as discussed in Chapter 4, is the practice of plea bargaining. Pleading guilty to a lesser charge than would be handed down for the alleged crime in hopes of receiving a more lenient sentence occurs in 80 percent of all cases. Eliminating the backlog of the courts would, it is to be hoped, lead to less of this practice and to a stronger reliance on petit juries for determining guilt.

Along with administrative-court reforms, experts see a need to update the jury system. Jury selection today is close to contemporary standards of democracy and equality. Congress, for example, enacted the Jury Selection and Service Act

[93] *Time* (May 6, 1972).
[94] *Time* (May 6, 1972).
[95] Maurice Rosenberg, "Court Congestion: Status, Causes and Proposed Remedies," in Jones, *The Courts, the Public and the Law Explosion*, pp. 35–37.
[96] Rosenberg, "Court Congestion," pp. 38–55.
[97] *Law and Order Reconsidered*, pp. 569–570.

in 1968 which prohibited racial discrimination in impaneling a federal jury.[98] However, the physical facilities and amenities most courthouses provide jurors are ancient, inadequate, and obsolete. Bureaucracy of the jury process results in very slow procedures, with prospective jurors sitting around for hours waiting. And the usual monetary compensation has fallen woefully behind current wage standards; in the federal courts, jurors receive only four dollars per day.[99] Yet the jury, by ensuring broad participation in the judicial process, plays an important role in bolstering public confidence in the administration of justice, especially in trials in which dissident critics are likely to question government credibility and the fairness of the judicial system.

Stripping away bureaucratic waste and instituting organization reform may be only one element in combating violence, but it remains an important one. In the words of the president of the American Bar Association, William T. Gossett: "Where violence threatens society, as it does today, one necessary response is clearly, forcefully and *efficiently* to enforce the criminal laws."[100] There are others, however, who after long study of court delay find that efficiency is the least of our problems. Maurice Rosenberg, professor of law at Columbia University and a long-time Director of the Project for Effective Justice, found the results of court cases more disheartening than the speed with which they are treated:

> *The deeper we probe into the problem of efficiency in court processes, the more apparent it becomes that the vital neglected problem is the quality, not the speed, of the processes. . . . In sum, among the costs of the obsession with speedier justice has been the erosion of the integrity of the judicial process from the viewpoint of the litigants and lawyers. . . . Slow justice is bad, but speedy injustice is not an admissible substitute.*[101]

The Problems of Correctional Institutions

Are We Successfully Rehabilitating the Criminal? In the American system of justice, the correctional institutions are treated as stepchildren. Because prisons are not politically glamourous issues and generate only the weakest support from legislators and the public, few inmates in the estimated 195,000 prison population[102] are suitably cared for or receive rehabilitation assistance. Overcrowded conditions are worst in the prisons located in the Northeast, where the facilities are overpopulated by 14 percent. Nationwide, the rate is 5.1 percent.

Prison statistics tell a story of neglect and indifference. Of the 4,037 prisons in the country, some 89 percent lack educational facilities, 86 percent cannot provide adequate recreation, and almost half lack appropriate medical services. When legislative bodies, prompted by the rising crime rates, appropriate funds to combat crime, the prisons frequently are overlooked. Only 25 percent of the money spent for criminal justice is used for correction.[103]

Given the alarming statistics that three-quarters of all prisoners convicted of committing felonies were previously convicted of committing misdemeanors,

---

[98] Richard Harris, *Justice, The Crisis of Law, Order and Freedom in America* (New York: Dutton, 1970), p. 71.
[99] *The Challenge of Crime in a Free Society,* p. 381.
[100] *Law and Order Reconsidered,* p. 559.
[101] Rosenberg, "Court Congestion," pp. 57, 58.
[102] Department of Justice, Bureau of Prisons, *National Prisoner Statistics,* bulletin no. 44.
[103] Clark, *Crime in America,* p. 217.

The drama is one rehabilitation method being used in some correctional institutions to help inmates develop a sense of involvement and self-awareness. This group of professional actors and prison inmates rehearses a play, **The Advocates,** *at New York City's Riker's Island prison.*

and that these convicts are responsible for four out of five serious crimes, it is clear that the ultimate goal of modern penology must be rehabilitation. As Ramsey Clark defined the word:

Rehabilitation means the purpose of law is justice — and that . . . we wish to give every individual his chance for fulfillment. The theory of rehabilitation is based on the belief that healthy, rational people will not injure others, that they will understand that the individual and his society are best served by conduct that does not inflict injury. . . . Rehabilitated, an individual will not have the capacity — cannot bring himself — to injure another or take or destroy property.[104]

Viewed as an apparatus for rehabilitation, the prison systems are resounding failures. Their objective, for the most part, is providing custodial care, and even this limited goal often is not met satisfactorily. Professional personnel such as teachers, vocational counselors, and psychologists, while dedicated and well-meaning, are too few in number to reach the inmate population with effective rehabilitative services. As visible in Table 9–3, a professional serving the prison system normally carries a staggering caseload. The President's Crime Commission

---

[104] Clark, *Crime in America*, p. 220.

Table 9-3   *Ratio of Rehabilitative Personnel to Prisoners*

Position	Number of Inmates per Staff Person
Classification worker	365
Counselor	758
Psychiatrist	1,140
Psychologist	803
Physician, surgeon	986
Social worker	295
Teacher:	
Academic	104
Vocational	181
Vocational rehabilitation counselor	2,172

Source: Joint Commission on Correctional Manpower and Training, Second Annual Report 1967–1968 (Washington, D.C.: Government Printing Office, 1968), pp. 2–3, as cited in Law and Order Reconsidered, a Staff Report to the National Commission on the Causes and Prevention of Violence (New York: Bantam, 1970), p. 625.

found a total complement of 2,685 case workers where 89,000 were needed by the prisons.

The Commission went on to estimate that only 20 percent of prison personnel make some kind of contribution to the inmate's rehabilitation. In 1965, for example, the nation's prisons employed over 121,000 persons, and, of these, 97,000 were guards, while only 24,000 had some duties related to rehabilitation. The situation in local jails is far worse.

Prison-reform advocates have suggested indeterminate sentences, or flexible jail terms, as a means for humanizing the prisons. This system provides for in-prison regular evaluations of an inmate's progress, and his release at any time at the discretion of correctional officials. The judge's sentence signifies the outer limit of incarceration, the clear goal of which is rehabilitation.[105] Others interested in prison reform suggest alternatives to imprisonment for offenders who are not habitual criminals. Objectors to military service, the youth arrested on a marijuana charge, the woman having an illegal abortion, and the respectable citizen involved in drunken driving would pay their debt to society in a meaningful program beyond prison walls, these reformers say.

Similarly, reform-minded penal experts urge more experimentation with limited confinement for criminals, such as work release and supervised correction within the community. Releasing inmates for several hours each day to work at an outside job has had encouraging results in the federal system; the state of California has experimented successfully with keeping youthful offenders in supervised community-residence centers.[106]

The Degrading Prison Environment While incarcerated in a penitentiary, a convict frequently lives through experiences that actually contribute to violent behavior instead of developing positive characteristics and personality traits leading to respect for law. It has been found that some prisons and jails warp

---

[105] Clark, *Crime in America*, pp. 222–226.
[106] Clark, *Crime in America*, pp. 228–234.

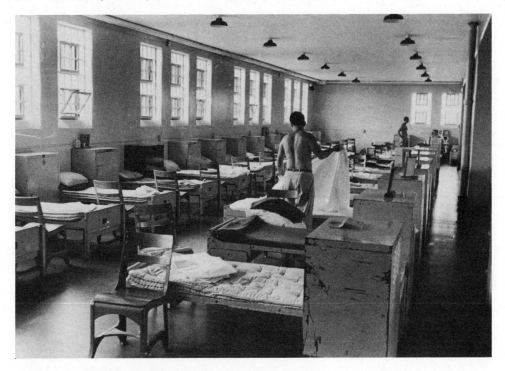

The depressing physical conditions at the vast majority of prisons make the dull life and threatening social atmosphere among prisoners hard to tolerate.

and demean the inmate. A Senate subcommittee investigating youth reformatories was told by one expert:

If someone suggested that we treat delinquents like animals, a lot of people would raise their eyebrows. . . . In many places throughout the country they have done a better job in meeting standards for the care and treatment of animals in zoos than we have for the care of [delinquent] children.[107]

Prisoners are often beaten, sexually assaulted, and terrorized by stronger "bully" inmates or by prison cliques. In the Philadelphia prison system, Police Department investigators found sexual attacks were endemic. Almost every slight young man became a potential target for homosexual aggression.[108] Even where the prisoners are not victimized by fellow inmates, physical torture, arbitrary solitary confinement and brutalizing overcrowding were reported. Not only are prison conditions frequently deplorable, but the state of the city jails and local workhouses used for detention while accused persons await trial are scandalous, in many instances. A Crime Commission consultant described them as "nothing more than steel cages in which people stay for periods of time up to a year."

Part of the answer to improved justice may lie in reducing incarceration of

[107] *Law and Order Reconsidered*, p. 633.
[108] *Law and Order Reconsidered*, p. 628.

"As a precedent, your honor, I offer a Perry Mason case first televised four years ago, in which. . . ."

Best Cartoons of 1970, edited by Lawrence Lariar (New York: Dodd, Mead, 1970).

accused persons to an absolute minimum. During the pretrial period when the defendant awaits his day in court, procedures can be instituted for keeping him in his community. In a New York City project, the courts released indigent defendants, who lacked the means to post bail but had strong roots in their communities, until the trial date. The "court summons" experiment has worked well in that community. Several studies have shown that parole could be utilized more widely and with better results by expanding supervisory staffs.

Is There Justice in the System?

The criminal-justice system in the United States—from the local police to the courts to the correctional institutions—suffers from inefficiency. Unfortunately, as has been discussed both in this chapter and in Chapter 4, the inefficiencies affect the poor, the black, and other minority groups far more than they affect the American white middle-class population. Justice, to the extent to which it means equal and impartial application of the laws, has not been fully achieved; until laws are fairly enforced, justice will remain an unfulfilled ideal.

SUGGESTED READING

Abraham, Henry J. *The Judicial Process* (New York: Oxford University Press, 1968). In paperback. An introductory analysis of both federal and local United States courts, with comparisons to England, France, and other countries, as the author deems appropriate. Abraham compares the various judicial processes in this country and analyzes and evaluates the main institutions and considerations affecting the administration of justice under law. The book is a comprehensive examination of law, the court systems, and judicial behavior.

Beard, Charles A. *The Supreme Court and the Constitution* (Englewood Cliffs, N.J.: Prentice-Hall, 1962). In paperback. (Originally published by Macmillan, 1912.) An examination of the historical documents of the men who wrote the Constitution. The author seeks to determine if the Framers intended the Supreme Court to possess the power to pass upon the constitutionality of acts of Congress, and he concludes that the Supreme Court did not arbitrarily assume the power of judicial review; rather, the men who framed and enacted the federal Constitution designed the federal system primarily to commit the established rights of property to the guardianship of a judiciary removed from direct contact with popular electorates.

Bickel, Alexander M. *The Supreme Court and the Idea of Progress* (New York: Harper & Row, 1970). In critical evaluation of the record of the Warren Court, Bickel accuses the Court of irrationality, inconsistency, overconfidence in itself and majority rule, and unwise decisions which lead to undue governmental centralization. He argues that the Warren Court intervened unwisely in social policy that should have been decided in the political arena. Included is a review of the Court's history, exploration of various legal philosophies that have motivated the Justices at significant periods, and the limitations on the Court in stimulating social progress.

Campbell, James S., Joseph R. Sahid, and David P. Stang. *Law and Order Reconsidered, A Staff Report to the National Commission on the Causes and Prevention of Violence* (Washington, D.C.: Government Printing Office, 1969; New York: Bantam, 1970). In paperback. The full government report that attempts to determine the extent to which violence is caused by the flaws of our nation's institutions and how these flaws can be eliminated. It deals with the rule of law, the political and social institutions of the country, and the agencies of law enforcement, including the police, the courts, and the correctional institutions.

Cox, Archibald. *The Warren Court: Constitutional Decision as an Instrument of Reform* (Cambridge, Mass.: Harvard University Press, 1968). In an examination of the main lines of constitutional development under the Warren Court, Cox considers questions raised by the extent and rapidity of the changes during that period. He analyzes the underlying pressures that produced the changes and the long-range institutional consequences in terms of the distribution of governmental power and the proper role of the Court. The author's conclusion is that the Warren's Court's rulings are in keeping with the mainstream of American history and within the genius of America's institutions.

Downie, Leonard, Jr. *Justice Denied: The Case for Reform of the Courts* (New York: Praeger, 1971). An examination of how badly American courts work, why they work badly, and what changes have been urged by those few brave lawyers who seek reform. Downie discusses the chaos and the bureaucratic expediency and inadequacy that plague the American court system, belie the nation's myth of justice, and threaten the nation's rule of law.

Forte, David F. (ed.). *The Supreme Court in American Politics: Judicial Activism vs. Judicial Restraint* (Lexington, Mass.: Heath, 1972). In paperback. This collection of articles and excerpts by leading judicial scholars and Supreme Court justices offers a wide variety of opinions on the topics of judicial review, judicial activism and restraint, neutral versus value-oriented decision-making, and the reality of a political Court as it exists today versus a nonpolitical Court.

Goldman, Sheldon, and Thomas P. Jahinge. *The Federal Courts as a Political System* (New York: Harper & Row, 1971). In paperback. Utilizing systems analysis of the workings of the federal courts within the context of the larger American political system, the authors examine the structure, process, and behavior of the federal courts. They also interpret two key events concerning the Supreme Court: the federal judiciary's handling of New Deal economic regulation cases and the transformation of the Warren Court to the Nixon Court.

Jacob, Herbert (ed.). *Law, Politics, and the Federal Courts* (Boston: Little, Brown, 1967). In paperback. A collection of readings that emphasize the political, vis-à-vis legal, aspects of adjudication, with the focus on judicial process rather than a single substantive area of decision-making. The political and governmental roles of the courts are viewed as a normal part of the American governmental process. The authors stress that trial and intermediate courts play significant roles in the federal judiciary.

Krislov, Samuel. *The Supreme Court in the Political Process* (New York: Macmillan, 1965). In paperback. An examination and analysis of the Supreme Court and its role in American politics. The author describes the internal processes of the Supreme Court and the major issues of constitutional law which concern it. He examines the recruitment of judges, the nature of the office, selection of cases, controversies surrounding court decisions, and the political and social forces which play an increasingly important role in the legal decision-making process.

Mayers, Lewis. *The American Legal System: The Administration of Justice in the United States by Judicial, Administrative, Military, and Arbitral Tribunals* (New York: Harper & Row, 1964). A systematic examination and evaluation of American legal institutions: the author describes the operation and functions of the city, state, and federal courts; administrative tribunals; voluntary arbitral tribunals; and several types of military tribunals. He traces the historical development of American legal institutions and discusses proposals for reform of the legal system.

McCloskey, Robert G. *The American Supreme Court* (Chicago: University of Chicago Press, 1960). A historical interpretation of the Supreme Court as a constitutional tribunal exercising the power of judicial review. McCloskey argues that the strength of the Court lies in its sensitivity to the changing political scene: the realization that judicial decisions should never be far removed from popular opinion. He contends that as the Court has made public policy through its judicial pronouncements, it has been a willingly active branch in the American governing process.

Pritchett, C. Herman. *The Roosevelt Court: A Study in Judicial Politics and Values, 1937–1947* (New York: Quadrangle, 1969). In paperback. (Reprint of original published by Macmillan.) Pritchett describes and analyzes the Justices of the Supreme Court and the decisions they handed down between the years 1937 and 1947, when Franklin Roosevelt was President. He includes the necessary historical background and judicial procedures for understanding the Court of that era, the liberal tone of the Court, and the leanings of the justices on important issues such as economic regulation (the Court vis-à-vis Congress), civil liberties, crime and punishment, labor, and the bureaucracy's place in adjudication.

Schubert, Glendon A. *Judicial Behavior* (Chicago: Rand McNally, 1964) and *Judicial Policy-Making* (Glenview, Ill.: Scott, Foresman, 1965). Schubert is an authority on the behavioral and systematic approach to the judiciary. The first of these works is a reader in theory and matters of judicial behavior, and the second a discussion of the role of the Supreme Court in the formation of public policy. In other books Schubert has described the judiciary of the federal government and the various states, compared the United States court system to that of other countries, and discussed the attitudes and ideologies of Supreme Court justices.

Shapiro, Martin. *Law and Politics in the Supreme Court: New Approaches to Political Jurisprudence* (New York: The Free Press, 1964). Shapiro shows precisely how much influence political, as distinct from constitutional, considerations have upon the Court's decisions. He examines the various roles the Court plays and explains how the federal courts are locked into the policy-making process. Demonstrating the artificiality of viewing the Supreme Court as a solely constitutional arbiter, he explains why an accurate understanding of the Supreme Court, without a political analysis, is impossible.

3

THE PEOPLE
IN POLITICS

One cannot understand politics by studying only the formal institutions and procedures of government, for sociological, psychological, and economic factors also have an important impact on power relations. This principle is particularly valid in discussing the role of the people in American politics. Although the Constitution states that everyone has the right to participate in politics, certain sociological, psychological, and economic factors may undercut the involvement of the people in the political process. Many critics of American society argue that the behavior of people in politics does not approximate the democratic ideal of enlightened, dispassionate, and objective decision-making. People do not get involved, are not well informed, and do not behave with consistency and rationality. There is a great gap between the ideal of democracy and the reality of popular participation in American politics.

The formal allocation of power and decision-making discussed in Part 2 establishes the rules of the game in American politics; it sets the broad limits within which politics is played. But it does not determine the outcome of the struggle for power, nor does it explain all of politics. For example, the formal power to pass laws resides in national, state, and local legislative bodies in the United States. But, in fact, public opinion has a direct and indirect influence on legislators, and interest groups play an important part in the making of laws, often actually writing the laws that will eventually apply to them.

The participation of people in politics through public opinion, political parties, interest groups, and voting is an extremely important aspect of politics in America. These are the topics of Part 3 of this book. Essentially, Part 3 addresses itself to the problem of representation in a mass society. Given the structures of power and decision-making that exist in the American political system, what role is left to the people? What channels for popular participation are available? Is popular involvement in the political process dominated by elites? Is the extent of popular participation that exists today compatible with the ideals of democratic government?

10
POLITICAL SOCIALIZATION
AND PUBLIC OPINION

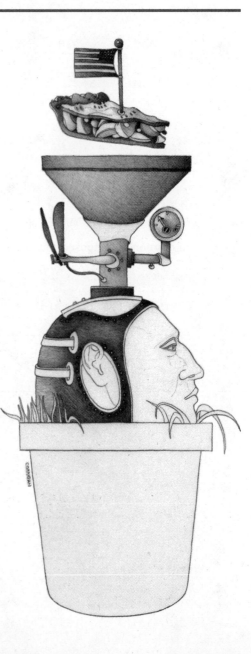

The image of the governmental official who genuinely tries to be attentive to public opinion corresponds with the democratic ideal that government is "of the people, by the people, for the people." In a democracy, the role of public opinion is supposedly elevated to a supreme position; the mass of people select political decision-makers and thus are expected to control, at least indirectly, the policies that will inevitably affect their lives.

Of course, in reality, public opinion does not always control political decisions, even indirectly. One reason is simply lack of information. In theory, the democratic system presupposes a public fully informed on the issues, and politicians aware of public sentiment on those issues. In practice, however, the public is often uninformed on an issue, or, indeed, unaware that there is one; politicians, in turn, do not always have knowledge of those opinions that do exist. But more important than simple lack of information is the fact that even if a politician wanted to follow "public opinion" in all his decisions, he would soon discover that there is no single "public opinion" on any issue. There is always a wide diversity of opinions, even among a small group of people in a geographically limited area. And there are always many people who have "no opinion" about a given issue. How, then, can a politician feel confident that the few people who write to him supporting a particular piece of legislation speak for his entire constituency? Obviously, he must attempt to strike a balance between acting upon his own ideas about what is the best course to take in a given situation, and basing his response on what his polls, letters, and other sources tell him that his "public" thinks about that issue.

A number of other developments also tend to undercut the primary role that public opinion is supposed to play in American democracy. One of these developments is the lack of interest which most Americans show concerning their own government and its activities. As early as the mid-1920s, Walter Lippmann pointed out this fact of American political life: the average American simply has neither the time nor the inclination to take an active role in political matters. Most people hold full-time jobs, and when they have free time, they prefer to spend it with their families, or in some form of recreation, rather than involve themselves in campaigns or other political activities. Few people see politics as having any direct bearing on their personal lives; and fewer, still, wish to make political activity a significant part of their daily activities.[1] Voting statistics seem to substantiate this viewpoint. Only about 60 percent of the eligible people in this country vote in presidential elections. And only about 30 to 35 percent take part in local elections.

Another factor that significantly limits the role of public opinion in American politics is the recent growth of the government itself. In the last forty years, American governmental institutions have greatly increased in both size and complexity, and they now deal with many issues of a highly technical nature. It is generally conceded that the resulting bewilderment of the average person has discouraged many from active participation in politics.

The growing size of government and the complexity of political decision-making undoubtedly have had an important impact on the ability of people to formulate knowledgeable opinions on many issues. But some contemporary political scientists offer still another explanation of why public opinion has so

[1] Walter Lippmann, *The Phantom Public* (New York: Macmillan, 1925).

little real significance in American politics today. They suggest that there is no such thing as truly autonomous public opinion, because the attitudes held by the mass of the people are molded far more by the manipulation of elites than by independent thought. If this is the case, mass public opinion is merely the echo of elite opinion and therefore is unable to serve any directing function in political decision-making; at best, the role of public opinion is merely a supportive one. This theory becomes all the more convincing when one considers the fact that most people do not know or care much about many political issues of the day. Obviously, then, since large segments of the population often fail to think about the issues at all, their political opinions might easily be molded by the combined influences of governmental leaders, the mass media, and other opinion elites.

In spite of these developments, however, one should not conclude that public opinion has no significance at all in American politics today. Public opinion may not have as great or as direct an influence on governmental activities as some might wish, but the political opinions held by a number of people have at least a limiting effect on policy decisions.

The purpose of this chapter is to explore the general characteristics of the beliefs and opinions held by Americans, how people acquire their beliefs, to what extent public opinion is influenced by political elites as well as by the mass media, and how much impact public opinion has on political decision-making and public policy.

The Nature of Public Opinion

If a person prefers blues to Beethoven, that preference is a reflection of his personal taste; it is his private opinion concerning music. But the opinion expressed by a large group of people about the desirability of extending foreign aid to another country is a public opinion. The term *public opinion* refers to opinions about issues of social concern that are expressed by a significant number of people. If the issue in question finds its way into the political arena, then the opinion expressed about it is called a *political opinion.*

Public opinion must concern an issue, or issues, of some significance to the well-being of a large segment of the population. The point at which an opinion is considered "public" is difficult to determine. If ten people in the United States are firmly convinced that the indecent exposure of animals is seriously undermining the moral fiber of American youth, their view would not normally be classified as a public opinion, unless, of course, such a view came to be held by a large segment of the American people. Thus, even an opinion that seems trivial or silly can become public opinion as long as a sufficiently large number of people believe it *and* express it in some way.

Conflict and Consensus in Public Opinion

Traditionally, Americans have been thought to have a consensus on a number of fundamental beliefs. We are said to agree on the importance and desirability of such institutions and basic rights as the free-enterprise system; free and open elections for selecting public officials; the freedoms of speech, religion, and assembly; and so forth. But, as many observers have pointed out, the political noninvolvement of most Americans, the fact that many do not bother to assert their opinions, if, indeed, they formulate opinions at all, creates the illusion of a consensus on certain fundamental political principles, when in fact there is none.

Even a very basic political value, which most people uphold when stated in a general way, will yield conflicting opinions when expressed in terms of a specific issue. Virtually every American would agree that freedom of speech – one of the essential rights guaranteed in the Constitution – is an important freedom which must be safeguarded. But a sizable number of people, when asked whether or not they would allow an avowed communist to teach in their high school, or to speak in the town assembly hall, would probably be upset by such a prospect; feeling threatened by the infiltration of "foreign ideas" into their community, they might well try to prevent that person from exercising his freedom of speech. In such an instance it is likely that the person opposing the communist's freedom of speech would not think that his actions infringed on the other person's civil rights.

This kind of paradox exists within many of us. It clearly demonstrates that public opinion in this country is not strongly ideological – that is, few Americans have well-integrated and highly consistent sets of ideals that guide their political views or behavior. Recent studies by Angus Campbell and his associates indicate that only 3 percent of Americans have a consistent ideology.[2] Thus, a poor person who feels strongly that his government should provide all of its citizens with adequate, low-cost medical care – regardless of their age or economic status – may, at the same time, be violently opposed to Medicaid and Medicare when such programs are lumped under the label "socialized medicine."

Some Basic Characteristics of Public Opinion

Degree of Political Knowledge Perhaps one reason most Americans are inconsistent in their political thinking is that a majority of the American public is not well informed about the structure of government or political issues. The late V. O. Key clearly pointed out this fact:

> *Much discussion of public opinion tacitly assumes a far more general focus of attention on political objects and a far wider distribution of political information among citizens than actually exists. The invention of sampling techniques and their application to the political attitudes of national populations have compelled revision of such suppositions. By these techniques substantial percentages of the population were shown to remain happily unaware even of issues that commanded the attention of Congress for weeks, provided screaming banners for the newspapers, and occupied the time of frenetic newscasters.[3]*

According to the results of numerous polls, the general population has extremely limited knowledge concerning even the most basic principles of our system of government. A poll taken by the National Opinion Research Center of the University of Chicago indicated that only 21 percent of the people queried knew what the Bill of Rights was. In similar studies, it was found that only 55 percent of the people knew how many senators their state had in Washington;

---

[2] See Angus Campbell, Philip E. Converse, Warren E. Miller, and Donald E. Stokes, *Elections and the Political Order* (New York: Wiley, 1966), for a definition of ideology.

[3] V. O. Key, *Public Opinion and American Democracy* (New York: Knopf, 1961), p. 78.

"I used to be a moderate, but Cambodia, the campus
rebellions and the subsequent repression of dissent
have polarized me to a point where now I only read the
sports page."

Playboy, *June 1971. Copyright © 1971 by* Playboy.

just 35 percent knew what the Electoral College was; and only 19 percent could
identify the three branches of the federal government.[4]

As a population, not only are we ill acquainted with the fundamental structures of our government, but most Americans are equally ill informed about
current political issues. A large proportion of Americans do not read about politics, a fact that helps explain why only a little over a third of the people know
the names of their congressmen, and a little less than half know which party
controls Congress.[5] Of those people who read a newspaper daily, many are interested only in the comics; and others confine their reading to the sports section
or the fashion page. Similarly, far more television viewers habitually turn to
situation comedies, sports coverage, and reruns of old movies, rather than to
news or public-affairs programs.

This low level of interest in politics leads to a habitual reluctance to become
informed about current events. As a result, when a political issue arises on which
people do have strong feelings, they may base their opinions on misinformation.
Take, for example, the issue of fluoridation. When scientists determined that
fluoridated water was helpful in the prevention of tooth decay and the strengthening of teeth, the discovery spawned a movement to introduce fluoride into the
water supplies of most American communities. But somehow a rumor began,
largely fed by right-wing extremist groups, that fluoridation was a dangerous
plot, designed to poison the national water supply. This "plot" theory was widely
believed; many people came to violently oppose fluoridation.[6] Had they been

---

[4] Robert E. Lave and David O. Sears, *Public Opinion* (Englewood Cliffs, N.J.: Prentice-Hall, 1964), p. 61.
[5] Lave and Sears, *Public Opinion*, p. 61.
[6] See Robert L. Crain et al., *Politics of Community Conflict: The Fluoridation Issue* (Indianapolis: Bobbs-
Merrill, 1968).

better informed of the facts about fluoridation, these people might have realized quickly that there was no basis for their fears.

Concentration of Opinion: Opinion Leaders and Followers Someone who grew up in a family where impassioned arguments about political issues were everyday occurrences, who has been involved in organizations in which political matters were central topics of discussion, or who is now an active follower of current events probably feels that just about everyone has a strong opinion about the significant issues of the day. But in fact, poll after poll has shown that there are very few questions on which many people are likely to express an opinion.

It is surprisingly difficult to determine how many people do and do not have opinions on a particular issue. Studies conducted by the American Institute of Public Opinion (AIPO) have demonstrated that, when asked specific questions, people do not always give honest answers. For example, in one study, the AIPO asked: Have you heard of the Tennessee Valley Authority—TVA? And 67 percent of the sample said that they had heard of it. But, when asked to describe briefly what the TVA was, another 12 percent of the total sample admitted that they did not know anything about it after all.[7] Similarly, people often say that they are strongly for or against specific acts which, it has turned out later, they cannot identify.

The fact that only a small percentage of the population has any opinion at all on most concrete and specific political issues means that public opinion is usually highly *concentrated*. The concentration of public opinion within a small group of people tends to produce *opinion leaders,* who, because of their access to channels of communication, exert a great deal of influence upon other people's opinions. This situation raises an important question: Is the small segment of the population expressing opinions representative of the public as a whole? Can this segment be said to accurately reflect the public will? For example, when the President proposes to cut back appropriations for a federal housing project, does his decision reflect the demands of a vocal and knowledgeable minority or the opinion of the public as a whole? Or when Congress passes a piece of civil-rights legislation, is its decision in keeping with the majority of the people?

Intensity of Opinion Even when people hold definite opinions about a particular issue, their opinions vary greatly in *intensity.* For instance, some people are mildly in favor of imposing a tariff on the importation of steel; others are mildly against it; still others are strongly for or against such a tariff. This variation in opinion intensity can have significant political results, because, as a general rule, the more intensely a person feels about an issue, the more likely he is to do something concrete about it. The people who organize and participate in lobbying activities or mass demonstrations in support of their political views are more likely to change other people's views—and, sometimes, to alter their votes—than are less politically active individuals.

There are a number of reasons for the wide variations in the intensity of opinions held by different people on specific issues. It seems probable that the more immediate an issue is to an individual—that is, the more personally it is likely to affect him—the more intensely he will voice his opinion on the matter. A person of draft age, for example, will be likely to have an intense opinion

---

[7] Key, *Public Opinion and American Democracy*, p. 79.

about the matter of draft reform (whatever his views may be concerning the military establishment in general, or some war in particular), because the issue directly affects his personal life. On the other hand, it is relatively difficult for most people to become really involved in a question such as whether or not the United States should give foreign aid to a particular country. Except under certain circumstances, the issue of foreign aid is merely an abstraction, and therefore it is difficult to develop intense opinions about it.

However, personal involvement does not entirely explain the intensity of people's opinions. If one has a close identification with a group that supports or opposes a particular issue, the intensity of one's opinions on that issue probably will be high. For example, a member of the League of Women Voters will presumably have stronger opinions about the programs the League supports than will a woman who is not affiliated with that particular organization. Furthermore, one's knowledge about an issue clearly affects one's opinion intensity, for it is unlikely that a person will feel strongly about a matter he knows very little about.

A major result of the variations in intensity of opinion has already been mentioned: often, a person who feels strongly about an issue is likely to be a participant in activities designed to implement his opinion. However, this is not always the case. Many persons with intense opinions do not participate to any significant degree in political activity. While it seems to be true that those people who do participate in political activity have strong opinions on the issues involved, it is not necessarily true that everyone who has a strong opinion on a given issue will act upon it. Those people who feel strongly but do not act may represent the segment of our society that feels frustrated and ineffective about being a participant in the political system.

Thus, intensity of opinion seems to depend on such factors as personal involvement in an issue, identification with the group affected, and knowledge of the subject. But intense views do not necessarily result in some form of political activity.

Stability of Opinion Although most Americans are ill informed about and unconcerned with politics, it can at least be said that, once they develop opinions on certain subjects, they tend to keep them. Public opinion about most important political issues dealing with basic political principles and practices appears to be quite *stable* — that is, resistant to change. One reason for this stability is that the strength of party identification, which develops early in life and which tends to be maintained throughout adulthood, is an important reference point which conditions people's opinions about particular issues and events. In other words, once a person decides that he is a Democrat (or a Republican, or a Socialist or whatever), his party affiliation will tend to influence the way in which he looks at various issues and candidates. For example, because the Democratic party has traditionally supported pro-labor legislation, a person who identifies himself as a Democrat may automatically support a bill increasing unemployment benefits, even without knowing a great deal about that bill, because of his party affiliation. If a loyal party supporter consistently views particular issues in party terms, a relatively high degree of stability in opinions prevails.

However, a person's opinions about the personalities of various political figures tend to be erratic. This unevenness occurs partly because personalities themselves are frequently inconsistent and partly because we have no common standard by which to judge them. In addition, the variability of public opinion concerning individual political figures is influenced by two other factors – the events that occur while they are in office, and the way these events are portrayed in the media. Lyndon Baines Johnson is a classic example of a President about whom the public's opinion changed drastically and quickly, during his tenure in office. Partly because of the circumstances under which LBJ first took office (the assassination of President Kennedy), the public was extremely sympathetic toward the new Chief Executive. But only a few years later, after the 1964 election, the situation had altered so greatly that – because of such issues as the still-escalating American involvement in the Vietnam War, and the negative treatment given President Johnson by a large segment of the country newsmen – public opinion was largely against him. In 1963, when he became President, 80 percent of the American people expressed their approval of Lyndon Johnson's performance in office. At the end of 1966, fewer than half the people approved of him; and, by 1969, the percentage of approvals had dropped to under 40.[8]

In general, the stability of public opinions depends on the nature of the stimuli – the events, issues, and problems that arise; how they relate to the public's preconceived attitudes and beliefs; and how deeply ingrained these preconceived attitudes are.

Latency of Opinion If a senator from New York, in taking stock of his constituents' views in preparation for his next election campaign, notices that few of the people from his state have expressed any opinion about a new proposal to establish a strategic missile base near Albany, does that mean that they have no opinions on that issue?

Public opinion on a given topic is often *latent* – that is, not crystallized or articulated – but, nevertheless, it is there, waiting to be tapped. Latent public opinion is a potentially important political force because a politician may be able to activate this latent opinion, when necessary, and perhaps receive the active support of a larger number of people. But the direction of latent public opinion is very difficult to interpret, and the latent opinion of the large "inattentive" segment of the public is even more difficult to predict than that of the smaller, "attentive" segment.

In our hypothetical case of the Albany missile base, suppose the New York senator wants to activate the latent opinion of his constituency, in order to gain its enthusiastic support in his upcoming campaign. He plans to base his campaign on the issue of preventing the establishment of the missile base, which he regards as an unnecessary expense and a significant risk to the people of the Albany area. He can be reasonably certain that the "attentive" residents of his state, those who have been keeping themselves informed on recent political developments, are at least somewhat familiar with the facts in this case. Thus, by taking into consideration their reactions to similar questions in the past, as well as the personal involvement they are likely to feel as residents of the state supposedly being threatened, the senator can predict that some members of the involved segment of his constituency would probably support his anti-missile fight. However, he cannot be sure about the uninformed voters in his state. They might be persuaded

---

[8] Harold Mendelsohn and Irving Crespi, *Polls, Television, and the New Politics* (San Francisco: Chandler, 1970), pp. 43–49.

by one of his political rivals into believing that the senator's position will leave the nation defenseless in the event of an enemy attack. Hence, having been exposed only to that point of view, they might well be against his anti-missile fight. Or, more likely, they might never hear enough about this issue to develop any real interest in it or opinions about it, a situation that could be just as harmful to the senator's campaign effort.

Part of the senator's problem may be the lack of urgency attached to the missile-base issue. In times of crisis, on the other hand, our political leaders—particularly the President—know that they can activate the latent opinion of the mass of the people. During wartime, for example, when it is important for the public to support the government actively, leaders can bring certain previously unexpressed opinions to the surface, to help strengthen the defense effort. Often, in such cases, the latent opinions need little coaxing to become activated. In his famous speech after the attack on Pearl Harbor, President Franklin D. Roosevelt was able to mobilize public opinion—quickly and quite enthusiastically—to support his decision to ask Congress for a declaration of war against Japan. Similarly, in August 1964, when the Johnson administration informed congressional leaders of an "unprovoked" attack on the *USS Maddox* in the Gulf of Tonkin, Congress gave its near-unanimous approval of a resolution requesting that the President take "all necessary measures" to prevent further aggression by North Vietnam. Thus, because it can often be tapped, latent public opinion is important—it sets the bounds within which political leaders operate.

Political Socialization

Public opinion, whether latent or actively expressed, is an important part of political life in America. But the opinions that people hold on particular issues usually depend on deeper factors—called political values and ideologies—that predispose individual views in one direction or another. What makes us essentially conservative or liberal? Through what process do we eventually become Republicans, Democrats, Socialist Laborites, or Communists? The process through which these basic political attitudes are inculcated in the individual is referred to as *political socialization*. The individual's opinions thus reflect, or are shaped by, the attitudes and beliefs he is taught to accept as a child.

The Role of the Family

The family is the first socializing agent in a child's life. As the child's major source of human contact through the preschool years, the family is the primary source of all cultural—including specifically political—socialization. Although recent study in this area suggests that the influence of school and other experiences on the individual is also extremely important, many researchers have concluded that the family is the most important agent in transmitting political beliefs to the individual.[9]

Children learn party identification from their parents at an early age—cases are often cited of four-year-olds who, when asked what they thought about some aspect of political life, answered firmly and without hesitation: "We're Republicans;

---

[9] Herbert H. Hyman, *Political Socialization* (New York: The Free Press, 1959), p. 69.

Flags and parades are major symbols in the patriotic imagery of white middle-class childhood.

that's all I know."[10] And, to a surprisingly large extent, this party identification tends to continue throughout the individual's life.

Working in the 1950s, Angus Campbell and his colleagues conducted a number of surveys to determine how consistent most people's partisan orientations are, from the time they enter the electorate throughout later life. The researchers found that "of those who can remember their first vote for President, two-thirds still identify with the same party they first voted for. A majority [56 percent] of these presidential voters have never crossed party lines; they have always supported their party's candidate."[11] All the data support the conclusion that people with strong party attachments tend to resist influences to change that attachment. Of course, as the Campbell study further pointed out, "Some members of the electorate do not form strong party attachments, . . . and they make up a sufficiently large proportion of the population to permit the short-term influence of political forces associated with issues and candidates to play a significant role in determining the outcome of specific elections."[12] In addition, more recent evi-

---

[10] Robert D. Hess and Judith U. Torney, *The Development of Political Attitudes in Children* (Garden City, N.Y.: Doubleday Anchor, 1968).

[11] Angus Campbell, Philip E. Converse, Warren E. Miller, and Donald E. Stokes, *The American Voter* (New York: Wiley, 1964), p. 87.

[12] Campbell, Converse, Miller, and Stokes, *The American Voter*, p. 87.

dence suggests that the number of "independent" voters may be increasing.[13]
Yet, regardless of the size of the independent segment of the electorate, it seems
true that those people whose families have identified themselves strongly with a
particular political party form a strong attachment for that party; on the other
hand, a person whose family has been more or less unaffiliated is likely to cross
party lines fairly frequently.

A number of different factors affect the strength of an individual's identification with the political party of his parents. Some observers argue that the family
structure is one such factor. The more autocratic the family structure—that is,
the less free a child is to participate in and criticize family decisions—the more
likely it is that, as a teenager, he will shift his support away from the party preference of his parents.

Kenneth P. Langton cited a number of comparative studies made among families in several countries.[14] In general, it was found that, because American families were less autocratic in structure than families studied in countries such as
Germany and Japan, American children were much less likely than the residents
of certain other nations to rebel by adopting political views different from those
held by their parents. Of course, one important reason for this might also be the
fact, already discussed, that American parents are not particularly concerned
about politics. Therefore, American adolescents seeking a form of rebellion against
their families would not be likely to pick the political arena for their protest. They
would be more likely to rebel in more tangible ways, that their parents would be
sure to notice and care about—such as manner of dress, hair styles, or patterns of
speech.

Langton also noted that the matter of adolescent rebellion should not be overstressed, since studies have suggested that "adolescent rebellion does not play an
important role in the formation of these types of political views [liberal versus
conservative orientations] in American society."[15] Herbert Hyman also found evidence in a study of family influence to the effect that "the almost complete absence of negative correlations provides considerable evidence against the theory
that political attitudes are formed generally in terms of rebellion and opposition
to parents."[16]

Although the strength of parental influence on children and young adults is
great, there are other factors which cause an erosion of parental partisanship in
later years. As V. O. Key pointed out, a tremendously strong force is not always
required to change an older person's party loyalty; often, "inherited identification
may . . . persist simply because no circumstance arises in conflict with it."[17] A
person brought up as a Presbyterian may never consider changing his religious
affiliation to another Protestant denomination unless there seems to be a good
reason for doing so—marriage to a devout Baptist, for example. Similarly, most
people are content to maintain their party affiliation, unless they think there is
something worthwhile to be gained by a shift. Particular events, such as the Great

[13] Milton C. Cummings, Jr. (ed.), *The National Election of 1964* (Washington, D.C.: The Brookings Institution,
1966), Table 8-11, "Distribution of Political Identification in the U.S., 1952–64," p. 278.

[14] Langton, *Political Socialization* (New York: Oxford University Press, 1969), pp. 24–25.

[15] Langton, *Political Socialization*, p. 24.

[16] Hyman, *Political Socialization*, p. 72.

[17] Key, *Public Opinion and American Democracy*, p. 298.

Depression, that have a strong impact on the party considered to be responsible, can cause widespread changes in party affiliation. Upward mobility (a rise in one's social class, due to a rise in income level and corresponding social status) may well have the same effect, as an individual comes into contact with persons of a different political outlook from that of his former friends. Women often change their parties when they marry, if their husbands' affiliation is different from that of the woman's own family. Another major factor in the shift in party identification is the individual's like or dislike of a particular party leader or candidate, or of a particular party policy.

In the United States, up to 80 percent of the persons who remember the party preferences of their parents, when both parents belonged to the same party, also support that party. But what happens in a family where the parents support different parties? Kenneth Langton and M. Kent Jennings stated, "When parental partisanship is mixed or inconsistent the identification of the offspring is more evenly divided between the parties."[18] Studies have shown that persons from families of split or inconsistent party loyalties are more likely to vote for split tickets (voting for the other party's candidate, when the candidate of one's own party seems less qualified) than are persons from politically homogeneous families.[19] Langton and Jennings also pointed out two major difficulties with the studies of political socialization and party identification that have been carried out thus far. One unavoidable problem is the necessity for the researchers to rely on their subjects' memories of the political situations existing in their families when they were children. It is likely that the respondent's recollection is often faulty. A second major difficulty is that past researchers have made no attempt to distinguish between the effects upon children of the political views of each parent; it was previously assumed that the parents influenced their offspring as a single unit. Recently, that assumption has been questioned. It had been widely believed that the child is most likely to follow the political preferences of his father. This viewpoint is based on the assumption that, since politics has been traditionally a male-dominated area of activity, a child would be more likely to know about his father's political preferences than about his mother's, hence to discuss political matters with him, and finally to imitate him. It was also traditionally believed that husbands dominated their wives' political preferences. But recent research indicates that, when a child's parents are split on party preferences, he is actually more likely to follow the views of his mother than those of his father.[20]

Research also indicates that children tend to acquire their general degree of interest in politics from their parents, as well as their sense of political efficacy.[21] Most of us have come to similar conclusions from observing the people around us. Generally speaking, children brought up by politically aware and active parents are more likely to engage in political activities themselves, or at least to follow political events more closely, than are children whose families showed no interest in political matters. Langton postulates a more specific effect upon the political interest and sense of political efficacy on a male child brought up with-

[18] M. Kent Jennings and Kenneth P. Langton, "Mothers vs. Fathers: The Formation of Political Orientations among Young Americans," *Journal of Politics,* vol. 31 (May 1969), p. 330.

[19] Key, *Public Opinion and American Democracy,* pp. 304–305.

[20] Jennings and Langton, "Mothers vs. Fathers."

[21] Key, *Public Opinion and American Democracy,* pp. 301–305.

out a father. He feels that, because the male-role model is absent, the son in a
father-absent family is more likely that the daughter (whose role model, the
mother, is still available) to have a lessened degree of political interest and a limited feeling of political efficacy.[22] This finding is particularly important in terms
of black Americans. Because fathers are absent in a higher percentage of black
families than white families, an unusually larger number of black children are
likely to be politically passive and apathetic. Thus, these children tend to grow up
into adults who are not motivated to participate in traditional channels of American political life. Moreover, their political apathy may also limit the extent to
which black leaders will be able to organize them successfully.

Recent research further shows that, although parents do tend, to some extent,
to transmit their orientations on specific issues to their offspring, this influence is
much less clear-cut than parental influence on their children's party identification.[23] V. O. Key hypothesized, "The odds are that conversation around the home
makes party identification far more visible than it does parental outlook on policy
questions. Nevertheless, children tend to take on their parents' views on current
issues, a type of influence that may decline in significance later in the child's life,
as new issues and new questions develop, and as the child becomes subject to
more nonparental influences."[24] At the same time, it must be remembered that
such factors as the parents' occupation, class, religion, and partisanship do seem
to affect the child's basic political orientation—in terms of identifying himself as
a liberal or a conservative.

Influence of the School

According to a comprehensive study by Robert Hess and Judith Torney, "The
public school appears to be the most important and effective instrument of political socialization in the United States."[25] Although it is becoming a widely held
opinion that the school, rather than the family, has the primary impact on the
formation of children's political beliefs, evidence concerning the relative importance of the school in this area is still inconclusive. In any case, it is clear that
the school has a critical impact on many aspects of the socialization process, since
it is the institution in which the child spends the largest portion of his time once
he reaches school age.

Hess and Torney identified three stages of conceptualization through which
young school children pass in the development of their political beliefs. During
the first stage, children attain a feeling of group identity as "Americans." This is
largely achieved through attachment to patriotic symbols employed in the classroom, such as display of the American flag, recitation of the Pledge of Allegiance,
the singing of patriotic songs, and the presence of photographs showing historical
figures or national monuments. At this point, the children do not understand the
symbolic content of these objects and activities, but they imitate the great defer-
ence clearly accorded them by adults. As one second-grade boy responded to the
question "What does the Statue of Liberty do?":

---

[22] Langton, *Political Socialization*, p. 32.
[23] M. Kent Jennings and Richard G. Niemi, "The Transmission of Political Values from Parent to Child," *American Political Science Review*, vol. 62 (March 1968), pp. 169–184.
[24] Key, *Public Opinion and American Democracy*, p. 306.
[25] Hess and Torney, *The Development of Political Attitudes in Children*, p. 120.

"Well, it keeps liberty."
"How does it do that?"
"Well, it doesn't do it, but there are some other guys that do it."
"Some other guys do it for the Statue of Liberty?"
"The Statue is not alive."
"Well, what does it do?"
"It has this torch in its hand, and sometimes they light up the torch. If the Statue was gone, there wouldn't be any liberty."[26]

Children at this early stage can visualize America only as a place that is good to live in, because they were born here, and because, they have been told, Americans enjoy a better material standard of living than do people in many other countries. Said another second-grade boy, when asked if he would prefer to be English:

Well, I wouldn't like to be an Englishman because I wouldn't like to talk their way, and I'd rather be an American because they have better toys, because they have better things, better stores, and better beds and blankets, and they have better play guns, and better boots, and mittens and coats, and better schools and teachers.[27]

At the second stage, children begin to think of America more in terms of abstract qualities—such as freedom and democracy. A fifth-grade boy offered this response in answer to the question "What is freedom?":

Well, to be free, you could vote any way you want. Like Khrushchev makes everybody vote for him, because he uses force. And in America, in a free country, you can do whatever you want. Free speech, I guess that's what it means.[28]

And finally, in the third stage, children are able to view the United States in relation to other countries.

In addition to encouraging a basic sense of national loyalty among children, elementary-school civics lessons emphasize the fact that it is the duty of every citizen to obey laws and figures of authority. Young children do not differentiate between rules laid down by their parents and those put forth by the government, but they learn at a very early age that it is important to obey all rules and that punishment of some sort is likely to follow any misdeed. In an interview with a third-grade girl the following exchange occurred:

"Well, what do you think about laws? Do you like them?"
"Well, it's for us to obey; it's for our safety. They're fair, and people who make them think of the people."
"Could there be bad laws?"
"I don't think there are any laws that would be cruel."[29]

It is interesting to note that, generally, the citizen's right to participate actively in politics, and his power to influence the government, are not stressed in the school curriculum until the fourth grade. And the matter of the citizen's right to participate is not given an equal emphasis with his duties (to obey all laws) until the eighth grade.[30]

---

[26] Hess and Torney, *The Development of Political Attitudes in Children*, p. 35.
[27] Hess and Torney, *The Development of Political Attitudes in Children*, p. 32.
[28] Hess and Torney, *The Development of Political Attitudes in Children*, p. 35.
[29] Hess and Torney, *The Development of Political Attitudes in Children*, p. 60.
[30] Hess and Torney, *The Development of Political Attitudes in Children*, pp. 126–127.

Furthermore, one study shows that the degree to which political participation is stressed in the school depends largely on the economic level and social class of the community in which the student lives. Edgar Litt reported that, in a comparison of civics programs in schools in three different communities in the Boston area, only the children in the schools in upper-middle-class communities were taught participation and conflict as part of politics. The lower-middle-class and working-class-community schools stressed the citizen's passive role in politics and emphasized the value of political harmony. As Litt said, ". . . students in the three communities are being trained to play different political roles and to respond to political phenomena in different ways."[31]

How long does the impact of the schools in the socialization process continue? While it is evident that the schools have a major impact on the process of socializing young children, research seems to indicate that much of the basic socialization of political attitudes takes place before the end of the elementary-school years. Although, clearly, students' political orientations are influenced by their studies after this time, the influence of the school on their attitudes declines rapidly after the eighth grade.[32]

Researchers debate the precise effect of high-school and college education on the political beliefs and behavior of students. A great many studies on this question indicate that there is a positive correlation between political orientation and years of education.[33] Such studies show that the level of education has a relationship to a person's sense of citizen duty and political efficacy, and also influences the extent of his psychological involvement and active participation in politics. However, recent studies indicate that the high-school civics curriculum has only limited impact—if, indeed, it has any—on the political beliefs, knowledge, and behavior of most students. These studies suggest that persons with more years of education tend to be more involved in politics because they are significantly different from persons with fewer years of education in other ways that affect their political attitudes.[34] In other words, it seems clear that most college-educated people have political attitudes that differ significantly from those of persons with only high-school educations. But it is not clear whether those extra years of education caused the college graduates to increase their political awareness and interest, or whether the persons who chose to attend college had already developed different political orientations, which were inculcated through means other than the schools.

Peer-group Influence

In addition to the influence of adults—notably, parents and teachers—children learn many social norms from their own peers. The influence of peer groups is particularly notable in terms of class status. For example, peer groups that are homogeneous in economic and social class tend to reinforce the political orientations and beliefs of that class. However, when peer groups are socially and eco-

---

[31] Edgar Litt, "Civics Education, Community Norms, and Political Indoctrination," *American Sociological Review*, vol. 28 (February 1963), pp. 69–75.

[32] Hess and Torney, *The Development of Political Attitudes in Children*, p. 131.

[33] See Key, *Public Opinion and American Democracy*, pp. 323–336.

[34] Kenneth P. Langton and M. Kent Jennings, "Political Socialization and the High School Civics Curriculum," *The American Political Science Review*, vol. 62 (September 1968), pp. 852–867.

nomically heterogeneous (as they often are in school), the working-class child is socialized toward the political norms of the middle class. Studies have shown that, in a heterogeneous peer group, the children from lower-income families are far more likely to defer to the opinions, and the leadership, of their higher-status peers in the group.[35]

Hess and Torney reported on the results of studies concerning the relationship between the degree of political interest and involvement of children and their membership in children's organizations—such as the YMCA, Scouts, school band, and so forth. They found that although politically involved children are, in fact, more likely to be members of groups (of both a political and a nonpolitical nature), children do not seem to acquire new political attitudes and beliefs from the act of participating in such groups.[36]

At later stages in the child's life, however, the influence of peer groups may increase. Theodore M. Newcomb's study of the changes in attitudes undergone by students at Bennington College has shown that the peer group, rather than the school itself, is the primary source of influence on the students' viewpoints. In referring to the Newcomb study, Robert A. Levine stated that peer groups have been clearly shown to be important shapers of student opinions, because it seemed evident from the study "that curriculum and faculty have little direct effect on student values at most colleges."[37]

The Socialization Process: An Overview

The socialization process in the United States clearly tends to build positive political images and attitudes among most children. Various sources cite countless examples of young children responding to queries by affirming that America is the "best" of all countries to live in, that the government exists to make laws which protect the citizens, and that the policemen are friendly and helpful gentlemen concerned almost exclusively with helping people. But these results were obtained largely from middle- and upper-middle-class white children. What about the other children?

Socialization and Subcultures A valid overview of the political-socialization process should recognize that there are significant exceptions to the positive images so easily absorbed by many white middle-class children. The subcultures generally considered to lie outside of the "normal" socialization process must also be considered. We shall consider here black children and poor children.

BLACK CHILDREN.   Schley R. Lyons reported on a study he made which compared children in an inner-city ghetto school with a control group of children in a more prosperous section of the same city. Eighty-three percent of the inner-city school children were black, while 92 percent of the control group children were white. Lyons found that the level of interest in the general subject of politics was almost identical in the two groups. However, he also discovered that, by age ten,

---

[35] Langton, *Political Socialization*, pp. 123–126.

[36] Hess and Torney, *The Development of Political Attitudes in Children*, pp. 137–143.

[37] Robert A. Levine, "American College Experience as a Socialization Process," in *College Peer Groups: Problems and Prospects for Research*, edited by Theodore M. Newcomb and Everett K. Wilson, (Chicago: Aldine, 1966), p. 117.

*If both her parents are Republicans,
she will probably be one, too.*

the children living in the slums were considerably more cynical about politics, and less sure of their own political efficacy, than were the children in the control group. In further studies, Lyons established again that black children were generally more cynical and tended to feel less politically effective than did white children, regardless of where they lived. In other words, relatively affluent black children had a more negative political outlook than did slum-dwelling white children.[38]

Edward S. Greenberg's study of the political socialization of black children in Philadelphia demonstrated, predictably, that "the 'normal' white pattern of patriotic leaning is not found in black children."[39] That is, white children, though they become more realistic and less idealistic about their government as they grow older, tend to retain a largely positive attitude toward local, state, and national

[38] Schley R. Lyons, "The Political Socialization of Ghetto Children: Efficacy and Cynicism," *Journal of Politics,* vol. 32 (May 1970), pp. 288–304.

[39] Edward S. Greenberg, "The Political Socialization of Black Children," in *Political Socialization,* edited by Edward S. Greenberg (New York: Atherton, 1970), p. 181.

governments. Black children also begin with an essentially positive view of the political world, as young children. But, between the third and ninth grades, the black child's opinion of government is seriously eroded. Older black children seem to retain a sense that the national government is important and basically benevolent, but they see this benevolence in terms of protecting the black community from essentially unhelpful state and, particularly, local governments. Again predictably, black children—whose youthful experience with law-enforcement agencies is likely to have been largely negative—have considerably less respect for the police than do white children.[40]

POOR CHILDREN.   Poor children, such as those in Appalachia, have much less positive attitudes toward politics in general than do more affluent children in other parts of the nation. In their study of Appalachian children, Dean Jaros and his co-workers pointed out that Appalachian children do not have highly positive views on politics at any stage in their development.

Moreover, the data indicate that the parents of Appalachian children have a great deal of influence on their children's political values, transmitting their own (largely negative) political feelings fairly directly to their offspring. Among Appalachian people, there is little feeling of parental authority; hence, little comparison is made between a child's father and the President, in contrast to the situation in more affluent families, in which the children generally see a strong resemblance between these two authority figures. Moreover, while in most other areas and situations children from father-absent families develop negative political evaluations (because of the absence of a strong, positive paternal role-model), Appalachian children from father-absent homes tend to have more favorable political views—presumably, because the child is receiving a less negative impression about the government.[41]

The Effects of Socialization   It is clear that the members of certain subcultures in our society do not learn the largely positive political attitudes acquired by the majority of Americans. Nevertheless, some observers maintain that the political-socialization process that exists in the United States has significant benefits: it reduces the possibility of conflict and contributes to the stability of the system. Others, however, argue that these effects of the socialization process are not necessarily desirable. As Fred I. Greenstein has stated,

> *To a considerable extent, political socialization seems to be conservative in its effects. Socialization processes foster the status quo through the perpetuation of class and sex differences in political participation, continuity between the generations in party preferences, continuation (and perhaps even strengthening) of adult assessments of the relative importance of political institutions.*[42]

Thus, although socialization seems to foster political continuity in the United States, it is a matter of judgment whether such continuity is an obstacle to desirable change.

---

[40] Greenberg, "The Political Socialization of Black Children," pp. 178–190.

[41] Dean Jaros, Herbert Hirsch, and Frederic J. Fleron, Jr., "The Malevolent Leader: Political Socialization in an American Sub-Culture," *American Political Science Review*, vol. 62 (June 1968), pp. 564–575.

[42] Fred I. Greenstein, *Children in Politics* (New Haven, Conn.: Yale University Press, 1965), p. 158.

Factors Affecting Opinions

Through the process of political socialization, a person acquires important and relatively permanent political values. But these values do not determine his opinions on particular issues. A number of factors influence the direction of public opinion, including place of residence, class status, ethnic background, and religion.

Place of Residence

A person's place of residence—the region in which he lives—is generally thought of as having a great deal to do with the kinds of opinions he will have, especially on political issues. The stereotyped images are that southerners are intolerant of new ideas, midwesterners are provincial in their overall outlook, easterners are extremely liberal, and so forth. But, in fact, "on most broad issues for which the data are available the mass of the people of all sections divide in approximately the same manner."[43] On more specific issues, however, it appears that region may still be an important factor. Thus, a recent Harris survey (see Table 10-1) showed that a greater proportion of residents in the South were opposed to the immediate integration of public schools than was the case in any other region of the country. Similarly, southerners and midwesterners were much less inclined to favor a coalition government in South Vietnam than were easterners and westerners.

Nevertheless, it is generally true that significant differences in political opinion based on place of residence are more closely related to community size than to region. And even differences between rural and urban opinions can be easily overstressed. People of all shades of opinion live in rural and urban areas. Only their averages in opinion are different; and on certain issues community size is not significantly related to public opinion at all.

However, studies have shown that residents of big cities tend to have the most "liberal" political opinions—that is, they support such issues as governmental action concerning matters like medical care or employment. Surprisingly, the most "conservative" opinions on these questions were found to exist among residents of small cities (with populations ranging from 10,000 to 50,000)—not, as might be expected, in rural areas.[44]

Class Status

A more generally recognized source of influence upon the political opinion of a person is his class status. Even though social classes are considerably less well defined and less important in the United States than they are, for example, in the European democracies, it appears that class status does have a significant impact on political opinion. However, it is always difficult to define a social class. Should we attempt to identify class in terms of some objective factor—such as level of income, education, or occupation? Or should class be defined by the subjective criterion of self-identification with a particular status? In spite of the difficulties involved, many political scientists conclude that the best criteria of class membership—that is, the ones most useful for the prediction of such things as political opinions—are the objective criteria of income, occupation, and education.

---

[43] Key, *Public Opinion and American Democracy*, p. 109.
[44] Key, *Public Opinion and American Democracy*, p. 112.

Table 10-1   **Harris Surveys Showing the Distribution of Political Opinion on Major Issues**

"The U.S. Supreme Court has ruled that public schools which are segregated must become integrated now without any further delay. In general, do you tend to approve or disapprove of this ruling for integration now by the U.S. Supreme Court?"

"Suppose the only way we could get peace in Vietnam were to agree to a coalition government which included the Communists in it. Would you favor or oppose such a coalition in Saigon?"

	Approve	Disapprove	Unsure		Favor	Oppose	Not Sure
Nationwide	55%	32%	13%	Nationwide	42%	39%	19%
By region:				*By region:*			
East	64	24	12	East	50	28	22
Midwest	53	32	15	Midwest	37	47	16
South	42	43	15	South	38	43	19
West	64	26	10	West	49	36	15
By race:				*By age:*			
White	53	34	13	18–29	47	39	14
Negro	69	16	15	30–49	46	38	16
By income:				50 and over	37	37	26
Under $5,000	48	35	17	*By race:*			
$5,000–9,999	53	35	12	Black	41	30	29
$10,000–14,999	56	32	12	White	43	40	17
$15,000+	69	24	7	*By income:*			
By 1968 vote:				Under $5,000	32	44	24
Nixon	52	34	14	$5,000–$9,999	40	40	20
Humphrey	67	19	14	$10,000–$14,999	45	39	16
Wallace	32	58	10	$15,000+	57	32	11

• Once social class has been defined, the implications it may have for American politics can be investigated. Research has shown that lower-status people tend to participate less in politics than higher-status people. This tendency holds true for relatively minor types of participation (such as voting, displaying a bumper sticker, or voicing a political opinion), as well as for major areas of participation (attending a political meeting, campaigning, or holding office). Some observers contend that the absence of lower-class participation in politics casts serious doubts on the efficacy of our democratic system, which is supposed to encourage, consider, and act upon the expression of all kinds of opinions, from all segments of society.

Class status, as seen in terms of occupational rank, has a significant effect on the direction of political opinion—that is, how "liberal" or "conservative" attitudes are. Traditionally, it has been assumed that the working class is less conservative than the middle and upper classes. The reasoning is that higher-status people have more of a vested interest in the existing system and therefore have far more to lose as a result of a significant change in the status quo. This assumption was validated primarily by evidence showing that a large proportion of workers vote for Democratic ("liberal") policies and candidates, while most upper-class people are ("conservative") Republicans. However, on taking a closer look at the matter, researchers have found that the direction of opinion of a given class varies, depending on the issue. On so-called "bread-and-butter" issues—economic questions which clearly center on improving the lot of the worker—lower-class groups do tend to be more "liberal" than the middle or upper classes. This is an understandable reaction, based primarily on self-interest. However, on other, more abstract issues, in which the benefits to the people are less readily apparent—such

Construction workers' demonstrations in support of the government's policies in Southeast Asia were a recent example of working-class "conservatism" on foreign affairs.

as foreign affairs or the defense of civil liberties—lower-class groups have tended to be more conservative.[45] The conservative attitude of the working class is evident, for example, in the large amount of support they gave to Governor George C. Wallace of Alabama in the 1972 presidential primaries. It is also revealed in widespread working-class opposition to the issue of busing school children in order to achieve racial integration in public schools, and especially on the question of improving job opportunities for blacks and other minority groups—due to white working-class fear that this will mean a loss in their own job security.

Ethnic Background

Continual references are still made, by optimistic but nearsighted civic leaders, to America as a "melting pot," in which immigrants from many different countries merge their life styles into the larger "American" culture. But recent events have indicated that members of most ethnic groups in this country are attempt-

[45] Key, *Public Opinion and American Democracy*, p. 150.

ing to find a new sense of their own identity—as Afro-Americans, Italian-Americans, Chinese-Americans. For these individuals, identification with their particular race and place of national origin has become a source of pride. Thus, the political opinions of many Americans today are tied up, to some extent at least, with their ethnic backgrounds. Generally, ethnic groups band together (engaging in practices such as "bloc" voting) only when a political issue or candidate emerges in which, or in whom, they have a particular interest.

For example, black city-dwellers are more likely to support a black candidate for mayor than a white candidate with equal qualifications. In fact, in recent years, a number of black mayors have been elected in large cities with heavily black populations—such as Newark, New Jersey; Cleveland, Ohio; and Gary, Indiana—because 95 percent of the black residents voted for the black candidate, while few whites did. Members of the Italian-American Civil Rights League have responded particularly favorably to public officials who help them de-emphasize the stereotyped association of many Italians, especially Sicilians, with the world of organized crime. Because politicians are aware of the effect of specifically racial- or ethnic-related issues in elections, particularly in those areas that have large numbers of residents from certain ethnic groups, special care is taken to put together a slate of candidates that will have "something for everyone"—an Italian, a black, an Irishman, and so forth—to appeal to the widest possible spectrum of voters.

Blacks are one of the most publicized of many groups that have formed political opinions along ethnic lines.

However, it is difficult to separate public opinion based on class status from that based on ethnic background. This is true because there is generally a correlation between class and ethnicity. Thus, except where specifically ethnic-related issues are involved, one cannot be certain which of the two factors has had a greater influence on the development of political viewpoints.

Religious Affiliation

To some extent, the same point can be made about the relationship of people's political opinions to their religious affiliations. It appears that Congregational, Presbyterian, and Episcopalian denominations are, as a rule, the most conservative religious groups, and the Jewish, Catholic, and Baptist groups are the most liberal. However, as in the case of ethnic background, this distinction seems to be based as much on class status as on religious affiliation. Generally, upper-class people of any religion tend to be more conservative on economic issues, and lower-class persons, no matter what their religious beliefs are, tend to be fairly liberal concerning economic policies. However, there are two major exceptions to this general rule. Many upper-class Jews are politically liberal on all issues, despite their class status; this is usually attributed to certain Jewish beliefs and experiences which place a high value on liberalism. The other notable exception is the tendency for upper-class Catholics to vote Democratic more often than the

When church and state collide on ethical questions, religious allegiance tends to preclude acceptance of the state position, as in Catholics' stand against recent laws legalizing abortion.

upper-class population at large. Although this tendency has not yet been explained, it is thought that most Catholic immigrants to the United States, predominantly from Italy, Ireland, and Poland, came to this country at a time of strong Democratic control in urban areas. Therefore, they tended to identify themselves as Democrats as well as Americans. And the descendants of these immigrants inherited their parents' Democratic party affiliation along with their religion and their sense of national origin.

Again, it should be emphasized that, class status aside, when a particular issue is viewed in religious terms, people are likely to take sides according to their religious beliefs—as, during the Second World War, when Jews gave their support to those politicians who responded quickly and strongly against Nazism. Similarly, many Catholics undoubtedly voted for John Kennedy simply because he was a Catholic.

Public Opinion and the Mass Media

In a nation such as ours, where virtually every citizen has constant and easy access to television and radio broadcasting, newspapers, and magazines, public opinion is obviously influenced to a significant extent by the mass media. However, the precise effect of the media on our political views and activities is not known.[46] Sometimes it seems that the media's influence has been grossly exaggerated. For example, it has been suggested for years that many big-city newspapers (notably the *Chicago Tribune*) have little effect on the politics of the cities in which they are published. And it is a well-documented fact that few people watch television news editorials, or read political endorsements in newspapers or magazines. On the other hand, some people say that the media have created "instant leaders"—such as Stokeley Carmichael and Abbie Hoffman—and that the media may have even encouraged the student riots of the 1960's, with student rioters taking over a dean's office in the morning and then running home to see themselves on the six-o'clock news that night. While it is unclear just how much influence the media do exercise in our society, many people have questioned the wisdom with which the media exercise their power.

Criticisms Raised against the Media

Criticism of our news media is hardly a recent development. Since the founding of the nation, the media have been the target of various kinds of attacks from many different segments of society.

Thomas Jefferson, a stout defender of the freedom of the press, bewailed its "falsehoods and errors." Succeeding Presidents—Abraham Lincoln, both Roosevelts, Dwight Eisenhower (who delivered a memorably intemperate attack on "sensation-seeking columnists and commentators" in the 1964 G.O.P. convention), John Kennedy (who once, in a huff at what he considered biased reportage, canceled the White House subscription to the late New York Herald Tribune*), Lyndon Johnson and Richard Nixon (whose notorious blast at newsmen in 1962, following his gubernatorial defeat in California, still*

---

[46] Nelson W. Polsby, "Political Science and the Press: Notes on Coverage of a Public Opinion Survey on the Vietnam War," *Western Political Quarterly,* vol. 22, no. 1 (March 1969), pp. 47–60.

haunts his relationship with the Washington press corps)—all regarded the media with more or less baleful eyes.[47]

Recent attacks from high-level politicians, notably the colorful speeches of Vice President Agnew, have emphasized three basic criticisms of the media: their commercialism, their high level of concentration, and their political bias.

Commercialism   In our economic system, where the media, in the main, are privately owned and therefore depend on selling their products, commercialism is unavoidable. This can be seen particularly well in the area of television news broadcasting, where the show-business appeal of personalities such as Walter Cronkite, Harry Reasoner, Eric Sevareid, and David Brinkley is sometimes more important in attracting viewers than the content of their reports. Moreover, the media, in general, pay less attention to national and international political events than they might. Rather than stressing news items, most weekly magazines emphasize colorful social and cultural affairs, exciting sports events, and other items of popular interest.

Television coverage of the news is severely limited, most of the prime-time slots being taken up with variety shows, situation comedies, and reruns of old movies. In light of the current ownership and control of television broadcasting, the lack of emphasis even on important news stories and editorial discussion is understandable. Television is, after all, a highly commercial industry which feels that in order to survive it must cater to the viewing tastes of the mass of the American people and advance whatever helps promote the sponsor's prosperity. And clearly, as has been shown by countless surveys, polls, and personal observation, most people are not terribly interested in politics. The results of a recent Gallup poll conducted for *Newsweek* magazine supports this contention: in general, "More than two out of three people were satisfied with the amount of news they were getting from the media. . . ."[48]

And yet, we must also take into account the success of such programs as the NBC "White Paper" specials on specific political and social problems, or the CBS program "60 Minutes," which presents shorter analyses of several different problems. Such successes seem to indicate that the interest of a fairly large proportion of the American public—many more people than had been assumed—can be stimulated.

Concentration   The issue of concentration—that is, the continued recent decline in the number of newspapers being published in the United States, along with an increase in joint ownership of newspapers or of various other means of mass communication—is an extremely important one. The trend toward an increasingly limited number of newspaper information sources is pronounced. Most of the nation's newspapers—well over 80 percent—receive most of their national and world news from only two wire services, the Associated Press (AP), and United Press International (UPI). Since 1910, the number of daily newspapers has declined consistently and drastically—as local papers went bankrupt because of rising costs, or as independent papers merged with one of the large newspaper

---

[47] *Newsweek,* "The People and the Press" (November 9, 1970), p. 22.
[48] *Newsweek,* "The People and the Press," p. 23.

chains. Today, almost half of our daily newspapers are owned by chains. Moreover, many companies that once specialized in a particular form of communication have grown into mammoth conglomerates that own and operate countless other businesses, including other media. For example, Time, Inc., now owns *Time, Life,* and *Sports Illustrated* magazines, along with numerous other firms—including several book publishing companies. And CBS owns the New York Yankees baseball team, the publishing firm of Holt, Rinehart and Winston, and many other assets—besides the various branches of CBS.

However, according to a 1970 Gallup poll, a large segment of the American people seem satisfied with the way in which the media are owned or run.[49] Sixty-four percent of the sample stated that they approved of the existence of newspaper chains (joint ownership of many papers by a single company). Half the people approving of chains agreed that a chain should be allowed to control broadcasting stations. And 41 percent supported the joint ownership of a newspaper and a television station in a city with only one newspaper.

Political Bias Apparently, the American public is not overly concerned about the increasing commercialism and concentration in our media. But the question of political bias in the media is a subject for more heated debate. While it is doubtful that such a thing as a completely unbiased newspaper, television program, or person could exist, there is a very real possibility that the political bias of the admittedly small number of people controlling the media can greatly influence the kind of news that gets reported. For example, the news media can prevent "the other side" from receiving fair exposure—by deciding which things will be covered in the evening news broadcasts, and which will be omitted—and it can determine the emphasis placed on, and the amount of time allotted to, particular news events. Biased presentation of the news may well have a negative impact on democracy—for open information is basic to any democratic government.

---

[49] *Newsweek,* "The People and the Press," p. 23.

Table 10-2   **Left or Right?**

Which point of view do you think is treated more fairly in the media?

	Newspapers by Readers	TV News by Viewers	Newsmagazines by Readers	Radio News by Listeners
Conservative	13%	8%	14%	9%
Liberal	22%	25%	21%	15%
Both equal	50%	52%	51%	52%
Don't know	15%	15%	13%	23%

Source: Newsweek, *"The People and the Press" (November 9, 1970), p. 24.*

In the previously cited Gallup poll, a large number of people said that they believed the owners of the media are conservative, and hence that their news reporting and editorials had a definite conservative bias. On the other hand, a large number of people also thought that the media are slanted, but toward a too-liberal position. Vice President Agnew is clearly one of those who feels that the media are run by a small group of leftists. In one of his famous attacks on television commentators, Agnew referred to them as "a tiny, enclosed fraternity of privileged men," and later dismissed them as the "super-sensitive, self-anointed, supercilious electronic barons of opinion."[50]

Nevertheless, the majority of the people seem to feel that both the conservative and liberal sides of political issues are treated fairly in the media, as indicated in Table 10-2. Among the minority who thought that the media were biased, pro-liberal bias was a more prevalent complaint than pro-conservative bias. The Gallup poll also pointed out that the people who are most critical about bias and inaccuracy in the press are those who are better educated and better informed about politics.

The Influence of Mass Media

In view of these criticisms, and the fundamental role of the media in a democracy, an important question is raised: To what extent are people really influenced by what they read or what they watch on television? Are their opinions really manipulated to the extent that many critics maintain?

The evidence collected thus far on this question is mixed. For example, it is true that many successful candidates for public office have received extensive support from the media. But no definite cause-and-effect relationship has been established between the political opinions expressed in the media and the voting behavior of the public. In fact, many candidates—including Mayors Richard Daley of Chicago and Frank Rizzo of Philadelphia—have won elections in spite of heavy opposition by the press.

While the degree of influence exercised by the media on public opinion has yet to be established, there are clearly a number of factors which significantly limit its impact. For one thing, not many people are careful followers of political events of any sort—whether local school budget cuts or presidential elections. Hence,

---

[50] Newsweek, "The People and the Press," p. 22.

most people are unaffected by whatever biases the media may express or can exert. Secondly, those people who are followers of political events tend to be selective in what they read or view—that is, they look at those presentations that agree with their viewpoints, and avoid those that disagree. In the summer of 1970, Fred W. Grupp conducted a series of studies on the frequency with which political activists (in this case, members of the conservative John Birch Society and the liberal Americans for Democratic Action) watched and listened to news broadcasts during a period of relative political calm (between national elections). Grupp found that the activists' level of newscast avoidance increased as their dissatisfaction with the political events being reported increased. That is, the subjects were attentive to news broadcasts only when they dealt with events and policies with which they agreed. Grupp further found that, in cases of dissatisfaction, television news coverage is more likely to be avoided than radio broadcasting—primarily because television presents a far more detailed, immediate, and graphic account of events.[51]

Another factor which tends to limit the impact of the media on public opinion is the two-step nature of information transmission—that is, from the media to opinion leaders (politicians, executives, and other influential figures), and then to opinion followers (the mass of the public). This two-step theory has been fully discussed by Joseph T. Klapper. Klapper suggested that whatever potential influences the media might have are largely neutralized by interpersonal influences—at home, in school, at work; therefore, media impact is indirect and weak.[52]

Finally, the effect of the media on people's political opinions is also limited by the healthy tendency of the public to be suspicious of what they read, see, and hear in the media. Of the subjects questioned in the Gallup survey, four out of five had heard of Vice President Agnew's criticism of the press. Forty-two percent of those people agreed with the Vice President; 53 percent felt that some viewpoints were not being covered adequately in news reportage; and 51 percent could recall some news event which they felt had been treated unfairly by the media.[53] An individual's suspicion of the news media increases in cases where he has actually witnessed or taken part in a given event which he later finds has been reported unfairly in the media.

Interaction between Political Leadership and Mass Opinion

According to one researcher,

All governments must concern themselves with public opinion. They do not maintain their authority by brute force alone; they must seek willing acceptance and conformity from most of their citizens. Popular government has its peculiarities, one of which is the basis for the exercise of its authority: that governors shall seek out popular opinion, that they shall give it weight, if not the determinative voice in decision, and that persons outside the government have a right to be heard.[54]

---

[51] Fred W. Grupp, Jr., "Newscast Avoidance Among Political Activists," *Public Opinion Quarterly*, vol. 34 (Summer 1970), pp. 262–266.

[52] Joseph T. Klapper, *The Effects of Mass Communication* (New York: The Free Press, 1960).

[53] *Newsweek*, "The People and the Press," p. 25.

[54] Key, *Public Opinion and American Democracy*, p. 412.

In order for this system of mutual influence to function properly, the interaction between our political leadership and public opinion must be two-way. The government, through the dissemination of information and its attempts at persuasion (using various means of propaganda, such as speeches and television broadcasts), tries to influence public opinion and gain public approval for the political course it intends to pursue. The public, in turn, having been influenced by the government and other sources of information and persuasion, transmits its opinion back to the political leaders – through polls, letter-writing, participation in interest groups, mass demonstrations, and voting. There are times when the force of public opinion in a particular case can exert a strong influence on our policy-makers; in other situations, the government will disregard the public's expression of a certain viewpoint. The basic question regarding this interaction is, How powerful is the influence in either direction? Is the influence primarily from leader to the public, or is it the other way around?

The Impact of Political Leaders on Public Opinion

Examples of the impact of political leaders on public opinion can be found in various branches of government. Of course, the President is in a position of unparalleled potential influence. He can call a press conference or give speeches on radio and television virtually whenever he chooses. Formal speeches are broadcast by heads of state in many countries (the Pope's addresses are broadcast from the Vatican, and Queen Elizabeth's annual Christmas message reaches the British people everywhere), but only in America does the President indulge in the public debate generally characteristic of the press conference.[55]

Theodore Roosevelt should perhaps be credited with originating the presidential press conference, with the informal talks he held with favorite reporters while shaving or eating. During World War I, President Wilson established a routine of regular conferences with the White House press corps; and FDR, because he was extremely close to the press, held informal sessions in his office twice a week. The presidential press conference, however, reached the height of spontaneity with Kennedy's live TV coverage of all his conferences. Since Kennedy, press conferences have been somewhat less frequent, with President Nixon holding fewer press talks during his first twenty months in office than any President since Hoover – about one every seven weeks.[56]

The personality of an individual President has an important impact on the frequency and the type of media broadcasts he employs; but the character of his administration is also influential. An administration which introduces few pieces of new and important legislation, and under which foreign involvements and domestic unrest are negligible, will have less need for utilizing the kinds of public broadcasting that a President in times of great crisis will typically use.

Federal bureaucrats have much less access to the means of mass communications than does the President, but every federal agency has a staff and some program for disseminating information. Of course, not all of these programs are designed specifically to influence public opinion. Some of the publicity material

[55] See Elmer E. Cornwell, Jr., *Presidential Leadership of Public Opinion* (Bloomington, Ind.: Indiana University Press, 1966).

[56] Jules Witcover, "Salvaging the Presidential Press Conference," *Columbia Journalism Review,* vol. 9 (Fall 1970), pp. 27–34.

Friends of President Lyndon B. Johnson claimed that TV press-conference coverage failed to convey Johnson's openness and geniality.

released by governmental agencies is simply factual material, such as census figures, announcements of decisions reached in certain cases, or the results of scientific research. These essentially informational publicity releases may help indirectly to change people's opinions. Often, however, certain officials and agencies try to influence public opinion openly. The Secretary of State, for example, may give a series of speeches to explain and attract support for a particular aspect of foreign policy. And, of late, the military has been particularly active in trying to reshape its image, to encourage the public to approve of military spending and activities. One estimate of the Pentagon's annual budget for self-advertisement is $190 million; this figure, however, is in sharp disagreement with the Pentagon's own estimate of $30 million.[57]

Congressmen also try to engender support for their activities, by sending out newsletters, having open meetings with their constituents, and publicizing their activities in the legislature by other similar means. Most of this information is straightforward reporting of a congressman's position on a particular issue. Occasionally, however, the information that a citizen receives from his representative or senator may involve a slight bending of the truth. Paul N. McCloskey, representative from California and unsuccessful contender for the Republican presidential nomination in 1972, made the following comment concerning the dissemination of information from legislator to the public:

[57] "Unmasking the Pentagon," *Newsweek* (March 8, 1971), p. 7.

The Congressional Record, *which purports to be a true rendering of congressional proceedings, is not that at all. Each Congressman and Senator is allowed to "revise and extend" his remarks at the end of each legislative day after having seen his actual spoken words in print. It is not uncommon for members to have second thoughts on their original utterances and thus to eliminate them or rewrite their role in actual House or Senate proceedings. Through seeking permission at the beginning of each day's legislative business "to revise and extend my remarks and to include extraneous matter," a legislator may later insert page after page of material leaving the impression that he made an impassioned speech on one burning issue or another when in truth he has not. If he wishes to carry his deception to the* nth *degree, he may then mail—postage free—that non-speech to his constituency.*[58]

Regardless, however, of such occasional distortions, all these forms of influence are, to some degree, essential. The army quite logically chooses to advertise itself as a newer, less rigid, more career-oriented organization, in order to bolster the falling rate of enlistment. An administration seeks to gain popular approval of a new program. A congressman attempts to elicit sufficient public support to pass a bill that he considers particularly important. However, a nation in which public opinion is merely a malleable substance, to be molded by political leaders for their own ends, is no longer a democratic system. Thus, it is important to investigate the extent to which our government manipulates public opinion.

In the United States, important limits are placed on the power of political leaders to control public opinion. For example, our officials do not have a monopoly on the dissemination of information; citizens are exposed to a diversity of opposing viewpoints, both public and private. For instance, although the government may well exert a significant influence in trying to justify the expense entailed by a new defense program, the public will also be exposed to opposite influences— from senators and congressmen opposed to the project, from peace groups protesting all military activities, and from numerous other sources, including the mass media.

Nevertheless, although the government has very real limitations on its power, its strength is still great enough to weight the battle heavily in its favor when an individual or a group disagrees with national policy.

The Impact of Public Opinion on Political Leaders

Yet public opinion also travels in the opposite direction—public officials are influenced by the political viewpoints of the mass public. Various institutionalized processes—the activities of interest groups and political parties, and the process of voting—are the primary channels through which the public influences its political leaders. These processes, which work on a long-range basis, are the topics of the following chapters in Part 3 of this book.

On a day-to-day basis, political leaders keep in touch with public opinion through citizen mail and through professional public-opinion polls, which have become extremely significant in recent years. The evidence indicates that polls often have a definite influence on political leaders. For example, it is widely believed that Lyndon Johnson's decision not to run for another term as President was influenced by the polls, as well as by the large-scale demonstrations held in opposition to his foreign policy, and the strong support given to Eugene McCarthy. Simi-

[58] Paul N. McCloskey, Jr., *Truth and Untruth: Political Deceit in America* (New York: Simon and Schuster, 1972), pp. 106–107.

larly, George Romney decided to drop out of the 1968 Republican presidential race on the basis of the poor showings he had had in the public-opinion polls, as did Edmund Muskie and John Lindsay in 1972.

In recent years, candidates for political office have watched the polls closely, because it is widely believed that polls tend to be an accurate reflection of public preferences. Opinion polls have become particularly important in predicting presidential elections. Recently, however, many critics suggest that the overuse and misuse of polls—especially early statewide polls taken before presidential primaries—are having a negative effect on our political system.

During the 1972 presidential primary elections, for example, six weeks before the vote in New Hampshire, a major Boston newspaper, the *Boston Globe*, published a poll that gave Senator Edmund Muskie of Maine 65 percent of the vote, with Senator George McGovern of South Dakota receiving only 18 percent. But, in the actual voting on March 7, Muskie received only 46 percent of the vote, and McGovern 37 percent. The effects of this discrepancy between projected and actual results were many and serious. First, the original estimate—of a 65-to-18 voting spread—made Muskie's actual performance appear much worse, and McGovern's much better, than they actually were. Even though there was no proof that Muskie *ever* held 65 percent of the vote in New Hampshire, his 46-percent return was widely regarded as a setback, a loss of support. And, as some observers have pointed out, in a political contest such as this, "the winner isn't necessarily the one with the most votes but the candidate who does better than expected. And expectations are built on polls."[59]

The already confused Democratic primary situation has been made even more chaotic by the announcement of contradictory poll results, many of which prove to have little relationship to the voting patterns of the people being polled. Polls become self-fulfilling prophecies in an important way: a candidate who consistently does poorly in the polls is likely to lose financial contributions to his campaign—for people are usually unwilling to "throw their money away on a loser," even when it is not certain that the candidate will lose.

Although the effects of polls have sometimes been criticized, the nationwide Gallup or Harris polls taken during the final presidential races have proved remarkably accurate in recent years, as survey techniques have become more and more sophisticated. In general—and particularly discounting surveys taken from a limited sample of people or a long time before the actual voting takes place—polls do frequently serve as a reliable indication of public-opinion trends on candidates and issues.

Assessing the impact of mass opinion on political leaders is thus not an easy task. Some observers believe that political leaders have a broad range of discretion in making policy decisions. For instance, as V. O. Key has pointed out, it seems clear that

> . . . *a wide range of discretion exists for whatever wisdom leadership echelons can muster in the public service. The generality of public preferences, the low intensity of the opinions of many people, the low level of political animosities of substantial sectors of the public, the tortuousness of the process of translation of disapproval of specific policies into electoral reprisal, and many other factors point to the existence of a wide latitude for the exercise of creative leadership.*[60]

[59] *Atlantic Monthly*, "Primaries and Opinion Polls" (May 1972), p. 8.
[60] Key, *Public Opinion and American Democracy*, p. 555.

Key's view seems to be substantiated by some of the evidence presented in the discussion of Congress in Chapter 6, where it was indicated that most congressmen could vote pretty much as they liked on many issues, as long as they did not defy their constituent's opinions concerning those issues on which there was a high degree of interest and consensus. Moreover, a leader can promise the public one thing and deliver another—Lyndon Johnson won the 1964 presidential election largely on the basis of a campaign pledge of nonescalation of United States activity in Vietnam; his victory presumably indicated that the majority of the public desired decreased American involvement in that war, but Johnson actually increased the extent of our involvement, on all levels. Thus, at times, a political leader may find it expedient or necessary to disregard an expressed public opinion.

However, other political analysts emphasize the fact that public opinion does set the broad limits within which political leaders can act. For example, a President would never entertain the thought of abolishing the present Social Security system, because public opinion would be too overwhelmingly in favor of maintaining it. Similarly, several Presidents were afraid of removing J. Edgar Hoover from his influential position as Director of the FBI, because public opinion so strongly supported him. Hoover was not replaced until he died, in May of 1972. In an extreme case, the force of public opinion might even be strong enough to unseat a political leader responsible for pursuing a highly unpopular policy.

SUGGESTED READING

Dawson, Richard E., and Kenneth Prewitt. *Political Socialization* (Boston: Little, Brown, 1969). In paperback. A discussion of the purposes, processes, and agents involved in the process of political socialization in the United States.

Free, Lloyd A., and Hadley Cantril. *The Political Beliefs of Americans* (New Brunswick, N.J.: Rutgers University Press, 1967). In paperback. A study based on extensive sampling of public opinion. Authors analyze public opinion in the United States, including opinions on specific issues as well as attitudes toward the political system in general.

Gallup, George, and Saul Forbes Rae. *The Pulse of Democracy: The Public-Opinion Poll and How it Works* (New York: Greenwood Press, 1968). Describes the development of polls in America, analyzes numerous polling techniques, and discusses the problems that face those who administer the polls. The authors argue that opinion surveys fill a real need in the existing structures of democracy insofar as they provide a channel for opinions to reach leaders.

Greenberg, Edward S., (ed.). *Political Socialization* (New York: Atherton, 1970). In paperback. Collection of essays covering diverse aspects of political socialization in the United States, including discussions of those groups largely excluded from the normal socialization process.

Greenstein, Fred I. *Children and Politics* (New Haven: Yale University Press, 1965). In paperback. An analysis of the political socialization of American elementary-school children. The author examines children's feelings toward political authority, the development of their political information and partisan identification, the relationship between social class and political learning, sex differences in political learning, and change and continuity over the years in children's political beliefs.

Hess, Robert D., and Judith U. Torney, *The Development of Political Attitudes in Children* (Garden City, N.Y.: Doubleday/Anchor, 1968). In paperback. A comprehensive study of the political attitudes, values, and beliefs of elementary school children.

Key, V. O., Jr. *Public Opinion and American Democracy* (New York: Knopf, 1961). The author discusses the distribution, properties, and formation of opinions, as well as how government affects the form and content of public opinion, and how public opinion may influence the manner, content, and timing of government action.

Lane, Robert E. *Political Ideology: Why the American Common Man Believes What He Does* (New York: Free Press, 1962). In paperback. Analysis of three aspects of political ideology: the latent political ideology of the American urban common man, the sources of this ideology, the way in which his ideology supports or weakens the institutions of democracy.

———. *Political Life: Why and How People Get Involved in Politics* (New York: Free Press, 1959). In paperback. In a comprehensive view of popular participation in American democracy, the author examines three kinds of phenomena: the political behavior of the American public, the attitudes and personality traits related to this behavior, and the environmental influences which affect political participation.

Lane, Robert E., and David O. Sears. *Public Opinion* (Englewood Cliffs, N.J.: Prentice-Hall, 1964). An examination and analysis of the formation of public opinion: the choice of group loyalties and identification, the choice of leaders, and views on public issues. The authors outline the nature of public opinion, discuss its formation, and analyze certain problems.

Langton, Kenneth P. *Political Socialization* (New York: Oxford University Press, 1969). In paperback. Overview of the influence of different social agencies in the process of political socialization. Includes data from several societies, but primary focus is on the United States.

Lippmann, Walter. *Public Opinion* (New York: The Free Press, 1965; originally published in 1922). Basic work on public opinion in the United States and its impact on government.

Milbrath, Lester W. *Political Participation* (Chicago: Rand McNally, 1971). In paperback. An analysis of how and why people become involved in politics.

Rosenau, James N. *Public Opinion and Foreign Policy* (New York: Random House, 1961). In paperback. A brief analysis of the relationship between public opinion and foreign policies, focusing on the role of opinion-makers.

11
INTEREST GROUPS AND THE POLITICAL PROCESS

As far back as Jackson's administration, a century and a half ago, the European observer Alexis de Tocqueville, much impressed by the tendency of Americans to form groups for a particular purpose, wrote:

As soon as several of the inhabitants of the United States have taken up an opinion or feeling they wish to promote in the world, they look out for mutual assistance; and as soon as they have found one another out, they combine. From that moment they are no longer isolated men, but a power seen from afar, whose actions serve for an example and whose language is listened to.[1]

The United States has changed enormously since de Tocqueville's visit, yet the tendency to form groups is stronger than ever. As many have observed, we seem indeed to be a "nation of joiners."[2] There are organizations for liberals and organizations for conservatives. There are societies to represent every conceivable sport and hobby—some, like the National Rifle Association, assuming national importance. And there are societies to promote the interests of nearly every national, racial, religious, and occupational group. The smallest minority has an organization to represent it. Somewhere there may even be a society for people who do not believe in joining societies.

David B. Truman, writing on the dynamics of interest-group behavior, defined a *group* as a collection of people who "interact with some frequency on the basis of their shared characteristics."[3] A group does not become an *interest group*, however, unless it has a particular goal that affects other members of society, and unless it takes steps to achieve that goal. Such a group, having specific shared attitudes, "makes certain claims on other groups in the society for the establishment, maintenance, or enhancement of forms of behavior that are implied by the shared attitudes."[4] The term *pressure group* is often used to designate an interest group whose principal reason for existence is to persuade government to act in support of its goals. Since government becomes involved in issues that affect the lives of everyone, it is the rare interest group that is not at least occasionally a pressure group.

Interest Groups and American Politics

Why is group activity so widespread in the United States? Why do groups grow and proliferate? Some groups, like the family, the neighborhood, the community, are not "political" associations at all; yet they foster strong loyalties and attitudes from which "issue groups" emerge. Many observers believe that groups proliferate as society and government grow more diverse and specialized. In other words, they may be seen as an attempt to cope with increased political complexity, an attempt made by groups of citizens who wish to protect and promote their own interests against those of competing groups.

The very nature of the American political system makes it responsive to pressures from interest groups. It is fertile ground for widespread group activity for three reasons: concern for constituency interests and support, the diffusion of political power, and the American party structure.

---

[1] Alexis de Tocqueville, *Democracy in America,* vol. II (New York: Vintage, 1945), pp. 117–118.

[2] Arthur M. Schlesinger, "Biography of a Nation of Joiners," *American Historical Review,* vol. 50 (1944), p. 1.

[3] David B. Truman, *The Governmental Process* (New York: Knopf, 1951), p. 24.

[4] Truman, *The Governmental Process,* p. 33.

Constituency Interest and the Politician

Political leaders in America cannot afford to ignore public opinion or the necessity for public support. Since a high percentage of government officials are elected rather than appointed, they must give some measure of consideration to the moods and concerns of the various interests that make up their constituencies. A political leader, perpetually facing the problem of reelection, is very much aware of the value of keeping important interest groups happy. As Abraham Holtzman puts it: "Because interest groups endeavor to make certain that the opinions of their publics are articulated, such groups fit legitimately into the framework of concern for public opinion within which public decision-makers operate."[5]

Diffusion of Political Power

The more centralized a government is, the greater the difficulty for interest groups to gain access to decision-makers. In the highly centralized political system of the Soviet Union, for example, interest-group activity is extremely limited. In contrast, the diffusion of political power in the United States makes for a great many channels of access to decision-makers, not only at the federal level but also at state and local levels. As a result, an interest group can work at one or more levels of government, according to its needs. Real-estate interests, for example, are more likely to concentrate at the state and local levels, since most legislation concerning property is enacted there; large manufacturing groups, on the other hand, will tend to focus on the federal level for the same reason. And if it fails at one level, an interest group may reorganize its forces and begin again at another. Moreover, fledgling groups, by working at local or state levels, can gain valuable experience for the more complex and demanding job of influencing the federal government.

The separation of powers within the various branches of government, and the system of checks and balances, are other factors that make it easier for interest groups to exert pressure on American politics. In both national and state governments, power is divided among the Executive, Legislative, and Judicial branches, with each branch acting as a check on the other two. As a result, if an interest group is not successful in the Congress, it may turn to the bureaucrats charged with enforcing the laws to try to get favorable action; if this effort fails too, they may still turn to the courts.

American Party Structure

Political parties in the United States, as noted in Chapter 6, are subject to much inner dissension and cannot maintain absolute control over the behavior of their members. Studies of American political parties have shown, moreover, that party leaders in Congress, as a rule, do not exert strong disciplinary power over congressional party members. Congressmen frequently disagree with party policies without fear of reprisal, when these policies conflict with the special interests of their constituencies. In general, the most severe punishment party leaders inflict on recalcitrant legislators is to hinder access to positions of influence. This lack of discipline makes for a very loose party structure, favoring the activity of interest groups.

---

[5] Abraham Holtzman, *Interest Groups and Lobbying* (New York: Macmillan, 1966), p. 58.

The additional fact that American political parties are not strongly ideological also facilitates access to government by interest groups. Interest groups are willing to work with and give support to either party; even those groups which predominantly favor one of the two political parties, do not hesitate to work with the other when it is in office. Thus, labor unions are closely allied with the Democrats, and the National Association of Manufacturers with the Republicans, but both groups are quite willing to cooperate with officials from the opposite party when it is to their advantage.

Interest-Group Power

The term *influence peddler* periodically comes to public attention, as in the 1950s when congressional investigators probed into some of the seamier aspects of lobbying, and the headlines gave fresh ammunition to muckrakers. Traditionally, pressure groups have often been viewed as representative of powerful, selfish interests unconcerned with the public and, at their worst, a source of spreading corruption. The Founding Fathers decried factions, fearing they would use government to their own ends. In *The Federalist*, No. 10, James Madison nevertheless saw them as the inevitable result of the diversity of interests within American society. Because factions could not be prevented, he argued, they required control by the Legislature.

The traditional view of interest groups as obstructive to public interest has been buttressed over the years by journalistic exposés. For example, in 1913 the National Association of Manufacturers was accused by one of its own lobbyists of widespread bribery in Congress and unfair intervention in politics and elections—charges that two years of congressional investigation failed to fully substantiate. In another major scandal during the 1920s—the Teapot Dome scandal—a number of major oil companies paid several hundred thousand dollars to Secretary of the Interior Albert Fall in order to obtain rights to lucrative oil reserves at Teapot Dome, Wyoming. Wrote one newspaper editor concerning the era: "The story of Babylon is a Sunday school story compared with the story of Washington. . . ."[6] In more recent times, scandals continue to flare up periodically. In 1958, the press carried banner headlines about gifts from the broadcasting industry to members of the Federal Communications Commission, and, later, about the vicuña overcoat and oriental rugs accepted by Sherman Adams, assistant to President Eisenhower, from industrialist Bernard Goldfine. Both scandals helped sustain the image of large interests as unscrupulous. In 1972, another tempest was stirred up by political columnist Jack Anderson when he revealed a memo allegedly written by a lobbyist for International Telephone & Telegraph which promised a four-hundred-thousand–dollar contribution to the Republican party in exchange for an abandonment of antitrust efforts against ITT by the Justice Department under the Nixon administration.

But there is another side to the picture of interest groups, fostered by political scientists, who take the pluralist position that democracy depends upon the effective expression of diverse interests made possible by interest-group politics. In the period after World War II, most political scientists were, in fact, convinced that group activity was the central force in American politics. The

[6] Morton Bordon, *The American Profile* (Lexington, Mass.: Heath, 1970), p. 234.

pluralist argument holds that diverse groups are beneficial because their activity safeguards democracy by dispersing power in society and maintaining a balance among conflicting interests. Like Madison, who would not deprive factions of liberty lest it be lost to all men, the pluralists have seen interest groups as an expression of freedom of association guaranteed by the Constitution. In addition, some argue that people unattached to an interest group are a disoriented mass, susceptible to demagogic appeals.

In reply to the charge that major interest groups possess unbridled power, pluralists contend that the influence of any single group or type of group is significantly restrained by the tendency of most people to belong to more than one group. This "overlapping membership" produces "cross-pressuring" in the individual—compelling him to make a choice between the aims of his different organizations. The freedom of members to make such choices prevents organizations from achieving the degree of cohesion they need to exert a controlling hand in the governmental decision-making process. The basic idea of a pluralist democracy is thus carried out: in a society where groups are continually in conflict, no single group is able to gain complete control.

In addition, pluralist theory holds that the latent power of "potential groups" also serves as a restraint against dominance by any single interest; in a democracy, powerful groups that go too far may arouse a public opinion that becomes organized and aggressive. Finally, there is the argument that pressure-group politics is essentially an open system and allows considerable room for change— one of the major reasons that group activity, all things considered, has acted as a workable means to achieve responsive government.

Today's political scientists, however, have raised some important issues concerning the impact of interest-group politics on the individual member, on the nature of public policy, and on the quality of leadership. They ask such questions as:

Do organized groups really represent the various kinds of interests in American society? Or do they, in fact, prevent "potential groups" from forming to act upon unrepresented grievances?

Do some groups have greater access than others to government, and, if so, why?

Do the leaders of groups accurately represent the diverse interests of members, or do the leaders of most groups pursue their own separate interests?

And, finally, do the powerful interest groups support movements for reform, or are they essentially conservative and dedicated to preserving the status quo?

The narrow basis of interests upon which the organized group is formed raises other questions—whether they encourage conformity, discrimination, and the judgment of political issues from the view of self-interest rather than the good of society in general. Later in this chapter we shall deal with such questions in more detail, for a deeper understanding of the role of group interaction in contemporary American politics.

Some Major Interest Groups in the United States

Interest groups in America are of many types and may be compared in several ways. Some are organized tightly, some loosely, and still others are merely "potential" groups. They may also be compared on the basis of their overall purpose; thus, some groups are specifically organized to influence public policy or advance a particular cause, such as the John Birch Society, the Southern Christian Leadership Conference, the Congress of Racial Equality, the Daughters of the American Revolution, the Americans for Democratic Action, and the League of Women Voters. There are other groups whose manifest purpose is not political, although they engage in lobbying activities, as, for example, the National Association of Manufacturers, the American Farm Bureau Federation, the American Medical Association, and Parent-Teacher Associations.

Groups may also be compared on the scope of their interests. Thus, the members of some groups share broad economic, ethnic, or occupational interests and take positions on a variety of issues. Other groups, however, such as antiwar groups or the American League to Abolish Capital Punishment are based on the sharing of a basic attitude or a particular position on a single issue. Such groups may dissolve after the issue is settled.

Business Groups

The term *businessman* covers a wide variety of Americans. The president of General Motors is a businessman. The land speculator, the contractor, the store owner, the restaurant proprietor, the importer, and the Wall Street broker are also businessmen. Thus, one would expect the business community to be heterogeneous, holding many conflicting opinions, and this is true to a large extent. But it is also true that most businessmen share certain concerns and attitudes. In a broad sense, it is thus possible to speak of the "business interest," or the opinion of businessmen.

Who Speaks for Businessmen? A vast number of interest groups represent business. They vary in size from small organizations managed by one person to large, highly structured groups with many full-time employees. Some dissolve within a few years after they are created, while others remain active for many years. On the national level there are an estimated two thousand organizations that represent business, and about eleven thousand on the state and local levels.[7] Among them are such diversified groups as the American Federation of Retail Kosher Butchers, the National Canners Association, the National Coal Association, the Pin Manufacturers Institute, and the American Newspaper Publishers Association. Such organizations engage not only in pressure activity, but often in public-relations activities which they call public education; they aid in the exchange of technical information and help to promote research—as a rule, market research. Or, as in the case of the tobacco industry, in defensive research—aimed at defending the industry against attacks from outside pressure groups.

In addition to groups that represent specific industries, there are organizations that attempt to speak for a wide segment of the nation's businesses. The largest and most encompassing is the Chamber of Commerce of the United States. Its members include about four thousand local chambers of commerce and trade associations and forty thousand business firms and individuals, and it claims to speak for an estimated five million firms and individuals.[8] Since the Chamber of Commerce purports to speak for American business as a whole, its policies tend to be a good deal more general than those of the specialized business groups,

---

[7] V. O. Key, *Politics, Parties, and Pressure Groups* (New York: Thomas Y. Crowell, 1964), p. 84.

[8] Margaret Fiske (ed.), *National Organizations of the United States* (Detroit: Gale Research Co., 1972).

President Nixon sipped coffee in a relaxed moment at the 1970 National Association of Manufacturers Convention, where he asked manufacturers for voluntary action to stem the tide of inflation.

making known the views of the business community on national issues. Through various media, it works to promote and protect the free-enterprise system. It also represents the American business world in matters of broad public policy.

In theory, the U.S. Chamber's annual national convention, composed of delegates from all of the local chambers, is responsible for controlling policy decisions. However, real power is lodged with the fifty-member board of directors. The board screens all policy issues to be considered at the annual convention. It also controls the association's finances, elects its officers, fills staff positions, and selects an executive committee from among its own members.[9]

A second business organization of national importance is the National Association of Manufacturers. Founded in 1895, the NAM represents the opinions of a broad spectrum of big manufacturing concerns. Because of the powerful interests it represents, it is able to take a definite and forceful position on many issues. Like the Chamber of Commerce, the NAM is controlled by a board of directors. The board of the NAM is composed of one hundred fifty members, most of them chosen at annual conventions. This board is vested with complete responsibility for making association policy. Selection of officers, appointment of committee and

[9] Holtzman, *Interest Groups and Lobbying,* p. 22.

staff members, and control over association finances and bylaws are also in the hands of the board.[10]

Evidence of the conservative position of the NAM is its recent support of a bill with right-to-work provisions, and its opposition to a bill to expand the federal manpower-training program, including provisions for public-service employment. In addition, the NAM has opposed establishment of a new, independent agency to represent consumers before existing federal agencies and the federal courts, as well as a bill permitting the Equal Opportunity Commission to issue cease-and-desist orders against employers guilty of discriminatory hiring practices.[11]

In addition to specialized business groups and the large federations of groups like the Chamber of Commerce and the National Association of Manufacturers, there are some one hundred or one hundred fifty giant corporations in the United States that act as interest groups in their own right. The typical large corporation enlists the aid of lawyers and specialists in presenting its position before the national legislature. And many, like International Telephone & Telegraph, hire professional lobbyists to look after their interests in Washington. Often a particular piece of legislation will have a powerful effect on a single company, although it leaves others relatively untouched. In such cases, collective organizations are not motivated strongly enough to intervene, so that it is up to the individual corporation to look after its own interests.

Agricultural Groups

In the first half of the nineteenth century the United States was still essentially an agrarian nation, with about 80 percent of the working force employed in farming. Fifty-seven percent of the nation's labor force was self-employed, with the major proportion being independent subsistence farmers, growing enough produce for their own use and selling the surplus. Agriculture was assured a position of high esteem within the society, upheld by the official priorities of government. Thomas Jefferson wrote that farmers were "the chosen people of God, if ever He had a chosen people," and that cities were "essentially evil" and "ulcers in the body politic."

After the Civil War, however, a great change transformed American society. Large numbers of people, forced to confront the evils of which Jefferson warned, migrated from the farms to the cities, swelling the ranks of industry. The number of people who gain their livelihood from farming has diminished drastically. In 1930, farmers made up over 25 percent of the total population; today, they total only about 5 percent.[12] At the same time, however, increases in the prices received by farmers for agricultural products have lagged far behind increases in the prices paid by farmers for other goods and services. Those who fare worst are the small, family-owned farms that are being forced out of business with the development of large-scale agri-business. The large farms (with sales over $20,000 per year) number only 17 percent of all farms but realize 54 percent of total farm income. The activities of a number of agricultural interest groups have contributed significantly to these developments.

---

[10] Holtzman, *Interest Groups and Lobbying*, p. 22.

[11] *Congressional Quarterly Weekly Report* (February 5, 1971), p. 330.

[12] U.S. Department of Commerce, *Agricultural Statistics* (Washington, D.C.: Department of Commerce, 1971).

Who Speaks for the Farmer? Like businessmen, farmers are an extremely varied lot. A New England dairy farmer has few problems in common with a southern cotton grower or a wheat farmer from the Plains States. Each faces problems which are uniquely his own and which bring him into conflict not only with other segments of society, but at times even with other farmers. As in the business world, a great variety of agricultural organizations have emerged, some of them in answer to local and specialized needs and others to promote the aims of farmers on a broader basis.

Some groups, known as commodity organizations, represent only the growers of a specific crop. They include such organizations as the American Cranberry Growers Association, the National Apple Institute, the National Beet Growers Federation, and the American Sugar Cane League. The broad interests shared by commodity groups are, however, represented by larger organizations which protect the interests of farmers in more general ways.

THE NATIONAL GRANGE.   Organized in 1867, the Grange is the oldest of the agricultural associations and is unique in that it functions not only as a political interest group but as a social and semireligious organization as well. The Grange considers itself a fraternal group and stresses "moral and spiritual idealism" along with farming interests. Its chief officer is known as the "National Master," and its ritualistic structure, which it has never changed, includes an "Assembly of Demeter," presided over by a "High Priest."

Despite its adherence to rituals of the past and the Jeffersonian mystique of the farmer as salt of the earth, the Grange, although less powerful than in the past, remains a force to be reckoned with in national politics. It is still fairly strong in the northeastern, Middle Atlantic, and northwestern states, particularly among the older farmers. The policies of the Grange have always been rather conservative, closely paralleling the platform of the Republican party. Recently, however, it has become more independent, gravitating toward more moderate positions, although it still opposes most of the government's attempts to control agricultural production. It also maintains a firm opposition to unionism. According to an official publication, the Grange opposes "all efforts of labor unions to organize farmers or farm workers," since it believes that the farmer has "all the headaches he can possibly bear" without having to worry about organized labor as well.[13]

AMERICAN FARM BUREAU FEDERATION.   Most powerful of the major agricultural groups, the AFBF derives its major strength from the Midwest and, to a lesser degree, the South and Southwest. Nevertheless, like the Grange, it has consistently portrayed itself as representative of American farming as a whole. The AFBF primarily supports the larger, more prosperous farmer interests. Since the New Deal, it has sided with the policies of the Republican party, opposing government control of farm production. In its self-help program, it offers low-cost loans and insurance policies. The AFBF cooperates closely with state university land-grant colleges and their extension services. It has also maintained friendly relations with certain business and professional groups—specifically, the Chamber of Commerce, the National Association of Manufacturers, and the American Medical Association—and has been treated preferentially by these groups in return.

---

[13] C. M. Gardner, *The Grange: Friend of the Farmer* (The National Grange, 1949), p. 170, as quoted in Key, *Politics, Parties, and Pressure Groups*, p. 33.

Although the AFBF has sometimes suffered serious inner divisions resulting from its uneasy coalition of midwestern corn growers with southern cotton farmers, its legislative influence remains great. After examining the organization's history, one commentator concluded that any measure "that is opposed by the AFBF is not likely to get far. On most agricultural matters . . . it is not too much to say that unless AFBF actively supports it the chances of its success are slight."[14]

NATIONAL FARMERS UNION.   In its liberal political orientation, the National Farmers Union is the maverick among the major agricultural organizations. Unlike the AFBF, it is unfriendly to the "factory farm" and views farming as a way of life, not simply as a way of making money. It pictures itself as carrying on "the tradition of old-fashioned, militant agrarian radicalism," a policy that has brought it harsh criticism from the other major farming groups, who regard some of its measures as dangerously "un-American." These measures include the proposed establishment of cooperative terminals, insurance agencies, and organizations to facilitate the purchase of farm machinery; and other plans leading to the socialization of farming. The National Farmers Union has stated that it supports such proposals in order that "the potential abundance of this Nation may be made available to all its people."

Founded in 1902 in Texas, the National Farmers Union now receives most of its support from the wheat-growing areas of Oklahoma, Nebraska, the Dakotas, Wisconsin, Minnesota, Montana, and Colorado. Unlike the other two major farm organizations, it has consistently supported the Democratic party in its policy decisions and has maintained friendly relations with labor unions. Although current trends seem to indicate that the future belongs to the big farms, the National Farmers Union remains a significant factor in national politics.

Labor Groups

Labor as a commodity, and as an organized group, is a recent phenomenon that has arisen out of industrial development. The concept of the working class sprang into being during the Industrial Revolution. Before then, there was no need to employ masses of people in factories and offices. Commodities were produced in small, owner-operated shops, and help was employed on a limited and personal basis. With the advent of industrialization, however, vast numbers of jobs needed to be filled. The workers who came forward to fill them lacked money, property, and organization. They were ideal victims for exploitation; and exploited they were, from the beginning of rapid industrial growth (about 1850) until they eventually won the right to bargain collectively under the Wagner Act of 1935. In the nearly one hundred years that intervened, however, the United States witnessed a bitter and often violent struggle between workers, fighting for fair treatment and better living conditions, and employers, who interpreted these demands as threats to their security.

Who Speaks for Labor?   In this struggle, workers have attempted to consolidate their strength through the formation of labor unions. In the late nineteenth century, a

---

[14] O. M. Kile, *The Farm Bureau Federation Through Three Decades* (Waverly Press, 1948), p. 389, as quoted in Key, *Politics, Parties, and Pressure Groups*, p. 34.

radical labor union, the Knights of Labor, was formed with the purpose of changing the American economic system. After long and bloody battles, it disappeared
from the scene and was replaced by the "bread-and-butter" unionism of various
craftsmen, such as electrical workers, carpenters, bricklayers, and plumbers.
These unions stressed better wages and working conditions rather than general
reform, and generally were more successful than their radical forerunners. In
1886, they formed the American Federation of Labor as a single organization of
all crafts and trades under the leadership of Samuel Gompers.

The AFL dominated the labor movement for the next fifty years, until a vocal
minority, led by John L. Lewis, agreed that "craft unionism" should be replaced
by "industrial unionism," or organization of the thousands of workers in mass-
production industries. The minority left the AFL in 1936 and established the Congress of Industrial Organizations, which grew into an organization of unskilled
and semiskilled industrial workers, principally in the auto and steel industries.
They were so successful that the AFL also started to move in the direction of
industrial unionism. In 1955, the AFL merged with the CIO. Today, although
there are several large and powerful independent unions, such as the United Mine
Workers or the Teamsters, the AFL-CIO is by far the largest and most powerful
labor organization in the United States.

The AFL-CIO is made up of over one hundred twenty independent national
labor unions and claims a total membership of approximately fifteen million. Although most of the unions that make up this figure are fairly small—40 percent
of them having fewer than twenty-five thousand members—a few, such as the
Electrical Workers and the Steel Workers, have memberships totaling over seven
hundred thousand. Each of these national unions is in turn composed of local
unions throughout the country, of which there are some eighty thousand.

Although each of the unions which constitute the AFL-CIO enjoys a high degree of autonomy, the governmental structure within the individual unions is
rarely egalitarian, tending mainly toward oligarchy or, in some cases, dictatorship.
In 1959, the Landrum-Griffin Act forced the unions to adopt certain democratic
practices, such as guarantee of free speech for members and protection from im-
proper disciplinary action by the union. Nevertheless, in most organizations a
small group of professional union workers still control the decision-making function.[15] A tradition of oligarchical union leadership was set by the late and formidable John L. Lewis of the United Mine Workers. James Hoffa, until his imprisonment ended his single-handed control over the Teamsters' Union, is a notable
recent example.

The AFL-CIO claims to be nonpartisan in that it promises to support any political candidate or public official who proves friendly to labor. In practice, however,
the AFL-CIO has sided so often with the Democratic party that their permanent
association seems to be almost accepted. In 1968, the United Auto Workers, under
the late Walter Reuther's leadership, spent $472,166 on Democratic election cam-
paigns through its newly established Community Action Program, part of a politi-
cal-action wing set up to manage UAW political affairs. And in 1972, despite his
deep antagonism to George McGovern, George Meany, chief of the AFL-CIO, did
not make an open break with the Democratic ticket by supporting Richard Nixon,
but followed McGovern's nomination with an announcement of neutrality. More-

[15] Seymour Martin Lipset, *Political Man* (New York: Doubleday Anchor, 1960), pp. 399–405.

In keeping with the time-honored association of organized labor with the Democratic Party, President Lyndon B. Johnson, the major Democratic figure of the time, was a featured speaker at a 1966 United Auto Workers Labor Day rally in Detroit. He winks at Walter Reuther, former union president, now deceased.

over, 74 percent of the leaders of unions within the AFL-CIO declared support for the Democratic presidential nominee.

Professional Groups

Doctors, lawyers, accountants, dentists, journalists, pilots, football players, actors — these professionals and others of all kinds have their own associations to speak for them. What they lack in numbers they more than make up for in cohesiveness, money, and prestige; consequently, they wield a considerable amount of power. A primary concern of professional interest groups is setting standards for licensing, and in this endeavor they maintain virtually unchecked control. Indeed, some commentators have described the professions as autonomous guild systems with cooperation from the government. Although, ultimately, legislators decide on the standards governing admission to the professions, in doing so they tend to rely so heavily on the superior technical knowledge of the members of the profession themselves that in reality legislative authority over the professions exists in name only. As V. O. Key remarked, a situation results "in which the profession controls itself in the name of the state."[16]

---

[16] Key, *Politics, Parties, and Pressure Groups*, p. 122.

The motives of the professional interest groups in lobbying for stricter licensing standards are twofold. True, they aim to protect the public from quacks and charlatans and thereby to prevent blemishes on the good name of the profession. But there is also the more selfish motive of limiting competition to keep fees at the highest possible level.

The American Medical Association   Perhaps the most powerful of the professional interest groups, the American Medical Association, representing 219,000 physicians and 1,966 medical societies,[17] has earned a reputation for conservatism and traditionally has aligned itself with the policies of the Republican party. In the 1930s it began a long, tenacious battle against proposals to provide some form of government-supported health care for the elderly—fearing that such plans meant the loss of control by doctors over their own profession. When President Truman proposed a health insurance plan in 1948, it touched off a large-scale propaganda campaign by the AMA which cost $4.5 million and was intended to "educate" the public into regarding socialized medicine as a dangerous threat to the American way of life. The AMA was successful in blocking the plan until the 1960s, when the idea surfaced again in the form of Medicare, which provides hospitalization for those over sixty-five through the Social Security system. Despite the AMA's strident objections, the influence of the lawmakers prevailed, and the Medicare Bill passed into law in 1965.[18]

The AMA has extensive fact-gathering facilities working in areas of professional interest to its members, keeps its members informed on proposed medical and health legislation on the state and national levels, aids in setting hospital and medical school standards, and produces two weekly and nine monthly publications.

The American Bar Association   The American Bar Association is not as powerful as the AMA, probably because lawyers, although they command great respect from the public, do not enjoy quite the prestige accorded to members of the medical profession. Nevertheless, the American Bar Association, which had 136,451 members in 1972,[19] does manage to exert a great deal of force on government chiefly by directing its efforts at the judiciary, rather than the legislature, the target of most other interest organizations. One factor which works in the ABA's favor is its members' familiarity with the governmental process. The training received by lawyers enables them to deal knowledgeably and effectively with the technical aspects of the decision-making process. Moreover, a high percentage of political leaders begin their careers as lawyers, and many retain their ABA membership. Thus, members of the ABA have the advantage of dealing with decision-makers who speak the same language that they do. The ABA maintains a library and publishes two monthly journals. Its numerous standing committees deal with a very broad range of legal matters. It is affiliated with many other legal organizations.

---

[17] *Congressional Quarterly Weekly Report* (February 15, 1971), p. 331.

[18] Oliver Garceau, *The Political Life of the AMA* (Cambridge, Mass.: Harvard University Press, 1941); and David R. Hyde and Payson Wolff, "The AMA: Power, Purpose and Politics in Organized Medicine," *Yale Law Journal*, vol. 63 (May 1954), pp. 938–1022.

[19] *Congressional Quarterly Weekly Report* (February 15, 1971).

Other Interest Groups

In addition to the kinds of groups already discussed, there are other categories of groups that may exert considerable influence over the American political process, although, in general, they have smaller memberships and less power.

Veterans' Groups The first powerful veterans' group to form in the United States was the Grand Old Army of the Republic, made up of Union soldiers who had served in the Civil War. The Union government was at the time controlled by the Republican party, and the GAR naturally took on a strong Republican bias. It exerted a powerful influence upon government during the latter half of the nineteenth century, but in the post–World War I years, its influence faded as its membership died, and the American Legion became the leading spokesman for veterans.

The American Legion maintains an official policy of nonpartisanship in politics, but in practice it supports the Republicans. It has directed its major political efforts toward obtaining higher pensions and medical insurance for veterans, but has also concerned itself with other issues, notably those bearing on the communist threat. It has taken a highly nationalistic stance on foreign policy issues, strongly supporting military leaders.

The Veterans of Foreign Wars, originally formed by soldiers who fought in the Spanish-American War, the second most powerful veterans' group in the country today, also supports United States military policy. Like the American Legion, it is interested primarily in increasing veterans' benefits. Both groups are highly oli-

Vietnam Veterans against the War here perform street theater to dramatize their antiwar protest.

garchical in structure. Rank-and-file members generally participate for social reasons, while official policies are formulated by an active minority.

Less broadly based, but with an essentially similar outlook on national policy, are the Catholic War Veterans and Jewish War Veterans groups. The Vietnam Veterans Against the War, a small but growing group, claiming twenty-five thousand membership nationally in the summer of 1972, stands in marked contrast to the older groups, many of its members having risked arrest in acts of civil disobedience to protest United States involvement in the Vietnam War. This organization, like the others, however, conducts drives to obtain jobs and hospital care for veterans.

Church Groups Churches, too, are involved in attempting to influence government. Churches in the United States not only speak out on various political issues, but they also engage in direct political action, some even maintaining organized lobbies in Washington to exert pressure on legislators. In addition, many interest groups in America have religious affiliations. Among the most prominent are the National Council of the Churches of Christ, the Women's Christian Temperance Union, the Friends Committee on National Legislation, the National Catholic Welfare Conference, and the National Conference of Catholic Charities. Their prestige and the high degree of zeal in their campaigns has enabled church-affiliated groups to influence presidential elections and to exert considerable influence on policies at the federal, state, and local levels. Issues have included school prayer, shared time for religious education for children in the public schools, aid to parochial schools, censorship, Sunday blue laws, abortion, and divorce.

In another day, the strength of church-affiliated groups in America was vividly demonstrated by the successful struggle of the Protestant-affiliated National Anti-Saloon League during the 1920s to prohibit the sale of alcoholic beverages. A highly organized, efficient group, the Anti-Saloon League concentrated first at the state level, perfecting its technique before moving on to Congress. The League was able to convert politicians into prohibitionists by its proven vote-getting ability; in its campaigns it encouraged voters to judge office-seekers *solely* by their stand on the liquor question. The group was primarily emotional in its appeal, gaining power through its insistent election-day slogan, "Mister, for God's sake don't vote for whiskey."[20] In more recent times as well, public officials find it advantageous to make concessions to religious-affiliated groups. Richard Nixon, for example, came out in opposition to abortion, a stance which clearly appealed to Catholic antiabortion groups.

Racial Minorities Most racial and ethnic groups form pressure organizations to combat prejudice and protest injustice against their members. Of these, groups representing American blacks have been among the most active groups working within the political system. The oldest and in some ways most conservative of black interest groups is the National Association for the Advancement of Colored People. Founded in 1909, the NAACP demanded full civil rights for blacks, breaking with the conciliatory policies of earlier leaders such as Booker T. Washington. The principal concerns of the NAACP have been to win political rights for blacks and, more recently, to achieve integration in education. Although it does not endorse

---

[20] Peter Odegard, *Pressures and Politics: The Story of the Anti-Saloon League* (New York: Octagon, 1967).

At the National Black Convention in Gary, Indiana, March 1972, Rev. Jesse Jackson (left), Gary Mayor Richard Hatcher, and other delegates give the Black Power salute.

candidates for public office, it has continued to conduct voter-registration drives in southern black communities.

Through its League Defense and Educational Fund, the NAACP achieved its greatest successes in the fifties and sixties, when its efforts were rewarded by a series of Supreme Court decisions opposing segregation. Once regarded as aggressive and daring, the NAACP now seems conservative and ineffective to those black people who want more rapid change than is possible through the necessarily slow-moving legal procedures and negotiations that have been NAACP policy. Nevertheless, the NAACP continues to be a force in American politics, and its vigorous campaigns against the nominations of Judges Clement F. Haynsworth, Jr., and G. Harrold Carswell to the Supreme Court in 1969 helped lead to their ultimate rejection.[21]

Consumers   Until recently, comsumer interests have gone largely unrepresented in American politics. However, as a growing number of Americans have become concerned over the deteriorating "quality of life," a variety of new groups has

[21] Douglass Lea, "Washington Pressures/NAACP Washington Bureau," *National Journal* (March 7, 1970), pp. 518–523.

"How will I recognize this Bess Myerson?"

New Yorker, *September 18, 1971*

come into being, dedicated to policing both business and government in an effort to keep unsafe products off the market and halt fraudulent or misleading advertising.

Typical of the new consumer activists is attorney Ralph Nader, who, with his team of student volunteers and other concerned citizens, has taken on the job of combating consumer abuses through the media and by means of legislative action. Nader's group has been successful not only in influencing legislation on such matters as automobile safety standards, food additives, pollution control, and care for the elderly, but has also heightened consumer awareness and sophistication. As a result, many consumers are no longer willing to accept the old adage "Let the buyer beware."

Environmentalist Groups Like the consumer activists, environmentalist groups bring pressure to bear against individuals and industries whose operations are deemed harmful—in this case, to the ecology or environment, by the careless use of technology. One such group is Friends of the Earth, led by David R. Brower, former executive director of the Sierra Club, another large environmental group. Friends of the Earth makes use of traditional lobbying techniques and public education to further the cause of conservation. Critics of Friends of the Earth, who believed the group lacked organization, were proved wrong in 1970 when it headed a coalition in a successful national drive to banish the proposed super-sonic transport, a giant passenger jet which, according to environmentalists,

Protection of the environment demands year-round watchfulness, as these clean-water demonstrators recognize.

would have wreaked havoc on the environment with its exhaust fumes and deafening sonic boom.[22]

The Sources of Group Power

Clearly, all interest groups are not equally influential in American politics. If they were, political decision-making would indeed become a hopeless stalemate. What, then, are some of the factors that contribute to the relative strength of particular interest groups in the political process?

Interest groups owe their influence to a host of factors, among them cohesiveness, leadership, size, prestige, geographical distribution, participation by members, and goals. None of these, however, can be isolated and measured to analyze its contribution to an organization's success as a pressure group. An interest group that rates high in one factor may be weakened by its low standing in another. Usually, the factors overlap and are difficult to disentangle. Also, it is necessary to consider such questions as: How much money does the group have? How much control does the group have over resources needed by its members—as, for example, the American Medical Association over medical schools, or the American

[22] Jamie Heard, "Washington Pressures/Friends of the Earth Give Environmental Interests an Active Voice," *National Journal* (August 8, 1970), pp. 1711–1718.

Bar Association over licensing? How close are the group's goals to American ideology? (Compare the Chamber of Commerce, in this regard, to the Black Panther Party.)

Cohesiveness, certainly, is a factor in the effectiveness of groups, but it is difficult to make comparisons between groups on this basis. Does the Catholic Church have more cohesion than the Chamber of Commerce? At a time when the Church is being torn by inner conflicts, it would be difficult to guess. In large measure, however, the power of both groups involves a cohesive spirit.

Although business groups represent an extremely diversified range of companies, in many cases directly in competition with one another, business as a whole represents a surprisingly cohesive and powerful force. Certain common interests serve to unite the business community on major issues, particularly when those interests are threatened. Moreover, a high degree of discipline prevails within the business groups. Representatives of different groups often work closely together to formulate general policies, and since it is possible for a majority of groups to impose economic sanctions on a deviant minority, dissension is kept to a minimum. Thus, business groups are able to maintain a greater cohesiveness than most other interest groups.

Labor groups, in contrast to business, though impressive in the size of their membership, are handicapped by their lack of cohesion. Cohesion depends on consensus within the group—a factor notably absent in labor as a whole, as pointed up by labor's mixed reaction to the presidential candidacy of George McGovern in 1972. Of the principal reasons for labor's failure to exert a decisive force upon government, its lack of unity is foremost. To influence government, a group must present a united front, and its leaders should be able to speak for all members of the group. Unless this is true, decision-makers will feel justified in voting against the leaders' proposals on grounds that the leaders do not really represent the opinion of the people for whom they profess to speak.

The scope of an organization is a major factor in its cohesiveness. A nationally organized group, for example, is more likely to face internal conflicts and may therefore be at a disadvantage. Moreover, the likelihood of conflict is increased when the member groups at the local level of a national organization have dissimilar problems, as in the case of the AFL-CIO, whose tremendous numerical strength masks inherent weakness. The AFL-CIO is a federation, and federations, by their very nature, cannot be highly unified. Each of the member unions that make up the massive organization has specific problems peculiar to itself; as these problems are passed along up the long hierarchical ladder, the odds increase against their reaching the attention of the national leadership.

Geographical dispersion, however, is not always a hindrance. The wide geographical dispersion of the farming community, for instance, though it does serve to divide farmers on issues, works in another way to their advantage: since farming goes on in all sections of America, agricultural interests play a constant part in the political process. Consequently, the interests of agriculture as a whole exert a steady force upon government, at both local and national levels.[23]

Leadership is another major factor in the cohesiveness of political interest groups.

---

[23] Wesley McCune, "Farmers in Politics," *Annals*, vol. 319 (1958), pp. 41–51; and Don F. Hadwiger and Ross B. Talbot, *Pressures and Protest: The Kennedy Farm Program and the Wheat Referendum of 1963* (San Francisco: Chandler, 1965), pp. 56–62.

In most groups, the leadership tends to be oligarchical: that is, an active minority within the group makes nearly all policy decisions, while the majority of members participates only in a peripheral way, approving automatically almost all the actions of the leaders.[24] Members sometimes are able to exert a limited influence upon leaders through such democratic methods as elections or debate, but, in general, interest-group leaders tend to be more high-handed than public officials in the way they treat members. To some extent, this oligarchical structure is beneficial, for too much control by members of a group may render the leadership unstable. Such a situation would limit the group's effectiveness, for its success depends on an experienced, smoothly working leadership that has the respect and confidence of governmental decision-makers. But the group cannot afford to allow its leadership to become too undemocratic. Despite their oligarchical prerogatives, the leaders must basically derive their power from the support of the membership. They can be dictatorial to a degree, but they cannot be capricious. Should they cease to express the attitudes of the people they are supposed to represent, they will not only risk losing the backing of the group's members, but will encourage inner divisions, weakening the group's power to influence the government.

The attitude of members is also a factor influencing the cohesiveness of an interest group. Apathy, for example, is a problem among union members. The rank and file of the major labor unions participate in decision-making processes at a very low level, or not at all.[25] A worker's decision to join a union, in fact, is motivated not so much by the desire to better his living and working conditions by participating in organized political activity, as simply by group pressure. One joins a union because everyone does, and, in many cases, because it is impossible to get work without a union membership. Members of church-affiliated groups, on the other hand, often take up a political cause with great zeal and dedication, a factor which increases their influence on public policy.

The prestige of a group, as indicated earlier, also gives it political influence. Naturally, a group with high social prestige, such as the AMA, will be listened to more readily than a less prestigious group. Moreover, a high-prestige group may be able to further a cause merely by giving it public support. The case for legalizing marijuana, for example, suffered a setback in 1972 when an AMA committee did not come out in favor of legalizing the drug even though the committee had concluded that it was not harmful. On the other hand, a group with little prestige may actually hinder a cause by espousing it; it has to work hard to attain the level of influence the high-prestige group achieves with no effort at all.

Business in general has high prestige among Americans, including public officials, many of whom share the values of businessmen. The influence of business groups is helped, too, by the fact that many political leaders began their careers as either businessmen or legal consultants and hold attitudes sympathetic to business. In the twenties, Calvin Coolidge asserted, "The business of America is business," and this ideology is still popular in America. Moreover, businessmen have more money to spend on extensive campaigns than do interest groups that run programs on the nickels and dimes of private contributors. When money and prestige are combined, the effect is often irresistible.

Prestige levels are not static, however, and a group may, by amassing broad

[24] Lipset, *Political Man*, pp. 417–424.
[25] Lipset, *Political Man*, pp. 405–410.

support, increase its prestige and, with it, its political advantage. Labor groups in America, for example, once had little more prestige than the Communist party, and the Knights of Labor was doomed because its radical outlook was not in accord with American ideology. But because the AFL-CIO made great advances in power and popularity during the twentieth century, its approval is widely sought by politicians running for office.

Finally, the goals sought by the group greatly influence its effectiveness. Groups that adopt popular goals tend, of course, to be more successful than groups whose goals run counter to prevailing moods. Yet even universal approval of objectives does not assure success. For example, groups devoted to eliminating certain fatal diseases often cannot muster support intense enough to obtain the financial backing they seek. Also important is the ability of an interest group to limit its goals to a definite area. A group that supports a broad spectrum of causes may spread itself too thin to exert effective pressure at any one point.

Evaluating Interest Groups:
In Whose Interest?

As the preceding analysis of major interest groups in American society shows, there are vast differences in power and influence among interest groups. Interest-group policies are biased in favor of the wealthiest and best-organized groups. The National Welfare Rights Association, for example, one of the few groups to represent the poor, is not very effective. The poor generally are left out of the system because they have neither the skills nor the resources to organize effectively.

Critics of the interest-group system argue that it contains built-in flaws that help perpetuate inequalities in American society. As one of these critics, David Ricci, has pointed out:

. . . certain important interests are persistently weak, continually ineffective, and repeatedly disregarded in the process of political bargaining. Consumers are in this category, since they lack powerful organizations, as do migrant farm laborers, white-collar workers, the poor, and "multitudes with an interest in peace."[26]

Ricci has further objected that traditional interest-group theorists tend to minimize the differences between powerful, well-organized groups and loosely organized or potential groups. These differences, some pluralists contend, are merely a matter of the degree of interaction within a particular group. Ricci has contended that it is precisely the degree of interaction, and its concomitant, cohesiveness, which determine whether a group will achieve the ends it seeks, or no ends at all. It is the difference, he says, "between a disciplined army and an anarchic mob."[27]

Other critics of interest-group theory argue that most groups are composed of members of the socioeconomic elite and therefore have a significant upper-class bias. As E. E. Schattschneider expressed it, "the flaw in the pluralist heaven is that the heavenly chorus sings with a strong upper-class accent. Probably about

---

[26] David Ricci, *Community Power and Democratic Theory: The Logic of Political Analysis* (New York: Random House, 1971), p. 79.
[27] Ricci, *Community Power and Democratic Theory*, p. 77.

90 percent of the people cannot get into the pressure system."[28] In other words, the pressure-group system does not represent all the interests of society. *"Pressure politics is a selective process* ill-designed to serve diffuse interests."[29] The notion that the interest-group system accounts for and serves all members of society on an equal basis simply does not stand up under close examination. Of the thousands of interest groups listed in the *National Associations of the United States* and the *Lobby Index,* the overwhelming majority are business organizations. Not only do businessmen dominate the system numerically, but, as a group, they participate politically more than other members of society. Studies have shown that businessmen write to their congressmen far more than do manual laborers by a ratio of about five to one. Even among farm owners, membership in interest groups is held by the more affluent, with most of the poorer farmers in America unaffiliated with a pressure group. According to some analysts, it is this bias of interest-group politics in America which is actually responsible for the effectiveness of the pressure-group system. As Schattschneider concluded, "The pressure system makes sense only as the political instrument of a segment of the community. It gets results by being selective and biased; if everybody got into the act the unique advantage of this form of organization would be destroyed, for it is possible that if all interests could be mobilized the result would be a stalemate."[30] To regard the upper-class bias among interest groups as direct rule over the American political system by a small elite is, however, an ill-considered judgment, in the opinion of some observers.

When a conflict becomes political, even powerful, organized business groups may lose out when smaller, less prestigious groups, motivated by strong convictions, mobilize public sympathy. This phenomenon is aided by the public image of big business as monopolistic—an image supported by the fact that some two hundred corporations own more than 50 percent of American industries.[31] The tendency by decision-makers to regard big business as villainous and small business as exemplifying the virtues of the American free-enterprise system was expressed by one writer when he noted that when big business limits production and fixes prices it is charged with "conspiracy in restraint of trade," while small businessmen who do the same thing are said to be practicing "fair trade."[32]

C. Wright Mills's concept of the United States as a political system ruled by an entrenched power elite, in which powerful business interests play a commanding role,[33] has been disputed by observers who maintain that power is dispersed among many businessmen, a pluralist elite whose interests may clash—as in the case of the airlines, the truckers, and the railroads—and that the sources of power change as the times change. Thus, although many people are not represented by interest groups, the end result nevertheless appears to be essentially democratic. The general public often makes its influence felt through channels other than group ac-

[28] E. E. Schattschneider, *The Semisovereign People: A Realist's View of Democracy in America* (New York: Holt, Rinehart and Winston, 1960), p. 35.

[29] Schattschneider, *The Semisovereign People,* p. 35.

[30] Schattschneider, *The Semisovereign People,* pp. 34–35.

[31] M. A. Adelman, "The Measurement of Industrial Concentration," *Review of Economic Statistics,* vol. 32 (November 1951), pp. 269–296.

[32] Claire Wilcox, "Concentration of Power in the American Economy," *Harvard Business Review,* vol. 38 (November 1950), p. 58.

[33] C. Wright Mills, *The Power Elite* (New York: Oxford University Press, 1956).

tivity: through political parties, for example, and the impact of public opinion. In addition, as indicated earlier, the latent power of "potential groups" also serves as a restraint against dominance by any single interest—in a democracy, a group that abuses its power runs the risk of stirring up new sources of opposition.

The Business of Lobbying: Tactics and Their Effectiveness

The structure of interest groups and their goals is one important aspect of interest-group politics in America. An analysis of the methods used by groups to influence public policy, however, is also important to an understanding of the pressure-group system. The remainder of this chapter will deal with the actual, day-to-day activities of pressure groups and, finally, will evaluate the theory and practice of interest group politics.

Direct Methods of Influence

Every interest group must decide whether it is to use "direct" or "indirect" methods to influence governmental decisions. That is, whether to exert pressure directly against the decision-makers by such means as conversations, letters, and the presentation of data; or, indirectly, by encouraging others to pressure them. Mobilization of public opinion is an indirect method. One poll of lobbyists revealed that about 80 percent believed the direct approach to be more effective.[34] The direct approach has obvious advantages; it is cheaper, simpler, and surer. Working through intermediaries makes the effort more expensive; also, there is the risk that the original message will be garbled by individuals who do not grasp its primary thrust. For these reasons, most interest groups consider direct confrontation with governmental officials the most efficient means of serving their clients' interests.

Backgrounds of Lobbyists Lobbying is the practice of trying to influence legislators to pass laws favorable to a group, and administrators to interpret the law favorably. The effectiveness of lobbyists varies widely. To some extent it is determined by their backgrounds, the experience and knowledge they bring to their jobs. Surveys show that while a small percentage of lobbyists are former members of Congress or persons who have been active in a political party, the great majority come from business or from the Executive branch of government and have had little active participation in party politics. Lobbyists may be heads of trade associations or of individual business firms; they may be elected officials of labor organizations; or they may be members of full-time lobbying staffs for such large organizations as the U.S. Chamber of Commerce or the American Farm Bureau Federation. Lobbying groups may be permanent and well established, or they may be *ad hoc* groups formed to exert pressure only on a specific bill. Another type of lobbyist is the attorney whose business is not primarily lobbying, but who may be engaged to present a client's case before the legislature, just as he might take on a client's defense in a court of law. Finally, there are individuals who function as lobbying agents for the President or for the executive departments, serving to further the proposals of the Executive in the halls of Congress.

---

[34] Lester Milbrath, *The Washington Lobbyists* (Chicago: Rand-McNally, 1963), p. 212.

Los Angeles Times *Syndicate*

Influencing Congressmen To be successful, the congressional lobbyist must be able to reach and convince key legislators. Access in itself is not difficult, since most legislators recognize that interest groups are necessary to the political process and are willing to spend some time listening to them. To establish friendly, favorable relationships with lawmakers requires effort, however, and interest groups use a variety of techniques. Trust is crucial to the endeavor, and in order to hold it, interest groups must provide information to legislators that is truthful and accurate, so that legislators may, in turn, present it with confidence to Congress and to their constituencies. Although interest groups use other techniques, such as donating services and campaign funds, and furnishing social entertainment, a reputation for reliability is probably the single most effective factor in winning a lawmaker's good will.

STRATEGIES: THE RULES OF THE GAME.   Many citizens believe lobbying a dirty business, an area where corruption runs rampant. But reliable sources indicate that this is not a very accurate representation of today's political reality. Stricter regulations and a vigilant press have effectively purged lobbying of most underhanded aspects. The strategies of today's lobbyists are in the main straightforward and aboveboard, not simply out of fear of discovery but because corrupt methods have proved to be rather ineffective. Threats and bribes, although they doubtless occur, are known to be less reliable than honest tactics. Most lobbyists lack the power to back up threats, so that when used they usually serve only to arouse hostility. Bribery is also a rather futile tactic. Surveys show that most congressmen cannot be bribed. Those who can do not carry enough power to override the influence of legislators whose votes are not for sale. The inefficiency of bribery as a lobbying tactic came to light in 1956 over the matter of the Natural Gas Bill. Having already passed the House of Representatives and expected to pass in the Senate, the bill was blocked when Senator Francis Case (R.-S. Dak.) accused a lobbyist working for its acceptance of having committed an act of bribery—offering him a $2500 "campaign contribution." Despite the scandal, the bill did pass in the Senate, but in the end President Eisenhower chose to veto it because of the "arrogant" lobbying tactic employed.

PROPONENTS, OPPONENTS, AND NEUTRALS.   In general, lobbyists do not try to force their attentions. Most congressional lobbying is aimed at activating proponents, or at convincing neutrals or undecided congressmen; lobbyists usually avoid opponents. They do so because a legislator's motives for opposing a particular issue are almost always based on solid political reasoning, not irrational prejudice. A lobbyist would have little to gain from a confrontation with such an antagonist; therefore, pressure groups usually work only where they already have a foot in the door.

COMMITTEES AND KEY LEGISLATORS.   Legislative committees are crucial links in the chain of events by which a bill becomes a law, and lobbyists recognize their importance. The findings and recommendations of committees have great weight with Congress; what committees support is usually acted upon favorably; what they oppose has little chance of passing. Committee hearings offer important opportunities for the lobbyist to exert influence. With his detailed knowledge of a given area, he can often help to impress a committee seeking information and to rally its support.

The shrewd lobbyist is aware of the prevailing mood of a committee—a mood usually determined by its chairman—and will be careful to take into account the predispositions and prejudices of such individuals when he presents his case.

TIMING.   The lobbyist must also adjust his strategy to the mood of Congress as a whole. Timing, as one observer has commented, "may often be more decisive for the fate of a bill than any other factor."[35] Governmental activity is a dynamic process and not a static balance of forces. Certain groups and individuals take definite stands on issues, but as new developments arise, the priorities of legislators are likely to shift, and proposals received favorably today may raise little enthusiasm tomorrow. Lobbyists must be sensitive to the changing pattern of events, or they may fail in their efforts for no other reason than that their timing was off.

LEGAL CONTROLS ON LOBBYING.   The right to lobby is assured by the Constitution. To do away with lobbying, or to impose such severe restrictions that lobbyists could not fulfill their functions, would be to cripple an important part of our democratic system. As a democratic function, however, the process of lobbying should be carried out in the open. To this end, Congress has passed a series of measures designed to bring congressional lobbying under governmental regulation.

The Federal Regulation of Lobbying Act of 1946 requires full-time lobbyists to register with certain congressional officials and to provide the following information: employer's name, salary, expenses, receipts, published material, and the particular piece of legislation whose passage or defeat they are trying to effect. Although this law has been used to punish lobbyists who fail to observe it, most observers agree that, basically, it is vague and ineffective. It does not adequately

---

[35] Milbrath, *The Washington Lobbyists*, p. 218.

Lending his expertise in the field of veterans' affairs at a hearing of the House Veterans Affairs Committee was American Legion National Commander J. Milton Patrick (with notebook open on table).

define what constitutes a full-time lobbyist, so that many borderline individuals don't know whether or not to register. The provisions calling for the reporting of income and expenditure are indefinite, leaving so much to the judgment of the lobbyist himself that the figures are virtually worthless. Moreover, the law does not provide for adequate enforcement. Information is filed, but it is not systematically reviewed and analyzed. Thus, it is rare that a lobbyist is brought to account for a transgression; numerous other infractions go undetected entirely.

Influencing Bureaucrats   Although the 1946 Lobbying Act makes no specific provision for lobbying in the Executive branch of government, it is an important political tool. Lobbyists hold a somewhat different place in the Executive branch, however, from the one they occupy in Congress. As in the Legislature, a reciprocal relationship of cooperation and mutual dependency develops between interest groups and government officials. But this relationship tends to be closer and more intense in the Executive branch. Many executive officials would not, in fact, be able to function without them. The U.S. Department of Labor, for example, depends on the help of the AFL-CIO in formulating its policies, and the major agricultural groups perform similar functions for the Department of Agriculture.

Interest groups, in turn, benefit substantially from their relationship with executive officials. They are likely to seek and receive such privileges as participating in executive decisions, affecting the appointment of officials, controlling the hiring of department staffs, and helping to formulate policy. To achieve these goals, interest groups may employ pressure tactics on executive officials. Not all interest groups have the resources to deal with executives successfully, but the larger groups are particularly well suited to exert substantial influences on the bureaucrat. Lobbyists may also appeal to the Legislature, to the public, or to executive officials higher up in the chain of command, in order to gain support from executive departments.

Interest groups that seek power in the Executive branch often angle for the right to appoint officials to executive departments, a particularly effective strategy. If the group is not permitted to actually name such officials itself, it may seek at least the privilege of vetoing appointments or setting up qualifications for appointees. When an interest group has been traditionally allied with a political party, its position is considerably strengthened when that party is in power in the Executive branch. The AFL-CIO, for example, had several of its members appointed to official positions under the Democratic Kennedy administration, and the American Farm Bureau Federation gained similar benefits during the Republican Eisenhower years.

Since executive officials are generally more vulnerable than legislators to interest-group pressure, they are far more likely to alter policy decisions at the behest of these groups. Therefore, a vigorous lobbying campaign launched against some executive policy is almost certain to bring results. This is not to say, however, that executive officials are the pawns of interest groups. Career officials have power and strategies of their own to keep the power of interest groups in check. The relationship can best be described as a close, somewhat competitive partnership, never as the total dominance of one over the other.

Influencing the Courts Compared with the Executive and Legislative branches of government, the Judiciary is quite well-protected against interest-group activity. Traditionally, the courts are viewed not as open marketplaces of ideas and interests, but as sacrosanct halls of justice from which outside influences must be excluded. However, there are certain ways in which interest groups are able to legally influence the Judicial branch, and many groups find these methods more effective for their purposes than appeals to other branches of government.[36]

The most significant influence groups can have on the Judiciary is in the selection of judges. The American Bar Association has been particularly active in this respect and on several occasions has used its influence to prevent the nomination of judges to the Supreme Court. Other groups, too, have worked to oppose the selection of judges they considered ideologically undesirable. In 1969, a number of legal, civil-rights, academic, and feminist groups successfully opposed the nomination of Clement F. Haynsworth, Jr., and G. Harrold Carswell to the Supreme Court.

Another method used by interest groups to influence the courts is by the presentation of *Amicus Curiae* briefs. *Amicus Curiae* means "friend of the court"— that is, an individual who offers information which may be of help to the court in reaching a decision. Such briefs allow interest groups to introduce their own points of view into the decision-making process. In the 1954 case of *Brown v. The Board of Education,* for example, Thurgood Marshall, then head of the NAACP Legal Defense and Education League and now Associate Justice of the Supreme Court, submitted arguments to the Court against school segregation. His efforts were influential in the Court's decision to overturn the earlier doctrine of "separate but equal" educational facilities.

---

[36] See Clement G. Vose, "Litigation as a Function of Pressure Group Activity," *Annals,* vol. 319 (1958), pp. 20–31.

Lastly, interest groups may initiate test cases. This tactic has proved very valuable for civil-rights groups, such as the NAACP, who find the Legislature, with its heavy concentration of southern representatives, difficult to win over. Time and time again the NAACP has won victories in test cases when other avenues to change were blocked.[37]

Indirect Methods of Influence

As already noted, direct methods of influence are favored by most interest groups. They are particularly favored by those groups that are well organized but short of money and other resources. Indirect methods, however, are also widely used to influence the decision-making process. Larger groups, especially, augment their lobbying efforts with such indirect techniques as appeals to the public or involvement in election campaigns. Indirect methods in pressure politics are largely a development of the twentieth century. The enormous scope of mass communication and modern advertising techniques help to make possible the types of indirect influence used by today's lobbyists.

Electioneering An indirect method used widely by interest groups is electioneering, which may involve campaign contributions to candidates sympathetic to their goals. Such contributions are generally nonpartisan in that they are not confined to representatives of one party but are distributed among politicians willing to support the aims of the group, regardless of party affiliation. Some of the larger interest groups spend huge sums on campaign contributions. For example, the American Medical Political Action Committee, a branch of the AMA, has spent over three million dollars to support candidates since 1962.[38] Electioneering may also involve endorsement or condemnation of a candidate as the case may be, and infiltration of political parties at the local level. On rare occasions, groups have gone so far as to form third parties to better represent their interests at the polls. This tactic is self-defeating, however, as even the largest interest groups are relatively helpless against the strength and organization of the major parties.

Grass-Roots Lobbying "Grass-roots" lobbying, a method used especially by large, well-financed groups, is another favored indirect technique. Here the lobbyist appeals directly to the people, with the expectation that they will relay his message back to government, amplified by their many voices. The appeal may entail a letter-writing campaign as well as the use of propaganda (or, as the groups prefer to call it, educational materials) in the form of advertising, films, publications, services, exhibits, and so on. The use of such methods, however, has been questioned, since — especially in the case of propaganda activity — their effectiveness is very hard to determine. Sometimes they may even be harmful, as may occur when a group that is making progress using direct methods suddenly arouses a host of vociferous enemies after it expands its efforts to the public level. Yet mass-media appeals and other indirect methods seem to be on the in-

---

[37] See Nathan Hakman, "Lobbying the Supreme Court — An Appraisal of Political Science Folklore," *Fordham Law Review*, vol. 35 (1966), pp. 15–50.

[38] Judith Robinson, "American Medical Political Action Committee," in *Political Brokers: Money Organizations, Power and People*, edited by the editors and reporters of *National Journal* (New York: Liveright, 1972), p. 69.

Using the technique of inviting arrest for the purpose of drawing attention to his cause, Rev. Ralph D. Abernathy here is led away during a protest against unfair food prices in New York City.

crease, as more and more groups become concerned with their "image" as well as with their status in government circles.

Protest as a Tactic of Influence

Protest, like grass-roots lobbying, uses the media to influence public opinion and thereby to affect lawmakers. Sometimes it is aimed at government, sometimes at other groups. Interestingly, it is a technique employed most often by small, relatively powerless groups to obtain free media coverage. Such groups are, in effect, carrying out the kind of propaganda campaigns run at great expense by the largest, best-financed groups.

Protest as a method of influence may take many forms. These range from small, peaceful, well-organized campaigns designed simply to draw attention to a particular problem, to large movements and confrontations, often spontaneous and unstable in nature, and sometimes leading to acts of violence. Whatever their nature, however, all protest activities depend heavily on publicity for their effectiveness. The march, picket, riot, or sit-in, as a rule, have significance only insofar as they influence public opinion after the event is reported in the media.[39]

Participation by the poor in protest movements is limited by the fear of consequences — the loss of a job, a police beating or arrest, or, as in the case of rent strikes in the slums, landlord retaliation.

One of the most successful ghetto-community organizers, the late Saul Alinsky, recommended protest as an effective means for building organization.[40] For example, his boycott in Montgomery, Alabama, which engaged a large number of blacks willing to risk retaliation, provided a base of support for the Southern Christian Leadership Conference, led by Martin Luther King, Jr., to grow into a leading voice for Negro rights.

Another example of the political use of protest movements has been the organization of constituencies from among antiwar protesters in support of peace candidates for Congress and, notably, the candidacies of Eugene McCarthy and Robert Kennedy for the Democratic presidential nomination in 1968, many of whose supporters turned to McGovern in the 1972 race.

Lobbying: Its Impact on Government

The average citizen tends to see lobbyists as extremely powerful entities whose influence in government vastly overshadows his own, but the evidence does not support this idea. In one survey aimed at assessing the importance of lobbying in American politics, both lobbyists and congressmen were almost unanimous in assigning lobbying a low place on the list of factors affecting government decisions.[41] It may even be true that interest groups, in their capacity as providers of information and services to government officials, serve the interests of those they seek to influence better than their own.

The power of interest groups is limited by a number of factors. First, even though government officials depend on groups for information, there are normally other sources within government to which they can turn. Secondly, decision-makers are approached by a great variety of interest groups. The various demands and pressures tend to cancel each other out, so that no one group is likely to gain absolute dominance. Finally, most political leaders come to office with very definite political leanings and commitments. These are not likely to be changed drastically through pressure activity.

The Pros and Cons of Interest Groups: A Summary

Interest groups provide an important source of information to decision-makers, though not the only source. Studies and reports prepared by interest groups to support their claims are often more detailed and complete than any the decision-maker can provide himself, and, though predictably biased, are valuable as a basis for action. In addition, interest groups donate other services to decision-

---

[39] Michael Lipsky, ''Protest as a Political Resource,'' *American Political Science Review*, vol. 62 (1968), pp. 1144–1158.

[40] Lipsky, ''Protest as a Political Resource,'' p. 1158.

[41] Milbrath, *The Washington Lobbyists*, p. 352.

makers, such as writing speeches, collecting data, drafting legislation, and so on. They may also function as an alternate constituency to the geographical one of elected officials—a constituency based upon shared interests.

On the negative side, interest groups have been charged with perpetuating certain inequalities in the political system, with failing to represent (or suppressing) certain points of view, and with exhibiting bias favoring the upper class, whose members are most likely to become involved in group activity. Upper-class attitudes in interest groups which exert a powerful influence on government have produced conservatism with regard to public policy. Interest groups are, with few exceptions, well-entrenched members of the establishment seeking to defend and reinforce the status quo. Finally, critics have questioned whether interest groups in America represent those who really deserve or need to be represented and, if they do not, whether the entire system is due for an extensive overhaul.

In reply to such criticism, it is pointed out that the interest-group system retains strongly democratic aspects. It is an open system; groups can form and take effective action for minority aims, as demonstrated, for example, by the NAACP and the National Welfare Rights Organization. Among the system's virtues is its dispersion of power—a dispersion which acts to modify the power of government officials in the Legislature, the bureaucracy, and the courts. Some observers have argued that interest-group influence is good because, without it, democratic participation would largely be confined to the vote—as in the Soviet Union, where 94 percent of the adult population votes, but where individuals are not allowed to form voluntary organizations. Thus, even though the system may be biased toward an elite and the status quo, it has room for conflicting interests and minorities, and permits accommodation to change.

SUGGESTED READING

Banfield, Edward C. *Political Influence: A New Theory of Urban Politics* (New York: The Free Press, 1961). In paperback. A study of the way influence works in a large American city. The author selects six representative political controversies from a two-year period in Chicago, describing those who actually made or influenced the decisions on these matters.

Bentley, Arthur F. *The Process of Government: A Study of Social Pressures* (Cambridge, Mass.: The Belknap Press of Harvard University Press, 1967. Originally published by University of Chicago Press, 1908). Intended as a scientific examination of human behavior, the book draws heavily on American history for illustrative data and focuses on group pressures as the dynamic factors at work in determining public policies.

Congressional Quarterly Service. *Legislators and Lobbyists,* 2nd edition (Washington, D.C.: Congressional Quarterly, 1968). A useful source book, containing a description of the unofficial role of lobbyists in the legislative process, an examination of the nature and extent of lobby activity, a review of the federal laws that regulate lobbying, and a discussion of particular lobby groups.

Engler, Robert. *The Politics of Oil: A Study of Private Power and Democratic Directions* (Chicago: University of Chicago Press, 1961). In paperback. A study of the nature of corporate power and its impact upon American political institutions. The author provides an overview of the political activity of the petroleum industry, documenting the methods used by that industry to influence law, governmental machinery, and public opinion.

Garceau, Oliver. *The Political Life of the American Medical Association* (Cambridge, Mass.: Harvard University Press, 1941). Description of how the AMA operates, what kinds of doctors become involved in the politics of the Association, and the impact of the AMA on public policy.

Hadwiger, Don F., and Ross B. Talbot. *Pressures and Protests: The Kennedy Farm Program and the Wheat Referendum of 1963* (San Francisco: Chandler, 1965). A case study of the Kennedy farm program, focusing on the pressure tactics of agricultural interest groups.

Holtzman, Abraham. *Interest Groups and Lobbying* (New York: Macmillan, 1966). In paperback. A brief examination of the organization and tactics of interest groups in America. The author explores the basis of interest-group power and the various ways in which interest groups promote the policies they favor.

Key, V. O., Jr. *Politics, Parties, and Pressure Groups.* 5th edition (New York: Thomas Y. Crowell, 1964). A classic description and analysis of American political parties and pressure groups. The author sees conflicting group interests and their mediation as the animating forces in the political process.

Lowi, Theodore J. *The End of Liberalism: Ideology, Policy, and the Crisis of Public Authority* (New York: Norton, 1969). In paperback. An examination and analysis of the political crisis of the 1960s—a crisis of public authority that, Lowi argues, arose from the failure of governmental and political institutions to cope with modern problems. At the root of the problem lies the liberal state, which is based on the assumption of pluralist theory that interest-group politics is the model of the good society.

Mahood, H. R. (ed.). *Pressure Groups in American Politics* (New York: Scribner, 1967). In paperback. A collection of readings dealing with the role of various types of pressure groups in public policy formation. The essays illustrate that because many nongovernmental organizations possess means of influencing the people and checking political decision-makers, they must be considered part of the governmental machinery.

McConnell, Grant. *Private Power and American Democracy* (New York: Knopf, 1967). In paperback. The author contends that public policy in America is made as much by private groups as by public officials and institutions. According to McConnell, a strong tradition of decentralization has fostered the development of an array of elite-based power structures, each with a narrow and specialized base of support, which exercise significant control over major areas of public policy.

Olson, Mancur, Jr. *The Logic of Collective Action, Public Goods and the Theory of Groups* (New York: Schocken, 1968). In paperback. A theory of group behavior, documented with empirical and historical studies of particular organizations. The author examines the extent to which the individuals who share a common interest find it in their individual interest to bear the costs of organizational effort.

Selznick, Philip. *TV and the Grass Roots.* (Berkeley, Calif.: University of California Press, 1949). A study of the impact of local power structure and interest groups on the development of a major public authority.

Truman, David B. *The Governmental Process: Political Interests and Public Opinion* (New York: Knopf, 1951). A systematic analysis and explanation of the political role of interests and interest groups in American politics. The author demonstrates how pressure groups influence, and are influenced by, the activities of political parties, legislatures, Presidents, governors, bureaucrats, judges, and the public; he also describes problems of organization and leadership within interest groups.

Wooton, Graham. *Interest Groups* (Englewood Cliffs, N.J.: Prentice-Hall, 1970). In paperback. A classification of interest groups, attempting to explain the different styles of behavior that interest groups exhibit. Wooton suggests four possible indicators of interest-group influence and examines the reasons why some interest groups are more influential than others.

Zeigler, Harmon. *Interest Groups in American Society* (Englewood Cliffs, N.J.: Prentice-Hall, 1964). In paperback. An interpretation of the role of formally organized interest groups in all branches, and at all levels, of government. The author discusses the development of group theory in political science.

12
POLITICAL PARTIES

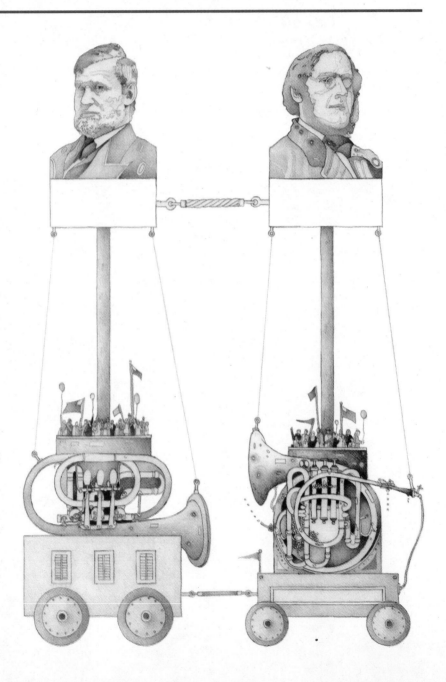

The Nature of American Party Politics

Why Have a Two-Party System?

Most Americans take the two-party political system of the United States for granted; in fact, the public even assumes it, somehow, to be the natural or logical ordering of politics. But actually, as compared to the party systems in many other countries, our political organization is quite unusual. For example, Canada has three major parties—the Progressive-Conservatives, the National Democrats, and the Liberals—in addition to a number of significant minor parties, such as the Social Credit party and the various separatist parties centered in Quebec. Italy has a multiparty system of government, where many different groups—from the Christian Democrats to the Communists—vie for power. In Japan and South Africa, there are two-party systems, but in both cases one of the parties is so strong as to make the second one into a token group. Why, then, do we in America have two major political parties—rather than forty, or seven, or one?

Many theories have been advanced on this subject through the years: the eighteenth-century Irish statesman and writer Edmund Burke claimed that everyone was born either a liberal or a conservative, and that the two main parties developed to serve as organizations designed to fit the lifelong needs of these two groups. Others believe in the "natural dualism" theory, which holds that all people naturally fall into one or another of various basic pairs of opposite traits—rich versus poor, weak versus strong, urban versus rural, North versus South—and that the inevitability of such splits requires the development and maintenance of two parties.[1] And yet others simply maintain that we have two political parties today because, traditionally, we have always had them.

More concrete theories about why the United States has developed a two-party system have also been suggested. For example, V. O. Key, Jr., has explained that our reason for having political parties in general is clear: it is the principal means for popular control of a government. Two parties developed largely because the government needed some machinery for winning votes once the United States' popular government was established and the ruling aristocrats of colonial times had lost their automatic authority.[2] Others point out that two parties generally allow for a more stable government than does a multiparty system, while a single party (such as that in Franco's Spain) is essentially the same as having no party at all, since the people have virtually no voice in their government's policy decisions, or in choosing public officials.

Democracy by its very nature seems to require at least two parties, so that the public is provided with viable alternatives. This arrangement, in America's case, seems to have led to stability in structure. England and the United States, two of the world's most enduring democracies, have long had two parties. On the other hand, the Weimar Republic of Germany (1921–1929), the Third Republic of France (1870–1940), and Italy since 1946 have all had multiple parties, and all have been extremely unstable politically. In fact, analysts believe that the

---

[1] Frank J. Sorauf, *Political Parties in the American System* (Boston: Little, Brown, 1964), p. 28.
[2] V. O. Key, Jr., *Politics, Parties, and Pressure Groups,* 5th edition (New York: Thomas Y. Crowell, 1962), p. 201. This source contains a detailed historical background on the development of American parties.

lack of political stability in Weimar Germany was the major reason for the rise of the Nazi party. Political systems with one active party are also incompatible with democracy. In the Soviet Union, for example, voting turnout is high, indicating popular participation, but the only choice is whether to accept or to reject the Communist party candidates. No alternatives are given.

Most political scientists believe America would be unlikely to develop a multiplicity of parties such as exists in certain European countries, because most of its citizens are relatively unconscious of class status, and do not consider politics in strong ideological terms.

Certain aspects of the American system of elections have also tended to limit its parties to two. According to the established system of election by single-member districts and pluralities of votes, only one officeholder can be elected in each district, and he need only get more votes than any of his opponents, not a majority of the total votes cast. Thus, third parties tend to atrophy within this system, because they cannot win elections often enough to build up political strength.

A different system of elections is used in countries such as France and Italy; there the system of proportional representation is used. Under this system, more than one person can represent a district, and the representatives reflect the proportion of the total number of votes they received in the election. That is, if the Communist party of Italy or France received 10 percent of the total vote, the Communists would get 10 percent of the total representatives, or seats. Some people argue that the system of proportional representation helps encourage multiple parties, since, under it, minorities are certain to win some seats and, thus, maintaining at least a little power in the government, can continue to exist as real forces. Proportional representation has not been used much in the United States; it was used in New York City from 1938 to 1946, and thereafter abandoned.

A final reason for our two-party system is explained by Clinton Rossiter: "One of the persistent qualities of the American two-party system is the way in which one of the major parties moves almost instinctively to absorb . . . the most challenging third party of the time."[3] For example, the Populist party, which developed and encouraged some important new ideas in the late nineteenth century was destroyed in 1892 when its primary platforms were taken over, in modified form, by the Democrats and Republicans.

The Function of Minor Parties

Despite the fact that our political process tends to limit their sphere of influence severely, minor parties have always existed in the United States, and will probably always continue to be a factor in our politics. V. O. Key, Jr., identified two types of minor parties: the *doctrinal parties*, such as the Socialists, who have a consistent philosophy and keep reappearing on the political scene, with various degrees of strength at various times; and the *transient parties*, based on faddish ideas—such as vegetarianism—which are generally short lived and politically insignificant.[4] More specifically, Clinton Rossiter divided minor parties into six

---

[3] Clinton Rossiter, *Parties and Politics in America* (Ithaca, N.Y.: Cornell University Press, 1968), p. 5.
[4] Key, *Politics, Parties, and Pressure Groups,* p. 255.

Robert M. LaFollette, who chalked up 16.7 percent of the vote as the Progressive party's 1924 presidential candidate, was second in history only to Theodore Roosevelt as a third-party presidential vote-getter.

types: *left-wing splinter groups* (such as the Socialists); *one-issue obsessionists* (like the Prohibitionists); *one-state party groups* (such as Minnesota's Farmer-Labor Party); *personal followings of the dissident hero* (such as the worshippers of Theodore Roosevelt and his Progressive Bull Moose party in 1912); *the dissident wings of a major party* (such as the Dixiecrats of 1948, a southern faction of the Democratic party); and *true minor parties* (such as the radical agrarian Populists).[5]

American third parties generally enter national and local elections in order to gain publicity for their causes; they seldom have any expectations of winning. Although the small parties which eventually merged into the Populist party in 1891 did, in fact, win considerable success in state and local elections in the southern and northwestern parts of the country in the 1890 election (including five seats in the Senate, forty-six in the House, and six governorships), strong support for their causes on the national level was not common. In 1972, however, there were predictions on the resurgence of the Populist party:[6]

---

[5] Rossiter, *Parties and Politics in America*, p. 4.

[6] The historian C. Vann Woodward has said that old political parties periodically revive. He discussed the history of the Populist party and the current populist movement. See C. Vann Woodward, "The Ghost of Populism Walks Again," *The New York Times Magazine* (June 4, 1972), pp. 16–17ff.

THE PEOPLE'S DEMOCRAT

Hubert Humphrey, long allied with civil-rights and labor advocates, listed his achievements in these fields under the heading Populism, a catchword for Democratic hopefuls in 1972.

It was just another week in American politics, 1972. John Lindsay called George Wallace a "phony Populist." George McGovern called John Lindsay a "Park Avenue Populist." Hubert Humphrey called himself "The People's Democrat," explaining at impressive length that the slogan meant he was and always has been a Populist. A New Jersey advertising man named Daniel Gaby went to an abandoned hotel ballroom in Newark to announce that he was the Populist candidate for the Democratic nomination for U.S. senator. . . . Jack Newfield and Jeff Greenfield, who used to compose rhetoric for Robert F. Kennedy, published a book called The Populist Manifesto.

Populism is in. It's what putting a little American flag in your lapel was a couple of years ago. Politicians of every stripe are discovering that by calling themselves Populists they can wrap themselves in all the right flags, Old Glory and the banners of Ralph Nader, George Wallace and the Sierra Club.[7]

But the infatuation with populism did not last long. In the final weeks of the 1972 campaign, there was very little mention of populism by either the Democratic

---

[7] Richard Reeves, "The New Populism and the Old: A Matter of Words," *Saturday Review* (April 8, 1972), p. 46.

Table 12–1   *Percentage of Popular Vote Gained by Third Parties in Presidential Elections since 1892*

Year	Candidate	Party	% of Vote
1892	James B. Weaver	People's	8.8
1904	Eugene V. Debs	Socialist	3.1
1908	Eugene V. Debs	Socialist	2.9
1912	Theodore Roosevelt	Progressive	27.8
	Eugene V. Debs	Socialist	6.1
1916	A. L. Benson	Socialist	2.2
1920	Eugene V. Debs	Socialist	3.5
1924	Robert M. LaFollette	Progressive	16.7
1928	Norman Thomas	Socialist	.7
1932	Norman Thomas	Socialist	2.2
1936	William Lemke	Union and others	1.9
1948	J. Strom Thurmond	States'-Rights Democrat (Dixiecrat)	2.4
	Henry A. Wallace	Progressive	2.4
1968	George C. Wallace	American Independent	13.6

or the Republican candidate. Some political observers attributed the short life of the new populism to its failure to develop workable means for achieving its goals.

A real Populism would be work, and would involve sacrifices in order to redistribute the benefits of an affluent society to all its citizens. Shouting at the Rockefellers and making them pay more taxes is fun, but that isn't going to bring a black family in Marianna, Florida, into the society and it isn't going to clean up the air over New York City.[8]

The largest percentage of the popular vote a third party has ever received is almost 28 percent, which was polled by Teddy Roosevelt as the Progressive candidate in 1912. Governor George C. Wallace of Alabama, who ran for the Presidency in 1968 on the American Independent Party ticket, won over 13 percent. In 1972, however, Wallace did not remain an American Independent, but ran in Democratic presidential primaries.

The Uniqueness of American Parties

Americans are generally inconsistent in their political attitudes, largely because they are not strongly ideological. Nor have strong ideological bases characterized the major parties in the United States, whereas parties in many other nations are strongly ideological. Marxist, Muslim, and Hindu parties, for example, tend to unite their members on many fundamental issues, values, and philosophies of life. In fact, religion has probably been the most frequent basis for the establishment of political parties throughout history and throughout the world.

Rather than encouraging members to think about positions on new issues according to established party lines and deep ideological commitment, parties in the United States espouse positions according to what issue the party leaders have been supporting or opposing, for whatever reasons.[9] Only in the United

---

[8] Reeves, "The New Populism and the Old," p. 47.
[9] Sorauf, *Political Parties in the American System,* p. 61.

States can one find so many voters fervently in favor and yet uninformed of a given measure—such as Medicare—simply because their party—in this case the Democratic—happens to be supporting that program at the time.

A barrier to ideological parties in the United States has been the need to win elections. This driving necessity also explains how our party leaders have consistently failed to fulfill their campaign promises. To win elections, a candidate must put together a coalition of diverse groups and interests. He cannot take too strong a stand on a given issue, for fear of alienating a large group of supporters. (Barry Goldwater's dramatic defeat in 1964 after he made statements that were construed as condoning nuclear war is a good example of this phenomenon.) Similarly, once elected, an officeholder cannot press too hard for fulfillment of campaign promises, if final achievement of the promised goal serves to alienate many of his constituents or potential sources of support for future elections. Since American politicians are subjected to frequent elections (every two years, for representatives), they must begin early in order to build support for their next election.

The structure of American political parties is designed to encourage frequent change in party membership. Unlike the party structure that exists in many other countries, ours is highly flexible. In the United States, a person who registers to vote as a Republican or Democrat pays no party dues, has to attend no party meetings, and can vote for the rival party or any one of several other minor parties in a given election, with no fear of reprisals, since his vote is secret. He can even change his party registration, merely by asking the voter-registration clerk to indicate his new affiliation on the proper forms. The frequency of switching one's vote from one party to another from election to election is quite common. Only about 34.8 percent of the electorate have strong party affiliations[10] (the figure for Republicans is 13.3 percent, for Democrats is 21.5 percent), and these people almost always (82 percent of the time) vote for the same party. An additional 39.6 percent of the public are classified as weak party identifiers, and they vote for their party 60 percent of the time. Since they do switch about 40 percent of the time, however, and are joined in their votes by independents who lean toward the Republican or Democratic party, and by pure independents (a category growing in recent years, as will be discussed later), there are all together quite a large number of Americans who cannot be said to support one party consistently. Their votes are cast for other reasons, including the personal appeal of candidates and issues.

What Is a Political Party?

After all this discussion of the nature and uniqueness of the American party system, it is time to ask just what a political party is and what it does. The term *political party* does not apply merely to a small group of high-level executives who make lengthy speeches around election time. A political party includes high- and low-level party leaders, a large corps of campaign workers, elected government officials, and ordinary voters who are loyal to the party. People often assume

---

[10] See Angus Campbell, Philip E. Converse, Warren E. Miller, and Donald E. Stokes, *The American Voter* (New York: Wiley, 1964), pp. 69–70, for all of the following statistics regarding party affiliation and voting patterns.

that high government officials are exclusively the leaders of parties, but party officials and elected officials are *not* the same; in fact, many of the strongest party leaders do not hold elective offices and are relatively unknown to the mass of the electorate. An assemblyman, for example, is an elected official and holds a government office, while the head of an assembly district, a party official, does not hold a government office. Jacob Arvey, a past chairman of the Regular Democratic Organization in Cook County, the county in which Chicago is situated, was an extremely powerful party official, although he did not hold a government office and was not widely known. Arvey, whose position is now held by Mayor Richard Daley, helped choose many Democratic nominees for the Presidency and Vice Presidency, while retaining his relative obscurity. Although the analogy is not perfect, Arvey's position was something like that of Joseph Stalin, who derived all his power from his position as Secretary of the Communist party but did not hold any government office.

A political party is usually defined as an organized group of people who are continually trying to place their own candidates in public office, so that they can control the government more effectively. In America, parties are seemingly necessary to set up and operate our government at four particularly important points in the system. When it is time for nominations to be made for government offices in an upcoming election, the party itself does the preliminary sifting and recruiting of likely candidates. Then, throughout a political campaign, party leaders and activists educate the voters, familiarizing them with the candidates' credentials. The party also provides workers—such as vote-counters—to help with the practical aspects of the actual election process; and when a party is victorious, its high-level members advise the newly elected official regarding those persons who are likely to be good appointees.

The Party
and Interest Groups

Some people see American political parties as mere interest groups, unable to govern the country effectively, squabbling among themselves, and wasting time and money. Of course, it is true that certain aspects of our party system tend to result in an inefficient government, but it should be made clear that there is an important difference between political parties and interest groups—interest groups cannot put candidates up for office under their interest-group name. The influential member of the group must align himself with a party. On the state and local level this alignment may result in such close identification of the interest group and party that the line of demarcation between the two becomes hazy. Political parties on the national level, however, are larger and more generalized organizations. Interest groups are usually smaller, more narrow and exclusive groups—such as the American Medical Association and the National Rifle Association; they concentrate their efforts on specific issues such as keeping health care in the private sector, or opposing gun-control legislation. In the United States, because parties are relatively weak and undisciplined, policy is not made according to deep party beliefs but according to which organized interests capture the party.[11] Theodore Lowi, a leading interest-group analyst,

[11] Frequently, minor parties, knowing they cannot win elections, act like organized interest groups, aligning themselves with the major party that best serves their interests, and vying for control within it.

has claimed that parties stand for nothing save these interest groups that capture them. He wrote:

The most important difference between Liberals and Conservatives, Republicans and Democrats—however they define themselves—is to be found in the interest groups they identify with. Congressmen are guided in their votes, Presidents in their programs, and administrators in their discretion by whatever organized interests they have taken for themselves as the most legitimate [at that time]; and that is the measure of the legitimacy of [the party's] demands.[12]

Lowi described this situation as unsatisfactory, since no one organized group represents the public and pushes for important national needs.

The Party and the Government

Why is there so much emphasis put on political parties if they are relatively weak and impotent? The answer is that political parties in America run elections, and the election of public officials is highly significant to a democracy. The Democratic and Republican parties, through the hullabaloo of nominations and campaigns, help the public change leadership peacefully and efficiently. This is no trivial matter: consider the bloodbaths and intrigue that accompany leadership changes in so many other countries. The election process presided over by the parties seems able to preserve the United States from military *coups d'état* and other difficulties which so often go along with the shift of government personnel.

Parties, which have been said to play a vital role in all areas—both tangible and intangible—in democracy, also link together the various levels of the government. Many experts hold that our political parties help to overcome the stalemate which might occur as a result of the separation of powers within the American government, because both parties have officials or strong supporters in each of the three branches of government who usually work together toward common goals. When the majority of Congress, for instance, is of the same party as the President, the Executive's legislative plan stands a good chance of being enacted exactly as he envisions it. When the majority of congressmen are of the opposing party, as has been the situation throughout the Nixon administration, bills usually get changed substantially before passage, if they are passed at all.

The History of American Political Parties

First Stage: The Origin of Parties

America has not always had organized political parties. In fact, with the founding of this country's permanent governmental structure, after the Revolution, many of our political leaders specifically counseled against the development of partisan politics or "factions." By 1787, however, James Madison, upset because all the states were acting independently of the national government, suggested that the national government check the states by balancing the factions that

---

[12] Theodore J. Lowi, *The End of Liberalism* (New York: Norton, 1969), p. 72.

had come to exist within each one and which, Madison said, were bound to always exist.[13] During the 1790s, both President Washington and his Vice President, John Adams, although realizing factions existed, voiced their suspicions about organized political parties. So did many others:

> *Most Americans in the early 1790's did not want parties. Not only the exalted George Washington, who was trying to be President of all the people, but Jefferson, Hamilton, and Madison railed against the spirit of party. . . . Party stood for selfish faction and petty maneuver. But the impulse toward political organization was inexorable.*[14]

The Constitution of the United States provided no rationale or regulation for the establishment of parties. On the contrary, parties are not even mentioned in the Constitution; the Founding Fathers apparently did not foresee the necessity for them. However, the split between Federalists and Anti-Federalists, which originated over whether or not to adopt the Constitution, is generally cited as the beginning of the American two-party system. In discussing the evolution of the American party system, Richard Hofstadter pointed out that the democratic system is based on a certain kind of opposition to government policies.[15] He argued that a democracy cannot be maintained unless there is a workable means for opposing government decisions. This opposition, in other words, must be articulate in criticizing existing doctrine and must be armed with alternatives to these programs. In addition it must be effective in winning offices, in order to carry out the changes it wishes to make. Hofstadter further pointed out that, in most other countries, organized opposition of the sort commonly practiced by American political parties is suppressed and regarded as intrinsically illegitimate and subversive. As recently as 1964, only 30 out of the 113 United Nations member countries had political systems with full legal opposition parties that had been in existence for a decade.[16] When the Founding Fathers contemplated such an opposition, wrote Hofstadter, they did so from their own particular historical perspective. They looked back on a history of England long filled with political parties and small factions involved in plots to murder the reigning monarch or perform other acts of treason. Sanctioning a similar opposition to established government did not seem reasonable to George Washington or to many other American leaders. In the past, opposition behavior had led only to irrational and generally unsuccessful action; they could not conceive of opposition in any other terms.

> *The idea of a legitimate opposition—recognized opposition, organized and free enough in its activities to be able to displace an existing government by peaceful means—is an immensely sophisticated idea, and it was not an idea that the Fathers found fully developed and ready to hand when they began their enterprise in republican constitutionalism in 1788.*[17]

Nevertheless, American political parties did develop. The first national party was the Federalist Party—founded by Alexander Hamilton (then Secretary of the Treasury) and dedicated to forming a strong central government, based

---

[13] James MacGregor Burns, *The Deadlock of Democracy* (Englewood Cliffs, N.J.: Prentice-Hall, 1963), p. 14.

[14] Burns, *The Deadlock of Democracy*, p. 27.

[15] This position is espoused by Richard Hofstadter in *The Idea of a Party System* (Los Angeles: University of California Press, 1969).

[16] Hofstadter, *The Idea of a Party System*, p. 7.

[17] Hofstadter, *The Idea of a Party System*, p. 8.

primarily on financial interests. The foes of the Federalists were Thomas Jefferson's Democratic-Republicans, basically an agrarian movement which also incorporated some urban strength, and which, in 1791, was in control of New York state through its Tammany Hall group. Modern terminology makes this history a bit confusing to follow, because the Democratic-Republicans, then referred to in short as the Republicans, were actually the forerunners of today's Democratic party. This first stage in the development of our party system ended in 1800 with the election of Thomas Jefferson as President; by this time the party divisions of weak central government (rural-agrarian interests) versus strong central government (urban-financial interests) became fairly clear.

Second Stage:
Free-Soilers and Civil War

The second stage in the development of our party system began in 1828, when Andrew Jackson, a hero from the War of 1812, was elected President. A new division occurred, completing the development of two major political parties such as we have today. The two new parties were the *Democrats* (led by Jackson), who were for popular rule, and their rivals the *Whigs*, a group of small bankers, merchants, and planters.

The 1848 election marked the emergence of a third party, the *Free-Soilers*, whose candidate, former President Van Buren, ran on a platform which seriously challenged that of the Democrats and the Whigs. The Free-Soilers were solid abolitionists and were the only significant political group to repudiate the controversial Compromise of 1850 between the states of the North and South. Further advocating free homesteads and a high tariff, the Free-Soilers lost the presidential election, but Van Buren probably pulled enough Democratic votes away from candidate Lewis Cass, a political nonentity, to throw the election to the Whigs' man, also an unfamiliar figure in politics, General Zachary Taylor.

By 1852, however, the political situation had splintered even further, and historical events had worsened. The Democrats were bitterly divided on the slavery issue between northern and southern membership; and it was obvious by then that the Civil War was on the horizon. The landslide victory of Franklin Pierce (a Democrat) in 1852 permanently crushed the Whigs, and left the political scene in chaos.

Out of that chaos, in 1854, came a new party to rival the Democrats. It was not merely the Whig party renamed, but rather a party born of protest against the extension of slavery into the newly acquired Western territories of the United States. This new rival party was the *Republican* party. Although they began slowly, the Republicans gathered enough strength so that their second presidential nominee, Abraham Lincoln, won the election of 1860 (albeit with only 39.8 percent of the popular vote), in which the Democrats ran two different candidates, one from the North and one from the South. Lincoln's victory meant future victory for the abolitionists in the Civil War. It began a period of Republican domination of the Executive branch of government which lasted until 1932 with only two interruptions (Grover Cleveland and Woodrow Wilson).

Republican Rule:
1860 to the New Deal

The period following the Civil War was marked by a rapid increase in industrialization, fed largely by an influx of immigrants. This industrialization resulted in the emergence of the financial "robber barons" and the formation of several minor political parties bent on fighting this new trend. Strongest of these parties was the *Populists* (the People's party), a radical agrarian movement founded in 1892. The Populists, whose rank-and-file membership was made up mostly of Western small farmers, nominated James B. Weaver, a former Democrat, as their presidential candidate in 1892. He lost, but received a solid amount of support (almost 9 percent of the popular vote); in that election the Populists also won a number of seats in Congress. Two other third parties which sprang up at that time were the *Grangers*—a group of discontented farmers—and the *Greenbackers* —who were against the government's proposed reduction of the amount of paper money in circulation.

The only other threat to this era of Republican rule came in 1912, when the party split into two factions, one supporting the *Progressive* party candidate, Theodore Roosevelt, for the Presidency, the other in favor of Robert Taft, a conservative. As a result of the split, the Democratic candidate, Woodrow Wilson, won that year, receiving 45.3 percent of the popular vote. However, even during Wilson's tenure of office, the major cities of political importance (Philadelphia, Pittsburgh, Chicago, and Cleveland) remained Republican, and World War I ended this brief interlude of Democratic authority.

The Democratic Coalition

Franklin D. Roosevelt broke the Republican monopoly and spearheaded a twenty-year period of Democratic control in America. His victory was largely due to the effects of the Great Depression, which caused many Republicans to switch their allegiance to the Democratic party. From 1935 to 1955, the Democrats added the support of minority groups and second-generation immigrants to their party, thereby making it much stronger and laying a solid base for the kind of party loyalty still seen among Democrats in many areas today.

The Breakdown of Party Loyalty

Although there are still large numbers of people who take the matter of party loyalty quite seriously (as discussed in Chapter 10), the trend since 1950 has been away from strong party allegiance. Since 1932 the United States has normally had a Democratic majority, with over 50 percent of its citizens declaring themselves Democrats. In the 1952 and 1956 elections, however, 55.1 percent and 57.4 percent, respectively, of the popular vote was cast for Dwight D. Eisenhower, a Republican. Clearly, then, Republicans acquired some support from declared Democrats in the fifties. Loyalty to party seems in fact to be breaking down among larger groups of people than ever before. After the 1960s, the coalition of diverse types of voters who had sustained the New Deal fell apart, as did their supportive organizations, the local political machines (powerful organized groups of local bosses who can virtually control the political activities of a given area). There are far fewer political machines and bosses today than there once were—Mayor Daley of Chicago is perhaps the best-known political boss still in evidence. New York City, once ruled with a strong fist by Tammany Hall, is an example *par excellence* of the decline of bossism. Edward Costikyan, a former leader of New York County's Democratic party, wrote:

1961 marked the end of the hurricane stirred up after World War II by the returning veterans, and the beginning of new and different competing forces . . . and on primary

Figure 12–1   **The Emergent Independent Majority, 1900–1968**

Third-party candidates often inspire voters to split their tickets, but the overall trend has been for voters to ignore party labels.

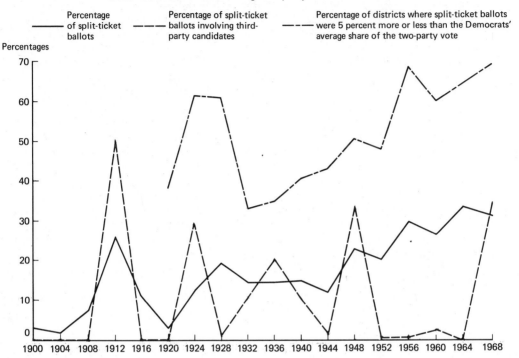

Source: Walter Dean Burnham, "The End of American Party Politics," Trans-Action, vol. 7, no. 2 (December 1969), p. 18.

day, September 5, 1961, the mayor [Robert F. Wagner, who successfully "wooed" the "reform" democrats and not the "regulars"] won. On the ballot with him and also successful were twenty-eight reform district leaders in Manhattan, the home of Tammany. Reform had triumphed and the bosses were dead![18]

The 1960s:
The Rise of the Independents

The 1960s, under the diverse leadership of Presidents Kennedy, Johnson, and Nixon, were another period of party realignment. In 1968 and 1972, increasing numbers of workers and union members abandoned their Democratic party allegiance and voted for Nixon and Wallace in presidential elections, and for Republican mayors and governors in many local elections.[19] Walter Dean Burnham attributed the breakdown of party loyalty, which he termed "electoral dis-

---

[18] Edward N. Costikyan, *Behind Closed Doors: Politics in the Public Interest* (New York: Harcourt Brace Jovanovich, 1966), pp. 27, 29.

[19] A good source for further details on the history of political parties in the United States is Wilfred E. Binkley, *American Political Parties: Their Natural History,* 4th edition (New York: Knopf, 1962).

aggregation," to a continuing increase in independents and ticket-splitters which began at the outset of the thirties.[20] He identified the New Deal as a force which halted this earlier move toward party breakdown. The New Deal, he pointed out, could control this tendency only as long as the issues generated by the Great Depression remained central to the majority of the electorate. As a result, he said, "Since 1952, electoral disaggregation has resumed, in many measurable dimensions" (see Figure 12–1).[21]

Similar observations were also noted by Richard M. Merelman, who in 1970 estimated that from 45 to 50 percent of American voters would change their political party alignments in the future.[22] The major participants in the independent movement, Merelman predicted, would be new voters and adults up to the age of thirty-four, who by 1985 will make up 44 percent and 82 percent, respectively, of the electorate.[23]

Even the most negative predictions about the future of American party loyalty—predictions that take into account factors such as the recent breakdown in party loyalty of voters and the no-longer-solid-Democratic South—must not underestimate the resiliency of parties in the United States. Throughout our history, political parties have been challenged, threatened, and near collapse—but the two major parties have not died. Despite the demise of numerous third parties, the Democrats have been around since about 1828, and the Republicans since 1854; and neither group seems about to expire. Rather, they seem to be changing. How have these institutions been able to maintain their remarkable longevity? While that question may not have a precise answer, examining the basic structure of American parties helps in understanding their stability.

The Structure of American Parties

The major American parties are both more and less than they seem, in terms of their organization. They are more, because there is a formal structure, from the grass roots of the rank-and-file members up to the Chief Executive (who is usually the strongest single individual of the party in power). This formal structure includes innumerable committees, officers, clerks, and such complex processes as the national Presidential convention. At the same time, however, our political parties are less than they seem, because, while in theory they are highly organized formal structures, in fact they have always been fragmented and decentralized. The recent breakdown of party loyalty may be an extension of this fragmentation in party structure. Our parties are seldom pictured any longer in the traditional structural "pyramid" (with a single, powerful leader at the top; a number of captains, lieutenants, and minor party officials beneath him; and myriad ordinary citizens forming the base), but rather as a series of separate and parallel layers or segments, none of them directly connected to any of the others.[24]

---

[20] Walter Dean Burnham, "The End of American Party Politics," *Trans-Action,* vol. 7 (December 1969), pp. 17–19.

[21] Burnham, "The End of American Party Politics," p. 18.

[22] Richard M. Merelman, "Electoral Instability and the American Party System," *The Journal of Politics,* vol. 32, no. 1 (February 1970), pp. 125, 139.

[23] Merelman, "Electoral Instability and the American Party System," p. 134.

[24] Key, *Politics, Parties and Pressure Groups,* p. 316.

Major political machines like that of Chicago's Mayor Richard Daley (right) are showing signs of wear, but conciliatory liberals like Senator Edward Kennedy court their support, vital to party unity.

Clearly, party decentralization has always been, and is likely always to be, a serious issue. Decentralization, in this case, means that, because of the strength of parties at the local level, the national party officials have very little control over political decisions made by the local party officials. This party localism is reinforced by the Constitution itself, which allows state legislatures to determine, within certain general guidelines, in what manner local elections shall be held. Frank Sorauf has called decentralization the most important aspect of our parties today.[25] Because state and local party representatives meet together only once every four years, in the national conventions (where state organizations do the party's national-level work), the parties do not really exist at a national level. Although the party organization has a great deal of power at the state level, and is extremely well organized at the city and county levels, there exists no real party power on a national scale.

The party boss, so common in America in past years, is another symptom of party decentralization. Political bosses are not found in other countries with well-developed party systems. In the United States there are still some state and local bosses (but none on the regional or national levels), all completely independent of each other, and all immune, for practical purposes, from any nationally based control or criticism. While this problem is becoming increas-

[25] Sorauf, *Political Parties in the American System*, pp. 39–43.

ingly less significant in current political dealings, the local or state party machines which continue to operate, such as those in Chicago and New Jersey, can still cause intraparty conflicts of great magnitude. For example, there was quite a stir created at the 1972 Democratic presidential convention when Chicago's mayor, Richard Daley, and the regular Democratic organization lost their seating bid to McGovern supporters.

The District, County, State, and National Committees

The organizational structures of the Democrats and Republicans are similar. Each party consists of committees at the various levels of government—district, county, state, and nation. Each level of organization has a chairman, and sometimes county or even district chairmen are more powerful than state chairmen. All but the national committee exist primarily for the purpose of picking nominees and candidates for office and for defining how state delegates to the national convention will be chosen; the result of this party structure is that the delegate-selection system varies from state to state.

The national committee is the most widely publicized of the party committees, although party organization is strongest and in tighter control at the district and county levels. Although most frequently discussed, the national committee is, in fact, a "non-thing," which seldom meets and has only a limited number of tasks to perform. National party committees consist of one man and one woman from each state and members from some of the United States territories such as Puerto Rico and the Virgin Islands.

In the Republican party, party loyalty is rewarded by making the state party chairman a national committeeman if his state has a Republican governor, a majority of its congressmen are from the Republican party, or his state has cast its electoral votes in the previous presidential election for the Republican candidate. When the national committee does meet, its primary job is to choose the city in which the national convention will be held. Considering how few American cities have sufficient hotel, restaurant, law-enforcement, and meeting-space facilities to accommodate all the people and paraphernalia of a presidential convention, this choice is far more limited than it might seem. Thus the national committee really becomes important only once every four years, when it organizes the convention for the purpose of choosing the party's presidential candidate. Between elections, the committee does various sorts of public-relations work for the party, such as putting out newsletters and advertising party-oriented legislation.

The chairmanship of the national committee is a much-sought-after position, which only sometimes confers real power on the person who holds it. According to party regulations, the national chairman should be elected by the members of the national committee. In fact, however, national chairmen are chosen by the party's presidential candidate. Party regulations also provide that the national chairman serve as the campaign manager of the party's presidential nominee. While it is by no means unreasonable for a presidential nominee to select his own campaign manager, the bypassing of rules in the choice of the campaign manager can strain party tempers. It seems ironic that parties, democratizing agents of our political system, do not operate democratically themselves.

Power comes to the national committee chairman only when his party occu-

Table 12–2   *Delegate Selection Systems in 1972*

Convention Systems		Committee Systems	Primary Systems	
Alaska	Mississippi	Arizona	Alabama	New Jersey
Canal Zone	Missouri	Georgia*	Arkansas	New Mexico
Colorado	Montana	Louisiana*	California	New York
Connecticut	Nevada	Puerto Rico	District of	North Carolina
Delaware	North Dakota		Columbia	Ohio
Guam	South Carolina		Florida	Oregon
Hawaii	Texas		Illinois	Pennsylvania
Idaho	Utah		Indiana	Rhode Island
Iowa	Vermont		Maryland	South Dakota
Kansas	Virginia		Massachusetts	Tennessee
Kentucky	Virgin Islands		Michigan	West Virginia
Maine	Wyoming		Nebraska	Wisconsin
Minnesota			New Hampshire	

* This placement pertains to the Democratic Party. The GOP utilized congressional district and state conventions.

Source: The New York Times *(July 23, 1971);* Congressional Quarterly Weekly Report, *vol. 30, no. 4 (January 22, 1972); p. 138; and various issues of* Congressional Quarterly Weekly Report *(January–June 1972).*

pies the White House. Backed by the President, a more than considerable source of support, the national chairman can hold out the promise of political appointments. When his party is not in power the national chairman's usefulness declines greatly, and the party is ruled by its congressional leaders. This situation, unfortunately, often leads to tension between party leaders in Congress and those on the national committee.

Congressional and Senatorial Campaign Committees

The other significant national party committees are the congressional and senatorial campaign committees. Both the Democrats and the Republicans have committees in the House and the Senate, the members of which are chosen by the party members in the appropriate branch of Congress. These committees channel money, advice, and other types of support to party members who are up for reelection to Congress.

The Party Structure and the Nominating Process

The process by which a politician becomes a nominee for any office is an intraparty procedure. Primaries were established as a means of taking the power to nominate candidates away from party leaders and giving it to the people. Direct primaries for congressional seats began in the early twentieth century. All primaries are independently regulated by the party structure of the state or territory. Their use has become widespread; almost all nominations on the state, county, and local levels for such offices as mayor, state legislator, senator, congressman, and governor are first submitted to the public through party or nonpartisan primary elections. Only candidates for the high office of President are not selected in this manner, but, instead, are chosen by a national convention of party delegates.

The enthusiastic Democratic-primary response to George C. Wallace in 1972 presidential primaries outside the South showed that the 1968 third-party presidential candidate had a national following, at the grass-roots if not at the committee level.

Electing the President: Presidential Primaries and Delegate Selection to the National Convention As indicated in Table 12–2, the national conventions which select their party's presidential nominee are chosen by various methods which differ from state to state. Many states do hold primaries, but others use state conventions or state committees for this purpose. Those that use committees are subject to strongest control by leading party members; it is believed that delegations to some national conventions from Louisiana and Georgia have been chosen entirely by the governors of those states. Richard Daley, mayor of Chicago, had absolute power over the choice of Democratic delegations to the conventions from 1956 to 1968. His power was upset by a dramatic change in delegate-selection procedures instituted by the supporters of George McGovern in 1972. The primary that year, conducted under new party regulations, gave greater representation to minority groups, youth, and women.

Why would a presidential candidate enter a state primary? John F. Kennedy's participation in the West Virginia primary of 1960 gave his candidacy a big boost, and certainly Eugene McCarthy's 1968 campaign was greatly helped by his primary victories in New Hampshire, Oregon, and California. On the other hand, Edmund Muskie's chances of winning the Democratic nomination

Table 12–3   Democratic Party Primaries, 1972[1]

State	Is There a Presidential-Preference Poll?	Are Delegates Bound at the Convention?	Is Primary Open or Closed?	Are Write-ins Allowed?	Number of Delegates	Method of Delegate Selection
Alabama	no	election of delegates who may be informally pledged	open	no	37	29 district delegates elected; 6 at-large delegates chosen by those elected; 2 at-large delegate seats filled automatically
Arkansas	no	election of unpledged delegates	closed	no	27	22 elected in primary; 5 chosen by elected delegates
California	yes—mandatory	binding till candidate releases; slates of delegates elected who may be pledged	closed	yes	271	238 elected in primary; 11 congressional delegates elected; 22 at-large delegates chosen by delegates
District of Columbia	yes—mandatory	slates of delegates list presidential choices; if pledged, a winning slate must vote for candidate for 2 ballots	closed	no	20	all elected in primary
Florida	yes—mandatory	binding for 2 ballots unless candidate releases or receives less than 35% of vote	closed	no	81	61 congressional district delegates chosen at district caucuses; 12 at-large delegates chosen at state caucus; 8 at-large delegates chosen by state Democratic committee
Illinois	yes—advisory	poll is nonbinding; election of delegates whose preferences are listed	closed	yes	170	160 delegates elected in primary; 10 at-large delegates chosen by elected delegates
Indiana	yes—mandatory	binding for 1 ballot	closed	no	76	57 congressional district delegates chosen by district caucuses; 19 at-large delegates chosen by state convention
Maryland	yes—mandatory	binding on delegates for 2 ballots unless candidate releases or receives less than 35% of vote	closed	no	53	48 congressional districts elected; 5 at-large delegates chosen by those elected
Massachusetts	yes—mandatory	binding on delegates for 1 ballot	closed	yes	102	82 delegates elected in primary; 20 at-large delegates elected
Michigan	yes—mandatory	binding for 2 ballots, or until released sooner	open	no	132	99 congressional district delegates chosen at district conventions; 33 at-large delegates chosen

State		Primary	Delegate binding		Delegates	Delegate selection
Nebraska	yes—mandatory	closed	election of delegates who may be pledged; pledged delegates must vote for candidate for 2 ballots, until released or candidate receives less than 35% of vote	yes	24	6 congressional district delegates elected; 16 at-large delegates elected in primary
New Hampshire	yes—mandatory	closed	election of delegates who may be pledged; pledged delegates bound till candidate releases	yes	20	all delegates elected in primary
New Jersey	yes—advisory	closed	nonbinding; election of delegates who may be pledged	yes	109	all delegates elected in primary
New Mexico	yes—mandatory	closed	binding for 1 ballot	no	20	all delegates chosen by state convention
New York	no	closed	election of unpledged delegates whose loyalties known to voters	yes, under certain conditions	278	congressional district 278 delegates elected in primary
North Carolina	yes—mandatory	closed	binding for 1 ballot	no	64	48 congressional district delegates chosen at district conventions; 14 at-large delegates chosen by state convention; 2 delegate seats filled automatically
Ohio	yes—advisory	closed	nonbinding election of delegates who specify 1st and 2nd presidential preferences	no	153	115 delegates elected by congressional district; 38 at-large delegates elected
Oregon	yes—mandatory	closed	binding for 2 ballots, unless candidate receives less than 35% of vote on first ballot or unless delegates released	yes	34	32 delegates elected by congressional district; 2 delegates named automatically

[1] Republican primaries were held in 1972 in each of these states under different regulations stipulated by the Republican party. These primaries, however, held far less significance than those of the Democrats; because President Nixon was up for reelection, few competitors entered the Republican contests, and none acquired any significant degree of Republican support.

(continued)

Table 12-3 **Democratic Party Primaries, 1972** (continued)

State	Is There a Presidential-Preference Poll?	Are Delegates Bound at the Convention?	Is Primary Open or Closed?	Are Write-ins Allowed?	Number of Delegates	Method of Delegate Selection
Pennsylvania	yes—advisory	election of delegates who may be pledged; pledged delegates bound for 1 ballot	closed	yes	182	137 delegates elected by state senatorial district; 27 at-large delegates chosen by those elected; 18 at-large delegates chosen by state committee
Rhode Island	yes—mandatory	binding for 1 ballot	closed	no	22	all delegates elected at large
South Dakota	yes—advisory	election of delegates who may be pledged; pledged delegates bound for 3 ballots	closed	no	20	all delegates elected at large
Tennessee	yes—mandatory	binding on delegates for 2 ballots, or until candidate gets less than 20% or releases sooner	closed	yes	49	most delegates chosen at congressional district conventions; a few at-large delegates chosen by state conventions
West Virginia	yes—advisory	nonbinding	closed	yes	35	26 congressional district delegates elected, 9 at-large delegates elected
Wisconsin	yes—mandatory	binding on delegates for 1 ballot, or until candidate releases or gets less than 1/3 of vote	open	no	67	56 congressional district delegates elected; 11 at-large delegates elected

in 1972 were blasted by his poor showing in New Hampshire's primary. But huge successes and debilitating failures are not always predictable. Candidates enter primaries so that they will become known to the public and to state conventions and so that they will gain sufficient support to make their nomination at the national convention inevitable. In addition, attempting to win primary support is almost always helpful as a gauge to winning a national election; a politician's inabilities and unpopularity are unavoidably revealed somewhere along the primary trail. Candidates who are not well known or who are far behind generally have little to risk in entering primaries, providing they can raise the funds to do so (see Chapter 13). Winning the contests demonstrates popularity, and losing them generally puts the candidate in no worse a position than he was in when he began.[26] Demonstrating popularity through the primaries does not, however, insure winning the nomination. Estes Kefauver, for example, not well known in 1952, entered fifteen out of sixteen primaries and won twelve of them; he then lost the nomination to Adlai E. Stevenson.

As Table 12–3 indicates, some states emphasize delegate selection, while others stress a presidential-preference poll; some hold both. In all but two states, the primary elections are closed. This means that only registered members of political parties can vote, and they can participate only in the primary of the party with which they are affiliated. Of the states that stress delegate selection in their primaries, there are four types of elections; each one uses different means of combining delegate selection with binding or nonbinding public commitments to candidates by each delegate.[27] Frequently, voting procedures in these primaries are confusing, and high percentages of voters go to the polls unaware that they will see no well-known names of candidates on the ballot.

Among the states that hold votes on the candidates themselves in presidential-preference polls, the resulting mandate for the delegates may be either advisory or mandatory. There is always the possibility, however, that when an advisory poll is conducted, the delegates can vote their own will at the convention, a will not reflected in the statewide poll. They have frequently done so; for this reason advisory polls are not utilized too widely, and harsh critics sarcastically refer to them as "beauty contests."[28] The presidential-primary system has become so complex that one critic has claimed:

They are bewilderingly varied in rules, techniques and significance and have in their totality no more relevance to the will of the people than the choice of a President by a combination of poker, chess and roulette.[29]

In addition to their differences in detail, all presidential primaries do not hold equal weight. The significance of each varies according to which state the pri-

---

[26] Robert Bendiner, in "Presidential Primaries," *The New York Times Magazine* (February 27, 1972), says the contrary. He notes that in the past some primaries have been "sudden-death." He cites Wendell Wilkie as having been defeated after losing the Wisconsin primary in 1944; Harold Stassen, defeated in the 1948 Oregon primary; Robert Taft, finished in the 1952 New Hampshire primary; Hubert Humphrey, wrecked in the 1960 West Virginia race; and Nelson Rockefeller, defeated in California's primary of 1964.

[27] This categorization of delegate-selection contests, as well as the classification of presidential-preference polls, can be found in Paul T. David, Ralph M. Goldman, and Richard C. Bain, *The Politics of National Party Conventions,* revised edition (New York: Vintage, 1964), pp. 193–205.

[28] James Michener, "One Man's Primary and How He Lost," *The New York Times Magazine* (May 21, 1972).

[29] Bendiner, "Presidential Primaries," p. 43.

mary is conducted in and who is on the ballot. For instance, any winner in a Republican primary in 1972 in which President Nixon's name was not on the ballot could hardly claim to be a leading contender for the Republican nomination. Because costs of contests are so exorbitant, it is not uncommon for politicians to pick and choose very carefully what races they enter. Thus, a little-known candidate can enter a poorly contested primary, get more votes than any other nominee on the ballot, and claim to have won. His victory is not really very significant.

The details of this hodgepodge system of presidential primaries can obscure recognition of how limited a place primaries hold in the final nomination of each party's candidate. In addition to the fact that not all states hold presidential primaries, the mean voter turnout in these primaries is, according to one study based on seventy-two primaries between 1948 and 1968, 27 percent of the population as compared to 62 percent who vote in the general election.[30] Another study reported similar findings, stating that primary turnout is 51 percent of the turnout for the general presidential election.[31] Such figures do not indicate very high voter participation on the average. Yet wide variance in the size of voter turnout does exist from state to state. In California, for example, voter turnout in primary elections is typically quite high. If primaries consistently attracted more voters, then supporters of presidential primaries could claim that primaries added to the popular choice of the President. One study asserted that voter turnout would improve if more primaries were binding and if two or more serious candidates were on every primary ballot. More precisely, the study concluded,

Evidence strongly suggests, but does not prove, that the number of candidates has more influence on the turnout than does the fact that a primary is binding. Nevertheless, the clear implication is that primaries might more nearly meet the first criterion of popular choice—high turnout—if more of them bound convention delegates to support the winner of a widely contested primary.[32]

The Democrats Select a Presidential Nominee: 1972 Although the delegate-selection procedures for presidential nominating conventions are not uniform and remain complicated in some states, the Democrats have attempted to make the process more equitable. A privately funded, unofficial study under the chairmanship of Senator Howard Hughes of Iowa was conducted before the 1968 convention. After presentation of recommendations to the convention, a resolution was passed calling for delegate-selection processes "in which all Democratic voters have had full and timely opportunity to participate." In ascertaining whether a state party has complied with this requirement, two criteria would be imposed: the unit rule (by which one candidate receives total delegate sup-

---

[30] Austin Ranney, "Turnout and Representation in Presidential Primary Elections," *American Political Science Review,* vol. 66 (March 1972), p. 23. Ranney also notes that three voter-turnout studies substantiate that over 20 percent more voters participate in general gubernatorial, congressional, and senatorial elections than in their respective primaries. Primary turnout is somewhat over 30 percent; general-election turnout over 50 percent.

[31] Harvey Zeidenstein, "Presidential Primaries—Reflections of 'The People's Choice'?," *The Journal of Politics,* vol. 32, no. 4 (November 1970), pp. 860–862.

[32] Zeidenstein, "Presidential Primaries—Reflections of 'The People's Choice'?," p. 872.

The new broadly based makeup of the 1972 Democratic convention was played up festively by delegates belonging to groups represented in large numbers for the first time.

port although he received only a majority or plurality of the state's support) could not have been used in any stage of the selection process; and all attempts to select delegates must have been made within one year before the convention by primary, convention, or committee procedures open to public participation. Such broad guidelines called for clarification; in February 1969 the Commission on Party Structure and Delegate Selection was formed, headed by Senator George McGovern of South Dakota. More than a dozen specific requirements were imposed on the states. In addition, the Commission urged the states to abolish all fees necessary for delegate selection and to ease any monetary burdens imposed on delegates or those running for delegate seats. Other pleas were made to end all committee appointments of delegates. The combined effects of the specific requirements and pleas was forceful prodding to dispense with electing delegations in a manner that would eliminate representation of minority views and pressure to permit fair access to the party, fair state apportionment to the convention, and fair representation of racial and ethnic minorities, women, and youth.

The 1972 Democratic convention saw a radical change in convention attendance. Of the delegates, 79 percent had never before been at a national party convention, 36 percent were women, 21 percent were members of minority groups, 21 percent were under thirty years of age.[33] Despite their newness to

[33] The source of these statistics is *Newsweek* (June 26, 1972), p. 22, which can be consulted for a state-by-state breakdown of the categories mentioned.

the convention system and their youthfulness, the group seemed to most commentators to be hard working and serious about their appointed or elected duty.

The National Convention   The event which is the focal point for both the Democratic and Republican national committees and the most widely followed part of our political process, save for the presidential election itself, is the national convention. National party conventions came into existence surprisingly late in our electoral history. And, while it may be difficult to imagine how a United States President could have been elected without the aid of these crowded, chaotic, and curious gatherings, in fact our Chief Executive's election was managed without it, and apparently rather well, for over forty years. Candidates for political office were originally selected by congressional caucus. The first true national conventions were held before the election of 1832, largely in response to the actions of Andrew Jackson, who, in 1824, knowing that he could not win his party's nomination, boycotted its caucus in Congress. It was decided that some sort of electoral reform was needed to insure a fair process of candidate selection, and the national convention was born.[34]

During modern conventions, which last three or four days, presidential and vice-presidential candidates are chosen, a party platform is agreed upon, and a campaign is launched. In addition to these time-consuming functions, the convention is the national governing body of each party. For all these purposes, four standing committees have been established: Credentials; Permanent Organization, which selects convention officials (the chairman, vice chairman, secretary, and sergeant-at-arms); Rules; and Resolutions.

The Republicans and Democrats employ different formulas for assigning delegate seats, resulting in 1,346 seats for the Republican party and 3,016 for the Democratic party. Both parties have provided for United States territories to be represented, with 16 delegate seats allocated to them by the Democrats and 11 by the Republicans. These figures, however, do not come near the total number of people who flock to the convention city. Aside from the delegates who are permitted on the convention floor, alternate delegates, selected or elected by each state, may attend, although they have no vote. In addition, there are hundreds of media people, party officials, and "whips" (strategy and liaison workers for each candidate) who have access to the hall. It is estimated that, in total, close to forty thousand people journeyed to Miami Beach for the 1972 Democratic convention. So that it will be clear exactly who is permitted on the floor, delegates, alternates, and others with official permission must wear identifying tags. Security is tight; so tight, in fact, that thousands of boxes of southern fried chicken donated to one party were X-rayed before they were permitted to be placed on the delegates' seats.

THE CREDENTIALS BATTLES.   The Credentials Committee is frequently the site of much heavy battle. In performing the function of certifying all delegates and alternates, the Committee must settle disputes between contesting delegations. While this procedure is generally regarded as a formality, groups dissatisfied with the Committee's dicta often take their cases to the convention floor. This kind of

---

[34] For a thorough discussion of the history of the national convention, see David, Goldman, and Bain, *The Politics of National Party Conventions*, pp. 39–80.

conflict has occurred most frequently, but not exclusively, among the Democrats. The 1912 and 1952 Republican conventions offered spectacular examples of such struggles, with results that directly influenced the choice of the party's nominee. In 1912, delegations supporting William Howard Taft were seated instead of those pledged to Theodore Roosevelt. The result gave Taft the nomination and led to the formation of Roosevelt's Progressive party. In 1952, delegations pledged to Senator Robert A. Taft were dislodged, Eisenhower delegates were substituted, and Eisenhower won the nomination.

Most of the Democratic credentials challenges up to 1972 have turned on the seating of southern delegations charged with party disloyalty and/or discrimination against blacks in their states. Prime examples were the battles over seating the Mississippi delegation in 1964 and the Georgia delegation in 1968.

The credentials controversies of the 1972 Democratic convention were of a different nature, however. They raged over the new Democratic reforms. One new rule had forbidden the winner-take-all policy (or unit rule) as applied in the California delegate-selection primary. California thus would have been forced to seat McGovern delegates in the same proportion as the amount of votes he won in the California primary, but the convention instead followed the winner-take-all seating policy. In October 1972 a Supreme Court decision was still pending on whether a convention is bound to follow its own rules.

Another heated controversy at this convention was the seating of the Illinois delegation, a battle that centered around Mayor Richard Daley of Chicago and how much power he, an old-time party boss, should hold. The Credentials Committee stripped what had come to be "Daley's delegation" of its seats because it was found in violation of reform guidelines.

The insurgent slate, which had organized to conform to the guidelines, included the highly visible and articulate Jesse Jackson and came to symbolize, in the minds of most delegates, a black alternative to the Daley slate. The issue was additionally complicated by the fact that Daley was a triple symbol: First, he was the symbol of the Chicago repression and the police riots of 1968; second, he was a symbol of the establishmentarian, old-line half of the party; and, third, he was a symbol of effective machine politics, of victory.[35]

When thrown open to the floor the Credentials Committee's decision was upheld, and Mayor Daley's delegation dislodged.

THE PLATFORM.   A recommended platform, representing the labor of the Resolutions Committee, is placed before the convention for approval. In most cases the formal presentation of the platform is a relatively minor part of the convention process, but the compromise and piecing together of the document in committee is a considerable task. The resultant document boasts of achievements if the party is in power and is highly critical if it is not. The platform, then, is a collection of political issues tied closely to the main business of the convention—more of an electioneering document than a blueprint for action.[36]

The adoption of the platform does not occur in isolation from the other activities of the convention but is ordinarily integrally related to the other major decisions of that body.

---

[35] Victor S. Navasky, "A Funny Thing Happened on the Way to the Coronation," *The New York Times Magazine* (July 23, 1972), pp. 37, 39.
[36] Key, *Politics, Parties, and Pressure Groups*, p. 421.

Usually the group that controls the nomination also controls the resolutions committee. Commonly the questions of policy that are intertwined with the nomination will also vex the platform drafters.[37]

There are numerous interesting cases of planks or sections of platforms dealing with specific issues being brought to the convention floor. In 1928, for example, a minority plank on agriculture supported by fifteen states was defeated by the Republicans; by 1932, this faction had rebelled against the rest of the party. Similarly, in 1948, the Democrats were faced with a civil-rights plank. The liberals of the North triumphed, with the result that sectional split within the party was widened. This particular struggle also pointed up the need for conciliatory politics in the American party system. As V. O. Key remarked, "The entire incident demonstrated, at least negatively, the uses of platform ambiguity in holding together party groups of divergent views."[38] In 1972, several minority planks relating to current social issues arose at the Democratic convention. Among the topics brought up were abortion, tax reform, gay liberation, and welfare rights. All four of these planks were defeated.

The result of the lengthy process by which platforms are passed is a rather noncommittal and unclear document. Although platforms reflect only moderate agreement between the two parties, one study revealed that the platform pledges of the two parties conflicted only about one-tenth of the time.[39]

The platform is direct on the issues that divide the parties and general on the issues that are divisive within the party. If this were not so, coalitions could never be formed and candidates never chosen. The importance of the platform to those who write it far surpasses the public's interest. It is not generally the inclusion or omission of a particular plank that determines whether a voter casts his ballot for the Republican or Democratic candidate.

WHO ATTENDS A CONVENTION.   The delegate-selection process, although greatly improved by the Democrats, has over the years been criticized for one inherently discriminatory aspect—the money factor. Persons selected to be delegates must pay their own way—transportation to and from the convention city, room and board, and other expenses while there. This stricture effectively prohibits a great many underprivileged persons from having a larger voice in their own party government. This criticism of elitism becomes even broader when one examines the delegate constituency of all conventions before 1972. In general, the delegations were far from representative of the states from which they came. They represented only the upper economic stratum; they tended to be almost all white even when the state had a large black population; largely male; and almost all composed of delegates a good deal older than twenty-one years old, denying young voters a fair say in party decisions. Some of these conditions, such as the token or unfair representation of blacks, women, and young people, have been rectified by the Democrats only. The major criticism, that economic considerations lead to discriminatory selection, remains valid.

---

[37] Austin Ranney and Wilmoore Kendall, *Democracy and the American Party System* (New York: Harcourt Brace Jovanovich, 1956), pp. 456–457.

[38] Key, *Politics, Parties, and Pressure Groups*, pp. 420–421.

[39] See Gerald M. Pomper, *Elections in America: Control and Influence in Democratic Politics* (New York: Dodd, Mead, 1968), pp. 193–194.

Table 12–4   **Number of Presidential Ballots in National Party Conventions, 1928–1968**

Year	Democrats	Republicans
1928	1	1
1932	4	1*
1936	1*	1
1940	1*	6
1944	1*	1
1948	1*	3
1952	3	1
1956	1	1*
1960	1	1
1964	1*	1
1968	1	1
First-ballot Total	9/11 (5 incumbents)	9/11 (2 incumbents)

First-Ballot Nominations: nonincumbents 11/15; incumbents 7/7

* Incumbents renominated.

Source: James W. Davis, National Conventions: Nominations under the Big Top *(Woodbury, N.Y.: Barron's Educational Series, Inc., 1972), p. 56.*

BALLOTING AT THE CONVENTION: THE SELECTION OF CANDIDATES.   The nomination and election of the presidential choice is the high point of each convention, with famous personages who ally themselves with the political position of the candidate delivering the speeches that place his name in nomination. Frequently one looks back on a congressman's participation at a convention or in an election as a gauge of what his early beliefs were in relation to his present position. Eugene McCarthy, for instance, delivered a nominating speech for Adlai Stevenson; the liberal views and calm, intellectual tone of the two seem quite similar. Governor Nelson Rockefeller, who competed with President Nixon for the Republican nomination in 1968, delivered the President's nomination address in 1972. Clearly this switch in position sheds light on the changing political alliances common in American politics.

Balloting at the convention is conducted by a roll-call vote. In both the Democratic and the Republican party conventions, a candidate need win only a simple majority of the delegate votes in order to win the nomination. However, this can be either a quick, simple process or an extremely time-consuming and exhausting one. Of course, it is the hope of every front-running candidate to win his party's nomination on the first ballot, as was accomplished by both McGovern and Nixon in 1972. However, at some conventions in the past, several ballots were required before a clear winner emerged. Table 12–4 shows how many ballots have been required to nominate candidates in the last eleven presidential elections. Perhaps the most famous case of a multiballot situation occurred at the 1924 Democratic convention, in which 103 ballots were taken before a majority of the voters went to John W. Davis, who eventually lost the election to Calvin Coolidge. Such extremes are, fortunately, quite rare. The last time more than one ballot was needed was for the Democratic nomination in 1952.

Once the party's presidential nominee has been determined, it has been customary for him to choose his vice-presidential running mate. In making this decision, the candidate must, of course, consider a number of factors (most important seems to be the goal of achieving a "balanced" ticket) without sacrificing too much harmony. That is, if the presidential nominee is a liberal from the Northeast, it might be wise for him to choose a relatively conservative running mate, preferably from the West or the South, in order to appeal to the widest possible spectrum of voters. At the same time, however, it would be political suicide for him to link himself with a politician whose views and goals were so diametrically opposed to his own that chaos would be the result if they were elected.

The vice-presidential choice made by the presidential nominee is placed in nomination for the Vice Presidency along with the names of others. It is conceivable that he can be defeated, but very unlikely. Those who have supported the presidential candidate courteously support his choice for the Vice Presidency. At the 1972 Democratic convention, there was some discussion of "throwing the vice-presidential choice open to the floor." This, however, would have required sanction by McGovern, who instead made the choice of Senator Thomas Eagleton of Missouri, thus avoiding a public statement on the topic, but clearly making his position known. About two weeks after the convention, however, Senator Eagleton withdrew from the nomination amid widespread publicity of past hospitalization for mental depressions. There were many expressions of doubt about the process by which vice-presidential candidates are chosen. The national committee met in a "mini-convention" and once again accepted a McGovern choice, officially approving R. Sargent Shriver, former head of the Peace Corps under President Kennedy and former head of the Office of Economic Opportunity under President Johnson, as their new candidate.

An Evaluation of
the American Party System

Elite Rule and American Parties

Criticisms leveled at the convention system reflect some of the larger political questions currently at issue in our country. One of the major criticisms of the American governmental system — and, in particular, of the structure of our parties — is that power is in the hands of elites. That is, too much of our political system is controlled by a very small, generally rich group of people who are often in a position to make decisions and to take action without consulting the opinions of the majority of citizens.[40] Our parties lack a mass base; they have no large, loyal active rank-and-file membership of voters who demand knowledge of their party leaders' actions.

Many political scientists contend that elite rule exists and is maintained in the United States because of nonpartisan and one-party political systems, which govern most American localities. Nonpartisan systems exist at present in over 80 percent of American cities, particularly those of small and medium size. In such communities, candidates for office cannot be identified with a party. This situation contributes to elite rule, because most people, unable to identify issues in the absence of party, do not turn out to vote. Those who do vote are dispropor-

[40] For a classic work that explains the inevitability of party officers monopolizing the power of their hierarchical organizations, see Robert Michels, *Political Parties: A Sociological Study of the Oligarchical Tendencies of Modern Democracy* (New York: The Free Press, 1962).

tionately middle-class Republicans, and thus they eventually come to control the politics of the city.[41] One-party systems affect elite rule because, as E. E. Schattschneider has pointed out, "one-party politics tends strongly to vest political power in the hands of people who already have economic power"[42] – that is, the rich. Many local areas have only one viable party and the second party (in some cases, Democrats, and in others, Republicans) has, for decades, been unable to win elections.

Some political theorists claim that elite rule of the sort in which the parties are run by a small group of interested activists is inevitable, and that, on the whole, it is acceptable. This holds true so long as there is a system of two competing elites which, as has been explained, is not always the case. If the two major parties are constantly trying to outdo one another by acting in accordance with the wishes of the voting majority, then the electorate may indeed be offered a real choice, which is one of the most important responsibilities of democracy.

Political Parties and American Democracy: Consensus and Unity

What is the relationship between American parties and the American system of democracy? It is relatively easy to detect inequities in specific aspects of our party system such as the national convention, and to suggest constructive reform. But the relationship between the party system as a whole and the governmental process is far more crucial, because the relationship will determine, in large part, the political future of our country. Some political analysts, after cataloguing many obvious criticisms, have come to the conclusion that our two major political parties are fragmented, chaotic, elitist institutions which do not seem to serve a significant positive purpose in government, and which, therefore, should be eliminated. Others, while admitting that some kinds of change have long been in order if our parties are to be improved, consider the two-party system to be an essential component of American democracy.

Pendleton Herring, asserting this point of view, has argued that one of the most important ideologies in the United States is the concept of consensus, or unity. Herring identified adjustment and compromise as the two major products of our party system and added that, because the United States glories in its diversity of viewpoints, we cannot expect, and should not desire, all Americans to agree on political issues. Rather, the parties exist to provide a means whereby bitter cleavages can be avoided, so that the country as a whole can become united in its general direction. Herring noted:

Our present party system is based on . . . mutual toleration of dissent. . . . The faith of democracy . . . is still based on the fundamental tenet that society can continue peacefully even though men agree to disagree. . . . Democracy provides an ideology conducive

---

[41] See Robert H. Salisbury and Gordon Black, "Class and Party in Partisan and Non-Partisan Elections: The Case of Des Moines," *American Political Science Review,* vol. 57, no. 3 (September 1963), pp. 584–592, and Oliver P. Williams and Charles R. Adrian, "The Insulation of Local Politics under the Non-Partisan Ballot," *American Political Science Review,* vol. 53, no. 4 (December 1959), pp. 1052–1063.

[42] E. E. Schattschneider, *The Semi-Sovereign People: A Realist's View of Democracy in America* (New York: Holt, Rinehart and Winston, 1961), p. 80.

to criticism, experimentation, and change. Our parties are perhaps to be judged finally in terms of their contribution to this flexibility. . . . Our present two-party system, with all its flaws, remains a useful implement for democracy.[43]

Similarly, Fred I. Greenstein has defended our party system, while recognizing its faults, on the basis that the parties aid both political stability and policy-making, two of the most important governmental functions. He pointed out that, while the parties do not always offer clear-cut policy differences to the voters, there is, in fact, a significant difference between the "midpoints" of the Republican and Democratic party programs.[44] Greenstein wrote that, since 1864, the United States has had no civil wars—a virtually unprecedented record for a democracy faced with the problem of holding together such a large and diverse population. This stability, he concluded, is the result of our two-party system, which requires flexibility and compromise despite the unfortunately slow bargaining methods of achieving new policies. Claiming that no viable alternative has yet been put forward, Greenstein continued, "The standard assumption is that parties make their contribution to policy-making by unifying governments—that is, by filling the major public offices with members of a team of like-minded partisans."[45] Since, in our system of separated powers, there are laws which make the three branches of the government independent of one another, and which prevent policy-making without their mutual cooperation, parties perform the essential task of unifying the government for compromise on policy decisions. The result is greater political stability.

From the pluralist point of view, then, political parties enhance majority rule. The nature of the political system, and the apparent centrist orientation of American voters, forces the parties to consolidate pluralities into absolute majorities. This process also enables parties to be instrumental in encouraging popular consultation. These two criteria, majority rule and popular consultation, are two of four minimum requisites for a democratic society advanced by Austin Ranney and Wilmoore Kendall.[46] The third is the ideal of popular sovereignty; parties, as has been discussed in Chapter 2, have widened the franchise. The last requirement of democracy is that it create equal political opportunity to participate in political decision-making. On this count Ranney and Kendall found that United States democracy has failed. Popular involvement in the parties themselves is discouraged. The lack of interest, whether attributable to party structure or to lack of voter interest, weakens parties in their potential role as recruiters of citizen participants in the political process.

A more far-reaching attitude on the positive nature of our parties has been expressed by Schattschneider. He wrote, "The rise of political parties is indubitably one of the principal distinguishing marks of modern government. . . . The political parties created democracy and modern democracy is unthinkable save in terms of the parties."[47] Schattschneider argued that our two-party system is effective because it automatically produces majorities. It does so because the

---

[43] Pendleton Herring, *The Politics of Democracy* (New York: Norton, 1965), pp. 431, 432, 434.

[44] Fred I. Greenstein, *The American Party System and the American People,* second edition (Englewood Cliffs, N.J.: Prentice-Hall, 1970), p. 110.

[45] Greenstein, *The American Party System and the American People,* p. 114.

[46] Ranney and Kendall, *Democracy and the American Party System,* Chapter 1.

[47] E. E. Schattschneider, *Party Government* (New York: Holt, Rinehart and Winston, 1942), p. 1.

voters really have only two reasonable choices. Generally one of the two will get a numerical majority of the votes in any election.

The kind of party compromise and moderation spoken of by Greenstein, Herring, Ranney, and Schattschneider can lead to more than just political stability. It can also lead to political stagnation, and encourage the maintenance of the economic and political status quo. As is true of so many apparently positive aspects of our government, this one actually works against those people who are already economically deprived.

The Problem of Responsible Parties

One of the most articulate critics of our current two-party system, James MacGregor Burns, has concentrated his arguments on the effect that parties have in Congress — and, thereby, on the government as a whole and on the people. Burns has argued that, ideally, the two-party system is a workable solution to the problem of how to exploit the underlying solidarity among a large group of people with very different interests. However, he pointed out, the American two-party system is far from ideal, because, in actuality, we do not have a two-party system in Congress. Instead, we have a kind of multiparty system, made up of a group of splinter parties representing a number of special-interest groups — such as southern Democrats, farmers, laborers, liberal Republicans, silver and cotton producers, and so forth. The problem, as Burns has viewed it, is that the members of these various groups tend to vote in Congress according to their own inter-

"*I just dreamed Barry Goldwater switched to the Democratic Party.*"

Saturday Review, *October 30, 1971*

ests, rather than by their party. "A President of the United States is a Democrat or a Republican, but key Senators and Representatives are more than likely to vote as members of a multi-party system."[48] Such party irresponsibility, with congressmen crossing party lines and sometimes ignoring the national platforms, cannot be disciplined or controlled by the party, which has no disciplinary machinery, and which would be unlikely to use it if it did exist.

In contrasting the British party system with our own, Burns noted that the former serves three cardinal purposes which the American system too often does not. The British political organization unites the various branches of the government, so that they can execute the will of the majority; it keeps minority groups from producing chaos in their attempts to gain power; and it offers the voters a genuine choice between two reasonably distinct programs.[49] British members of Parliament do not cross party lines, for in England "the party is supreme." Because British voters can make a real choice, they generally vote in terms of the party's record and program, rather than according to the personality and campaign promises of an individual candidate. "They do not elect Tom Brown or Sir Wyatt Smith, but the Labour or Conservative candidates." Such a system, Burns has said, while it may seem authoritarian to some of us, is in fact "an almost ideal form of representative government," which leads to a real choice for the voter and to assurance that the successful Prime Minister will continue to support his party's programs throughout his tenure in office.[50]

The dodging of party responsibility in the Congress of the United States has, according to Burns, at least two serious negative results. The first is that close cooperation for effective action becomes increasingly difficult; and the second, that the public, being so frequently ignored, begins to wonder how meaningful and how honest our parties are. Important questions arise in the minds of the voters: "Does the party really mean what it says, or is its program simply a means of enlisting popular support without assuming responsibility for action?"

The desire for party responsibility as expressed by Burns was first advocated at the beginning of the 1950s.[51] Although Burns has held fast to his view, many other political scientists since that time have claimed the British model invalid, impossible, or undesirable for the United States.[52] These experts have explained that the studies of the early fifties linked citizens to party only through policies, when, in fact, many nonrational bases for political behavior (such as ethnic, economic, religious, and sectional identification) existed at that time and continue to exist today. It is invalid, in the opinion of these experts, to assume that

---

[48] James MacGregor Burns, *Congress on Trial* (New York: Gordian Press, 1966), p. 36, "The Impotence of Party."

[49] Burns's comparison of American to British parties can be found in Burns, *Congress on Trial*, pp. 36–39. All quotations on the topic come from these pages.

[50] Hugh A. Bone has concurred with Burns that Americans are given no clear-cut policy alternatives and that their parties provide no assurances of promises being carried out. See Hugh A. Bone, *American Politics and the Party System* (New York: McGraw-Hill, 1965), pp. 647–663.

[51] See "Toward a More Responsible Two-Party System: The Report of the Commission on Political Parties of the American Political Science Association," *American Political Science Review*, Supplement, vol. 44, no. 3, part 2 (September 1950), pp. 1–99.

[52] For a comprehensive review and analysis of the 1950 Report of the American Political Science Association, in light of all significant research on the topic of responsible American parties since that time, see Evron M. Kirkpatrick, "Toward a More Responsible Two-Party System: Political Science, Policy Science, or Pseudo-Science?," *American Political Science Review*, vol. 65 (January 1971). All points made in this paragraph are derived from this article.

voters make choices simply according to rational policy offerings and not according to their stable, enduring other party affiliations. The critics of the theory of responsible parties look back on Britain after World War II and claim that only the first election after the war offered true party choices. To have assumed, they have said, that, because of the policy orientation, interest groups were not operative then was simply erroneous. In reality, interest-group activity has strongly affected British elections since that time, just as it has affected American elections. More general criticism of the early theorists has taken issue with those who would have society adapt to a superimposed party system. Recent evaluations of the party in society conclude that parties are interrelated with political culture, institutions, and constitutional order. Parties are, in fact, dependent on these variables. Lastly, numerous studies have shown that responsible parties as outlined in the early fifties do not exist anywhere in Western European or Anglo-Saxon democracies. Instead, parties which are loosely organized, broadly based, and clientele-oriented for the purpose of seeking a middle ground to gain majorities have proliferated throughout the democratic world.

Republicans or Democrats: What's the Difference?

The "irresponsibility" of parties, the "client-orientation," and the flaws in party structure have resulted not only in a lack of choice between candidates and policies, but also in a tendency for both major parties to be as bland and as noncommital as possible.

The parties, moderate and tolerant and self-contradictory to a fault, are interested in the votes of men, not in their principles, and they care not at all whether the votes they gather are bestowed with passion or with indifference — so long as they are bestowed and counted. The task that they have uppermost in mind is the construction of a victorious majority, and in a country as large and diverse as ours this calls for programs and candidates having as nearly universal an appeal as the imperatives of politics will permit.[53]

The "universal appeal" of the two major American parties makes them so similar that the differences between them are not always so distinct as many would like them to be. Clinton Rossiter noted that, during a series of lectures he delivered in South Africa on American politics, the first question invariably asked him was, "What is the difference between a Democrat and a Republican?"[54] Although Rossiter had a hard time explaining this difference, there is, for most Americans, a significant difference between the Republican and the Democratic parties, even if they cannot always describe this distinction in concrete or ideological, political terms.

The traditional images of our two major parties are built around the people who vote for candidates nominated by the parties.[55] Historically, "typical" Republicans are relatively wealthy, predominantly white, Protestant, and either mem-

[53] Rossiter, *Parties and Politics in America*, p. 11.

[54] Rossiter, *Parties and Politics in America*, p. 107.

[55] See Richard Rose and Derek Urwin, "Social Cohesion, Political Parties, and Strains in Regimes," *Comparative Political Studies*, vol. 2 (April 1969), pp. 7–44. This article discusses various aspects of social cohesion in political parties, here and in seventeen other Western countries with similarly competitive political systems. The authors determined that, in the United States, religion is the most important single determinant of party identification, and social class the next in importance.

Governors Ronald Reagan of California (left) and Nelson A. Rockefeller of New York both fall within the tradition associated with Republicans, but Reagan is known for his relatively conservative leanings, compared with the more liberal tendencies of Rockefeller.

bers or supporters of big business. The Republican self-image is one of a relatively sedate group of hardworking people. "Typical" Democrats, in contrast, are working-class people, largely members of minority groups, who are primarily concerned with getting the federal government to allocate money for projects aimed at alleviating the plight of the lower classes. The Democrats' self-image, somewhat exaggerated, to be sure, is of a party filled with highly idealistic heroes and professionals, working to achieve all the important goals for the common people, who they feel are neglected by their political rivals. On the other hand, the self-image of the Republicans is of a group of men following in the footsteps of Abraham Lincoln, promoting individualism and free enterprise, and devoted to fighting off the evil, radical, socialistic, un-American projects of the Democrats.

The Democratic party is the oldest existing political party in the world; it is also the toughest, in terms of survival; and it has in its ranks a majority (54 percent) of citizens who have declared their party affiliation. If the President is not a Democrat, that is true because of the particular candidates that were presented to the public in that election and does not indicate a decrease in the party's strength. In contrast to this situation, the Republican party (which now attracts about 42 percent of party affiliates) was born spontaneously, as a sectional protest against the extension of slavery in the United States. Thus, from its inception, the Republicans have been regarded as anti-South; and, perhaps surprisingly, because now the party is conservative in many respects, it was once considered an extremely radical organization.

A short glance at the voting behavior and issue orientation of the two parties can further clarify their differences. The Republicans ran the so-called Age of Enterprise, between 1900 and 1925, when the wealthy and powerful families— such as the Carnegies, the Rockefellers, and the Fords—were developing our industrial powers. But the Democrats ruled over the Age of FDR, ushering in his new economy and the new theory of Internationalism. The two parties have also been clearly divided on certain specific issues. For example, from the late

1800s to the 1930s, the question of a higher or a lower protective tariff was a party issue – the Democrats advocated a lower tariff, the Republicans a higher one. The Republicans have also traditionally favored more isolationist foreign policies than have the Democrats.

In an attempt to establish statistical proof regarding the differences or similarities between the two parties, Herbert McCloskey, Paul J. Hoffmann, and Rosemary O'Hara conducted a field study to determine the relation of political ideology to party membership. Large samples were taken of both Democratic and Republican party "leaders" and "followers"; their responses to questionnaires were compared on twenty-four key issues and on a number of attitudes, questions, and scales. According to the data compiled, "the belief that the two American parties are identical in principle and doctrine has little foundation in fact."[56]

The researchers discovered that the Democratic and Republican leaders did disagree strongly on many important issues. It was further apparent that Republican leaders, in particular, often hold positions with which a number of their constituents disagree strongly – a sign that party leaders are less easily swayed by other people's opinions than is often supposed. Perhaps predictably, the leaders of the two parties disagreed most strongly about the issues on which their parties' identities have always been based – such as big business and services for working people. An interesting corollary to this finding was the discovery that, while the leaders of the parties diverge strongly on many issues, their followers disagree only moderately in their attitudes toward the same issues. "Republican followers, in fact, disagree far more with their own leaders than with the leaders of the Democratic party."[57] It was also found that the parties are internally united on some issues but divided on others, and that "the parties achieve greatest internal consensus on the issues which principally divide them from their opponents."[58]

In addition, then, to the differences between the Republican and Democratic parties, there are significant splits within each of the parties. These splits have widened recently, and some people have predicted that they might eventually threaten the existence of the two-party system.

Internal Discord
in the Parties

One of the most important of the internal party splits is also one of the most obvious differences – that which exists between the left- and the right-wing elements of each party. While all Republicans undoubtedly share certain basic party attitudes, there is obviously a wide ideological gulf separating such political figures as Republican Senators Edward Brooke (a liberal black from Massachusetts) and Barry Goldwater (a long-time Arizona conservative). The variety of viewpoints within the Democratic party is even more pronounced – compare, for example, two more senators – Adlai Stevenson III (an Illinois liberal), and Harry Byrd (a staunch conservative from West Virginia). This deep Democratic cleavage is visible when one compares two traditional Democrats – the

---

[56] Herbert McCloskey, Paul J. Hoffmann, and Rosemary O'Hara, "Issue Conflict and Consensus among Party Leaders and Followers," *American Political Science Review*, vol. 54, no. 2 (June 1960), p. 425.

[57] McCloskey et al., "Issue Conflict and Consensus," p. 426.

[58] McCloskey et al., "Issue Conflict and Consensus," p. 427.

urban, immigrant, Catholic, laborer of the North and the rural, white, Protestant, farmer of the South. There is also a long-standing Republican split,
essentially an ideological chasm, between sophisticated, big-business conservatives of the East and small-town traditional conservatives of the Midwest.

The Unsolid South   The political split which has attracted a great deal of attention
recently is one within the Democratic party—the rebellion of the previously "solid"
South. The eleven states of the old Confederacy (Alabama, Arkansas, Florida,
Georgia, Louisiana, Mississippi, North Carolina, South Carolina, Tennessee,
Texas, and Virginia) have always been aligned against the northern part of the
nation to some extent. But, since the 1930s, when the Democrats became the
national majority party, the South began to ally itself with the Democratic
North. And, in fact, these eleven states have been consistently run by a single
party, the Democrats, for over a hundred years. Until 1970 no Republican governor had been elected in any of the eleven states since Reconstruction (save in
Tennessee, where a Republican was elected governor in 1920).[59] The Solid South
went Democratic because of the force of tradition, various vested interests, and
the memory of the Civil War. When Eisenhower, a Republican who was born in
Texas, won half of the South in the presidential election of 1952, his Republicanism
was declared not to be an issue; rather, his personality was said to have "risen
above" the dirt of partisan politics.[60]

Today, however, these same eleven states, plus six other border states (Delaware, Kentucky, Maryland, Missouri, Oklahoma, and West Virginia), have developed, regardless of the party affiliation of their governors, a kind of southern
bloc, which is the most obvious and powerful factional interest in national politics. Why and how did this change occur? Allan P. Sindler traced the present
rebellion to the 1952 Democratic convention, which took place just after the
Republicans announced their choice of Dwight D. Eisenhower as a presidential
nominee. The Democrats at the convention were worried about Ike's strength;
President Truman had already announced his intention of refusing a second
term; a North-South split over the issue of civil rights seemed imminent; and
the Democrats had no strong, unifying candidate. They eventually nominated
Adlai Stevenson, who was unsuccessful in the general election, and the dissident
southern Democrats felt it was time to stop compromising with the North. Thus
ended the South's political "solidarity."[61] By the early 1970s it was clear that
Nixon had attracted many southerners. His Supreme Court appointments have
generally pleased the South, and southern congressmen usually align themselves
with northern Republicans in opposition to northern Democratic liberal positions.
It is suspected that if George Wallace had not run on a third-party ticket in the
1968 election, taking five southern states, Nixon would have won more than the
few borderline southern states that he did capture. To many observers the contemporary political scene appears to be on the verge of a major crisis. A number
of changes seem bound to occur in the near future to the individual parties, to
the party system, to the government as a whole. Endless opinions are offered
on what should happen, and what can be done now to avoid chaos later.

---

[59] In 1970, Virginia elected a Republican governor, and Tennessee did so, once again, in 1971.
[60] Rossiter, *Parties and Politics in America*, p. 138.
[61] Allan P. Sindler, "The Unsolid South," in *The Uses of Power*, edited by Alan F. Westin (New York: Harcourt
Brace Jovanovich, 1962).

The Future
of American Partisan Politics

A frequent and major criticism of the American party system has been the inability of third parties to make any significant headway on the national political level. Because our two major parties form a loose coalition of contending forces at the national level, third parties generally have no real chance to enter the big-time political arena. This barrier, many people feel, invalidates the professed American ideal that even the smallest political groupings have the opportunity to participate in elections with a reasonable chance of winning.

Walter Dean Burnham has pointed out that there seems to be a tendency for our political parties to cease functioning as links between the government and the people, and to continue being of use merely as office-filling organizations. If this trend were to continue, our need for parties might end. However, Burnham has conceded, it is possible that the political realignments likely to occur in the future may instead "serve to recrystallize and revitalize political parties in the American system." Welcoming this trend, he asserted:

Political parties, with all their well-known human and structural shortcomings, are the only devices thus far invented by the wit of Western man that can, with some effectiveness, generate countervailing collective power on behalf of the many individually powerless against the relatively few who are individually or organizationally powerful.[62]

Along with this optimism, however, Burnham was careful to note that the sphere of party politics – that is, the parties' range of activity – is becoming narrower, as more and more of their functions are taken over by other agencies.[63]

Some analysts have predicted that a consensus of the middle class is likely to come to dominate American politics in the near future; others hope a dissident minority will unite, in order to upset the current party system.

Most of the criticisms of the American party system are based on the "rational man" model of democracy – a model that assumes a well-informed electorate will make choices on the basis of reasoned arguments. But it is quite possible that this goal will never be realized; experience with universal suffrage in the United States in the last half-century demonstrates that most people will continue to be ill-informed and lacking motivation to participate in politics. Schattschneider has suggested that this situation may not be as bad as the theorists contend it is:

The tendency of the literature of politics is to place a tremendous premium on the role of the interested and to treat indifference as a mortal sin, but the reluctance of the public to press its opinions on the government concerning a great multitude of issues is really not as bad a thing as we have been led to think: it is a mark of reasonableness and common sense. The public is far too sensible to attempt to play the preposterous role assigned to it by the theorists. We have tended to undervalue this attitude because we have labored under an illusion about democracy.

We have become cynical about democracy because the public does not act the way the simplistic definition of democracy says it should act, or we try to whip the public into

---

[62] Burnham, "The End of American Party Politics," p. 20.

[63] Walter Dean Burnham, "Party Systems and the Political Process," in *The American Party Systems,* edited by William Nisbit Chambers and Walter Dean Burnham (New York: Oxford University Press, 1967), pp. 205–207.

doing things it does not want to do, is unable to do and has too much sense to do. The crisis here is not a crisis in democracy but a crisis in theory. . . . The power of the people in a democracy depends on the importance *of the decisions made by the electorate, not the* number *of decisions they make. . . . In the interests of clarity and the survival of the political system we need a definition of democracy that recognizes the limitations [on political action] that nature imposes on large numbers.*

A working definition must capitalize on the limitations of the people as well as their powers. . . .[64]

In concluding any discussion on American parties, it is important to note Schattschneider's view. For the reality is that it is the criticism of the political structure in the United States which is not rational, whether the people act rationally or not. A more realistic outlook must be adopted by the pedagogues in defining democracy and the party system, one that takes the actual political behavior of Americans into account.

SUGGESTED READING

Agar, Herbert. *The Price of Union* (Boston: Houghton Mifflin, 1966). A historical examination of the origins and developments of the American party system which explores the reasons for its long-term stability and coherence. Agar finds that the apparent irrationality, slowness, compromise, and dearth of principles of the American party system have in reality enabled the system to work. He concludes that coalition politics, in which the major competing parties offer echoes instead of choices, has been the price of union in the United States.

Bailey, Thomas A. *Democrats vs. Republicans: The Continuing Clash* (New York: Meredith Press, 1968). In examining the history of America's two major political parties with particular attention to successive presidential elections, Bailey argues that, from their beginnings, differing adherents, techniques, and goals have distinguished American parties. He demonstrates how and why these divergences developed and continued, and defends the American two-party system as the oldest continuous structure of its kind in the world and the most successful.

Binkley, Wilfred E. *American Political Parties: Their Natural History,* 4th edition (New York: Knopf, 1962). A comprehensive history of American political parties in which the author ascertains and accounts for the social or group composition of each of our major political parties. Binkley demonstrates the art of group diplomacy played by national political leaders in building the great political coalitions.

Bone, Hugh A. *American Politics and the Party System* (New York: McGraw-Hill, 1971). In this textbook on political parties and the party system in American politics, the author examines the various theories on political parties, the genesis and development of American parties, their characteristics and bases of electoral support. He discusses individual participation in politics in light of the pluralist nature of American society and the traditional means of access to government that it affords. He concludes by analyzing the new political challenges to American society.

Chambers, William N., and Walter D. Burnham (eds.). *The American Party Systems: Stages of Political Development* (New York: Oxford University Press, 1967). In paperback. A systematic explanation of what American political parties are today and an analysis of how they got that way. These essays examine the concept of political development through an analysis of the patterns of organization and activity in the several

---

[64] Schattschneider, *The Semi-Sovereign People,* pp. 134, 140, 141.

national party systems that have existed during the history of the United States, and exist today. The authors raise important questions about the origins, characteristics, and functions of the American political party systems.

Eldersveld, Samuel J. *Political Parties: A Behavioral Analysis* (Chicago: Rand McNally, 1964). A study of the American party process through a case study of the Detroit metropolitan area. The author employs behavioral techniques and methods of analysis to examine party structures, political perspectives of party leaders, the party as an organizational system, and the functional relationships between the parties and the public. Eldersveld describes the party as an open and plural group that performs important tasks, strengthening the foundations for political consensus.

Greenstein, Fred I. *The American Party System and the American People* (Englewood Cliffs, N.J.: Prentice-Hall, 1970). In paperback. In a description, analysis, and evaluation of party politics and electoral behavior in the United States, Greenstein sets up criteria for judging the party system: Does it contribute to the degree to which the political system is democratic? Does it foster or hamper the stability of the political system? How, if at all, does the institution affect the adequacy of governmental policy-making? After examining the role of parties in the electorate, in organized party politics, in the diverse state party systems, and in national parties, the author concludes that American parties make a substantial, but far from perfect, contribution on the basis of all three criteria.

Herring, Pendleton. *The Politics of Democracy: American Parties in Action* (New York: Norton, 1965). In paperback. In an analysis of the American party system originally published in 1940, Herring identifies what the utility of American parties appears to be in the light of their actual functioning and suggests the value this utility has, as a part of the larger political process, for reconciling change with stability. He argues that machine control, pressure politics, propaganda, money, patronage, and bureaucracy all pose threats to democracy, but that they are also elements natural and necessary to the democratic system.

Hofstadter, Richard. *The Idea of a Party System: The Rise of Legitimate Opposition in the United States, 1780–1840* (Berkeley, Calif.: University of California Press, 1972). In paperback. An examination of the historical thought processes by which American political leaders slowly edged away from their complete philosophical rejection of a party and hesitatingly began to embrace a party system. Hofstadter analyzes the emergence of legitimate party opposition and the theory of politics that accepted it.

James, Judson L. *American Political Parties: Potential and Performance* (New York: Pegasus, 1969). In paperback. In describing and evaluating American political parties, James concentrates on the continuities in partisanship and presents a unified empirical description of current party performance to which he relates a doctrinal analysis of democratic theory and political-party functions. He concludes that the American party system is more coherent, democratic, and responsible than it is often given credit for, and that, although the internal structure and organization of political parties have not been thoroughly democratic, they have effectively contributed to the goal of democratic government.

Key, V. O., Jr. *Southern Politics* (New York: Random House, 1949). In paperback. In this classic work Key examines the character and structure of southern politics and the deep political problems of that region. He analyzes the nature of the South's one-party political systems and the effect they have on the internal politics of the state and on the politics of the nation as a whole. He explains the political patterns and trends of the region, stressing that its foremost problem is race.

Lubell, Samuel. *The Future of American Politics*, revised edition (New York: Harper & Row, 1965). In paperback. This book is a description of the New Deal coalition, its various components, and how it was held together. In evaluating the coalition, Lubell stresses the implications it holds for American politics.

Ranney, Austin. *The Doctrine of Responsible Party Government* (Urbana, Ill.: University of Illinois Press, 1962). In paperback. Ranney examines and analyzes the doctrines of responsible party government espoused between 1870 and 1915, and their criticisms. He relates these doctrines to present-day discussions of the function of political parties in the American system and demonstrates why the responsible-party doctrine cannot become a reality until the American people have fully accepted the doctrine of majority-rule democracy and until certain political structures, such as the Senate filibuster, staggered elections, and life-tenure Court appointments, are altered.

Schattschneider, E. E. *Party Government* (New York: Holt, Rinehart and Winston, 1942). Schattschneider examines the rise of political parties in modern governments and the relationships between parties and democratic government. In maintaining that political parties created democracy and that modern democracy is unthinkable except in terms of the parties, he offers a polemic in defense of party government, as the democratic and liberal solution to the problem of reconciling authority and liberty.

Sorauf, Frank J. *Political Parties in the American System* (Boston: Little, Brown, 1964). In paperback. In an analysis and interpretation of the nature and operations of American political parties, Sorauf uses the concept of a system to suggest the way in which the two major parties operate, what functions they perform, how they interact with each other, and what their place is within the larger framework of political institutions and processes. He claims parties contribute to political stability and conservatism in America while furnishing a vital mechanism through which Americans make many crucial choices. Recognizing the valuable roles parties perform in the American system, he disputes the claim that they are the key or creators of modern democratic systems.

13
CAMPAIGNS AND CANDIDATES: THE IMAGE OF DEMOCRACY

Never has a national political convention been so carefully staged as one was in 1972 when, in a smoothly scripted production geared to the television audience, the Republican Party nominated the incumbent for President among hundreds of cheering youths. Nixon's staff, already carrying out a campaign theme based on the lofty image of a candidate as The President, arranged for Nixon to appear on the convention platform, where he strove to show the public that he was not just a dignified President, but also a regular fellow, at ease exchanging quips with comedian Sammy Davis, Jr., before television cameras.

Senator George McGovern, fresh from his nomination as the Democratic candidate, swam, rode a horse, and went camping to help his television image. When he started on the primary campaign trail, he took to wearing sideburns, bolder neckties, and suits tailored with a "mod" look to make him look less like the professor and son of a small-town minister that he had once been, and more like a dynamic national leader. But when the presidential campaign itself got under way, McGovern, eager to please future supporters, appeared on Wall Street wearing a white shirt, dark suit, navy-blue tie, and shorter hair.

Regardless of party or qualifications, both Nixon and McGovern, as well as every other person who sought office in the United States in 1972, knew that the image they projected to the American public was crucial to victory—probably more crucial than their views on any of the issues. With the assistance of professional consultants, party advisers, and huge sums of money, each was prepared to take fullest advantage of all media to appeal to as many segments of the voting public as possible.

Joseph Napolitan, a professional consultant who managed the advertising in Hubert Humphrey's 1968 presidential campaign, has compiled a list of campaign media, or "vehicles of communication," that a candidate for office may utilize. He included "television, radio, print advertising and brochures, billboards, direct mail, computers, professional telephone campaigns, rallies, meetings, speeches, and the junk: buttons, streamers, nail files, shopping bags, and ball-point pens."[1] This chapter will examine some of the more widely favored methods used by the candidate to communicate with voters, to convince them that he is more deserving of government office than those who oppose him.

Mass Media and Campaigning

Opinions vary about the degree to which voting habits are affected by the communications media. Some observers believe the media can put a candidate in office. Others, like David Garth, who engineered John Lindsay's 1972 television campaign for the Democratic presidential nomination, give them less importance. Garth has estimated that a successful campaign is based only one-fourth on the media. The other important considerations, those that make up three-fourths of a campaign, are organization, the issues, and the candidate himself.[2] No one can deny, however, that even if media are only a part of the campaign, they exert a considerable effect on the whole.

[1] Joseph Napolitan, *The Election Game and How to Win It* (New York: Doubleday, 1972), p. 3.
[2] Victor S. Navasky, "The Making of a Candidate," *The New York Times Magazine* (May 7, 1972), p. 80.

The New Propagandists

A small group known as the International Society of Political Campaign Consultants met in London in 1972 for its annual meeting, held to exchange ideas and hear talks delivered by members. Few people outside the group were aware of this meeting, yet it would probably affect the politics of many nations, for the members of the group serve as media directors for most of the political candidates in the world. They are so influential that some observers believe that it is they, and not the actual candidates, who will do most to determine future voting patterns. As Nicholas Johnson, Commissioner of the Federal Communications Commission, remarked about the 1972 election, "Our Presidential campaign is really going to be waged between two television consultants nobody knows."[3]

These consultants are not political figures in the traditional sense of the word. Though they may have favorites among the candidates, they are primarily hired professionals whose services are available for a price. And there is nothing to prevent them from becoming the permanent employees of an incumbent President. Herb Klein, for example, an expert on media who has become President Nixon's Director of Communications, has had tremendous power to direct and control the media. This power, combined with the time privileges generally accorded a President by television executives, gives the President substantial means for influencing public opinion. Some critics have expressed alarm over this development and warned that it has the potential for becoming the kind of thought control predicted in Aldous Huxley's *Brave New World* or George Orwell's *1984*.

Who are the new propagandists? Most are highly talented individuals with impressive credentials as media experts. As might be expected, many come from the advertising world. Harry Treleaven, for example, one of Nixon's consultants, was a vice president of J. Walter Thompson, one of the nation's largest advertising agencies. Charles Guggenheim, Senator George McGovern's chief media consultant, was a documentary filmmaker who had received five Academy Award nominations and won two. William Gavin was less renowned than these others when, as a young high-school teacher with interests in politics and the media, he wrote an incisive letter to Richard Nixon which resulted in his appointment to the Nixon campaign team of 1968 as one of its guiding intelligences.[4] Of crucial importance on any political media-team is the specialist known as a "time buyer," whose responsibility it is to see that the candidate's message is aired at the proper time. Nixon's time buyer has been Ruth Jones, a woman paramount in this field. Her knowledge of TV programming and viewing habits across the country is so extensive that at least one observer feels that had she been in the employ of Hubert Humphrey in 1968, the outcome of that election might have been reversed.[5]

The Press

The press in America, long an influence on public opinion, began to take a new place in political campaigns in recent decades as public relations grew into a major American industry and public figures became more conscious of the uses

---

[3] Navasky, "The Making of a Candidate," p. 79.

[4] Joe McGinniss, *The Selling of the President, 1968* (New York: Pocket Books, 1970), pp. 28–29.

[5] Navasky, "The Making of a Candidate," p. 81.

they might make of the news media. Earlier politicians had tended to shun reporters as trouble-makers, but this tendency changed; while they still worried about the potential enmity of such muckraking journalists as the late Drew Pearson and his successor, Jack Anderson, they began to recognize that such influential newsmen could also be useful allies. Edward N. Costikyan, a journalist and politician, wrote of these practical alliances:

> *Today the press is one of the principal tools of a political leader. He uses it as he uses his captains and district leaders, or money, or campaign literature. For the market has shifted: where once reporters and politicians were essentially antagonists, the former snooping into the private conduct of the latter—who wanted no publicity—now reporters and politicians sometimes seem to be co-practitioners of the same trade.*[6]

Costikyan noted that political figures utilize the press in many ways. They often manage to get an announcement of their candidacies into the newspaper by arranging that a rumor leak out from a "reliable source." By spreading the rumor before the formal announcement, the aspiring officeholder can gauge the public's reaction to his candidacy before actually committing himself. In addition to planting stories in papers, candidates arrange for informative, supportive letters to appear in the letters-to-the-editor column. Thus, what readers accept as a random sampling of public opinion is often a dialogue between political forces moderated by the newspaper's editorial board. Some of the letters that appear in an effort to create a favorable political climate for the candidate are solicited from well-known persons in the community; others may originate within the party organization and are sent to the paper under false signatures.[7] Newspapers, unaware and unconcerned about a letter's origin, simply print an equal number from each political camp. In this way they can remain unbiased until close to election day, when they customarily come out in support of one of the contenders.

Newspapers generally attempt to be objective in reporting news of the campaign while it is in progress. Sometimes, however, they are not. Candidates, when they fear an impending defeat or have already lost an election, claim newsmen write their biases directly into their news reports or indirectly make their political feelings known by excluding from their news stories some public addresses or actions made by candidates. Richard Nixon, after losing his bid for Governor of California in 1962 to the incumbent Democrat, Pat Brown, protested that the press hadn't given him a fair shake. In a news conference the morning after his defeat, he scolded the press for "its lack of objectivity." Repeatedly asserting that a reporter is free to write and interpret as he "feels it" and that metropolitan newspapers have the "right to take every position they want to on the editorial page,"[8] he nevertheless blamed the press, and specifically the *Los Angeles Times*, for not asking the same questions of each candidate and for neglecting to report some of his important campaign statements. He said a paper must recognize that although it has the right to be against a candidate and

---

[6] Edward N. Costikyan, *Behind Closed Doors: Politics in the Public Interest* (New York: Harcourt Brace Jovanovich, 1966), p. 220.

[7] Costikyan, *Behind Closed Doors*, pp. 226–227.

[8] This quotation and all the others from the news conference can be found in the full transcript of it in the *New York Times* (November 9, 1962), p. 18.

give him "the shaft," it must at the same time "put one lonely reporter on the campaign who will report what the candidate says now and then." He noted that a television "flub" he had made immediately got into print, while a similarly embarrassing "flub" of Governor Brown's was never printed. He summed up his views on press coverage in general as follows:

I think that it's time that our great newspapers have at least the same objectivity, the same fullness of coverage, that television has. And I can only say thank God for television and radio for keeping the newspapers a little more honest.

Then, in a soulful farewell statement in which he inaccurately predicted that this was his last news conference, he said, ". . . as I leave you I want you to know — just think how much you're going to be missing. You won't have Nixon to kick around any more."

Whether large metropolitan newspapers report objectively or not, it has been shown that their editorial support exerts little or no impact on the outcome of elections. The *Chicago Tribune,* for instance, despite its large circulation and years of vigorous support for Republican candidates, has had no apparent effect on the voting habits of most Chicagoans, who consistently vote Democratic. Many politicians are aware of how insignificant mere editorial support can be. One of them noted that "editorial backing does not help unless they give you a story every day and push it. Five percent of the readers read the editorial page. And when it comes out two or three days before the election, it doesn't help much."[9]

Radio

When radio was first used in a presidential campaign in 1924, many observers believed that it would soon change the whole character of campaigning. They foresaw that, given the ability to reach millions through the airwaves, a presidential candidate would no longer have to expend large amounts of time, money, and energy to appear in person in every state in the union. But the prediction was wrong. A decade later, Will Rogers was to comment, "We thought that when the radio was perfected and everybody could hear a speech, that it wouldn't be necessary to drag the candidate around the country, like a circus. But no, the State Leaders must satisfy their vanity by having him appear in person in the State."[10]

The introduction of radio, however, did have a perceptible effect on political campaigns. For one thing, radio brought the candidate's voice into the homes of the public. The voter who wanted a firsthand impression was no longer compelled to stand in a noisy crowd at some whistle-stop along the candidate's campaign trail. For the first time he could hear a candidate's words distinctly and without distractions. Moreover, because radio had no time for long-winded speeches, the candidate had to get to the point faster than he might in person. The voter no longer had to rely solely on the press for accounts of all major speeches and could make a more personal assessment of the candidate and his stand on issues. Radio began a trend toward subjectivity in voting in national elections that was heightened by the advent of television. The Democratic candi-

[9] Quoted in John W. Kingdon, *Candidates for Office: Beliefs and Strategies* (New York: Random House, 1968), p. 51.

[10] Jules Abels, *The Degeneration of Our Presidential Election* (New York: Macmillan, 1968), p. 35.

The pre-radio presidential campaigns of Theodore Roosevelt, who ran in 1904 as a Republican and in 1912 as a Progressive, relied like its predecessors on live appearances before crowds.

date in the 1920 campaign, John W. Davis, was not too far wrong, it seems, when he predicted, "Some day candidates for President will be chosen on the basis of how they sound and look."[11]

In 1948 the power of radio as a political instrument was brought home by the consequences of the network debates between Harold Stassen and Thomas E. Dewey, both contenders for the Republican party's presidential nomination. The subject of their debates was whether or not the Communist party should be outlawed, with Stassen asserting that it should, Dewey that it should not. The debate soon degenerated into a squabble which did little to clarify the issue. Dewey, with a superior speaking style, was popularly considered the winner, and did in fact win the nomination. Although the debate did not win an ultimate victory for the Republicans, it apparently had great influence on a bill then pending in Congress. The Mundt-Nixon Bill then under consideration was aimed not at outlawing the Communist party outright, but at placing it under regulations which would greatly hinder its activities. Because the Dewey-

---

[11] Abels, *The Degeneration of Our Presidential Election,* p. 45.

Stassen debates created substantial support for the bill (both candidates supported it, but for different reasons), it was subsequently passed by Congress and enacted into law.[12]

Despite the eclipse of radio by the more powerful medium of television, it still has an important place in campaigning. Since many people listen to radio regularly and in many cases through large portions of their day, media experts consider a well-placed political message an effective way to keep a candidate in the public mind. In 1972, for example, in an article detailing a campaign strategy for the Democrats to unseat Richard Nixon in 1972, one political theorist recommended "a series of low-key, factual five-minute radio programs on important issues." As he pointed out, "The cost is low, and the impact can be high."[13]

Television: The Influence of the Visual Medium

Television's potential for influencing the thinking of Americans is supported by impressive figures. More American families own at least one television set than have telephones or indoor plumbing. These sets, which are in 95 percent of American homes, are in operation for an average of five and one-half hours per day, making television viewing the third most time-consuming American pastime, after working and sleeping. A poll conducted by Roper Research Associates in 1968 showed that 65 percent of those questioned named television as their chief source of political information, while only 24 percent named newspapers, 5 percent magazines, and 4 percent radio.[14]

Theories about the impact of television as expressed by Marshall McLuhan, a Canadian English professor, in his best-selling book, *Understanding Media*,[15] received so much attention that Richard Nixon distributed excerpts from the book to his 1968 campaign staff. According to McLuhan, the pervasiveness of television in American life has had a significant effect on the American electoral process. It has, he said, created an obsession with image. Because television concentrates on how a candidate looks, sounds, and conducts himself, it distracts the viewer from the content of his speech. Voters are now less likely to cast their ballots for a particular candidate on the basis of class interests or the urgings of such authority figures as employers, union leaders, and clergymen. Instead they vote for a candidate because he appeals to them in some vague, subjective way, because he is "their sort of man." Thus, McLuhan maintained, "with T.V. came the end of bloc voting in politics, a form of specialism and fragmentation that won't work since T.V. Instead of the voting bloc, we have the icon, the inclusive image. Instead of a political viewpoint or platform, the inclusive political posture or stance. Instead of the product, the process."[16]

Concentration on image has produced a strange new brand of campaign tactics. Today's candidate is packaged and promoted through the media with the kind of calculation once reserved for building Hollywood stars. Even the cam-

---

[12] Abels, *The Degeneration of Our Presidential Election*, p. 26.

[13] Joseph Napolitan, "Yes, the Democrats *Can* Beat Richard Nixon," *Saturday Review* (April 1, 1972), p. 27.

[14] *Voters' Time: Report of the Twentieth Century Fund Commission on Campaign Costs in the Electronic Era* (New York: The Twentieth Century Fund, 1969), pp. 6–7.

[15] Marshall McLuhan, *Understanding Media: The Extensions of Man* (New York: Signet Books, 1968). In paperback.

[16] McLuhan, *Understanding Media*, p. 280.

Actions such as George McGovern's autographing of a hard hat in the 1972 presidential campaign are designed to promote a "regular guy" image as much as to woo a certain bloc vote.

paign slogan has changed from being simply catchy, like "Win With Wilkie," or "I Like Ike," to word combinations designed to exploit more emotional reactions: "Nixon's the One," and "Trust Muskie." The aim of the phrase-makers and image-builders is to produce a certain kind of picture in the minds of voters—to mold the public perception of the candidate to their specifications.

Image first came to the fore as a major factor in the presidential race of 1960. It has generally been conceded that one of the deciding factors in that election was the series of TV debates between Kennedy and Nixon in which Kennedy somehow seemed to come across better than his opponent.[17] Philip Deane, a British journalist, drew on McLuhan's ideas in attempting to explain why the debates had tipped the scales of public opinion in Kennedy's favor. Nixon, he said, had defended his opinions "with too much flourish for the T.V. medium." Kennedy, he went on to say, "presents an image closer to the T.V. hero . . . —something like the shy young Sheriff—while Mr. Nixon with his very dark eyes that tend to stare, with his slicker circumlocution, has resembled more

---

[17] For a discussion of the impact the Kennedy-Nixon debates had on the public, see Kurt Lang and Gladys Engel Lang, "Ordeal by Debate: View Reactions," *Public Opinion Quarterly,* vol. 25, no. 2 (Summer 1961), pp. 276–288.

the railway lawyer who signs leases that are not in the interests of the folks in the little town."[18]

Nixon applied the lesson of these debates to the 1968 campaign. As his advisers realized, he needed to appeal to both the over-thirty and under-thirty segments of the electorate, "groups . . . conditioned by two different worlds, the pre-tv and the post-tv environments." The staff discerned from McLuhan and the political scene that older voters are characterized by "linear rationality," while the younger generation is "emotional, unstructured, uncompartmented, direct."[19] Nixon advisers recognized the effectiveness of Robert Kennedy, a leading contender in the 1968 Democratic primaries, and his "screaming appeal to the tv generation."[20] They maintained that this appeal had "nothing to do with logical persuasion; it's a total *experience,* a tactile sense—thousands of little girls who want him to be president so they can have him on the T.V. screen and run their fingers through the image of his hair."[21] While no amount of media manipulation could give Nixon's hair the presumed tactile appeal of Robert Kennedy's, Nixon advisers did find it possible to create the image of a "new Nixon" by emphasizing all the resources of radio and television—the filmed message, the live presentation, the sixty-second spot. Their tactics appear to have paid off on election day, when a slight majority of American voters did indeed decide that "Nixon's the One."

The artfulness of a presentation on television or in another medium is not the only criterion that governs the public's acceptance of political messages offered through the media. The weight given to a political message is also affected by the context in which it appears. The voting public evidently trusts certain media more than others, because it believes in their relative impartiality and resistance to manipulation. Media men have learned to exploit this faith by making maximum use of the most trusted means of communication.

Walter DeVries and V. Lance Tarrance discovered through surveys that the average voter trusts information presented in television news programs above all other sources, while paid political TV announcements are about twenty-fourth on the credibility list.[22] This assessment of the credibility of television news over television advertisements was supported by a 1960 study conducted by Alan L. Clem of voting patterns among residents of Spirit Mound Township, South Dakota. Clem found that voters in this rural district believed that newspapers were the most reliable source of news. However, they ranked television news second, radio news third, and paid television ads fourth. One inference Clem drew from this study was that those media forms which are most effective are beyond a candidate's control. He wrote, "few, if any, candidates can order the newspapers or radio or television stations to insert plugs for him in their news reports. The candidate can control the advertising, but he cannot control the news."[23]

---

[18] As quoted in McLuhan, *Understanding Media,* p. 287.

[19] These thoughts on the two necessary types of appeal are contained in an analysis of McLuhan written for practical campaign purposes by William Gavin of Nixon's staff. The three short passages just quoted can be found in McGinniss, *The Selling of the President, 1968,* pp. 197 and 198.

[20] Gavin in McGinniss, *The Selling of the President, 1968,* p. 197.

[21] Gavin in McGinniss, *The Selling of the President, 1968,* p. 197.

[22] Navasky, "The Making of a Candidate," p. 84.

[23] Alan L. Clem, *Spirit Mound Township in 1960 Election: Government Research Bureau Report No. 44* (Vermillion, S. Dak.: University of South Dakota, 1961).

Techniques of TV Politics

Political campaign specialists avail themselves of the known techniques of advertising and public relations in preparing a television campaign. But because a candidate is much harder to sell than a bar of soap, the media men must invent increasingly sophisticated techniques.

Today's media consultants have proved that it is not so difficult to manipulate the news as Clem supposed. True, candidates cannot dictate what goes into news programs, but they can use certain techniques to assure news coverage of their activities, and they can also appear on news-type shows. For instance, Edmund Muskie's media consultant, Robert Squier, pursued a policy in 1972 of booking appearances for his candidate on all the major television talk shows. In addition, Muskie's paid advertisements were designed to resemble news shots, and Muskie workers kept local stations supplied with a constant stream of videotape releases covering the candidate's campaign activities. Muskie consultants went on the assumption that, if it was not possible to control news programs, they could at least benefit from the credibility of these shows by working their promotional efforts around them. McGovern used similar informal clips of himself talking to groups of prospective supporters for his short television ads.

A candidate who adjusts his campaign to the news media must, however, make some concessions. Like radio, television must edit out large sections of political speeches, often shortening them to a fraction of their original length. Half-hour or fifteen-minute news programs, which endeavor to report a wide range of events in a manner designed to hold the attention of audiences, are not likely to devote more than a few minutes of air time to any one news item. If the editor who whittles down the speech does not support the candidate, it is also possible that the resulting news clip will not be as favorable as the candidate would like. Consequently, politicians have learned to make their newsworthy campaign speeches as short as possible. As Tom Schwartz, a media consultant, wrote, "It makes sense . . . to use a 45-to-50-second speech when announcing one's candidacy. This way the speech will be covered in its entirety in the evening news."[24]

Aware of television's power over public opinion, politicians usually attempt to cooperate with its newsmen in the interest of their future careers. One notable exception has been Spiro T. Agnew. During the early Nixon years, the Vice President bitterly attacked the press, and television news programs in particular, for what he charged as liberal bias against the Nixon war policies in the presentation of news. While many newsmen reacted angrily to what they regarded as a threat by an administration spokesman to freedom of speech and the press, there followed a noticeable decline in criticism of the administration by television newscasters and commentators. Generally speaking, however, political leaders prefer to stay on the good side of newsmen, to insure favorable coverage.

Convention Coverage The greatest opportunity for the television medium to show off the scope and sophistication of its technique is in its live coverage of the two national nominating conventions. Viewers have come to expect the networks to provide not only continuous coverage of the events on the convention floor, but to do it in such a way that the coverage makes them feel they are actually present

---

[24] Quoted by Navasky, "The Making of a Candidate," p. 84.

as participating and informed observers. Accordingly, thousands of technicians, analysts, and announcers must be brought to the convention site, as well as millions of dollars' worth of equipment assembled in a monumental feat of communications.

The 1968 Democratic convention in Chicago presented special problems for this expensive and highly organized team effort. Fearing possible violence by the thousands of protesters who had gathered to express their opposition to the Vietnam War, convention organizers mobilized a huge security network consisting of over ten thousand heavily armed Chicago police, and a reserve of riot squads, national guard, and regular army contingents. The presence of these forces, along with the taxi and telephone strikes which hit the city as the convention opened, hampered television crews. Denied full access to the convention floor, they concentrated their cameras on the violent clashes between protesters and police outside the hall. Millions of viewers across the country were thereby given the impression that the convention was a woefully mismanaged circus under siege by the forces of chaos. Although there were many who held fast to the opinion that the convention itself was well run and that the conflict on the streets could not have been avoided by better party planning, sympathizers with the protesters supported the media's implication that a badly run and undemocratic convention was, to a great extent, responsible for the tension and violence. In the end, television's coverage of this particular convention served to discredit the Democratic party sufficiently so that, in combination with a series of events occurring after it, it contributed to Hubert Humphrey's ultimate defeat.

Like the parties and candidates, the television networks compete fiercely in presidential conventions and elections to anticipate what the public wants to see and hear.

Paid Political Announcements: The Long and Short of It In planning a television advertising campaign, candidates must decide how much to spend on half-hour or hour-long programs (some, such as telethons, may last even longer) and how much on one-minute spots. Each form of political programming offers distinct advantages and disadvantages which a candidate must weigh according to their vote-getting potential and the sort of image he wishes to project.

In general, the sixty-second spot is considered more desirable in terms of the number of people reached in proportion to the money spent. In 1968, a one-minute network spot during the show *Gunsmoke*, which appeared in prime time, would have cost about fifty thousand dollars exclusive of production costs and reached approximately nineteen million people of voting age. By contrast, a half-hour program at a similar time would cost about eighty thousand dollars, exclusive of its production costs, and would only be seen in about six to eight million homes.[25] The half-hour show, however, does offer certain advantages which make it nearly as popular as the spot with most candidates.

Although the audience for a half-hour show is likely to be composed primarily of viewers who have already made up their minds to vote for the candidate, the show serves as an effective way to reinforce the candidate's popularity with these people. The longer format gives the candidate a chance to express his position on the issues at greater length and an opportunity to create a favorable impression on uncommitted voters or those who are leaning in his direction. It also stands a better chance than a spot of being picked up and reported by other news media. Half-hour programs may be films, or live presentations in which the candidate answers questions from members of a panel or from viewers who telephone the channel. Although a live format may seem to expose the candidate to unrehearsed, possibly hostile challenges, in reality there is little risk. Media consultants usually take every precaution to assure that nothing will happen to make their candidate look bad. In 1968, for example, Richard Nixon held a half-hour panel show to be broadcast from Chicago. Before the show, Nixon consultants issued a memorandum explicitly describing the sort of people who should appear on the six-man panel. Staff workers were instructed to find people of a certain age and race (three twenty-five to thirty-five, three thirty-five to fifty, all of them white), in specific occupations and of a certain psychological temperament. "Find business and professional people, housewives, etc. Look for extroverts who will not be intimidated by a television studio environment. There will be no studio audience; nevertheless, we want to be careful we don't recruit anybody who'll freeze in front of the camera."[26]

Despite the advantages of half-hour shows as a reinforcement technique, the sixty-second spot remains more widely used as an advertising strategy, primarily because of the enormous numbers of people it reaches. It has been estimated that in the 1968 campaign a single spot might have been seen by as many as twenty-three million voting-age viewers, almost a third of the number who cast votes in the election.[27] Many of these spots do not discuss the issues; they merely allude to them, striving to strike a responsive emotional chord in the viewer, in much the same manner as the television commercial attempts to sell soft drinks

---

[25] *Voters' Time*, pp. 15–16. A footnote in this source notes that an advertising agency representative claimed that "almost the worst prime-time 20-second spot got a larger audience than the best half-hour program."
[26] Quoted in McGinniss, *The Selling of the President, 1968*, p. 250.
[27] *Voters' Time*, p. 7.

or the latest model of an automobile. For example, one spot in Nixon's 1968 campaign focused attention on the law-and-order issue by showing a middle-aged woman walking alone down a dark, deserted city street with a shadowy figure trailing her. Meanwhile, the announcer quoted figures on the rising crime rate in urban areas, and ended with the assertion: "Freedom from fear is a basic right of every American. We must restore it." The woman walked down a sidewalk and slowly disappeared from view. Would she reach her home and family in safety? The screen then flashed a slogan already widely advertised to Americans: "This time vote like your whole world depended on it," dissolving into the single word, "Nixon."

Many have criticized the use of spots to advertise presidential candidates. F.C.C. Commissioner Nicholas Johnson called them "immoral—too short for any serious discussion of the issues."[28] Frank Reynolds, a top executive of the ABC television network, used even stronger language, asserting that "the slick political spots now polluting the air are no less injurious to public health than cigarette advertising."[29] Despite such criticism, the sixty-second spot is probably here to stay.

Can a Candidate Be Sold?

Just how effective can the various media be in winning an election, and are the ethics employed by their practitioners in the interests of the democratic system? One ethical problem is that the high cost of television time gives an advantage to candidates with large campaign treasuries. Lacking such resources, minor-party candidates cannot get the necessary television exposure to compete equally, and even major-party candidates with limited funds are often forced to quit a race when they have run out of funds for television time. Thus, the dominance of television has made presidential campaigning, more than ever, a rich man's game.

As for the question of just how important television has become to national politics—whether image alone, projected on the home screen, can put a candidate over the top—there are arguments on both sides. Marshall McLuhan, as well as Joe McGinniss, the author of *The Selling of the President, 1968*, would claim that the media have this power. Richard Nixon, in a televised question-and-answer session in Oregon, said during the 1968 campaign, "People are much less impressed with image arguments than are columnists, commentators, and pollsters. And I for one rejected the advice of the public relations experts who say that I've got to sit by the hour and watch myself. The American people may not like my face but they're going to listen to what I have to say."[30] Nevertheless, Nixon's success in 1968 has been largely attributed to one of the most expertly planned and executed television campaigns ever used by a presidential candidate.

Evidence of the power of image in presidential campaigns has come from a study made by the Survey Research Center at the University of Michigan. The study argued that, since 1952, candidate image has been the most important factor in deciding presidential elections. Eisenhower's appeal, "already personal

---

[28] Navasky, "The Making of a Candidate," p. 84.
[29] Navasky, "The Making of a Candidate," p. 88.
[30] McGinniss, *The Selling of the President, 1968*, pp. 174–175.

in 1952, became overwhelmingly so in 1956."[31] The American public was highly susceptible to his sincerity, his virtues as a family man, his churchgoing, and his "sheer likeableness." It must be noted that the attractiveness of a candidate "implies more than something about the candidate himself; it also implies something about the response dispositions of the electorate."[32] In competition with Eisenhower's likeableness in the 1952 and 1956 elections was Adlai Stevenson's urbanity and intellectualism, which, although likeable attributes to some smaller sectors of the electorate, became insurmountable liabilities in the general population, as did the circumstance of his divorce.

In the matter of image, television has clearly shown its power to hurt a candidate's chances for nomination or election by revealing things which ordinarily would have gone unnoticed. Most commentators agree that in the 1960 presidential race Nixon was badly hurt by his poor appearance in the televised debates. What he said, or even how he said it were not deciding factors; rather, how he was viewed by the public at the other end of the television camera was the crucial factor. Looking gaunt and strained, with darkly bearded jowls, inadequate makeup, and a light-colored jacket that blended with the background, the personal appearance of the man was a disappointment to many viewers. Nixon did not seem to fit the part of a President. Kennedy, on the other hand, with his youthful good looks and self-confidence, impressed many viewers as superior presidential material.

The media can hurt a candidate badly by magnifying some human behavior, such as a lapse of self-control, into a mark of shame. Such behavior is believed to have gravely damaged Senator Edmund Muskie's chances for the Democratic nomination in 1972. Muskie made a good showing early in the campaign and was considered by many to be the strongest contender for the nomination. But he lost his image of strength when he wept while defending his wife against an attack on her character made by publisher William Loeb. The incident was widely reported in the press and on radio and television. Soon people all over the country were reported to be asking, "Do you want a President who weeps?"[33] and Muskie's prestige took a drop from which it never recovered. A similar event occurred in 1969, when Mario Procaccino, the Democratic candidate in the New York City mayoral race, cried on TV in a speech accepting the Democratic nomination, virtually destroying his chances against the incumbent, John Lindsay.[34]

If television can act as a potent force to defeat a candidate, it is reasonable to infer that it can also contribute greatly to a victory. As noted, most Americans live in the almost constant presence of television. For many, the images on the screen are the only direct contact with the candidates. Clearly, any candidate who can manipulate this medium to his own ends commands a very powerful

[31] Donald E. Stokes, Angus Campbell, and Warren E. Miller, "Components of Electoral Decision," *American Political Science Review*, vol. 52, no. 2 (June 1958), p. 377.

[32] Donald E. Stokes, "Some Dynamic Elements of Contests for the Presidency," *American Political Science Review*, vol. 60, no. 1 (March 1966), p. 25.

[33] James A. Michener, "One Man's Primary—and How He Lost It," *The New York Times Magazine* (May 21, 1972), p. 99.

[34] Although the excessive display of emotion can be harmful to a candidate, some political analysts hold that a good bit of common sentimentality attests to "basic self-esteem." For a discussion of the sentimentality of George McGovern and other contrasts between his and Nixon's characters, see James David Barber, "The Question of Presidential Character," *Saturday Review* (October 1972), pp. 62–66.

Much of Edmund Muskie's favorable preconvention showing in 1972 was attributed by political observers to his minority-group origins (Polish Catholic) and his expertise in urban problems.

ally. But some media experts contend that the political power of television has been overrated. Among them is Fred Papert, an ad man who has worked for Senator Robert Kennedy, Senator Jacob Javits, and former Senator Charles Goodell. Papert has asserted that, "the notion that we are able to 'create' winners, or even to remove warts, is nonsense."[35] Yet one must question whether this statement reflects an unbiased assessment or whether it reflects a media man on the defensive. Perhaps the media experts cannot remove warts, but, as we have seen, they can find ways of distracting the voter from any warts, or negative personality traits, that do exist.

Campaign Strategy: The Technique of Being a Winner

The Advantage of Charisma

Ever since television changed the complexion of campaign politics, substituting revealing close-ups of candidates for more removed, traditional media techniques, we have been hearing more and more about something called "charisma." The word first entered the political vocabulary with Eisenhower's 1952 campaign,

---

[35] Navasky, "The Making of a Candidate," p. 80.

when it was used to describe the aura of greatness of the fatherly military hero who promised, "I will go to Korea." Since then it has come to be almost a prerequisite for a presidential candidate, so that where it does not exist, the candidate's managers find it necessary to invent it. The indiscriminate labeling of politicians as charismatic has tended to obscure the word's real meaning, making the word little more than a synonym for *glamour*.

A lofty conception of political charisma was offered by Max Weber, the nineteenth-century father of sociology. Weber identified charisma as one of the three basic principles on which authority may be based. He wrote that people obey a guide of rational rules for the good of the society, or they become ruled by custom, generally under a hereditary leader. The third choice open to them is a break from tradition and a "surrender to the extraordinary, the belief in *charisma*, i.e., actual revelation or grace resting in such a person as a saviour, a prophet, or a hero."[36]

Charismatic leadership, according to Weber's definition, has certain risks. Usually arising in times of crisis, when society is beset by extraordinary problems, the charismatic leader is embraced precisely because he offers to overturn the status quo. In the American political system, such an offer often serves to split the leader's party, creating factions as strongly opposed to each other as they are to the major opposition party. If, by chance, two charismatic leaders should rise to prominence at the same time, a battle for supremacy is inevitable, often at the expense of both their programs.

In recent times, however, the focus on charisma spurred by the advent of television has had at least one significant effect on the American political process. By tremendously increasing the importance of a candidate's image, the public-relations man has hastened the decline of political bosses who work behind the scenes to select and dominate candidates.[37] Today, the candidate for high office is not always the obedient party member who has carefully avoided making enemies. He is more likely to be someone who, through use of the media, has won popularity and confidence by appealing directly to the people. At the same time, the power of the political boss, with his record of back-room manipulation and ambiguous official standing, has diminished.

The 1968 Democratic convention saw a struggle between old-style politics dominated by bosses and their strong party organizations, and new, more crusading figures. Senator Eugene McCarthy, a man with little power within the party, had captured the enthusiastic approval of many liberals and a body of young people who opposed the Vietnam War and were eager to change the political system. Hubert Humphrey had the backing of the party leaders and represented a continuation of the policies of the Johnson administration. Humphrey won the nomination, but not without a demonstration of extreme disappointment by those who had committed themselves to McCarthy and who felt that the Democratic machine had betrayed them by acting against the best interests of the people. In 1972, Senator George McGovern won the nomination that had eluded McCarthy four years earlier and, in a strong blow to machine politics, gained a victory that attested to the growing power of the media to create leaders and bring them to positions of authority.

---

[36] Quoted in Lewis Chester, Godfrey Hodgson, and Bruce Page, *An American Melodrama: The Presidential Campaign of 1968* (New York: Viking, 1969), p. 308.

[37] Stanley Kelley, Jr., *Public Relations and Political Power* (Baltimore: Johns Hopkins Press, 1969), p. 206.

Forming a Strategy

Although up to this point the crucial role of the media in projecting image has been emphasized, it should be recognized that there are other very significant elements that are dealt with in general campaign strategy. A candidate's strategy is his overall plan of attack, consisting of moves and alternative moves aimed at winning the election. Positions on the issues, regional affiliations if he is running for the Presidency, image, reputation, present political office, all affect a candidate's strategy. As one study of the electoral process put it, "The strategies of participants in a Presidential election make sense once we understand the web of circumstances in which they operate. . . . Strategies are courses of action consciously pursued toward well-understood goals. Watching strategies show how political leaders use the constraints and opportunities of the environment to achieve their goals."[38]

While campaigning has changed drastically in many respects, in other ways it has remained the same. Constitutional and traditional factors, such as the two-party system, the nominating and electoral processes, and certain long-standing and predictable antagonisms between regions and interest groups continue to exert a strong influence on strategy in presidential campaigns. Through these relatively unchanging factors, certain recognizable patterns in strategy have become established.

Challengers and Incumbents In any election there are really two distinct campaigns, one for the party nomination and one for election by the people. Because the aim of each campaign differs, different strategies are involved. During the prenomination period, strategies tend to vary most widely, because at this point the field is likely to be occupied by many candidates of unlike backgrounds and with varying advantages. Some may be familiar, popular figures, while others may be obscure hopefuls—"dark horses." When one of the candidates is the incumbent, the variations in strategy will be especially wide. It is customary, for example, for an incumbent President's party to award him the nomination without question, if he desires it, and this is almost always true for governors and congressmen as well. Thus, a presidential candidate who is already in office need not campaign at all prior to the national party convention, and incumbents on other levels of government need not neglect their duties to muster state or local party support. These officials must, however, guard and work to bolster their popularity. The incumbent's campaign is usually waged unofficially through the sponsorship of legislation in the public interest and spectacular executive decisions calculated to gain popular approval. Many observers considered Nixon's peace-seeking journeys to Moscow and Peking, prior to the 1972 election, examples of such tactics.

The nomination of the incumbent may be challenged, however, by political leaders within the party who differ with the policies of the man in office. Paul McCloskey, a liberal Republican from California, and John Ashbrook, a conservative Republican from Ohio, both made such challenges to Nixon early in 1972. Nixon defeated them both by decisive margins in the two primaries in which they ran, eliminating both men from the race. So great are the odds against a

[38] Nelson W. Polsby and Aaron B. Wildavsky, *Presidential Elections* (New York: Scribner, 1971), p. 3.

candidate trying to wrest the nomination from an incumbent President, that no experienced politician undertakes such a campaign with the serious intention of winning. Rather, such battles are usually waged to win national exposure for the challengers and to pressure the President to adjust policies of his which have caused dissension in the party.

Who Are the Strategy-Makers?

At the annual presentation of awards by the Academy of Motion Picture Arts and Sciences, stars who receive an Oscar usually make a little speech in which they thank by name "all the people who made this possible"—the director, producer, writer, technicians, and others. Presidents and other officials elected to high office also have a long list of people who helped put them into office. It would not serve the winners' public images, however, to make post-election speeches thanking them for making victory possible. Nevertheless, these people are the unheralded individuals who give each candidate for political office guidance, information, organization, encouragement, and, above all, loyalty. In concert with the candidate himself, they are the molders of campaign strategy.

The makeup of strategy teams varies with the personality and background of the candidate. The group that guided John Kennedy to the White House in 1960 was made up of nine key figures. Of these, only two, John Kennedy himself and his brother Robert, had had any direct experience in presidential politics before that time. The rest were largely ambitious political amateurs of keen intelligence. Among the team members were Kenneth O'Donnell, a former football teammate of Robert Kennedy at Harvard, and Lawrence O'Brien, a man who was later to act as the Democratic national chairman and national campaign director for McGovern. These two men became Kennedy's chief directors of operations. Other key figures were Pierre Salinger, a newspaperman who later became Kennedy's press agent, and Theodore Sorenson, a scholarly young historian whom Kennedy once described as his "intellectual blood-bank."[39] Richard Nixon's staff in that election was smaller, built around a core of two trusted men: Leonard W. Hall, a former congressman from New York, and Robert H. Finch, a young California lawyer.

While some candidates are able to assemble their own strategy staffs, others must accept choices made for them. This is almost always true of a Vice President who has assumed the Executive Office upon the death of a President. Lyndon B. Johnson, for example, was aided in his 1964 campaign by a coalition of old Kennedy men, who worked with such Johnson faithfuls as Bill Moyers and Jack Valenti. Some friction did develop between the two camps, but in general the coalition operated efficiently, guiding Johnson to a landslide victory over Barry Goldwater.

Nixon's 1968 campaign, which stands as one of the best planned and most efficient campaigns in presidential history, succeeded only after he amended an earlier strategy marked by old-fashioned ideas and underpreparation. Nixon succeeded by relying heavily on a well-integrated staff of seasoned professionals— men like Leonard Garment, Harry Treleaven, Ronald Ziegler, and Herbert Klein. A close personal friend and law associate, John Mitchell, who later became Attorney General, was Nixon's campaign manager. In 1972 the President's staff re-

---

[39] Theodore H. White, *The Making of the President, 1960* (New York: Pocket Books, 1961), p. 61.

mained pretty much the same. Upon the resignation of Mitchell, who had acted in that year as Chairman of the Committee to Re-elect the President, Nixon appointed Clark MacGregor, whose warm, outgoing personality was in marked contrast to the cool reserve of his predecessor.

Responsibilities of the Campaign Manager The campaign manager is by far the most important figure in the candidate's staff of strategists whether the election is on the local, state, or national level. His role has grown in recent years, as the importance of image has grown. Because a candidate is usually unable to see himself as others see him, he relies on his manager to detect his most "salable" characteristics and present them effectively to the public.

As a strategist, the campaign manager must make decisions in three broad areas: attack, theme, and pace.[40] *Attack* defines the candidate's offensive against his opponent. Since nothing hurts a candidate more than to be put on the defensive by his opponent, a campaign manager will try to think of ways in which his candidate can come out early in the campaign with cogent criticism of his opponent's record and positions, as well as with a definite program of his own.

Theme also becomes important early in the campaign; in fact, it forms the substance of the attack. As defined by one commentator, "The purpose of the campaign theme is to simplify complex public issues into brief, clear, recognizable statements to the advantage of the candidate. The Theme should run through all rallies, television performances, brochures, billboard ads, publicity releases, and other forms of communicating with the electorate."[41] Themes, at least effective ones, can usually be expressed in a single phrase; for example, Kennedy's "Get America Moving Again," was directed against the stagnation of the Eisenhower years, and Nixon's "This Time Vote Like Your Whole World Depended on It" offered salvation in time of crisis. Hubert Humphrey's failure in 1968 was in some measure attributed to his lack of theme. Unable to coordinate his positions on the issues into a unified theme, he was forced to rely wholly on melodramatic pleas for party unity and a challenge to Nixon to state *his* positions more clearly.

Pace refers to the ordering of activities from the time the campaign gets under way to the eve of the election. Given a specific amount of time and money, the campaign manager must decide how and when they should be spent. Rallies, television campaigning, registration drives, and the like must all be planned and correlated to get the most out of available resources. Work begins on a campaign behind the scenes, and eventually a politician makes a formal statement of candidacy. This formal declaration is carefully timed in the context of the general pace of the campaign. Often, as has been discussed, incumbents can pace their official actions so as to aid their forthcoming or ongoing campaigns. These carefully timed events become a significant part of a reelection campaign strategy. Occasionally, however, events occur close to election time which are detrimental to the incumbent's image. When possible, the incumbent, from his influential position, overshadows them by other actions or manages them to his advantage. For example, in June 1972 the now-famous "Watergate Caper" made headlines.

---

[40] This discussion and the opinions offered in it are taken from Dan Nimmo, *The Political Persuaders: The Techniques of Modern Election Campaigns* (Englewood Cliffs, N.J.: Prentice-Hall, 1970), pp. 52–56.

[41] Nimmo, *The Political Persuaders*, p. 54.

Seven men who were linked to President Nixon's reelection campaign were discovered attempting to bug the office of the Democratic National Committee. The consensus of political analysts and the widely publicized opinion of the Democrats was that administration officials had done everything possible to prevent the case from going to court before the election. A thorough public examination of the occurrence before the election could only have been detrimental to the President and the general pacing of his campaign strategy.

Presidential Strategy
and the National Convention

Although only aspirants for the Presidency must concern themselves with a strategy to capture the nomination at their national party conventions, the long and intricate machinations required to accomplish this feat are interesting and show quite vividly the necessity for presidential candidates to form large, well-organized, and capable campaign staffs far before the general election. The makeup and mechanics of the national convention itself have already been discussed in Chapter 12. But pertinent to this strategy discussion is the fact that delegates to the convention are in general formally or informally pledged to vote on the first ballot for a particular candidate. In order to win the nomination on the first ballot, a candidate must secure the support of a certain predetermined number of these delegates; in 1972 the necessary number for the Democrats was 1,509, for the Republicans 674. The quest for a first-ballot nomination has led candidates to engage in what is known as "the numbers game" — the calculated effort to secure the support of those state delegations whose total number of votes will add up to a victory.

In playing the numbers game, a candidate must first determine where his strength lies. He plays on traditional political loyalties in certain sections of the country, concentrating on those areas where support is strongest and writing off areas where there is no chance of winning. He may also exploit certain regional opinions in order to reverse traditional voting trends in his favor.[42] For instance, after Richard Nixon was nominated in 1968, he promised southern leaders that, if elected, he would ease up on school desegregation. And Senator McGovern, in his primary and election campaigns, concentrated on large, liberal states, such as New York.

Primaries   As Nixon's "southern strategy" showed, traditional regional allegiances are no longer fixed. Not only have some sections, like the South, started to change their loyalties in national elections, but groups defined by socioeconomic criteria and by age — such as the blue-collar vote or the youth vote — have become less predictable than before. In view of this change, many presidential candidates have come to recognize the increasing importance of state primaries as a guide to campaign strategy. Primaries, like public-opinion polls, which will soon be discussed, provide a picture of voting trends throughout the country and also give lesser-known or less popular candidates an opportunity to build national

---

[42] For a comprehensive look at the strategy used by Presidents and presidential hopefuls to capture southern support in the 1960s and early 1970s, see the book written by editors of *The Atlantic Constitution*, Reg Murphy and Hall Gulliver, *The Southern Strategy* (New York: Scribner, 1971).

support, as well as the immediate, crucial support of convention delegates.[43] The impact of a candidate's victory in an important primary may often be enough to catapult him to the front ranks. Such was clearly the case when John Kennedy beat Hubert Humphrey in the 1960 Democratic West Virginia primary, a precedent that established primary participation and victories as significant in gaining presidential nominations.[44] And Eugene McCarthy's impressive showing in the New Hampshire primary in 1968 turned him overnight from a maverick peace candidate to a leading contender for the nomination.[45]

Primaries can be risky affairs, however, and despite the growing attention given to them, they are still shunned by some candidates. Many politicians prefer to rely on support from the party machinery. Such candidates look upon primaries as potentially dangerous contests "in which victory guarantees nothing . . . but in which defeat kills. . . ."[46] For example, in 1960, Stuart Symington, one of the contenders for the Democratic nomination, chose to avoid engaging in primaries against crowd-pleasers like Kennedy and Humphrey, preferring instead to rely on his campaign managers' manipulation of powerful party bosses. Unfortunately for Symington, the negotiations fell through, and he was defeated at the convention by candidates who had taken the primary route.

Another factor that makes primaries unpopular with some candidates is their high cost. Astronomical sums are required to finance campaigns in one state after another. Nixon spent half a million dollars in the Oregon primary alone in 1968, a figure that represented only a small part of his total prenomination expenditure. Robert Kennedy spent $2 million in the California primary of that same year. The primary system is hardest on candidates who have to struggle on a shoestring budget. This was the case when Humphrey ran against the wealthy John Kennedy in the 1960 West Virginia primary. Having run out of campaign funds, Humphrey was forced to pay for desperately needed television time entirely out of his own limited personal resources. Because he lacked money to buy the services of technical experts, his television presentations turned out to be dismal failures, and he was roundly defeated. Thus primaries have become part of a political system that prevents any but the wealthy from running successfully for President, a fact that has concerned many but has only very recently led to substantial changes in campaign-spending regulations.

Intraparty Support Primary victories result from a variety of circumstances. A candidate's primary campaign often enjoys a substantial boost when another candidate leaves the race and offers him his support. In this case all the delegates committed to the retiring candidate are turned over to the man he chooses to support. In this way, Henry Cabot Lodge threw his support to Governor Nelson

---

[43] The mayor of New York City, John V. Lindsay, long a very liberal Republican, announced in August 1971 that he had switched his political affiliation to the Democratic party. Then he proceeded to enter Democratic presidential primaries to gain national exposure. Most commentators agreed that the switch was part of a long-term strategy to eventually put him in the White House.

[44] See John W. Davis, *Springboard to the White House: Presidential Primaries, How They are Fought and Won* (New York: Thomas Y. Crowell, 1967), pp. 1–2. This book is an excellent general source for information on presidential primaries.

[45] See Ben Stavis, *We Were the Campaign: New Hampshire to Chicago for McCarthy* (Boston: Beacon Press, 1969) for a readable account of McCarthy's bid for the Presidency in 1968, written by a campaign worker who followed the candidate along the campaign trail.

[46] White, *The Making of the President, 1960*, p. 47.

A. Rockefeller in 1968, and Eugene McCarthy released his supporters to George McGovern in 1972. Candidates, however, are often reluctant to admit defeat and may withhold political support from a more successful contender, particularly if they are not in agreement over policies. If the nomination at the national convention should go to a second ballot, however, such candidates often change their minds and release their committed delegates to one of the front runners.

Another way candidates gain strength is by enlisting the support of party leaders. Because most convention delegates are either very minor political figures or merely politically involved private citizens, they generally do as they are told. At the convention such individuals are out of their element, overwhelmed, even intimidated by the noise and frenzied activity, and are likely to follow party discipline rather than act independently.[47] Thus, candidates usually concentrate on swaying the leaders who control these delegates or, at times, the leaders who control the leaders. Efficient communications networks are essential for such activity, and along with technical equipment, a carefully drilled corps of lieutenants stands ready to carry out instructions on the floor at a moment's notice. These lieutenants help candidates in the complex task of turning the follow-the-leader game in their favor. A biographer of President Nixon wrote that his "command post" at the 1968 Republican convention resembled the "operating room of a great hospital."[48] Goldwater's superb convention communications network in 1964 was described by Theodore H. White as follows:

Floor control of the convention . . . had been given to Clifton White, who had meticulously studied the Kennedy communications planning of the 1960 Democratic Convention — and bettered it. In his green-and-white trailer behind the convention hall, White sat at a web of some sixteen walkie-talkies and thirty telephone lines. From the twin consoles of his telephone board, he could reach seventeen phones strategically placed at the aisle seats of his floor managers; two more were "hot" lines to Goldwater's suite . . . two more to headquarters of the Southern delegates . . . two more to the main Goldwater switchboard. One white button (the "all-call" button) could reach every phone with its attendant monitor all through the convention hall and the city. An antenna, located jam-proof at the very pinnacle of the auditorium, reached the walkie-talkies, deploying men to any necessary point instantly. Higher powered walkie-talkies of newest manufacture, delivered just before the convention, were on standby at the control wagon, able to communicate for twenty miles from base. (Goldwater, a devoted ham radio operator and fascinated by electronics, regretted later that if they had had just a few more weeks to prepare, they could have put a pocket telephone in the shirt pocket of every single delegate on the floor.)[49]

Considerations in Strategy Formation

Time of Voter Decision The impact of political campaigns on voters is still unclear. A study of voting habits conducted by Paul Lazarsfeld, Bernard Berelson, and Hazel Gaudet divided voters into three groups, according to when during the campaign they reach their final decision. There are the "May Voters," the "June-to-August Voters," and the "September-to-November Voters." The study showed, further, that those who decide late in the campaign fall into one of two groups those who are subjected to cross-pressures (for example — Catholics tend to vote

---

[47] Costikyan, *Behind Closed Doors,* p. 167.
[48] Earl Mazo and Stephen Hess, *Nixon: A Political Portrait* (New York: Harper & Row, 1968), p. 318.
[49] Theodore H. White, *The Making of the President, 1964* (New York: Signet, 1965), pp. 243–244.

Democratic, while the rich tend to vote Republican—hence, a rich Catholic may be subject to cross-pressure); and those who are simply not very interested in the election outcome and let friends or circumstances make up their minds. Since those who decide early in the campaign are not especially subject to campaign appeals, no matter how persuasive, campaigners concentrate on the second two groups in an effort to bring wavering voters over to their side.[50]

Increased Voter Turnout How many votes can a campaign bring in? Most estimates on this point tend to be low. All that can be said with certainty is that a vigorous campaign increases voter turnout. But then, those who have been persuaded to vote and do not generally do so are usually independents and weak partisans. Whom they will cast their ballots for is unpredictable. Edward N. Costikyan, who took part in Johnson's 1964 campaign against Goldwater, estimated that if Johnson's staff had done nothing to promote their candidate, his victory might have been significantly less than the 61.1 percent by which Johnson won. Costikyan concluded that "10 to 15 percent (probably closer to 10) is about the maximum that any political organization can contribute to a campaign . . . usually 5 percent is a fairer figure."[51] Yet, even 5 percent is a decisive margin in a national election, as shown by Kennedy's narrow victory over Nixon, and Nixon's narrow victory over Humphrey. For this reason, campaigning can be crucial in swaying the vote.

The Basic Functions of a Campaign Lazarsfeld, Berelson, and Gaudet, in another study of voting patterns, have analyzed the impact of presidential campaigns through a classification of their functions: activation, conversion, and reinforcement. *Activation* is the ability of campaign propaganda to awaken voters to the candidates' positions on the issues and to motivate them to align themselves actively with the candidate who best represents their interests. "What the political campaign did, so to speak, was not to form new opinions, but to raise old opinions over the thresholds of awareness and decision."[52]

Conversion of voters from one party to the other is infrequent, because those whose political interest is highest are usually party members who are most exposed to political propaganda and hence least likely to be swayed by it. This kind of voter is also most likely to have formed distinct opinions about the candidates early in the campaign, and is thus more likely to listen only to supportive propaganda of their own party. On the other hand, voters most open to conversion are those who are politically indifferent and have "read and listened least."[53] The fact that propagandists must aim their conversion attempts at this politically ignorant segment accounts, perhaps, for the prevalence of such emotionally oriented techniques as the sixty-second spot. Given an opportunity to educate the public politically, campaign managers appeared to have opted for novel, eye-catching ways to snare the unsophisticated voter.

By far the most important effect of political campaigns takes place through the *reinforcement* of established preferences. While campaigners realize that

---

[50] Paul Lazarsfeld, Bernard Berelson, and Hazel Gaudet, *The People's Choice: How the Voter Makes Up His Mind in a Presidential Campaign,* 3rd edition (New York: Columbia University Press, 1968), pp. 52–64.

[51] Costikyan, *Behind Closed Doors,* p. 275.

[52] Lazarsfeld, Berelson, and Gaudet, *The People's Choice,* p. 74.

[53] Lazarsfeld, Berelson, and Gaudet, *The People's Choice,* p. 94.

most people decide their vote long before the election, or at least show strong tendencies one way or the other, it is recognized that these preferences must be reinforced along the way, or they will be subject to capture by the opposing party. Most people, even those who are the most independent, need to be re-assured that their choice is the right one. If they are exposed only to opposing arguments, they may begin to have doubts about the candidate of their choice. Campaign workers therefore keep their partisans supplied with a steady stream of information and arguments to use in defending their choice against the propaganda of the opposing camp.

The Use of Public-Opinion Polls One of the most powerful tools acquired by campaign managers has been the public-opinion poll. Although polls have been used in presidential elections since William McKinley's campaign of 1896, in recent years they have become much more complex and sophisticated. Numerous private polling organizations serve politicians, and they have progressed far from the rather crude polls of the past, which made such blunders as picking Alf Landon over Roosevelt in 1936 and Thomas E. Dewey over Truman in 1948. Today's public-opinion polls, based on more sophisticated interviewing and interpreting techniques and aided by computer technology, are capable of predicting within a 2- or 3-percent margin of error.

Despite the increased precision of poll-taking methods since 1948, campaign underdogs still cite Harry S Truman's upset of Thomas E. Dewey in the 1948 presidential election as an example of the unreliability of polls in predicting election results.

Modern polling systems concentrate on parts rather than the whole, and most political professionals consider national polls—the same questionnaire administered nationwide—useless.[54] Therefore, they concentrate on regional responses to specific questions in an effort to measure voter tendency. When used in this way, polls serve as thermometers of public response, and as indicators of the people's awareness, predilections, and dissatisfactions. The type of poll commonly called the "laundry list," which ranks candidates in order according to national popularity, is the poll least useful to politicians in planning their campaigns, although it is the kind most frequently reprinted in newspapers and probably most interesting to the average voter. Properly used, polls can make campaigning more effective. Many media experts recommend them as the first step in a politician's candidacy; an early poll, Edward Costikyan has written, helps the candidate "to find out who he is."[55] Louis Harris points out that polls are helpful in breaking down the political composition of a constituency.[56] Once the poll has informed the candidate of how well he is known, what positions he is identified with, and how well he is trusted and liked, he can then use this information in designing a more effective campaign. Poll findings can, of course, be misused, as they were when the New York state Democratic party attempted to defeat Governor Nelson A. Rockefeller in 1962. Polls taken in April and May revealed that many of Rockefeller's 1958 supporters—chiefly liberal Jewish Democrats who had turned Republican in opposition to Democratic political boss Carmine DeSapio—were now disenchanted with the governor and ready to return to the Democrats. To assure their support, the party sought a candidate who would appeal to their interests, settling finally on Appellate Judge Bernard Botein. News of this strategem leaked to the press, resulting in a headline similar to: "New York Democrats Seek Jewish Candidate for Governor." Jewish voters resented this attempt to manipulate their ethnic loyalties, and, in an effort to show that there was no "Jewish vote," that Jews do not support candidates merely because they are Jewish, they gave their support to Rockefeller.[57]

Poll-taking may be aided by various sophisticated data-processing devices. Such devices have also come to play a growing role in other aspects of campaigning, as in the compilation of lists of potential contributors. Joseph Napolitan has recommended another use for sophisticated equipment: the replacement of old-fashioned newspaper-clipping files with computer banks containing not only printed matter, but tapes of radio and television programs. This resource gives the candidate's speechwriters access to information on past events in all sections of the country with possible political importance—"to capitalize on the information already inside everyone's brain."[58]

[54] For one expert's opinion see Napolitan, "Yes, the Democrats *Can* Beat Richard Nixon," p. 24.

[55] Costikyan, *Behind Closed Doors*, p. 219.

[56] Louis Harris, "Polls and Politics in the United States," in *American Party Politics*, edited by Donald G. Hertzberg and Gerald M. Pomper (New York: Holt, Rinehart and Winston, 1966), p. 176.

[57] This analysis of the misuse of a poll is drawn from Costikyan, *Behind Closed Doors*, pp. 213–215.

[58] "For example, no one who lived in New York in July 1970 is likely to forget the suffocating smog that smothered the city for a few days during the middle of that month. Utilization of newsfilm clips and commentaries would instantly recall those horrendous conditions and could trigger the rage and frustration New Yorkers felt during those days." Napolitan, "Yes, the Democrats *Can* Beat Richard Nixon," p. 27.

The huddle of demoralized supporters around a TV in the aftermath of an assault on a public figure has become an all-too-familiar sight in the last decade.

On the Campaign Trail

When primaries are over and national-convention excitement has subsided, political contests are marked by a dramatic rise in intensity as the field for every elective office narrows down to the two leading teams. People with only slight interest in politics now suddenly take notice. Who is leading the race? What will happen next to change the tide of events? For many months, Americans are caught up in the emotionally charged atmosphere of a contest, a monumental contest if a President is to be chosen. For the candidate, it is one of the most grueling experiences he has ever known, so much so that his health and strength must be carefully protected lest he collapse under the tremendous strain of campaigning.

In addition to travel and exhausting work, which involve predictable and thus manageable campaign concerns, candidates on the campaign trail must cope with a violent trend which places them in constant jeopardy. The assassination of Robert Kennedy the night he won the 1968 California primary and the attempted assassination of George Wallace before the 1972 Maryland primary have made the reality of this danger very clear. Now, part of a campaign manager's job is to make certain his man has adequate protection. Under a law passed by Congress in 1968, hours after Kennedy's death, Secret Service protection is offered to presidential and vice-presidential candidates.[59] Although the law does not specifically provide protection for candidates prior to the conventions, the Secret Service set a precedent in 1968 by guarding the twelve candidates who ran in the primaries. Protection for candidates in other than the presidential and vice-presidential races is provided, as deemed necessary, by each state.

The Advance Men at Work

An enormous amount of advance work is necessary to launch a full-scale campaign that will run smoothly. Advance work means the difference between a well-organized, efficient campaign such as Nixon's in 1968, and an erratic one, such as Humphrey's of the same year. One of Humphrey's managers has spoken of lack of preparation as the most significant factor in his 1968 defeat:

> [Humphrey] approved the campaign plan in Chicago on August 30. That was the Friday before Labor Day, which is the day the campaign begins, traditionally. Instead of having three or four weeks to mount a campaign, we had three days. And so the candidate went on the road, and he was a disaster.[60]

Campaign workers attend to the infinite number of details involved in carrying out the campaign. While media men deal in broad effects, workers deal with the practical considerations necessary to the success of rallies or television shows, speaking engagements, and benefit dinners. So-called advance men take care of such tasks as renting appropriate halls for rallies, placing microphones where needed, checking to make sure that a candidate's speaking engagement does not conflict with his appearance at an important football game. The attention of campaign workers is always on the details, the battle rather than the war.[61] They are concerned primarily with how many votes the candidate can draw out of a particular appearance or action, a criterion that is usually the determining factor in their decision-making.[62]

Other campaign workers—often unpaid volunteers—do even more basic work: they phone registered voters to remind them to vote for the candidate, canvass neighborhoods, distribute literature on the streets, drive people to the polls. Campaign workers may also participate in registration drives—ostensibly non-partisan, but actually calculated to get out those sectors of the population most likely to vote for the candidate.

Campaign Literature

The literature distributed by campaign workers usually contains slogans blaring the candidate's campaign theme, statements made by him, a recounting of his political record, and the endorsements of influential figures. Literature of this sort is problematic for campaign planners and workers, because most people simply do not bother to read it. When read, the material can be very useful; if not read, it is not worth the effort and money invested in writing and printing it. Most commentators agree that the key to successful campaign literature is

[59] *Congressional Quarterly Weekly Report*, vol. 30, no. 21 (May 20, 1972), p. 1124.
[60] Quoted in Chester, Hodgson, and Page, *An American Melodrama*, p. 632.
[61] For an interesting personal account of advance work see Jerry Bruno and Jeff Greenfield, *The Advance Man* (New York: Bantam, 1971).
[62] Costikyan, *Behind Closed Doors*, pp. 269–278.

brevity. "Almost every piece of political literature is too long," one authority observes.[63] If this fault is true of handouts and mailed literature, it is doubly true of the flocks of political books published every presidential-election year. These books, both by and about the candidates, are written with varying degrees of objectivity and have at least one thing in common: they have more to say than most people are interested in knowing. The June 4, 1972, edition of the *New York Times Book Review* carried writeups of a book on George McGovern, one on Henry M. Jackson, and one on Edmund Muskie, all in the running at that time for the Democratic presidential nomination. In the same issue there were reviews of three new books on Edward Kennedy, two on Nixon, and one astrological guide to the candidates by a self-proclaimed witch, Sybil Leek. While such books rarely get to be best-sellers, they do accomplish a useful service: for those who read them, they often show how the candidates stand in relation to each other and the government.

Issue Orientation

The kind of arguments or voter appeals used by candidates and their staffs in speeches or printed matter depends heavily on whether the candidate is the challenger or the incumbent; the challenger attacks, the incumbent defends. And the incumbent is more likely than the challenger to win. In the campaign battle, he can extol his achievements in office, while the challenger can only criticize and promise. Each candidate will discuss his views on the issues he believes will win him support and attempt to conceal his less popular opinions.

Circumstances vary, but over the years certain broad party stances have been noted. For example, it has been noted that the Democrats, being the majority party nationally, call for a vote for the party in presidential elections, while Republicans tend to urge voting for the man.[64] Republicans in running for President and Congress have emphasized foreign-policy issues, pointing to the fact that, starting with World War I, a Democratic President has been in power whenever America has become embroiled in a war. At the 1972 Republican convention, keynote speakers hailed Nixon as a peacemaker because he had made conciliatory moves toward China and the USSR. They ignored the unsolved problems of the domestic economy and urban decay and crime. Democratic campaigns, however, stressed that these problems had grown worse during Nixon's administration. In this election year, as in others before it, the Democrats emphasized their own concern with the interests of the poor and the middle class.

Incumbents who can usually save campaign costs and energies by not entering primaries, also benefit by avoiding the interparty conflicts generated in these contests. In contrast, one who is a primary candidate, in the effort to distinguish his position from that of other candidates of his party, may make statements that may help him to win the nomination, but which hurt him in the general election that follows. This phenomenon was strikingly illustrated in 1972 when George McGovern embraced the policies suggested by his advisers on welfare and tax reform and thereby placed himself politically to the left of the two other leading contestants, Edmund Muskie and Hubert Humphrey. With the aid of a well-organized campaign, he won the nomination, but his proposals were

---

[63] Costikyan, *Behind Closed Doors*, p. 240.
[64] David A. Leuthold, *Electioneering in America: Campaigns for Congress* (New York: Wiley, 1968), p. 112.

". . . And if I am re-elected Senator I solemnly promise to keep all those promises I made six years ago."

Saturday Review, *September 13, 1969*

widely attacked as unworkable, not only by the opposition but by members of his own party. This development caused him considerable embarrassment, making it necessary for him to revise his proposals in an effort to recover his lost prestige.

The incumbent also has an advantage in ascertaining what the voters want, because his office receives large amounts of mail from the public. In fact, an incumbent has been receiving mail from the public throughout his term and thus is able to gauge trends in voter desires and beliefs more accurately than his challengers. If he should need more information, he has many available resources in government. This same information is often unavailable to the challenger, or is difficult, time-consuming, and expensive to research.[65]

In most elections, the incumbent bases his campaign on his status as President, governor, senator, congressman, or the like, and in effect makes his political status or experience an issue. Just a glance at the 1972 Republican presidential campaign reveals this tactic: bumper stickers and other advertising devices carried the message "Reelect the President" across the country. The technique is just as pervasively used in the states to reelect mayors, governors, and others, who almost always put the magic word *reelect* on campaign paraphernalia. Challengers are often made into issues by incumbents. Keeping "a Goldwater" or "a

[65] Leuthold, *Electioneering in America*, p. 59.

McGovern" from becoming President was crucial to Democrats in 1964, who dubbed Goldwater a warhawk, and to Republicans in 1972, who tagged McGovern a radical.

Aside from the issue of the candidates themselves, the 1972 campaign showed a clear division between the two candidates on almost every point of national policy: continuation of military alliances, defense spending, the size of the federal budget and allocation of funds within that budget, the needs of the poor versus the tax burden on those who are well off.

Alarmism, one of the oldest ploys of politicians, is generally injected into every campaign through manipulation of issues. The poet and novelist Robert Penn Warren has remarked that candidates offer imaginary solutions to imaginary problems of imaginary people. The issue of school busing, for example, which many saw as a smokescreen for strong racial prejudices, continued to be used by Republican campaigners in 1972 to strike an emotional response in the electorate. With characteristic cynicism, H. L. Mencken once put it this way: "The whole aim of practical politics is to keep the populace alarmed (and hence clamorous to be led to safety) by an endless series of hobgoblins."

Regardless of how carefully the candidate approaches the issues, every campaign carries the possibility that an unforeseen event, particularly in the area of foreign relations, or some rumor or scandal, will cause a sharp swing in voter sentiment. To voters, scandal is often of greater interest than the more routine political issues. A classic illustration is the campaign of 1884, which was enlivened with charges and countercharges of scandal. Grover Cleveland, still a bachelor, had accepted responsibility for fathering an illegitimate child, and Republicans gleefully roamed the streets chanting, "Ma, ma, where's my pa?" The Democrats countered by accusing the Republican candidate, James G. Blaine, of accepting bribes from the "money men" of the railroads. Ironically, these same industrialists gave Blaine little support during his campaign and had no fear of Cleveland. Scandal, however, is not always taken so lightly. Despite Senator Edward M. Kennedy's record as a strong congressional leader and his popularity in the public opinion polls, in the opinion of many observers the Chappaquiddick affair, in which he was involved in the accidental drowning of a young woman who had worked on his brother Robert's staff, will shadow his political career for as long as he chooses to be in public office.

The Electoral College in the Presidential Election

The Framers of the Constitution were concerned about two eventualities: mob rule, and the capture of government power by extremist factions. To insure against these possibilities, they adopted, among other things, the system of the Electoral College. According to the Constitution, senators, congressmen, and holders of local offices are elected by popular vote, but the President is not; instead, he is chosen by groups of electors from each state who convene at their state capitols some time after election day and cast their votes. There are as many electors in each state as there are senators and representatives. Although no constitutional provision compels them to do so, electors have traditionally cast their votes on a winner-take-all basis. If a candidate has won the majority of the popular vote in a state, by no matter how narrow a margin, all the electoral votes of that state are his. This system has peculiarities which affect the way campaigns are run.

For one thing, candidates tend to concentrate on winning majorities in the most populous states, such as California, Illinois, New York, Ohio, Pennsylvania, and Texas, because these states, even if they support a candidate by only a small majority, can often yield him so many electoral votes that victory is assured. Candidates invariably calculate which combination of large states, bolstered by which small ones, will total the number of electoral votes needed to win; they then plan their campaigns accordingly. Thus, a candidate might get a smaller popular vote than his opponent and yet win the election on electoral votes. This peculiarity has actually occurred twice: both Rutherford B. Hayes in 1876 and Benjamin Harrison in 1888 had smaller popular votes than their opponents, yet won their elections. Hayes was victorious by only one electoral vote, but Harrison had a substantial lead of sixty-five.

Another effect of the electoral system is the possibility that a third-party candidate may win so many electoral votes that neither of the two leading candidates has a majority. In this case, according to the Twelfth Amendment, the election is decided in the House of Representatives, and the preference of the third-party candidate may become the deciding factor in "swinging" the election. An example of an election decided in the House is the now-famous election of 1824, which Andrew Jackson called a "corrupt bargain." In this instance there were four candidates in the general election, all Democratic Republicans.[66] One of them, Henry Clay, was also Speaker of the House. When forced to back either Jackson or John Quincy Adams, the candidates who, in that order, had received the largest fractions of the popular vote, Clay chose Adams as the lesser of two evils, sending Jackson to Tennessee to begin a three-year-long presidential campaign.

The Electoral College Controversy

Critics of the Electoral College have proposed that it be abolished in favor of some other system. They point out the danger inherent in the electoral system: it can produce a President who does not have a majority of the popular vote and is not truly representative of the people; if an election should be thrown into the House, the influence and bargaining power of a minor-party candidate might control the election. In either case, the result would be an unpopular and ineffectual President.

The major proposal for reform is elimination of the Electoral College and election of the President by direct, popular vote. Adherence to the strict principle of rule by majority, it is argued, would mean more democratic representation for the individual voter. Campaigns would no longer necessarily be geared to states with the largest number of electors, and the nation would be assured of a President who truly held the mandate of the people. Other commentators, however, feel that the popular election of the President is not necessarily the more "democratic" alternative, and call it "government by adding machine."[67] As these critics see it, popular election would bring undesirable changes in its wake. For exam-

---

[66] The Federalist party offered no candidate in 1824 and by 1828 had no national organization. The Democratic Republican party noted here had split by 1828 into Democratic Republicans (the Jacksonians) and National Republicans (the Adamsites). The Republican party of today did not originate until 1854.

[67] The source of the comments on the Electoral College is Irving Kristol and Paul Weaver, "A Bad Idea Whose Time Has Come," *The New York Times Magazine* (November 23, 1969), p. 43.

ple, if the large states ceased to be the prizes of the election, candidates would have to adjust their campaigns to appeal equally to all sections of the country. This effort would send the cost of campaigns far above their already fantastic figures. Television, as the medium best able to reach large numbers of people, would exert even more power in politics, creating a new tradition of "studio politicians." The popular-election proposal has also been seen as the death of the two-party system, because it would offer third parties the opportunity to make their strength more apparent at the national level. Finally, critics point out that popular election would act against the interest of the working class and urban minorities: under the present electoral system, presidential candidates must gear their appeals to such constituencies to win over states with large electoral votes.

In recent decades, two other suggestions for electoral reform have received wide attention. One is a plan advocated by Senator Karl E. Mundt (R.-S. Dak.), which would provide for two presidential electors to be chosen at large in each state, like senators, and the rest in congressional districts. The other plan, introduced in 1948 by former Senator Henry Cabot Lodge of Massachusetts and former Representative Ed Gossett of Texas, proposes the division of each state's electoral votes in proportion to the popular vote.[68] Alexander Bickel has pointed out that either of these plans could be adopted by state legislatures "at any time, since the practice of awarding the entire electoral vote to the popular winner rests on custom. But most large states will not soon abandon the custom voluntarily, understanding that it works to their advantage, and so long as some states continue to cast a bloc electoral vote, it is unprofitable for the others not to do so." Therefore, either of these methods "would have to be imposed by constitutional mandate."[69]

The High Cost of Democracy

As already noted, campaign expenditures have risen steadily, reaching shocking proportions, particularly in presidential elections, which must be conducted nationwide. Table 13-1 shows how rapidly expenses of this kind have accelerated in recent years. In the twelve years from 1952 to 1964, there was a 43-percent increase in these expenditures, raising the costs from $140 to $200 million. Then, in one four-year period alone, between 1964 and 1968, costs rose 50 percent, the total expenditure soaring to $300 million. Why does it cost so much for the United States to elect its prominent officials?

To begin with, a politician's time while he is campaigning is precious. To move himself and his staff rapidly to speaking engagements throughout the state or the country, he requires a private plane or one to which he has frequent access. For a presidential candidate, this one expense can be very great. In addition, pri-

---

[68] Allan P. Sindler in 1962 found most suggestions for Electoral College reform anti-urban in nature. The proportional plan, in particular, was held to be adverse to the maintenance of the two-party system, as it would produce "one-partyism in presidential politics, namely facilitating Democratic control of the White House by means which would reflect and contribute to the heightened influence of the southern faction of the Democratic Party. . . ." See Allan P. Sindler, "Presidential Election Methods and Urban-Ethnic Interests," in Herzberg and Pomper, *American Party Politics*, pp. 410–417. The quotation is from page 414.

[69] Alexander M. Bickel, *Reform and Continuity: The Electoral College, The Convention, and the Party System* (New York: Harper & Row, 1971).

Table 13-1   **Political Expenditures**

All Levels of Government, 1952–1968 (in Millions)

Year	Cost	Increase	% Increase
1952[1]	$140	—	—
1956	155	$ 15	11
1960	175	20	13
1964	200	25	15
1968	300	100	50
1972*	400	100	33

[1] Data for 1952 and 1956 from Alexander Heard, *The Costs of Democracy* (Chapel Hill, N.C.: University of North Carolina Press, 1960), pp. 7–8. For 1960 and 1964, see Herbert E. Alexander, *Financing the 1960 Election* and *Financing the 1964 Election* (Princeton, N.J.: Citizens Research Foundation, 1962 and 1966).
* Estimated costs.

Source: Herbert E. Alexander, "Financing Parties in Campaigns in 1968," *in* Political Parties and Political Behavior, *edited by William J. Crotty, Donald M. Freeman, and Douglas S. Gatlin (Boston: Allyn & Bacon, 1971), p. 316. Data for 1972 added by author.

vate polling companies charge steep fees to carry out large-scale public-opinion surveys, and expensive computer services are needed to collate and analyze this information. Media strategy must be planned by high-priced experts, and television and radio time call for huge outlays, as illustrated in Figure 13-1. In 1968, with ten candidates vying for the presidential nomination, costs reached an all-time high. The total expenditures of all presidential hopefuls on their pre- and post-nomination campaigns was $100 million, while similar costs in 1964 had been $60 million.[70] Nixon, the biggest spender, spent more than $10 million on prenomination costs alone; even Ronald Reagan's staff spent a total of $700,000 on "a non-campaign for a non-candidate."[71] In 1972 George McGovern stated at the time of the Democratic national convention that his goal was to raise $36.5 million, an amount that was, no doubt, meant to defray both primary- and general-election costs. One commentator has seen the reasons for these increases in the nature of the Presidency itself, noting: "The Presidency is more important today than previously, and therefore the stakes for achieving it are greater."[72] But costs for other elective offices are also very steep. Governor Nelson A. Rockefeller of New York, aided by vast personal resources, spent $6.9 million for his reelection in 1968—a figure which is almost as much as the combined totals of his opponent and the three senatorial candidates from that state. Senator Wayne Morse's campaign for the Senate in Oregon cost him only $300,000, but each similar candidate in California was reported to have spent $1 million, and one candidate in New York, Democrat Richard Ottinger, spent $2.5 million. House races were variously reported at $50,000 and $75,000.[73]

Where does the money come from? The popular belief that contributors come

---

[70] Herbert E. Alexander, "Financing Parties in Campaigns in 1968," in *Political Parties and Political Behavior*, 2nd edition, edited by William J. Crotty, Donald M. Freeman, and Douglas S. Gatlin (Boston: Allyn & Bacon, 1971), p. 317.

[71] Alexander, "Financing Parties in Campaigns in 1968," pp. 319, 324. For a discussion of the Republican financial advantage in 1968 see Herbert E. Alexander and Harold B. Meyers, "A Financial Landslide for the G.O.P.," *Fortune* (March 1970), pp. 104ff.

[72] Alexander, "Financing Parties in Campaigns in 1968," p. 318.

[73] All these statistics are from "Campaign Spending in the 1968 Election," *Congressional Quarterly Weekly Report,* vol. 27, no. 49 (December 5, 1969), p. 2438.

Figure 13–1   **Charges for Broadcasts, All Candidates and Presidential and Vice-Presidential Candidates, General Election Campaigns, 1956–1968**

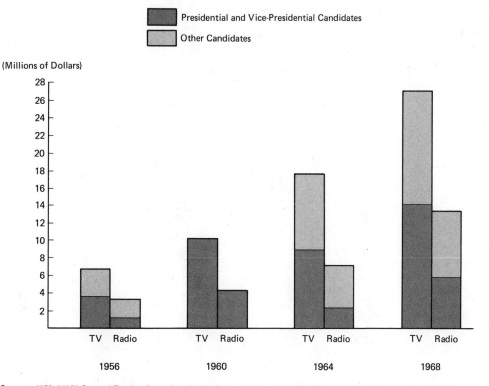

Sources: *1956, "1956 General Election Campaigns," 85th Cong., 1st sess. 1960, 1964, and 1968, FCC, Survey of Public Broadcasting. From* Voters' Time: Report of the Twentieth-Century Fund Commission on Campaign Costs in the Electronic Era *(New York: Twentieth-Century Fund, 1969).*

from only the wealthy classes is not entirely true. Recent studies show that approximately 10 to 12 percent of the population contributes to campaigns. This figure bears out the results of an experiment in Pennsylvania in 1956, which showed that small, individual contributors can add substantially to campaign funds. In a heavily Republican area of the state, the Democrats decided to appeal to party supporters for contributions. The appeal garnered 10 to 15 percent of the amount needed to finance the campaign, and, in addition, served to build party spirit.[74] Small contributors are particularly important in financing the campaigns of new grass-roots candidates. George Wallace, for example, collected $9 million in 1968, mostly from individuals who contributed $10 and less to his campaign.

The bulk of campaign funds in presidential elections, however, comes from contributors who each give at least $100 (see Figure 13-2). In fact, in the Democratic party in 1968, 5 percent of the contributors gave more than $100, and this

---

[74] See Richard F. Schier, "Political Fund Raising and the Small Contributor," in Herzberg and Pomper, *American Party Politics,* pp. 168–174.

Figure 13–2   **Contributions of $500 or More as Percent of All Contributions by Individuals to National-Level Committees, Democratic and Republican Parties, 1952–1968**

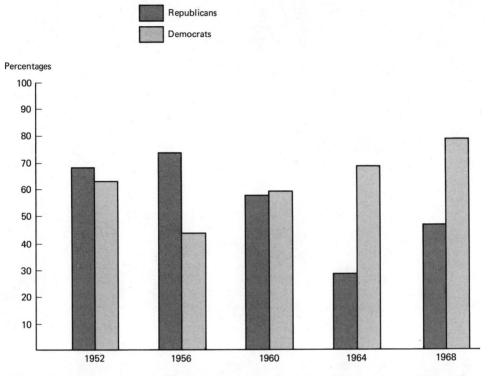

■ Republicans

▨ Democrats

Sources: *1952 and 1956 derived from Alexander Heard,* The Costs of Democracy *(Chapel Hill, N.C.: University of North Carolina Press, 1960), pp. 48, 51. 1960 from Herbert E. Alexander,* Financing the 1960 Election *(Princeton, N.J.: Citizens' Research Foundation, 1962), p. 58. 1964 from Herbert E. Alexander,* Financing the 1964 Election *(Princeton, N.J.: Citizens' Research Foundation, 1966), p. 85. 1968 estimated on the basis of preliminary data. From* Voters' Time: Report of the Twentieth Century Fund Commission on Campaign Costs in the Electronic Era *(New York: Twentieth Century Fund, 1969).*

5 percent financed the bulk of the campaign.[75] In the prenomination campaign of that year, there were three individual contributions of $500,000, one to McCarthy, one to Nixon, and one to Robert Kennedy.[76] In total, that same year, over four hundred contributions of $10,000 or more were made to Republicans and Democrats combined.[77] Contributions from wealthy families often amount to sizable fortunes (for example, some sources report that one Rockefeller family member gave over $1 million to the governor's presidential nomination campaign in 1968). Labor is also a great contributor. The AFL-CIO donated enormous amounts in 1968 to Humphrey's campaign. Special party organizations such as the Republican President's Club are used to drum up financial support. On September 19, 1968, fund-raising dinners held in twenty-two cities grossed almost $6 million for Richard Nixon. The Republicans, in fact, grossed more

[75] Herbert E. Alexander, *Financing the 1968 Election* (Lexington, Mass.: Heath, 1971), p. 151.

[76] Alexander, "Financing Parties in Campaigns in 1968," p. 320.

[77] Alexander, *Financing the 1968 Election,* p. 301.

"They say to get elected to public office in America one must be rich. Well, my friends, I'm rich. I'm very rich."

New Yorker, *October 3, 1970*

money in 1968 than the Democrats, and they got it from fewer contributors.

Although rich men obviously have an advantage when running for office in high-level politics, a strange combination of forces often makes it difficult for them to win broad financial support. The facts seem to indicate that, while it is possible for a poor candidate to attract the nickels and dimes of a broad-based following, men with money and connections, like the Kennedys and the Rockefellers, are "handicapped by the feeling of many that they can afford to spend their own money. Then, ironically, if they do spend substantially their own, they are criticized for it."[78]

The Controls on Campaign Spending

Theoretically, campaign expenditures are controlled under the Corrupt Practices Act of 1925 (which limits campaign costs of congressmen) and the Act to Prevent Pernicious Political Practices of 1939 (which deals with presidential campaigns). Under the first act, a candidate for the House of Representatives may spend no more than five thousand dollars, a candidate for the Senate, no more than twenty-five thousand. A presidential candidate is limited to three million. This limit is clearly unreasonable, in light of current costs. As one columnist wrote:

[78] Alexander, "Financing Parties in Campaigns in 1968," p. 320.

Since it costs a minimum of ten million dollars for a Presidential candidate who has any chance of being nominated to reach the Convention and then as much as thirty million dollars to run a campaign, the man who finally becomes President of the United States violates either the spirit of the law, as Mr. Humphrey did, or the spirit and the letter of the law, as Mr. Nixon did.[79]

Campaign costs regularly exceed the allotted figures. In fact, most politicians spend from ten to two hundred times the allowed amounts to get themselves elected. They do this through loopholes in the law. For example, the Corrupt Practices Act stipulates that a candidate must report all funds collected or spent "with his knowledge or consent." Thus, many candidates simply let a staff member handle all their financial transactions, which technically allows them to report their funds as "none." George McGovern did this after his senatorial race in 1968. In addition, the Hatch Act of 1940 prohibited an individual from donating more than $5,000 to a candidate or campaign committee. Many circumvented this prohibition giving $5,000 on behalf of themselves and other members of their families to numerous candidate and party committees on all levels of government, the number of which proliferated freely. Even campaign spending by labor unions and private and government corporations, which has been expressly forbidden since 1947, has not deterred labor and the heads of corporations from donating to their favored candidates. The trouble with the laws governing campaign spending before 1972 was that they were unenforceable and that nearly all candidates were forced to break them. Thus, under the letter of the law, the President and nearly every member of Congress are guilty of criminal acts.

The dysfunction of campaign-spending laws also points to a basic and serious flaw in our democratic system—the granting of privileged access to power to persons of wealth. Few contributors to campaigns give money out of purely charitable impulses. In return for their contributions, they expect the opportunity to influence lawmakers. As one lobbyist said, "Half an hour or an hour [with a congressman] can be worth many, many thousands of dollars."[80] Thus, the present system of campaign financing leads to the "buying" of lawmakers by wealthy political contributors. Not only is access bought, but positions in new administrations are bought. This is true for Democrats and Republicans. A report on campaign funding in the 1968 election lists the fashionable diplomatic posts assigned after Nixon took office. Coincidentally, half a dozen ambassadorships were assigned to men who had donated over $22,000 to Nixon's campaign![81]

There have been some efforts at reform. Dennis J. Morrisseau, a candidate for the House from Vermont, sent a letter to the Clerk of the House stating that he refused to reveal his expenditures for this 1970 campaign. He hoped, by this act of civil disobedience, to force the government to publicly acknowledge the inadequacies of the law. So far there has been no official action on Morrisseau's challenge.[82]

One substantial effort in the direction of reform has been passage of the new Federal Election Campaign Act of 1971, which went into effect in April 1972. Under the new law, which repealed the Federal Corrupt Practices Act of 1925,

---

[79] Richard Harris, "A Fundamental Hoax," *New Yorker* (August 7, 1971), p. 37.
[80] Harris, "A Fundamental Hoax," p. 55.
[81] Alexander, *Financing the 1968 Election*, pp. 353–354.
[82] For a full description of Morrisseau's challenge see Harris, "A Fundamental Hoax," pp. 38–48.

a contributor's name, occupation, and address must be reported when a contribution is made. The law also places limits on the amounts candidates may spend on specific campaign items, such as television, radio, newspaper, billboard, and telephone advertising. In addition, the law restricts the amount candidates can contribute to their own campaigns, in either their own or their relatives' names, thus placing limitations on the millionaire politicians. The only campaign expenditure not limited is money allocated to direct-mail appeal to the voters. The ceilings on media advertising will vary depending on the size of the constituency that must be reached. Each candidate for the Presidency or for Congress can spend ten cents for each resident over eighteen years old in the jurisdiction of the race. None, however, will be denied spending at least $50,000, though no more than 60 percent of the total may be used on broadcast spending. The new law had an impact on the 1972 nominating campaign when McGovern made public all of his contributions and forced the other candidates to do the same.

Is It All Worth It?

Considering all the absurdities and questionable practices that go into a presidential campaign in the United States, one might ask whether we need such a

Richard M. Nixon's well-planned 1968 presidential campaign no doubt helped him gain victory, which eluded him in the face of John F. Kennedy's massive campaign organization in 1960.

practice at all. Might it not be better to scrap the election campaigns and substitute some calmer, more rational method? The government might, for instance,
administer various tests—intelligence, psychological, physical, and the like—and
publish the results along with the candidate's political record. Such a method,
however, would serve to eliminate one aspect of the campaign importance to a
democracy. If it does nothing else, the presidential campaign forces the candidates to go out among the people and relate to them by shaking hands, kissing
babies, and making speeches. This is an important test for a man who aspires
to be an elected representative, for, as one commentator puts it: "The sweaty,
grasping people are the taproot of power, and if a politician cannot cope with or
relate to a crowd, he is in political trouble. . . ."[83] Campaigns create a rapport
between the candidates and the public, and despite the machinations of the
media people, they show us, perhaps better than any other method, the kind of
men being offered us as leaders. True, campaigns are expensive, boisterous, and
ever occasionally scandalous. Yet it is quite possible that without them our country
would be less than it is.

SUGGESTED READINGS

Alexander, Herbert E. *Financing the 1968 Election* (Lexington, Mass.: Heath, 1971). In
the third study of presidential-election finances under the auspices of the Citizens' Research Foundation, Alexander analyzes the political, scientific, and technological reasons
for the most expensive campaign on record. He shows how financing changes, what
sources candidates try to tap, and the development, new to 1968, of significant liberal
money to finance New Politics primary campaigns.

————. *Money in Politics* (Washington, D.C.: Public Affairs Press, 1972). In this fourth
study, Alexander carries the question of campaign finance through the 1972 primaries.
The book includes information concerning the amount of money each candidate obtained
from small contributors. It also analyzes the impact of the Federal Election Campaign
Act of 1971 on campaign finance.

Bruno, Jerry, and Jeff Greenfield. *The Advance Man* (New York: Bantam, 1971). In paperback. Bruno began working as an advance man for JFK's presidential campaign in 1960
and has become one of the best in the business. He and Greenfield write humorously and
insightfully about busy days on the campaign trail scouting ahead of the candidate,
scheduling stops, and organizing rallies. They discuss the differences between campaign
and presidential visits and the increasing specialization of campaign politics.

Chester, Lewis, Godfrey Hodgson, and Bruce Page. *An American Melodrama: The Presidential Campaign of 1968* (New York: Dell, 1969). This thorough, incisive, and compelling account of the 1968 presidential campaign was written by three American-based
journalists of the Sunday *Times* of London. The authors trace the contest for the presidency through the primaries, conventions, and November election. Their work provides
an interesting contrast to the better-known account written by Theodore H. White.

Leuthold, David A. *Electioneering in a Democracy: Campaigns for Congress* (New York:
Wiley, 1968). In paperback. Leuthold studied congressional campaigns in ten San Francisco Bay districts in 1962, a year when there was no presidential race, but when Cali-

[83] Richard M. Scammon and Ben J. Wattenberg, *The Real Majority: How the Silent Center of the American
Electorate Chooses Its President* (New York: Coward, McCann & Geoghegan, 1970), p. 2.

fornians were voting for governor and other state offices. He sees campaigning as a process by which ambitious candidates acquire and make use of political resources to influence votes. Conclusions are drawn about the efficacy of party in a state where parties are traditionally weak, about the value of incumbency, and about the degree of competitiveness in congressional campaigns.

Mailer, Norman. *Miami and the Siege of Chicago* (New York: New American Library, 1968). In paperback. In this book a novelist's eye captures the hoopla, color, and human interest of the 1968 national conventions. Norman Mailer gives his personal account of the rather calm Republican conclave of Miami and the chaotic scene and cast of characters assembled in Mayor Daley's Chicago for the Democratic convention.

McGinniss, Joe. *The Selling of the President, 1968* (New York: Pocket Books, 1968). In paperback. McGinniss has written a highly entertaining, media-oriented account of the 1968 election. He is frank and extremely revealing, delving into the image-makers and how they packaged Richard Nixon so successfully that the American public bought him. The book thus asserts that Presidents *can* be sold and that the success of media campaigning is the determining factor in an election.

O'Connor, Edwin. *The Last Hurrah* (New York: Bantam, 1956). In paperback. O'Connor's novel tells the story of Frank Skeffington's last campaign and his tumultuous passing from the political scene. The affectionate portrait of an old-time Irish political boss, which may well have been patterned on Boston's former mayor, James Michael Curley, explores how big-city bosses governed cities under turbulent social and economic conditions, and how the voters' loyalties to them formed the solid foundations of political parties active in state and national politics.

Pierce, Neal R. *The People's President* (New York: Simon and Schuster, 1968). A history of the Electoral College and a statement of the major concerns—constitutional, political, and social—that Americans and their leaders must consider as they decide the best way to elect their President. The author argues against the Electoral College, which he says has thwarted the will of the majority of Americans, and supports the election of the Chief Executive by the direct vote.

Polsby, Nelson W., and Aaron B. Wildavsky. *Presidential Elections: Strategies of American Electoral Politics* (New York: Scribner, 1972). In paperback. A study of presidential elections which integrates recent research on electoral behavior into the evolving structure of competition for winning the Presidency. Polsby and Wildavsky describe the context within which the battle for presidential office is waged, discuss the strategies of contending parties and, through example, explain why such strategies are used by some contestants and other strategies by others. They also discuss the possibility and desirability of presidential-election reform.

Riordan, William L. (ed.). *Plunkitt of Tammany Hall* (New York: Dutton, 1963). In paperback. Senator George Washington Plunkitt delivers himself of keen and often hilarious sermons on how to win elections in turn-of-the-century New York City. He describes his own rise to Tammany district leader through the acquisition of a loyal following of voters, his career in Tammany, and his tenure in public office.

Sayre, Wallace S., and Judith H. Parris. *Voting for President: The Electoral College and the American Political System* (Washington, D.C.: The Brookings Institution, 1970). In paperback. A comprehensive analysis of the existing electoral system of presidential election. The authors compare the results of the present system with the likely impact of four leading alternatives—the direct vote, the automatic plan, the district plan, and the proportional plan. They argue that the present electoral system manages to give appropriate weight to a great many of the relevant factors in American political life and therefore should be retained, although with minor improvements.

White, Theodore H. *The Making of the President, 1960* (New York: Atheneum, 1961). In paperback. Although White has written about each presidential campaign since 1960, his first book is still the best. He begins with the primaries, including an excellent account of the make-or-break West Virginia contest, and moves through the November election. Since the 1960 election, White himself has become a celebrity. Leading candidates have actually come to judge their success in mid-campaign by whether White is concentrating on them or on the opposition. In conjunction with a version of the 1968 election, this book is useful for several comparisons: the use of volunteers by JFK in 1960 and by RFK and McCarthy in 1968; the tone and strategy of the presidential campaigns waged by Richard Nixon in 1960 and 1968.

Williams, T. Harry. *Huey Long* (New York: Bantam, 1970). In paperback. Williams's biography of the Kingfish, Huey P. Long of Louisiana, illustrates how difficult it is to separate electioneering and its strategy from the everyday life of any politician, let alone one of the most flamboyantly successful. From the time Long began his law practice and ran for his first office, commissioner of the state railroad regulatory commission, he was always campaigning. He even claimed to know what offices he wanted to hold and in what order: governor, senator, and President of the United States.

14
VOTING BEHAVIOR
AND ELECTIONS

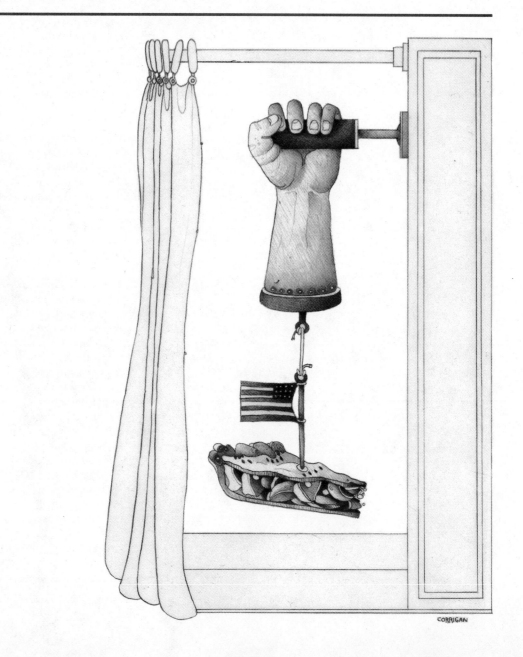

CORRIGAN

Americans, because of their democratic system of government, are denied many of the political glories witnessed by citizens of certain other countries. The swearing in of an American President, for example, while impressive and exciting in its way, hardly rivals the coronation of the British monarchs, or the elaborate and costly investiture ceremonies of the rulers in many Asian nations, in terms of pomp, color, size, or sheer duration. On the whole, however, whatever our lives lack in governmental splendor on many state occasions is more than compensated for by the excitement our system of elections generates. "Elections are the great public ceremonies of American life."[1]

Voting, in fact, is the American way of deciding nearly everything—from the person to head the country, to the high-school student-body president, to the best-dressed man and woman of the year, to the champion canine at the dog show. The importance of the voting process in American politics can be clearly seen on a presidential election night, when most of the people in the country cluster around their radios and television sets to hear the election returns. The votes they cast that day will have an enormous impact on their lives for the next four years.

The United States Constitution, though it neglects to mention anything about political parties, does detail the process by which our various public officials are to be selected. Constitutional provisions are made for the popular, direct election of members of the House of Representatives; the Seventeenth Amendment (ratified in 1913) also provides for the popular election of senators (previously senators had been appointed by the state legislatures). And, although the American President is not elected directly by the people, he is chosen by electors who in turn are chosen by the people, and who are pledged (by tradition, not law) to a particular presidential candidate. This method of presidential elections is described in the Constitution.

The Constitution also determines who shall be permitted to vote. The lengthy and oftentimes bloody struggles that accompanied the fight of various groups of Americans to extend the suffrage to more and more people may also be viewed as evidence of the importance Americans attach to the right to vote. Today, most American citizens over the age of eighteen are legally entitled to vote in all local, state, and national elections. This widened electorate is the result of a recent constitutional amendment, the Twenty-sixth, which for the first time adds to the Constitution mention of a specific age requirement for voting. Previous to the passage of this amendment (which was formally ratified by the states in 1971), the decision of the age at which Americans could vote was left up to the discretion of the individual states. This practice, however, resulted in some inconsistency. Although the vast majority of states did not allow their residents to vote until age twenty-one, eighteen-year-olds could vote in Kentucky and Georgia, nineteen-year-olds in Alaska, and twenty-year-olds in Hawaii. Because of a rising feeling of discontent with this inequity, in addition to the opinion held by many people that a young man who was old enough to be drafted to serve in the armed services should be allowed to help select public officials, the voting age requirement was made consistently eighteen throughout the nation.

Because it has already been discussed elsewhere in this book (see Chapters 2

[1] Gerald M. Pomper, *Elections in America: Control and Influence in Democratic Politics* (New York: Dodd, Mead, 1968), p. 41.

"Right on, Pop! I'm home to vote."

New Yorker, *October 30, 1971*

and 3), the historical background of the extension of suffrage in the United States will be discussed only briefly here. V. O. Key summarized the gradual movement toward universal suffrage:

> *Universal suffrage, now regarded as commonplace, did not come about in a day. Popular governments at first allowed only a small part of the populace to vote. In western democratic societies the suffrage has been gradually extended to new groups; each extension has been in response to demands by or on behalf of a group emerging from political subordination and seeking a voice in the management of public affairs. Whether by the acquisition of suffrage these new groups always gained power and influence or merely won a symbol of emancipation may be questioned. Nevertheless, the step-by-step extension of the suffrage has brought with it far-reaching changes in the methods and strategy of politics.*[2]

The success of the American Revolution did not immediately ensure the right of all Americans to vote. On the contrary, until the emergence of Jacksonian democracy (in the 1830s), the American government continued to emulate the suffrage rules of Great Britain, which held that only men who owned property could vote. This requirement was believed justified on the basis that voting was a privilege to be reserved for those people whose choice would not be controlled

---

[2] V. O. Key, Jr., *Politics, Parties, and Pressure Groups,* 5th edition (New York: Thomas Y. Crowell, 1964), p. 597.

by others. Therefore, the reasoning continued, since non-property-owners could never be completely free of coercive influence from the owner of the land on which they lived and worked, they were denied the right to vote. Giving them that right would be, in effect, the same as giving their landlords an extra vote of their own. Of course, a large part of this anti–universal-suffrage feeling on the part of the wealthy landowners was undoubtedly aimed at preserving their own interests; if the masses were given the right to vote, they might well support policies detrimental to the interests of the propertied classes. In any case, during the nineteenth century, after a lengthy and complicated process of rulings and counter-rulings, the property qualifications for voting privileges were eventually removed.

The second major change in suffrage rules was the extension of the right to vote to women, a privilege which was not given them until the Nineteenth Amendment to the Constitution was ratified in 1920. Commenting on the legal rights of women in nineteenth-century America, V. O. Key stated:

The crusade for woman suffrage in the beginning was closely related to the abolition movement. Woman, because of her extensive legal disabilities under the common law, was compared with the slave. And, in truth, the legal rights of the married woman were closer to those of the slave than to those of free white men.[3]

Basically, the opponents of woman suffrage in the 1880s felt that a woman's place was in the home—that she was intellectually, emotionally, and biologically unfit for participating in politics. Key has pointed out that, in addition to this basic attitude toward women, there was fear on the part of certain business owners that their interests would be endangered by enfranchising women; the liquor interests, in particular, were partially correct in this fear, since women have always been less than favorably disposed toward increasing the free flow of liquor. Between 1913 and 1919, a group of women (the "suffragettes," as they were called) adopted relatively militant tactics, including picketing the White House, going to jail and actually serving long sentences, and engaging in hunger strikes in the jails, as well as other kinds of demonstrations. Because many women of some wealth and social importance engaged in these activities, because they were carried on over an extended period of time, and because of other, more intangible factors, woman suffrage was finally instituted.

Black Americans—that is, black *male* Americans—were technically granted the right to vote by the Fifteenth Amendment (adopted in 1870). However, until very recently, such legal restraints as poll taxes and literacy tests effectively prevented large groups of blacks from exercising their right to vote, particularly in the South. Social and economic factors still exist that discourage black voters; for example, because many blacks are poor, they often fear losing salary to leave work early in order to vote. (Although there are legal provisions stating that employers cannot, in fact, penalize their workers in this way, the fear persists in many cases.) The reality and importance of the "social pressures" that militate against blacks voting in many southern areas was demonstrated during the 1960s, when groups of civil-rights workers, both white and black, went south to initiate black registration drives; violence flared on many occasions, proving that black southerners had had very real reasons for not voting in the past. But this situa-

---

[3] Key, *Politics, Parties, and Pressure Groups*, p. 612.

Election-day scenes in the South like this one in Alabama have multiplied since the early 1960s.

tion has improved in recent years. The voting-rights laws have been given stronger teeth, and the courts today are more likely than before to intervene in cases of racial discrimination in terms of voting and other activities.

After winning the right to vote, however, disillusionment set in among many formerly disenfranchised groups, for they came to realize that voting does not necessarily effect change in social and economic conditions. Although the right to vote is supposed to grant people political power, American women, enfranchised since 1920, are still clearly discriminated against in business and the professions; and government-funded day-care centers, which allow married women to have both a family and a career, remain few in number. Similarly, although legal barriers to black voting have been lifted since the 1960s, and blacks have won several impressive victories at the polls, they are still discriminated against in many areas. Even though blacks have far more opportunities to succeed in America than they have ever had before, they are certainly still not "equal" to most whites in terms of opportunities. As these two examples clearly demonstrate, the right to vote is not necessarily synonymous with real political power.

Voting: The Voice of the People

Theoretically, the electorate is supreme in a democracy. The voters are supposed to have the ultimate control over their political decision-makers, and public officials are supposed to pay attention to their constituents, because they depend on the voters for reelection. The theoretical power of the American electorate is demonstrated by the fact that we do, in fact, select by secret ballots in relatively free and open elections over one half-million public officials of various ranks and positions. Despite this apparently tremendous and direct influence on who obtains government office, the role of the electorate in American democracy remains ambiguous, for it is still unclear just how much effect, if any, the popular vote has on governmental policies.

> *To choose a government is not to choose governmental policies. Whereas the voters largely do determine the players in the game of American politics, they have far less control over the signals the players will call, the strategies they will employ, or the final score. The popular will, as represented by a majority of voters, does not determine public policy.*[4]

This point seems verified by the significant discrepancies that may occur between elections and public policy. In the 1964 presidential election, for example, Lyndon Johnson's large margin of victory over Barry Goldwater was presumed to indicate a popular "mandate" against a further extension of the war in Vietnam, as advocated by Goldwater. However, during his term in office, Johnson did not follow this "mandate"; the war was escalated, and many opponents of our involvement in Southeast Asia felt that their vote had had no appreciable effect on the outcome of the war or on their government's foreign policy. Similarly, studies indicate that constituency influence has relatively little impact on congressional decision-making. Warren E. Miller and Donald E. Stokes, for example, reported that there is practically no correlation between constituency attitude and how representatives vote on foreign-relations and welfare issues, and only a mild correlation on civil-rights legislation.[5]

Because public officials do not always follow constituency preferences, many critics of the American political system charge that the role of the voter is much less important than it appears to be in theory—that the significant policy decisions are made by a small group of "elite" politicians, who do not have to answer to the people and who can and often do ignore their clear-cut wishes. These critics argue that the voters seldom have a meaningful choice between candidates, and that frequently the major parties' candidates, even for the Presidency, demonstrate no clear differences on major policy questions. In addition, some observers contend that the voters are often manipulated by certain superficial elements projected by the candidates—such as their "images," as created by professional advertising agencies, or their physical appearances, personalities, and so forth. These observers conclude, therefore, that elections in America have little influence over public policies.

Today, then, there is some discontent over the American electoral process precisely because the electorate is limited to selecting officials and has little influence over the policies these officials institute once in power. But other political observers answer that, although the people do not have direct control over the details of governmental policy, they do enjoy indirect influence. Thus, while public influence is limited by the decentralized structure of the major political parties, by the complexity of governmental bodies, and by certain social conditions, these same factors help to give the people more than one chance to influence

---

[4] Pomper, *Elections in America*, p. 51.
[5] Angus Campbell, Philip E. Converse, Warren E. Miller, and Donald E. Stokes, *Elections and The Political Order* (New York: Wiley, 1966), Chapter 16, "Constituency Influence in Congress."

Figure 14–1   *Voter Participation in Presidential Elections, 1880–1968*

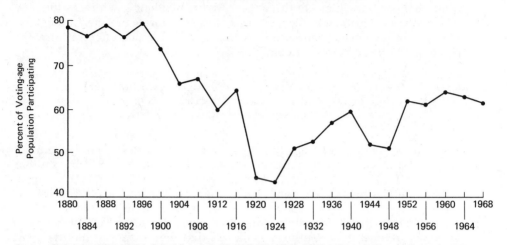

Sources: Figures for 1880 to 1916 in Robert E. Lane, Political Life (New York: The Free Press, 1965), p. 20; figures for 1920 to 1968 in Bureau of the Census, Statistical Abstract of the United States, 1969 (Washington, D.C.: Department of Commerce, 1969), p. 368. Reprinted with permission of The Macmillan Company from Political Life by Robert E. Lane. © The Free Press, a Corporation, 1959.

government. That is, since there are so many different levels of government in this country, and so many elections, the opportunities for effectively bargaining and protesting are increased.

One way to determine how much effect elections have on policy and on the people who win public office is to examine the facts of average voter turnout for various types of elections in America. After all, no matter how effective the election system might be in theory, it becomes a moot question unless a significant portion of the country's elegible voters actually mark their ballots on election day.

Voter Participation in America

Americans are not famous for turning out to vote. In fact, in recent years, approximately 40 percent of the eligible voters in America have failed to vote in presidential elections; in congressional elections, fully half of our eligible voters do not vote; and in state and local elections, the percentage of people not voting frequently reaches 70 percent, or in some cases even higher. However, the American electorate has not always been so apathetic about exercising its voting rights.

Voter turnout in America was extremely high in the mid-nineteenth century. In the presidential election of 1860, for example, close to 85 percent of the residents in non-southern states voted, and more than 75 percent of southerners also voted. From the 1860s through the 1920s, a clear decline in voter participation occurred in both presidential and off-year elections. In most states, a resurgence seems to have occured starting with the early 1930s—although this is not clear in all cases. What is clear, however, is the fact that Americans of the 1970s participate less in the election of their President than did their nineteenth-century counterparts, as shown in Figure 14-1.

Some observers contend that this trend is the inevitable result of urbanization and the transition to an industrialized society in which the individual is more alienated from the political process than ever before. Clearly, there is some truth

Table 14-1   **Voter Participation in Other Industrialized Nations**

Country	Year	Turnout
Canada	1968	75.7%
Denmark	1968	89.3
France	1968	80.0
West Germany	1969	86.8
Norway	1969	82.5

Source: Walter Dean Burnham and Richard Scammon in the Freedom to Vote Task Force Report, That All May Vote *(Washington, D.C.: Democratic National Committee, December 1969), App. VIII.*

in this explanation. However, as Table 14-1 indicates, there are other highly industrialized nations, notably those of Western Europe, which nevertheless have significantly higher rates of voter participation than does the United States. To help explain this downward trend in American voter participation, we must therefore look for factors which tend to affect voter participation, at any time and in any place.

Factors Affecting Voter Participation

There are two basic kinds of factors which significantly influence voter participation in this country—institutional factors and personal factors. It is easier to distinguish and analyze the first type of influence, since the decision to vote or not to vote is clearly affected by the structure and operation of the electoral system. Article I, Section 4 of the Constitution gives to the states the power to prescribe the time, place, and manner of holding elections. Typically, therefore, different states have established different systems for qualifying, registering, and actually voting. This situation has had both good and bad consequences—good, in that it allows for experimentation and diversity (several states gave women the right to vote long before the Nineteenth Amendment was ratified); and bad in that it has traditionally enabled some states to discriminate against certain voters (not until the 1970 amendments to the Voting Rights Act of 1965, for example, were literacy and character tests, which had formerly prevented thousands of southern blacks from voting, prohibited).

Several observers have emphasized institutional factors in explaining the decline in voter participation in the United States since the nineteenth century. Walter Dean Burnham, for example, stressed the fact that the American electoral system has created a "double hurdle" for American voters which Western European voters need not clear: Americans must often meet residency and registration requirements (registering sometimes as often as once a year), and American elections are held on working days, whereas election day is a national holiday (or else it is held on a Sunday) in many other countries.[6] Linking the hurdle of registration to the long-term trend in voter participation in the United States, Stanley Kelley and his associates found that in the late nineteenth century, when voter turnout in presidential elections ranged between 75 and 85 percent, registration was not required in many parts of the country, and in many other parts, systems

---

[6] Walter Dean Burnham, "The Changing Shape of the American Political Universe," *The American Political Science Review,* vol. 59 (March 1965), p. 12.

of automatic registration existed. Between 1896 and 1924, many states enacted restrictive registration requirements, and there was a steady decline in voter turnout. Then, in the period from 1924 to the present, when the turnout has gradually increased, most states have liberalized their registration laws.[7] The investigators concluded "that registration requirements are a more effective deterrent to voting than anything that normally operates to deter citizens from voting once they have registered, at least in presidential elections."[8]

Voter registration is required in almost all the fifty states, but the requirements for registration vary widely from state to state. For example, voter registration can be *permanent* or *periodic*. That is, the voter may be required to register only once for as long as he lives (provided he does not move or become disqualified in some other way), or else he may have to reregister once a year, once every two years, or every four years. Permanent registration is more common in the United States than periodic registration. Voter registration can be *personal*—in which case, the voter must appear in person and apply to have his name added to the registration list; or it can be *nonpersonal,* in which case an official governmental agency prepares the registration lists from the information available to it regarding who in its district is and who is not eligible to vote, according to local requirements. There is also *compulsory* registration and *noncompulsory* registration. In the former, a person must have his name entered on the voting list before election day in order to be allowed to vote, whereas, in the latter, he can vote if he proves to the clerk on election day that he fulfills all the necessary registration requirements.

A carefully planned and regulated voter-registration system is important in that it reduces the incidence of fraud in American elections. According to V. O. Key, "the American election system has gained an unenviable reputation for fraud."[9] While reports of election fraud are undoubtedly exaggerated in many cases, it is true that our voting system cannot seem to cope with, or to prevent, a certain amount of fraud. Much of the fault lies in registration systems which cannot be adequately supervised. Some of the most common forms of trickery, which are extremely difficult to detect or correct, include "repeating"—that is, the same person votes more than one time, generally under several different names, often imaginary ones, which have been placed on the registration list and which, therefore, are not questioned; and "tombstone voting," in which someone votes more than one time, using the name of a legitimately registered local voter who has died since the previous election but whose name has not yet been removed from the official registration list.

What are some of the specific requirements for voter registration? In addition to the requirement that the person be at least eighteen years old, the principal restrictions are those regarding residency. In the past, residency requirements varied from state to state, with some states (such as Minnesota) requiring only that a person live in that state for thirty days before being able to register to vote there; other states (including New York) required at least a three-month residency; and still others required as much as six months or a year. Stringent resi-

---

[7] Stanley Kelley, Jr., Richard E. Ayres, and William G. Bowen, "Registration and Voting: Putting First Things First," *American Political Science Review* (1967), p. 374.

[8] Kelley et al., "Registration and Voting," p. 362.

[9] Key, *Politics, Parties, and Pressure Groups,* p. 636.

dency requirements often had a discriminatory impact on the poor, because the poor tend to be the most transient; however, since there is now a great deal of mobility in all of American society, such requirements would have a significant effect on all economic classes.

In 1970, Congress passed legislation forbidding any residency requirements of more than thirty days for voting in presidential elections. This action did not forbid longer residency requirements for voting in state and local elections, technically leaving them up to the individual states. But in March of 1972, the Supreme Court declared unconstitutional a Tennessee law requiring three months' residency to vote in state and local elections, stating that "30 days appears to be an ample period of time" to register new arrivals. This ruling does not make it completely clear whether thirty days is the maximum residency requirement to be allowed under the Constitution, but a tendency to do away with unduly restrictive registration laws is clearly evident here. It is estimated that this new ruling will give the vote to as many as 5.6 million people, judging from the number who were ineligible to vote in 1968 elections because they had moved too recently to register.[10]

In addition to residency requirements, there are special regulations for absentee voting, which are also regulated by the individual states. Even if you are a registered voter in a given state, you can still lose your chance to vote if you are away from home, or ill, on election day. To accommodate mainly those persons who know in advance that they will have to be away from home at election time — because of a business trip, for example, or because they are in the military services, or attending school away from home — various absentee voting procedures have been established by the states. Nevertheless, many states effectively prohibit military personnel stationed away from home from voting, by technically permitting absentee voting but requiring, for example, that an individual register in person. In many states, too, college students eighteen and over find that they are effectively prevented from voting. Often their home states do not allow them to vote without registering in person, or performing other inconvenient tasks, and because they are not considered "residents" of their college towns, they are unable to register there either. However, recent lower-court rulings have eliminated this "disenfranchisement" of college students, allowing them to vote in the city in which they attend school. Thus, college students in Berkeley, California, had a tremendous impact on that city's government in 1972 by electing students to several key local offices.

Another "structural" factor which significantly affects voter participation is the *form of the ballot* the voters have to cast. Recently, in the 1972 spring primary in New York state, the voters were confused and angered by the unclear ballot they had to use in order to register their choice for various offices, particularly the presidential electors. A great many people had no idea who or what they were voting for, since the electors' names were printed on the ballot, without any information identifying which presidential candidate they were pledged to support. As a result, many people refused to vote, or voted without being sure of their own choices. Although this is an extreme case, it serves to illustrate the kind of confusion that can result from the variety of ballots currently in use.

---

[10] Fred P. Graham, "Long Residency for Voting Upset by Supreme Court," in the *New York Times* (March 22, 1972).

The ballot used today in American elections is the so-called "Australian" secret ballot, which all the states had adopted by 1950. During the colonial period and the early history of the United States, the customary form of balloting was by voice vote, where the voter simply told the recording clerk which candidate he supported. Gradually, oral ballots were replaced by a system of paper ballots—still hardly secret, since each party supplied its own ballots, which were printed privately, often on different-colored paper. Soon after the Civil War, the secrecy of the vote became an important issue, because many voters were being bribed and intimidated. These factors led to the eventual adoption of the Australian ballot.

Our present ballot has two forms, the *party-column* (or "Indiana") ballot, and the *office-column* (or "Massachusetts") ballot. The party-column ballot is more common; it has the various candidates arranged according to party. Because the party-column ballot enables voters to vote for all the candidates of a party by pulling a single voting-machine lever, or by marking a single X in the party column, this ballot form encourages people to vote a straight party ticket. On the other hand, the office-column ballot, which tends to discourage straight-ticket voting, has the candidates' names arranged under the title of the office to be filled.

Both types of ballots can be either *long-form* or *short-form* ballots. Long-form ballots include a large number of candidates' names and, often, constitutional amendments or other proposed legislative measures that must be voted on; short ballots contain fewer names and propositions. The long ballot was particularly common during the early part of the twentieth century when it was used by machine politicians as a way of discouraging people from splitting their tickets and making their own choices. Since many voters were uninformed, for one reason or another, about some of the many names and propositions listed on the long-form ballot, they frequently voted only for the major offices listed. In this way, many people confronted with long-form ballots in presidential elections merely marked their choices for President and Vice President, leaving the spaces for state and local officials blank. Because not all voters can be expected to know or care very much about all the items listed on the long ballot, and because many others become tired of voting long before they finish the ballot, there has been a strong movement established to abolish the long-form ballot, in favor of the shorter version.

The voting machine, first used in an 1892 election at Lockport, New York, has gradually become a widespread phenomenon, and has by now replaced the paper ballot in most states. Voting machines represent a major breakthrough in the physical process of voting. They have eliminated many possibilities for election fraud, and are also much faster, far more accurate, and more consistent than human vote-counters.

All these structural factors have an effect on voter participation in this country. However, such institutional and structural factors alone can hardly account for the widespread nonvoter phenomenon. The main reason for the failure of many Americans to vote is not built into the electoral system; instead, nonparticipation is primarily attributed to a personal feeling of apathy on the part of many citizens. Many eligible voters simply neglect to register to vote; many others who do register become disinterested during the actual campaign; and still others, finding themselves faced with a choice among several candidates for a particular office, none of whom they like, decide not to vote at all.

Of course, there are also people who have legitimate reasons for not voting—sickness, disability, work requirements, unexpected absence from home. A Gallup poll of the 1968 presidential election estimated that at least 10 million such people existed.[11] Thus, in calculating the percentage of the "eligible" voters who actually turned out to vote in a given election, this group of people should perhaps be taken into account; subtracting them from the voting-age population in the country would substantially increase the percentage of voter turnout recorded. In other words, there are often valid reasons why individuals may be unable to vote in a particular election. But what about the majority of the people, most of whom are either consistently voters or nonvoters? What determines who votes and who does not?

To Vote or Not to Vote

The Voter: Who Votes and Why?

It has been said that "the act of voting requires the citizen to make not a single choice but two. He must choose between rival parties or candidates. He must also decide whether to vote at all."[12] And, as Angus Campbell and his associates have pointed out in their analysis of voter turnout in America, "The really extraordinary aspect of our presidential elections is that tens of millions of people *do* expend the energy required to reach their polling-places and register their votes."[13]

What generalizations, if any, can be made about those Americans who habitually exercise their right to vote? V. O. Key contended that "if one approaches [voter] participation from the standpoint of the individual . . . it turns out that persons with specified characteristics, regardless of the nature of the general situation, are more likely to vote than are persons without those attributes."[14] The "attributes" which seem to affect voter participation in America tend to be of two basic types—a person's socioeconomic background, and certain psychological characteristics.

Socioeconomic Background A particular kind of socioeconomic background is not a cause of higher voter participation. Rather, there are certain demographic factors which correlate with a high frequency and consistency of voting.

The two factors which seem to be most significantly associated with voter participation are *class status* and *level of education*. In this case, "class status" refers both to a person's level of income and to his type of occupation. In general, upper-class status—including those who are in higher income brackets and are professional workers or white-collar employees—is correlated with greater voter participation. This correlation is partially explained by the fact that upper-class persons do not have to worry about losing business, or money, by spending time away from work at the polls. Furthermore, because of their background, they are also more likely to be interested in political matters and to have a greater sense of political efficacy—that is, to believe that their votes make a difference. The more *education* a person has had, the more likely he is to vote. College-educated per-

[11] Gallup Poll (December 10, 1968).

[12] Angus Campbell, Philip E. Converse, Warren E. Miller, and Donald E. Stokes, *The American Voter* (New York: Wiley, 1964), p. 49.

[13] Campbell et al., *The American Voter*, p. 50.

[14] Key, *Politics, Parties, and Pressure Groups*, p. 585.

sons, in particular, tend to vote regularly—probably because their education has brought them more into contact than the average person with political ideas and issues. Better-educated people are more likely to be interested in politics, because they tend to know more about it.

Age is another significant sociological factor affecting voter participation. Perhaps surprisingly, young people are not noted for their participation in the voting process. In fact, in the 1964 and 1968 presidential elections, the eighteen-to-twenty-year-olds turned out to vote in the lowest percentage of any age group, in the states where they were permitted to vote. Generally, middle-aged people are far more likely to vote than either young or old people. This phenomenon is generally thought to exist because the average young person is likely to be so busy with personal activities—taking care of young children, setting up a newly established household, finishing college or graduate school, beginning in a career, and so forth—that his interest in and time for political activity is often severely limited. Also, young people tend to move more frequently than older people; their mobility puts them at a second disadvantage, in that they are frequently unable to meet the residency requirements necessary for registering to vote before a given election.[15] Elderly people tend not to vote because of a combination of factors—physical disability, geographical and economic inconvenience, and a feeling that they have little to do with the country's political life once they are retired from the business world and their children have grown up. Therefore, it is assumed that middle-aged people vote more than other age groups primarily because they tend to be economically and socially more secure than either young or elderly people.

Ethnic background and *religious affiliation* are also related to voter participation. It is widely believed that America's famous "melting pot" has led to the cultural assimilation of the approximately sixty-five million Americans who can be classified as "ethnics" (blacks, and all the so-called "hyphenated Americans"— the Italian-Americans, Irish-Americans, and so forth). In fact, however, ethnic minorities in the United States have not undergone complete political assimilation. Ethnicity seems to be a factor affecting voting behavior, including the level of voter participation. Jews, for example, tend to turn out to vote in greater percentages than any other ethnic group—a primary source of their political effectiveness. Similarly, Protestants have a higher rate of voter participation than do Catholics, and whites a higher rate than nonwhites. Thus, although black Americans may be generally aware of their tremendous potential political power as an ethnic bloc, they seldom turn out to vote in large numbers, and so this potential strength is dissipated. In recent years, however, blacks have turned out to vote in large numbers when there is a black candidate on the ballot, as in Newark, New Jersey; Gary, Indiana; and Cleveland, Ohio. As a group, Spanish-speaking Americans (primarily including Puerto Ricans and Chicanos) are also characterized by low voter turnout.[16]

Sex is another factor associated with voter participation. Traditionally, men

---

[15] See Philip E. Converse, with the assistance of Richard Niemi, "Non-Voting among Young Adults in the United States," in *Political Parties and Political Behavior,* edited by William J. Crotty, Donald M. Freeman, and Douglas S. Gatlin (Boston: Allyn and Bacon, 1971), pp. 453–466.

[16] See Mark R. Levy and Michael S. Kramer, *The Ethnic Factor: How America's Minorities Decide Elections* (New York: Simon and Schuster, 1972).

"I always wait until my husband decides on a candidate—then I vote for his opponent."

Parade, *September 1968*

have voted more than women, supposedly because women felt less social pressure to vote and tended to be less well-informed about or interested in politics. But the gap between the sexes has been closing since 1920, probably, in part, because of the increasing number of women joining the work force, and the increased availability of child-care facilities on election day. In any case, the difference between the percentage of eligible men and women voters who do vote is not very large, and women have always tended to vote in relatively large numbers when specifically female-oriented issues such as abortion and divorce laws were on the ballot.

One other demographic factor affecting voter participation is *geographic location.* The place where one lives may influence one's social and economic background, and hence one's voting participation. Generally, people who live in the North and the West are more likely to vote than are southerners. City-dwellers tend to vote more often than rural residents, and people who have lived in their current place of residence for a long time have better voting records than do relative newcomers to the area.[17] Interestingly, these patterns of voter turnout do not

---

[17] Levy and Kramer, *The Ethnic Factor,* p. 586.

Figure 14-2   *Intensity of Party Identification and Voter Turnout*

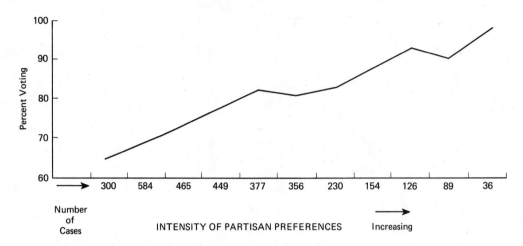

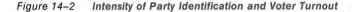

Source: Angus Campbell, Philip E. Converse, Warren E. Miller, and Donald E. Stokes, The American Voter *(New York: Wiley, 1964), p. 53. Copyright © 1964. Reprinted by permission of John Wiley & Sons, Inc.*

necessarily hold constant for other countries. For example, in Canada rural residents have a significantly higher voter participation rate than urbanites.[18]

Finally, it has been found that people who are affiliated with various *groups* — whether labor unions, church groups, sports clubs, or whatever—are more likely to vote. Perhaps this happens because such people feel themselves more closely linked with the life of their communities—which, in turn, gives them more reason for participating in the political life of that community.[19]

Psychological Characteristics In addition to socioeconomic factors such as class status, education level, age, ethnic and religious background, sex, and geographical location, there are several psychological characteristics which seem to be associated with voter participation. These motivational factors are closely intertwined with the socioeconomic factors previously discussed, and have recently been studied rather extensively to determine to what extent they influence voter turnout.

According to Angus Campbell and his co-workers, a greater intensity of *partisanship* is correlated to greater voter participation, as shown in Figure 14-2. In other words, "the greater the strength of the individual's preference [for a particular party, or a particular candidate], the greater the likelihood he would vote."[20] In addition to strength of partisan preference, a person's decision to vote tends to be affected by whether or not he feels the upcoming election will be a close one. A person with weak partisan preference is not likely to be significantly affected

[18] Howard A. Scarrow, "Patterns of Voter Turnout in Canada," *Midwest Journal of Political Science,* vol. 5 (1961) pp. 351–364.
[19] Key, *Politics, Parties, and Pressure Groups,* p. 589.
[20] Campbell et al., *The American Voter,* p. 53.

in either case, but a person with stronger preferences is likely to be influenced a great deal—that is, he will be more likely to vote if he thinks the election will be close.

A person who has greater *interest* in a political campaign and who is concerned about the outcome of that election is more likely to vote. The Campbell study found that "the rate of turnout among persons of high interest exceeded that among persons of low interest by nearly 30 percent."[21] Predictably, data also confirm that people who are personally concerned about the outcome of an election tend to vote more. This conclusion is not surprising; for example, a person who works for his city government is more likely to vote in a local election than is someone who feels that the election's results will not directly affect him.

A greater *sense of political efficacy* also increases the likelihood of voter participation. If a person feels that an election is already a lost cause, and that his individual vote can do no good, he is hardly likely to bother going to the polls. The voter, then, is someone who believes that his vote can help to elect the candidate he supports, or at least that it can help defeat the rival candidate. That is why in apparently close elections there is often a higher voter turnout than at other times —it is easier to feel that one's own vote will have a significant effect in an election where only a few thousand votes separate two rival politicians.

People who are *nonauthoritarian,* who are supportive of democratic ideals, and tolerant of different views, are more likely to vote than people who lack these characteristics. Also, people with a greater sense of *citizen duty,* those who feel they are expected to vote, tend to vote more than those who do not consider voting a duty.

The Nonvoter:
Who Does Not Vote and Why?

It is reasonably clear what attributes characterize the typical American voter. But what about the person who does not vote: what factors influence his decision to remain outside the electoral process? Essentially, those people who do not vote, and the reasons why they do not vote, are the opposites of those which apply for the voter. We have established that the typical American voter is a white, middle-aged, middle-to-upper-class person, with a college education, and lives in a city; the typical voter is also somewhat more likely to be male and Jewish or Protestant than female and Catholic. If these things are true, then the typical American nonvoter must tend to be either rather young or rather old, nonwhite, and lower class. The nonvoter probably did not go to college, lives in a rural area, is female, and is Catholic. Of course, these characteristics are only statistical generalizations; no one would assert that they always hold true, or that there is any cause-and-effect relationship between, say, sex or religion, or class status and voter participation.

In addition, a small part of the nonvoting public in America are those who, by law, cannot vote. Since 1928, for example, people who are resident aliens have been prohibited from voting in our elections; only American citizens can vote in American elections. Moreover, in many places prisoners, as well as persons who are not now in prison but who were once convicted of certain types of crimes,

---

[21] Campbell et al., *The American Voter,* p. 56.

Table 14-2   **Characteristic of High- and Low-Turnout Voters**

Higher Turnout	**Lower Turnout**
High income	Low income
High education	Low education
Occupational groups:	Occupational groups:
Businessmen	Unskilled workers
White-collar employees	Servants
Government employees	Service workers
Commercial-crop farmers	Peasants, subsistence farmers
Miners	
Whites	Negroes
Men	Women
Middle-aged people (35–55)	Young people (under 35)
Older people (over 55)	
Old residents in community	Newcomers in community
Workers in western Europe	Workers in United States
Crisis situations	Normal situations
Married people	Single
Members of organizations	Isolated individuals

Source: *From* Political Man *by Seymour Martin Lipset. Copyright © 1959, 1960 by Seymour Martin Lipset. Reprinted by permission of Doubleday & Company, Inc.*

and persons who are in mental institutions or who have been declared mentally incompetent or legally insane are likewise not allowed to vote.

Finally, there are political factors that influence nonvoting. The type of election, for example, affects the level of voter turnout, with the highest participation reserved primarily for national contests. Within national elections, there is greater participation in presidential elections than in congressional off-year elections; there are more nonvoters in state and local elections than in national elections; and participation in primary elections is lowest of all.

Another important political factor influencing voter turnout is the extent of two-party competition in a given area. Data reveals that nonvoting is greatest in areas with little such competition.

An Evaluation of the Nonvoting Phenomenon

Four out of every ten adults in America do not vote in presidential elections. While no political system could expect to achieve 100-percent voter participation in any election, our rate of turnout is still inexplicably low. As E. E. Schattschneider stressed, the phenomenon of nonvoting in America seems to be voluntary—that is, there are no laws prohibiting American nonvoters from exercising their legal rights. Why, then, do they choose not to vote?

It is profoundly characteristic of the behavior of the more fortunate strata of the community that responsibility for widespread nonparticipation is attributed wholly to the ignorance, indifference and shiftlessness of the people. This has always been the rationalization used to justify the exclusion of the lower classes from any political system. There is a better explanation. Abstention reflects the suppression of the options and alternatives that reflect the needs of the nonparticipants. It is not necessarily true that the people with the greatest need participate in politics most actively.[22]

---

[22] E. E. Schattschneider, *The Semi-Sovereign People* (New York: Holt, Rinehart and Winston, 1960), pp. 104–105.

Thus, according to Schattschneider, many people are effectively excluded from voting by extralegal processes, social pressures, and "by the way the political system is organized and structured."[23] He argues, as do other political observers, that low voter turnout indicates a serious upper-class bias in the electoral system that hinders substantial change in public policies. Moreover, those who are left out of the electoral processes reflect a widespread rejection of the American political system. As Schattschneider indicated, if the nonvoting public could somehow be mobilized into exercising that right, all existing political alignments could be overturned, because "In the past seven presidential elections the average difference in the vote cast for the winning and losing candidates was about one-fifth as large as the total number of nonvoters."[24]

However, while analysts like Schattschneider claim that the low voter turnout indicates a rejection of the American political system by a relatively large number of citizens who find that system unresponsive to their needs, other observers disagree. For example, Eugene Burdick has suggested that voter apathy may actually have an opposite influence—it may help to promote a stable democracy. He cites the well-documented uninvolvement of most of the American electorate, concluding that "concord . . . flows from simple disinterest in politics."[25]

Some people say that, because those Americans who do not vote tend to be more authoritarian and less tolerant in their viewpoints than those people who do vote, the participation of these nonvoters would undercut democratic norms. Moreover, others suggest that those who do not vote, far from representing a wholesale rejection of the system, reflect a widespread satisfaction with the political process. Thus, Americans are said to vote only when they are dissatisfied with their government's policies; widespread nonparticipation in the election process is taken to represent widespread approval.

Regardless of which one of the many sides of this argument has the greatest validity, it is still necessary to consider the question: How much voter participation is enough? Some people suggest that our standards of the "democratic" level of voter participation are too high; they claim that the voter-turnout rate that now exists might well be the best we can expect, given contemporary conditions. E. E. Schattschneider pointed out:

> The tendency of the literature of politics is to place a tremendous premium on the role of the interested and to treat indifference as a mortal sin, but the reluctance of the public to press its opinions on the government concerning a great multitude of issues is really not as bad a thing as we may have been led to think; it is a mark of reasonableness and common sense.[26]

As Schattschneider has said, "nobody knows enough to run the government."[27] The political experts may know more about politics than the members of the general public, but the people must still have a say in what these educated elites decide. "The problem is not how 180 million Aristotles can run a democracy, but how we can organize a political community of 180 million ordinary people so that

---

[23] Schattschneider, *The Semi-Sovereign People,* p. 111.

[24] Schattschneider, *The Semi-Sovereign People,* p. 99.

[25] Eugene Burdick and Arthur J. Brodbeck, *American Voting Behavior* (New York: The Free Press, 1959), pp. 138–141, 144–148.

[26] Schattschneider, *The Semi-Sovereign People,* p. 134.

[27] Schattschneider, *The Semi-Sovereign People,* p. 136.

it remains sensitive to their needs."[28] In other words, Schattschneider takes the position, as do a number of other observers, that there is nothing inherently wrong with a system like ours in which a large proportion of the ordinary people do not choose to vote, as long as the educated elite that govern the country continue to take their wishes into consideration.

The Voter's Choice

In attempting to win an election, a candidate will not be particularly concerned about the nonvoters; it is the voting public's preferences that will decide whether or not he is elected. It is extremely difficult to identify precisely why a particular individual votes as he does — often even the voter himself does not know why he votes a given way. Nevertheless, political scientists have been able to identify various types of factors that seem to influence (or at least to be associated with) voter preference.

The two basic types of factors are essentially the same as those which we saw tend to influence voter participation. There are both *sociological* and *psychological* factors at work in determining what candidates each individual voter will support at the polls.

Sociological Factors

Social Class A primary sociological influence upon voter preference has always been social class. In general, members of the upper class — those with higher incomes, and higher-status occupations — are more likely to vote Republican. The Democratic party, on the other hand, has traditionally been identified as the party of the "little man," whose ranks included most of the economically underprivileged voters in America, as well as many of the immigrants and most southerners. In the 1930s, these categories of people provided the Democratic party's major source of support, but between the 1930s and the late 1960s, many aspects of American politics have changed, and with them, many aspects of party alignment by class, income, and status. For example, from 1940 through the end of the 1960s, "as the middle class grew in size, so did the proportion of it supporting the Democratic party." Thus, whereas the middle class had formerly been primarily Republican, by the late 1960s a majority of middle-class Americans were Democrats.[29] This shift toward greater Democratic identification among the middle class has been explained by several factors. First, as large numbers of people who had always identified themselves as Democrats became increasingly affluent, they retained their identities as Democrats, despite their change to an essentially "Republican" status. In addition, as many of the Democrats became increasingly prosperous, the actual character of the party was transformed. Finally, since so many members of the present middle class are "new" middle-class people, they are receptive to government programs and policies concerned with the industrialism which gave them entry into their new class status.[30]

This shift in party support, however, in no way negates the traditional truism

---

[28] Schattschneider, *The Semi-Sovereign People*, p. 138.
[29] Everett Carll Todd, Jr., *American Political Parties* (New York: Norton, 1970), p. 285.
[30] Todd, *American Political Parties*, pp. 286–287.

that middle- and upper-class people tend to vote according to the party which they feel best represents their economic interests. Although social class and party identification are not so closely linked in the United States as they are in many European nations, the electorate does tend to see the major parties as associated with specific class interests, and they vote accordingly.[31]

Education In addition to the relationship between class status and voter preference, it appears that level of education and voter choice are also related. In general, college-educated people are more likely to vote Republican than Democratic. This tendency is consistent with the association between class status and party preference, for it is likely that the more education one has, the higher the social class he will belong to.

Ethnic Background and Religious Affiliation In terms of ethnic background, it is generally true that blacks, Irish, Poles, and Eastern European ethnic groups are more likely to vote Democratic than Republican. In terms of religious affiliation, data indicate that Jews and Catholics are more likely to vote Democratic than are Protestants. At times, religion may have an important influence on the outcome of an election. It is clear, for example, that religion played a significant role in shaping voting behavior in the Kennedy election of 1960.[32]

Seymour Martin Lipset analyzed data from the 1964 presidential election in order to determine whether or not "bloc" voting (that is, a group of people sharing the same ethnic or religious characteristics who tend to vote in accordance with the interests of their group) was a significant factor in that election.[33] He traced the alignment of Catholics to the Democratic party back to the early nineteenth century, when many of the immigrant Catholics joined the Democratic party because it was of great assistance to immigrants in finding jobs and in giving them other benefits. Lipset stated that this identification of Catholic voters as Democrats had relatively little political importance in the nineteenth century, because the Catholics at that time constituted only a very small part of the American electorate. Today, however, Catholics make up more than one-fourth of the eligible voters, giving them considerable political clout. Yet the traditional identification of Catholic voters with the Democratic party is not secure; in recent years, many Catholics have shifted their allegiance to the Republican party.

Lipset points out that, while Jews constitute only 3 to 4 percent of the electorate, their high concentration in states with large numbers of electoral votes (such as New York, California, Pennsylvania, and Illinois) gives them a great deal of political influence. Most Jews vote Democratic—even well-to-do Jewish people. This apparent contradiction is explained by Lipset as the reaction of the Jews as a people who are frequently the target of social discrimination, even when they are wealthy and powerful members of a community. This feeling of discrimination helps Jews to identify with the underprivileged groups who have traditionally supported Democratic candidates and policies.

[31] Robert R. Alford, "The Role of Social Class in American Voting Behavior," *Western Political Quarterly*, vol. 26 (March 1963), pp. 180–194.

[32] Converse and Niemi, "Non-Voting among Young Adults in the United States," p. 97.

[33] Seymour Martin Lipset, "How Big is the Bloc Vote?" in *American Party Politics*, edited by Donald G. Herzberg and Gerald M. Pomper, pp. 390–394.

Blacks, who constitute about 12 percent of the U.S. population, have recently become an extremely important political "bloc" to contend with. Race has been a significant factor in many local elections since the late 1960s and in recent presidential elections. Naturally, the civil-rights issues are of the utmost importance to black voters, as are other measures directed at improving the lot of economically and socially underprivileged Americans. Therefore, it is not surprising to find that most blacks support the Democratic party. However, this pattern of black Democratic support is relatively new. The Republican party was originally the one that promoted the civil rights of black people: the G.O.P. was Lincoln's party, and the Republicans were viewed as responsible for freeing the slaves. Thus, the Republican party continued to win strong support from black voters, from the Civil War to 1932, when a dramatic shift in black partisanship occurred. As the Roosevelt administration began to establish federally financed relief and public-works programs, labor unions started to organize large groups of black workers, and the Democratic party gradually took over the role as advocate of black civil rights.

Pollsters have predicted that liberalism in the "youth vote" at prestigious universities like Columbia, pictured here, will be offset by the votes of more conservative students at smaller schools, and the votes of nonstudent youth.

Since Catholics, Jews, and blacks make up about 40 percent of the American population today, the votes of these groups continue to be highly significant.[34] However, members of these groups can no longer be counted on to form a cohesive bloc.

Age   Age has long been considered an important sociological factor that influences voter preference. The general rule is that young voters are more likely to support Democratic candidates than are older voters. But in the past year or so, much excitement has been generated by the Twenty-sixth Amendment to the Constitution, which lowered the voting age to eighteen. Although it is still too early to be able to tell with any real certainty, political analysts and laymen, as well as the political candidates themselves, are still trying to determine what changes, if any, will result from the influx of new, younger voters, whose numbers have been estimated at about twenty-five million. (Although there will be.approximately twenty-five million eligible young voters, it is generally estimated that only about 42 percent of them will actually vote in presidential elections.)[35] Because political office-holders and candidates alike expect significant changes to result from the new youth vote, they directed a large amount of their campaigning efforts, particularly prior to the 1972 presidential election, toward the youthful electorate. Voter registration drives were especially popular—eager registrars set up tables and registration lists virtually everywhere, on college campuses, at beach resorts, even outside Madison Square Garden in New York City, where crowds of young people had gathered in late July of 1972 to hear the Rolling Stones' series of rock concerts.

However, many analysts now judge that there will be little overall difference between the votes cast by these young people and those of older voters. This belief is supported by data gathered in a Gallup poll of young voters conducted in 1971. The poll determined that, although young voters are certainly numerous, their tendency to stay away from the polls in relatively large percentages may well offset their potential numerical strength. It also showed that the newcomers, by and large, have characteristics similar to those of older voters. That is, the young voters are only slightly better educated, and just a bit more liberal, than are the older voters.[36] And, whereas the rate of young people registering as Democrats versus Republicans was roughly two to one, this is the same general proportion of registration partisanship that has traditionally been observed among older voters. Furthermore, a greater percentage of youth have identified themselves as independents.

Sex   It appears that the sex of the voter has little influence on the party he chooses to support. Data indicate that 3 to 5 percent more women than men identify with the Republican party. However, this discrepancy is probably due to general differences in the social characteristics of men and women. For example, the average age of women is slightly greater than that of men, and, as we have seen, older voters are more likely to be Republican than Democratic.[37] Of course, strong party

---

[34] Lipset, "How Big Is the Bloc Vote?," p. 394.

[35] "How Will Youth Vote?," *Newsweek* (October 25, 1971), p. 28.

[36] "How Will Youth Vote?," *Newsweek* (October 25, 1971), p. 28.

[37] Campbell et al., *The American Voter*, p. 261.

Table 14-3   **Group Voting Trends in Presidential Elections, 1948–1968
(Percentage Voting for the Democratic Party in a Two-Party Vote)**

	1948	1952	1956	1960	1964	1968[d]
Female	49	40	37	46	68	42
Negro	68[a]	76[a]	63[a]	66[a]	98	94
Under 34	57	45	41	52	71	40
35–44	57	45	41	50	67	44
45–54	44	42	39	54	68	36
55–64	40[a]	34	32	43	68	37
65 or over	46[a]	36	43	37	53	40
Metropolitan areas	56	42	44	57	71	45
Cities over 50,000	[c]	51	33	50	66	50
Towns, 2,500–50,000	[c]	37	36[b]	40	60	40
Rural	61	39	42	47	67	29
Protestant	43	36	35	36	61	32
Catholic	62	51	45	82	79	54
Jewish	[b]	71[a]	77[a]	89[a]	89[a]	85
Business and professional	19[a]	31	31	44	57	34
White-collar	47[a]	35	39	48	63	38
Skilled and semiskilled	72	51	44	57	76	43
Unskilled	67	67	47	59	80	53
Farm operator	59[a]	37	46	33	63	34
Union member	76[a]	55	51	62	83	46
Grade school	63	48	41	54	78	48
High school	51	43	43	52	68	40
College	22[a]	26	31	35	53	33

[a] Because these percentages were computed on the basis of fewer than 100 cases, sampling error may be sizable.
[b] Too few cases to compute a stable proportion.
[c] Data not available.
[d] Takes into account a three-party split.
Source: Center for Political Studies, University of Michigan.

identification along sexual lines may occur in cases where a particular party or candidate strongly advocates a specifically sex-related issue, such as abortion.

Geographical Region Geographical regions are still associated with a particular party, at least to some extent. For example, the South—although this pattern has changed in recent years—has traditionally been a stronghold for the Democratic party; and residents of the urban areas of the Northeast still vote predominantly Democratic. Likewise, rural areas still tend to support the Republicans. Suburban areas are becoming a mixture of Republicans and Democrats, whereas formerly they were predominantly Republican regions.

Psychological Factors

The sociological factors affecting voter preference—such as class status, level of education, ethnic and religious background, age, sex, and geographical region—

Table 14-4   ***Party Identification Among the American Electorate, 1940–1971***

	Percentage of Voters Identifying Themselves as:		
Year	*Democrats*	*Republicans*	*Independents*
1940	42	38	20
1950	45	33	22
1960	47	30	23
1964	53	25	22
1966	48	27	25
June 1968	46	27	27
Oct. 1971:			
Voters 21 and over	45	27	28
New voters	38	18	42

Sources: Gallup Opinion Index, *Report No. 28, October 1967, for 1940–1966 data;*
Congressional Quarterly, *Weekly Report (August 23, 1968), for June 1968 data;*
Newsweek *(October 25, 1971), for October 1971 data.*

were the focus for early studies of voting behavior. However, recent analysts have criticized such studies, because they feel sociological approaches tend to present a rather static picture of voting preference. Instead, later studies have tended to focus on long- and short-term psychological factors affecting voter preference, particularly party identification.

Party Identification   Party identification—the tendency of a person to consistently consider himself either a Democrat or a Republican—is the single most important factor in predicting individual voter choice (see Table 14-4):

Few factors are of greater importance for our national elections than the lasting attachment of tens of millions of Americans to one of the parties. These loyalties establish a basic division of electoral strength within which the competition of particular campaigns takes place.[38]

It is undoubtedly true that "an individual's vote can be predicted more accurately from his party affiliation than from any other personal characteristic such as race, religion, or social class. Moreover, it is a better predictor than attitudes on any of the political issues of the day."[39] Why is this so? Some observers believe it is because most Americans, being ill-informed and uninterested in politics in general, need the security of a party label to tell them which candidates to support and what measures to vote for. As discussed in Chapter 10, party identification is a habit which most people acquire from their parents and tend to keep throughout their lives. The strength of the party-identification "habit" is indicated by the fact that "almost three-quarters of adult Americans consider themselves Republicans or Democrats; and an additional eleven to nineteen percent say that they lean toward one party or another."[40] In addition, 70 percent of party identifiers say they have always or usually voted for their party's presidential candidates, and even those people who cross party lines in a given election generally

[38] Campbell et al., *The American Voter,* p. 67.

[39] Benjamin I. Page and Raymond E. Wolfinger, "Party Identification," Chapter 19 of *Readings in American Political Behavior,* 2nd edition, edited by Raymond E. Wolfinger (Englewood Cliffs, N.J.: Prentice-Hall, 1970), p. 291.

[40] Page and Wolfinger, "Party Identification," p. 290.

tend to continue thinking of themselves as supporters of "their" party. This explains how a large number of staunch Democrats could vote for Eisenhower in 1952 and 1956, while continuing to retain their Democratic indentification.

THE INDEPENDENT VOTER.   The American voter's loyalty to "his" particular party is an extremely strong characteristic. However, there is evidence that the number of independent voters is increasing today.

Political analysts, in attempting to gauge the effects of independent voters, are divided mainly into two camps. The problem hinges on what kind of people one thinks these independents are, as a group. Some observers, for example, believe that independent voters are less involved in politics than are strong party identifiers. According to Angus Campbell,

Independents . . . have somewhat poorer knowledge of the issues, their image of the candidates is fainter, their interest in the campaign is less, their concern over the outcome is relatively slight, and their choice between competing candidates, although made later in the campaign, seems much less to spring from discoverable evaluations of the elements of national politics.[41]

Other political observers, however, disagree with Campbell's analysis of the independent voter. They feel that, often, the independent refuses to align himself with either major party because he feels that neither party's platform offers him anything. As Walter Dean Burnham pointed out:

. . . the pattern of change in recent years seems fairly clear. The political parties are progressively losing their hold upon the electorate. A new breed of independent seems to be emerging as well—a person with a better-than-average education, making a better-than-average income in a better-than-average occupation, and, very possibly, a person whose political cognitions and awareness keep him from making identifications with either old party.[42]

THE NORMAL VOTE.   Despite the unquestioned increase in the number of independent voters, and whichever side one feels is most valid in the debate over the independents' degree of political involvement, the majority of Americans continue to identify with either the Democratic or the Republican party. Since, in the last four decades, there have been substantially more Democrats than Republicans within the American electorate, political scientists at the Survey Research Center conclude that, in the absence of short-term influences, the "normal vote" could be predicted to be predominantly Democratic.

The "normal vote" is a concept developed on the basis of data collected in a series of election studies undertaken by the Survey Research Center. From this data, a "normal" vote—the voting pattern that can generally be expected from a particular group of voters, or from the nation as a whole—can be predicted. The "normal" vote, once determined, can help political scientists in assessing what kinds of changes are occurring in voting behavior in each election.

If party identification persists over long periods of time, and if most voters, since 1932, have identified themselves with the Democratic party, how then have

---

[41] Campbell et al., *The American Voter*, p. 83.

[42] Walter Dean Burnham, *Critical Elections and the Mainsprings of American Politics* (New York: Norton, 1970), p. 127.

Republicans been elected in recent years? The answer lies in the short-term influences — namely, specific candidates and issues — which generally cause party voters to defect.

Candidates According to one political analyst, "attitudes toward the candidates are the major statistical explanation of voting defection."[43] One reason for the strong influence of candidates on voting behavior may be that voters simply find it easier to formulate attitudes toward candidates than toward specific issues. In particular, negative attitudes toward candidates are readily formulated. Many people, for example, may vote for one candidate simply because they wish to voice strong dissatisfaction with the candidate of the opposite party.[44] In any case, it seems apparent that a candidate's personality, physical appearance, "image," and so forth, are all factors that influence voters and may cause party supporters to defect in their voting. Classic examples of voter defection due largely to the personality of a presidential candidate are the cases of Dwight Eisenhower, who received a great deal of Democratic support, and that of a particularly attractive candidate, John Kennedy, who likewise gained a significant amount of support from voters who identified themselves with the Republican party. The tremendous influence that certain types of candidates can have on voter defection is a well-known fact to campaign managers and party administrators, who attempt to use the generally successful "strategy" of running candidates who are not only qualified and experienced, but also attractive to the voters in both parties.

Issues Similarly, particular issues which are salient, and on which voters perceive a different stand on the parts of the various candidates, affect voter choice. It is relatively easy to see how a particular issue that is prominent, and which directly affects a number of people in the electorate, can cause an informed voter to change parties. However, as has been documented countless times, the vast majority of American voters are not informed about politics, and in fact most voters are unlikely to know much about even the most widely publicized issue. Furthermore, it is particularly ironic to find that "it is the least informed members within the electorate who seem to hold the critical balance of power, in the sense that alternations in governing party depend disproportionately on shifts in their sentiment."[45] That is, the baseline of voters that can generally be expected to vote for a particular party is not critical in determining the outcome of an election; it is rather the undecided voter — the one who continually shifts his vote from party to party — who seems to be most important. And these so-called floating voters tend to be those people who have the least interest in and information about politics.

After presenting and analyzing statistics on the behavior of floating voters in recent presidential elections, Philip E. Converse concluded, as have other political scientists, that nonpartisanship is closely linked with a considerable lack of political information.[46] This link is understandable when one considers that most Amer-

---

[43] Richard W. Boyd, "Presidential Elections: An Explanation of Voting Defection," *American Political Science Review*, vol. 62 (June 1969), p. 504.

[44] Boyd, "Presidential Elections," p. 504.

[45] Campbell et al., *Elections and the Political Order*, p. 136.

[46] Campbell et al., *Elections and the Political Order*, p. 137.

icans are not strongly ideological. Lacking a unified political philosophy, most nonpartisans have no cues to which to turn in evaluating issues and selecting candidates. A critical segment of our electorate, then, must depend upon the current flow of political information to the voter, in order to be able to make decisions, and to vote.

Voting Patterns in Presidential Elections

One of the most interesting, and also most important, patterns of voting behavior to study are those that emerge in elections for the Presidency. Naturally, these elections assume greater importance, in general, than do off-year elections; in national politics, the electoral "prize" is always control of the Presidency.

The fact that presidential and congressional elections frequently occur at different times, while it allows for a degree of independence between these two branches of our federal government, also causes serious problems in the workings of government. As V. O. Key noted,

The electorate must choose, not an assortment of unrelated functionaries, but a government. Yet on the day of a presidential election not one but around 500 elections occur. Fifty states choose presidential electors, 435 districts elect Representatives, and a third of the states designate Senators.[47]

Key further pointed out that this independence often "assures that elections will produce a mixed mandate."[48] And, of course, there have been many cases in which, for example, a Democrat is elected President in one year, by a considerable margin of votes; but where his party loses strength in the Congress during the following off-year election. In such cases, many difficulties occur, and much delay is caused, by the continuous friction between the President and the congressional majority, each working toward different goals.

An interesting phenomenon in presidential elections is what is known as the coattails effect. This term refers to what frequently happens when a popular presidential candidate is elected by a landslide of votes, carrying with him into office other candidates from his party—for Congress, as well as for state and local offices. The coattails effect occurs because of the tendency for many people to vote a straight ticket—a practice which is sometimes encouraged when party-column ballots are being used, because a straight ticket can be voted with the move of just one lever. But there are also other reasons for straight-ticket voting: a loyal partisan who is not familiar with all the names that appear on the ballot may well choose to vote a straight party ticket because he supports and knows the presidential candidate.

While its effect is often seen, and while it can have a significant impact on national-level politics, the importance of the coattails effect can be overstated. The incidence of ticket-splitting has increased in recent years, tending to dissipate the effect. Some people, in response to the recent increase in split-ticket voting, are calling for structural reform in government. They propose the establishment of a disciplined two-party system so that it will no longer be possible to

---

[47] Key, *Politics, Parties, and Pressure Groups*, p. 545.
[48] Key, *Politics, Parties, and Pressure Groups*, p. 545.

elect a divided government, as we so often do now, which will waste much of its time and energy fighting within its various branches.

Another important voting pattern which has been closely observed is the geographical one. Long-term sectional voting patterns can be observed in presidential elections. Until recently, the South was the famous example of solid Democratic voting. Generally, northern New England and parts of the Midwest have been Republican strongholds; Democratic strength has tended to be consistent in the industrial states. The maps in Figure 14-3 illustrate the breakdown of partisan votes, by region, in a series of presidential elections.

Short-term coalitions also form among various groups of states, in different elections. For example, although Maine and Vermont are traditionally Republican states, when Franklin Roosevelt ran for President an unusually large number of people from those two states supported him, despite his being a Democrat. Similar kinds of short-term coalitions among generally Democratic states helped give Eisenhower his large majorities of the popular vote. More recently, in the 1964 presidential contest, Republican Barry Goldwater, an unusually conservative candidate, drove several traditionally Republican sections of the country to support Lyndon Johnson, whose popularity among many voters had already been ensured by the dramatic manner in which he took office in 1963 after President Kennedy was assassinated. Thus, in 1964, Johnson won considerable strength from voters living in the East, the West, and the Midwest—while Goldwater's only strength lay in the South. Because he felt fairly certain that he could carry essentially the same states that Nixon had won in the 1960 election, Goldwater's carefully thought-out campaign strategy had been to win strength in the South, counting primarily on his civil-rights stance to give him strong support there. The difficulty was that Goldwater was able to attract strong support only in the South; and even there, many voters, feeling that his position on civil rights was the only part of his platform they wanted to support, decided not to vote for him. Statistical comparisons demonstrate that the regional variations in voting patterns, caused by short-term factors (in this case, both candidates and issues), that occurred in 1964 were of an unusually large magnitude.[49]

The most significant short-term factor influencing regional voting patterns in the 1968 presidential election was, of course, the third-party candidacy of George Wallace. Studies have shown that the shift in popular preferences that occurred between 1964 and 1968 was massive.

It is likely that the proportion of voters casting presidential ballots for the same party in these two successive elections was lower than at any time in recent American history.[50]

Types of Presidential Elections

V. O. Key prefers to look at voting patterns in terms of what he has identified as the four basic types of presidential elections.[51] The first of these is the *reaffirmation* election, in which a "vote of confidence" is essentially given to the party, the candidate, and the policies that have dominated federal-government actions dur-

---

[49] Philip E. Converse, "Social Cleavages in the 1964 Election," in Crotty et al., *Political Parties and Political Behavior*, p. 429.

[50] Converse, "Social Cleavages in the 1964 Election," p. 360.

[51] Key, *Politics, Parties, and Pressure Groups*, Chapter 19.

Figure 14–3   **Presidential Elections, 1928–1968**

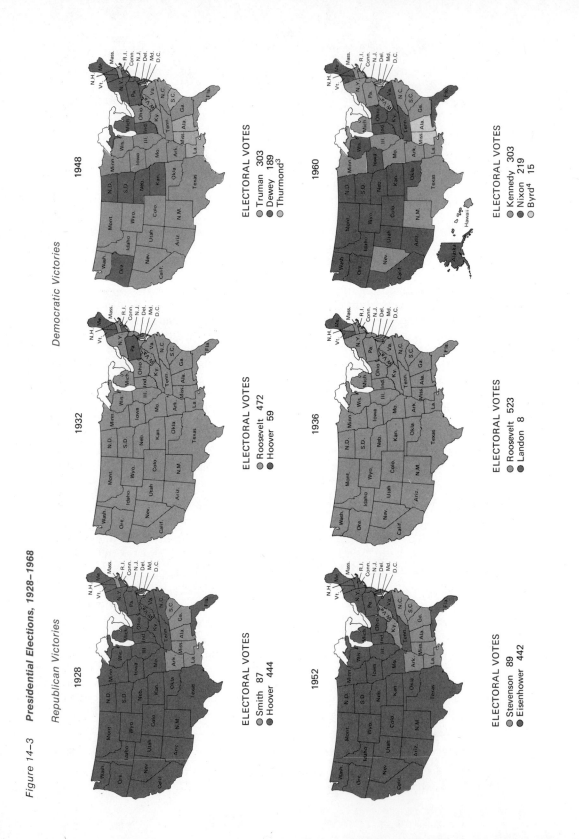

Republican Victories

Democratic Victories

1948

ELECTORAL VOTES
Truman 303
Dewey 189
Thurmond[3]

1960

ELECTORAL VOTES
Kennedy 303
Nixon 219
Byrd[4] 15

1932

ELECTORAL VOTES
Roosevelt 472
Hoover 59

1936

ELECTORAL VOTES
Roosevelt 523
Landon 8

1928

ELECTORAL VOTES
Smith 87
Hoover 444

1952

ELECTORAL VOTES
Stevenson 89
Eisenhower 442

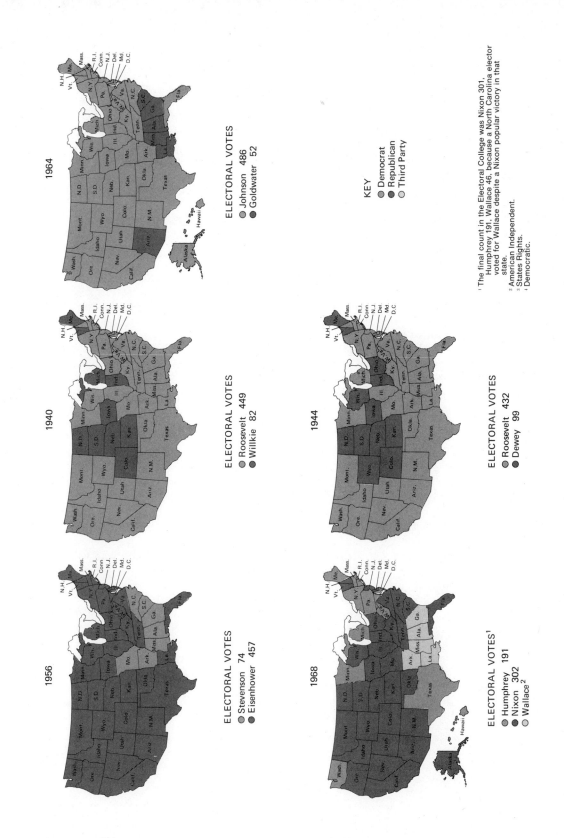

1964

ELECTORAL VOTES

● Johnson 486
● Goldwater 52

1940

ELECTORAL VOTES

● Roosevelt 449
● Willkie 82

1956

ELECTORAL VOTES

● Stevenson 74
● Eisenhower 457

1944

ELECTORAL VOTES

● Roosevelt 432
● Dewey 99

1968

ELECTORAL VOTES[1]

● Humphrey 191
● Nixon 302
● Wallace[2]

KEY

● Democrat
● Republican
● Third Party

[1] The final count in the Electoral College was Nixon 301, Humphrey 191, Wallace 46, because a North Carolina elector voted for Wallace despite a Nixon popular victory in that state.
[2] American Independent.
[3] States Rights.
[4] Democratic.

ing the preceding presidential term. Examples of reaffirmation elections are the reelection of William McKinley in 1900, the election of Theodore Roosevelt in 1904, and the election of William Taft in 1908, all of which broadly reaffirmed the "vote of confidence" won by the Republicans in the 1896 election.

Landslide elections, or what Key referred to as "votes of lack of confidence," are cases in which one candidate receives an overwhelming majority of the popular vote, as did Franklin Roosevelt in 1932, and Lyndon Johnson in 1964. Landslides generally seem to occur in situations where there is widespread discontent — as there was during the Great Depression — or a threatening force to contend with — such as the conservatism of Goldwater in 1964.

The third type of presidential election, as identified by Key, is the *realignment* election. In realignment elections, generally the administration is returned to power, but by virtue of the support of a different coalition than that which made up its primary base of support in the previous election. In other words, a significant shift has taken place in the opinions of many voters, alienating some and attracting others. Such shifts can be caused by a number of different factors. Key considered the election of 1928 a realignment type, because Hoover won the Presidency in 1928 through support of quite different groups from those who had given the office to Coolidge in 1924.

Critical elections are the most rare; these are the elections which mark a major change in party domination on the national level. The presidential election of 1896 between William McKinley and William Jennings Bryan was a "critical" election, in Key's view, since it marked the end of a lengthy period of Democratic domination.

Angus Campbell and his co-workers have devised a somewhat different system of classification for types of presidential elections, roughly corresponding to that of Key. Campbell divided presidential elections into three types: maintaining, deviating, and realigning. *Maintaining* elections are those in which "the pattern of partisan attachments prevailing in the preceding period persists, and the majority party wins the Presidency."[52] Truman's victory in the 1948 election could be termed an example of a "maintaining" election. In 1948, an unprecedentedly low percentage of the electorate (51.5 percent) turned out to vote; and the Democrats remained in power.

An example of a *deviating* election is the 1916 election, which was won by Woodrow Wilson. "In a deviating election the basic division of party loyalties is not seriously disturbed, but the influence of short-term forces on the vote is such that it brings about the defeat of the majority party."[53]

In those infrequent cases where "popular feeling associated with politics is sufficiently intense that the basic partisan commitments of a portion of the electorate change, and a new party balance is created," a *realigning* election occurs.[54] Since realigning elections have historically been associated with major periods of national crisis, it is not surprising that Campbell repeats Key's example of the election of 1932 as probably the most dramatic reversal of party alignments in American electoral history.

---

[52] Angus Campbell, "A Classification of the Presidential Elections," in Campbell et al., *Elections and the Political Order,* p. 64.

[53] Campbell, "A Classification of the Presidential Elections," p. 69.

[54] Campbell, "A Classification of the Presidential Elections," p. 74.

The 1970s Realignment

In the 1970s, we may be in a period of major party realignment. The primary shift at present seems to be from the Democratic to the Republican party. Recently, a number of observers have written about this phenomenon of the emergent Republican majority.

One of the bases for this apparent shift began in the late 1960s, when blacks and upper-middle-class (so-called limousine) liberals became united against the white lower middle class. This new coalition amassed power, eventually succeeding in electing mayors in several significant cities—such as Atlanta and New York. Blacks in other cities were also able to vote as a solid bloc, electing black mayors in places such as Cleveland, Newark, and Gary.

These patterns, plus the racial riots of the late 1960s, produced a countermobilization of the "middle Americans," who have since elected a number of mayors who they feel will support their own needs and positions—mayors such as Frank Rizzo of Philadelphia, Charles Stenvig of Minneapolis, Los Angeles's Sam Yorty, and Chicago's Richard Daley. These counter-mobilized middle Americans have also joined forces in terms of their national voting patterns, with a substantial vote for either Nixon or Wallace in 1968. The Wallace phenomenon, in particular, has been taken by many political analysts as a harbinger of things to come in American politics.

There is a strong feeling of disagreement about the direction in which American politics will be heading in the near future. Kevin P. Phillips is one of those political scientists who say that there is clear evidence to indicate that a Republican majority is emerging, a majority which is likely to dominate the political scene in the 1970s. Phillips cited the presidential election of 1968 as "the end of the New Deal Democratic hegemony and the beginning of a new era in American politics."[55] He has called the upheaval in party dominance that took place between 1964 and 1968 equal in scope and overall political importance to that which occurred between 1928 and 1932. The 1932 election marked the deposition of the old Republicans, and the emergence of a strong Democratic party, based on Roosevelt's New Deal programs and philosophies. The reversal of voting strength, from Democrats supporting Johnson in 1964 to Republicans against Humphrey in 1968, is said to demonstrate the power of the "new" Republican majority.

According to Phillips, and certain other political analysts, the 57 percent of the vote given to the Republicans and to George Wallace's American Independent party in 1968 indicates a new coalition of conservative Republicans, united in their protest against the Democrats' failure to deal successfully with social questions such as the urban and black "revolutions" of the 1960s. Phillips holds that the strong feeling of alienation from the Democratic party held in common by a large number of Americans, including a significant number of Democrats who have been leaning more and more toward Republicanism in the recent election years, will change regional partisan trends. "The upcoming cycle of American politics is likely to match a dominant Republican Party based in the Heartland, South and California against a minority Democratic Party based in the Northeast and the Pacific Northwest. . . ."[56] Furthermore, Phillips maintains that increasing

---

[55] Kevin P. Phillips, *The Emerging Republican Majority* (New York: Doubleday Anchor, 1970), p. 25.
[56] Phillips, *The Emerging Republican Majority*, p. 465.

urbanization in America, generally conceived of as a boon to the Democratic party and a problem for Republicans, is in fact just the opposite, because the "new" urbanization taking place in America can better be termed "suburbanization." The suburbanization trend is a basically conservative one, which is resulting in increasing Republican majorities in significant cities, even in such places as Boston, where the Democrats have traditionally been in control.

Richard M. Scammon and Ben J. Wattenberg essentially support Phillips's conclusion. They have argued that, in terms of socioeconomic background, the new winning coalition in American politics will be "unyoung, unpoor, and unblack" — that is, middle aged, middle class, and white. Furthermore, in terms of its attitudes toward basic social and economic issues, this new coalition will be very much at the center of the ideological spectrum.[57]

Elections and Democratic Politics

How Rational Is the American Voter?

The American electoral process does seem to be important to most people. But how much do elections really mean? In considering this question, one must first take another look at the American voter, for if the voters in this country are not fairly rational in their voting choice, then the electoral process itself cannot be very meaningful.

How rational is the American voter? As one might expect, even the experts are strongly divided on this question. Traditionally, political analysts have looked to one of two sharply diverging descriptions, or models, of our electorate.[58] One model is that of the philosophical citizen, the ideal democratic voter; the other is that of the voter as a manipulated subject, more or less entirely at the mercy of people and forces beyond his interest or control. Political analysts have attempted to determine which of these two models is the most accurate.

Clearly, the model of the American voter as a political philosopher does not very often apply. According to this description, citizens in their voting behavior seek the common good, not their group or personal interests; they are concerned about political activities; they are well-informed about politics; and they participate in the political system. Perhaps most important, each voter is believed to cast his vote as an individual, entirely upon the basis of his own well-educated opinion, ignoring all outside pressures. As already discussed, data indicate that very few Americans are politically well informed — only about 3 percent of the electorate can be said to have a consistent political ideology. And although most Americans vote as individuals, their decisions are still greatly influenced, both directly and indirectly, by many forces. These influences include their socioeconomic backgrounds, certain psychological factors, and, probably most important, the political party with which they identify.

What about the concept of the American voter as a political "sheep," who is manipulated by his party, by Madison Avenue advertising agencies, by his family, by his church, and who has no real opinions of his own? Not surprisingly, this

---

[57] Richard M. Scammon and Ben J. Wattenberg, *The Real Majority* (New York: Coward, McCann & Geoghegan, 1970), p. 307.
[58] See Pomper, *Elections in America*, Ch. 4.

point of view has tended to be exaggerated too. Recent studies have shown that sociological influences, while important, are not all-powerful or completely determining. Within almost any social grouping, the membership will be split between the two major political parties. Furthermore, many Americans belong to several groups, which often have conflicting allegiances, thus subjecting a large proportion of the supposedly "manipulated" electorate to cross-pressures, which can greatly alter their voting patterns. In addition, recent evidence demonstrates that the stability of party loyalty, once taken for granted, is no longer predictable, at least in terms of individual behavior. The relative rise in political interest and education, as well as the recent increase in the number of independent voters, have tended to make partisan identification a less powerful factor in voting behavior than before.

Taking into consideration these two models and the facts that contradict them, it seems clear that the vast majority of American voters are neither sages nor fools. To be sure, many individual voters act in odd ways indeed; yet in the main the electorate behaves about as rationally and responsibly as we should expect, given the clarity of the alternatives presented to it and the character of the information available to it.[59]

How Meaningful Are Elections?

Since the American voter is clearly not the ideal, concerned citizen envisioned by many proponents of democracy, we must ask whether or not our electoral system is still meaningful. Just how meaningful can our elections be when the people participating in them are not motivated by the common good, are not necessarily intelligent, or even particularly interested in what happens regarding the issues and candidates on the ballot? Many political observers agree that "traditional assumptions about the character of voting in a democracy have not been demonstrated in practice. But popular elections have also failed to confirm the fears of the opponents of democracy."[60] In other words, our elections are neither as meaningful as we would like them to be, nor as meaningless as many cynics like to imply. This chapter has shown that many aspects of our electoral system prevent the mass of the people from exercising a direct influence on government. Voter-registration regulations, the system of choosing a President through the Electoral College rather than directly by popular vote, the great sums of money necessary to finance even the most modest campaign efforts—all these factors, and many more, tend to reinforce what is an essentially elitist political system.

Yet although it may be true that elections have little direct impact on the policies of government, it is also rather unrealistic to expect that they should. It is virtually impossible for the people to directly determine all the policy questions that political decision-makers face each day: whether a new welfare system should be created, and if so, what type of system it should be; whether expenditures for aircraft carriers should be curtailed; whether a new drug should be allowed on the market; and innumerable other questions, many extremely technical and complex. The important things, then, are that people have the right to vote—a right which took them much time and often bloodshed to acquire—and that they have

---

[59] V. O. Key, *The Responsible Electorate* (Cambridge, Mass.: Harvard University Press, 1966).
[60] Pomper, *Elections in America*, p. 357.

real alternatives in elections. As discussed in Chapter 12, while the choices may not always be the best in every election, there are real choices to be made in most. Thus, elections and voting remain crucial elements in American democracy.

SUGGESTED READING

Berelson, B. R., P. F. Lazarsfeld, and W. N. McPhee. *Voting: A Study of Opinion Formation in a Presidential Campaign* (Chicago: University of Chicago Press, 1954). In paperback. A pioneer study of voting in America. Both an analysis of the ways in which individuals and groups form preferences and make choices in elections, and a study of the behavior of the electorate in a democratic society.

Campbell, Angus, P. E. Converse, W. E. Miller, and D. E. Stokes. *The American Voter* (New York: Wiley, 1960). An analysis of voting behavior in United States presidential elections. Based on the results of the 1952 and 1956 elections, the book is an examination of the relationships among the political, psychological, social, and economic factors determining the vote.

————. *Elections and the Political Order* (New York: Wiley, 1966). A successor to *The American Voter,* with a focus on the behavior of the electorate as a whole rather than on individual voter choice.

De Sola Pool, Ithie *et al. Candidates, Issues and Strategies: A Computer Simulation of the 1960 and 1964 Presidential Elections* (Cambridge, Mass.: Massachusetts Institute of Technology Press, 1965). Investigates the extent to which various issues, such as anti-Catholicism, civil rights, and foreign policy, contributed to the outcomes of the presidential elections of 1960 and 1964.

Flanigan, William H. *Political Behavior of the American Electorate* (Boston: Allyn and Bacon, 1972). In paperback. An analysis and description of the American electorate and an exploration of voting behavior during the past two decades.

Jennings, M. Kent, and Harmon L. Zeigler. *The Electoral Process* (Englewood Cliffs, N.J.: Prentice-Hall, 1966). A collection of essays dealing with various aspects of voting and elections, including the role of the campaign in congressional politics, consequences of ethnic politics, organized labor, electoral strategies and voting patterns in southern elections, latent partisanship in nonpartisan elections, and reactions to the presidential nominations in 1960.

Key, V. O. *The Responsible Electorate: Rationality in Presidential Voting 1936–1960* (New York: Vintage, 1966). In paperback. An analysis of aggregate voting statistics and survey research data on voting behavior. The author presents a new portrait of the American voter, who he claims is neither straitjacketed by social determinants nor manipulated by skillful propagandists.

Lazarsfeld, Paul F., Bernard Berelson, and Hazel Gaudet. *The People's Choice: How the Voter Makes Up His Mind in Presidential Elections* (New York: Columbia University Press, 1968; originally published in 1944). In paperback. A classic study of voting behavior focusing on the relationship between socioeconomic background and voter choice. Based on data collected in Erie County, Ohio, during the presidential contest between Wendell Wilkie and Franklin D. Roosevelt.

Levy, Mark R., and Michael S. Kramer. *The Ethnic Factor: How American Minorities Decide Elections* (New York: Simon and Schuster, 1972). A comprehensive study of voting patterns among ethnic groups in the United States.

Phillips, Kevin P. *The Emerging Republican Majority* (New York: Doubleday Anchor, 1969). In paperback. Phillips argues that a new Republican coalition is likely to dominate national elections after 1968, replacing the old Democratic coalition that has led since FDR.

Pomper, Gerald M. *Elections in America: Control and Influence in Democratic Politics* (New York: Dodd, Mead, 1968). In paperback. Analysis of the relationship between the behavior of the American electorate and the actions of government leaders.

Scammon, Richard M., and Ben J. Wattenberg. *The Real Majority* (New York: Coward, McCann & Geoghegan, 1970). In paperback. The authors argue that the new winning coalition in American politics is middle aged, middle class, and white, and that candidates adopting a moderate position on issues are more likely to win.

Schaffer, William R. *Computer Simulations of Voting Behavior* (New York: Oxford University Press, 1972). A study, using sophisticated methodology and computer simulation, of how a voter decides. The author presents and evaluates various models of the voter's decision-making processes.

4

PUBLIC POLICY

Political ideology, the structure of power and decision-making, and the actual distribution of power in a political system all have one important reason for existing: the making of public policy. Public policy comprises governmental positions, actions, and legitimate spheres of influence on issues that vitally affect the daily lives of the people. Public policy includes questions about war and peace, environmental pollution, education, health, crime, justice, safety, and sanitation, among many others. What the government does or fails to do in these areas has a great impact on how people live. Public policy, therefore, is the payoff in the game of politics, for, if the system operates well, the lives of citizens will be improved.

Public policy, of course, cannot completely determine how people live. There are some things government cannot accomplish. But over the course of human history government has become an increasingly important factor in the lives of people. In socialist and communist countries, the government attains the apex of its influence, because it can reach into every realm of life.

For most of American history, the formation of public policy has been conducted under the pluralist system of government described in the preceding three parts of this book. There is considerable question about how far the United States government should go in regulating or influencing the lives of those it governs. There is also a great deal of debate concerning how fair and how effective existing public policies and programs are. This final part of the book will evaluate the outcomes of the American political system, focusing on public policy in the areas of economic affairs, urban renewal, welfare, environmental pollution, defense, and national security. The aim is to go beyond a mere description of existing legislation, in an effort to understand what the actual consequences of government activities are. For example, this part will show that, even though the laws may forbid racial discrimination in housing, such discrimination exists. The social, psychological, economic, and cultural factors that have produced housing discrimination are at times more important in determining who gets what, when, and how, than the legal system itself.

15
PROMOTING THE GENERAL WELFARE

Increasingly, over the years, the federal government has become involved in a wide range of activities—regulating business, promoting economic prosperity, safeguarding the environment—in an attempt to "promote the general welfare." This chapter will examine not only the procedures that the federal government uses to accomplish these ends, but also the more basic questions of what, exactly, should be the government's role, and how well it is performing this role. The chapter will be concerned primarily with the problem of the extent to which it is desirable for the government to involve itself in various aspects of American life, and the very controversial subject of how effective its policies and programs have been.

Government Regulation of Business

The Fight Against Monopolies

Through most of our history traditional American values have favored an attitude of "laissez faire" toward business—an approach which opposes government intervention in economic matters beyond the minimum necessary for the maintenance of order. Until the late 1800s, the federal government generally maintained a hands-off attitude regarding the conduct of business. The post–Civil War period, however, saw the development of huge business trusts, which, by controlling sources of supply and transportation, could set prices and make it impossible for small firms to compete. In 1879, John D. Rockefeller established the Standard Oil Trust, under which thirty-nine separate oil-refining companies were combined into one company, thus monopolizing the production, refining, and marketing of almost all the oil in the nation. Shortly thereafter, similar trusts were formed in the sugar, tobacco, whiskey, and meat-packing industries. Widespread public reaction to some of the less attractive practices of these trusts—bribery, rebates on railroad rates, price-fixing, and so on—led to a cry for government regulation, and the subsequent passage of the Sherman Anti-Trust Act of 1890. On paper, the Act sounded like a workable trust-busting measure. It stated that "every . . . combination in the form of trust or otherwise, in restraint of commerce . . . is illegal." In practice, however, during its early years, the Sherman Act was ineffective.[1] From 1890 to 1903, only twenty-three cases were prosecuted. One Attorney General, Richard Olney, declared flatly that he believed the Act was "no good"; and with an 1895 Supreme Court ruling (*United States* v. *E. C. Knight Co.*) which declared that the Sherman Act could not be applied to companies involved in manufacturing, monopolies continued to flourish.[2]

More vigorous enforcement of the Sherman Act began with Theodore Roosevelt in 1904. In 1911, the Supreme Court ordered the dissolution of both Standard Oil (which controlled 91 percent of the oil-refining industry in the United States at the time) and American Tobacco (with 80 percent of the tobacco business). The

---

[1] The Sherman Act had actually been passed with the tacit approval of a pro-business Congress which believed (as later events proved true) that it would not be enforced. Passage was part of a compromise under which the Sherman Act was approved to help appease agricultural and consumer interests, while a protective tariff, which was the real concern of the business community, was enacted at the same time.

[2] In a later (1899) case involving the Addyson Pipe and Steel Company, however, the Court reversed itself in part, ruling that a company engaged in the manufacture of merchandise for delivery beyond state borders was subject to the Sherman Act.

Clayton Anti-Trust Act of 1914 went a step beyond the Sherman Act, for rather than merely outlawing "combinations . . . in restraint of commerce," it also outlawed a number of business practices which "substantially lessen competition or tend to create a monopoly."[3] Simultaneously, Congress also passed the Federal Trade Commission Act, establishing the five-man Federal Trade Commission to prevent "unfair methods of competition" in American business and to help enforce the Clayton Act. Two later Amendments to the Clayton Act have been particularly significant: the Robinson Patman Amendment of 1936, designed to help small retailers by prohibiting a manufacturer from selling his goods more cheaply to one customer than to another, unless there are actual differences in costs; and the Celler Amendment of 1950, which forbids one corporation from buying stock or acquiring the assets of another firm, when the effect would be to lessen competition.

Although much of our antimonopoly legislation has been on the books for a considerable period of time, implementation has been spotty. Originally, both the courts and the administrators seemed to differentiate between "good" trusts and "bad" trusts—Theodore Roosevelt prosecuted Standard Oil, but left undisturbed the International Harvester Company; and the Supreme Court, in both the Standard Oil and American Tobacco cases, suggested that only "bad" trusts, which achieved their bigness through unreasonable restraints of trade, should be dissolved, while those that had used fair means were legal. This approach was spelled out in the 1920 U.S. Steel case, in which the Supreme Court ruled that "the law does not make mere size an offense." In other words, a merger resulting in a big company or even a monopoly was not illegal per se, for the question of inter-industry competition—such as competition between the plastic industry and the steel industry—also had to be considered.

Since World War II, a completely new factor has entered the picture. Earlier mergers were largely among competitors—the meat-packing trust involved a merger of many independent meat-packing companies and was obviously monopolistic as far as the meat-packing industry was concerned. But the new wave of mergers involved conglomerates—a single company acquiring many other businesses in noncompetitive industries. Ford Motor Company, for example, acquired the Philco appliance company; and CIT, a loan company, aware of the fact that the Justice Department would not permit it to make new acquisitions in the finance field, bought an X-ray company, an office-furniture company, a department store, and a greeting-card company. Recent Department of Justice rulings, however, now suggest that the government will go to court to fight conglomerate-type mergers too, on the grounds that such mergers create huge companies with the potential to reduce either present or future competition; the Courts have generally agreed with the Justice Department's view. In 1968, for example, after a protracted battle with the FTC and in the courts, Proctor and Gamble (a leading soap and toiletries company) was forced to relinquish its acquisition of Clorox (a laundry-bleach company); and in 1972, bowing to the threat of court

---

[3] Such outlawed practices included price discrimination (selling goods below cost for a period of time to drive competitors out of business), interlocking directorates among firms in the same business, contracts under which a customer was forced to buy certain goods in order to receive others, and purchase of stock by one corporation in another (competing) firm when the effect might be a reduction in competition.

Defense-appropriation cutbacks since the late 1960s have hurt the economy, because corporations like Martin-Marietta, which manufactured these missiles, had grown so dependent on defense contracts.

action, International Telephone and Telegraph agreed to dispose of its Avis Rent-a-Car and Levitt (home building) acquisitions.

No one can argue with the fact that the American business community is dominated by a relatively small number of giant firms: the five hundred largest corporations in America own over two-thirds of U.S. manufacturing assets, and in 1969, the three largest corporations—General Motors, Standard Oil of New Jersey, and Ford—had total revenues equal to those of all the states in the Union combined, excluding California and New York. Does this concentration of economic power represent a danger to the American system? Should the government be taking even stronger steps to fight "bigness," or does big business, as one writer claimed, provide not only "an efficient way to produce and distribute basic commodities and to strengthen the nation's security," but also "a social institution that promotes human freedom and individualism"?[4]

Much of current thinking would disagree with the latter view. Today, many observers accuse the largest corporations of irresponsible behavior, especially concerning pollution and the production of shoddy or dangerous goods. Moreover, the close connection between the largest U.S. companies and the Department of

---

[4] David E. Lilienthal, *Big Business: A New Era* (New York: Harper & Row, 1953), p. ix.

Table 15-1   **Total Business from Defense Contracts**

	Defense Contracts 1961–1967 (in millions)	% of Total Sales		Defense Contracts 1961–1967 (in millions)	% of Total Sales
Lockheed Aircraft	$10,619	88	Textron	1,798	36
General Dynamics	8,824	67	Ling-Temco-Vought	1,744	70
McDonnell Douglas	7,681	75	Internat. Tel. & Tel.	1,650	19
Boeing Co.	7,183	54	I.B.M.	1,583	7
General Electric	7,066	19	Raymond International*	1,568	u
North American-Rockwell	6,265	57	Newport News Shipbuilding	1,520	90
United Aircraft	5,311	57	Northrop	1,434	61
American Tel. & Tel.	4,167	9	Thiokol	1,301	96
Martin-Marietta	3,682	62	Standard Oil of N.J.	1,277	2
Sperry-Rand	2,923	35	Kaiser Industries	1,255	45
General Motors	2,818	2	Honeywell	1,129	24
Grumman Aircraft	2,492	67	General Tel.	1,124	25
General Tire	2,347	37	Collins Radio	1,105	65
Raytheon	2,324	55	Chrysler	1,091	4
AVCO	2,295	75	Litton	1,085	25
Hughes	2,200	u	Pan. Am. World Air.	1,046	44
Westinghouse Electric	2,177	13	F.M.C.	1,045	21
Ford (Philco)	2,064	3	Hercules	1,035	31
RCA	2,019	16			
Bendix	1,915	42			

u-unavailable
* Includes Morrison-Knudsen, Brown & Root, and J. A. Jones Construction Co.
Source: Ralph E. Lapp, The Weapons Culture *(New York: Norton, 1968), pp. 186–187.*

Defense is also a topic of criticism. (Table 15-1 shows those American firms that were awarded military contracts totaling more than $1 billion between the years 1961 and 1967.) President Eisenhower first emphasized the enormous power which this "military-industrial complex" could wield, suggesting that it could someday grow beyond the bounds of democratic control. Soon afterward his fears seemed to be materializing. In 1970–1971, for example, an alliance of huge business firms and the armed forces exerted tremendous pressure to obtain billions of dollars of public money to finance the continued development of a supersonic airplane. Although defeated by the counter efforts of taxpayer, consumer, and environmental groups, the experience illustrated the financial power and political influence available to major U.S. corporations, and the potential dangers to the rest of our society when this power is combined with the authority and prestige of the military establishment.

Ralph Nader, the consumer advocate, has suggested that the government break up the approximately one hundred U.S. companies with assets of over $2 billion. Although it is unlikely that such drastic measures will be undertaken in the foreseeable future, it is clear that the government has attempted to control the growth of big business to some extent over the years by bringing suit under various antitrust laws. (Table 15-2 gives some idea of the number of antitrust cases instituted since 1890.) Nevertheless, concentration of industrial power has actually accelerated in the post–World War II period as a whole. In 1967, the two hundred largest

Table 15-2   **Number of Antitrust Cases, 1890–1969**

Years	Antitrust Cases Instituted by the Department of Justice	Federal Trade Commission Restraint-of-Trade Cases
1890–1894	9	
1895–1899	7	
1900–1904	6	
1905–1909	39	
1910–1914	91	
1915–1919	43	206
1920–1924	66	177
1925–1929	59	60
1930–1934	30	37
1935–1939	57	140
1940–1944	223	103
1945–1949	157	47
1950–1954	159	57
1955–1959	195	92
1960–1964	215	69
1965–1969	195	76
Total	1551	1064

Source: Richard A. Posner, "A Statistical Study of Antitrust Enforcement," Tables 1 and 2, Journal of Law and Economics, vol. 13 (October 1970), pp. 365–419.

corporations in America held 59 percent of the total manufacturing assets, as compared with only 49 percent in 1950.[5]

The New Consumerism

There are now more than three dozen federal agencies involved in one way or another with protection of consumers, including HEW's Food and Drug Administration, the Federal Communications Commission, and the Office of Consumer Affairs in the Executive Office of the President. The most important, however, is the Federal Trade Commission. Dating back to 1915, the FTC has, for most of its life, been primarily concerned with enforcing the Clayton Act by preventing unfair competition. Although in 1938 it was also given the power to prevent and prosecute deceptive selling practices as they affect consumers, the FTC did almost nothing in this area for thirty years. Finally, in 1970, following one widely publicized exposé of the Commission by Ralph Nader and another by Miles W. Kirkpatrick, chief of the American Bar Association's Anti-Trust Section, President Nixon appointed Kirkpatrick to the chairmanship of the FTC.

Since that time, the Commission has expanded the use of its power to deal with unfair and deceptive selling, advertising, packaging, and lending practices. It follows a simple procedure: after a preliminary investigation reveals what the Commission's Bureau of Consumer Protection considers an unfair or deceptive practice, the FTC issues a "proposed" complaint. The company involved may "consent"

[5] U.S. Department of Commerce, Bureau of the Census, *1967 Census of Manufacturers, Concentration Ratios in Manufacturing* (Washington, D.C.: Government Printing Office, 1967).

and a settlement will be negotiated, under which the company will promise to stop committing the offense and perhaps take specified remedial measures. If a company does not consent, the FTC may resort to litigation.

The procedure seems straightforward, but companies often object to the publicity given by the media to the "proposed" complaint. Although the Commission carefully specifies that a complaint merely indicates that there is reason to believe that the law has been violated, the news stories resulting from such announcements are often written in such a way as to suggest that the company has no defense at all. However, in a two-year period in which the Commission issued more than four hundred fifty complaints, only forty were contested, suggesting that many of the complaints have been justified.

Commission activities have been concerned with many different kinds of companies. It has objected, for example, to selling procedures used by door-to-door encyclopedia salesmen, to unproven claims concerning significant differences in headache remedies, and to the use by certain automobile dealers of such nebulous phrases as "pre-driven" in their attempts to sell used cars as practically new. Not only has the Commission required the offending corporations to cease such deceptive advertising, but in a new approach, it now requires offenders to engage in "corrective advertising"—the firms are required to make amends by issuing a specific amount of new advertising in which they admit their previous errors.

Bess Myerson Grant, Commissioner of Consumer Affairs for New York City, has been a staunch advocate of fair pricing and clear labeling of food packages and other consumer goods.

Recent developments suggest that the FTC may go even farther than merely questioning the honesty or accuracy of selling practices: it now appears prepared to take on the problem of the costs of advertising, when such costs seem unfair to consumers. In 1971, following this line of reasoning, the Commission issued a complaint against the four largest cereal manufacturers in the United States, accusing them of using exorbitant advertising outlays (20 percent of each sales dollar) to corner the market, and thus realize monopoly profits. The Commission claimed that breakfast cereal prices were 15 to 25 percent higher than they should have been, and threatened court action to divide the four offenders into more competitive smaller companies.

Obviously, those businesses that are the targets of specific FTC decisions are disturbed by its new activism. But objections are not confined only to those directly affected by FTC complaints. Other more impartial observers challenge the Commission's approach, claiming that by its very nature, advertising must be permitted to take "the same liberties with reality and literality as the artist." As one observer explained, "the purpose [of advertising] is to influence the audience by creating illusions. . . . The consumer . . . wants 'truth,' but he also wants and needs the alleviating imagery and tantalizing promises of the advertiser."[6] And still others fear that if the FTC persists in its refusal to let manufacturers advertise product differentiation, merely because such differentiation is trivial (as in the headache-remedy case), the long-run effect will be to drive some manufacturers out of business, reducing competition and doing the consumer more harm than good. Finally, there is a group of sociologists that claims that although the consumer does indeed need some protection against fraud, what he more urgently requires is the education to judge intelligently among products when all the facts are given. For example, Dr. Lewis Mandell of the University of Michigan's Institute for Social Research reported on a study he made after passage of the Truth in Lending Law—theoretically a major accomplishment of the "new consumerism." This 1968 act requires that lenders (banks, small loan companies, department stores that sell on credit) publicize the true cost of credit both in percentage rates and in dollar totals. Mandell found, however, that most consumers did not take the trouble to understand the meaning of the percentage figures and did not shop around for the best buy; he blamed our education system for this failure: "College students who have counted all the commas in *Hamlet* and harangue their parents on the tragedy of Vietnam, don't know the differences between interest rates of 8 and 18 percent," he said, suggesting that the government should concentrate more on increasing the consumer's economic knowledge, so that all can become intelligent buyers.[7]

Most Americans would approve of the FTC regulations that protect the consumer from unsafe products—flammable kitchen aprons, children's toys decorated with lead paint, TV sets that emit large amounts of radiation—or with Food and Drug Administration rulings that prohibit the marketing of potentially dangerous substances. They would also encourage enforcement of the tighter meat and poultry inspection laws passed in 1967 and 1968, of truth-in-lending legislation, and of pollution-emission and safety regulations for automobiles. Some, however, feel that the government should go even further, and that there should be a formal

---

[6] Theodore Levitt, *Harvard Business Review* (July-August 1970).

[7] Gilbert Burck, "High Pressure Consumerism at the Salesman's Door," *Fortune* (July 1972), p. 94.

consumer's representative or "ombudsman" (perhaps in the form of an independent Consumer Protection Agency) to speak for consumers at the highest government levels. Nevertheless, there are others who fear the eventual consequences of some of the forms the "new consumerism" now appears to be taking. They ask how far the government's responsibility towards the consumer should extend, and to what extent the government should be permitted to decide which products are suitable and how they should be presented to potential customers. These are questions which policy-makers must confront in the years to come.

Full Employment, Price Stability, and Economic Growth

Although the federal government has been concerned from its earliest days with the economic well-being of the nation (tariff acts to protect our infant industries were among the first measures passed in the first session of Congress), the broadest implications of this responsibility were not recognized until the Employment Act of 1946. Under this legislation, the government assumed an obligation to pro-

Growing inflation and rising interest rates contributed to mass layoffs in the late 1960s.

vide full employment and a stable price level for the nation. The Act reads, in part:

The Congress declares that it is the continuing policy and responsibility of the Federal Government to use all practicable means . . . for the purpose of creating and maintaining . . . conditions under which there will be afforded useful employment opportunities . . . for those able, willing and seeking to work, and to promote maximum employment, production, and purchasing power.

The thinking behind the Employment Act of 1946 was greatly influenced by the experiences of the 1930s, when unemployment rose to nearly 25 percent and national income dropped to less than half its 1929 level. During that era, the British economist John Maynard Keynes suggested that if private individuals and businesses did not spend enough to stimulate the economy and increase the level of employment, then the government should act. Keynes and his later followers (who included many prominent New Dealers) recommended, for example, that under such circumstances, the government should increase its own expenditures to create new jobs; it should cut taxes so that the private sector would have more money to spend; it should force interest rates down so that business would find it attractive to borrow money to expand production and thus create new job opportunities. In all, the Keynesian economists believed that it is at times necessary for the government to take an active role in managing the economy. Today, politicians and economists alike agree that the federal government should not sit by while the nation is confronted with cycles of recession and inflation. Instead, by judicious use of various economic tools, the government can, in theory, provide the full employment and stable purchasing power mandated by the Full Employment Act.

In formulating an economic policy which will accomplish the aims of the Act, the government relies on information and procedures developed by many different bodies. Among the most important are the Council of Economic Advisers, a three-person team which advises the President directly; a Joint Economic Committee consisting of members from both the House and the Senate; the Office of Management and Budget, which devises taxing and spending plans; and the Federal Reserve Board, which regulates the nation's monetary system. The tools which the government has at its disposal are of two kinds—monetary and fiscal. Broadly speaking, Democratic administrations beginning with President Kennedy have generally tended to emphasize the forceful use of fiscal tools, while the Nixon administration has recently revived interest in monetary methods. However, most authorities would probably agree that a mix of the two is, and will continue to be, standard government economic policy under any administration.

Fiscal Tools

Fiscal policy involves the use of government spending and taxing as a means of regulating the level of employment and prices. Essentially, an economy can be faced with one of two ailments: a recession, which is characterized by a high level of unemployment; or a period of too-rapid acceleration, which is generally accompanied by inflation.[8] To remedy recession, fiscal policy requires that more money be pumped into the economy—either through an increase in government

---

[8] In recent years, however, the United States has experienced both unemployment and inflation simultaneously.

or public spending, or through a tax cut which would put more money into the hands of consumers and businesses and thus increase private spending. In a similar way, fiscal measures can be used to help control rising prices. In an inflationary period, the government can cut (or postpone) its own spending programs, or it can raise taxes in order to reduce the expenditures of individual consumers and businessmen.

Nondiscretionary versus Discretionary Fiscal Tools   In our economy today there are certain fiscal tools which are built into the system and do not require any specific government action to become activated. These are called the "automatic stabilizers" (or nondiscretionary fiscal tools). They go to work automatically, modifying tax collections or government spending whenever changes in economic activity threaten the nation with unacceptable increases in unemployment or prices.

Perhaps the most effective of these automatic stabilizers is our federal income-tax system. In the United States, income is taxed progressively—that is, taxpayers pay proportionately (as well as absolutely) more in taxes as their incomes increase. For example, in 1971, a married wage-earner was taxed 15 percent on his first $1000 of taxable income; but that same individual was taxed at the rate of 32 percent on income between $20,000 and $24,000, and 70 percent for any income over $200,000. Because of such a graduated tax schedule, when the economy is in a recession and total national income declines, income-tax collections decline both absolutely and as a percentage of national income. As a result, consumers' after-tax income does not decline as much as the drop in national income, thus counteracting some of the bad effects of the recession.[9]

In times of too-rapid economic acceleration, when inflation is a problem, our progressive tax system also has a stabiliziing effect. As paychecks increase (because there is full employment and employers are under pressure to give raises to keep their employees and attract new ones), an increasing percentage of these higher incomes are paid in taxes. As a result, consumers do not have quite so many after-tax dollars to spend, and prices are less likely to increase.

Federal transfer payments (public funds "transferred" to certain segments of the population through unemployment insurance, welfare payments, Social Security, and so on) are another important automatic stabilizer. In times of economic decline, businessmen cut back their levels of employment, and income in the hands of workers decreases. If there were no offsetting government activity, these workers would buy less and there would then be additional layoffs in other businesses, resulting ultimately in widespread recession. However, it is precisely at this point that unemployment insurance and welfare benefits are paid, providing consumers with a source of income and thus cushioning to some extent the effects of the downturn in business activity. In other words, if employment declines by 5 percent, income in the hands of consumers will not decline by a comparable amount, because of transfer payments. Of course, when business picks up, these payments stop automatically.

---

[9] The example of an individual taxpayer will clarify this. In 1971, a wage-earner with two children earning $9000 and taking the standard deduction paid a federal income tax of $1230, leaving him with after-federal-tax income of $7770. If his earnings were cut 10 percent to $8100, he would pay a tax of $1051, leaving him with $7049. Thus, although his gross earnings declined by 10 percent, his after-tax earnings declined by only 9.2 percent.

In addition to these automatic, or nondiscretionary, fiscal tools, the government also has at its disposal various discretionary fiscal devices. These differ from the automatic stabilizers in that they do not go to work automatically; specific government action (usually congressional approval) is required to authorize them, and for that reason they are subject to time-lags or political compromise that often limits their effectiveness. Discretionary measures include changes in the entire schedule of tax rates, as, for example, in 1964, when a substantial tax cut for every income level was passed in order to cut unemployment and speed up economic growth; or in 1967, when the Johnson administration increased taxes by imposing a 10-percent surtax in an attempt to control inflation. Other discretionary tools include altering government spending plans: for example, the government can embark on a road-building program during a period when unemployment is high, and cut back on such construction oulays during an inflationary period.

Monetary Policy

The government also uses monetary policy in its attempts to regulate the economy, under the theory that changes in the amount of money available, and the rate of interest charged to borrow money, can affect total spending and hence the levels of employment and prices. To simplify: monetary policy is based on the understanding that business and consumer borrowing and spending (and eventually employment) will be encouraged if money is plentiful and interest rates are low; conversely, such borrowing and spending will be cut back if money is scarce and loans are expensive.

The Federal Reserve Board, often referred to as the Fed, is the government agency responsible for formulating and carrying out monetary policy in the United States. The relationship between the Board and the rest of the government is an interesting one: although its seven members are appointed by the President (for fourteen-year terms) and frequently testify before Congress, the Board is completely independent of both congressional and presidential control. Thus, there have been times in the past when it appeared as if the Fed (and its monetary policies) were working at cross purposes with some of the fiscal policies of the President. From 1966 to 1969, for example, the Fed raised interest rates in an attempt to slow down the economy and restrain inflation. But during the same period, administration spending (particularly to finance the war in Vietnam) increased rapidly, thus stimulating the economy; and Congress refused during a large part of those years to raise taxes.

The Federal Reserve System includes the seven-man Board of Governors and a network of twelve regional Federal Reserve Banks across the nation; practically all the important commercial banks in the United States are members of the System. It is the lending activities of the individual member banks that the Fed attempts to regulate, for collectively they provide an enormous source of credit to businesses and individuals across the country. The Federal Reserve has four main methods which it can use to regulate the amount of credit (and hence the money supply) available in the economy.

Open-Market Operations Through the buying and selling of government bonds in the open market, the Fed can regulate the supply of bank credit available. In brief, the Federal Reserve will sell government bonds when it wishes to reduce the level of loanable funds and will buy them when it wishes to increase the supply of loanable funds.[10]

Changes in Reserve Requirements Each member bank of the Federal Reserve System is required to keep on deposit with its regional Federal Reserve Bank a sum equal to a specified percentage of its total deposits. This percentage is called "the reserve requirement." By cutting reserve requirements, the Fed can make it possible for member banks to increase their loans. Raising reserve requirements has the opposite effect: it will cause banks to contract their loans outstanding. Thus, the Fed will cut reserve requirements in order to stimulate credit (and eventually spending and employment), and it will raise reserve requirements in order to reduce bank lending activity and control inflation.

Changes in the Discount Rate Member banks which need additional funds in order to make loans to customers can, under certain circumstances, borrow from the regional Federal Reserve Banks. The interest rate charged by the Federal Reserve Bank is called the "discount rate," and obviously this discount rate will closely affect the interest rate charged by banks to their customers. Therefore, in times of high unemployment, the Fed will cut the discount rate; this cut in turn will result in lower member-bank interest charges, and, it is hoped, will encourage borrowing by bank customers. Conversely, an increase in the discount rate will be used to discourage customer borrowing in an inflationary period.

Selective Credit Controls The Federal Reserve Board has the power to set credit terms on various kinds of loans and establish interest-rate ceilings for different kinds of savings institutions. It can specify downpayment requirements and repayment periods on consumer instalment loans. During World War II and the Korean War, for example, it raised the down-payment and shortened the repayment period on car and appliance loans in order to discourage such consumer purchases. The Fed can also establish the amount of money (margin requirements) investors may borrow in order to buy stocks and bonds, and it will limit such borrowing in inflationary periods. Finally, the Fed can specify interest rates which various kinds of banks can pay to their depositors. In the late 1960s, for example, the Fed permitted savings banks to pay higher interest rates to depositors than commercial banks, because savings banks generally invest most of their depositors' funds in home mortgages, and the Fed wished to stimulate home building.

How Effective Are Government Attempts to Stabilize the Economy?

If we consider two basic criteria—the unemployment rate and the price level—it appears that the government has had considerable success during the post–World War II period in preventing both extreme depressions (like that experienced in the United States in the 1930s) and runaway inflations (like that of Germany during the post–World War I period, when between 1919 and 1923 the mark declined

---

[10] For further details see *The Federal Reserve System: Purposes and Functions* (Washington, D.C.: Board of Governors of the Federal Reserve System, 1963), Chapter 15, "The Open Market Policy Process."

"Our President has frozen all allowances."

New Yorker, *November 6, 1971*

to less than 1 billionth of its former value). However, in terms of milder economic fluctuations, the record is not as impressive. Unemployment rates have reached levels of 6 to 7 percent several times during the last twenty-five years, and in a nation as big as the United States, a 6-percent unemployment rate in 1972 meant that five million people were out of jobs. Moreover, persistent and accelerating inflation from the mid-1960s to the early 1970s was particularly problematic (a 5-percent annual inflation rate means money loses half its buying power in about fifteen years). The period since 1969 has been especially difficult, with the nation plagued by an unusual combination of unemployment and inflation; the government was reluctant to embark on those measures usually taken to restrain price increases because of the fear that such activities would depress employment even further. Finally, in August 1971 — in a move which dramatically demonstrated American acceptance of the concept that the government has a right and a duty to interfere in economic affairs in order to promote prosperity — President Nixon proposed the 1971 Economic Stabilization Act, which was promptly passed by Congress. The plan involved severe measures previously acceptable in the United States only under wartime conditions: wage and price controls.

Passage of the Economic Stabilization Act of 1971 illustrates one of the key issues concerning government economic policy: there is almost universal approval of stabilization objectives, but considerable controversy about the choice of methods. Such controversies take numerous forms. Many people, for example, would question the extended use of price and wage controls as a permanent anti-inflation device, believing that they are neither effective nor appropriate in a democracy. Others would advocate increasing the variety of automatic stabilizers available so that fiscal tools could be brought into action more quickly, rather than waiting for congressional action; President Kennedy, for example, at one time requested the authority to raise or lower overall income-tax rates by 5 percent, but he did not obtain it. Another expert, Milton Friedman, a prominent economist at the University of Chicago, has argued that the single most important factor governing economic activity is the money supply; he holds that manipulation of fiscal devices (government spending and taxes) is not significantly effective.[11]

In addition to the issue of the choice of monetary and fiscal tools, there is also the problem of conflict between economic-stabilization goals and political considerations. If, for example, public officials decide that the need for increased military spending is of primary importance, then efforts to halt inflation must often take second place. Such a conflict between economic and political goals occurred during the Vietnam War, when rapidly escalating defense expenditures seemed to counteract all efforts to curb inflation. Certain political realities can also make it difficult to successfully employ various stabilization tools. A President, for instance, will clearly be reluctant to propose a tax increase during an election year, even if rising inflation seems to warrant it. For these and many other reasons, the record of monetary and fiscal policy in the United States has not been as successful as many would wish. In general, it is often our involvement in wars, and the increased military spending that accompanies it, which largely accounts for periods of widespread prosperity, rather than the effective use of monetary and fiscal policy.

Housing and Urban Development

Housing is one of the most important ways in which a government can affect the life style of its citizens, the character of their environment, even the employment and educational opportunities they have. Poor housing correlates with physical illness and a high death rate, with juvenile delinquency, chronic alcoholism, broken families, and so on.[12] This does not mean that poor housing *causes* these conditions, but rather that poor housing tends to be associated with a wide diversity of social ills. In urban areas, substandard housing often leads to the deterioration of entire neighborhoods, and sometimes (as in the case of Bedford-Stuyvesant or the East Bronx in New York City) to ghetto areas the size of individual cities which are subject to the whole range of urban problems: crime; fear; inadequate health, educational, and sanitation facilities; and drug addiction.

Since the mid-1930s, housing experts have become increasingly aware that "housing is the field in which private enterprise has turned in [one of its] sorriest performances."[13] Of all the goods the average American uses, housing has perhaps been least affected by the technological revolution: standardization, new materials, and factory assembly are feasible only for mobile homes and prefabricated housing, while, as late as 1971, more than two-thirds of all dwellings built were still conventional housing—put up on the site, subject to weather risks, and involving high labor costs. The result has been that the cost of housing has increased rapidly, and it is generally agreed that private industry on its own is not able to provide a supply of housing that is within the economic reach of a large part of the American population, both the very poor and those of moderate income.

---

[11] Milton Friedman has suggested that a plan allowing for a steady growth of the money supply at a constant rate would be the most successful stabilizing tool.

[12] Alvin L. Schorr, *Slums and Social Insecurity* (London: Thomas Nelson, 1964), p. 143.

[13] Claire Wilcox, *Toward Social Welfare* (Homewood, Ill.: Richard D. Irwin, 1969), p. 270.

Government Efforts to Help Private Housing

Since the 1930s, the federal government has played an important, though indirect, role in providing much of the middle- and upper-middle-income housing built in the nation. It has accomplished this without becoming involved in the actual construction process, nor has any significant outlay of public money been required. Instead, government policy has been to concentrate on a series of measures designed to increase the availability of long-term mortgage credit to private home buyers, enabling them to purchase and maintain the housing produced by the private sector of the economy. During the 1930s, the Home Owners Loan Corporation (a government-owned lending agency) refinanced the mortgages of home owners who were temporarily unable to meet their mortgage payments. In later years, the Federal Housing Administration (FHA) and the Veterans Administration (VA) provided government guarantees for home mortgages so that banks were willing to make long-term mortgage loans to private individuals with relatively modest incomes. In addition, the federal government has worked to provide banks with large sums of loanable funds: by offering Federal Deposit Insurance Corporation (FDIC) insurance on savings-account deposits, the government has encouraged individual savers to deposit their funds in savings institutions, and it is these dollars that have provided most of the mortgage funds obtained by private home buyers during the last thirty years. Most authorities agree that these programs have been notably successful in increasing the supply of new homes available for purchase by middle-income groups. On the other hand, however, the programs have not encouraged the construction of low-cost housing for purchase or rent. Thus, government programs have contributed very little as far as improving housing conditions among the poor is concerned.

Public Housing

Most public housing occupied by lower-income families in the United States has been built under a formula in which the federal government pays for most of the costs involved in constructing the housing, and rents paid by tenants to the local housing authorities cover operating costs. The federal government establishes site and construction standards, and together with the municipal housing authority, also sets standards of eligibility for prospective tenants. (For example, they must be citizens, now living in substandard housing, with incomes not above a certain stated amount; they must not represent a health or safety risk to the community, and so on.) About three million Americans now live in public housing projects built and operated under such a formula.[14]

Housing Act of 1937 The first major piece of public-housing legislation was the Housing Act of 1937. This Act was essentially a slum-clearance measure—an attempt to eliminate the slums that local housing codes and local regulation of slumlords had failed to remove.[15] Passage of the Act was facilitated by support from organized labor; because the country was still in the Depression, labor viewed the Act as a job-creating measure.

---

[14] The *New York Times* (July 24, 1972), p. 52.
[15] The Act originally required the demolition of an old building for every new one built. This requirement was changed when the national housing shortage became acute.

Housing Act of 1949 By 1949, emphasis shifted from slum clearance to urban renewal. The objective of federal housing programs was no longer merely to improve housing available to the poor, but to rebuild whole areas of cities afflicted
with urban blight. Under the Housing Act of 1949 and the Urban Renewal Act
of 1954, a local public agency submits a renewal plan for a blighted area to the
federal Urban Renewal Administration. Once the plan is approved, the local agency
acquires all the land which is to be included in the project through direct purchase or exercise of the right of eminent domain. It then evicts local inhabitants,[16]
tears down all the old buildings, provides new streets and public utilities, and
finally, sells or leases most of the land to a private developer. Some new public
housing projects are also included in the redeveloped area.

At every step of the way, federal government money is available to the local
public agency. The Urban Renewal Agency will provide funds for drawing up
plans, for buying out and relocating residents and businesses who are forced to
move, and for construction of utilities, such as sewers and water mains. In addition, the federal government makes a major contribution by subsidizing the overall cost of acquiring the property. In a typical case, the cleared land may be valued
at only 30 percent of the acquisition cost, and the federal government will supply
the money to compensate for most of this loss.[17]

Failures of Public Housing and Urban Renewal

Both the public-housing and the urban-renewal approaches to solving the housing
problem in the United States have come under heavy attack. Neither program has
provided enough housing for all who require it. Both ignore, to some extent, the
housing needs of the very poor; and in the opinion of some experts, both have
tended to exacerbate the very problems they were intended to solve, and to create
new problems as well. For example, in many cases, as a direct consequence of
urban renewal, urban blight has moved from the center of the city to a wider area
in its outskirts. Thus, new and even more highly segregated ghettos have replaced
the old ones.

Problems with Public Housing A basic failure of public housing is that the supply
falls short of the demand: there are far too few units for those to whom public
housing represents the only adequate housing they can afford. In New York City,
for example, it has been estimated that at the present rate of turnover, a person
placing his name at the end of the current waiting list for public housing would
have to wait more than thirty years before being offered an apartment. There has
also been considerable criticism of the physical design of many of the larger housing projects. City planners frequently describe the acres of concrete high-rise
public-housing apartments as "standardized and cheerless." Moreover, administrative procedures practiced by local public-housing agencies have often been
offensive to tenants and of questionable value. For example, a tenant must report
every income increase to the Public Housing Authority; as family income in-

---

[16] In theory, the law requires that occupants evicted must be offered safe and sanitary housing, in good loca-
tions at rents they can afford, before eviction.

[17] In most instances, a third of the loss is assumed by the city itself, except in the case of economically depressed cities, in which case the city is required to provide only one-fourth. The city's contribution may be
in the form of land, streets, schools, or other site improvements.

The activism that came of age in the 1960s has found one of its voices in cities among tenants battling rising rents and deteriorating conditions in buildings.

creases, rents are raised, and eventually, a family whose income exceeds certain standards will be forced to leave. This provision discourages many tenants from seeking better jobs or prompts them to lie about their actual incomes. Housing-authority personnel are also accused of invading the privacy of tenants in their efforts to obtain accurate income information. Other invasions of tenant privacy occur when housing authorities routinely check apartments to see that tenants do not, for example, paint their own quarters, hammer nails into the wall, own pets, keep bicycles on the sidewalks, shake mops out of windows, or maintain more than a stated number of people within each dwelling unit. Entire families are subject to eviction under certain conditions—as when they continue to house a child convicted of certain crimes. Moreover, before a family can be admitted to a housing project, it must provide extensive information to the housing authority about all sorts of very personal matters, and in some cases having illegitimate children, a common-law marriage, or a record of drug addiction can be grounds for being refused admission.

A fundamental objection to inner-city public housing projects concerns the fact that many of them tend by their very nature to create or perpetuate ghettos. The residents of most projects have common backgrounds: one-fourth of them receive public assistance, half are black, many are members of broken families. "A typical tenant is a black woman, without a husband, supporting a family with help from ADC."[18] In addition, it is possible that the impersonal monolithic buildings themselves encourage the development of segregated ghetto cultures; housing projects,

---

[18] Wilcox, *Toward Social Welfare*, p. 285.

for example, may inhibit the development of a full neighborhood life, because they lack the diversity that characterize traditional city streets, where shops, churches, and movie houses stood side by side with residential dwellings and provide a measure of interest and safety for the inhabitants of the block. Instead, project tenants often live secluded in their own apartments, in fear of crime in their hallways and stairwells, with limited opportunities to meet other people and engage in other social activities. Neighborhood schools, attended largely by project children, reinforce isolation, and thus the housing project, originally intended to provide safe and decent new housing for the poor as a first step in facilitating their entrance into the mainstream of American life, ends up being an important factor in reinforcing the self-perpetuating life styles of those who live there. Moreover, if the only decent housing available to minority groups is located within these central-city housing projects, this limits minority group access to jobs available outside the city, makes school integration impossible and, in general, promotes the continuance of a segregated society.

Problems with Urban Renewal Individual tenants have objected to the practices involved in public housing, and entire communities have often fought urban renewal. A major complaint concerns what happens to the people who are displaced when land is acquired. In theory, the law requires that those evicted must be provided with suitably located decent housing at prices they can afford. In practice, however, many tenants are forced into more expensive dwellings which are often worse than those they left. Many must leave the community (a particular hardship for the elderly), and few are able to return to the area afterwards, since most urban-renewal areas include fewer dwelling units after renewal is completed, and many of these are generally high-rent units.[19] One evaluation of the situation is that urban-renewal programs have destroyed twice as many dwellings as they have built, and that the new housing has been primarily luxury apartments for the rich.[20]

In brief, most authorities agree that urban renewal has done almost nothing to house the poor. It is true that it has removed some inadequate urban housing, in which the poor lived under conditions that were often unsafe, unsanitary, and unattractive. But it has replaced this housing with sparkling new downtown areas, to the delight and profit of real-estate operators, office builders, commercial developers, and tenants who can afford high rents. It has not provided low-cost replacement housing for the dispossessed poor; instead, many of them have been driven into the surrounding area, creating new conditions of overcrowding, new slums, new urban blight. Eventually, these peripheral areas become the next candidates for urban renewal, and a new round of eviction begins.

Recent Innovations
in Solving the Housing Problem

Model Cities Act Objections to the traditional urban-renewal and public-housing approaches to solving the housing crisis in the United States have resulted in a

---

[19] Land cleared for urban-renewal projects is generally more than four-fifths residential before clearance, but only three-fifths residential afterwards, with commercial office buildings, large retail stores, community facilities, and the the like replacing the former housing units. See Herbert Gans, *The Urban Villagers* (New York: The Free Press, 1962).

[20] Wilcox, *Toward Social Welfare*, p. 282.

number of new programs introduced in recent years. In 1966, Congress passed the Model Cities Act (Demonstration Cities and Metropolitan Development Act) under which urban-renewal–type projects would be conducted in a select group of cities, with two important innovations. First, emphasis would be placed on obtaining the cooperation of the poor people in the neighborhood, both in planning and in running the renewal operation. Second, each project would represent a coordinated attack on all the problems of the area – not just housing, but also educational, health, sanitation, and recreational problems. It was hoped that such an approach would result in a truly improved urban environment, one which would be designed for and made available to the former residents. Particular care was to be taken in providing homes for those temporarily dispossessed, and for their eventual resettlement in new but low-cost public housing within the area.

Housing and Urban Development Act of 1968   An even broader attack on the housing problem was envisioned in the Housing and Urban Development Act of 1968. This Act set as its goal the building of twenty-five million new housing units in the 10-year period 1969-1978, of which six million would be government-supported units built for low- and moderate-income families. As part of this program, in fiscal 1972 alone, the federal government spent almost $2 billion on 478,000 housing units.[21]

What was new about the HUD Act of 1968, however, was not merely the ambitions and costly scope of the program, or the fact that long-range planning was involved; the legislation included some new measures to provide low- and middle-cost housing for citizens. It is true that a substantial part of federal funds for housing low-income families will still go to the conventional low-rent public-housing projects built by local housing authorities, but more promising for the future are the mortgage-guarantee and rent-subsidy programs provided under the Act. For example, poor families are aided by a rent supplement program, under which they pay one-fourth of their income in rent, if they agree to move into certain approved new projects; the federal government pays the difference. Similarly, moderate-income families have been helped by federal rent and mortgage subsidies when they buy or rent certain approved new housing under these subsidies, the government paying the difference between the rent or mortgage payments and a certain stated percentage of the participants' income.[22] These moderate-income programs are intended to help families whose incomes are generally too high for admission to public housing projects, but too low to afford adequate housing without some form of assistance. The theory has been that low-income groups will benefit indirectly because as moderate-income families move into these subsidized housing units, their vacated homes will become available to the poor.

New Directions for Public Housing

By mid-1972, however, it was becoming clear that some of our national housing programs were facing significant problems on many fronts. An increasing number

---

[21] Charles L. Schultze, Edward R. Fried, Alice M. Rivlin, Nancy H. Teeters, *Setting National Priorities: The 1972 Budget* (Washington, D.C.: The Brookings Institution, 1971), p. 278.

[22] For example, under Section 235 of the Act, the federal government pays the difference between 20 percent of family income and mortgage payments. Under Section 236, it pays the difference between 25 percent of family income and fair market rents in certain special projects.

of "old" subsidized public-housing projects operated by local public-housing authorities were confronted with rising levels of crime and vandalism; in addition, they were running into financial difficulties. Despite the original federal-government contribution to construction costs, tenant rents were inadequate to maintain the projects in acceptable condition. A 1972 House of Representatives Subcommittee report indicated that fifty-nine local housing authorities were experiencing "serious financial problems" and that seven were "verging on insolvency."[23] These included housing projects in Washington, Detroit, Kansas City, Newark, and San Francisco. One multimillion-dollar project in St. Louis was actually abandoned, and in the Detroit area, where the government was promoting moderate-income housing through subsidies and mortgage guarantees on new homes as provided in the 1968 HUD Act, 8500 homes had been repossessed by the federal government because of defaults and abandonments.[24]

Housing Allowances A possible alternative to present housing programs lies in a system of direct cash subsidies which would be paid to low- and moderate-income families; these families could then use the allotments to obtain better housing as they pleased in the open market, instead of being restricted to certain approved new housing projects as they are under the 1968 Act. The housing obtained could be new, or it could be existing housing. Since it is usually cheaper to obtain older housing than new housing, this approach might provide an economical way of capitalizing on the existing stock of homes. One estimate is that such an "open-market housing allowance" could provide housing for low- and moderate-income groups at 50 to 60 percent of the present cost of 1968 HUD rent and mortgage subsidy plans.[25] A trial program of this nature has been operated in Kansas City,[26] where the federal government took 205 families from some of the worst slums in the city, gave them rent-money supplements, and allowed them to find better housing of their own choice anywhere within the seven-county area surrounding the city. Families were predominantly black and Mexican-American, all were from inner-city neighborhoods, and some had lived before in high-rise public-housing apartment projects. The program has been judged a success: one hundred fifty out of one hundred seventy families interviewed preferred the direct-housing allowance to public housing, and Kansas City officials estimate it would have cost $25,000 per unit to build traditional public housing for them, as compared with an average subsidy of less than $1,500 per family per year required under the direct-subsidy plan.

Scatter-Site Housing Even if such a system of housing allowances is expanded, it is probable, because of housing shortages, that new conventional public housing projects will continue to play an important role. There has, however, been new interest in the question of where such housing should be located. In the past, most public housing projects have replaced slum housing; thus, they have generally been located in inner cities and have tended to create or perpetuate minority segregation. Recently, however, attempts have been made to locate public

---

[23] The *New York Times* (July 24, 1972), p. 1.
[24] The *New York Times* (July 24, 1972), p. 52.
[25] Schultze et al., *Setting National Priorities: The 1972 Budget*, p. 294.
[26] Plans for a larger experiment, involving one thousand Pittsburgh families, were announced in mid-1972.

housing outside the ghetto. This concept of "scatter-site housing" has attracted interest, partly in response to the Kerner Commission, which called for a reorientation of "federally aided low and moderate income housing programs . . . so that the major thrust is in nonghetto areas," and partly in response to several court decisions which held that construction of federally assisted housing "in areas where it would intensify segregation" was in direct violation of the 1964 Civil Rights Act and the due-process clause of the Fifth Amendment.[27]

Since that time, various city, state, and federal housing agencies have attempted to build scatter-site housing, but have met with overwhelming opposition in most communities. One civil-rights leader has remarked in despair that if such efforts persist, they will "kill this nation's public housing program," and that the more the federal government attempts to impose scatter-site housing on reluctant communities, "the less likely it is that any public housing will be built."[28] Liberal organizations and leaders may agree that subsidized housing scattered throughout the community will help to eliminate de facto segregation and the educational, vocational, and cultural inequities that such segregation brings, but middle-class communities fear scatter-site housing and have shown a willingness to use any available method to prevent it from being constructed in their own neighborhoods.

The government's role in housing its citizens is at an important crossroads at this time. Earlier approaches to the problem face serious limitations: giant-sized public housing projects within the inner city no longer appear to be a viable solution to the problem of housing the poor; the inequities of many urban-renewal programs are also becoming more apparent. New programs, including direct cash allowances, increasing emphasis on use of existing housing rather than new housing, construction of entire "new towns" with government assistance, and improved financing and more liberalized zoning for low-cost mobile houses are now being considered. Equally important are attempts to simplify and unify the entire complicated network of housing legislation that has developed more or less piecemeal since the 1930s. In mid-1972, an omnibus housing bill, the HUD Act of 1972, directed toward this end, was before Congress, but passage was uncertain.

Social Welfare Programs

The federal government has developed a number of programs through which it tries to help those who are unable, for one reason or another, to support themselves. These social-welfare programs may be divided into two basic categories: social insurance plans (Social Security, unemployment insurance, Medicare), and direct public assistance or "welfare" payments.

Social Insurance Plans

Social Security In 1971, some 26 million retired or disabled Americans, or their survivors, received over $36 billion in Social Security payments. Since its creation almost forty years ago (the Social Security Act of 1935), Social Security has be-

---

[27] *Gautreaux* v. *United States Department of Housing and Urban Development,* 7th Circuit Court of Appeals (1971).

[28] Martin Hochbaum, "Scatter-Site Approach is Faulty," the *New York Times* (June 18, 1972).

come such an integral part of the American way of life that it is hard to imagine that in the 1936 presidential election, the Republican candidate, Alf Landon, actually campaigned on a platform calling for its repeal. (Landon lost, carrying only Maine and Vermont.) The original Act provided benefits only to those who retired because of age, and many groups of workers – such as household employees and agricultural workers – were excluded from coverage. Today, however, Social Security covers almost all workers, and guarantees not only retirement benefits to the aged, but also payments to dependents and survivors of covered persons and to disabled workers. Payments vary depending on years of employment and wages earned. The system is financed by regular contributions from workers and their employers; in 1973, the worker and his employer were each paying a tax of 5.5 percent of his first $10,800 of earnings.[29] Over the years, the level of benefits received under social security has increased significantly: as recently as 1956, the average monthly benefit received by a single person was $63.09; by 1973, it had increased to an average $161. Congress, which sets the benefit schedule, has generally been under great political pressure to approve increases, because the continuing inflation of the sixties and seventies has made it impossible for many retired workers to maintain adequate standards of living. There was a 10-percent increase in benefits in 1971, and an additional 20-percent boost in September of 1972. These benefit increases have been financed partly through larger collections reflecting the increased number of new workers who have entered the system recently, partly by virtue of the higher wage level now enjoyed by most workers, and partly through continuous increases in both the taxable base and the rate of taxation.

Medicare The Medicare program, added to the Social Security system in 1965, covers all those over sixty-five who receive Social Security old-age benefits, plus many others over sixty-five who are not eligible for these benefits. It pays for a very large portion of substantial medical expenses – hospital costs, nursing-home care, and so on – incurred by those covered. The recipient over sixty-five pays no current insurance premium in order to be eligible for the Medicare insurance program: it is financed (just like regular Social Security payments) by the Social Security tax paid by all workers during their working years. However, those receiving Medicare can elect to pay a small monthly sum to enroll in a program that will also pay most of their bills for doctors' services outside of hospitals.

Unemployment Insurance By 1937, urged by the federal government, all the states had established unemployment-insurance programs under which benefits are paid to those who are out of work.[30] Today about sixty million workers (80 percent of the American labor force) are covered under such plans. Typically, benefits are

---

[29] Beginning in 1974, the tax base will be $12,000.

[30] In 1935, when the Social Security Act was passed, there was considerable pressure for a federal system of unemployment insurance, but for several reasons, including the fear that such a program would be ruled unconstitutional, it was left to the states. In some states, however, local businessmen fought passage of such programs, believing that an unemployment-insurance package, financed by employers, would put them at a disadvantage in terms of costs vis à vis businessmen operating in states without such programs.

   At this point, Congress cleverly imposed a nationwide employers' payroll tax, but included a provision that most of the tax would be refunded to the states in those states imposing an unemployment-insurance tax of equal magnitude. As a result, within two years, all the states had unemployment-insurance programs.

paid for six months, although when unemployment in a particular state exceeds a certain level (usually 6 percent), payments are sometimes extended to nine months or more. States set the level of unemployment benefits, and they vary widely from state to state: in 1970, West Virginia paid an average weekly benefit of $33.50, or nearly half the maximum payment in Connecticut of $60.26. In 1971, in an average week, 2.1 million people collected unemployment checks, averaging $55.49.[31] The programs are financed primarily by payroll taxes paid by employers.

Problems of Social Insurance Programs There are a variety of relatively minor procedural objections to present social-insurance practices. For example, those affected argue that it is unfair for retired married women workers under some conditions to receive smaller benefits than married men or unmarried women workers with identical contribution records. Unemployment benefits are attacked by labor groups as inadequate both in amount and in duration; on the other hand, employer groups object to the practice in some states of paying unemployment-insurance benefits to workers who go out on strike. Others are worried about the growing cost of the Medicare program: there have been substantial and in some cases apparently unjustified increases in doctor and hospital fees since Medicare was introduced. Finally, there has been some feeling that Social Security recipients are always one step behind in an inflationary economy—that because benefit increases perpetually trail cost-of-living increases, they should instead be tied automatically to the cost of living. Consequently, in 1972 a new cost-of-living clause was added to the Social Security Act, which provides for automatic increases in benefits beginning in 1975 whenever the consumer price index rises by 3 percent or more. Over all, the old-age and Medicare provisions of our social-insurance programs have generally been approved by most Americans, who feel that they provide a dignified and respectable way for workers to maintain an adequate standard of living after retirement. It is only recently that some authorities have raised basic questions about the use of Social Security as the best and cheapest way through which a society can provide protection for its citizens against the economic hazards of old age. These questions involve two matters: how the system is financed, and to whom the benefits are paid.

As we have seen, the system is financed through a fixed percentage tax on the first $10,800 of income, and nothing on income over $10,800. This means that in 1973 a worker earning $10,800 a year had an out-of-pocket cost of 5.5 percent of his total income, or $594. A worker earning $20,000 paid the same $594, but it amounted to only about 3 percent of his income, and a worker earning $50,000 paid a Social Security tax of a little over 1 percent. Moreover, most economists agree that the entire payroll tax really falls on wages—that the employers' contribution is viewed by businesses as a labor cost, and that the wages of workers would be higher by the amount of the employers' contribution if such a contribution were not required.[32] Thus, in 1972, a married worker with three children earning $10,800 was actually paying a Social Security tax of 11 percent or $1,188 —more than he paid in federal income tax.

As a result, in terms of providing services in accordance with ability to pay, the

[31] *Economic Report of the President, 1972* (Washington, D.C.: Government Printing Office, 1972), p. 225.

[32] Brookings Institution study as quoted in Schultze et al., *Setting National Priorities*, p. 212.

Social Security system seems unfair, for its fees are regressive—those in the lower income groups pay the highest percentage rates. Moreover, some observers also view the system as economically unsound, especially in periods of high unemployment and low economic growth, for dollars taken from the paychecks of the low-income workers by increases in Social Security taxes are most likely to be the very dollars that would otherwise be spent immediately and thus help stimulate the economy.

Critics of Social Security have also raised questions about the distribution of benefits. The original concept of Social Security was primarily to provide decent retirement for the aged, and to accomplish this aim, it was decided that Social Security payments would be made to all participants in the plan, regardless of their other resources. However, a retired worker under age seventy-two was not permitted to earn more than $1800 without losing part of his benefits, although there was no ceiling on unearned income—a recipient could collect unlimited amounts of dividends, interest, rents, private pension payments, and so on without losing a penny of his monthly Social Security check. As a result of these inequities, Congress in 1972 altered the Social Security rules so that beginning in 1973, there is no ceiling on the amount that a retired worker can earn after age seventy-two without losing any of his benefits.

In brief, then, many authorities agree that Social Security is a relatively inefficient way of providing minimum incomes to the elderly. Recommendations for changes include reforming the payroll tax to take some of the burden off low-income workers, or perhaps shifting at least part of the source of funds from Social Security tax receipts to the general revenues. Other suggestions include transferring more responsibility of providing income for the elderly poor away from the Social Security system to other forms of public assistance; in this way cash payments to the truly needy among the elderly could be increased as required, without simultaneous increases to all aged recipients, including those with adequate outside income.

Public Assistance or Welfare

While the various social-insurance programs provide some of the supplementary income required by different segments of the population, in 1972 about fifteen million Americans obtained additional public assistance, involving federal, state, and local expenditures of over $18 billion. Almost all public assistance goes to two general categories: the elderly and/or disabled who either are not eligible for Social Security or do not receive enough to live on from such payments, and those qualifying under Aid For Dependent Children.

This distribution of public assistance is particularly interesting in the light of the various programs introduced since the early 1960s aimed at reducing the welfare rolls by providing employment-opportunity information, training programs, vocational guidance, and so on. The public-assistance law enacted by Congress in 1962, for example, provided federal support for such programs, and President Kennedy described it at the time as "a new approach, stressing services in addition to support, rehabilitation instead of relief, and training for useful work instead of for prolonged dependency."[33] At the present time, however, many author-

---

[33] *Social Security Bulletin No. 25* (1962), as quoted in Wilcox, *Toward Social Welfare*, p. 241.

ities are growing doubtful about the ultimate success of these programs as the answer to the expanding welfare rolls. It is true that there is a certain relatively small percentage of welfare recipients who might be able to become self-supporting through vocational training, but by any standards it will be difficult to find suitable employment for the blind, the aged, the disabled, and the millions of children who make up most of those on welfare. Moreover, from the point of view of society as a whole, there is some question whether it is really desirable to find jobs for those on welfare; the costs in terms of alternative care for their children, possible increases in juvenile delinquency, drug addiction, and so on could outweigh the money saved in direct welfare payments. Thus, the statistics suggest that job-training programs are not necessarily directly and immediately relevant to the problems of the millions of Americans who swell our welfare lists.

Anyone who attempts to make sense out of the bewildering pattern of federal public-assistance programs will have a difficult time of it. The system is organized on the basis of personal characteristics of the recipient — whether he is blind or old or a dependent child — and also on the basis of what state the recipient lives in. In most cases, the federal government shares the cost with the states (and sometimes with the localities), and Congress determines the percentage of the federal contribution. Different types of recipients receive different amounts in benefits: the blind have always had a higher benefit scale than the disabled, and both have received more than the aged and almost twice as much as dependent children. Moreover, since eligibility requirements and actual benefit levels have traditionally been left to the individual states to determine, with the federal government paying a stated percentage of whatever levels each state establishes, dollar payments vary tremendously among the states. In the Aid For Dependent Children program in June of 1971, for example, the average monthly family benefit was $183.40, but state averages ranged from $52.45 in Mississippi to $265.65 in Hawaii. Although most of the benefit money (and a substantial part of the administrative costs) are met by the federal government, state and local welfare departments administer the programs.

The largest, most costly, and most controversial of the public assistance programs involves Aid For Dependent Children. This program, introduced as part of the Social Security Act of 1935, was designed to help women with children but no husbands. Over the years, however, a series of objectionable practices has resulted from its implementation. First, because no federal aid is provided under AFDC for families with an employed male breadwinner, regardless of how little he earns, there is an incentive for fathers with low-paying jobs to desert their families, so that their wives and children may receive more income from AFDC than the father could earn. Secondly, until a 1970 Supreme Court decision ruled otherwise, many states had rules forbidding AFDC payments to be made to families in which the mother was living with a man who was not her husband, regardless of whether or not he was supporting the children. This rule led to midnight raids on welfare recipients' apartments and similar practices not likely to foster confidence or trust between social workers and those they were supposed to be helping; nor was it a particularly efficient and sensible use of social workers' time and energy. Third, until 1967, all earnings by recipients were subtracted from their welfare payments. In other words, a mother receiving the average of $2000 a year in AFDC benefits paid in 1966 would have had no incentive to go out and get a job for $50 or even $60 or $70 a week, for such a job would have added nothing to her total income, once she deducted social security, traveling

Among children whose parents receive AFDC benefits, the ability to attend school often hinges on whether payments allow enough for children's clothing.

expenses, child care, and so on. Since 1967, federal law has permitted recipients to keep some of their earnings ($30 a month plus an allowance for work-related expenses, and one third of any income over $30 a month), but there are still some aspects of the present AFDC system that discourage welfare mothers from working.[34]

However, the most vocal objections to AFDC have come from taxpayers, disturbed by the rapidly growing numbers involved. From 1955 to 1972, the number of AFDC children more than quadrupled, resulting in enormous increases not only in the federal welfare budget, but also in the budgets of states and localities where the effect was felt immediately and directly in sharply higher local taxes. In New York City, for example, the budget of the Department of Social Services was over $2.2. billion for fiscal year 1973, a sum larger than the individual budgets of 43 of the 50 states. Probably racial prejudice was also involved in objections to the welfare system, as about half of all AFDC recipients are black. Newspaper stories appeared telling of three-generation AFDC families in which

---

[34] A typical example concerns an AFDC mother with three children living in Chicago in 1971 and earning $3000 a year. Under current benefit standards, her AFDC payments and food stamps (minus Social Security and other taxes) would bring her total income to $5,067. If she got a much better job and began earning $5000, her benefits would fall, her taxes would rise, and her net disposable income would be $5310. Her additional $2000 of earned income would make her only $243 better off. Schultze et al., *Setting National Priorities,* p. 181.

illegitimate daughters produced illegitimate grandchildren, with AFDC benefit checks financing welfare as a permanent way of life. Widespread resentment led to a series of attempts to cut down on the number of people receiving welfare who did not actually deserve it. The 1967 federal public-assistance law included a number of provisions intended to compel AFDC parents to accept work or job training or else lose benefits, and similar provisions were included in various state laws. In practice, however, although there have been a few spectacular successes where AFDC mothers were sent to college or given job training and are now self-supporting, in most cases, the government has been able to provide neither job opportunities, nor meaningful job training, nor satisfactory day-care facilities which would lead to a significant decrease in AFDC rolls.

Reforming the Present Welfare System It seems, then, that the present welfare system pleases no one. Recipients complain that benefits are inadequate, inequitable, and administered in a demeaning manner. Social workers feel that they are so caught up with the mechanics of determining eligibility and preventing fraud that they have no time for the counseling which they are professionally trained to offer welfare clients. Taxpayers criticize welfare costs, charging that nothing is being accomplished with the expenditures. And politicians worry about the growing militancy of the poor, who for the first time are now organizing themselves into a vocal constituency which demands to be heard. Various suggestions for improvement of the program have been offered—such as a nationwide scale of benefits, or one that eliminates features that discourage recipients from seeking employment. But many feel that only a far-reaching overhaul of the entire system will be effective.

The most widely discussed alternative is some version of the Family Assistance Program sent to Congress by President Nixon in 1969, but still not passed by mid-1972. Under the FAP, the federal government would guarantee a minimum income for all families with children. The original Nixon plan, for example, called for a basic benefit of $500 for each of the first two people in a welfare family, and $300 for each additional person (a family of four would receive $600). The family could keep the first $72 of additional income earned with no cut in benefits; it would lose 50¢ of each dollar it earned over $720, and all benefits would stop when an earned income of $3920 was reached.

The most important innovations of the FAP include the facts that it would establish nationwide benefit standards in place of current state standards[35] and would introduce the concept of income support to a new group—the working poor —by providing additional income for perhaps fifteen million or more Americans who, though they have incomes below the official poverty line, have never qualified before under any other federal assistance program. The plan has been praised as one that attacks the problem of nationwide poverty while at the same time providing incentives for those who can work, and promoting family stability by paying benefits without encouraging fathers to desert their families. Nevertheless, liberals have attacked Nixon's FAP as extremely inadequate ($1,600 for a family of four is hardly enough to provide a decent standard of living), and con-

---

[35] The new benefit levels would be sharply higher than those presently in force in many Southern states (Arkansas, Alabama, Georgia, Mississippi, South Carolina, and Texas, among others). Any states wishing to maintain higher levels could, of course, do so.

servatives have criticized it as an enormous burden on the middle-income tax-payer. One observer estimated that President Nixon's very modest benefit schedule would cost an additional $3.4 billion annually over the costs of the present wel-fare system in 1972; raising the minimum to a higher level, such as $3,600, would cost an additional $21 billion.[36] In the 1972 presidential campaign, Senator George McGovern offered various alternative minimum-income plans with similar objec-tives but sharply higher minimums than the Nixon plan offered; the questions of the costs of such programs and their effect on the nation were an important cam-paign issue. Such bipartisan support—from both Nixon and McGovern—would suggest, however, that it is only a matter of time until some kind of an FAP pro-gram, largely financed by the federal government, will be introduced as an alter-native to our present welfare system.

Technology, Growth, and Environmental Pollution

Traditionally, Americans have had great confidence in the concept of economic growth; they have maintained a firm conviction that the ability to produce more and better goods was the key to prosperity and to a better life; through growth, it was argued, we would have the wealth needed to eventually solve whatever prob-lems were confronting us at any particular time. Thus, we tended to read each new record-breaking production statistic with pride and pleasure as a sign that conditions were improving and that life was becoming easier and better. Within the last few years, however, we have begun to recognize that growth is not an unmixed blessing—that in the search for growth we may be destroying our en-vironment, irrevocably spoiling the quality of life for ourselves and our children, and perhaps even threatening our very existence.

Prosperity and Pollution

The prosperity that Americans have pursued so energetically and so successfully during the post–World War II period has been achieved both through growth (in-creasing production levels) and through developing improved technology. It now appears clear that an important by-product of both factors has been a sharply higher level of environmental pollution. Some authorities place most of the blame on growth. For example, in 1940, electric utility companies burned oil and coal containing about three million tons of sulfur, but by the late 1960s they were releasing fifteen million tons of sulfur into the air each year. Similarly, in 1940, sixteen billion gallons of gasoline were consumed in automobiles in the United States, as contrasted with over fifty billion by the late 1960s.[37] Other people, how-ever, believe that the radical changes in our technology will prove more detri-mental to the environment than absolute growth. For example, we do not know at this point what the potential dangers are of the thermal pollution released into our waters from nuclear-powered electric-utility plants, or the amounts of radia-tion that may or may not escape from the nuclear fuels used in them. Barry

---

[36] Schultze et al., *Setting National Priorities*, p. 179.
[37] Schultze et al., *Setting National Priorities*, p. 254.

"Goodness me! You mean my little pie shop is polluting the air?"

New Yorker, *October 9, 1971*

Commoner has written of risks posed by many of these new technologies: nuclear fallout that poisons the air, synthetic chemicals that remain in the soil or water for years, excess carbon dioxide released into the atmosphere from fuel consumption. He has called man a "sorcerer's apprentice . . . acting upon dangerously incomplete knowledge,"[38] with potentially disastrous results. "The environment," he said, "is a complex, subtly balanced system, and it is this integrated whole which receives the impact of all the separate insults inflicted by pollutants. Never before in the history of this planet has its thin life supporting surface been subjected to such diverse, novel and potent agents. . . . The cumulative effects of these pollutants . . . can be fatal to the complex fabric of the biosphere . . . and if unchecked, will eventually destroy the fitness of this planet as a place for human life."[39]

Commoner emphasized the environmental consequences of technology; others have noted that equally important are the sociopolitical consequences. Alvin Toffler has written of "future shock" — the difficulties many of us have in coping with the rapidly accelerating number of physical and social changes that the new technology brings with it.[40] One reaction is a wistful desire to return to the "good

---

[38] Barry Commoner, *Science and Survival* (New York: Viking, 1967), p. 28.
[39] Commoner, *Science and Survival*, p. 122.
[40] Alvin Toffler, *Future Shock* (New York: Random House, 1970).

old days," when life was simpler and the threatening social problems created in the wake of the new technology nonexistent; it can be seen as an attempt to escape the problems of technology through an emphasis on "natural" goods—organic foods, hand-woven fabrics. Another reaction is the alienation that characterizes some forms of youth culture, often accompanied by a desire to "drop out" of a society so threatened by environmental risks.

On the other hand, many reject the propositions that technology and growth are inherently destructive. Pointing to the past record, they claim that it is only through more and better technology that the living standards in most of the advanced nations of the world have achieved their current high levels. In addition, many argue that, as a practical matter, it would appear almost impossible to turn the clock back—to reverse our present dependence on advanced technology. The cost would be too great; the dislocations in terms of living patterns would be unacceptable for too many people if major cutbacks were made in our use of electric power, fertilizers, and insecticides, to say nothing of automobiles.

The federal government has based its environmental-protection activities on recognition of the fact that technology and growth are both inescapable; instead it has devoted its efforts to developing methods to eliminate the worst effects of modern technology. Most of these efforts are very new and quite modest. As recently as the period from 1957 to 1965, for example, the average annual appropriation in the biggest federal environmental program—waste-treatment facilities to improve our water supply—was less than seventy million dollars.[41] Progress accelerated in 1970 with the creation of the Environmental Protection Agency, which now has primary responsibility for all federal antipollution efforts. Since then, the government has become increasingly involved in various ways of controlling and eliminating water- and air-pollution damage.

The federal government's general approach to the problem of pollution has been two-pronged. First, the government has authorized substantial expenditures for research and development and for construction of pollution-control facilities. Most of the money is allocated to the states, on a matching-fund basis, primarily for building municipal waste-treatment facilities to clean up rivers, harbors, and lakes, and to prevent future pollution. The second part of the government's efforts has involved passage of laws which establish standards for air and water purity,[42] and the enforcement of these laws with fines or court orders imposed through the judicial process. Under such measures, paper companies, printers and dyers, primary metal and petroleum companies, and so on have been persuaded to sign consent agreements under which they promise to stop polluting activities, or have been sued by the Justice Department and fined by the courts. Because court procedures to enforce antipollution laws are lengthy and provide many opportunities for delay while pollution continues, many observers now argue that there is a better way to attack the problem. They recommend the use of "emission charges" or "effluent fees"—that is, a stiff tax to be paid by the polluter on each unit of pollutant he discharges into the air or the waters. A company faced with such charges would have an immediate economic incentive to improve its waste-disposal procedures, whereas under the present enforcement system "the primary

---

[41] Schultze et al., *Setting National Priorities*, p. 246.
[42] Among the most important antipollution measures of recent years have been the 1965 Water Quality Act, the 1966 Clear Water Restoration Act, the Water Quality Improvement Act of 1970, the Air Quality Act of 1967, the Clear Air Amendments of 1970, and the Clean Air Standards Act of 1971.

A phenomenon of the last two decades, the no-deposit soft-drink bottle has been criticized by environmentalists, who advocate recycling—collecting the bottles, grinding them up, and re-using the glass—instead of allowing the bottles to pile up as waste.

incentive . . . is for industrial pollutors to hire lawyers to delay administrative and court action."[43] Although the "emission charge" approach has not yet been tried as far as water resources are concerned, in his 1972 message on the environment President Nixon did propose the imposition of such a tax on the emission of sulfur oxide by electric utility plants, smelters, and other industrial concerns that emit large quantities of sulfur oxide waste.

Protecting the Environment: A Look to the Future

It is likely that the federal government's role in protecting and improving the environment will expand over the coming years. Although current efforts have been restricted largely to air and water pollution, it is possible that interest will include eliminating noise pollution, beautification of recreational and national scenic resources, and other areas of environmental improvement. In all cases, some methods will have to be found under which private individuals and industries can be restrained from causing further damage to the environment, and we will have to accept the idea that these methods may involve personal inconveniences. Moreover, it seems clear that the international nature of environmental pollution—from ocean oil spills to high-altitude nuclear-device explosions to emissions of mercury wastes into international fishing waters—has consequences that cannot be controlled by any one nation acting by itself.

---

[43] Schultze et al., *Setting National Priorities*, p. 242.

SUGGESTED READING

Anderson, Martin. *The Federal Bulldozer* (New York: McGraw-Hill, 1964). A critical evaluation of the federal urban-renewal program, arguing that the program is extremely costly and destructive of personal liberty.

Commoner, Barry. *Science and Survival* (New York: Viking, 1963). An analysis of the interactions between science and society. The author argues that Americans tend to use modern large-scale technology before fully understanding its consequences.

Davies, J. Clarence, III. *The Politics of Pollution* (New York: Pegasus, 1970). In paperback. An analysis of the political considerations involved in the problem of environmental pollution. The author discusses federal antipollution laws as well as the activity of Congress, interest groups, and the general public regarding the issue.

Dubos, René. *Reason Awake: Science for Man* (New York: Columbia University Press, 1970). In paperback. A collection of readings focusing on the problems resulting from rapidly advancing technology and population growth.

Erlich, Paul R., and Ann H. Erlich. *Population, Resources, Environment: Issues in Human Ecology* (San Francisco: W. H. Freeman, 1970). A discussion of the worldwide threat posed by the related problems of environmental pollution, overpopulation, and limited food resources. The authors contend that the only solution to these problems is a dramatic change in human attitudes regarding reproduction, economic growth, technology, and the environment.

Heller, Walter W. *New Dimensions of Political Economy* (New York: Norton, 1967). In paperback. Discusses the contribution of modern economics to the improvement of society.

Moynihan, Daniel Patrick. *Maximum Feasible Misunderstanding* (New York: The Free Press, 1969). In paperback. A discussion of the War on Poverty initiated under the Johnson administration. The author analyzes some of the problems involved in the attempt to encourage maximum feasible participation of the poor in Community Action Programs.

Okun, Arthur M. (ed.). *The Battle Against Unemployment* (New York: Norton, 1965). A collection of readings by economists and public officials discussing the political values and economic concepts involved in making monetary and fiscal policy.

Schorr, Alvin. *Slums and Social Insecurity* (London: Thomas Nelson, 1964). In paperback. An evaluation of public housing programs and their effectiveness in alleviating poverty and insecurity.

Schultze, Charles L., Edward R. Fried, Alice M. Rivlin, and Nancy H. Teeters. *Setting National Priorities: The 1972 Budget* (Washington, D.C.: The Brookings Institution, 1971). The second in a series of annual books written by the staff members of the Brookings Institution analyzing the major issues in the President's national budget.

Steiner, Gilbert. *Social Insecurity: The Politics of Welfare* (Chicago: Rand McNally, 1966). A discussion of the political circumstances that produce particular welfare policies. The author addresses the question of whether welfare clients are provided an adequate voice in the formulation of policies that affect their lives.

Wilcox, Claire. *Toward Social Welfare* (Homewood, Ill.: Richard D. Irwin, 1969). A discussion of the problems of poverty, insecurity, and inequality of opportunity, and an analysis of present programs and proposals designed to alleviate these problems.

Zwick, David, and Marcy Benstock. *Water Wasteland* (New York: Grossman, 1971). In paperback. Ralph Nader's study-group report on water pollution. Discusses the magnitude of the water-pollution problem and the ineffectiveness of governmental action.

16
FOREIGN POLICY: PROVIDING FOR NATIONAL SECURITY

Insuring the national security of the United States is one of the vitally important tasks of the federal government. During most of the last decade, over 40 percent of our total annual federal budget has been devoted to military and diplomatic expenses, and the methods and objectives of our foreign policy have been major political issues in every election since World War II. Moreover, the close relationship between foreign-policy spending and domestic spending has made the conduct of United States foreign policy inescapably and immediately related to the everyday affairs of every American citizen.

Ideals and Reality in American Foreign Policy

The Moralistic Approach to Foreign Affairs

One of the basic themes underlying the conduct of United States foreign policy has been what Eugene V. Rostow, former Under Secretary of State, called the "School of Wilsonian Virtue,"[1] or what Senator J. William Fulbright, chairman of the Senate Foreign Relations Committee, described as "the missionary instinct in foreign affairs."[2] Both of these statements refer to the strong moralistic tone which has characterized many of the pronouncements and policies of the United States government since the late 1800s, a tone epitomized in Wilson's 1917 request to Congress for a declaration of war against Germany in order to "make the world safe for democracy." Such an approach involves looking at the world "in moralistic rather than empirical terms";[3] it implies that the primary objectives of United States foreign policy are to protect and foster good or virtuous nations, and to oppose relentlessly those peoples or governments that do not meet with our particular standards and brand of morality.

Many examples of this moralistic thinking highlight the record of United States involvement with foreign nations over the years. In 1898, the United States went to war with Spain with the professed aim of liberating Cuba from Spanish tyranny";[4] in fact, before hostilities started, President McKinley announced to the world that any armed United States intervention in the island, if it came, would be in the interest of humanity. The same tone is apparent in McKinley's explanation of American annexation of the Philippines shortly thereafter. It was America's duty, he said, "to educate the Filipinos, and uplift and civilize and Christianize them, and by God's grace do the very best we could by them, as our fellowmen for whom Christ also died."[5] A similar note was sounded a few years later in 1905 by President Theodore Roosevelt in justifying past and future United States intervention in Latin-American affairs; he referred to our role as a "burden," a "responsibility," and an obligation to "international equity."[6]

This pattern of explaining American foreign-policy decisions in moralistic terms

[1] Eugene V. Rostow, "Eight Foreign Policies for the United States—Which is Yours?," *The New York Times Magazine* (April 23, 1972), p. 66.
[2] J. William Fulbright, *The Arrogance of Power* (New York: Vintage, 1966), p. 21.
[3] J. William Fulbright, *Old Myths and New Realities* (New York: Vintage, 1964), p. 6.
[4] Fulbright, *The Arrogance of Power*, p. 6.
[5] Samuel Flagg Bemis, *A Diplomatic History of the United States*, 5th edition (New York: Holt, Rinehart and Winston, 1965), p. 472, as quoted in Fulbright, *The Arrogance of Power*, p. 6.
[6] Quoted in Fulbright, *The Arrogance of Power*, p. 6.

has persisted well into the twentieth century. After World War II, Secretary of State George C. Marshall called for aid to Europe on the grounds that "it is right" that the United States use its wealth to help others.[7] Similarly, President Harry S Truman, asking Congress for funds to provide assistance to Greece in the spring of 1947, did not emphasize the potential military or economic threats to the United States posed by any increase in Soviet influence in this part of the world; instead, he spoke of the appropriations as a measure designed to create "conditions in which . . . nations will be able to work out a way of life free from coercion."[8] Even more recently, the war in Korea was justified as necessary to insure that nation's survival as a "free society,"[9] and the original congressional resolution authorizing escalation of the war in Vietnam (the Tonkin Bay Resolution, 1964) stated the United States' goal as "assisting the peoples of Southeast Asia to protect their freedom."[10]

Objections to such a moralistic approach to foreign policy are several. Critics argue that moralizing is an attempt to conceal part, if not all, of the facts from the world and, particularly, from the American people. This criticism is not unjustified; despite the elevated language used, there has been a good deal of self-interest involved in United States policies.[11] United States concern for the Philippines was based on more than a sense of duty toward the Filipinos; it was closely related to the possibility of future trade opportunities with China. The Marshall Plan and the Truman Doctrine unquestionably restored the economic well-being and stability of Western Europe, but our interest in Western Europe was not merely charitable; it was also part of a broad anticommunist policy providing important military and political benefits to the United States. In addition, there is considerable doubt how "free" the peoples of South Korea or South Vietnam have been under their U.S.-sponsored governments, or whether, indeed, the restoration of domestic freedoms was ever a *primary* aim of United States policy.

Even more troublesome than moralistic aims have been the extreme positions to which this approach has led the United States. The government of the United States has tended to equate virtue with the American way of life and to believe that the Communist U.S.S.R. is therefore, by definition, evil. Thus, as Fulbright phrased it, the Cold War period since 1947 has been marked by a conviction that "just as the President resides in Washington and the Pope in Rome, the Devil resides immutably in Moscow."[12] In his estimation, this conviction or "old myth" has led America to oversimplify, and to base its entire foreign policy on the primacy and seriousness of the communist threat. The myth has led the United States into many strange compromises: although a peace-loving nation, it spends eighty billion dollars a year on national defense; although a democracy, it supports a variety of undemocratic, possibly fascist, but *firmly anticommunist* allies (Spain, South Vietnam). Moreover, because the United States for a long time persisted in

---

[7] Quoted in Howard Furnas, "The President, A Changing Role," *The Annals of the American Academy*, vol. 380 (November 1968), p. 10.

[8] Samuel Eliot Morison, *The Oxford History of American People* (New York: Oxford University Press, 1965), p. 1058.

[9] Quoted in Fulbright, *The Arrogance of Power*, p. 14.

[10] *Global Defense: U.S. Military Commitments Abroad* (Washington, D.C.: Congressional Quarterly, 1969), p. 23.

[11] In this connection, a statement by Henry Kissinger, President Nixon's chief foreign-policy adviser, is particularly interesting: "Countries do not assume burdens because it is fair," said Dr. Kissinger, "only because it is necessary." Henry A. Kissinger, *American Foreign Policy: Three Essays* (New York: Norton, 1969), p. 71.

[12] Fulbright, *Old Myths and New Realities*, p. 7.

In the famous "Kitchen Debate" in Moscow with Soviet Premier Nikita S. Khrushchev, Richard M. Nixon, then Vice President, expressed the U.S.-Soviet antagonism that generated American containment policy.

viewing communism as a single monolithic evil, it has been very slow to take advantage of divisions within the communist camp itself, as between China and the U.S.S.R. Recently, however, U.S. foreign policy appears to have adopted a somewhat more pragmatic tone, and, on various occasions since 1969, President Nixon has admitted that perhaps it is no longer necessary, desirable, or possible for the United States to impose its own form of democracy all over the globe.

Containment

Since 1947, the motif underlying most United States national-security decisions has been the policy of containment of the Soviet Union. The policy was first spelled out in an article in *Foreign Affairs* published anonymously in July 1947. Very soon, however, it was an open secret in Washington that the anonymous writer was George Kennan, an important State Department policy-maker. And as time went on (especially after Kennan was appointed United States Ambassador to Russia in 1952), it became clear that containment, as described and justified by Kennan, was indeed official policy.

Kennan saw all U.S.-Soviet relationships in terms of what he considered "a basic antagonism between the capitalist and socialist worlds,"[13] with the unrelenting goal of the Soviets being "the submission or destruction of all competing powers.[14] He noted, however, that the Russians would be in no hurry to precipitate

---

[13] George Kennan, "Sources of Soviet Conduct," reprinted in George Kennan, *American Diplomacy: Nineteen Hundred to Nineteen Fifty* (New York: Mentor, 1951), p. 94.
[14] Kennan, "Sources of Soviet Conduct," p. 92.

the destruction of their enemies, as they believe their goal to be historically inevitable but not necessarily imminent. Over the years there would probably even be times when it would appear that the Soviet government was changing, was becoming more amenable to compromise and to cooperation with capitalist nations. Kennan observed, however, that such developments were merely "tactical maneuvers," and that we should not be misled by them or lulled into a sense of false security. Instead, he advocated an unswerving United States policy toward the Soviet Union based on "a long-term, patient but firm and vigilant containment of Russian expansive tendencies."[15] Accordingly, the United States should "confront the Russians with unalterable counterforce at every point where they show signs of encroaching upon the interests of a peaceful and stable world."[16] The policy of containment as developed and applied by United States diplomats since 1947 expanded upon Kennan's guidelines and gradually assumed that all communism as practiced by nations anywhere in the world was monolithic (that is, the same everywhere, because it was everywhere under the immediate direction of the "masters" in the Kremlin), and therefore, *a priori,* inimical to the interests of the United States. Thus the United States in effect adopted a global commitment to restrain the expansion of Soviet power by guaranteeing help to any nation threatened, internally or externally, by communism.

The Tools of Containment The instruments through which the United States carries out its containment policy all involve commitment of funds extensive enough to make the United States an obtrusive presence. Chief among the tools are foreign-aid programs, security pacts, and overseas troop deployment. These categories overlap; the presence of one often implies that one or both of the others are also present.

FOREIGN-AID PROGRAMS. The United States has given substantial military and economic help to nations threatened by communist takeovers. In 1947, for example, when the Near East was confronted with Soviet pressures, Congress, at President Truman's request, authorized sizable appropriations to aid Greece and Turkey. Truman's message to Congress at the time dealt with more than the specific Soviet threat to these two nations; the presidential address actually enunciated a general principle, which later came to be known as the Truman Doctrine: "I believe," Truman said, "that it must be the policy of the United States to support freed people who are resisting attempted subjugation by armed minorities or by outside pressures."[17] The Truman Doctrine was to dominate United States foreign-policy thinking for two decades. The first financial-aid plan initiated was the Marshall Plan,[18] through which $13 billion was given to Western European nations between 1947 and 1951 as part of a successful campaign to strengthen their economies and military forces. Subsequently, many other programs with similar objectives were developed. The United States has supplied direct military assistance to some nations by outfitting those countries' armed forces; to others, it has provided nonmilitary financial and technical assistance, so that they could

---

[15] Kennan, "Sources of Soviet Conduct," p. 99.

[16] Kennan, "Sources of Soviet Conduct," p. 104.

[17] Quoted in Morison, *The Oxford History of the American People,* p. 108.

[18] The Marshall Plan was named for George C. Marshall, Commander-in-Chief of U.S. Armed Forces during World War II, Secretary of State at the time this aid program was introduced, and architect of the plan.

Thirty-five million dollars' worth of food was sent to Greece as foreign aid in the first year after the Truman Doctrine was enunciated in 1947.

concentrate their own resources on defense needs; and to still others the United States has offered a variety of economic goods and services such as outright grants, loans, and loan guarantees. During most of the 1960s, foreign aid of one sort or another ran over $3 billion annually (from 1968 to 1970 it was about $2.5 billion), and it is estimated that, in all, since the start of the various aid programs initiated under the Truman Doctrine in 1947, total United States aid has been approximated at $88.6 billion.[19]

SECURITY PACTS. Another approach to containing the Soviet threat is formal United States commitment to other countries through a series of security pacts and treaties which put the communist world on notice that the United States or any signatory will defend any other against communist aggression. Among the formal commitments are collective-security pacts involving the United States and several other nations. Perhaps the most successful of these has been NATO (North Atlantic Treaty Alliance), signed in 1949. Under NATO, eleven European nations (later expanded to fourteen) and the United States agreed that "an armed

[19] For a variety of views about the purposes and effectiveness of United States foreign aid, see Robert A. Goldwin (ed.), *Why Foreign Aid?* (Chicago: Rand McNally, 1963).

attack against one or more of them . . . shall be considered an attack against them all," and if such an armed attack occurs, each of them . . . will assist the party . . . so attacked, by taking . . . such action as it deems necessary, including the use of armed force. . . ."[20] Other collective pacts with similar provisions include the ANZUS Pact (1951), among Australia, New Zealand, and the United States; SEATO (1954), among the United States and a handful of Southeast Asian Nations; and the Rio Pact (1947), among the United States and twenty Latin American countries.

In addition to collective-security pacts, the United States has signed bilateral mutual-defense treaties with the Philippines (1951), South Korea (1953), Taiwan (1954), and Japan (1960) and has entered into defense arrangements with about a dozen other countries, such as Denmark, Canada, and Spain, through executive agreements. Finally, as a result of various congressional resolutions, such as the Formosa Straits Resolution of 1954, the Middle East Resolution of 1957, and the Berlin Resolution of 1962, the United States has committed itself in one way or another to the defense of many other areas around the world.

OVERSEAS TROOP DEPLOYMENT. The United States has also demonstrated its determination to defend noncommunist nations through the deployment of its own troops abroad. At the height of the Vietnam War (1968), there were about 1.2 million United States military personnel stationed overseas, including not only 500,000 in Vietnam, but almost a quarter of a million in West Germany, 82,000 in other NATO nations, and 10,000 in Spain.[21] By 1972, the number had been reduced substantially to about 650,000 men, primarily because of reduction of United States forces in Vietnam to about 40,000, and some withdrawals from Western Europe which were effected as a dollar-saving device in the face of the United States balance-of-payments crisis of 1971–1972.

Containment in Practice: 1947–1973 United States foreign policy, as practiced under the philosophy of containment, has used various methods to achieve its ends. In Europe, containment has been implemented through the Marshall Plan and subsequent economic help to NATO nations, both of which provided the United States with potent and reliable allies and prevented any further expansion of communism in Europe. In 1962, to prevent communism from gaining a foothold in the Western Hemisphere, President Kennedy ordered a naval blockade of Cuba, preventing Russia from installing missile sites on the island. In two other instances, in Lebanon in 1958 and in the Dominican Republic in 1965, communist-inspired forces attempted to take over established pro-United States governments. In each case, the United States sent in troops (5,000 marines to Lebanon, 30,200 men to the Dominican Republic), and although there was almost no actual fighting in either case, the United States' presence was adequate to insure the survival of the existing governments.

The implementation of these various tactics seems to imply that containment, as practiced, has been uniformly successful. In fact, policies of containment have

---

[20] *Global Defense,* p. 7.

[21] *Global Defense,* p. 38. The same source also notes that in 1968, the Soviet Union, the nation with the next-highest number of military personnel stationed abroad, had a total of only 250,000 troops deployed outside its own frontiers.

not always been eagerly accepted, nor have they always achieved their desired goals very rapidly. The Berlin Airlift of 1948–1949 and the Korean War, which lasted from 1950 to 1953, are examples of successes after long, arduous military struggles. The Vietnam War, a struggle in which Americans actively engaged for over eight years, is another conflict which grew directly out of containment policy. This particular conflict concerns us today more than Berlin or Korea, and consensus is not at all unanimous that it represents a success for American containment policy.

As a result of military operations during the last few weeks of World War II, Berlin, though jointly administered at the end of the war by France, Britain, the U.S.S.R., and the United States, was located deep within the Eastern Zone, controlled by the Soviet Union. The city was therefore completely surrounded by Soviet troops. In 1948, the Soviets attempted to assume control of Berlin by blockading all freight shipments to the city via roads or rails passing through the outlying Soviet-controlled territory. The United States responded with a vast airlift by which about a hundred airplanes a day kept forces in the city and supplied 2.5 million Berliners with food, fuel, and medical supplies. After ten months, the Soviets finally lifted their blockade, opening the city to normal freight deliveries. It was clear that only this firm United States action had kept Berlin from falling to the U.S.S.R.

In 1950, North Koreans, armed with Soviet equipment and joined by Communist Chinese "volunteers," attempted a military conquest of the United States–backed Republic of South Korea. Taking immediate measures to defend South Korea, the United States sent massive shipments of men and equipment to bolster the faltering South Korean army. In addition, it asked for and obtained United Nations approval of its military endeavors (the Soviet Union was absent from the Security Council at the time and thus could not veto the resolution), and eventually fourteen other U.N. member nations sent troops to fight alongside the American and South Korean forces. However, the bulk of the personnel, money, and material for the difficult and expensive war was supplied by the United States, which ultimately suffered more than 150,000 casualties, including 24,000 fatalities. A truce, finally signed in 1953, returned conditions to the status quo that had existed before the war, with the thirty-eighth parallel once again dividing North and South Korea. Since that time the United States has supported South Korea with huge amounts of military and economic aid; United States grants and credits to South Korea between 1945 and 1970 totaled 4.8 billion.[22]

American involvement in Vietnam can be traced back to the period following the Geneva Conference of 1954, under which France, the former colonial power, withdrew from South Vietnam. Almost immediately, Americans moved in with substantial economic and military aid in order to protect successive Saigon governments from Communist-supported attacks. As early as 1955, President Eisenhower sent United States military advisers to South Vietnam to help train its armies; by 1961 these advisers numbered six hundred. Despite such assistance, the military situation continued to deteriorate, and the South Vietnamese government, faced with one coup d'état after another, appeared unable to withstand either the internal subversion fomented by the Vietcong (revolutionary South

[22] *Statistical Abstract of the United States, 1971* (Washington, D.C.: Department of Commerce, 1971), p. 761.

The United States air base on Guam has served as a jumping-off place for giant B-52 bombers like these sent on air missions in Indochina.

Vietnamese forces supported by the North Vietnamese) or the external military efforts of North Vietnam. After a North Vietnamese attack on a United States destroyer in the Gulf of Tonkin in 1964, Congress quickly passed the Tonkin Bay Resolution, authorizing the President to take "all necessary measures to repel any armed attack against the forces of the United States . . . and to assist any member or protocol state of the Southeast Asia Collective Defense Treaty [South Vietnam is a protocol state] requesting assistance."[23] Almost immediately the United States proceeded to increase its commitment. At the beginning of 1964 there were 23,000 American troops in Vietnam, although at that time they were still officially described as "advisers" to South Vietnamese forces; by the end of the year there were 184,000, and they were admittedly engaged in direct combat as well as in an advise-and-support capacity. Escalation continued, until by 1968 more than half a million Americans were fighting in Southeast Asia.

The first major United States attempt to end the war occurred in March 1968, when President Johnson ordered a halt to United States bombing over most of North Vietnam and offered to begin negotiations for a peaceful settlement. Petty procedural difficulties, such as arguments over the shape of the conference table, delayed the start of talks until early 1969. Once begun, they continued inter-mittently in Paris over the next several years. In Vietnam itself, American participation in the war slowly declined. In 1969, President Nixon, in his first tele-vised address to the nation after assuming the Presidency, announced a program of "Vietnamization" of the war, a process by which South Vietnamese troops

---

[23] The attacks occurred on August 2 and August 4, 1964. The congressional resolution was offered and passed with a minimum of debate on August 7, by a vote of 414 to 0 in the House of Representatives and 88 to 2 in the Senate. Only Senators Wayne Morse, (D.-Ore.) and Ernest Gruening (D.-Alaska) opposed.

would replace American troops in "winding down" of the war. As a result of a
phased withdrawal of all American ground combat forces, fewer than forty
thousand American soldiers remained in Vietnam by the end of 1972. Concurrently, President Nixon and his chief foreign-policy adviser, Henry Kissinger,
explored many different channels (including use of Soviet and/or mainland
Chinese intermediaries) in an attempt to achieve a formal diplomatic peace
settlement. Such a settlement appeared imminent by late 1972.

The Future of Containment in the 1970s   As the preceding examples indicate,
the United States has practiced the policy of containment with almost relentless
consistency during the post–World War II period: the long and costly war in Vietnam was based on the same containment ideology as the Berlin Airlift twenty
years earlier. Today, however, many foreign-policy experts question the assumptions on which containment is based. First, there is a growing recognition that
communism is not monolithic, and that, therefore, it is not necessarily true that
any "accretion of communist influence *anywhere* must redound to the direct
benefit of . . . Moscow and Peking."[24] Hans Morgenthau, for example, has suggested that perhaps the containment of Vietnam is *not* "essential" to the interests
of the United States. It is likely, in his judgment, that the communism that would
develop there would be an independent national communism in the Yugoslavian
mold, rather than a satellite government subservient to Communist China the
Soviet Union.[25] Secondly, many critics now doubt the actual ability of the United
States to contain communism on a worldwide basis. President Nixon sounded this
theme as early as 1969, when he said that in the future the United States would
encourage Asian nations to assume more responsibility for their own defense,
and that the United States would henceforth try to "limit [its] own involvement."[26]
Thirdly, it appears that the United States no longer sees its foreign-policy options
in terms of the moral absolutes of earlier years, absolutes that in the past made
any meaningful cooperation or compromise with communist nations impossible.
In 1972, President Nixon visited mainland China, and, for the first time in more
than twenty years, some normalization of trade and tourist relationships between
the two nations now appears possible. Several months later, Nixon went to the
U.S.S.R., emerging with a significant arms-limitation treaty. Shortly thereafter,
Secretary of Commerce Peter G. Peterson announced plans for substantial expansion of trade between the United States and the Soviet Union, including
perhaps the extension of U.S.-government credits to the Soviets for the purchase
of American goods, and the granting of tariff concessions favorable to the Soviet
Union, like those extended to other nations that export goods to the United States.
 At this point, it is difficult to determine the future direction of United States
foreign policy. Although those in control of policy-making appear to be moving
away from containment, no clear-cut policy has as yet emerged to replace it.
It seems probable, however, that any new policy developed for the seventies will
no longer try to deal with communism as a monolithic whole but will instead
recognize the different levels of threat posed by the various kinds of communism
as they exist in different nations. It will also try to turn to its own advantage, in

---

[24] Townsend Hoopes, *The Limits of Intervention* (New York: McKay, 1969), p. 8.
[25] Hans Morgenthau, *A New Foreign Policy for the United States* (New York: Praeger, 1969), p. 10.
[26] *National Diplomacy: 1965–1970* (Washington, D.C.: Congressional Quarterly, 1970), p. 128.

one way or another, the major split in the communist world, between mainland China and the Soviet Union. Along with this philosophical change and the probable new direction of future policy, the United States has begun to recognize the growing importance of the Third World powers and has diminished somewhat its previous almost exclusive concern with Europe.

The Nuclear Arms Race and Mutual Deterrence

Although containment has been practiced exclusively through the use of conventional military tools – such as airplanes in Berlin; tanks, infantry, and airplanes in Korea and Vietnam; a naval blockade in Cuba; and marines in Lebanon – the United States has come to recognize that such conventional weaponry is inadequate in dealing with certain kinds of wars. The Vietnam War, for example, is a perfect illustration of an armed conflict in which conventional weapons have not been successful. Yet the United States and its enemy in Vietnam have been cautious to keep the war limited and avoid a worldwide conflagration. In pursuit of this aim, both the Soviets and the Chinese have supplied only defensive weapons to the North Vietnamese, so that the United States would not feel pressured into using anything but conventional weapons.

Many experts believe that modern war or military conflict has been kept limited because the huge stocks of nuclear arms held by the United States, the Soviet Union, and a handful of other nations have in effect created an "automatic and naked balance of terror."[27] These weapons are not merely a "quantitative extension of conventional weapons, but are qualitatively different from them,"[28] and hold destructive consequences of a nature that is both immediate (through their blast effect) and long term (through radiation fallout). If utilized, they could kill perhaps one hundred twenty million Americans or Soviets in a few afternoons of thermonuclear war.[29] Thus, in every confrontation between the U.S.S.R. and the United States in the Cold War period, each of the two nations has apparently ruled out – either tacitly or openly – the use of such weapons. In one instance in 1956, the United States refused any intervention during the anti-Soviet Hungarian Revolution on the grounds that such action might precipitate a nuclear war.

Nuclear Weapons and Foreign Policy

Once the tremendous destructive capacity of nuclear weapons is recognized, some of the traditional tools, goals, and rules of foreign policy become practically meaningless. For example, treaties and alliances no longer provide the same measure of security as before. Hans Morgenthau conceptualized this situation as follows:

In the pre-nuclear age, ally A could have been expected with a high degree of certainty to come to the aid of ally B at the risk of defeat in war. In the nuclear age, ally A cannot

---

[27] Herman Kahn, "The Missile Defense Debate in Perspective," in *Why ABM?*, edited by John J. Holst and William Schneider, Jr. (Elmsford, N.Y.: Pergamon Press, 1969), p. 292.

[28] Morgenthau, *A New Foreign Policy for the United States*, p. 207.

[29] Kissinger, *American Foreign Policy*, p. 69.

Table 16-1   **Major United States Military Installations Abroad**[1]

Location	Service	Number
Canal Zone	Army	7
	Navy	4
	Air Force	2
Germany	Army	124
	Air Force	8
Italy	Army	5
	Navy	3
	Air Force	1
Japan	Army	28
	Navy	6
	Air Force	6
South Korea	Army	52
	Air Force	2
Marianas	Navy	5
	Air Force	1
Philippines	Navy	5
	Air Force	1
Puerto Rico	Army	2
	Navy	3
	Air Force	1
Ryukyus	Army	11
	Navy	3
	Air Force	2
Spain	Navy	5
	Air Force	3
Thailand	Air Force	7
United Kingdom	Navy	4
	Air Force	8

[1] Listed here are countries with a minimum of six major United States military installations as of September 1969. The total number of major bases at that time was 340, a figure which did not include the 59 bases then in Vietnam. Other major bases were located in the Azores, Bermuda, the British West Indies, Canada, Crete, Cuba, Ethiopia, Greece, Greenland, Iceland, Libya, the Marshall Islands, Midway, Morocco, the Netherlands, Newfoundland, Pakistan, Taiwan, Turkey, and the Virgin Islands.

Source: Department of Defense.

be expected with the same degree of certainty to come to the aid of ally B at the risk of its own destruction.[30]

If one substitutes the United States for ally A and France for ally B, it becomes understandable why General Charles de Gaulle repeatedly declared that he believed all alliances in the modern world were obsolete for all practical purposes,[31] or why Henry Kissinger has commented that "the more NATO relies on strategic nuclear war as a counter to all forms of attack, the less credible its pledges will be.[32]

[30] Morgenthau, *A New Foreign Policy for the United States*, p. 234 (italics added).

[31] President de Gaulle's news conference January 14, 1963, quoted in Morgenthau, *A New Foreign Policy for the United States*, p. 235.

[32] Kissinger, *American Foreign Policy*, p. 69.

In addition to the weakening of treaty agreements, the acquisition of additional territory, often considered to be logistically valuable in prenuclear days, becomes unimportant in light of nuclear war. If one assumes that any direct conflict between the United States and the U.S.S.R. or China is likely to be an all-out war, then possession of American bases in South Vietnam or Greece, or Soviet bases in Cuba or North Vietnam becomes irrelevant because of the long-range ballistic technology each nation now possesses.

Two other concepts widely accepted in the era of conventional weapons must also be rethought in the age of nuclear capacity. The first is the current need for weapons storage: arms races were justified in prenuclear times because it appeared clear that a nation with twice as many guns, soldiers, or airplanes as its enemy was more likely to emerge victorious from any conflict. Today, however, both the United States and the U.S.S.R. possess more than enough weapons to destroy the other completely—the United States having been especially insistent in describing its "overkill" capacity—although there appears to be no rational explanation for continuing to stockpile nuclear weapons once this point has been reached. A second problem concerns the search for a way of defending oneself against the nuclear threat. In the past, sufficient quantities of defensive weapons often made it too expensive or too difficult for an aggressor to proceed indefinitely. Today, however, in an age of nuclear war, the mere quantity of defense is useless: if 90 percent of the nuclear warheads aimed at a target are destroyed by an antiballistic-missile (ABM) system, and only 10 percent succeed in reaching their target, the defender, although statistically doing a brilliant job of defense, might nevertheless find half his population destroyed by the one or two missiles that eluded the defense shield. To be successful, then, any technologically oriented defense against nuclear weapons must be practically 100 percent effective, and even the most sanguine supporters of the various ABM systems are hesitant to make such a claim.

If nuclear weapons are too dangerous to use and their very existence nullifies many of the traditional tools of conventional diplomacy and conventional war, what then is their actual role in terms of national-security policy? The answer is clear: the power of nuclear weapons lies in their deterrent force. What has actually localized recent wars such as those in the Middle East, Korea, and Vietnam (which has never actually been a declared war), and contained the Soviet Union, China, or the United States from expanding their territory has not been the conventional diplomatic and military channels outlined in the preceding section, but the mutual-deterrent effect of the nuclear threat. This threat may prove to be the most effective peace-keeping device man has ever discovered, for, as former Secretary of Defense Robert S. McNamara has said of our growing nuclear arsenal, "We are giving a possible opponent the strongest imaginable incentive to refrain from striking our own cities."[33]

National Security in a Nuclear Age

Experts emphasize that although we now have extensive nuclear capability, national-security efforts cannot deal only with nuclear capability, ignoring limited-warfare strategies and equipment. The United States must continue to prepare

[33] Quoted in Morgenthau, *A New Foreign Policy for the United States,* p. 223.

for limited wars even in a nuclear world, for if nuclear war is "unthinkable,"[34] then limited war will inevitably be the accepted medium for achieving desirable goals.[35] This is the rationale for keeping two and a half million men and women in the United States armed forces and spending billions every year on other than nuclear weapons, while at the same time stockpiling the infinitely more potent nuclear devices which can be monitored by a handful of experts.

Despite the fact that a majority of the scientists across the nation are dubious about the possibility of developing effective nuclear defenses (Herman Kahn estimated that ninety percent of those who spoke out on the subject were opposed to it[36]), the government in 1971 proceeded with elaborate antiballistic-missile programs. These ABM systems are designed to use radar to detect any nuclear warhead delivered by an enemy missile at the United States, and then to destroy it through the use of an interceptor-missile warhead exploding in the vicinity of the oncoming warhead, or, as one authority has described it, by "hitting a bullet with a bullet."[37] Work on such plans began as early as 1956. The Zeus Nike system was developed in the early 1960s as a defense against possible Soviet attack; the Sentinel system was designed in the late sixties in response to the successful firing of a thermonuclear device by the Chinese; and since then, several expensive elaborations of both systems have been undertaken.

Los Angeles Times *Syndicate, October 4, 1967*

---

[34] Herman Kahn has written on war in the nuclear age in *Thinking the Unthinkable* (New York: Avon, 1969).

[35] Morgenthau, *A New Foreign Policy for the United States,* p. 213.

[36] Kahn, "The Missile Defense Debate in Perspective," p. 295.

[37] William Schneider, Jr., "Missile Defense Systems: Past, Present, and Future," in Holst and Schneider, *Why ABM?,* p. 3.

Limitations on Nuclear Armaments Along with development and refinement
of offensive and defensive conventional and nuclear weapons, survival in the
nuclear world involves the search for nuclear arms-limitation agreements among
nations. In 1962 the United States signed a treaty with the Soviet Union banning
nuclear tests in the air, under water, and in outer space; in 1968 the United Nations
approved a treaty banning the spread of nuclear weapons to nations which did
not possess them at the time (the United States Senate ratified it in 1969); and
in 1972 President Nixon, during his visit to the U.S.S.R., concluded an arms-
control agreement with the Soviet Union placing a five-year freeze on the number
of offensive nuclear missiles possessed by both the Soviets and the United States.
The Senate approved the agreement in September of that year.

In the view of many experts, the attempts to rationalize the existence of nuclear
weapons in terms of traditional diplomatic concepts—arms limitation, elaborate
defensive shields, and the like—are worth exploring. However, it must be remembered that the cost of nuclear weapons is tremendous (the price tag for the early
Nike system alone was estimated at $20 billion),[38] and the government must
decide whether huge expenditures of this sort hold high priority and whether
the economy can handle them. In addition, there is always the danger that in its
concern with any one of these alternatives, the United States may be lulled into
a false sense of security and ignore or forget the major goal of deterrence and
the inescapable horror of nuclear war if deterrence fails.

Foreign Policy:
The President versus the Congress

According to the Constitution, the President is preeminent in the conduct of foreign
affairs, and in modern times his power has been growing, while that of Congress
has been declining. The President is Commander-in-Chief of the Armed Forces,
and he has the power, with the advice and consent of the Senate, to nominate
ambassadors and to make treaties, although the latter also requires two-thirds
approval by the Senate. To Congress is reserved the right "to declare war," "provide for the common defense," "raise and support armies," and "provide and
maintain a navy." In recent years, however, the lines have tended to blur between
congressional and presidential responsibility. In particular, the power to declare
and approve treaties, which theoretically gave the Congress, and especially the
Senate, a significant role in the conduct of foreign affairs, has become almost
irrelevant. No longer is a declaration of war necessary to commit American armed
forces or resources to foreign campaigns; every American President since World
War II has sent substantial contingents of American troops abroad without requesting such a declaration.[39] Moreover, there have been many executive arrangements between the United States and foreign governments drawn up outside the
usual treaty-making channels, and thus bypassing the Senate completely, which

---

[38] Schneider, "Missile Defense Systems," p. 6.

[39] President Truman sent troops to Korea; President Eisenhower to Lebanon; President Kennedy ordered
U. S. ships to blockade Cuba and increased the troop commitment in Southeast Asia; President Johnson
escalated the war in Vietnam to the point where 550,000 American troops were stationed there, and, in
addition, sent U. S. armed forces to the Dominican Republic. President Nixon ordered invasion of Cambodia
in 1970, and increased U.S. troop levels in other Southeast Asian nations (Cambodia, Laos) while decreasing
forces in Vietnam.

have committed the United States to extensive responsibilities abroad. The overall result has been a decline in the use of the foreign-policy prerogatives reserved to Congress, and an increase in presidential options.

There have been periods of American history in which Congress played a central role in shaping United States foreign policy. The Senate, in particular, showed its independence on numerous occasions by rejecting treaties proposed by the President,[40] including the 1920 Versailles Treaty, which contained provision that would have made the United States a member of the League of Nations. Since 1935, however, no major treaty has been defeated in the Senate, and Congress in general has confined its policy-making activities to reducing the size of the annual foreign-aid appropriations requested by the administration and to providing, from time to time, a public forum for discussion of administration policy — almost inevitably, however, after the policy has been executed. Some argue that speedy, secret presidential action is essential in today's world, and there is neither the time nor the opportunity to permit Congress to debate conditions or suggest solutions. Roger Hilsman, a former Assistant Secretary of State, gave the following example of this problem, on the basis of his own service in the Kennedy administration during the Cuban Missile Crisis of 1962:

The Soviet missiles were discovered on October 14. If it were to be effective, action had to be taken before they became operational, which was about October 26th in the case of the medium range missiles. . . . This means that President Kennedy had only a week or so to explore the alternatives and decide what to do, and it had to be done in secrecy. Most Congressmen feel that there is simply no practical way that Congress could be brought into such a decision.[41]

Other foreign-policy specialists have observed that, once decisions have been made and action taken, there is some reluctance, at least initially, to criticize, even if individual congressmen disagree with the line of action adopted by the President. Political scientist Kenneth Waltz has suggested a reason: inevitably a President's popularity increases during an international crisis, *regardless of what action he takes.* "In the face of such an event, the people rally round their chief executive,"[42] reflected Waltz. It is true that if military action taken during an emergency drags on, presidential popularity may decline substantially, but in the initial stages, when the decisions that will affect the long-range direction of United States foreign policy are first taken, it appears that public opinion will support *whatever the President does,* and congressmen, as practical politicians, hesitate to criticize in the face of such widespread popular acceptance.

Congress may also be reluctant to engage in public debate of presidential action

---

[40] Royden J. Dangerfield listed seven treaties defeated through 1928 under the two-thirds-vote rule, to which Kenneth N. Waltz added the 1935 defeat of the protocol through which the United States would have become a member of the Permanent Court of International Justice. See Kenneth N. Waltz, *Foreign Policy and Democratic Politics* (Boston: Little, Brown, 1967), p. 96.

[41] Roger Hilsman, *The Politics of Policy Making in Defense and Foreign Affairs* (New York: Harper & Row, 1971), p. 27.

[42] Waltz, *Foreign Policy and Democratic Politics,* p. 274. Waltz reached this conclusion after a study of public-opinion polls going back to President Franklin Roosevelt's administration. For example, in June of 1950, before the United States attacked Korea, polls indicated that only 37 percent of the American public approved of the way President Truman was handling his job; one month later, after the attack, 46 percent approved. Similarly, President Kennedy's popular standing reached its highest point ever, 83 percent, immediately after the Bay of Pigs fiasco in Cuba — as contrasted with an average of 70 percent during his entire time in office.

for fear that such action may be misunderstood abroad. Senator Fulbright, for example, a leading critic of administration policy in Vietnam, has admitted that "it seems reasonable to suppose that the debate on Vietnam has given the Viet-cong, the North Vietnamese, and the Chinese a distorted impression of internal divisions within the United States."[43] Moreover, even if a congressman is willing to accept this risk and wishes to take positive action to alter United States policy, there are few actions he can take. For example, although a senator may feel that a particular war is unwise, he may hesitate to end it by voting against mili-tary appropriations, for in doing so he is taking "weapons and ammunition out of the hands of men already being shot at,"[44] and to him such a measure seems rather callous and unfair. Thus, the vaunted congressional power of the purse tends to become ineffective as a realistic device to force withdrawal, once a Presi-dent has committed United States troops abroad.

Another reason for the decline of congressional power involves the fact that the President alone has access to much of the information needed to make sensible decisions: the Central Intelligence Agency, the intelligence divisions of the State Department, and the military are all executive agencies, reporting to the Presi-dent. Recognizing this reality, conscientious congressmen who might otherwise question the wisdom of a particular line of action are reluctant to do so for fear that they may be reasoning without complete knowledge of the solution. Thus, the expansion of the President's staff; the multiplication in the size, funding, and number of executive intelligence agencies; and the increasing scope and com-plexity of foreign affairs have all worked toward giving the President a virtual monopoly on information, while leaving Congress unsure of itself in times of emergency.[45]

In addition, the unique position of the President vis à vis the media should be noted. A President can preempt prime-time television and, sitting behind the imposing presidential desk against the backdrop of the Great Seal of the United States, can offer his policy in a setting that predisposes an audience toward ac-ceptance and support. Similarly, calling press conferences, dominating news-paper headlines, and making use of top-level speechwriters are all powerful means available to him. Congress, however, cannot speak in unison; opposition to the President, if it exists, is fragmented and less newsworthy. Indeed, as Theodore Roosevelt observed early in the century, the Presidency is a "bully pulpit" from which to persuade.

In brief, it appears clear that responsibility for leadership in the conduct of United States foreign affairs cannot reside to any significant extent with the Congress. The procedure through which Congress has lost almost all power was summarized by Senator J. William Fulbright, who, as a senator since 1944 and Chairman of the Senate Committee on Foreign Relations since 1959, has had a unique opportunity to observe the rise of executive dominance. The Senator has

---

[43] Fulbright, The Arrogance of Power, p. 55.

[44] Hilsman, The Politics of Policy Making in Defense and Foreign Affairs, p. 27.

[45] Robert Kennedy's description of the Cuban Missile Crisis illustrates this point. On October 16, 1962, the CIA showed the National Security Council Executive Committee photographs taken by U-2 planes of Russian missile bases under construction in Cuba. Kennedy lists the handful of men who listened to the CIA pres-entation; not a single congressman was included among the almost two dozen who had sole access to the information upon which final United States action toward the Russians was based. Robert Kennedy, Thir-teen Days (New York: Norton, 1971), pp. 2, 8.

ascribed the decline of senatorial power to the "shattering series of crises" which have characterized American relations with the rest of the world during the last twenty-five years. "The effort to cope with these," he said, "has been Executive effort, while the Congress, inspired by patriotism, importuned by Presidents, and deterred by lack of information, has tended to fall in line behind the Executive."[46]

Is Foreign Policy Made by an American Elite?

In examining who makes United States foreign policy, some observers claim that the decision-makers in the executive bureaucracy are almost exclusively drawn from the wealthy classes of America, which constitute a power elite. G. William Domhoff wrote:

. . . American foreign policy is initiated, planned, and carried out by members and organizations of a power elite that is rooted in and serves the interests of an upper class of rich businessmen and their descendants. . . . None of the factors often of importance in domestic issues — Congress, labor, public opinion — has anything but an occasional and minor effect on foreign policy. If there is one issue-area truly and solely the domain of the power elite, it is foreign policy. Given the great importance of foreign policy in determining the framework within which all types of policy-making take place, power elite dominance of this single issue-area gives them a great influence on all aspects of the political process.[47]

Domhoff then went on to describe the "most important institutions in foreign policy decision-making," noting those institutions which are clearly discernible as being used for this purpose: the National Security Council, which was formed in 1947 as part of the Executive Office of the President and used in varying ways by Presidents since that time (see Chapter 7); the Department of State; and the Department of Defense. But he also cited as "most important" other institutions not so obvious to the general public. These include "large corporations and banks, closely intertwined charitable foundations, two or three discussion and research associations financed by these corporations and foundations [such as the Carnegie, Ford, and Rockefeller Foundations] . . . and specially appointed committees of the federal government" (such as commissions and task forces).[48]

Discussed by Domhoff are the Council on Foreign Relations, a nonpartisan research and discussion group which has been called a "school for statesmen"; the Committee for Economic Development; the RAND Corporation; and some institutes affiliated with elite universities. It appears that much of United States foreign policy is thrashed out by reputed experts in quiet meetings of these organizations before it receives official status. In addition, the same wealthy industrialists, joined by an occasional college president, who dominate all these organizations serve together in government positions. They can be found in quantity in the State Department, in the Defense Department, on the National Security Council, and on government commissions. Although Domhoff has not demonstrated that these men operate solely, or even primarily, in the interests of their

---

[46] Fulbright, *The Arrogance of Power*, p. 45.

[47] See G. William Domhoff, "How the Power Elite Make Foreign Policy," in G. William Domhoff, *Higher Circles: The Governing Class in America* (New York: Vintage, 1970), pp. 111–112.

[48] Domhoff, *Higher Circles*, p. 112.

Figure 16–1 *International Affairs and Finance Outlays*

Billions of Dollars

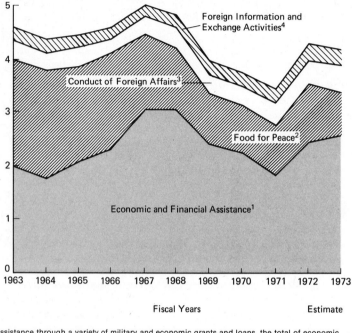

Fiscal Years   Estimate

[1] Assistance through a variety of military and economic grants and loans, the total of economic aid exceeding military aid each year. Includes multilateral and bilateral development agreements, many channeled through the Agency for International Development.
[2] The selling and donating of surplus American agricultural commodities on favorable terms to friendly nations.
[3] Operation of United States government offices abroad and annual assessed contributions to international organizations.
[4] Educational and cultural exchange activities between the United States and other countries. Includes activities of the United States Information Agency abroad.

Source: *Executive Office of the President, Office of Management and Budget,* The U.S. Budget in Brief, Fiscal Year 1973 *(Washington, D.C.: Government Printing Office, 1972), p. 47.*

corporations, he has suggested that current sociological, psychological, and economic research indicate that it would be natural for them to act in their self-interest and interpret the world from their "individual upbringing, cultural background and occupational roles."[49]

The Instruments of Foreign Policy

The State Department

The State Department is the oldest executive agency in the government. It was established in 1789 as the Department of Foreign Affairs, under an act instructing its Secretary to conduct the business of his department "in such manner as the President of the United States shall from time to time order or instruct." In theory,

[49] Domhoff, *Higher Circles,* pp. 154–155.

such a mandate should mean that there is a close working relationship between the President and the Department of State; in practice, however, most Presidents have had great difficulties in using the facilities of the State Department effectively in the conduct of foreign relations, and have tended, increasingly, to work outside its normal channels. Arthur Schlesinger, Jr., for example, reported that President Kennedy "used to divert himself with the dream of establishing a secret office of thirty people . . . to run foreign policy, while maintaining the State Department as a facade in which people might contendedly carry papers from bureau to bureau."[50]

Department Organization Some critics maintain that the problems of the State Department stem in part from its organization. At State Department headquarters in Washington, the top administrative level consists of the Secretary of State, two Under Secretaries, two Deputy Under Secretaries, and the Counselor of the Department. Each of these officers has a staff of special assistants. On the second level are five regional Assistant Secretaries (the five regions are Europe, East Asia and the Pacific, Africa, Inter-America, and the Near East and South Asia), each of whom heads up a Bureau (such as the Bureau of East Asian and Pacific Affairs) which are then further subdivided. Next down the line are the "country desks" or "teams," and in addition to this chain of command, there are about six other Assistant Secretaries and several other functional bureaus dealing with such chores as administration, legal advice, issuance of passports, education, economic affairs, intelligence, and liaison with Congress. The State Department also administers some semiautonomous agencies, which will soon be discussed, as well as the United States Mission to the United Nations and the Permanent Mission of the United States of America to the Organization of American States. Some nine thousand men and women serve abroad in the State Department. Only a handful of these people are in top, politically appointed positions, which are often given to politicians and to those who have contributed to successful presidential campaigns. For example, Arthur K. Watson, former president of IBM, was appointed ambassador to France by President Nixon. Occasionally men from academia with outstanding qualifications are appointed: President Kennedy chose Edwin O. Reischauer, an expert on Japanese culture and society from Harvard University, to be his ambassador to Japan and John Kenneth Galbraith, a Harvard economist, to be ambassador to India.

The Inefficiency of State Department Bureaucracy Critics complain that the highly structured State Department organization has resulted in built-in inefficiencies which make policy-making a tortuously slow procedure. Arthur Schlesinger, Jr., has written that "every proposal [must] run a hopelessly intricate obstacle course before it [can] become policy."[51] Obviously, some bureaucratic checks are necessary in order to run a large organization and to see that a consistent policy is being maintained. Nevertheless, some authorities argue that the State Department has become so slow-moving and unwieldy that, as George Kennan concluded, "American statesmen will have to take refuge in a

---

[50] Arthur M. Schlesinger, Jr., *A Thousand Days: John Kennedy in the White House* (Boston: Houghton Mifflin, 1965), p. 413.
[51] Schlesinger, *A Thousand Days*, p. 410.

bypassing of the regular machinery and in the creation of ad hoc devices—kitchen cabinets, personal envoys, foreign offices within foreign offices, and personal diplomacy—to assure . . . any effective diplomacy."[52]

Complaints about the inefficiency of the State Department are not new: in 1961, President Kennedy characterized the Department as a "bowl of jelly"; a quarter of a century earlier, his father, Joseph Kennedy, while United States ambassador in England, had similar complaints, insisting that "the State Department did not know what was going on . . . that nothing got to the President straight unless he sent it to the President direct."[53] The result has been a continuing commitment on the part of Presidents to the use of resources outside the State Department. President Woodrow Wilson's staff at the 1919 peace conference at Paris included some State Department people, but Secretary of State Lansing disliked the whole idea of the League of Nations, and so Wilson relied primarily on a corps of experts outside the Department, recruited by Colonel House, his personal adviser. President Franklin Roosevelt referred to United States ambassadors stationed abroad as "my" ambassadors, and encouraged them to send personal evaluations and communications directly to him in addition to their regular reports to the State Department. President Kennedy chose Robert S. McNamara, Roswell Gilpatrick, and Paul H. Nitze from the Defense Department to chair important foreign-policy task forces, and President Nixon sent Secretary of the Treasury Connally on various missions to NATO and SEATO nations, while his own specially appointed national-security adviser, Henry Kissinger, has handled most of the negotiations on ending the war in Vietnam.

Semiautonomous State Department Agencies Surprising as it may seem, only about one-fifth of the personnel in many of the larger United States embassies abroad are actually State Department officials. Joining them are large numbers of employees of semiautonomous agencies, loosely tied on paper to the State Department, but often operating quite independently. These include the Agency for International Development (AID), the Peace Corps, the United States Information Agency (USIA), and the Arms Control and Disarmament Agency (ACDA).

The *Agency for International Development,* known commonly as AID, is responsible for channeling most of the economic- and technical-assistance funds appropriated by Congress for foreign nations, and in some cases it also plays a role in administering military assistance. Many AID personnel stationed overseas work directly as technical advisers in the field, helping lower-income nations to accomplish such tasks as building roads and operating development programs in agriculture and rural health and education.

The *Peace Corps* was established by President Kennedy in 1961 in an effort to harness some of the idealism of America's youth and demonstrate this idealism to the rest of the world. The goals of the Peace Corps, from its inception, were to contribute to the development of nations whose friendship was of critical importance, to promote international cooperation and good will toward the United States, and to contribute to the education of America and to intelligent participation in the world. Sargent Shriver, the first chairman of the Peace Corps,

---

[52] Kennan as quoted in Schlesinger, *A Thousand Days,* p. 410.
[53] Schlesinger, *A Thousand Days,* p. 407.

Togo, in western Africa, is one of the nations where Peace Corps activities are carried out.

successfully fought to keep the new organization free from diplomatic and intelligence activities, a position it has maintained to this day. By 1972 the Peace Corps, a highly successful operation, had about 9000 volunteers of all ages serving in sixty countries, and its budget was $106 million.

The *United States Information Agency* (USIA), founded in 1953 as a successor to the World War II Office of War Information, operates libraries, information services, radio broadcasting (the Voice of America), and other propaganda services in over a hundred nations throughout the world. There is a USIA staff in almost every embassy, with some ten thousand employees serving abroad in all.

The *Arms Control and Disarmament Agency* (ACDA), established by President Kennedy in 1961, is responsible for research and development of arms-control devices and programs and also participates directly in international or bilateral arms-control and arms-limitation negotiations such as those that resulted in the "hot line" between Washington and Moscow, and the treaty banning use of nuclear devices in outer space.

Although these four agencies nominally operate under the aegis of the State Department, the exact nature of State Department control is sometimes difficult to ascertain, because of the size and scope of agency activities. AID, for example, has a budget that far exceeds the State Department's ($1.7 billion for AID in 1971 versus only $406 million for State), and even the USIA had almost $200 million to spend in that year. Moreover, the chiefs of these agencies often have direct access to the President: for example, Don Wilson, Deputy Director of the USIA in 1962, was a member of that inner group of the National Security Council which produced the Cuban missile-crisis policy, and similarly, the directors of AID and ACDA are usually members of top-level policy-making groups. In the past, some sensitive and controversial situations have developed out of the lack of policy-making coordination between the State Department and these agencies. During the early stages of the Hungarian uprising in 1957, for example, Voice of America broadcasts were so encouraging that they suggested to the Hungarian people that the United States might officially help them. At the same time, the State Department was working out a policy that precluded any direct American involvement.

The Central Intelligence Agency

It was not until fairly late that the United States accepted the need for a powerful and effective intelligence service. As recently as the 1920s, for example, the Secretary of State, Henry Stimson, broke up the cryptographic section of his department, declaring, "Gentlemen do not read each other's mail."[54] During World War II, President Roosevelt established the Office of Strategic Service (OSS), with responsibility for all phases of espionage, under General "Wild Bill" Donovan, but as soon as the war was over, there was considerable pressure in Washington to eliminate any such agency. In 1947, however, as part of the National Security Act, which created the National Security Council (NSC), a permanent independent intelligence organization reporting to the NSC was created. It was called the Central Intelligence Agency (CIA) and was given a virtual monopoly over the control of all government espionage activities.

The CIA's dominant position in intelligence results from the double role assumed by its director. Not only does the chief of the CIA control all of the Agency's intelligence activities, but he also sits simultaneously as the chairman of the United States Intelligence Board and in this capacity operates the intelligence branches of the State Department, the FBI, and the military, as well as the CIA. The resources of the CIA are formidable: estimates of its annual budget are about two billion dollars,[55] and, when necessary, it operates its own military-training centers, airplanes, pilots, naval vessels, and radio transmitters. In Washington, the CIA staff assigned to cover a particular nation may be larger than that available to the State Department: Roger Hilsman has mentioned, for example, that at one time the CIA had six persons working on its sensitive Laos desk, while the State Department had only three.[56] The Agency may also have more operatives stationed abroad in a particular post; moreover, because it is not subject to the same rotation requirements as the State Department, CIA officials may develop closer, longer-term relationships with the local power establishment. As a result of this flexibility, some have claimed that the CIA was responsible for the overthrow of President Ngo Dinh Diem in South Vietnam and that it may well have dabbled in the internal politics of a number of countries.

For a long time, the CIA had tremendous political appeal and great support in Congress, similar to that enjoyed by the FBI and earned as a result of capable

---

[54] Hilsman, *The Politics of Policy Making in Defense and Foreign Affairs,* p. 56.

[55] Hilsman, *The Politics of Policy Making in Defense and Foreign Affairs,* p. 63.

[56] Hilsman, *The Politics of Policy Making in Defense and Foreign Affairs,* p. 63. Hilsman also mentioned that the CIA pays better salaries than the State Department.

staff, good administration, and innovative activity. In fact, the first two men that President Kennedy believed it necessary to carry over into his new administration in 1960 were Directors J. Edgar Hoover of the FBI and Allen W. Dulles of the CIA. The CIA, however, has recently had many critics. One reason for the criticism was the series of fiascos attributed to it. In 1960, for example, it was the CIA's decision to send a U-2 high-altitude photographic "spy plane" over the Soviet Union just before a scheduled summit conference between President Eisenhower and Chairman Nikita Khrushchev.[57] It was also instrumental in planning the unsuccessful Golfo de Cocheros (Bay of Pigs) invasion.[58] More serious, however, was a growing feeling that the CIA was not merely functioning as an intelligence tool, but was moving increasingly into the area of policy-making. In a book published in 1964, the charge was made that there were "two governments in the United States today," one visible, the other invisible, and that this invisible government (the CIA), with a "quasi-independent status and a power of its own" was often working secretly "in just the opposite direction" of the publicly announced government policies, even, perhaps, against the wishes of the President himself.[59]

Major efforts to limit CIA power were taken by President Kennedy. Early in his administration he sent a letter to all ambassadors giving them top authority to "oversee and coordinate all activities of the US Government" in their countries, including the activities of the CIA. After the Bay of Pigs, Robert Kennedy was assigned as an informal presidential watchdog over all espionage activities, and the President also made some tentative stabs at reducing the CIA budget.[60] In addition, Allen Dulles, who had headed the Agency since its inception, was replaced by John McCone, a more cautious, self-effacing individual, and at least some progress was made in reducing the scope of CIA activities. Realistically, however, it must be recognized that national security requires not only armies and navies, but also intelligence agencies; that secrecy is essential to intelligence operations, and that the line between carrying out policy and creating policy may become blurred when zealous men operate under conditions of danger where speed and decisiveness are essential. For this reason, it appears that the CIA will continue to operate very much as it has in the past, despite the risks such an "invisible government" presents to an open, democratic society. As recently as 1966 the Senate recognized this reality and killed a bill proposing the creation of a formal watchdog committee to oversee the CIA.

The Military

There is a fundamental American conviction, written into the Constitution, that the military must always be under civilian control. Thus the military establishment in the United States should be restricted to carrying out policies developed

---

[57] The plane was shot down, and in the resulting hard feelings, the summit meeting was canceled.

[58] A force of about 1500 anti-Castro Cubans, trained and equipped by the CIA, was routed by Cuban forces when they attempted a landing on the island. For a full discussion of this crisis see Schlesinger, *A Thousand Days*, pp. 233–266.

[59] See David Wise and Thomas B. Ross, *The Invisible Government* (New York: Random House, 1964), as quoted in Hilsman, *The Politics of Policy Making in Defense and Foreign Affairs*, p. 60.

[60] Schlesinger, *A Thousand Days*, pp. 426–428. Schlesinger also noted that after the Bay of Pigs fiasco Kennedy relied more on foreign-policy generalists than on specialists from the Departments of State and Defense. In this way he hoped to get a better balance of ideas.

by other branches of the government. Realistically, however, most foreign-policy decisions today involve military considerations, and some sort of military advice is therefore essential in reaching them. For this reason the choice of military advisers and the channels through which their advice reaches top civilian policy-makers becomes an important factor in how national-security policy is made.

Civilian control of the military rests in the President and the Secretary of Defense. The Joint Chiefs of Staff, who are military men, and the civilian secretaries of each of the services (Army, Navy, and Air Force) serve under the Secretary of Defense. Within the Department of Defense, a tradition of strong civilian leadership has developed, reflecting in part the outstanding caliber of some of the men who have filled the top post. The first Secretary, James V. Forrestal, who served in Truman's Cabinet, had wide experience in both business and foreign affairs and had drafted the original plans which established the single Department of Defense; Robert S. McNamara, who served in the Kennedy and Johnson Cabinets, was President of the Ford Motor Company before assuming the post; and Melvin Laird, Nixon's appointee, had been a forceful and powerful member of the House. In spite of the strength of these civilian leaders, the power of the military men as opposed to civilians has always been formid-

In September 1963, Vietnam was already a serious problem to be weighed by President John F. Kennedy, Secretary of Defense Robert S. McNamara, and General Maxwell Taylor, then Chairman of the Joint Chiefs of Staff.

able, and in a nation where 40 percent of the national budget is spent by the military, this power represents a continuing threat to other institutions of government.

The Roots of Military Power   The actual power of the military in connection with national-security issues emanates in part from its broad constituency.[61] Various elements of the public and of Congress tend to equate patriotism with support of the military and will therefore rally behind any suggestions put forth by it. In addition, the armed forces have many allies in business (see Chapter 15 for a discussion of the military-industrial complex), who have a natural interest in supporting them. In many ways, however, it is the full potential of the military, unused to date, which is most frightening, for since the armed forces have legal control of most of the weapons within our society, there is always the fear that a strong military man will appear, and, backed by the military establishment, take over the nation. The American public's admiration for military figures is evidenced by the number of Presidents who have been generals and by the great adoration accorded men like Generals Douglas MacArthur and Dwight D. Eisenhower. The fear that these men will become too powerful is not a new one, nor is it confined only to the United States. Julius Caesar, Napoleon, and Gamal Abdel Nasser, to name only a few historical figures, have managed to subvert the loyalties of the armed forces within which they served and overthrow their countries' legitimate governments. The fear that military force will be used against the societies they are sworn to defend is one that every democratic society faces.

Civilian control of the military is designed to fight such threats. It is difficult, however, to devise any system through which the principle of civilian supremacy can be insured under all conditions. Basically, it depends on the general attitudes of the society and the military men, and how the military sees its role vis à vis the entire community. The United States, to date, has been lucky on both counts. A healthy suspicion of the military, a feeling that it may be too nationalistic, aggressive, and undemocratic, has always existed. The American antimilitary tradition goes back to the nineteenth century, and most historians attribute it to the fact that the country was geographically isolated by two oceans and did not need strong military forces. Furthermore, the experiences of American immigrants, now parents and grandparents in the United States, before they came to this country have led to much suspicion of the military. Many of these people had either served in the military or suffered at its hands, and most of them had seen destruction in Europe. Thus there are many in America who may be reluctant to support militarism and the military hero.

The United States Army has attracted good military men. The officer corps has always been drawn from a wide base, and not from an aristocracy, as, for example, was the case with the Prussian military elite in Germany. Moreover, because West Point appointments are made by congressmen, wide geographic representation is insured, and the military does not have the opportunity to perpetuate a particular type or class, as part of the selection process is out of its hands. Perhaps most important, however, is the American tradition that its

---

[61] The discussion of military power and the maintenance of civilian control are drawn from Hilsman, *The Politics of Policy Making in Defense and Foreign Affairs*, pp. 49–56.

"Are other countries allowed to do things for reasons of overriding national security?"

New Yorker, *December 4, 1971*

military-officer corps should be apolitical and reflect the ethics and mores of society at large, not a special military mentality.[62]

There is much to suggest, then, that our system has been successful in preserving respect for American democratic traditions and values and discouraging a national military mentality. Nevertheless, recently Americans have become increasingly aware of the vast power the military can wield without being held unaccountable to any branch of government. First, the Pentagon Papers indicated the military's success in selling four Presidents on the wisdom of committing United States resources to major military involvements against the judgment of many of the top civilian advisers. Then, again, in 1972, reports from Vietnam indicated that Air Force General John D. Lavelle had ordered bombing missions against targets outside those authorized by President Nixon. In addition to these particular instances there has been some evidence to suggest that the size of the military has enabled it to form its own standards of justice, not up to the standards of the civilian society. Military training and military punishment can be brutal and unjust. In 1969 an article appeared which described rioting and brutalities—much of it directed against racial minorities—in a California Marine Corps prison. The major source for the article was the testimony of a former prison doctor which had appeared in a leaked official memo. Revelations such as this one call attention to the fact that America may indeed have a military

---

[62] Hilsman, *The Politics of Policy Making in Defense and Foreign Affairs*, p. 52.

standard different from its civilian standard.[63]

All of these experiences indicate that the power of the military has grown tremendously in the United States; the Vietnam War even suggests that it may have gotten out of control of the Commander-in-Chief. One of the continuing problems of the future, then, will be how civilians can keep the military in check in a world in which the military is essential to national security.

The United States and the Third World

Preoccupation with the containment of communism has been the major goal of United States foreign policy since World War II. As a result, the United States has not been greatly concerned with the Third World—those ninety or so nations which are not closely aligned with either the United States and its allies or the Second World of the Sino-Soviet Bloc[64]—and routinely has allocated only small amounts of economic and military aid to it. The only occasions on which Third World nations have been able to attract significant United States attention have been the times they appeared to be on the verge of joining the communist camp. When such threats materialized, either through external attack (South Korea), internal political change (Lebanon), or a combination of the two (Vietnam), there has been a sizable infusion of United States concern, money, arms, and troops. Driven by an overriding concern to prevent the spread of communism, the United States has often found itself aligned with the most reactionary elements within a country.[65] As a result, America's image in the Third World has suffered.

Although the Third World today consists of mostly poor and industrially underdeveloped nations, it contains the bulk of the world's population and thus it may very likely hold economic and military importance in the future. With this fact in mind, some experts maintain that the United States has erred in concentrating its primary foreign-policy efforts in Europe, giving only a peripheral and occasional glance at the Third World. Even in cases in which the United States has formed relationships with Third World nations, many critics question the nature and viability of these international bonds.

The Nature of the Third World

Third World nations, although they differ in many ways, share certain characteristics. Most of them were at one time colonies. Some, such as many African nations, have only recently gained independence.[66] Others, such as most South

---

[63] See Robert G. Sherrill, ''The Pendleton Brig: Andersonville-by-the-Sea,'' *The Nation* (September 15, 1969), pp. 239–242.

[64] The term ''Sino-Soviet bloc'' is a misnomer, implying as it does a unity of interests between the Soviets and the Chinese, who since the late 1960s have been bitter enemies and rivals. However, many political scientists continue to use it as a catch-all phrase for the major communist nations and their allies.

[65] Events in Korea, Taiwan, the Dominican Republic, Peru, Pakistan, and Vietnam all provide examples of occasions when the United States has supported governments opposed by the more liberal local elements.

[66] Between 1959 and 1969, thirty-two countries, covering five-sixths of the African continent, achieved their independence.

American countries, have been independent for many years. As a result of their common colonial past, Third World nations are vehemently anticolonialist. In addition, because they are generally nonwhite nations that have been subjugated by whites, they all take a strong stand against racial discrimination. They also share a common economic condition: they are largely nonindustrial and very poor, with economies based either on subsistence agriculture or on the raising, gathering, or mining for export of a single commodity such as cocoa, tin, fish meal, rubber, or coffee. As such, these countries are too poor to accumulate the large amounts of capital, raised in more highly developed areas through savings and taxation, needed to become more industrialized by building electric plants, roads, or manufacturing facilities. At the same time, other problems, such as social unrest, internal conflicts between ethnic or religious groups, and the coexistence of small enormously wealthy elites with vast poverty-stricken masses provide an unstable political climate which frightens away private investors from abroad. The Third World nations need outside assistance if they are to achieve economic progress, and since this help will probably not be available through the usual private channels, they must depend either on international sources, such as the various United Nations–sponsored economic-aid organizations, or on bilateral agreements with individual foreign nations.

Although there are many similarities among Third World nations, there are also conflicts and differences of view among them. At the United Nations, for example, except on those issues involving obvious questions of colonialism or racial discrimination, such as sanctions against apartheid policies in Rhodesia

Mrs. Indira Gandhi (second from left) greeted President and Mrs. Nixon in 1969 when they visited India, largest of the Third World nations and the one to which the rest of the Third World looks for guidance.

or South Africa, they rarely vote as a bloc.[67] The African nations, for instance, were split over the issue of United Nations action during the civil wars in the Congo and Nigeria; and the various Third World nations took opposite sides in UN attempts to settle the disputes between India and Pakistan over Kashmir in 1952 and 1965, and in the Pakistani Civil War of 1971, when India went to the assistance of Pakistan's rebellious eastern province, now the separate nation of Bangladesh. One of the sensitive issues among these nations includes the relationship between the Asians who have settled over the years in Africa and the native Africans themselves; in 1972, for example, Uganda ordered most of its Indian and Pakistani inhabitants to leave the country in ninety days. There are also border disputes between neighbors, such as the Algeria-Morocco and Ghana-Togo disputes, and hard feelings arising from competition to sell the same commodities in world markets.

The absence of harmony within the Third World must be emphasized because of the recurring notion, frequently expressed at high government levels, that perhaps the guiding principle behind United States policy toward the Third World should be the fear that they some day will unite in a battle against us. Such reasoning has occasionally been used to justify United States foreign aid, although considering both the poverty and the diversity of interests among Third World nations, this risk does not appear great at the present time. But the Third World countries may find it advantageous to bind themselves closer. Imamu Amari Baraka (Le Roi Jones), a black militant and poet, has encouraged blacks in America to unite with brothers and sisters in the Third World. Together they comprise well over half of the world's population, and, if effectively aligned, they could be a powerful world force.

The Major Powers and the Third World

In describing the overall relationship between the major powers and the Third World, it is necessary to examine the situation from the points of view of both America and the Communist Bloc. The major powers have attempted in various ways to cultivate the good will (if not the close alliance) of those nations that make up the Third World. Confronted with these attempts, the Third World countries have "picked [their] way through the advantages offered by [each of] the . . . major powers . . . ,"[68] moving warily so as not to forfeit good relations with either side, and striving at all costs to maintain their nonaligned status. Some Third World nations have proved particularly adept at this technique and have placed themselves in the position of graciously accepting help from both sides simultaneously. In Afghanistan, for example, the Soviet Union was busy paving the streets of the capital city, Kabul, while the United States built the Afghans a hydroelectric plant.[69] Other countries, because of their difficult politi-

---

[67] For a discussion of the Third World in the United Nations see J. D. B. Miller, *Politics of the Third World* (New York: Oxford University Press, 1967), pp. 18–42.

[68] Miller, *Politics of the Third World*, p. 65.

[69] Hans Morgenthau distinguished the types of aid the major powers give to Third World nations, placing the Soviet aid in the instance of Afghanistan in the category of prestige aid, offering quick political results, and the American aid in the category of aid for economic development, which offers slower results. See Morgenthau, *A New Foreign Policy for the United States*, pp. 88–106.

cal situations, have relied too heavily on the aid of only one superpower. The Vietnam War, with its attendant destruction, has provided a valuable lesson to many smaller Afro-Asian states in the dangers of accepting too much help from one of the major powers.

The exact basis of the arrangement between Third World nations and major powers has varied according to the major power involved. Former colonialist states such as France, England, and the Netherlands have in many ways remained on close terms with their former colonies because of the social and economic ties that persist. England, for example, offers trade advantages to members of the Commonwealth, countries which at one time were British colonies. In most former French colonies, French is still spoken and thus a natural link exists between France and these nations.

Communist states, never having been colonial powers, claim a special relationship with the Third World. They assert they are free from the colonial economic and governmental ties and the discrimination which characterized the French and British experiences in Africa and Asia. During the early years of the Cold War, Soviet efforts to win Third World friends were hampered by an ideological reluctance to help Third World nations not already under control of orthodox Communist parties. Rapidly, however, the Soviet Union moved to a more realistic position in which it was willing to support any government which, although noncommunist, followed policies acceptable to the Soviets, and it was under these ground rules that support to such obviously noncommunist leaders as Jawaharlal Nehru of India and Gamal Abdel Nasser of Egypt ensued.[70] The U.S.S.R. now provides trade concessions, military assistance, and technical aid to its friends (it bought Egyptian cotton, provided the Egyptian air force with airplanes, and built the Aswan Dam). In addition the Soviet Union occasionally executes a brilliant propaganda coup, such as the establishment of the Patrice Lumumba Friendship Institute in Moscow.[71]

In recent years, however, the Soviets have been stiffly rivaled by the Chinese. The Chinese argue that as non-Europeans they have a special claim to the friendship of the Third World. In addition, they contend that they are better prepared to understand and help developing nations because the economic conditions in China are closer to those of Third World nations than are the already developed conditions of the Soviet economy. Lastly, China criticizes the ideological ambiguity of the Soviet Union, accusing it of being more interested in coexisting with the United States than in fostering the revolutionary struggle for world communism. Chinese influence has been successful to some extent in various African countries, including Tanzania and Burundi, where it has gained a foothold through the use of technical, economic, and military aid. In fact, latest statistics show that China has negotiated or renewed aid or trade agreements with twenty-four African nations.[72] The success of these efforts in wooing the Third World can be seen in the large number of Third World nations that supported the admittance of the People's Republic of China to the United Nations in 1971.

---

[70] See Miller, *Politics of the Third World,* pp. 49–55, for a discussion on the transformation of Soviet foreign policy.

[71] Lumumba was the first Prime Minister of the Congo when it achieved its independence in 1960; at the time, he was a charismatic figure throughout Africa.

[72] The *New York Times* (September 4, 1972), p. 2.

The Role of the United States in the Third World

Because the United States was itself a former colony and successfully fought a revolution which established its independence, for many years Third World countries believed that the United States supported their common goals. As early as 1956, however, Tom Mboya of Kenya described the growing feeling of "puzzled disappointment" felt by Africans as they compared the actual policies of the United States against its claim to represent the spirit of the anticolonial movement.[73] It is easy to understand Mboya's disenchantment when the objectives of United States policy during the Cold War period are considered: in dealing with the Third World, just as in dealing with every other foreign nation, the primary concern of the United States has been to insure its own national security through the containment of communism, almost without regard to what the side effects might be. Often a side effect has been the support of the conservative elements in foreign revolutionary struggles, a fact that most current Third World leaders cannot condone. In addition, United States intervention in the internal affairs of Third World nations such as Lebanon, the Dominican Republic, and Vietnam has hurt America's reputation, for while our leaders saw United States involvement in Vietnam as an attempt to stop the spread of worldwide communism, many Third World leaders saw it as merely an example of unwarranted American interference.

Nor have American economic activities in the Third World been totally successful. This deficiency is partially due to the fact that the United States has tried to do too much in too many places with too little money. During the period when American foreign-aid expenditures were at their highest levels (1954–1962), the Soviet aid program involved only a total of 24 countries, with seven receiving most of the help. The United States was busy extending economic help in one form or another to 104 countries.[74] Moreover, the actual amounts of aid received by individual countries from the United States, although large in an absolute sense, have tended to be fairly small in terms of the overall economy of each recipient nation. Aid in 1961, totaling 1.9 percent of India's Gross National Product, 2.5 percent of Colombia's, and 2.3 percent of Pakistan's, represents typical amounts of United States assistance. Two countries, South Korea and South Vietnam, were both recipients of unusually large amounts of aid because of extraordinary problems; they received help representing significant proportions of their total GNPs, 16.8 percent and 12.3 percent respectively.[75] Considering these statistics, it is probably unrealistic for the United States to expect that its modest efforts will guarantee totally friendly and supportive foreign policy from the recipient nations.

Recently, some observers, both American and foreign, have raised additional questions about American economic policy toward the Third World. The Prebisch Thesis (named for the Argentinian economist who developed it) hypothesized that during the post–World War II period, despite all the help from eager suitors on both sides, the Third World has made little economic progress, and that, in

---

[73] Rupert Emerson, *Africa and United States Policy* (Englewood Cliffs, N. J.: Prentice-Hall, 1967), p. 104.

[74] Waltz, *Foreign Policy and Democratic Politics,* p. 190.

[75] Waltz, *Foreign Policy and Democratic Politics,* p. 194.

"I wonder what Rice Krispies taste like?"

Saturday Review, *March 18, 1972*

fact, the gap between the major economically advanced nations and the Third World has actually widened.[76] The Thesis also asserts that certain very specific United States activities have been directly responsible for this gap. One socialist expert claims that a capitalist nation such as the United States has no choice but to exploit the Third World if it wishes to maintain its own prosperity. Because the United States needs raw materials, investment opportunities, and the markets provided by Third World nations, it has structured its economic-aid policies so as to insure that these are available to it on favorable terms.[77] Such a rationale would explain United States reluctance to channel aid through international organizations, preferring instead to use bilateral arrangements. It would also explain the United States' desire to maintain control of world credit facilities, its reluctance to establish favorable tariff and quota arrangements, and its willingness to support any government in the Third World which is prepared to protect American business within its borders, regardless of the desires of local citizens.

Such a view of the economic relationship of the United States with the Third World would be considered too radical by many observers. However, even more conservative observers agree that we do not have "much to show for [our] expenditures and efforts either in the economic development of the [Third World] . . .

---

[76] See Raul Prebisch, *Towards a New Trade Policy for Development* (New York: United Nations Publishers, 1964).

[77] See Harry Magdoff, *The Age of Imperialism: The Economics of U. S. Foreign Policy* (New York: Monthly Review Press, 1969).

or in political advantages to [ourselves],"[78] and that after twenty-five years of containment politics accompanied by foreign aid, we have managed only to exhaust much of the reservoir of good feeling with which we entered the Cold War. It is, therefore, encouraging that there are now indications that policy changes may be under way. Many foreign-aid programs are being restructured so as to permit recipients to use the funds more independently and effectively. In 1969, for example, President Nixon lifted restrictions on AID dollars lent to Latin American countries so that these dollars no longer had to be spent in the United States (where prices might be higher) but could be used anywhere in Latin America,[79] and on various occasions the President has indicated his desire to channel American aid increasingly through multilateral or international agencies.[80]

The United States appears to be reaching toward a new interpretation of the communist threat, one which would decrease the pressure exerted by the United States on those Third World nations which are developing indigenous communist governments. It is intriguing to speculate about what effects friendlier U.S.-Soviet and U.S.-Chinese relationships, established since President Nixon's journeys to those countries, will have on the Third World. Will the détente among the major powers mean that they will no longer feel obliged to compete for Third World good will through foreign aid? Much, of course, depends on attitudes and events in the Sino-Soviet world. But it is hoped that the détente will mark the beginnings of more effective joint efforts to assist developing nations in ways the Third World nations find beneficial and which, in the long run, will serve the world community.

SUGGESTED READINGS

Barnet, Richard J. *The Economy of Death* (New York: Atheneum, 1969). In paperback. Barnet examines the defense budget to see what the taxpayer has gotten for his more than one-trillion–dollar investments (since 1946) and demonstrates how the public has been consistently shortchanged. He argues that the military-industrial complex wastefully and irrationally sets national priorities and undermines America's capacity to solve its real problems. He offers a political strategy for shifting from an economy of death to an economy of life.

Chomsky, Noam. *American Power and the New Mandarins* (New York: Random House, 1967). In paperback. A collection of political and historical essays which point the way to a new analysis of America's present course. Chomsky examines the dual role of American liberal intellectuals in representing a society with incomparable wealth and power while at the same time sharing in the use of that power. He shows how these new mandarins construct an ideology that justifies their claim to power, and reinterpret both past and present to support that claim.

Emerson, Rupert. *Africa and United States Policy* (Englewood Cliffs, N. J.: Prentice-Hall, 1967). In paperback. An examination of the highly complex, diverse, and even contradictory relations between the United States and African governments. Emerson discusses past Afro-American relations, United States interests and activities in Africa, potentially

---

[78] Morgenthau, *A New Foreign Policy for the United States,* p. 110.

[79] See President Nixon's remarks at the annual meeting of the Inter-American Press Association, October 31, 1969, as reprinted in *National Diplomacy,* pp. 125–127.

[80] *National Diplomacy,* p. 18.

troublesome issues and areas, and future courses that African governments may pursue. Throughout, the author emphasizes that Afro-American relations have taken on almost totally new dimensions in the last decade with the demise of colonialism in Africa.

Fulbright, J. William. *The Pentagon Propaganda Machine* (New York: Random House, 1971). In paperback. In an expanded version of a series of speeches given on the Senate floor in December 1969, Senator Fulbright illustrates the multifaceted and quietly pervasive nature of the Defense Department's public-relations activity. He discusses the threats that such militarism poses for democracy and argues that Americans must halt and then turn back the incursions the military has made into the United States' civilian political system.

Galbraith, John Kenneth. *Ambassador's Journal* (New York: New American Library, 1970). In paperback. As John F. Kennedy's ambassador to India, Galbraith kept a journal which also includes some letters he wrote to the President outside of his official duties. In addition to Galbraith's likes and dislikes, wittily described, he offers insights into the job of filling important posts between election and inauguration, relations between the man in the field and the bureaucracy at home (in this case, the highly typical Department of State), and the personal diplomacy of visits to India by First Lady Jacqueline Kennedy and Vice President Lyndon Johnson.

Hilsman, Roger. *The Politics of Policy Making in Defense and Foreign Affairs* (New York: Harper & Row, 1971). In paperback. Hilsman examines foreign and defense policy-making and establishes a theory of policy-making as a political process. He discusses the functions and powers of the President, Congress, the military, the CIA, the State Department, the press, interest groups, and the electorate in this process and concludes by suggesting how policy making might be improved.

Hoffman, Stanley. *Gulliver's Troubles or the Setting of American Foreign Policy* (New York: McGraw-Hill, 1968). In paperback. An examination of the constraints, particularly domestic, on United States policy in Atlantic affairs and its significance for future policy. The author examines the present international system as a whole, the domestic setting of American policy, and the impact of the former on political relations between the United States and its European allies. He tries to determine what the United States, with its enormous power, can attempt and expect to achieve in the Atlantic area, given the kind of nation it is and the way the world is.

Kahn, Herman. *On Thermonuclear War* (New York: The Free Press, 1969). In paperback. A sober examination of the military side of what the author believes may be the major problem that faces civilization—namely, the threat of thermonuclear war. The author adopts the systems-analysis point of view and employs quantitative analysis wherever possible to examine the probability, consequences, and possibilities of deterrence of a thermonuclear catastrophe.

Kennedy, Robert F. *Thirteen Days: A Memoir of the Cuban Missile Crisis* (New York: Norton, 1969). In paperback. An eyewitness account written by President John F. Kennedy's late brother, at that time Attorney General of the United States, describing the 1962 Caribbean confrontation between two atomic powers, which brought the world to the edge of the nuclear abyss. Kennedy traces the events that occurred during those days of crisis, describes the personalities involved, and provides insights into the executive decision-making process in the United States. He also probes the awesome responsibility and moral burden of two super-nations holding the fate of the world in their hands.

Kissinger, Henry A. *American Foreign Policy: Three Essays* (New York: Norton, 1969). In paperback. A volume of essays in which the author examines the framework of United States foreign policy, the stresses to which that framework is being subjected, and the prospects for world order in an era of high international tension. He argues that overwhelming military strength in a nuclear age is no guarantee that a nation can act with decisiveness on the international stage, and he uses the American involvement in Vietnam to illustrate this point.

Magdoff, Harry. *The Age of Imperialism: The Economics of United States Foreign Policy* (New York: Monthly Review Press, 1969). In paperback. In response to the escalation of the war in Vietnam, the author analyzes the United States as a major capitalist economic power in the world today. He demonstrates the falsity in the assumption that United States foreign policy is isolationist, and he identifies a close parallel between aggressive American foreign policy aimed at controlling as much of the globe as possible, and the energetic international expansionist policy of American business. His point is that imperialism is not a matter of choice, but rather a way of life, for a capitalist nation.

Miller, J. D. B. *The Politics of the Third World* (New York: Oxford University Press, 1967). In paperback. An examination of the countries of Asia and Africa which are not currently under the control of Europeans and do not have communist governments. The essay is concerned with international behavior and those aspects of a state's domestic affairs that contribute to its foreign policy. The author argues that, although these nations have created the impression of a common political front, political agreement and unity have neither been shown in past practice nor are likely to reveal themselves in the future.

Morgenthau, Hans J. *A New Foreign Policy for the United States* (New York: Praeger, 1969). In paperback. An examination of United States foreign policy—its objectives, its principles, and the assumptions about the world on which it has been formed—by one of the world's most distinguished professors of international politics. Morgenthau's purpose is to contribute to the development of an empirical and conceptual framework from which the outlines of a new and relevant policy may be constructed. He argues that America may be doomed unless it radically reorients its thinking to the world as it actually is in the 1970s.

Parenti, Michael. *The Anti-Communist Impulse* (New York: Random House, 1969). In an examination of American ideology, the author inquires into the origins, the development, and the domestic and overseas manifestations of American anticommunism, as well as the cultural predispositions leading to it. Disturbed at what anticommunists do in the name of freedom, he explains how the United States' obsession with anticommunism has warped its commitments to freedom and prosperity, immobilized its efforts to remedy national ills, and caused the pursuit of a foreign policy that has led to the death and maiming of thousands of persons, Americans and others.

EPILOGUE: PROSPECTS FOR POLITICAL CHANGE

Many observers felt that the landslide victory for Nixon in 1972 indicated not so much that the majority of Americans were unaware of the need for change, as that they feared what would happen if change took place too rapidly. For almost two hundred years the political system established by the Constitution has operated tolerably well. But a feeling is growing that the nation's problems have gotten out of hand and that the government, within its present structure, is incapable of solving them. A deteriorating environment, inequality and injustice, racism and war, a breakdown of the old social and moral values, alienation and boredom, all seem to plague the United States in the midst of material affluence.

Several problems of government in the United States that have been cited repeatedly in this book are related to the broader ills facing American society today. One such problem concerns representation. The decline in the power of the Legislative branch at all levels of government has made it difficult for the people to exert a significant influence on public policy. This situation raises important questions concerning how to achieve representative government in an age of executive and bureaucratic domination.

A second problem is related to democratic theory and the realities of political life in a modern industrialized society. The classical ideal holds that all citizens, or at least a majority of them, should be well informed about issues, interested and willing to participate in politics, and able to make rational decisions concerning candidates and policies. Such an ideal, however, is far from an accurate description of how the American electorate actually behaves. Voters, it is argued, are concerned more with personalities than with issues. As Adlai Stevenson once commented, ". . . to the extent we must unavoidably get into issues at all we like to weave them all into a single sort of brightly colored cloak which will fit each man completely and distinguish him clearly from his competitors."[1] The inability to implement the classical ideal of democracy has had dysfunctional consequences for American democracy and has contributed to elitism in American government.

A third problem of government in the United States concerns political ideology. Liberalism, which for almost half a century has been the dominant American political ideology, now faces a crisis of major dimensions. Liberal government programs have fallen far short of their intended goals. The failure has left America adrift, in search of a new ideology to replace the now-questioned ideals of liberalism.

Proposals for Constitutional Reform

As America approaches its bicentennial celebration, many thoughtful people are talking about constitutional reform as a political solution to the difficulties of American society in the modern world. Although many illnesses of modern society cannot be cured by political remedies, those that might respond to such treatment are frequently prevented from doing so by the obsolete machinery of government established by an eighteenth-century constitution. The American Constitution has undergone few changes in the last two centuries, its twenty-six amendments having done little to alter our basic political institutions. This fact

---

[1] Statement by Stevenson made in 1956, quoted in the *New York Times* (November 7, 1972), p. 35.

is remarkable in view of the responsibilities of modern government—ranging from moon exploration to Medicare, and undreamed of by the Framers of the Constitution.

If a constitutional convention were called today, it would be drastically different from the one held in Philadelphia in 1787, but the focus, as when the Framers met, would be on where to delegate power most effectively within a democratic framework and in the light of a rapidly changing society. It is impossible to tell what kind of constitution might emerge. The essential debate, however, would probably take place between those who want a stronger federal government, although not necessarily more power for the Chief Executive, and those seeking more local control.

Most proposals for changing the Constitution have dealt merely with parts of it. Few have approached the scope of those offered by Rexford Guy Tugwell and his co-workers at the Center for the Study of Democratic Institutions.[2] The proposed Tugwell constitution, a highly detailed model for a fundamentally new framework of government, has attracted considerable attention. Tugwell, a member of Franklin D. Roosevelt's original "brain trust" and Governor of Puerto Rico, has spent much time and effort on the study of constitutional reform.

The Tugwell proposals give the central government far more power and unity than it has now. Tugwell suggests that the states be replaced by "republics" (each with no more than 5 percent of the total population) having less power than the present state governments; his plan also favors giving more power to the federal government. The Tugwell proposals would change the structure and function of the present three branches of government—Legislative, Executive, and Judicial—and create an Electoral branch, a Planning branch, and a Regulatory branch. The Regulatory branch would take away the President's authority over the bureaucracy and leave him to concentrate his efforts instead on foreign-policy matters and domestic affairs. Among other changes, Tugwell proposes a national convention to nominate presidential candidates for a single, nine-year term.

Tugwell and his co-workers assume that their proposals offer the best ways to deal with problems now facing the country. In short, his model constitution may be called a planner's dream, for, through it, planners like Tugwell would be given extensive power to apply what Walter Lippmann has termed a strong public philosophy to try to change the direction of our lives.[3]

Are Americans ready for such extreme changes in the structure of government? The 1972 presidential election showed that, if anything, they are in a mood for only cautious change. According to a late 1972 poll conducted by Daniel Yankelovich, 40 percent of Americans, divided equally between Democrats and Republicans, saw themselves as "conservative." The year before, only 25 percent described themselves in this way.[4] It seems, therefore, that unless there is a sudden and marked reversal of the trend, Americans would reject such fundamental changes as those embodied in the Tugwell proposals. In the unlikely event of a new constitutional convention, however, Tugwell's proposals or others similar to them would probably be introduced into the debate.

---

[2] Rexford Guy Tugwell, *Model for a New Constitution* (Palo Alto, Calif.: James E. Freel Associates, 1970).

[3] Walter Lippmann, *The Public Philosophy* (Boston: Little, Brown, 1955).

[4] *Time* (November 20, 1972), p. 14.

We might speculate further that other proposals for a new constitution would take the opposite direction. For example, those who favor community control and are against bureaucracy might draft a constitution that greatly limits the powers of the national government and establishes small community units as the basis for the representative system.

Many questions directly related to current problems would be brought to the floor of a new constitutional convention. Should the President have the right to order any military engagement that might result in an undeclared war? Is the existing process of constitutional amendment too cumbersome? Should the distribution of funds for education and welfare be federal or local responsibilities? Should the concepts of church and state as they apply to public education be rethought? Should nominees for the office of President be chosen by direct primaries rather than party conventions? Should the President be elected by popular vote rather than by the Electoral College? What are the civil rights of prisoners and people in military service? The list of issues is long. Every case ever brought before the Supreme Court on constitutional grounds is related to the discussion.

Regardless of specific issues, the great constitutional debate, now as it was two hundred years ago, is probably that of centralization versus decentralization. The present system is considerably decentralized—too decentralized, according to Tugwell and people with similar views. Opinions on reform differ widely; the only opinion that appears to have a growing consensus is that there is a pressing need to alter some of the serious deficiencies of the existing system of government. Advocates of reform felt that there was much at stake in the 1972 presidential election.

Political Change: The 1972 Election

Presidential Primaries

President Nixon had formidable resources at his disposal in his bid for reelection. Republican campaign literature asked the American voter to "re-elect the President," a slogan that made good use of Nixon's accomplishments and the prestige of his office. The Democrats might make promises, but Nixon had a record of four years of service. He had negotiated arms control, installed wage and price controls, and held back tax increases. He could point with justifiable pride to his trips to Peking and Moscow. Moreover, as the incumbent he had a historical advantage: incumbent Presidents have failed to win reelection only twice in this century, in 1912 when Taft was defeated by Wilson, and in 1932 when Hoover lost to Franklin D. Roosevelt.

The tremendous advantage an incumbent has was demonstrated by the hopeless bids for nomination made by two Republican challengers, both aiming to dramatize their differences with the President. One was the liberal Representative Paul McCloskey of California, who protested Nixon's war policy; the other was Representative John Ashbrook of Oregon, who expressed the uneasiness of party conservatives over the President's China trip, his wage and price controls, and other issues. Few observers at any time regarded either contender as a threat to the President. McCloskey left the contest after the New Hampshire primary, where he received 20.2 percent of the vote to Nixon's 69.2 percent. Ashbrook scored 9.6 percent in New Hampshire and also ran in the Florida primary, where Nixon carried 87.1 percent of the vote.

Long before Republican presidential hopefuls emerged, a contest for the Democratic nomination had begun. On the eve of the congressional election of 1970, Senator Edmund S. Muskie of Maine appeared as spokesman for the Democratic Party on a telecast in which he sharply criticized President Nixon's participation in a San Diego rally that had been staged by Republican strategists. Muskie handled the assignment with an air of statesmanship that won approval from many Democrats who already regarded him as the party's first choice for the nomination. By the time earnest campaigning began, the field was crowded with Democratic challengers. Serious divisions in the party were already apparent.

In January 1971, the polls showed Muskie as the most popular choice of Democratic voters, with Senator Edward M. Kennedy of Massachusetts second, despite his decision not to run, and former Vice President Hubert Humphrey a close third. At that time, Senator George McGovern of South Dakota had a 3-percent rating in the polls, and most observers dismissed him as a serious contender. Muskie moved to solidify his lead in 1971 by collecting endorsements from prominent Democrats and tapping various sources of campaign money. He planned to enter all of the first eight primaries and hoped to knock most of his opponents out early so that he could face the most formidable one, Humphrey, from a position of strength. Humphrey stayed out of the New Hampshire race, where he expected Muskie to be strong. He planned to concentrate on selected primaries in the large industrial states, where he could count on his long-standing trade-union, black, and ethnic-group support.

When campaigning began in New Hampshire in February, traditionally the kickoff of presidential campaigns, the Democratic cast of characters had changed several times and was only then beginning to take shape for the months ahead. Senators Harold Hughes of Iowa and Birch Bayh of Indiana had tried and failed to win the necessary financial and political support to launch candidacies, and Senator Fred Harris of Oklahoma had raised the banners of a populist campaign and then withdrawn.

In addition to Muskie, Humphrey, and McGovern, the list of Democratic candidates included Senator Henry M. Jackson of Washington, Senator Eugene J. McCarthy of Minnesota, Senator Vance Hartke of Indiana, Representative Shirley Chisholm of New York, chairman of the House Ways and Means Committee Wilbur Mills, Governor George Wallace of Alabama, Mayor John V. Lindsay of New York, and Mayor Sam Yorty of Los Angeles.

Even before New Hampshire, Democrats had begun to keep a close watch on Iowa, one of the states that does not hold primaries but chooses delegates at party caucuses. In Iowa, precinct caucuses were being held throughout the state, preliminary to the state convention on May 30, where the delegates to the national convention would be selected. At these precinct caucuses, McGovern's strength first became apparent. Despite his low showing in the national polls, McGovern scored 27.6 percent to Muskie's 35.5 percent, an "unexpectedly strong showing."[5] A week later in Arizona, Muskie again led in the voting for delegates at the caucus level, with 37.8 percent, Lindsay ran second with 23.6 percent, and McGovern ran third, with 20.4 percent. Although Muskie was the apparent victor, Lindsay and McGovern together received over 40 percent of the vote.

Once the primaries began, however, they took the spotlight away from contests in such nonprimary states as Iowa and Arizona. In New Hampshire, McGovern, with 37.6 percent, ran second to Muskie's 47.8 percent. A week later in the Florida primary, which hinged on the busing issue, George Wallace scored a stunning victory. He received 41 percent of the vote, gaining almost all of the delegates. His lead was followed by Humphrey, with 18 percent; Jackson, 13.5 percent; Muskie, 8.8 percent; Lindsay, 6.1 percent; and McGovern, 6.1 percent.[6] The real losers were Muskie and Lindsay, for McGovern had largely avoided the Florida primary campaign.

The Wisconsin primary in April settled the question of who was to be the lib-

---

[5] R. W. Apple, Jr., "Muskie is Victor in Iowa," the *New York Times* (January 26, 1972), p. 15.
[6] *Congressional Quarterly Weekly Review*, vol. 30, no. 11 (March 11, 1972), p. 549.

eral candidate, Lindsay or McGovern. Here McGovern won his first clear victory, receiving 30 percent of the vote to Lindsay's 7 percent. It was only then that observers began to take him seriously as a contender.

It was also in the Wisconsin primary that all the Democratic candidates began to talk about economic issues—unemployment, taxes, and inflation—each striving to be more of a populist than the others.[7] McGovern's support in Wisconsin, one survey showed, came from a wider spectrum than expected. As in Manchester, New Hampshire, he did well in the blue-collar wards, where he had gone into the factories to shake hands and discuss with workers their grievances against the American system.

There was evidence, however, that in Wisconsin the Republicans had encouraged registered Republicans to cross over in the primaries to help defeat the candidates believed to be strongest. And by this time it was clear that Muskie was in trouble for other reasons as well. In an unguarded moment, he had wept before reporters after a critical attack was made on his wife by the publisher of the *Manchester Union Leader.* He made another political error after his Florida defeat by denouncing Wallace in terms that also indicted the governor's supporters. Muskie's support was viewed as broad but not deep, and his strategy of trying to be all things to all Democrats may have hurt him in a series of primaries where several contenders took turns attacking him. In Pennsylvania Muskie left the race, saying he had run out of resources.

Wallace, meanwhile, surprised Democrats with the dimensions implicit in his Florida victory. In Wisconsin, he came in second to McGovern, with the help of numerous cross-over voters. Wallace seemed content to score high in preference polls while showing little interest in organizing delegate slates and getting them elected. It is significant that he received only two delegates in Pennsylvania, although he came in second in the primary: the Democrats in that state had long regarded him as a renegade. When he was knocked out of the campaign by an attempted assassination, it was on the eve of expected primary victories in Maryland and Michigan, where court orders had made busing the major issue. Ironically, he was then at the peak of his success with nowhere to go as a Democratic candidate. He had not been entered in any of the remaining primaries.

McGovern and his campaign workers were tireless delegate-hunters. To their high-yield wins in California and New York they added impressive totals in the nonprimary states.[8] When delegates previously committed to Muskie were free to be courted again, the McGovern organization made capital of the opportunity. In the twenty-eight state conventions, McGovern garnered about 400 of the 1,009 delegates, to Humphrey's total of about 100.

In his phenomenal advance, McGovern was aided by a grass-roots organization containing many political reformers who had worked for McCarthy in the 1968 primaries, and enthusiastic young volunteers drawn to McGovern's idealism.

---

[7] Douglas Robinson, "Economy is Key in Wisconsin," the *New York Times* (April 1, 1972), p. 1.

[8] Jon Nordheimer, "16 Georgia Blacks Named Delegates," the *New York Times* (March 12, 1972), pp. 1, 35. Probably most striking was the voting in Georgia on March 11. In 1968 Governor Lester Maddox's hand-picked delegation had been denied their seats while the Credentials Committee examined charges that blacks had been seriously discriminated against and were underrepresented in the delegation. In the end a compromise had been reached seating half of the Maddox and half of the reform delegations. In this election sixteen of the forty elected were blacks, and Chisholm and McGovern forces scored upsets in the Atlanta area.

They spread over voting precincts like "a major land army on the move."[9] They canvassed, distributed literature, telephoned voters, and packed caucuses, politicking with a zeal reminiscent of the old ward professionals. Not surprisingly, McGovern's preconvention campaign evoked deep resentment in party regulars, who saw young insurgents appearing at caucuses who had never shown up at regular party meetings.

By early May the field had been narrowed down to two active candidates, Humphrey and McGovern, who battled it out in a series of televised debates in California, hitting at issues of jobs, welfare, and taxes. The debates deepened the party rift and provided ammunition for the Republicans in the later campaign. McGovern's plans to cut the Pentagon budget and redistribute income were attacked vigorously by Humphrey, whose words would later be quoted by Republican campaign literature. To those whose livelihood depended on defense-related industries, McGovern's proposals were threatening, and middle-class wage-earners saw themselves paying for more grants to the poor.

The Humphrey forces, joined by a number of the other candidates, moved to contest the winner-take-all feature of the California primary, which had handed McGovern a bonanza. They brought a case to the federal courts and embarked on a last-ditch "stop McGovern" movement that dominated the period from that primary to the convention in July.

The Democratic Convention

Planning, Preparation, and Reform In the four years after the 1968 Democratic Convention, party officials and planners were concerned with taking steps to prevent a repetition of the debacle at Chicago. Clearly reforms were needed, and even before the party had left the convention in Chicago it had named a reform commission to make changes in the delegate-selection procedure. The Commission on Party Structure and Delegate Selection, headed by Senator George McGovern, had been charged with making the 1972 Convention more representative of Democrats as a whole than the one in Chicago. In 1968, for example, antiwar candidates had won several primaries, but most of the convention delegates had not been chosen in primaries. Insurgents were dissatisfied because they had failed in their attempts to keep the nomination from Vice President Hubert Humphrey and to secure an antiwar plank in the party platform. After McGovern resigned from the reform commission to pursue his presidential campaign, his place was taken by Representative Donald Fraser (D.-Minn.), but McGovern's imprint remained on the finished commission report.

A major thrust of the McGovern delegate-selection reforms was to take "affirmative steps to encourage the participation" of blacks, Chicanos, women, and youth "in reasonable relation to their presence in the population."[10] The goal was to establish procedures maximizing the participation of the rank and file in delegate selection at all levels and in the makeup of the state delegations in Miami Beach. A direct result of these reforms was the increase in the number of primaries in 1972 over 1968. In 1972 twenty-three presidential primaries chose 65 percent of the delegate strength or 1,900 votes, as compared to the twelve pri-

[9] *Newsweek* (May 8, 1972), p. 24.
[10] *Congressional Quarterly Weekly Report*, vol. 30, no. 12 (March 18, 1972), p. 581.

maries in 1968 that had chosen 42 percent of the delegates.

Beginning in June, the Credentials Committee dealt with eighty-two challenges of 1,289 delegates from thirty different states and representing 41.5 percent of all the delegates.[11] The most important challenges, however, were those to California and Illinois. The chairwoman chosen by the Democratic national committee to preside over the Credentials Committee was Patricia Roberts Harris, a black lawyer. A staff of thirty-six lawyers would sit as hearing officers for the credentials challenges.

Although four states retained winner-take-all primaries, only California became an issue, and that was closely tied up with the late-blooming "stop McGovern" coalition. On June 29 the Credentials Committee overturned the report of its hearing officer and voted to strip McGovern of 151 of his 271 California delegates and award them instead to the other California contestants in proportion to their standing in the primary. A few days later, McGovern retorted in a *Life* interview that he would not let "a bunch of established politicians gang up to prevent me from getting the nomination because I didn't come to them for help. . . ."[12] He directed his attorneys to challenge the Committee's action in the federal courts, arguing basically that it is not permissible to change the rules after the game has been played. On July 5, a United States Appeals Court, in a two-to-one decision, ordered the reinstatement of McGovern's delegates.

At issue in Illinois were the fifty-nine delegates closely allied with the archenemy of reformers, Mayor Richard Daley of Chicago. While the party reforms had discouraged but not forbidden winner-take-all primaries, their intent hit directly at practices long associated with choosing delegates in Illinois. Although the delegates were elected in a party primary, the slates had been formed secretly, without widespread participation. Challengers argued that their meetings were forcibly broken up, and the resulting delegation did not comply with the newly adopted guidelines for representation. In the end, the Daley delegation was unseated in favor of the challenging delegation led by a young black alderman, William S. Singer.

Some observers had already noted in April and May that the reforms were failing to have the effects widely attributed to them—many of the delegate slates in the primary were highly unrepresentative. Voters seemed to vote for white, middle-aged men. Delegates were often chosen from the ranks of the alternates. And, indeed, many of the credentials challenges were made over these very issues.

Thus, by July, this much was known: nine out of ten of the delegates had not been to a national convention before;[13] 1,173, or 38 percent, were women, compared with 13 percent in 1968); 649, or 21 percent, were youths, compared with 4 percent in 1968; and 468, or 15 percent, were black, the same figure as in 1968.[14] With all of the challenges finally settled, they listed themselves by occupation as follows:[15]

---

[11] "Campaign '72: Democratic Convention Commissions," *Congressional Quarterly Weekly Report*, vol. 30, no. 27 (July 1, 1972), p. 1575.

[12] Cited in "Democratic Convention: New Faces and New Rules," *Congressional Quarterly Weekly Report*, vol. 30, no. 28 (July 8, 1972), p. 1635.

[13] "Democratic Convention: New Faces and New Rules," p. 1637.

[14] "Democratic Ticket: Two Liberal Midwestern Senators," *Congressional Quarterly Weekly Report*, vol. 30, no. 29 (July 15, 1972), p. 1721.

[15] "Democratic Ticket," p. 1723.

10% "politicians"
 5   union leaders
22   professional jobs
10   teachers
 9   students
13   housewives
13   business
 1   farmers
 4   laborers
 4   clerical
14   union members

What everyone was speculating on before the delegates assembled was, What kind of impact would these newcomers make?

At the same time that the Credentials Committee grappled with its job, the Platform Committee, under the direction of Richard E. Neustadt of Harvard University, professor and former Kennedy adviser, was trying to find some common ground among the badly splintered Democratic hopefuls and their followers. In those states that held state conventions, platforms were being adopted. These deliberations and the series of regional platform-committee hearings held by Neustadt present a fascinating picture of the Democratic party in 1972—who its activists were and what concerned them. Iowa, at its convention, adopted planks favoring amnesty for war resisters, legalized abortion, legalization of marijuana, and repeal of laws concerning homosexuality. Similarly, Maine supported abortion reform, and the platform adopted in Wyoming was too liberal for some state politicians to support. These and other states expressing similar views at the state conventions are not usually seen as hotbeds of radicalism.[16]

The Democrats staged Neustadt's regional hearings for maximum media coverage and carefully matched moderators and subjects: former Senator Wayne Morse (D.-Ore.) on foreign policy, Senator Edward Kennedy on the economy. After amassing a formidable list of proposals, a smaller drafting committee, with Kenneth Gibson, the black mayor of Newark, New Jersey, as chairman and composed of representatives of the major Democratic contenders, succeeded in drawing up a document that struck a populist tone, modified McGovern's call for major defense cuts, and had the following major features: a call for abolition of the draft and amnesty for war resisters, a guarantee of jobs for all Americans, a guaranteed income above the poverty line, and a promise to break up corporate monopolies. The language about busing is indicative: it approved busing as one tool to be used where segregation has been legally imposed.[17] Minorities promised to carry their losing causes to the floor: the Wallace planks condemning busing, gun control, the ban on prayer in the schools; and liberal planks favoring equal rights for homosexuals, repeal of restrictions on abortions, and a minimum income of $6,500.[18]

Late Nights in Miami Beach: The Apogee of the McGovern Campaign The chief business of the first day of the Democratic convention was the credentials fight.

---

[16] John Herbers, "Activist Planks Stir Democrats," the *New York Times* (May 30, 1972), p. 30.

[17] John Herbers, "Democrats Vote Pro-Busing Plank," the *New York Times* (June 27, 1972), pp. 1, 30.

[18] "Campaign '72: Democratic Convention Commissions," pp. 1569–1570.

The day before, Senator Muskie had suggested that all of the major contenders meet to iron out credentials problems, but the meeting never came about after McGovern refused to attend. Meeting for nine hours in full session, the convention first considered the question of sex and racial representation, with the McGovern forces giving up principle for parliamentary advantage. It then turned to the California challenge, which was solved to McGovern's satisfaction, by a vote of 1,618 to 1,238, and his nomination seemed secure. All attempts to compromise on Illinois went by the board, and the Daley delegation was unseated, 1,372 to 1,486.[19]

On the second night the convention adopted a platform. Two changes were made which modified the original draft, one pledging support to Israel and one promising to return surplus federal lands to Indians. The Wallace planks were voted down by voice vote, as was Senator Fred Harris's tax-reform plan. Two roll-call votes disposed of other minority planks: liberalization of abortion went down, 1,591 to 1,103; the liberal $6,500 minimum income was defeated, 1,853 to 1,000.[20] Much has been said about the discipline and organization of McGovern's supporters who wished to vote their consciences on the sex-race credentials issue and the various liberal minority platform planks but did not.

The third day was devoted to presidential nominations and voting. Most of the other candidates asked that their names not be put in nomination, or that they be withdrawn. Governor George Wallace, former North Carolina Governor Terry Sanford, Representative Shirley Chisholm, Senator Henry Jackson, and Senator McGovern were nominated. McGovern was nominated by Senator Abraham S. Ribicoff (D.-Conn.) and seconded by Valerie Kushner, wife of a prisoner of war in Vietnam, and Representative Walter Fauntroy (D.-D.C.). California was the first to be polled, and, ironically, the newly seated reform Illinois delegation clinched it for McGovern. Before the switches began, McGovern had 1,715.35 votes.[21] The magic number for winning the nomination was 1,509.

During the next day, Senator McGovern spent the afternoon choosing a running mate, calling first Senator Edward Kennedy, who had thus far stayed away from the convention, trying to maintain the credibility of his disclaimers to interest in any position on the ticket for 1972. Again, he said no. Others considered, according to most accounts, included Senator Ribicoff, Senator Muskie, Mayor Kevin White of Boston, and Senator Thomas F. Eagleton (D.-Mo.). Late in the afternoon McGovern announced that Eagleton had accepted. That evening some of the delegates broke their closely held ranks, and state representative Frances Farenthold (D.-Tex.), who had made a strong run for governor of Texas in the primary, challenged McGovern's choice. Others who entered as candidates were former Governor Endicott Peabody of Massachusetts; Stanley Arnold, a New York businessman, who had campaigned for the office on the theory that more attention should be placed on choosing a Vice President; Senator Mike Gravel (D.-Alaska), Representative Peter Rodino (D.-N.J.), and Clay Smothers, a black Wallace supporter.[22]

---

[19] "Democratic Ticket," p. 1723.

[20] "The Platform: Few Changes Made in Original Draft," *Congressional Quarterly Weekly Report*, vol. 30, no. 29 (July 15, 1972), p. 1724.

[21] "The Platform," p. 1719.

[22] "Democratic Ticket," p. 1713.

The session dragged on into the next morning, but finally Eagleton was nominated and the time for speeches arrived. Eagleton attacked the Nixon administration with partisan fervor and promised to set a contrast to what he saw as Agnew's low style. Then, as the delegates settled in to savor their victory, Kennedy delivered a rousing introduction, and the defeated presidential candidates, save for the absent Wallace, stood with candidate McGovern in a show of unity as he launched his campaign by urging the country to "come home."

The Republican Convention

The Switch from San Diego to Miami Beach By all accounts, President Nixon wanted the 1972 Republican convention near his California White House, and his friends had prevailed on the reluctant city of San Diego to be his host. Early in the spring, however, columnist Jack Anderson began publishing information including an incriminating memorandum, supposedly written by one of International Telephone and Telegraph's top lobbyists, Mrs. Dita Beard, who was subsequently traced to a hospital bed where she was sequestered for a time from all questioning. While details are still not clear, allegations were made about the impropriety of an ITT promise to underwrite expenses for the convention, allegedly in return for favorable treatment from the Justice Department in its antitrust suit. The ITT story broke at a time when Richard Kleindienst was expecting confirmation as Attorney General, and former Attorney General John Mitchell had recently become head of the President's reelection effort. The Republicans pulled out of San Diego and quickly made plans to follow the Democrats into Miami Beach in August.

"Four More Years": The Republicans in Miami Beach Both conventions in Miami Beach coexisted with what the city euphemistically called "non-delegates," groups which ranged along several political and social spectra. Antiwar protesters, Yippies, and Vietnam Veterans Against the War, among others, secured campgrounds and areas in which to demonstrate. Miami Beach police were specially trained, and reserves of Florida state police, national guardsmen, and army troops could be called up "in case of trouble." But although protesters attempted to prevent delegates from entering the Republican convention (for the most part, unsuccessfully), and a few fracases with police resulted in arrests, major trouble did not materialize.

In contrast to the Democrats and their inability to keep to a schedule, the Republicans had a well-organized, predictable, and largely placid time at their convention. Taking only three days to the Democrats' four, they began with a temporary chairman, Governor Ronald Reagan of California, making the first address. Saving the afternoon for committee work, they were able to make nominations on the second night. The choice of President Nixon was unanimous, save for a lone vote for McCloskey, mandated by the results of the primary, in the New Mexico delegation.

Nominated by his old adversary, Governor Nelson Rockefeller (N.Y.), Nixon was seconded by eleven people chosen to represent various parts of the population. They included Senator James Buckley, the New York conservative; Frank Borman, the astronaut; former Secretary of the Interior Walter Hickel; and individuals representing youth, labor, Chicanos, Vietnam veterans, blacks, southerners,

ethnic minority groups, and disaffected Democrats.[23] The Nixon platform, largely drawn up by the White House, saw the opposition captured by an ideological extreme:

It pictured those supporting Senator George McGovern as promoting a "hand-out economy in which the idle live at ease," "fiscal folly," a policy of "begging with adversary nations," and allowing those "in a distant bureaucracy" to run the lives of the people for them.[24]

The President himself was more conciliatory in his acceptance speech, which sought to welcome disaffected Democrats to his "new majority."

Maneuvering for control of the Republican party for 1976 also went on in Miami Beach. Such efforts arose in the Rules Committee as it considered various proposals for redistributing delegates to the next convention. The various proposals reflected a struggle between the party's liberal and conservative wings, the latter eager to smooth the way for an Agnew-for-President campaign in 1976. Although a compromise was reached, the liberals were regarded as the losers. Variations on the liberal-conservative struggle included cold-shoulder treatment of congressional liberals Paul McCloskey (Cal.) and Donald Riegle (Mich.), and only perfunctory consideration of proposals to open the delegate-selection procedures for 1976 to permit more young people, women, and minorities—questions which had greatly preoccupied the Democrats.[25] Much of this debate, however, went on below a surface kept calm by a watchful White House intent on the here and now.

The Campaign

"For the first time in the history of this country, we have a presidential campaign with only one candidate," charged George McGovern.[26] Traditionally, the American presidential campaign runs from Labor Day to Election Day, about two months. But in 1972 there was not a campaign in the usual sense. While the Democratic nominee crisscrossed the country, his opponent campaigned hardly at all, until the last ten days before the election. McGovern's charges were either answered by presidential substitutes or ignored. Tom Wicker, writing just before the election, described the tone of what some political observers dubbed a "non-campaign." The spring and, indeed, the whole year told "one of the most dramatic stories in our political history."

Then the myth-makers botched the job. Having risen to the pinnacle, the same mild-mannered Goerge McGovern with the same splendid organization and the same political base toppled right off again, into one of the deepest pits ever seen in a presidential campaign.[27]

Richard Nixon, a not unbiased observer, remarked in an interview published the

---

[23] "Campaign '72: An Optimistic Republican Take-Off," *Congressional Quarterly Weekly Report,* vol. 30, no. 35 (August 26, 1972), pp. 2115–2118.

[24] "The 1972 Platforms: A Real Choice for the Voters," *Congressional Quarterly Weekly Report,* vol. 30, no. 35 (August 26, 1972), p. 2146.

[25] "Republican Convention: Almost Undisturbed Harmony," *Congressional Quarterly Weekly Report,* vol. 30, no. 34 (August 19, 1972), pp. 2043–2049.

[26] Douglas E. Kneeland, "McGovern Assails Nixon as Elusive," the *New York Times* (October 31, 1972), pp. 1, 36.

[27] "McGovern with Tears" *The New York Times Magazine* (November 5, 1972), p. 36.

day after his reelection: "This election was decided the day he [McGovern] was nominated. The issue in this election was his views."[28]

Democratic planners had set the date of their national convention six weeks earlier than the 1968 convention, feeling that they had started out several weeks too late in the last campaign. Soon, however, Democrats were conceding that they had lost practically the whole month of August over the "Eagleton Affair" and were no better off than they had been in 1968. The original vice-presidential nominee, Thomas Eagleton, whose political career had included many elective offices in Missouri and who had been elected to the Senate in 1968 after unseating a Democratic incumbent in the primary and defeating a popular Republican congressman in the general election, was thought to be a highly effective campaigner. A Roman Catholic with labor and big-city ties, but not far from McGovern on many issues, Eagleton, it was thought, would complement McGovern without any sacrifice of principles.

Eagleton's fall from grace began when he appeared with McGovern on July 25 to announce that although he had voluntarily hospitalized himself three times between 1960 and 1966 and submitted to shock and drug therapy for "nervous exhaustion and fatigue," he was now fit to hold high office. McGovern asserted that he would stand behind Eagleton "1,000 percent." In the next week, Eagleton denied unsubstantiated rumors of alcoholism published by columnist Jack Anderson, and defended himself for not discussing his treatment for emotional problems when McGovern first talked with him about the nomination. As the furor built and newspapers demanded Eagleton's resignation, McGovern defended his choice while the Republicans maintained silence. Then, on July 31, under severe pressure from Democrats, including McGovern, Eagleton withdrew, and McGovern set about finding another running mate, beginning by asking most of those he had asked before.[29]

On August 5, McGovern took national television time from a major campaign address to announce that his new vice-presidential choice was R. Sargent Shriver, now a Washington lawyer, formerly the first head of the Peace Corps, head of the Office of Economic Opportunity, and an ambassador to France under Lyndon Johnson. Shriver, a Maryland Catholic, was also connected in the public mind with the Kennedy family by virtue of his marriage to Eunice Kennedy. He was approved by a special meeting of the Democratic National Committee, where Senator Mike Mansfield (Mont.) noted, during his introduction of Shriver, "We are, in all bluntness, off to a bad start. Let us face that honestly."[30]

McGovern began his formal campaign on Labor Day before a labor audience in Ohio, not Detroit, the traditional kickoff site of Democratic presidential campaigns. During September he spoke on the following subjects, among others: a new program for space, the recent deal to sell wheat to the U.S.S.R., the wiretapping of Democratic headquarters by Republican spies caught in the Watergate building complex, the administration's wage-and-price policy, strip mining and an Ap-

---

[28] Garnett O. Horner, "Statements from Pre-Election Interview with Nixon Outlining Second-Term Plans," the New York Times (November 10, 1972), p. 20.

[29] "Democratic Ticket: Furor over Eagleton's Illness," Congressional Quarterly Weekly Report, vol. 30, no. 31 (July 29, 1972), pp. 1851–1852; and "Democrats: Search for New Vice Presidential Nominee," Congressional Quarterly Weekly Report, vol. 30, no. 31 (July 29, 1972), pp. 1915–1917.

[30] "The Vice Presidency: Shriver, with Little Dissent," Congressional Quarterly Weekly Report, vol. 30, no. 33 (August 12, 1972), p. 1982.

palachian program, aid to nonpublic schools, Israel and national defense, the prisoner-of-war question, narcotics traffic and drug abuse, and urban policy.

In contrast to McGovern, Nixon made three political appearances all month, a surprise visit to an Italian-American picnic, a New York speech and dinner, and a barbecue held by John Connally in Texas. Aides let it be known that the Nixon administration would not raise taxes after the election; the President defended his drug program and criticized "permissive judges."

In addition, "surrogates," as White House planners called them—Republicans who spoke in Nixon's place—were answering McGovern's charges. In speech after speech, McGovern began hitting at economic issues and the need for tax reform. He declared that while executives could deduct the cost of their lunches, complete with martinis, on their tax returns, the working man could not deduct the price of a "bologna sandwich." The Administration countered with a press appearance by the Chairman of the Council of Economic Advisers, Herbert Stein, who held up a chuck roast and proclaimed that there had been an eleven-cent-per-pound drop in meat prices. Stein had begun to attack McGovern's economic program in June, and the White House tax promise was part of a strategy picturing McGovern as an extremist. "He'll double taxes," the Republicans charged.[31]

McGovern's amended economic program emphasized full employment, tax reform, and income redistribution, but the Republicans kept bringing up the discarded McGovern proposal that everyone be given a minimum income grant of $1,000. McGovern proposed to enact $268 savings in taxes by slowly eliminating tax preferences for capital gains and abolishing those in real estate and oil depletion. He would further eliminate accelerated depreciation rates and tax privileges for foreign trade. Having withdrawn his plan to cut the defense budget at once by $55 billion, McGovern proposed instead three cuts for the next three years at $10 billion a year.[32]

Republican strategy was to send out a milder-toned Vice President Agnew, to meet McGovern's issues by trying to put him on the defensive, and to keep Nixon "presidential" until nearly the end.[33] Instead of the partisan campaigning of the 1970 congressional elections, Republicans would be reaching for disaffected Democrats. As Republican congressional and state candidates began to perceive the extent of the President's lead, they exerted pressure to get him to do more campaigning, but the original script was largely adhered to.

By the end of September, the polls continued to show Nixon leading with approximately 61 percent of the vote, and McGovern's advisers were searching for a way to reverse the campaign's fortunes. They concentrated on some twenty of the largest states, which together would yield 328 electoral votes. For example, the candidate had already been to Ohio five times. In a tacit admission that the Republicans had made McGovern's personality an issue, McGovern's staff would put McGovern forward as a "moral leader"[34] and hit hard at the President's refusal to debate, his "hiding" in the White House, and the issues of corruption and de-

---

[31] John F. Busby, "Report/Complex McGovern Election Plan Dissolves in Campaign Heat," *National Journal*, vol. 4, no. 38 (September 16, 1972), p. 1452.

[32] Busby, "Report/Complex McGovern Election Plan Dissolves in Campaign Heat," p. 1450.

[33] "Report Nixon Buoyed by Early Leads, Plans Elaborate Campaign Under White House Mantle," *National Journal*, vol. 4, no. 36 (September 2, 1972), pp. 1381–1393.

[34] "McGovern Seeks Moral Leader's Role," the *New York Times* (September 24, 1972), p. 46.

ceit on the war, campaign finances, the Watergate episode, and the grain deal. McGovern began a series of "fireside chats" on television. His campaign had always been geared to the media, hitting a certain number of media markets a day. But these speeches, on Vietnam, on foreign policy, or on corruption, would attempt to contrast the candidate's personality with that of his opponent. His charges of corruption in the Nixon administration brought a speedy denial from Republican campaign director Clark MacGregor, and his Vietnam speech was immediately attacked by Secretary of Defense Melvin Laird. By the end of October, McGovern's charges were summed up in an admonition to the American people of what the next four years would be like: "Watergate corruption, Nixon recession, Connally oil, and Republican reaction."[35]

In October, Nixon held his only news conference since August and journeyed to Philadelphia to sign his revenue-sharing bill. He also made an unannounced speech before a meeting of wives of prisoners of war and began a series of radio addresses, one a week until the election. Before the election he had journeyed once to the South, to Atlanta; once to Cleveland and the Midwest; once to aid Senate candidates in Illinois, Michigan, Oklahoma, and Rhode Island; and to California for the weekend of November 4–5 to vote from his California home.[36] Campaigning in Michigan, and in Ohio at Cleveland and Youngstown, Nixon spoke to enthusiastic blue-collar crowds. Judging his audience well, the President predicted economic expansion and success in his efforts to stem the illegal flow of drugs. And he told them what they wanted to hear, that theirs was not "a sick society."[37]

McGovern continually attempted to make an issue of the Watergate affair. During the fall, a series of newspaper disclosures implicated high White House aides in a plan to recruit political spies and saboteurs to collect information, sow confusion, and raise obstructions in the spring primary campaigns. The Democrats were puzzled at the seeming public apathy and willingness to believe that this kind of activity was widespread in all election campaigns. McGovern's charges became increasingly bitter, and Democrats could only hope that by the time the election arrived, political corruption would be a prime factor influencing voter choice.

While political corruption was an issue which came late to the campaign, Vietnam and national-defense policy had been there from the beginning, and on these topics the two candidates held views as well defined as those they held on economic issues. McGovern's national-defense advisers had been increased in number after he won the nomination in order to bring in men such as former Defense Secretary Clark Clifford and Paul Warnke, who was Assistant Secretary of Defense for International Security Affairs under Clifford. The themes they stressed in a report to McGovern made public in late September were that the United States was overextended abroad and that it was shortchanging its citizens at home. "No foreign government should look to the United States for protection from internal

---

[35] Kneeland, "McGovern Assails Nixon as Elusive," the *New York Times* (October 31, 1972), pp. 1, 36.

[36] Linda Charlton, "Nixon Holds Strategy Meetings: More Appearances Seen," the *New York Times* (October 5, 1972), p. 52; and Robert B. Semple, Jr., "Nixon Is Widening Campaign Effort," the *New York Times* (November 1, 1972), p. 1.

[37] Douglas E. Kneeland, "President Woos Blue-Collar Votes—Sees Economic Surge across Nation," the *New York Times* (October 29, 1972), pp. 1, 50.

change," they argued.[38] We should dismantle our Asian bases and concentrate instead on our "special responsibilities" in Europe and Israel. Specifically, the report said, promises to abandon "useless new nuclear weapons systems" should be backed up by ceasing development on any more MIRVs, and eliminating B-1 bombers or Trident submarines completely. Instead, McGovern outlined a foreign policy tied to "idealism."[39] And there was Vietnam. McGovern timed a major speech on Vietnam for the same day on which Nixon, as a candidate in the 1968 campaign, had charged that an administration which had had four years to solve that war should not be awarded another four. Then, during October, when Henry Kissinger returned from negotiations with the North Vietnamese bringing the promise of "peace at hand," McGovern welcomed it. He turned instead to domestic issues, and then returned to the original subject of the war during the campaign's waning days, asking why the same peace could not have been achieved in 1969.

Election Results

Long before Election Day, Republicans were confident of a landslide victory. The final count showed that the President carried forty-nine states for a total of 521 electoral votes, receiving 60.89 percent of the popular vote, a figure exceeded only by Lyndon Johnson's 61.09 percent in 1964. McGovern won only in Massachusetts and the District of Columbia. In three states, his native South Dakota, Rhode Island, and Minnesota, he received over 45 percent of the vote. The *New York Times* noted that Nixon's victory "marked an increase in support from 1968 that cut across all geographic regions and major ethnic groups."[40]

The seven largest states, where McGovern had concentrated most of his campaign efforts, showed the following Nixon majorities: California and Michigan, 51 percent; Illinois, New York, Ohio, and Pennsylvania, 60 percent; Texas, 67 percent. Producing even larger majorities, the South for the first time went solidly Republican.

Who Voted? When the returns were all in, four leading political-survey organizations[41] concurred that one-third of all Democrats had voted for Nixon, and that he had retained virtually all Republican voters. They also found that Nixon had had the support of two large traditionally Democratic groups—Catholics and blue-collar workers. Catholics voted for him by about 53 to 46 percent. Blue-collar workers, who had voted Democratic by five to four in the last five elections, in 1972 voted for Nixon by five to four. The votes of union members, however, seemed split about evenly between Nixon and McGovern.

Black Americans, who had much to gain from McGovern's proposals, gave him almost 90 percent of their votes, a somewhat smaller percentage than that received by Humphrey in 1968. A shift of the traditionally Democratic Jewish vote was evident early in the campaign. Although Jewish voters gave McGovern

---

[38] "McGovern Unit Says Defense Can Be Cut," the *New York Times* (September 22, 1972), p. 30.

[39] "McGovern Details a Foreign Policy Tied to 'Idealism'," the *New York Times* (October 6, 1972), p. 1.

[40] The *New York Times* (November 9, 1972), p. 1.

[41] CBS, Harris, Gallup, and Yankelovich. The *New York Times* (November 9, 1972), p. 1.

a majority on Election Day, Nixon received nearly 40 percent of their votes, as compared with 15 percent in 1968.[42]

The total size of the vote was one of the smallest in recent decades. The 75 million votes cast represented only 55 percent of eligible voters, the lowest proportion since 1948. Over half the new young voters, the eighteen-to-twenty-four-year-old group, numbering 25.7 million Americans, did not vote at all. Only 47 percent of this group went to the polls or cast absentee ballots. Their votes gave McGovern only a slight edge, contrary to expectations.

Two reasons were given for the low voter turnout: first, that many people were dissatisfied with both candidates, and second, that the polls, which had emphasized a major victory for Nixon, made some voters think their vote would make little difference to the outcome. In assessing the turnout, however, it should be noted that a great many citizens are still unregistered. Of the registered voters, about 80 percent exercised their franchise.

A Mandate for Nixon? To obtain a more accurate picture of the national temper than was shown by the presidential returns, political analysts carefully examined congressional, state, and local contests for coattails effects. Were Nixon's coattails long and strong enough to carry Republicans to a victory that would shift the balance in Congress? The answer was negative. Democratic candidates for the United States Senate carried six states that were previously held by Republican senators—Colorado, Delaware, Iowa, Kentucky, Maine, and South Dakota. In a notable upset, the seventy-four-year-old Margaret Chase Smith (R.-Me.) lost her seat to William Hathaway, a moderate Democrat, leaving the Senate without a single woman in office. Republican senatorial candidates replaced Democrats in only four states—New Mexico, North Carolina, Oklahoma, and Virginia. The Democrats were therefore left with a Senate majority of fifty-four to forty-three, an increase of two seats. One of the few instances where a coattails effect appeared to work was in North Carolina, where the President's 70-percent majority was accompanied by the election of a Republican governor and senator.

In the House of Representatives, the net gain to Republicans of thirteen seats was far short of the forty-one they needed for control. Moreover, the new House would have more black and more young members, not simply because of the November election but because of earlier primary victories and the departure of many powerful elderly leaders.

In the eighteen gubernatorial contests, liberals in general made a good showing. Democrats gained governors in three states, Delaware, Illinois, and Vermont, and lost Missouri and North Carolina.

The President's large majority appeared to mean that many Americans had turned themselves off to the issues raised by McGovern, that an affluent middle class did not wish to risk a change in the status quo. However, the ineptness of the McGovern campaign and the low voter turnout offered reason to doubt that the majority had as much significance as was apparent on the surface. The returns in other contests, moreover, made it possible to say that the voters had given the President a mixed mandate.

---

[42] *Time* (November 20, 1972), p. 17.

The Road Ahead Nixon's reelection made the long-range prospects for change uncertain, although certain immediate prospects were clear. The people who voted for him, including a large number of those who had switched from Wallace, apparently were not troubled about the threats to civil rights and the Bill of Rights, about tax inequities, racial inequality, the power of the military-industrial complex, the concentration of executive power, the massive bombings of North Vietnam, and what has been called "the creaking disability of government on all levels."[43] But some of them had also voted for legislators and governors who had addressed themselves to such concerns.

After the election, the problems on which McGovern had focused were still there, and many were part of the daily lives of people. For the most part, the states and cities had so far been unable to deal effectively with the growing problems of welfare, crime, narcotics, education, urban deterioration, and environmental pollution. (In a number of state referenda, a wide variety of environmental measures were approved by the voters on Election Day.) Many people believed that the solutions had to come at the highest levels of government. At the same time, community control was still being demanded by such disparate groups as ghetto blacks and ultraconservatives such as William F. Buckley, Jr., who sounded off on a familiar note by writing a column after the election in which he called for "a genuine rediscovery of the ideal of the community, of the primacy of the individual, of the spontaneity of the private sector."[44] Nixon himself had been speaking up for decentralization as he prepared to tighten the federal budget.

There was no immediate response from blacks to an election that was interpreted by a number of analysts as an expression of racism. Only 29 percent of white voters voted for McGovern, which was even lower than the 35 percent of the white vote cast for Humphrey in 1968. To some observers, the 1972 election was one of the most racially polarized in American history. But white racism came as no surprise to black Americans. The busing issue still loomed, with the Supreme Court decision on busing standing between the President and his expressed desire for a busing amendment.

When the election was over, the Democratic party was left with a power struggle between the McGovern supporters and the groups determined to erase the stamp of McGovernism from the party. Immediately, action began to oust Jean Westwood from the chairmanship and replace her with another chairman to wipe out the memories of 1972.

As Richard Nixon began his second term in office, the issue of constitutional reform, basic to real change, was ignored in the clamor of problems that vied for attention. For, as the election figures had shown, the American people were in no great hurry for change.

---

43 *Time* (November 20, 1972), p. 22.
44 The *New York Post* (November 14, 1972), p. 38.

APPENDIXES
INDEXES

1 THE DECLARATION OF INDEPENDENCE

When in the course of human events, it becomes necessary for one people to dissolve the political bands which have connected them with another, and to assume among the Powers of the earth, the separate and equal station to which the Laws of Nature and of Nature's God entitle them, a decent respect to the opinions of mankind requires that they should declare the causes which impel them to the separation.

We hold these truths to be self-evident, that all men are created equal, that they are endowed by their Creator with certain unalienable Rights, that among these are Life, Liberty and the pursuit of Happiness.—That to secure these rights, Governments are instituted among Men, deriving their just powers from the consent of the governed, That whenever any Form of Government becomes destructive of these ends, it is the Right of the People to alter or to abolish it, and to institute new Government, laying its foundation on such principles and organizing its powers in such form, as to them shall seem most likely to effect their Safety and Happiness. Prudence, indeed, will dictate that Governments long established should not be changed for light and transient causes; and accordingly all experience hath shown, that mankind are more disposed to suffer, while evils are sufferable, than to right themselves by abolishing the forms to which they are accustomed. But when a long train of abuses and usurpations, pursuing invariably the same Object evinces a design to reduce them under absolute Despotism, it is their right, it is their duty, to throw off such Government, and to provide new Guards for their future security.—Such has been the patient sufferance of these Colonies; and such is now the necessity which constrains them to alter their former Systems of Government. The history of the present King of Great Britain is a history of repeated injuries and usurpations, all having in direct object the establishment of an absolute Tyranny over these States. To prove this, let Facts be submitted to a candid world.[1]

He has refused his Assent to Laws,[2] the most wholesome and necessary for the public good.

He has forbidden his Governors to pass Laws of immediate and pressing importance, unless suspended in their operation till his Assent should be obtained; and when so suspended, he has utterly neglected to attend to them.

He has refused to pass other Laws for the accommodation of large districts of people, unless those people would relinquish the right of Representation in the Legislature, a right inestimable to them and formidable to tyrants only.

He has called together legislative bodies at places unusual, uncomfortable, and distant from the depository of their Public Records, for the sole purpose of fatiguing them into compliance with his measures.

---

[1] To those countries not involved in the conflict and, therefore, unbiased.

[2] In some of the colonies, laws passed by the legislatures had to be approved by the King.

He has dissolved Representative Houses repeatedly, for opposing with manly firmness his invasions on the rights of the people.

He has refused for a long time, after such dissolutions, to cause others to be elected; whereby the Legislative Powers, incapable of Annihilation, have returned to the People at large for their exercise; the State remaining in the mean time exposed to all the dangers of invasion from without, and convulsions within.

He has endeavoured to prevent the population of these States; for that purpose obstructing the Laws of Naturalization of Foreigners;[3] refusing to pass others to encourage their migration hither, and raising the conditions of new Appropriations of Lands.

He has obstructed the Administration of Justice, by refusing his Assent to Laws for establishing Judiciary Powers.

He has made Judges dependent on his Will alone, for the tenure of their offices, and the amount and payment of their salaries.

He has erected a multitude of New Offices, and sent hither swarms of Officers to harass our People, and eat out their substance.[4]

He has kept among us, in times of peace, Standing Armies without the Consent of our legislature.

He has affected to render the Military independent of and superior to the Civil Power.

He has combined with others to subject us to a jurisdiction foreign to our constitution, and unacknowledged by our laws giving his Assent to their acts of pretended legislation:

For quartering large bodies of armed troops among us:

For protecting them, by a mock Trial, from Punishment for any Murders which they should commit on the Inhabitants of these States:

For cutting off our Trade with all parts of the world:

For imposing taxes on us without our Consent:

For depriving us in many cases, of the benefits of Trial by Jury:

For transporting us beyond Seas to be tried for pretended offences:

For abolishing the free System of English Laws in a neighboring Province,[5] establishing therein an Arbitrary government, and enlarging its Boundaries so as to render it at once an example and fit instrument for introducing the same absolute rule into these Colonies:[6]

For taking away our Charters; abolishing our most valuable Laws, and altering fundamentally the Forms of our Governments:

For suspending our own Legislature, and declaring themselves invested with Power to legislate for us in all cases whatsoever.

He has abdicated Government here, by declaring us out of his Protection and waging War against us.

He has plundered our seas, ravaged our Coasts, burnt our towns, and destroyed the lives of our people.

---

[3] Laws by which immigrants obtained the privileges and immunities of natural citizens of the states.

[4] To deprive the colonists of their possessions and wealth, either by confiscation or by requiring them to cooperate in bringing about these results.

[5] The Quebec Act of 1774 provided, among other things, that French law be adopted in civil trials, thereby denying trial by jury.

[6] The Quebec Act also extended the boundaries of the province of Quebec to the west, thus including within it some land claimed by eastern colonies.

He is at this time transporting large armies of foreign mercenaries to compleat the works of death, desolation and tyranny, already begun with circumstances of Cruelty & perfidy scarcely paralleled in the most barbarous ages, and totally unworthy the Head of a civilized nation.

He has constrained our fellow Citizens taken Captive on the high Seas to bear Arms against their Country, to become the executioners of their friends and Brethren, or to fall themselves by their Hands.

He has excited domestic insurrections amongst us, and has endeavoured to bring on the inhabitants of our frontiers, the merciless Indian Savages, whose known rule of warfare, is an undistinguished destruction of all ages, sexes and conditions.

In every stage of these Oppressions We have Petitioned for Redress[7] in the most humble terms: Our repeated Petitions have been answered only by repeated injury. A Prince, whose character is thus marked by every act which may define a Tyrant, is unfit to be the ruler of a free People.

Nor have We been wanting in attention to our British brethren. We have warned them from time to time of attempts by their legislature to extend an unwarrantable jurisdiction over us. We have reminded them of the circumstances of our emigration and settlement here. We have appealed to their native justice and magnanimity, and we have conjured them by the ties of our common kindred to disavow these usurpations, which, would inevitably interrupt our connections and correspondence. They too have been deaf to the voice of justice and of consanguinity.[8] We must, therefore, acquiesce in the necessity, which denounces our Separation, and hold them, as we hold the rest of mankind, Enemies in War, in Peace, Friends.

We, therefore, the Representatives of the united States of America, in General Congress, Assembled, appealing to the Supreme Judge of the world for the rectitude of our intentions, do, in the Name, and by Authority of the good People of these Colonies, solemnly publish and declare, That these United Colonies are, and of Right ought to be Free and Independent States; that they are Absolved from all allegiance to the British Crown, and that all political connection between them and the State of Great Britain, is and ought to be totally dissolved; and that as Free and Independent States, they have full Power to levy War, conclude Peace, contract Alliances, establish Commerce, and to do all other Acts and Things which Independent States may of right do. And for the support of this Declaration, with a firm reliance on the Protection of Divine Providence, we mutually pledge to each other our Lives, our Fortunes and our sacred Honor.

---

[7] Made formal requests that the King repeal the arbitrary policies and thus correct the injustices.

[8] A relationship based on descent; the term here refers to the English ancestry of many of the colonists.

2 THE CONSTITUTION OF THE UNITED STATES OF AMERICA

We the People of the United States, in Order to form a more perfect Union, establish Justice, insure domestic Tranquility, provide for the common defence, promote the general Welfare, and secure the Blessings of Liberty to ourselves and our Posterity, do ordain and establish this Constitution for the United States of America.

Article I

Section 1

[GENERAL LEGISLATIVE POWERS]
All legislative Powers herein granted shall be vested in a Congress of the United States, which shall consist of a Senate and House of Representatives.

Section 2

[HOUSE OF REPRESENTATIVES, ELECTIONS, QUALIFICATIONS, OFFICERS, AND IMPEACHMENT POWER]
The House of Representatives shall be composed of Members chosen every second Year by the People of the several States, and the Electors in each State shall have the Qualifications requisite for Electors of the most numerous Branch of the State Legislature.

No Person shall be a Representative who shall not have attained to the Age of twenty-five Years, and been seven Years a Citizen of the United States, and who shall not, when elected, be an Inhabitant of that State in which he shall be chosen.

Representatives and direct Taxes shall be apportioned among the several States which may be included within this Union,[1] according to their respective Numbers, which shall be determined by adding to the whole Number of free Persons, including those bound to Service for a Term of Years, and excluding Indians not taxed, three fifths of all other Persons.[2] The actual Enumeration shall be made within three Years after the first Meeting of the Congress of the United States, and within every subsequent Term of ten Years, in such Manner as they shall by Law direct. The Number of Representatives shall not exceed one for every thirty Thousand, but each State shall have at Least one Representative; and until each enumeration shall be made, the State of New Hampshire shall be entitled to chuse three, Massachusetts eight, Rhode-Island and Providence Plantations one, Connecticut five, New-York six, New Jersey four,

---

[1] The Sixteenth Amendment (1913) abolished the requirement that taxes must be apportioned among the states.

[2] Section 2 of the Fourteenth Amendment (1868) modified this provision, stating: ". . . the whole number of persons in each State, excluding Indians not taxed."

Pennsylvania eight, Delaware one, Maryland six, Virginia ten, North Carolina five, South Carolina five, and Georgia three.

When vacancies happen in the Representation from any State, the Executive Authority thereof shall issue Writs of Election to fill such Vacancies.

The House of Representatives shall chuse their Speaker and other Officers; and shall have the sole Power of Impeachment.

Section 3

[THE SENATE: ELECTION, QUALIFICATIONS, OFFICERS, AND IMPEACHMENT TRIALS]

The Senate of the United States shall be composed of two Senators from each State, chosen by the Legislature thereof,[3] for six Years; and each Senator shall have one Vote.

Immediately after they shall be assembled in Consequence of the first Election, they shall be divided as equally as may be into three Classes. The Seats of the Senators of the first Class shall be vacated at the Expiration of the second Year, of the second Class at the Expiration of the fourth Year, and of the third Class at the Expiration of the sixth Year, so that one third may be chosen every second Year; and if Vacancies happen by Resignation, or otherwise, during the Recess of the Legislature of any State, the Executive thereof may make temporary Appointments until the next Meeting of the Legislature, which shall then fill such Vacancies.

No person shall be a Senator who shall not have attained to the Age of thirty Years, and been nine Years a Citizen of the United States, and who shall not, when elected, be an Inhabitant of that State for which he shall be chosen.

The Vice President of the United States shall be President of the Senate, but shall have no Vote, unless they be equally divided.

The Senate shall chuse their other Officers, and also a President pro tempore, in the Absence of the Vice President, or when he shall exercise the Office of President of the United States.

The Senate shall have the sole Power to try all Impeachments. When sitting for that Purpose, they shall be on Oath or Affirmation. When the President of the United States is tried, the Chief Justice shall preside: And no Person shall be convicted without the Concurrence of two thirds of the Members present.

Judgment in Cases of Impeachment shall not extend further than to removal from Office and disqualification to hold and enjoy any Office of honor, Trust or Profit under the United States: but the Party convicted shall nevertheless be liable and subject to Indictment, Trial, Judgment and Punishment, according to Law.

Section 4

[STATE REGULATION OF CONGRESSIONAL ELECTIONS]

The Times, Places and Manner of holding Elections for Senators and Representatives, shall be prescribed in each State by the Legislature thereof; but the Congress may at any time by Law make or alter such Regulations, except as to the Places of chusing Senators.

---

[3] The Seventeenth Amendment (1913) changed this method of selecting senators, calling for their direct election.

The Congress shall assemble at least once in every Year, and such Meeting shall be on the first Monday in December, unless they shall by Law appoint a different Day.[4]

Section 5

[CONGRESSIONAL RULES AND PROCEDURES]
Each House shall be the Judge of the Elections, Returns and Qualifications of its own Members,[5] and a Majority of each shall constitute a Quorum to do Business; but a smaller Number may adjourn from day to day, and may be authorized to compel the Attendance of absent Members, in such Manner, and under the Penalties as each House may provide.

Each House may determine the Rules of its Proceedings, punish its Members for disorderly Behavior, and, with the Concurrence of two thirds, expel a Member.

Each House shall keep a Journal of its Proceedings, and from time to time publish the same, excepting such Parts as may in their Judgment require Secrecy; and the Yeas and Nays of the Members of either House on any question shall, at the Desire of one fifth of the present, be entered on the Journal.

Neither House, during the Session of Congress, shall, without the Consent of the other, adjourn for more than three days, nor to any other Place than that in which the two Houses shall be sitting.

Section 6

[CONGRESSIONAL PAY, PRIVILEGES, AND RESTRICTIONS]
The Senators and Representatives shall receive a Compensation for their Services, to be ascertained by Law, and paid out of the Treasury of the United States. They shall in all Cases, except Treason, Felony and Breach of the Peace, be privileged from Arrest during their Attendance at the Session of their respective Houses,[6] and in going to and returning from the same; and for any Speech or Debate in either House, they shall not be questioned in any other Place.

No Senator or Representative, shall, during the time for which he was elected, be appointed to any civil Office under the authority of the United States, which shall have been created, or the Emoluments[7] whereof shall have been encreased during such time; and no Person holding any Office under the United States, shall be a Member of either House during his Continuance in Office.

Section 7

[LEGISLATIVE PROCEDURES]
All Bills for raising Revenue shall originate in the House of Representatives; but the Senate may propose or concur with Amendments as on other Bills.

Every Bill which shall have passed the House of Representatives and the Senate, shall, before it become a Law, be presented to the President of the United States; if he approve he shall sign it, but if not he shall return it, with

---

[4] The Twentieth Amendment (1933) changed this date to January 3 of every year.

[5] The houses of Congress can act as judicial tribunals and bar congressmen-elect from being seated if a two-thirds vote of the chamber involved is obtained. The Supreme Court, however, has held that a member-elect can be banned only for failing to meet constitutional requirements as delineated in Article I, Sections 2 and 3.

[6] This privilege is known commonly as congressional immunity.

[7] Salaries or fees.

his Objections to that House in which it shall have originated,[8] who shall enter the Objections at large on their Journal, and proceed to reconsider it. If after such Reconsideration two thirds of that House shall agree to pass the Bill, it shall be sent, together with the Objections, to the other House, by which it shall likewise be reconsidered, and if approved by two thirds of that House, it shall become a Law. But in all such Cases the Votes of both Houses shall be determined by Yeas and Nays, and the Names of the Persons voting for and against the Bill shall be entered on the Journal of each House respectively. If any Bill shall not be returned by the President within ten Days (Sundays excepted) after it shall have been presented to him, the Same shall be a Law, in like Manner as if he had signed it, unless the Congress by their Adjournment prevent its Return, in which Case it shall not be a Law.[9]

Every Order, Resolution, or Vote to which the Concurrence of the Senate and House of Representatives may be necessary (except on a question of Adjournment) shall be presented to the President of the United States; and before the Same shall take Effect, shall be approved by him, or being disapproved by him, shall be repassed by two thirds of the Senate and House of Representatives, according to the Rules and Limitations prescribed in the Case of a Bill.

Section 8

[POWERS OF CONGRESS]
The Congress shall have Power

To lay and collect Taxes, Duties, Imposts and Excises, to pay the Debts and provide for the common Defence and general Welfare of the United States; but all Duties, Imposts and excises shall be uniform throughout the United States;

To borrow Money on the Credit of the United States;

To regulate Commerce with foreign Nations, and among the several States, and with the Indian Tribes;

To establish an uniform Rule of Naturalization, and uniform Laws on the subject of Bankruptcies throughout the United States;

To coin Money, regulate the Value thereof, and of foreign Coin, and fix the Standard of Weights and Measures;

To provide for the Punishment of counterfeiting the Securities and current Coin of the United States;

To establish Post Offices and post Roads;

To promote the Progress of Science and useful Arts, by securing for limited Times to Authors and Inventors the exclusive Right to their respective Writings and Discoveries,

To constitute Tribunals inferior to the supreme Court, [10]

To define and Punish Piracies and Felonies committed on the high Seas, and Offences against the Law of Nations;

To declare War, grant Letters of Marque and Reprisal,[11] and make Rules concerning Captures on Land and Water;

---

[8] This action is commonly called a presidential veto.

[9] This procedure is called the pocket veto.

[10] This provision permitted the establishment of the entire federal court system.

[11] Commissions granted to private citizens by the government which authorize them to capture ships of foreign nations.

To raise and support Armies, but no Appropriation of Money to that Use shall be for a longer Term than two Years;

To provide and maintain a Navy;

To make Rules for the Government and Regulation of the land and naval forces;

To provide for calling for the Militia to execute the Laws of the Union, suppress Insurrections and repel Invasions;

To provide for organizing, arming, and disciplining, the Militia, and for governing such Part of them as may be employed in the Service of the United States, reserving to the States respectively, the Appointment of the Officers, and the Authority of training the Militia according to the discipline prescribed by Congress;

To exercise exclusive Legislation in all Cases whatsoever, over such District (not exceeding ten Miles square) as may, by Cession of particular States, and the Acceptance of Congress, become the Seat of the Government of the United States, and to exercise like Authority over all Places purchased by the Consent of the Legislature of the State in which the Same shall be, for the Erection of Forts, Magazines, Arsenals, dock-Yards, and other needful Buildings;—And

To make all Laws which shall be necessary and proper for carrying into Execution the foregoing Powers, and all other Powers vested by this Constitution in the Government of the United States, or in any Department or Officer thereof.[12]

Section 9

[RESTRICTIONS ON CONGRESSIONAL POWER]

The Migration or Importation of such Persons as any of the States now existing shall think proper to admit, shall not be prohibited by the Congress prior to the Year one thousand eight hundred and eight, but a Tax or Duty may be imposed on such Importation, not exceeding ten dollars for each Person.

The privilege of the Writ of Habeas Corpus[13] shall not be suspended, unless when in Cases of Rebellion or Invasion the public Safety may require it.

No Bill of Attainder[14] or ex post facto Laws[15] shall be passed.

No Capitation, or other direct, Tax shall be laid, unless in Proportion to the Census or Enumeration herein before directed to be taken.[16]

No Tax or Duty shall be laid on Articles exported from any State.

No Preference shall be given by any Regulation of Commerce or Revenue to the Ports of one State over those of another: nor shall Vessels bound to, or from, one State, be obliged to enter, clear, or pay Duties in another.

No Money shall be drawn from the Treasury, but in Consequence of Appropriations made by Law; and a regular Statement and Account of the Receipts and Expenditures of all public Money shall be published from time to time.

---

[12] This provision is known as the "elastic" clause or the "necessary and proper" clause.

[13] A writ of habeas corpus is a written instruction protecting a citizen from arbitrary arrest and punishment by demanding that authorities take the prisoner before a judge and there state the reasons for arrest.

[14] An act of Congress which singles out a person or group and orders punishment without trial.

[15] Laws which impose penalties for acts that were not illegal when performed or increase punishment for a crime after it has been committed.

[16] The requirement that all taxes be equally apportioned among the states according to population was eliminated by the Sixteenth Amendment (1913), which granted Congress the power to levy a tax on incomes.

No Title of Nobility shall be granted by the United States: And no Person holding any Office of Profit or Trust under them, shall, without the Consent of the Congress, accept of any present, Emolument, Office, or Title, of any kind whatever, from any King, Prince, or foreign State.

Section 10

[RESTRICTION ON THE POWERS OF THE STATES]
No State shall enter into any Treaty, Alliance, or Confederation; grant Letters of Marque and Reprisal; coin Money; emit Bills of Credit; make any Thing but gold and silver Coin a Tender in Payment of Debts; pass any Bill of Attainder, ex post facto Law, or Law impairing the Obligation of Contracts, or grant any Title of Nobility.

No State shall, without the Consent of the Congress, lay any Imposts or Duties on Imports or Exports, except what may be absolutely necessary for executing its inspection Laws: and the net Produce of all Duties and Imposts, laid by any State on Imports or Exports, shall be for the Use of the Treasury of the United States; and all such Laws shall be subject to the Revision and Control of the Congress.

No State shall, without the Consent of Congress, lay any Duty of Tonnage,[17] keep Troops, or Ships of War in time of Peace, enter into any Agreement or Compact with another State, or with a foreign Power, or engage in War, unless actually invaded, or in such imminent Danger as will not admit of Delay.

Article II

Section 1

[PRESIDENTIAL POWER, ELECTION, AND QUALIFICATIONS]
The executive Power shall be vested in a President of the United States of America. He shall hold his Office during the Term of four Years[18] and, together with the Vice President, chosen for the same Term, be elected, as follows:

Each State shall appoint, in such Manner as the Legislature thereof may direct, a Number of Electors, equal to the whole Number of Senators and Representatives to which the State may be entitled in the Congress: but no Senator or Representative, or Person holding an Office of Trust or Profit under the United States, shall be appointed an Elector.

The electors shall meet in their respective States, and vote by ballot for two Persons, of whom one at least shall not be an Inhabitant of the same State with themselves. And they shall make a List of all the Persons voted for, and of the Number of Votes for each; which List they shall sign and certify, and transmit sealed to the Seat of the Government of the United States, directed to the President of the Senate. The President of the Senate shall, in the Presence of the Senate and House of Representatives, open all the Certificates, and the Votes shall then be counted. The Person having the greatest Number of Votes shall be the President, if such Number be a Majority of the whole Number of Elec-

---

[17] A tax levied on a seagoing vessel when entering, using, or leaving a port.

[18] A President was limited to serving two terms (or ten years under certain circumstances) by the Twenty-second Amendment (1951).

tors appointed; and if there be more than one who have such Majority and have an equal Number of Votes, then the House of Representatives shall immediately chuse by Ballot one of them for President; and if no person have a Majority, then from the five highest on the List the said House shall in like Manner chuse the President. But in chusing the President, the Votes shall be taken by States, the Representation from each State having one Vote; A quorum for this Purpose shall consist of a Member or Members from two-thirds of the States, and a Majority of all the States shall be necessary to a Choice. In every Case, after the Choice of the President, the person having the greatest Number of Votes of the Electors shall be the Vice President. But if there should remain two or more who have equal vote, the Senate shall chuse from them by Ballot the Vice President.[19]

The Congress may determine the Time of chusing the Electors, and the Day on which they shall give their Votes; which Day shall be the same throughout the United States.

No Person except a natural born Citizen, or a Citizen of the United States, at the time of the Adoption of this Constitution, shall be eligible to the Office of President; neither shall any Person be eligible to that Office who shall not have attained to the Age of thirty-five Years, and been fourteen Years a Resident within the United States.

In Case of the Removal of the President from Office, or of his Death, Resignation, or Inability to discharge the Powers and Duties of the said Office, the same shall devolve on the Vice President, and the Congress may by Law provide for the Case of Removal, Death, Resignation, or Inability, both of the President and Vice President, declaring what Officer shall then act as President, and such Officer shall act accordingly, until the Disability be removed, or a President shall be elected.[20]

The President shall, at stated Times, receive for his Services, a Compensation, which shall neither be increased nor diminished during the Period of which he shall have been elected, and he shall not receive within that Period any other Emolument from the United States, or any of them.

Before he enter on the Execution of his Office, he shall take the following oath or Affirmation: — "I do solemnly swear (or affirm) that I will faithfully execute the Office of the President of the United States, and will to the best of my Ability, preserve, protect and defend the Constitution of the United States."

Section 2

[POWERS OF THE PRESIDENT]
The President shall be the Commander in Chief of the Army and Navy of the United States, and of the Militia of the several States, when called into the actual Service of the United States, he may require the Opinion, in writing, of the principal Officer in each of the executive Departments, upon any Subject

---

[19] The procedures of the Electoral College were changed by the Twelfth Amendment (1804), which adapted the Electoral College to the party system. Candidates for President and Vice President were listed separately, but voting for the two men took place together as a party ticket.

[20] The Twenty-fifth Amendment (1967) provides for the Vice President to become President if the President dies, resigns, or is removed from office. It also delineates presidential disability and provides for nominating and confirming a new Vice President.

relating to the Duties of their respective Offices, and he shall have Power to grant Reprieves and Pardons for Offences against the United States, except in Cases of Impeachment.

He shall have Power, by and with the Advice and Consent of the Senate to make Treaties, provided two thirds of the Senators present concur; and he shall nominate, and by and with the Advice and Consent of the Senate, shall appoint Ambassadors, other public Ministers and Consuls, Judges of the supreme Court, and all other Offices of the United States, whose Appointments are not herein otherwise provided for, and which shall be established by Law: but the Congress may by Law vest the Appointment of such inferior Offices, as they think proper, in the President alone, in the Courts of Law, or in the Heads of Departments.

The President shall have Power to fill up all Vacancies that may happen during the Recess of the Senate, by granting Commissions which shall expire at the End of their next Session.

Section 3

[PRESIDENTIAL/CONGRESSIONAL RELATIONSHIP]
He shall from time to time give to the Congress Information of the State of the Union, and recommend to their Consideration such Measures as he shall judge necessary and expedient; he may, on extraordinary Occasions, convene both Houses, or either of them, and in Case of Disagreement between them, with Respect to the Time of Adjournment, he may adjourn them to such Time as he shall think proper, he shall receive Ambassadors and other public Ministers; he shall take Care that the Laws be faithfully executed, and shall Commission all the Officers of the United States.

Section 4

[IMPEACHMENT]
The President, Vice President and all civil Officers of the United States shall be removed from Office on Impeachment for, and Conviction of, Treason, Bribery, or other high Crimes and Misdemeanors.

Article III

Section 1

[STRUCTURE OF THE JUDICIARY]
The judicial Power of the United States, shall be vested in one supreme Court, and in such inferior Courts as the Congress may from time to time ordain and establish. The Judges, both of the supreme and inferior Courts, shall hold their Offices during good Behavior,[21] and shall, at stated Times, receive for their Services, a Compensation, which shall not be diminished during their Continuance in Office.

Section 2

[JURISDICTION OF FEDERAL COURTS]
The judicial Power shall extend to all Cases, in Law and Equity, arising under

---

[21] "During good Behavior" generally means life tenure unless a flagrant crime is committed.

this Constitution, the Laws of the United States, and Treaties made, or which shall be made, under their Authority;—to all Cases affecting Ambassadors, other public Ministers and Consuls;—to all Cases of admiralty and maritime Jurisdiction;—to Controversies to which the United States shall be a party;—to Controversies between two or more States;—between a State and Citizens of another State;—between Citizens of different States;—between Citizens of the same State claiming Lands under Grants of different States, and between a State, or the Citizens thereof, and foreign States, Citizens or Subjects.[22]

In all Cases affecting Ambassadors, other public Ministers and Consuls, and those in which a State shall be Party, the supreme Court shall have original Jurisdiction. In all the other Cases before mentioned, the supreme Court shall have appellate Jurisdiction, both as to Law and Fact, with such Exceptions, and under such Regulations as Congress shall make.

The Trial of all Crimes, except in Cases of Impeachment, shall be by Jury; and such Trial shall be held in the State where the said Crimes shall have been committed; but when not committed within any State, the Trial shall be at such Place or Places as the Congress may by Law have directed.

Section 3

[TREASON]
Treason against the United States, shall consist only in levying War against them, or in adhering to their Enemies, giving them Aid and Comfort. No Person shall be convicted of Treason unless on the Testimony of two Witnesses to the the same overt Act, or on Confession in open Court.

The Congress shall have Power to declare the Punishment of Treason, but no Attainder of Treason[23] shall work Corruption of Blood, or Forfeiture except during the Life of the Person attained.[24]

Article IV

Section 1

[FAITH AND CREDIT AMONG STATES]
Full Faith and Credit shall be given in each State to the public Acts, Records, and judicial Proceedings of every other State.[25] And the Congress may by general Laws prescribe the Manner in which such Acts, Records and Proceedings shall be proved, and the Effect thereof.

Section 2

[PRIVILEGES AND IMMUNITIES]
The Citizens of each State shall be entitled to all Privileges and Immunities of Citizens in the several States.[26]

---

[22] The Eleventh Amendment (1798) suspended judicial power of the federal courts over cases between a state and citizens of another state, or between a state and foreign nations.

[23] Attainder of treason is the elimination of civil rights, resulting from a conviction for treason.

[24] An attainder of treason shall not apply to the traitor's descendants.

[25] This provision applies only to civil, not to criminal, laws.

[26] Known as the comity clause, this one protects citizens when in a state other than their home state.

A person charged in any State with Treason, Felony or other Crime, who shall flee from Justice, and be found in another State, shall on Demand of the executive Authority of the State from which he fled, be delivered up to be removed to the State having Jurisdiction of the Crime.[27]

No person held to Service or Labour in one State, under the Laws thereof, escaping into another, shall, in Consequence of any Law or Regulation therein, be discharged from such Service or Labour, but shall be delivered up on Claim of the Party to whom such Service or Labour may be due.[28]

Section 3

[ADMISSION OF NEW STATES]
New States may be admitted by the Congress into this Union; but no new State shall be formed or erected within the Jurisdiction of any other State; nor any State be formed by the Junction of two or more States, or Parts of States, without the Consent of the Legislatures of the States concerned as well as of the Congress.

The Congress shall have Power to dispose of and make all needful Rules and Regulations respecting the Territory or other Property belonging to the United States; and nothing in this Constitution shall be so construed as to Prejudice any Claims of the United States, or of any particular State.

Section 4

[THE STATES AS REPUBLICAN GOVERNMENTS]
The United States shall guarantee to every State in this Union a Republican Form of Government, and shall protect each of them against Invasion; and on Application of the Legislature, or of the Executive (when the Legislature cannot be convened) against domestic Violence.

Article V

[AMENDING THE CONSTITUTION]
The Congress, whenever two thirds of both Houses shall deem it necessary, shall propose Amendments to this Constitution, or, on the Application of the Legislatures of two thirds of several States, shall call a Convention for proposing Amendments, which, in either Case, shall be valid to all Intents and Purposes, as Part of this Constitution, when ratified by the Legislatures of three fourths of the several States, or by Conventions in three fourths thereof, as the one or the other Mode of Ratification may be proposed by the Congress; Provided that no Amendment which may be made prior to the Year One thousand eight hundred and eight shall in any Manner affect the first and fourth Clauses in the Ninth Section of the first Article; and that no State, without its Consent, shall be deprived of its equal Suffrage in the Senate.

---

[27] The process is known as extradition.
[28] The Thirteenth Amendment (1865) repealed this provision.

Article VI

[DEBTS, SUPREMACY, AND OATH]

All Debts contracted and Engagements entered into, before the Adoption of this Constitution, shall be as valid against the United States under this Constitution, as under the Confederation.

This Constitution, and the Laws of the United States which shall be made in Pursuance thereof; and all Treaties made, or which shall be made, under the Authority of the United States, shall be the supreme Law of the Land; and the Judges in every State shall be bound thereby, any Thing in the Constitution or Laws of any State to the Contrary notwithstanding.[29]

The Senators and Representatives before mentioned, and the Members of the several State Legislatures, and all executive and judicial Officers, both of the United States and of the several States, shall be bound by Oath or Affirmation, to support this Constitution; but no religious Test shall ever be required as a Qualification to any Office or public Trust under the United States.

Article VII

[RATIFICATION]

The Ratification of the Conventions of nine States, shall be sufficient for the Establishment of this Constitution between the States so ratifying the Same.

Done in Convention by the Unanimous Consent of the States present the Seventeenth Day of September in the Year of our Lord one thousand seven hundred and Eighty seven and of the Independence of the United States of America the Twelfth. In Witness whereof We have hereunto subscribed our Names,

G:⁰ WASHINGTON — Presidt, and Deputy from Virginia

New Hampshire
  John Langdon
  Nicholas Gilman
Massachusetts
  Nathaniel Gorham
  Rufus King
Connecticut
  Wm Saml Johnson
  Roger Sherman
New York
  Alexander Hamilton
New Jersey
  Wil: Livingston
  David Brearley
  Wm Paterson
  Jona: Dayton

Pennsylvania
  B Franklin
  Thomas Mifflin
  Robt Morris
  Geo. Clymer
  Thos. FitzSimons
  Jared Ingersoll
  James Wilson
  Gouv Morris
Delaware
  Geo Read
  Gunning Bedfor Jun
  John Dickinson
  Richard Bassett
  Jaco: Broom

---

[29] This is the supremacy clause, which establishes the supremacy of the national government over the states.

Maryland
  James McHenry
  Dan of St Thos. Jenifer
  Danl Carroll
Virginia
  John Blair—
  James Madison Jr.
North Carolina
  Wm Blount
  Richd Dobbs Spaight
  Hu Williamson

South Carolina
  J. Rutledge
  Charles Cotesworth Pinckney
  Charles Pinckney
  Pierce Butler
Georgia
  William Few
  Abr Baldwin

Amendments to the Constitution

Amendments I through X, known collectively as the Bill of Rights, were ratified on December 15, 1791.

Amendment I

[FREEDOM OF RELIGION, SPEECH, PRESS, ASSEMBLY, AND PETITION]
Congress shall make no law respecting an establishment of religion, or prohibiting the free exercise thereof; or abridging the freedom of speech, or of the press; or the right of the people peaceably to assemble, and to petition the Government for a redress of grievances.

Amendment II

[FREEDOM TO KEEP AND BEAR ARMS]
A well regulated Militia, being necessary to the security of a free State, the right of the people to keep and bear Arms, shall not be infringed.

Amendment III

[QUARTERING OF SOLDIERS]
No Soldier shall, in time of peace be quartered in any house, without the consent of the Owner, nor in time of war, but in a manner to be prescribed by law.

Amendment IV

[SECURITY FROM UNREASONABLE SEARCHES AND SEIZURES]
The right of the people to be secure in their persons, houses, papers, and effects, against unreasonable searches and seizures, shall not be violated, and no Warrants shall issue, but upon probable cause, supported by Oath or affirmation, and particularly describing the place to be searched, and the persons or things to be seized.

Amendment V

[RIGHTS OF ACCUSED PERSONS IN CRIMINAL CASES]
No person shall be held to answer for a capital, or otherwise infamous crime,

unless on a presentment or indictment of a Grand Jury, except in cases arising in the land or naval forces, or in the Militia, when in actual service in time of War or in public danger; not shall any person be subject for the same offence to be twice put in jeopardy of life or limb; nor shall be compelled in any Criminal Case to be a witness against himself,[30] nor be deprived of life, liberty, or property, without due process of law; nor shall private property be taken for public use, without just compensation.

Amendment VI

[ADDITIONAL RIGHTS OF THE ACCUSED]
In all criminal prosecutions, the accused shall enjoy the right to a speedy and public trial, by an impartial jury of the State and district wherein the crime shall have been committed, which district shall have been previously ascertained by law, and to be informed of the nature and cause of the accusation; to be confronted with the witnesses against him; to have compulsory process for obtaining Witnesses in his favor, and to have the Assistance of Counsel for his defence.

Amendment VII

[CIVIL RIGHTS IN COMMON LAW]
In suits at common law, where the value in controversy shall exceed twenty dollars, the right of trial by jury shall be preserved, and no fact tried by a jury shall be otherwise re-examined in any Court of the United States, than according to the rules of the common law.

Amendment VIII

[BAILS, FINES, AND PUNISHMENTS]
Excessive bail shall not be required, nor excessive fines imposed, nor cruel and unusual punishments inflicted.

Amendment IX

[RETENTION OF RIGHTS OF THE PEOPLE][31]
The enumeration in the Constitution, of certain rights, shall not be construed to deny or disparage others retained by the people.

Amendment X

[RESERVATION OF POWERS TO THE STATES OR PEOPLE]
The powers not delegated to the United States by the Constitution, nor prohibited by it to the States, are reserved to the States respectively, or to the people.

---

[30] This provision protects a citizen against self-incrimination.
[31] These retained rights are the ones referred to in the Declaration of Independence.

Amendment XI

[RESTRICTION OF JUDICIAL POWER][32]
[*Ratified on January 8, 1798*]
The Judicial power of the United States shall not be construed to extend to any suit in law or equity, commenced or prosecuted against one of the United States by Citizens of another State, or by Citizens or Subjects of any Foreign State.

Amendment XII

[ELECTION OF PRESIDENT AND VICE PRESIDENT][33]
[*Ratified on September 25, 1804*]
The Electors shall meet in their respective states, and vote by ballot for President and Vice-President, one of whom, at least, shall not be an inhabitant of the same state with themselves; they shall name in their ballots the person voted for as President, and in distinct ballots the person voted for as Vice-President, and they shall make distinct lists of all persons voted for as President, and of all persons voted for as Vice-President, and of the number of votes for each, which lists they shall sign and certify, and transmit sealed to the seat of the government of the United States, directed to the President of the Senate;—The President of the Senate shall, in presence of the Senate and House of Representatives, open all the certificates and the votes shall then be counted;—The person having the greatest number of votes for President, shall be the President, if such number be a majority of the whole number of Electors appointed; and if no person have such majority, then from the persons having the highest numbers not exceeding three on the list of those voted for as President, the House of Representatives shall choose immediately, by ballot, the President. But in choosing the President, the votes shall be taken by states, the representation from each state having one vote; a quorum for this purpose shall consist of a member or members from two-thirds of the states, and a majority of all states shall be necessary to a choice. And if the House of Representatives shall not choose a President whenever the right of choice shall devolve upon them, before the fourth day of March next following, then the Vice-President shall act as President, as in the case of the death or other constitutional disability of the President. The person having the greatest number of votes as Vice-President, shall be the Vice-President, if such number be a majority of the whole number of Electors appointed, and if no person have a majority, then from the two highest numbers on the list, the Senate shall choose the Vice-President; a quorum for the purpose shall consist of two-thirds of the whole number of Senators, and a majority of the whole number shall be necessary to a choice. But no person constitutionally ineligible to the office of President shall be eligible to that of Vice-President of the United States.

Amendment XIII

[*Ratified on December 18, 1865*]

---

[32] Revision of part of Article III, Section 2.
[33] Revision of part of Article II, Section 1.

Section 1

[ABOLITION OF SLAVERY][34]
Neither slavery nor involuntary servitude, except as a punishment for crime whereof the party shall have been duly convicted, shall exist within the United States, or any place subject to their jurisdiction.

Section 2

Congress shall have power to enforce this article by appropriate legislation.

Amendment XIV [35]

[*Ratified on July 28, 1868*]

Section 1

[RIGHT OF CITIZENSHIP]
All persons born or naturalized in the United States, and subject to the jurisdiction thereof, are citizens of the United States and of the State wherein they reside. No State shall make or enforce any law which shall abridge the privileges or immunities of citizens of the United States; nor shall any State deprive any person of life, liberty, or property, without due process of law,[36] nor deny to any person within its jurisdiction the equal protection of the laws.

Section 2

[REPRESENTATION IN CONGRESS]
Representatives shall be apportioned among the several States according to their respective numbers, counting the whole number of persons in each State, excluding Indians not taxed. But when the right to vote at any election for the choice of electors for President and Vice-President of the United States, Representatives in Congress, the Executive and Judicial officers of a State, or the members of the Legislature thereof, is denied to any of the male inhabitants of such State, being twenty-one years of age, and citizens of the United States, or in any way abridged, except for participation in rebellion, or other crime, the basis of representation therein shall be reduced in the proportion which the number of such male citizens shall bear to the whole number of male citizens twenty-one years of age in such State.[37]

Section 3

[RESTRICTION ON ELEGIBILITY TO HOLD OFFICE]
No person shall be a Senator or Representative in Congress, or elector of President and Vice-President, or hold any office, civil or military, under the United States, or under any State, who, having previously taken an oath, as a member of Congress, or as an officer of the United States, or as a member of any State legis-

---

[34] Repeals part of Article IV, Section 2.

[35] Sections 1 and 2 of this amendment revise parts of Article I, Section 2.

[36] This due-process clause, when combined with the Fifth Amendment, provides uniform civil rights for all United States citizens.

[37] Changed by the Nineteenth (1920) and Twenty-sixth (1971) Amendments so that women citizens and citizens over eighteen years old are included each time "male citizen" is mentioned here.

lature, or as an executive or judicial officer of any State, to support the Constitution of the United States, shall have engaged in insurrection or rebellion against the same, or given aid or comfort to the enemies thereof. But Congress may by a vote of two-thirds of each House, remove such disability.

Section 4

[DEFINITION OF PUBLIC DEBTS]
The validity of the public debt of the United States, authorized by law, including debts incurred for payment of pensions and bounties for services in suppressing insurrection or rebellion, shall not be questioned. But neither the United States nor any State shall assume or pay any debt or obligation incurred in aid of insurrection or rebellion against the United States, or any claim for the loss or emancipation of any slave; but all such debts, obligations and claims shall be held illegal and void.

Section 5

The Congress shall have power to enforce, by appropriate legislation, the provisions of this article.

Amendment XV

[*Ratified on March 30, 1870*]

Section 1

[BLACK SUFFRAGE]
The right of citizens of the United States to vote shall not be denied or abridged by the United States or by any State on account of race, color, or previous condition of servitude.

Section 2

The Congress shall have power to enforce this article by appropriate legislation.

Amendment XVI

[PERSONAL INCOME TAXES][38]
[*Ratified on February 25, 1913*]
The Congress shall have power to lay and collect taxes on incomes, from whatever source derived, without apportionment among the several States, and without regard to any census or enumeration.

Amendment XVII

[POPULAR ELECTION OF SENATORS][39]
[*Ratified on May 31, 1913*]
The Senate of the United States shall be composed of two Senators from each

---

[38] Revision of the type of taxes and their method of collection as noted in parts of Article I, Sections 2 and 9.
[39] Revision of part of Article I, Section 3.

State, elected by the people thereof, for six years; and each Senator shall have one vote. The electors in each State shall have the qualifications requisite for electors of the most numerous branch of the State Legislature.

When vacancies happen in the representation of any State in the Senate, the executive authority of such State shall issue writs of election to fill such vacancies: Provided, That the Legislature of any State may empower the executive thereof to make temporary appointment until the people fill the vacancies by election as the Legislature may direct.

This amendment shall not be so construed as to affect the election or term of any Senator chosen before it becomes valid as part of the Constitution.

Amendment XVIII

[Ratified on January 29, 1919]

Section 1

[PROHIBITION OF LIQUOR]
After one year from the ratification of this article the manufacture, sale, or transportation of intoxicating liquors within, the importation thereof into, or the exportation thereof from the United States and all territory subject to the jurisdiction thereof for beverage purposes is hereby prohibited.

Section 2

[ENFORCEMENT POWER]
The Congress and the several states shall have concurrent power to enforce this article by appropriate legislation.

Section 3

[PROVISION FOR RATIFICATION]
This article shall be inoperative unless it shall have been ratified as an amendment to the Constitution by the legislatures of the several states, as provided in the Constitution, within seven years from the date of the submission hereof to the states by the Congress.

Amendment XIX

[WOMAN SUFFRAGE]
[Ratified on August 26, 1920]
The right of the citizens of the United States to vote shall not be denied or abridged by the United States or by any state on account of sex.

Congress shall have power, by appropriate legislation, to enforce the provision of this article.

Amendment XX

[Ratified on February 6, 1933]

Section 1

[TERMS OF PRESIDENTIAL AND VICE-PRESIDENTIAL OFFICE]
The terms of the President and Vice-President shall end at noon on the 20th

day of January, and the terms of the Senators and Representatives at noon on the 3rd day of January, of the years in which such terms would have ended if this article had not been ratified; and the terms of their successors shall then begin.

Section 2

[TIME OF CONVENING CONGRESS][40]
The Congress shall assemble at least once in every year, and such meeting shall begin at noon on the 3rd day of January, unless they shall by law appoint a different day.

Section 3

[DEATH OF PRESIDENT-ELECT]
If, at the time fixed for the beginning of the term of the President, the President elect shall have died, the Vice-President elect shall become President. If a President shall not have been chosen before the time fixed for the beginning of his term, or if the President elect shall have failed to qualify, then the Vice-President elect shall act as President until a President shall have qualified; and the Congress may by law provide for the case wherein neither a President elect nor a Vice-President elect shall have qualified declaring who shall then act as President, or the manner in which one who is to act shall be selected, and such person shall act accordingly until a President or Vice-President shall have qualified.

Section 4

[PRESIDENTIAL SUCCESSION][41]
The Congress may by law provide for the case of the death of any of the persons from whom the House of Representatives may choose a President whenever the right of choice shall have devolved upon them, and for the case of the death of any of the persons from whom the Senate may choose a Vice-President whenever the right of choice shall have devolved upon them.

Section 5

Sections 1 and 2 shall take effect on the 15th day of October following the ratification of this article.

Section 6

This article shall be inoperative unless it shall have been ratified as an amendment to the Constitution by the legislatures of three-fourths of the several States within seven years from the date of its submission.

Amendment XXI

[Ratified on December 5, 1933]

---

[40] Revision of part of Article I, Section 4, so that the beginning of the congressional session corresponds closely to the time the President takes office.

[41] Revision of part of Article II, Section 1. This amendment is further changed by the Twenty-fifth Amendment (1967).

Section 1

[REPEAL OF LIQUOR PROHIBITION]
The eighteenth article of amendment to the Constitution of the United States is hereby repealed.

Section 2

["DRY" STATES]
The transportation or importation into any State, Territory, or Possession of the United States for delivery or use therein of intoxicating liquors, in violation of the laws thereof, is hereby prohibited.

Section 3

This article shall be inoperative unless it shall have been ratified as an amendment to the Constitution by conventions in the several States, as provided in the Constitution, within seven years from the date of the submission hereof to the States by the Congress.

Amendment XXII

[Ratified on February 26, 1951]

Section 1

[LIMITATION ON PRESIDENTIAL TERM IN OFFICE][42]
No person shall be elected to the office of the President more than twice, and no person who has held the office of President, or acted as President, for more than two years of a term to which some other person was elected President shall be elected to the Office of the President more than once. But this Article shall not apply to any person holding the office of President when this Article was proposed by the Congress, and shall not prevent any person who may be holding the office of President, or acting as President, during the term within which this Article becomes operative from holding the office of President or acting as President during the remainder of such term.

Section 2

This Article shall be inoperative unless it shall have been ratified as an amendment to the Constitution by the legislatures of three-fourths of the several states within seven years from the date of its submission to the States by the Congress.

Amendment XXIII

[Ratified on March 29, 1961]

Section 1

[ELECTORAL VOTES FOR THE DISTRICT OF COLUMBIA][43]
The District constituting the seat of Government of the United States shall appoint in such manner as the Congress may direct:

---

[42] This section expands on Article II, Section 1.

[43] Until 1961, the residents of the District of Columbia could not vote in national elections.

A number of electors of President and Vice-President equal to the whole number of Senators and Representatives in Congress to which the District would be entitled if it were a State, but in no event more than the least populous State; they shall be in addition to those appointed by the States, but they shall be considered, for the purposes of the election of President and Vice-President, to be electors appointed by a State; and they shall meet in the District and perform such duties as provided by the twelfth article of amendment.

Section 2

The Congress shall have power to enforce this article by appropriate legislation.

Amendment XXIV

[*Ratified on January 23, 1964*]

Section 1

[POLL TAX ABOLISHED]
The right of citizens of the United States to vote in any primary or other election for President or Vice-President, for electors for President or Vice-President, or for Senator or Representative in Congress, shall not be denied or abridged by the United States or any State by reasons of failure to pay any poll tax or other tax.

Section 2

The Congress shall have power to enforce this article by appropriate legislation.

Amendment XXV [44]

[*Ratified on February 10, 1967*]

Section 1

[PRESIDENTIAL SUCCESSION]
In case of the removal of the President from office or his death or resignation, the Vice-President shall become President.

Section 2

[VICE-PRESIDENTIAL SUCCESSION]
Whenever there is a vacancy in the office of the Vice-President, the President shall nominate a Vice-President who shall take the office upon confirmation by a majority vote of both houses of Congress.

Section 3

[PRESIDENTIAL DISABILITY]
Whenever the President transmits to the President pro tempore of the Senate and the Speaker of the House of Representatives his written declaration that he is unable to discharge the powers and duties of his office, and until he transmits

---

[44] Changes and expands on part of Article II, Section 1.

to them a written declaration to the contrary, such powers and duties shall be discharged by the Vice-President as Acting President.

Section 4

[CONGRESSIONAL POWER TO DECLARE AND TO END PRESIDENTIAL DISABILITY] Whenever the Vice-President and a majority of either the principal officers of the executive departments, or of such other body as Congress may by law provide, transmit to the President pro tempore of the Senate and the Speaker of the House of Representatives their written declaration that the President is unable to discharge the powers and duties of his office, the Vice-President shall immediately assume the powers and duties of the office as Acting President.

Thereafter, when the President transmits to the President pro tempore of the Senate and the Speaker of the House of Representatives his written declaration that no inability exists, he shall resume the powers and duties of his office unless the Vice-President and a majority of either the principal officers of the executive department, or of such other body as Congress may by law provide, transmit within four days to the President pro tempore of the Senate and the Speaker of the House of Representatives their written declaration that the President is unable to discharge the powers and duties of his office. Thereupon Congress shall decide the issue, assembling within 48 hours for that purpose if not in session. If the Congress, within 21 days after receipt of the latter written declaration, or, if Congress is not in session, within 21 days after Congress is required to assemble, determines by two-thirds vote of both houses that the President is unable to discharge the powers and duties of his office, the Vice-President shall continue to discharge the same as Acting President; otherwise, the President shall resume the powers and duties of his office.

Amendment XXVI

[Ratified on June 30, 1971]

Section 1[45]

The right of citizens of the United States, who are eighteen years of age, or older, to vote shall not be denied or abridged by the United States or by any state on account of age.

Section 2

The Congress shall have power to enforce this article by appropriate legislation.

---

[45] Prior to ratification of this amendment, no age requirement for voting was specified in the Constitution.

NAME INDEX

SUBJECT INDEX

Tables

Page 170: Adapted from *Facts and Figures on Government Finance,* 16th Edition, 1971, by permission of Tax Foundation, Inc. *Page 206:* Reprinted from *1971 Congressional Quarterly Almanac* ©, p. 1140. *Page 373:* Harris Survey: December 28, 1970, May 3, 1971; copyright 1970 and 1971 Chicago Tribune Co.-New York Daily News Syndicate. *Page 380:* Newsweek, Copyright, 1970. *Page 451:* Reprinted from John W. Davis, *National Conventions: Nominations Under the Big Top;* copyright 1972 Barron's Educational Series, Inc. *Page 498:* From Herbert E. Alexander, "Financing Parties in Campaigns in 1968," in *Political Parties and Political Behavior,* Second Edition, edited by Crotty, William J., Freeman, Donald M., and Gatlin, Douglas S.; © Copyright 1971 by Allyn and Bacon, Inc., Boston, Mass. Reprinted by permission. *Page 524:* From *Political Man* by Seymour Martin Lipset; copyright © 1959, 1960 by Seymour Martin Lipset. Reprinted by permission of Doubleday and Company, Inc. *Page 530:* Reprinted by permission of Center for Political Studies, University of Michigan. *Page 531:* 1940–1966 data by permission of the Gallup Organization, Inc.; 1968 data by permission of Congressional Quarterly, Inc.; 1971 data by permission of Newsweek, Copyright, 1971.
Page 552: Reprinted from Ralph E. Lapp, *The Weapons Culture* (1968) by permission of W. W. Norton & Company, Inc. *Page 553:* Reprinted from Richard A. Posner, "A Statistical Study of Antitrust Enforcement," *Journal of Law and Economics,* vol. 13, October, 1970, by permission of *Journal of Law and Economics.*